Catalogue

of Medieval and Renaissance Manuscripts

in the Beinecke Rare Book

and Manuscript Library

Yale University

VOLUME IV: MSS 481–485

Medieval and Renaissance Texts and Studies

Volume 176

Arizona Studies in the Middle Ages

and the Renaissance

Volume 11

Catalogue

of Medieval and Renaissance Manuscripts

in the Beinecke Rare Book

and Manuscript Library

Yale University

VOLUME IV: MSS 481–485

BY

Robert G. Babcock
Lisa Fagin Davis
Philip G. Rusche

Arizona Center for Medieval and Renaissance Studies
Tempe, Arizona
in collaboration with
BREPOLS
2004

Support for this publication was provided by the
H. P. Kraus Fellowship in Early Books and Manuscripts.

© Copyright 2004
Arizona Board of Regents for Arizona State University
and Brepols Publishers n.v., Turnhout, Belgium

ASMAR Volume 11: ISBN 2-503-514405 and D/2004/0095/58

Library of Congress Cataloging-in-Publication Data
Beinecke Rare Book and Manuscript Library.
    Catalogue of Medieval and Renaissance manuscripts in the Beinecke Rare Book and Manu-script Library, Yale University.
    (Medieval & Renaissance texts & studies ; v. 34, 48, 100, 176)
    Includes bibliographical references and indexes.
    Contents: v. 1. MSS 1–250—v. 2. MSS 251–500—v. 3. Marston manuscripts.—v. 4. MSS 481–485.
    1. Beinecke Rare Book and Manuscript Library—Catalogs.
    2. Manuscripts—Connecticut—New Haven—Catalogs.
    3. Manuscripts, Latin (Medieval and modern)—Catalogs.
    4. Manuscripts, Greek (Medieval and modern)—Catalogs.
    5. Manuscripts, Medieval—Connecticut—New Haven—Catalogs.
    6. Manuscripts, Renaissance—Connecticut—New Haven—Catalogs.
        I. Shailor, Barbara A., 1948— . II. Title. III. Title: Catalog of Medieval and Renaissance manuscripts in the Beinecke Rare Book and Manuscript Library, Yale University. IV. Series.
    V. Series: Medieval & Renaissance texts & studies ; v. 34, etc.
Z6621.B4213   1984   011'.31   84–667
ISBN 0–86698–065–2 (v. 1)   ISBN 0–86698–115–2 (v. 3)
ISBN 0–86698–030–X (v. 2)   ISBN 0–86698–218–3 (v. 4)

This book is made to last.
It is set in Carnegie, smythe-sewn
and printed on acid-free paper
to library specifications

Printed in the United States of America

Board of Advisors

Contents

Foreword

THE FOURTH VOLUME OF THE *Catalogue of Medieval and Renaissance Manuscripts in the Beinecke Rare Book and Manuscript Library of Yale University* is devoted to the items in the general collection with the shelf numbers MS 481, 482, 483, 484, and 485, each a discrete collection of manuscript fragments. The second volume of the Beinecke catalogue, where one might have expected to find the items described here, reports: "MSS 481–485. Five collections of fragments that will be published separately."[1] This is the promised publication.

This is not a catalogue of all of the Western medieval and Renaissance manuscript fragments in the Beinecke Library. Many individual fragments have separate shelf numbers and are described (or will be described) in the appropriate place in the Beinecke catalogues. Many other fragments are preserved in the bindings of printed books and manuscript codices; there is at present no listing of these. Nor is this a catalogue of all of the fragment *collections* in the Beinecke Library: the collection MS 3 is described in volume 1 of this series; MS 525, MS 712, and MS 748 will be included in the fifth volume; MS 785 and MS 804 in the sixth.

The fragment collections MS 481–485 were omitted from the second volume of the Beinecke catalogue for several reasons. First, describing the contents of these fragment collections required two hundred and eighty-five separate entries, a larger number of entries than are included in the second volume otherwise. Second, it became clear that full, descriptive cataloguing of fragments could be a more time-consuming process than the cataloguing of codices, in large part because of the difficulty of identifying the texts. The inclusion of the fragment collections in volume two would have more than doubled the size of that volume and substantially delayed its publication. Finally, it also became clear that, if the fragments were to be given full catalogue descriptions, the style of the entries ideally would be somewhat different from that used for describing codices. Our intentions and procedures are described below in the section labeled "Format of the Entries."

---

[1] Barbara A. Shailor, *Catalogue of the Medieval and Renaissance Manuscripts in the Beinecke Rare Book and Manuscript Library, Yale University*. Volume II: *MSS 251–500*, MRTS vol. 48 (Binghamton, NY, 1987), 459.

The production of this catalogue was from beginning to end a collaborative effort. Brief preliminary descriptions for some of the items were made by Cora Lutz, with the assistance of Barbara Shailor, beginning more than thirty years ago. To some extent, these descriptions were based on the ones provided by book dealers, especially H. P. Kraus, who in turn had the assistance of various scholars, notably Bernhard Bischoff. A plan to produce a full descriptive catalogue was made by Barbara Shailor in the course of her work on the second volume of the Beinecke catalogue. A template for the descriptions was produced by Shailor, with the assistance of Richard Rouse, and this served as the original basis for the descriptions here. The amount of information eventually included in the descriptions, however, far exceeds the original plan. To some extent, the order of presentation of the information has also been altered. The full-scale cataloguing of the collections was begun about 1990 by Robert Babcock, who is responsible for the final editing and form of this catalogue. Lisa Davis produced the original drafts of entries for MS 482, and Philip Rusche those for the other collections; he also made the transcriptions of incipits and rubrics from the manuscripts, added the information about punctuation, and described the display scripts and initials. Babcock assigned the dates and localizations. The identification of texts was done by all three of the authors, though Rusche alone identified most of the liturgical and homiletic texts.

Over the years, several graduate students at Yale have assisted in various ways with this catalogue, including researching and drafting individual descriptions or categories of descriptions. Among these (in chronological order) Nancy Seybold, Mark Rabuck, Laura Williams, Andrea Rossol Usami, and John Anderson deserve special notice. Williams contributed especially to the description of manuscripts for the Mass and produced the bibliography. Usami added the information on accents and hyphens and produced most of the indices. Anderson selected and organized the production of the plates. All three contributed countless hours to copy-editing and proofreading.

Special thanks are also owed to many other Yale students who enrolled in Babcock's graduate seminar in Latin Paleography. Their studies of many of these fragments, and especially the questions they raised about them, led to many improvements in the final descriptions. Other individuals who provided specific assistance are cited under the appropriate entries. We sincerely regret any omissions that may have occurred.

Introduction

THIS CATALOGUE IS DEVOTED TO THE description of fragments—single leaves, groups of leaves, or pieces of leaves—of medieval and Renaissance manuscripts written between the seventh and the sixteenth centuries in Western Europe. They are, for the most part, the battered remnants of otherwise lost books from the Middle Ages.

Paleographers have long recognized the importance of manuscript fragments for the study of medieval writing, especially in the earliest periods of the Middle Ages from which few complete codices survive. Manuscript fragments comprise a significant portion of the items described in such fundamental works as E. A. Lowe's *Codices Latini Antiquiores*, Bernhard Bischoff's *Die südostdeutschen Schreibschulen und Bibliotheken in der Karolingerzeit*, and Klaus Gamber's *Codices Latini Liturgici Antiquiores*. Scholarly articles and monographs devoted to individual fragments or groups of fragments are legion. One thinks especially of the pioneering studies of palimpsests by Alban Dold,[2] and of Neil Ker's seminal monographs on manuscript fragments from St. Augustine's, Canterbury, and from Oxford.[3]

Manuscript fragments have also played an important role in literary history. The *Ruodlieb*, a chivalric epic of the eleventh century that is one of the most widely studied works of medieval Latin literature, was reconstructed from the fragments of a manuscript that was dismembered by a fifteenth-century bookbinder at the abbey of Tegernsee.[4] The leaves of an important manuscript of a fourteenth-century commentary on Dante were used in the eighteenth century to bind archival

---

[2] A bibliography of Dold's studies is found in *Colligere Fragmenta. Festschrift Alban Dold zum 70. Geburtstag*, ed. Bonifatius Fischer and Virgil Fiala (Beuron, 1955).

[3] N. R. Ker, "The Migration of Manuscripts from the English Medieval Libraries," *The Library*, ser. 4, 23 (1943): 6ff.; idem, *Fragments of Medieval Manuscripts Used as Pastedowns in Oxford Bindings, with a Survey of Oxford Bindings, c. 1515–1620*, Oxford Bibliographical Society Publications, n.s. 5 (Oxford, 1954). Among the more interesting recent publications, one might cite the collection of essays on manuscript fragments published as *Fragmenta Darmstadiensia*, ed. Walter Berschin and Kurt Hans Staub (Darmstadt, 1997).

[4] A concise account of the history of the text of *Ruodlieb* is given by Benedikt Konrad Vollmann, *Ruodlieb*, Erträge der Forschung 283 (Darmstadt, 1993), 3–8.

registers. The manuscript was recently reconstructed from fragments scattered be-tween Italy and North America.[5] New information about Boccaccio's early studies was gained by analyzing the dismembered leaves of a twelfth-century manuscript that he reused to make commonplace books in which he copied extracts from a variety of literary works as he read them.[6]

In spite of the importance of manuscript fragments in these and countless other studies, few catalogues devoted exclusively to fragments have been published.[7] We hope that this catalogue might encourage further work in this area.

The fragments described here bear little relation, in their appearance or in their history, to the illuminated leaves or cuttings commonly sold on the antiquarian book market as miniature works of art.[8] With few exceptions, we are not describing leaves that were removed from books in the modern period for decorative purposes. They are mostly derived from manuscripts that were dismembered already in the Middle Ages or Renaissance because they were worn out or because their texts were outdated. Most of them were recycled by bookbinders and survived into the twentieth century as flyleaves or pastedowns in fifteenth- or sixteenth-century bindings. They were removed from these bindings in the twentieth century[9] and collected for their script or their text. They are rarely of interest for their artistic merit. But they have considerable value for the study of Latin paleography and codicology, as well as for the history of the book, the history of libraries, the trans-mission of texts, and medieval liturgy and music.

Almost all of the fragments included in this catalogue are in Latin, though there are a few items in Middle High German and in Hebrew. The two larger groups of fragments described here (MS 481 and MS 482) were assembled originally as a paleographical collection documenting a wide range of Latin bookscripts used dur-ing the Middle Ages and Renaissance. They serve that purpose admirably well. In-cluded are specimens in Uncial, Visigothic, Merovingian, Beneventan, and human-ist scripts, as well as numerous examples of Caroline minuscule and Gothic book

---

[5] Fabrizio Franceschini, _Dante, il Buti e gli Appiani. Un codice tra Piombino, Piacenza e il Massachusetts_ (Pisa, 1998).

[6] Virginia Brown, "Boccaccio in Naples: The Beneventan Liturgical Palimpsest of the Laurentian Autographs (MSS. 29.8 and 33.31)," _Italia Medioevale e Umanistica_ 34 (1991): 41–126.

[7] A rare exception is Ambros Kocher, _Mittelalterliche Handschriften aus dem Staatsarchiv Solothurn_, Veröffentlichungen des Solothurner Staatsarchivs 7 (Solothurn, 1974).

[8] This is not true of items in MSS 483 and 485. The collecting of manuscript miniatures is the subject of the introductory essay by William Voelkle and Roger Wieck in _The Bernard H. Breslauer Collection of Manuscript Illuminations_ (New York, 1992), 13–16.

[9] It cannot be stressed strongly enough how destructive it is to remove and alienate fragments from bindings. In addition to destroying the integrity of the bindings, the removal of fragments obliterates the most important available information on their provenance.

hands, with a particular richness in eleventh- and twelfth-century manuscripts from Southern Germany.

Several items are of unusual codicological interest, including a seventh-century leaf containing the Gospel of Luke written *per cola et commata* (481.1); several leaves of Notker Balbulus's sequences, with the musical notation written in the margins instead of above the text (481.39); and a Pilgrim's Guide to Jerusalem, which may have originally been rolled or folded for transport as an amulet (481.77).

The fragments described in this catalogue are almost all derived from books,[10] and they provide a good selection of the most common types of books produced in the Middle Ages. There are manuscripts of biblical texts (with and without glosses), classical and patristic authors, exegetical treatises, sermons, liturgical works, monastic rules, medieval encyclopedias, legal works, scholastic treatises, schoolbooks, grammatical works, medieval chronicles, calendars, and medieval poetry. Classical authors are represented by manuscripts of Vergil and Cicero; the Greek fathers by Basil and Origen (in Latin translation); the Latin fathers by Augustine, Jerome, and Gregory. Medieval writers include Isidore, Bede, Paul the Deacon, Notker Balbulus, Bern of Reichenau, and Thomas Aquinas; and on the secular side, Boethius, Priscian, Wirnt von Gravenburg, Eberhard of Béthune, and Ludolphus de Luco. There are numerous liturgical manuscripts, many of them with early examples of musical notation, including a substantial portion of an eleventh-century breviary (481.25); sequentiaries with works by Notker Balbulus and Gottschalk (481.39 and 481.40); and seventeen leaves of a twelfth-century antiphonary from Lambach that shed new light on the performance there of a Magi play (481.51).[11]

Manuscripts written in Italy, Spain, France, England, Germany, Switzerland, Austria, and the Low Countries are represented. A few items can be attributed to specific writing centers, including scriptoria in Luxeuil, Rheims, Tours, Freising, Fulda, Schaffhausen, Lambach, Kremsmünster, and Melk. The complete manuscripts from which these fragments derive were preserved in the Middle Ages in libraries in Tours, Fulda, Lambach, Kremsmünster, Melk, Klosterneuberg, and Brixen, and provide new evidence about the medieval collections of these libraries.

Some of the fragments described here preserve texts of uncommon interest. An example already cited is the apparently unique Pilgrim's Guide to Jerusalem. Other rarities include a leaf from a pre-Vulgate Latin translation of Judges; one from the *Ars Laureshamensis*, an uncommon medieval grammatical treatise; and one from a portion of Dynus de Mugello's *Super Infortiato* that, so far as we know, is not attested elsewhere. Some of the fragments are among the earliest surviving witnesses

---

[10] Excepting the aforementioned Pilgrim's Guide and a few documents in MSS 481 and 482; these are not fragments at all, but complete single-sheet texts, presumably included in the collections by Zinniker as examples of notarial scripts.

[11] On the Lambach Antiphonary, cf. Davis, *Epiphany*.

to the texts they bear; included in this group are the leaves from Origen's *Peri archon* (481.7), from the *Vitae* of Sts. Ulrich and Afra by Bern of Reichenau (481.23), from the *Liber Constitutionum Sororum Ordinis Praedicatorum* of Humbert of Romans (482.91), from Leonardo Bruni's Latin translation of Aristotle's *Nicomachean Ethics* (481.123), and from a Ps.-Augustinian Christmas sermon (481.2).

This catalogue is intended to make available to a wide range of scholars some of the paleographical treasures of the Beinecke collection. We hope that it encourages further research on and publication of these manuscripts.

Format of the Entries

The description of each manuscript in the fragment collections MS 481—MS 485 follows, for the most part, the methodological considerations and explanations of format as presented in volume 1 of this series of Beinecke catalogues (pp. xix–xxi of the Introduction). But there are some changes as well. In some ways the descriptions here are longer than those for complete codices described in the previous Beinecke catalogues. Our guiding principle in making these descriptions was to present the researcher with as much information as possible that might help in identifying other surviving fragments from the same original manuscripts. It is our belief that every such leaf that can be identified will add to our knowledge of the original, and otherwise lost, medieval books from which these fragments derive. In particular, we hope that a leaf elsewhere might provide information about origin or provenance that is lacking in our leaf. To facilitate the identification of other fragments, we provide more extensive physical descriptions and a more detailed discussion of display scripts, minor initials, correcting hand(s), and punctuation than will be found in the descriptions in the first three volumes of the Beinecke catalogues. We have also added to each entry, where applicable, a section listing other fragments of the same manuscripts, to the extent that they are known to us. In some cases, we provide a more detailed description of contents than that found in the earlier volumes of this series. This is particularly true for the liturgical fragments, for which we identify, if possible, each piece of the Mass or divine office.

The descriptions in this volume differ from those in the previous Beinecke catalogues in other ways. The fragments are not bound, so there is no description of their bindings;[12] we rarely know much about provenance; and there is, in general, little or no bibliography—scholarship on these fragments having been limited by the fact that they were until now uncatalogued and largely unknown.

To facilitate the identification of related fragments elsewhere, we include for each manuscript a plate, reproducing it, unless otherwise specified, at life-size.

---

[12] But see below, paragraph 5: *Other Information.*

We have attempted to provide in every description a consistent selection of data. It might well be argued that some of these data (e.g., the placement of capitals, the type of punctuation, the characteristics of the display scripts) is of interest only for manuscripts from certain periods or places, and so should not have been included for others. It is also undoubtedly true that some of the fragments described here are more interesting than others, and it might be argued that the less interesting ones should have been only briefly described (or omitted altogether). But we decided not to allow our own prejudices, or those of our age, to determine which manuscripts are important and which are not, but rather to present, to the extent that we could, the same information in the same order for each fragment:

I. Heading

The first line of the heading of each entry consists of the **call number**, in bold type, on the left; and the known or probable place of origin along with the date, known or approximate, on the right. The presumed place of **origin**, typically assigned on the basis of paleographical criteria and hence open in many cases to debate, is normally given according to modern political boundaries, except that "Southern Germany" should be understood in a broad sense to include German-speaking areas adjacent to Bavaria, including parts of Switzerland, the Tyrol, and Austria. We do, however, frequently specify one or another of these regions when we feel that a particular manuscript can be more narrowly localized (so, e.g., we write "Southern Germany or Austria"). For the Italian manuscripts in Caroline script, an attribution to "Central Italy" should be understood to exclude the Beneventan zone. A more precise localization is given (e.g., a region, city or monastery) where possible. In most cases the **date** is based on paleographical criteria and is, consequently, often open to debate. Dates are given, in general, by century, in Roman numerals. The suprascript notations *in*, 1, *med*, 2, *ex* refer to the beginning, first half, middle, second half, and end of the century; suprascript notations like 2/3, 2/4, or 4/4 denote, respectively, the second third, the second quarter, or the fourth quarter of a century. XI–XII indicates a manuscript of either the eleventh or twelfth century, whereas s. XI/XII denotes the period around the turn of the century.

The second line provides, on the left, an **author** and/or short **title** (and, in parentheses, the language if it is not Latin), and, on the right, a reference to the plates at the end of the volume. Our practice has been to describe, in the first instance, the author and/or title of the text actually contained on the leaf, rather than the author or title of the complete manuscript from which the fragment may derive. So, for instance, a passage from the Bible is described as a Bible, although the complete manuscript from which the leaf derives may not have been a Bible, but a lectionary, breviary, missal, or even a homiletic, exegetical or other work in which the biblical passage was quoted. Names of biblical books follow the Latin Vulgate. If we think the author/title given in the heading might not accurately reflect the contents of the entire volume from which the fragment derives, we indicate this in the body of the description. In the case of **sermons**, we generally supply not only the author or title of the sermon, but also the name of the compiler of the collection of sermons from which we suspect the fragment derives. So, for instance, a fragment containing only a sermon by St. Augustine will be labeled as such in the heading, but perhaps qualified by a suggestion that the leaf derives not from a manuscript devoted to Augustine's sermons, but from the homiliary of Paul the Deacon or that of Alan of Farfa. For **liturgical** fragments, we give the title (in English or Latin) of the type of liturgical book from which we believe the fragment derives. Especially in the case of small fragments, it is often difficult, sometimes impossible, to be absolutely certain about the contents of the original manuscript.

II. *Contents*

As a rule we record texts in the sequence in which they occur in the manuscript and cite the folio number for the beginning and conclusion of each article. Text identifications and bibliographical citations, when needed, follow immediately the incipits and explicits for an article. In the case of some texts, especially where we cannot be sure how they began or ended, a brief identification (and bibliographical citation, if appropriate) is given instead.

The description of contents is preceded in a few cases by comments that might assist in understanding the contents or nature of the complete manuscript from which the fragment derives.

The manuscripts are in **Latin** unless otherwise stated.

We began this catalogue, and had completed most of it, before electronic resources became available that would have greatly simplified the task of identifying texts. We were, however, able to benefit from some of these resources in the final stages of our work, especially the on-line *Cantus* databank and the CETEDOC and *Patrologia Latina* CD-ROMs. For many medieval texts, however, especially the exegetical, homiletic, liturgical, legal, and philosophical works of the thirteenth century and later, there are still very few electronic aids available. We were able, in the end, to identify most of the texts on our fragments, but will be grateful for any information on the items that escaped us or for corrections to our identifications.

Rubrics and headings written in display script are here printed in italics. Transcriptions of incipits and explicits attempt to retain the original orthography of the text; abbreviations and ligatures are expanded silently. Our practice with abbreviations has been to expand them into the classical Latin spelling (e.g., *quaesumus, praestans*), even though we reproduce the orthography of the manuscripts when these same words are written out in the manuscripts. For rubrics in liturgical manuscripts, our guides have been the *Cantus* online database, CAO, and the modern Roman missal. In general, the original orthography of the manuscript has been maintained when words in the rubrics are written in full in the manuscript; when the words are abbreviated in the manuscript, we have generally standardized the abbreviations following the practices in the above-cited sources. We have followed the *Cantus* online database in using V. for verses and *v.* for versicles; abbreviations of *antiphona* that include, in whatever form, a single *a* have been uniformly transcribed as A.; various abbreviations for *psalmus* have been condensed into Ps.; the abbreviation *Ad B. A.* (*Ad "Benedictus" Antiphona*), when used in the manuscripts, appears for *in ev. A.* for lauds; abbreviations for *dominica* and *feria* have been silently expanded. The abbreviations for *uitatorium* (alternative form of *inuitatorium*) *vit.* and *vitor.* have been retained as in the manuscripts.

Parallel oblique lines "//" indicate that the text begins or ends imperfectly. Square brackets "[ ]" denote editorial intervention or problems of interpretation (e.g., [?]), as well as physical losses within the manuscript. The use of [*sic*] is restricted to readings that may appear peculiar to the modern reader but which do, in fact, appear in the text.

III. *Physical Description*

The physical description of each leaf or group of leaves appears next; the information is usually recorded in the following order:

a. **Material** on which a manuscript is written. A description of the quality of the parchment or its physical condition and defects may follow in parentheses. Next follows the **number of leaves** and foliation (when present), or information about the position of a leaf within its original quire. The numbering of the leaves in the descriptions reflects our best guess at the *order* of the leaves in the original manuscript, *not* the original numbering of the leaves within that manuscript.

b. The **dimensions** of the folio(s)—the height and width, respectively, in millimeters—occur next. It should be noted that the dimensions of the surviving fragment are recorded here, not the original dimensions of the complete leaf nor those of the book from which the fragment comes. In a few cases, where it is possible to estimate with some degree of certainty the original dimensions of the leaf, we record this estimation immediately following the actual current dimensions. The dimensions of the **written space** on the surviving fragment follow in parentheses. For fragments smaller than a complete leaf, we include also an estimate of the original dimensions of the written space, when it is possible to do so with some degree of certainty.

c. Next appears the number of **columns** and of **lines**; for partial leaves we also include, where possible, the estimated number of lines of the original. Aspects of the physical arrangement of the page are described next: **ruling**, bounding lines (rulings that delineate the written space), the instruments or materials used for ruling (dry-point, crayon, lead, ink), and prickings.

IV. *Scribes, Scripts*

An identification of the principal script (or scripts) found on the fragment is followed by a date and localization of the writing, usually based on paleographical criteria. The display scripts are described next, then the initials and other *litterae notabiliores*. The description specifies the scripts used for display purposes or *litterae notabiliores* and the size of the letters, as well as the colors and style of **decoration**, where present. Since many of the manuscripts described here are from the twelfth century, we frequently confronted the problem of whether to call a particular script "late Caroline" or "early Gothic". In general, we have labeled a script Gothic if it combined an organized baseline with the gabling of curved strokes and the fusion of adjacent round letters. Undoubtedly some scholars will disagree with our labeling of some scripts, but the plates will make up for any confusion about our terminology. The **nomenclature** for the various types of Gothic scripts was supplied by Albert Derolez, following, essentially, the system of G. I. Lieftinck, "Pour une nomenclature de l'écriture de la période dite gothique," in *Nomenclature des écritures livresques du IXe au XVIe siècle*, ed. B. Bischoff, G. I. Lieftinck, and G. Battelli (Paris, 1954).

Next follows a description of the **punctuation** present on the leaf, for which we have adopted the terminology of M. B. Parkes, *Pause and Effect: An Introduction to the History of Punctuation in the West* (Aldershot, 1992). We also note here the presence of accent or inflexion marks, and of hyphens. For punctuation marks, accent marks, and hyphenation, we generally record our impression of whether it is in the same ink or a different ink from that of the text. Corrections on the manuscript and other later marginalia or inscriptions may be described next.

V. *Other Information*

The next paragraph provides other information about the fragment or the manuscript from which it derives. This might include, in the case of **fragments recovered from bindings**, information about the way the fragment appears to have been used in the binding (e.g., as a flyleaf, pastedown, wrapper, etc.), and any data we can extract from the fragment about the binding, such as its size, the presence of inscriptions on it, etc. We also include in this section, to the extent that the information is known to us, a list of **other fragments from the same original manuscript**, recording their location and, often, their contents, especially where the latter is crucial for understanding the contents of our leaves.

VI. *Modern Inscriptions*

The following paragraph records modern notes and inscriptions. We include these because they provide information about the more recent provenance of the fragments, though we rarely know who the writers of these notes were or what their original significance might have been.

VII. *Provenance*

The provenance, to the extent to which it is known to us, comes next, except that the information about provenance provided in the following paragraphs is not repeated in every entry.

MS 481 and MS 482 are separate portions of a fragment collection compiled by the Rev. Franz-Josef Zinniker of Lucerne, Switzerland. Zinniker's collection was acquired by the firm of H.P. Kraus in New York City in the early 1960s. Kraus divided the Zinniker collection into two large groups (and also dispersed a few leaves separately; see e.g., the description of MS 481.25). The group that became MS 481 was acquired for the Beinecke Library by Edwin J. Beinecke in 1965. Mr. Kraus gave the remainder of the Zinniker collection to the Beinecke Library the same year, and it became MS 482. In many cases, different leaves from the same original manuscript were divided between the two groups (or under separate numbers within the same group). We have reunited these under a single shelf number and a single entry. Unfortunately, almost nothing is known about the sources from which Zinniker acquired his fragments, though it is likely that he acquired many of them from the firm L'Art Ancien. An employee of this firm named Frauendorfer, who was involved in the firm's acquisition of manuscripts and early printed books from Lambach Abbey (Upper Austria) in the 1950s, resided in Lucerne.[13] Some of the Lambach items in the Zinniker collection were among those that passed through Frauendorfer's hands. A detailed study of the dispersal of Lambach manuscripts and printed books in the twentieth century remains to be written; it would undoubtedly shed some light on Zinniker's sources. At least one of Zinniker's fragments, MS 481.72, was earlier in a catalogue of the Leiden dealer Eric von Scherling (whether Zinniker acquired it directly from von Scherling or through an intermediary is not known to us). For each of the fragments in MS 481 and MS 482, Zinniker's shelf number(s) is given, as is any earlier shelf number assigned by the Beinecke Library. Where we have been able to discover any earlier provenance, this is recorded as well.

MS 483 was the gift of Henrietta C. Bartlett to the Yale University Library in 1954. The leaves were listed and numbered in DeRicci's *Census*, and we have retained the DeRicci numbering.

The leaves in **MS 484** were acquired by the Yale University Library Associates and by individual friends of the Yale University Library around 1947 from the firm

---

[13] On the Zinniker fragments from Lambach, cf. Babcock, *Reconstructing a Medieval Library*.

of H. P. Kraus, which offered them for sale in its *List 109*. The donors of the individual leaves are listed in each description.

VIII. *Bibliography*

The bibliography section records publications known to us where our manuscript is mentioned, but this listing does not repeat bibliography already cited in the description, nor does it include general bibliography related to the catalogue description. The latter (e.g., printed versions of the texts cited, information on the author, title, or other general aspects of the manuscript, script, or text) is found within the body of each description if it seemed to us essential for understanding the entry. A bibliography and list of the abbreviations used in bibliographic citations follows the introduction to this catalogue.

Indices

Multiple indices (1–7) provide access to information in the descriptions:

1. MSS arranged by country (or region) of origin and by century.

2. Dated MSS.

3. General Index: persons, places, authors, etc. Works by a known author are listed under the author's name. Anonymous works are listed by title.

4. Illuminators and Scribes.

5. Provenance: individuals and institutions that previously owned the manuscripts.

6. Other MSS cited.

7. Incipits: there are separate indices for liturgical and non-liturgical (excepting biblical) texts.

Plates

Each manuscript is illustrated with a plate, normally showing only a small portion of the fragment, at actual size (unless otherwise specified). Additional illustrations will be available soon by Internet through the home page of the Beinecke Library. The plates are arranged in the order of the catalogue entries.

Acknowledgments

WE ARE GRATEFUL TO MANY INDIVIDUALS for their continuing help and support during this long project. Our greatest debt is to the members of our Board of Advisors, who offered invaluable assistance in many ways. In particular we are grateful to Albert Derolez for supplying the nomenclature for Gothic scripts, for proofreading the transcriptions, and for advising on the date and localization of manuscripts from France and the Low Countries (he also heroically read through drafts of all of the descriptions, preventing us from making untold errors); to Alois Haidinger for providing expertise on the manuscripts of German and Austrian origin, and in particular for identifying the provenance of many of the Austrian fragments; to Paola Supino Martini for providing expertise on the Italian fragments, and especially on the Italian documents; and to James Grier for advising us on the descriptions for the musical and other liturgical fragments.

In addition to the members of the Advisory Board, many other scholars have shared their expertise with us, either during visits to the Library or through personal correspondence. First among these must be mentioned Professor Hartmut Hoffmann of Göttingen, who generously provided information on many of the fragments. His attributions of date and origin will be found in many of the descriptions. We are also indebted for their assistance to: Bernhard Bischoff (whose opinions about the ninth-century fragments are cited in the appropriate descriptions), David Brafman (for information about the fragments that passed through the firm of H. P. Kraus), Virginia Brown, Walter Cahn, Margot Fassler, Hugh Feiss, Kurt Holter, Maija Jansson, Ivan Marcus (who described the Hebrew fragments), Alfred Mueller (who coordinated the photographic work), Timothy Noone, Richard Rouse (who originally drafted the template we have used for the entries), Rega Wood, and Craig Wright.

Ralph Franklin, the director of the Beinecke Library, provided encouragement to this project for many years, as well as the financial support that allowed Lisa Davis, Philip Rusche, and the graduate students listed above (p. x) to contribute to this project.

Bibliography & Abbreviations

Acta Sanctorum	*Acta sanctorum quotquot toto orbe coluntur . . . editio novissima,* curante Joanne Carnandet (Paris, 1863–1940).
AH	*Analecta hymnica medii aevi* (Leipzig, 1886–1922).
Babcock, *Reconstructing a Medieval Library*	Robert G. Babcock, *Reconstructing a Medieval Library: Fragments from Lambach* (New Haven, 1993).
Barré, "Mondsee"	H. Barré, "L'Homéliaire carolingien de Mondsee," *Revue Bénédictine* 71 (1961): 71–107.
Barré, *Homéliaires*	H. Barré, *Les Homéliaires carolingiens de l'école carolingien d'Auxerre,* Studi e testi 225 (Vatican City, 1962).
BHL	*Bibliotheca hagiographica latina,* ediderunt Socii Bollandiani.
Bischoff, *Schreibschulen*	Bernhard Bischoff, *Die südostdeutschen Schreibschulen und Bibliotheken in der Karolingerzeit,* 2 vols. (Wiesbaden, 1960–1980).
B.N.	Bibliothèque Nationale.
Bourque	Emmanuel Bourque, *Étude sur les sacramentaires Romains,* Studi di antichità cristiana 20 and 25 (Rome, 1948 and 1958).
Bruylants	Placide Bruylants, *Les Oraisons du missel Romain,* 2 vols. (Louvain, 1952).
CAO	*Corpus Antiphonalium Officii,* ed. Renatus-Johannes Hesbert, 6 vols. (Rome, 1963).
CCCM	Corpus christianorum: Continuatio mediaevalis (Turnhout).
CLA	E. A. Lowe, *Codices Latini Antiquiores* (Oxford, 1934–72).

CLLA	Klaus Gamber, *Codices Liturgici Latini Antiquiores* (Freiburg, 1968).
CPL	*Clavis patrum latinorum*, ed. E. Dekkers, 3rd edition (Steenbrugge, 1995).
CSEL	Corpus scriptorum ecclesiasticorum latinorum.
CCSL	Corpus christianorum: Series latina (Turnhout).
Davis, *Epiphany*	Lisa Fagin Davis, *Epiphany at Lambach: The Evidence of the Gottschalk Antiphonary*, Ph.D. dissertation, Yale University, 1993.
De Ricci	S. De Ricci, *Census of Medieval and Renaissance Manuscripts in the United States and Canada* (New York, 1935–40).
Deshusses (1982–83)	Jean Deshusses and Benoit Darragon, *Concordances et tableaux pour l'étude des grands sacramentaires* (Fribourg, 1982–83).
Deshusses (1988)	Jean Deshusses, *Le Sacramentaire Grégorien: ses principales formes d'après les plus anciens manuscrits* (Fribourg, 1988).
Dold, *Palimpsest-Studien*	Alban Dold, *Palimpsest-Studien II: altertümliche Sakramentar- und Litanei-Fragmente im Cod. Lat. Monac. 6333*, Texte und Arbeiten 48 (Hohenzollern, 1957).
Dold, *Monza*	Alban Dold and Klaus Gamber, *Das Sakramentar von Monza* (Hohenzollern, 1957).
Dold, *Salzburg*	Alban Dold and Klaus Gamber, *Das Sakramentar von Salzburg* (Hohenzollern, 1960).
Faye and Bond	C. U. Faye, *Supplement to the Census of Medieval and Renaissance Manuscripts in the United States and Canada*, continued and edited by W. H. Bond (New York, 1962).
Gamber, *Sakramentartypen*	Klaus Gamber, *Sakramentartypen*, Texte und Arbeiten 49–50 (Hohenzollern, 1959).
Gamber, *Sakramentar-Pontifikale*	Klaus Gamber and Sieghild Rehle, *Das Sakramentar-Pontifikale des Bischofs Wolfgang von Regensburg (Verona, Bibl. Cap., Cod. LXXXVII)* (Regensburg, 1985).
Gazette	*Yale University Library Gazette.*

Gerbertus   Martinus Gerbertus, *Monumenta veteris liturgiae aleman-*
                     nicae (St. Blasien, 1777).

GKW   *Gesamtkatalog der Wiegendrucke* (1925–).

Grégoire   Reginald Grégoire, *Homéliaires liturgiques médiévaux.*
                     Analyse de manuscrits (Spoleto, 1980).

Grotefend   Hermann Grotefend, *Zeitrechnung des deutschen Mittel-*
                     alters und der Neuzeit (Hannover, 1891–98).

Hain   L. F. T. Hain, *Repertorium bibliographicum . . . ab arte*
                     typographicum inventa usque ad annum MD (Stuttgart,
                     1826–38).

Hänggi   Anton Hänggi, *Der Rheinauer Liber Ordinarius (Zürich*
                     Rh. 80 Anfang 12. Jh.) (Freiburg, 1957).

HC   Walter Copinger, *Supplement to Hain's Repertorium bib-*
                     liographicum (London, 1895–1902).

Holter (1989)   Kurt Holter, "Mittelalterliche Buchkunst in Lambach,"
                     198–226 and "Das mittelalterliche Buchwesen des
                     Benediktinerstiftes Lambach," 53–64 in *900 Jahre Klos-*
                     terkirche Lambach (Linz, 1989).

Holter (1959)   Kurt Holter, "Die Handschriften und Inkunabeln,"
                     213–70 in *Die Kunstdenkmäler des Gerichtsbezirkes Lam-*
                     bach, Österreichische Kunsttopographie 34 (Vienna,
                     1959).

Holter (1957)   Kurt Holter, "Zu einem Verzeichnis der frühmittelal-
                     terlichen Handschriften," 434–42 in *Karolingische und*
                     Ottonische Kunst: Werden, Wesen, Wirkung, ed. Her-
                     mann Aubin et al. (Wiesbaden, 1957).

Holter (1956)   Kurt Holter, "Zwei Lambacher Bibliotheks-verzeich-
                     nisse des 13. Jahrhunderts," *Mitteilungen des Instituts für*
                     Österreichische Geschichtsforschung 64 (1956): 262–76.

Hürlimann   Gebhard Hürlimann, *Das Rheinauer Rituale (Zürich Rh.*
                     14 Anfang 12. Jh) (Freiburg, 1959).

Keil   Heinrich Keil, ed., *Grammatici latini* (Leipzig, 1855–).
                     [All references are to vol. 2.]

Kraus, *List no. 109* H. P. Kraus, Inc., *List no. 109, Monuments of Palaeogra-*
                     phy (New York, [1947]).

Liber Usualis	*Liber usualis*, ed. Benedictines of Solesmes (Tournai and New York, 1962).
Mai	Angelo Mai, ed., *Novae Patrum Bibliothecae* (Rome, 1852–). [All references are to vol. 1.]
MBKÖ	*Mittelalterliche Bibliothekskataloge Österreichs*, ed. T. Gottlieb et al. (Vienna, 1915–).
MGH	Monumenta Germaniae Historica.
Missale Romanum	*Missale Romanum Mediolani 1474*, ed. R. Lippe, Henry Bradshaw Society 17 and 33 (London, 1899, 1907).
Mohlberg	Kunibert Mohlberg, *Das fränkische Sacramentarium Gelasianum in alamannischer Überlieferung (Codex Sangall. no. 348)*, St. Galler Sakramentar-Forschungen 1 (Münster, 1971).
Mombritius	Boninus Mombritius, *Sanctuarium seu Vitae Sanctorum* (Paris, 1910–). [All references are to vol. 2.]
OCT	Oxford Classical Texts.
Parkes	M. B. Parkes, *Pause and Effect: An Introduction to the History of Punctuation in the West* (Cambridge, 1992).
PL	*Patrologiae cursus completus, series latina*, accurante J.-P. Migne.
PLS	*Patrologiae cursus completus, series latina*, accurante J.-P. Migne. Supplement.
RH	U. Chevalier, *Repertorium hymnologicum* vols. 1–4 (Louvain, 1892–1921); vols. 5–6 (Brussels, 1920–21).
Richter	Gregor Richter, Albert Schönfelder, *Sacramentarium Fuldense saeculi X* (Fulda, 1912).
Sacramentorum Gellonensis	*Liber sacramentorum Gellonensis*, ed. A. Dumas, CCSL 159, 159A (Turnhout, 1981).
Sarum Missal	J. W. Legg, *The Sarum Missal, edited from three early manuscripts* (Oxford, 1916).
Schaller-Könsgen	Dieter Schaller and Ewald Könsgen, *Initia carminum Latinorum saeculo undecimo antiquiorum* (Göttingen, 1977).

Shailor, *The Medieval Book*	Barbara A. Shailor, *The Medieval Book* (New Haven, 1988; reprinted Toronto, 1991).
Stegmüller	Friedrich Stegmüller, *Repertorium biblicum medii aevi* (Madrid, 1950–).
Verfasserlexikon	Kurt Ruh et al., *Die deutsche Literatur des Mittelalters: Verfasserlexikon*[2] (Berlin, 1977–).
von den Steinen	W. von den Steinen, *Notker der Dichter und seine geistige Welt*, 2 vols. (Bern, 1948). All references are to the Editionsband.
Walther, *Initia*	H. Walther, *Initia carminum ac versuum medii aevi posterioris latinorum*, Carmina medii aevi posterioris latina i, 2nd ed. (Göttingen, 1969).
Walther, *Sprichwörter*	H. Walther, *Lateinische Sprichwörter und Sentenzen des Mittelalters*, Carmina medii aevi posterioris latina ii (Göttingen, 1963–86).

MSS 481–485

MS 481.1
Bible, Luke (Vulgate)

f. 1ra   //dicebat autem et . . . faciem terrae et cæ//[li]

Luke 12.54–56. The lower portion of the leaf is trimmed with loss of text.

f. 1rb   //dico tibi non . . . et respondens//

Luke 12.59–13.2. The lower portion of the leaf is trimmed with loss of text.

f. 1va   //homines habitantes . . . et uenit quaerens//

Luke 13.4–6. The lower portion of the leaf is trimmed with loss of text.

f. 1vb   //et mittam stercora . . . decem et octo//

Luke 13.8–11. The lower portion of the leaf is trimmed with loss of text.

Parchment. 1 folio. 110 x 216 mm (written space originally ca. 250 x 160 mm). 2 columns. 13 lines remaining of an original ca. 31 lines. Dry-point ruling on the hair side before folding; double vertical bounding lines surround each column.

Written in uncial script, with the minuscule form of *e*. Lowe dated the script to the late seventh century (CLA 7:16, no. **141, with plate of recto; Lowe saw the fragment while it was in the Zinniker collection in Lucerne). The initials are slightly enlarged and are written on the inner vertical bounding line; one initial "E" ("Erat"; Luke 13.10) is filled with orange. The Eusebian chapter and canon numbers are added in a lighter ink, but perhaps in the same hand, in the margins. The text is written *per cola et commata*, and is occasionally punctuated with a punctus, placed medially; a later hand has added a punctus versus after "Non" (Luke 13.5). Nomina sacra ("spm") are abbreviated.

Five other leaves from this manuscript were formerly in the collection of Sir Thomas Phillipps, MS 1329, 1–10 (CLA 2:7, no. 141). Lowe reports the dimensions of the complete leaves formerly in the Phillipps collection as 290 x 215 mm (240 x 160 mm) and the number of lines as 31, and the contents as portions of Matthew, Mark, and John.

Modern notations in pencil identify the text on the recto and verso. The number "IX" is also written in pencil in the upper margin of the recto.

Zinniker 203. The number "3" is written in ink in the upper margin of the recto.

Bibliography:
Shailor, *The Medieval Book*, 25, no. 25 (with plate).

MS 481.2   Luxeuil, France, s. VIII[in]
Pseudo-Augustine, Sermon 190 (from a Homiliary)   Pl. 2

f. 1   [Inc: Dominus noster Iesus qui erat apud patrem antequam natus esset ...] //creauit utrumque sexum etiam nascendo . . . ad praesepe accedamus//

Pseudo-Augustine, Sermon 190 (Christmas); B. M. Peebles, "St. Augustine, Sermo 190: The Newberry-Yale Text," in *Corona gratiarum, miscellanea patristica, historica et liturgica Eligio Dekkers, O.S.B.* (Brugge, 1975), 339–51, here 346.82–348.153. The sermon, a reworking of Augustine's Sermon 190 (PL 38.1007–9), is also preserved in Chicago, Newberry Library, MS 1, art. 16 (Southwestern France, s. XI[1], formerly Sir Thomas Phillipps MS 1326); see P. Saenger, *A Catalogue of the Pre-1500 Western Manuscript Books at the Newberry Library* (Chicago, 1989), 4, MS. 1, art. 16.

Parchment (recto is badly stained; the fragment is torn is several places, including the upper corner of the recto where a few letters of text are lost). 1 folio. 212 x 132 mm (written space 180 x 108 mm). 1 column. 20 lines, recto, and 21, verso. No visible ruling; if any was once present, the scribe did not observe it, for the number of lines on each side of the leaf, within the same written space, differs.

Written in Luxeuil minuscule which Lowe dated to the beginning of the eighth century (CLA 7:16, no. **173 with plate of verso; see also the description in P. Salmon, *Le lectionnaire de Luxeuil*, 2 vols. [Rome, 1944], 2:10–11 and pl. II). 1-line capitals are written in brown uncials and are not set apart from the text. There is only minimal word separation and no punctuation.

Fourteen other leaves from this manuscript survive: London, British Library, Add. MS 29972 (13 folios; CLA 2:16, no. 173) and Metz, Bibliothèque Municipale, Salis 140, 1 (1 folio; CLA 6:27, no. **173, where Lowe incorrectly reports that the leaf was destroyed in 1944). The manuscript was broken up before 17 September 1831, when a transcript of the London leaves was made that does not include the Metz or Yale leaves.

Lowe suggested that these fragments may have been part of the manuscript now in New York, Pierpont Morgan Library, MS 17 (plate in CLA 11:23, no. 1658 and in Salmon, pl. III). They are of similar size, format and content and seem to be written by the same scribe (see also Etaix, 8–9).

A modern hand has written "VIII" (for "saec. VIII"?) in pencil in the upper margin of the recto.

Zinniker 201. The number "1" is written in ink in the upper margin of the recto.

Bibliography:

> Etaix, R., "Sermon pour l'Épiphanie tiré d'un Homiliaire en écriture de Luxeuil," *Revue Bénédictine* 81 (1971): 7–13.
>
> Grégoire, 51–53.
>
> Tribout de Morembert, M. H., "Le plus ancien manuscrit de Luxeuil (VIIᵉ siècle): les fragments de Metz et de Yale," *Mémoires de l'Académie Nationale de Metz*, 5th ser., vol. 14 (1969–71): 87–98.
>
> Shailor, *The Medieval Book*, 26, no. 26 (with plate).
>
> Xerox Corporation, *Ten Thousand Years of Recorded Information*. Exhibition Catalogue (Stamford, Conn., n.d.), 25.

MS 481.3
Basil of Caesarea, *Regula ad Monachos*

Northeastern Spain, s. IX/X
Pl. 3

f. 1   //uel male comedet [*sic*] maledicus est . . . huiusmodi autem necessitates//

Basil of Caesarea, *Regula ad Monachos* (translated into Latin by Rufinus of Aquileia), Interrogatio 41.1–42.6; K. Zelzer, ed., CSEL 86 (Vienna, 1986), 86–87; PL 103.513.

Parchment. 1 folio. 182 x 112 mm (written space 145 x 80 mm). 1 column. 18 lines. Dry-point ruling on the flesh side; single vertical bounding lines. Prickings in upper and outer margins.

Written in Visigothic minuscule, dated to the end of the ninth or begining of the tenth century by B. A. Shailor, "Corrections and Additions to the Catalogue of Visigothic Manuscripts," *Scriptorium* 32 (1978): 310–12. E. A. Lowe dated the script to the end of the ninth century in "Studia Palaeographica," *Sitzungsberichte der Königlichen Bayerischen Akademie der Wissenschaften*, Philosophisch-philologische und historische Klasse, Jahrgang 10, 12. Abhandlung (Munich, 1910): 1–87 (rpt. in idem, *Palaeographical Papers, 1907–1965*, ed. L. Bieler, 2 vols. [Oxford, 1972], 1:2–65, here 49). L. Delisle, *Mélanges de paléographie et de bibliographie* (Paris, 1880), 54, assigned it to the the beginning of the tenth century.

The 2-line initials of the interrogatio and the responsio are written in brown uncials with the sides of the "Q" and the ascender of the "D" filled with orange-red; they are not set apart from the text. 1-line initials are in brown uncials, with one use of a minuscule *e*, and are not set apart from the text. The chapter headings are written in a script with Visigothic and uncial (i.e., round *d*, uncial *a*) elements, slightly larger than the text script. Punctuation consists primarily of the punctus, placed medially, with a larger space indicating a major pause. There is occasional use of the punctus elevatus and a similar sign, consisting of a punctus with a wavy line above it (cf. A. Millares Carlo, *Tratado de paleografía española*, 3rd ed., 3 vols. [Madrid, 1983], 1:283). Word-spacing is irregular.

Fragments from the same manuscript are preserved as Paris, Bibliothèque Nationale, lat. 10876 and 10877, containing the Rules of Isidore and Fructuosus, and Tours, Bibliothèque Municipale, 615, containing the Rule of Basil. The manuscript was brought from Toulouse by the monks of the abbey of Marmoutier near Tours around the beginning of the eighteenth century (see Delisle, *Mélanges*, 54).

Zinniker 202. The number "2" is written in ink in the upper margin of both sides.

Bibliography:
Millares Carlo, A., *Tratado de paleografía española*, 3rd ed., 3 vols. (Madrid, 1983), 1:337, no. 251.
Shailor, *The Medieval Book*, 27, no. 27 (with plate).

MS 481.4   Northeastern France (Rheims?), s. IX^{in}
Bible, Esther (Vulgate)   Pl. 4

f. 1   //tempus [singularem per ordinem] puellarum ut intrarent . . . in unum
          Mardoche//[um]

          Esther 2.12–3.6. The upper margin has been trimmed with the loss of the
          first line and a portion of second line of text.

f. 2ra   [hieru]//salem cum iechonia rege . . . fons paruus [*corrected from:* paruos]//

Esther 11.4–10. The inner and upper margins have been trimmed with loss of text.

f. 2rb   [uel]//let, et fixum habebat . . . praecepitque ei//

Esther 11.12–12.5. The upper margin has been trimmed with loss of text.

f. 2va   [fu]//erant interfecti . . . nequaquam abuti//

Esther 12.6–13.2. The upper margin has been trimmed with loss of text.

f. 2vb   [consili]//ariis meis . . . turbare subiectaru//[m]

Esther 13.3–5. The inner and upper margins have been trimmed with loss of text.

Parchment. 2 folios (probably once formed the outer bifolium of a quire). Fol. 1 measures 264 x 226 mm; fol. 2 measures 200 x 210 mm (written space originally ca. 245 x 210 mm). 2 columns. Fol. 1 has 25 lines, and fol. 2 has 19 of an original 26 lines. Dry-point ruling on the flesh side; single vertical bounding lines. Prickings at corners of written space.

Written by several scribes in Caroline minuscule, dated by Bischoff to the beginning of the ninth century and attributed to northeastern France, perhaps Rheims (Bischoff, *Schreibschulen*, 2:40). 1-line capitals are written in brown uncials with occasional use of minuscule *e*, and are usually not set apart from the text. Part of chap. 12.6 and the beginning of chap. 13 are written in orange-red uncials with square capital forms of *A*, *E*, and *M* beside the uncial forms of *A* and *M* and round forms of *E*. Punctuation consists of the punctus, punctus elevatus, and virgule. Corrections have been added by contemporary hands, including superscript letters, erasures and the addition of cauda on *e*; punctuation has also been altered or added, including the introduction of the punctus versus. Word spacing is inconsistent.

Other fragments from this manuscript are preserved in Lambach, Stiftsbibliothek, Fragment 3 (3 folios). These leaves contain Esther 5.14–6.10 and 6.10–7.4; 9.12–19 and 9.20–27; 14.8–19 and 14.19–15.10 (see the descriptions in Bischoff, *Schreibschulen*, 2:40, and in Holter [1989], 211, cat. no. IX.06; the Kraus leaves described by Holter and Bischoff are now the Beinecke fragments).

Another leaf is preserved as a flyleaf in the back cover of Kremsmünster, Stiftsbibliothek, CC 246a (formerly Lambach Ccl 246; the manuscript is briefly described in Holter [1959], 262). This flyleaf is mentioned in the Hauswedell Catalogue, *Wertvolle Bücher des 15.–20. Jahrhunderts Autographen* Auction 56 (Hamburg, 5–6 May 1954), no. 1, which lists the contents of the flyleaf as the Vetus Latina version of Judith 13.31 and 14.7–8; the catalogue also records that an offprint from a pastedown contains Judith 13.31 and 14.12–14. That pastedown is now Hannover, Kestner-Museum, Inv. 3990 (Cul. I, 80), whose contents include the Vetus Latina version of Judith 13.31–14.6 and 14.11–14. Further fragments removed from Kremsmünster CC 246a are preserved at Kremsmünster (information kindly provided by Haucke Fill). A leaf containing Esther 8.10–9.12 was sold by Hartung & Hartung, Munich, Auktion 103 (6./7. November 2001) lot 39. This leaf was acquired by the Beinecke Library, where it is now MS 965.

The Lambach library catalogue in Lambach Cml XIX includes a manuscript containing the books of Tobias, Macchabees, Judith, Esther and Esdras (see Holter [1956], 274, no. 107 and MBKÖ, 5:57). Holter identifies this item as Lambach Cml LXI, a manuscript of the late twelfth or early thirteenth century. Because of its similar contents, it is possible that Cml LXI is a copy of the manuscript preserved in the Beinecke, Hannover, Kremsmünster and Lambach fragments. There is a brief description of Cml LXI, which is no longer at Lambach, in Holter (1959), 241.

Fol. 1 was formerly used as a flyleaf in the binding of Lambach, Stiftsbibliothek, Ccl 86 (the notation "86P" is written in pencil in the lower right corner of the recto). Fol. 2 was used as a flyleaf in Lambach Cml CXXVI (shelf number "126" written in the upper center of the verso; faded notation "126" in pencil in lower right margin of verso). It was briefly described while still in Lambach by Holter (1957), 440, no. 2b.

Fol. 1 was formerly Zinniker 265. Fol. 2 was formerly Beinecke MS 482.1B, Zinniker 60.

Bibliography:
Babcock, *Reconstructing a Medieval Library*, 8–7, 87, and fig. 45.

MS 481.5   Tours, France, s. IX$^{2/4}$
Bible, Job (Vulgate)   Pl. 5

f. 1ra   //Apud ipsum est . . . in lucem umbram//

           Job 12.16–22. The lower portion of the leaf has been trimmed with loss of text.

f. 1rb   //meus, et audiuit . . . ut pro illo lo//[quamini]

           Job 13.1–7. The lower portion of the leaf has been trimmed with loss of text.

f. 1va   [in]//ruet super uos . . . et enigmata//

Job 13.11–17. The lower portion of the leaf has been trimmed with loss of text.

f. 1vb   //et respondebo tibi . . . omnes semitas//

Job 13.22–27. The lower portion of the leaf has been trimmed with loss of text.

Parchment. 1 folio. 200 x 265 mm (written space originally ca. 265 x 197 mm). 2 columns. 16 lines remaining of an original ca. 25. Dry-point ruling on the flesh side; double vertical bounding lines surrounding both columns. Single horizontal bounding lines; additional, short horizontal ruling for running titles. Additional vertical ruling in outer margin.

Written in Caroline minuscule, which Bischoff dated to the second quarter of the ninth century and attributed to Tours (letter of 9 December 1985). 2-line initials are written in brown uncials, and are written between the vertical bounding lines when they occur at the beginning of a line. 1-line initials within text are in brown uncials. Running titles (Liber/Iob) are written in the upper center in brown rustic capitals. Punctuation consists of the punctus elevatus, punctus versus, and punctus interrogativus. A later hand has made some corrections and altered the punctuation.

The Roman numerals "iiii" and "v" appear with a cross in the margins next to Job 13.14 and 13.23, perhaps signifying lessons.

Zinniker 205. The number "5" is written in ink in the upper margin of both sides (erased on verso).

Bibliography:
Shailor, *The Medieval Book*, 70, no. 71 (with plate).
Ganz, David, "Mass Production of Early Medieval Manuscripts: The Carolingian Bibles from Tours," in *The Early Medieval Bible. Its Production, Decoration and Use*, ed. Richard Gameson (Cambridge, 1994), 53–62, here 60 (mentioned without shelf number).

MS 481.6   Northeastern France, s. IX$^{3/3}$
Bible, Prophets (Vulgate)   Pl. 6

f. 1   [ini]//quitatibus suis et . . . atrii interior//[is]

Ezechiel 43.10–17. The inner margin at the bottom of the leaf has been trimmed with loss of text.

f. 2ra   //in [lumbis eorum] et non accingentur in sudore ... emundatus, sep//[tem]

          Ezechiel 44.18–26. The upper and lower margins have been trimmed with loss of text.

f. 2rb   //offeret pro peccato ... sanctitatis uig//[inti]

          Ezechiel 44.27–45.4. The upper, lower, and outer margins have been trimmed with loss of text.

f. 2va   [uig]//inti gazofilacia ... et hae sunt//

          Ezechiel 45.5–13. The upper, lower, and outer margins have been trimmed with loss of text.

f. 2vb   [quo]//que olei, batus ... arietes in//[maculatos]

          Ezechiel 45.14–23. The upper and lower margins have been trimmed with loss of text.

f. 3ra   //regio et sicut ... conuocarentur harioli,//

          Daniel 1.13–2.2. The upper and lower margins have been trimmed with loss of text.

f. 3rb   //rex; Uidi somnium ... nec repperietur//

          Daniel 2.3–11. The upper, lower, and outer margins have been trimmed with loss of text.

f. 3va   //ut perirent omnes ... deus patrum meorum//

          Daniel 2.12–23. The upper, lower, and outer margins have been trimmed with loss of text.

f. 3vb   [ser]//mone[m] regis ... et ecce q[ua]si sta//[tua]

          Daniel 2.23–31. The upper and lower margins have been trimmed with loss of text.

f. 4   //et intuitus eius erat ... deos tuos non colimus//

          Daniel 2.31–3.18.

f. 5ra   //ut ligatis pedibus . . . quia in ueritate//

              Daniel 3.20–28. The upper and inner margins have been trimmed with
              loss of text.

f. 5rb   [uniuer]//sa quae fecisti . . . anima contrita e//[t]

              Daniel 3.31–39. The upper and outer margins have been trimmed with
              loss of text.

f. 5va   [n]//os, Sed fac nobis . . . benedicebant deum in for[nace dicen]tes//

              Daniel 3.41–51. The upper and outer margins have been trimmed with
              loss of text.

f. 5vb   //supergloriosus in saecula . . . ẹstus dominum, laudate et super//[exaltate]

              Daniel 3.53–66. The upper and inner margins have been trimmed with
              loss of text.

f. 6ra   //dominum laudate et superexaltate . . . hominum dominum laud//[ate]

              Daniel 3.68–82. The upper and lower margins have been trimmed with
              loss of text.

f. 6rb   [superexalta]//te eum in saecula . . . ignis. et nihil cor//[ruptionis]

              Daniel 3.85–92. The upper and lower margins have been trimmed with
              loss of text.

f. 6va   //misac et abednago de medio ignis . . . babylonis; Nabuchodonosor//

              Daniel 3.93–98. The upper and lower margins have been trimmed with
              loss of text.

f. 6vb   //et mirabilia eius . . . somniorum meorum//

              Daniel 3.100–4.6. The upper and lower margins have been trimmed with
              loss of text.

f. 7ra   [fac]//ta est, et sanctuarium . . . reges de gente//

Daniel 8.13–22. The upper and lower margins have been trimmed with loss of text.

f. 7rb　　//suam. et dirigetur . . . pactum et misericordiam//

Daniel 8.24–9.4. The upper and lower margins have been trimmed with loss of text.

f. 7va　　//prope sunt et his . . . ueritatem tuam//

Daniel 9.7–13. The upper and lower margins have been trimmed with loss of text.

f. 7vb　　//ira tua et furor tuus . . . quem uideram//

Daniel 9.16–21. The upper and lower margins have been trimmed with loss of text.

f. 8ra　　[septu]//aginta ebdomades adbreuiatæ . . . uerum uerbum//

Daniel 9.24–10.1. The upper and inner margins have been trimmed with loss of text.

f. 8rb　　//autem uicesima et . . . Intellege uerba//

Daniel 10.4–11. The upper and outer margins have been trimmed with loss of text.

f. 8va　　[uen]//i [added suprascript: propter] sermones . . . Cumque loqueretur//

Daniel 10.12–15. The upper and outer margins have been trimmed with loss of text.

f. 8vb　　//in scriptura ueritatis . . . ipsa et qui addu//[xerunt]

Daniel 10.21–11.6. The upper and inner margins have been trimmed with loss of text.

ff. 9r–10v　　[trans]//gressi sunt pactum . . . frustra erant in gal//[gal]

Hosea 6.7–12.11.

f. 11r   //fundauit. qui uocat ... dominus deus tuus.
          Explicit Amos Propheta

          Amos 9.6–15 (end).

f. 11r–v *Incipit Prologus Abdie Propheta*
          Abdias qui interpraetatur seruus ... sonat eloquio.

          Prologue to Abdias (from Jerome, *Epistola ad Paulinum*; PL 22.546); Steg-
          müller 516.

f. 11v   *Incipit Abdias Propheta*
          Visio Abdię. haec dicit ... Tu quoque eras quasi//

          Abdias 1–11.

f. 12r–v //super uos probiti sunt ... dicit dominus exercituum. Amen. Explicit.

          Aggeus 1.10–2.24 (end).

f. 12v   *Incipit Zacharias propheta*
          Zacharias memor domini sui multiplex ... sub iugalis. Explicit.

          Prologue to Zacharias (from Jerome, *Epistola ad Paulinum*; PL 22.547);
          Stegmüller 540.

ff. 12v–13 In mense octauo ... quę sunt iuxta duo//

          Zachariah 1.1–4.12. The upper right portion of fol. 13 has been torn with
          loss of text.

f. 14   [fac]//tum est uerbum ... et saluabit eos//

          Zachariah 8.1–9.16. The upper right corner of the leaf has been torn with
          loss of text.

f. 15   //Et erit qui offenderit ... exercituum in die illa.
          Explicit Zacharias Propheta.
          Incipit Prologus Malachię Prophetę.

          Zachariah 12.8–14.21 (end).

f. 16   //ita ut ultra non . . . terram anathemate.
          Explicit Malachias Propheta.

          Malachi 2.13–4.6 (end). The remainder of the verso (half of col. 1 and all
          of col. 2) is blank.

Parchment. 16 folios (fols. 2–3 and 5–8 are partial). The measurements of the fragments are as follows: fol. 1, 271 x 201 mm; fol. 2, 210 x 186 mm; fol. 3, 210 x 173
mm; fol. 4, 280 x 203 mm; fol. 5, 203 x 135 mm; fol. 6, 194 x 215 mm; fol. 7, 172
x 215 mm; fol. 8, 202 x 133 mm; fol. 9, 276 x 215 mm; fol. 10, 273 x 225 mm
(portion of conjugate leaf attached, measuring 264 x 17 mm); fol. 11, 274 x 225
mm; fol. 12, 279 x 205 mm; fol. 13, 278 x 223 mm; fol. 14, 274 x 203 mm; fol. 15,
272 x 199 mm; fol. 16, 271 x 205 mm (written space 223–230 x 173 mm; the horizontal text rulings are not consistently spaced). 2 columns. 31-32 lines. Dry-point
ruling on the hair side; single vertical and horizontal bounding lines. Pricking preserved in lower margins.
    Written in Caroline minuscule, which Bischoff has dated to the last third of the
ninth century (letter of 5 October 1985). 1-line initials are written in brown uncials, with occasional use of minuscule or rustic capital *E*, and are not set apart
from the text. The end of Daniel 3.23 (fol. 5r) is written in brown rustic capitals.
The end of Daniel 3.90 (fol. 6r) is written in orange-red rustic capitals, and the 2-
line initial "T" ("Tunc") of 3.91 is in orange-red. The rubric of the Prologue to Abdias (fol. 11r) is written in orange-red uncials, and the first six lines of the prologue
alternate in orange-red and brown uncials. The rubric and first three lines of the
text of Abdias (fol. 11v) are written in orange-red uncials. The entire prologue to
Zacharias (fol. 12v) is written in brown rustic capitals.
    Punctuation consists of the punctus, punctus elevatus, punctus versus, and
punctus interrogativus. A later hand has altered some of the punctuation. The text
scribe has added in the lower margins passages that were originally omitted, indicating the suppletions (at Daniel 3.3 and at Aggeus 2.9–10) with a tie mark " ˙/."
(fols. 4r and 12v). The numeral "viiii" appears in the margin next to Daniel 3.91
(fol. 6r), perhaps signifying a lesson.
    The quire signatures "v" (fol. 4v), "vi" (fol. 8v), and "vii" (fol. 10v) appear in
the center of the lower margin in the same ink as the text. The fragments preserve
portions of the last five quires of a ten-quire manuscript. Fols. 1 and 4 were the
outer bifolium of quire V; fols. 2 and 3 formed the second bifolium. Similarly, fols.
5 and 8 and fols. 6 and 7 formed the outer and the second bifolia of quire VI. Fols.
9 and 10 were the last two leaves in quire VII. Fol. 11 came near the end of quire
VIII or perhaps, since it does not bear a quire signature, the beginning of quire IX.
Fols. 12 and 13 formed the first two leaves of quire X; fol. 14 was the fourth, fol. 15
the sixth and fol. 16 the eighth leaf of quire X. The Beals fragment (see below) was
the the fifth and the Lambach fragment (see below) the seventh leaf of this quire.

Quires I–IV, now missing, would have contained the first forty-two chapters of Ezechiel.

Fols. 1 and 4 were formerly used in the binding of Lambach, Stiftsbibliothek, Ccl 113. Fols. 2, 3, 5 and 8 were used in the binding of Lambach Ccl 344. Fols. 6 and 7 were used in the binding of Lambach Ccl 256. Fols. 12, 15 and 16 were used in the binding of Lambach Ccl 185.

When these leaves were still in Lambach, they were seen by Holter who briefly described them in Holter (1957), 440–41, no. 2c (Beinecke fols. 2, 3, 5 and 8), no. 2d (Beinecke fols. 6 and 7), no. 2e (Beinecke fols. 12, 15 and 16), and fn. 14 (Beinecke fols. 1 and 4). Holter briefly described Lambach Ccl 113 and Ccl 344 in Holter (1959), 259 and 263, where he noted that the binding fragments were missing.

Fol. 9 was used as the flyleaf in the binding of a volume measuring ca. 275 x 205 mm. Fol. 10 was used as the flyleaf in the binding of a volume measuring ca. 275 x 225 mm, possibly Lambach Ccl 86. Holter records that a leaf bound in this volume had the quire signature "vii", 2 columns and 31 lines (see Holter [1957], 441, no. 2g); these details accurately describe fol. 10. Fols. 11, 13 and 14 were used as flyleaves in the binding of volumes measuring ca. 275 x 210 mm, but not necessarily the same volume.

Another leaf from the same manuscript, formerly owned by Walter B. Beals of Olympia, Washington (see De Ricci, 2:2188, no. 1), is listed as lot 3 in the Sotheby's Sale Catalogue for 14 July 1981. This leaf contains Zachariah 9.16–12.8 and fits between Beinecke fols. 14 and 15. The binding of Lambach Ccl 444 contains a leaf with the Prologue and text of Malachi that fits between Beinecke fols. 15 and 16 (Holter [1957], 441, no. 2f and Bischoff, *Schreibschulen*, II.40). Strips from this manuscript are in the binding of Lambach Ccl 87 (see Holter [1957], 441, no. 2h; he does not record what text they contain).

The Lambach library catalogue in Cml XIX includes the item "Prophetia nova et vetus" (Holter [1956], 274, nos. 100–1, and *MBKÖ*, 5:57). Holter identifies the "vetus" manuscript as "Fragm. s. IX"; these are now the Beinecke fragments; according to Holter, the "nova" manuscript refers to the manuscript that was formerly Lambach Cml XXII (see Sotheby's Sale Catalogue, 11–14 November 1929, lot 393).

Modern hands writing in pencil or in ink have written the textual identifications on several leaves. Another modern hand has written the following numbers in pencil in the lower right corner (recto or verso) of the leaves: fol. 1, "20"; fol. 2, no number; fol. 3, "23"; fol. 4, "12"; fol. 5, "24"; fol. 6, "27"; fol. 7, "22"; fol. 8, "25"; fol. 9, "18"; fol. 10, "14"; fol. 11, "28"; fol. 12, "15"; fol. 13, "13"; fol. 14, "19"; fol. 15, "16"; fol. 16, "17".

Fols. 1–5, 7–8, 10–11, 13 and 16 were formerly distinguished by the following letters in order: G, F, C, A, J, D, I, H, B, K, and E. Fols. 6, 9, 12, 14, and 15 were formerly Beinecke MS 482.5, distinguished by the following letters: E, B, D, A, and C. These leaves were formerly in the collection of Rev. Zinniker under the following numbers in order: 251, 250, 221, 121, 262, 66, 222, [no known number for fol. 8], 69, 260, 200, 86, 269, 68, 85, and 225.

Bibliography:
   Babcock, *Reconstructing a Medieval Library*, 87–88 and figs. 5 and 18.

MS 481.7   Fulda, Germany, s. IX$^{2/3}$
Origen, *Peri Archon (De principiis)*   Pl. 7

f. 1   //nihil prius geri quam anima . . . Uideamus quomodo etiam paulus apos-
           tolus ut potestatem//

           Origen, *Peri Archon* (translated into Latin by Rufinus of Aquileia), III.1.4–
           III.1.6; H. Görgemanns and H. Karpp, eds., *Origenes vier Bücher von den
           Prinzipien*, 2nd ed. (Darmstadt, 1985), 468–78; P. Koetschau, ed., *Origenes
           Werke*, vol. 5, *De principiis* (Leipzig, 1913), 198–203. The upper corner of
           the leaf is torn with loss of text.

Parchment (recto stained and covered with glue from use as a pastedown; the upper center and corner are torn). 1 folio. 270 x 187 mm (written space 205 x 167 mm). 1 column. 27 lines. Dry-point ruling on the hair side; text surrounded by double ruling lines.

   Written in Caroline minuscule by the same scribe who copied a manuscript of Sedulius Scotus's *Expositio in epistolam Hieronymi ad Damasum papam* now in Basel, Universitätsbibliothek, F V 33. See R. G. Babcock, *Gazette* 64 (1989/90): 83-85, rpt. in German in *Fuldaer Geschichtsblätter* 68 (1992): 156–59; Babcock, "Häresie und Bibliothek: Die Fuldaer Handschrift von Origenes' Περὶ ἀρχῶν," in *Kloster Fulda in der Welt der Karolinger und Ottonen*, ed. G. Schrimpf, Fuldaer Studien 7 (Frankfurt a.M., 1996), 277–90; and for the Sedulius manuscript, see Hartmut Hoffmann, *Buchkunst und Königtum im ottonischen und frühsalischen Reich*, 2 vols. (Stuttgart, 1986), 1:141 and 2: pl. 32. Hoffmann attributes the Sedulius manuscript to Fulda and suggests that it was written around 880. Bernhard Bischoff, in his *expertise* for H. P. Kraus Inc., attributed MS 481.7 to Northeast France.

   1-line capitals are in brown uncials, with occasional use of an enlarged minuscule *e*, and are written within the text. Punctuation is by *distinctiones*, here a twofold system in which a punctus is placed low (*subdistinctio*) for a minor pause or high (*distinctio*) for a major pause (see Parkes, 31–32); the scribe uses the same system in the Basel manuscript. Word-spacing is irregular. Corrections have been added in a late fourteenth- or early fifteenth-century hand.

   This leaf was used as a pastedown in the binding of a volume measuring ca. 270

x 187 mm. A modern hand has added a partially undeciphered annotation in pencil in the lower margin of the verso, ". . . Lor. 20.6.92."

Zinniker 107.

MS 481.8   Southeastern Germany, s. IX$^{1/3}$
South German Homiliary   Pl. 8

The sermons preserved here and in the Schøyen leaves (see below) are from a homiliary that circulated in southern Germany in the Carolingian period (see J.-P. Bouhot, "Un sermonnaire carolingien," *Revue d'Histoire des Textes* 4 [1974]: 181–223, and G. Folliet, "Deux nouveaux témoins du sermonnaire carolingien récemment reconstitué," *Revue des Études Augustiniennes* 23 [1977]: 155–98). They are found here in the same order as in Munich, Bayerische Staatsbibliothek, Clm 6310 (Freising, s. IX^1) where they are homilies 1–3 (see Bouhot, 209), and in Berlin, Preussische Staatsbibliothek, Hamilton 56 (s. XII; see Bouhot, 215–16 and Folliet, 178–79). Another copy of this homiliary is found in Beinecke MSS 482.4 and 484.2, both originally part of the same manuscript, also from Lambach.

f. 1r–v   [Inc: Saluator noster fratres carissimi natus de Patre . . .] //nulla utiliora possunt inueniri . . . feliciter ueniemus Praestante et auxiliante domino nostro iesu christo cui sit honor et gloria in saecula. Amen.

South German Homiliary, Homily I.1 (Circumcision, 1 January) = Caesarius, *Sermo* 191; G. Morin, ed., CCSL 104 (1953), 778–79.

f. 1v   Epiphaniam id est apparitionem domini saluatoris . . . omnium regum monstrauit//

South German Homiliary, Homily I.2 (Epiphany, 6 January) = Pseudo-Augustine, Sermon 140; Mai, 1:329; CPL 372. Antiphons and responses for the Circumcision and for Epiphany have been added in an early eleventh-century hand in the margins of both the Beinecke and the Schøyen leaves (see below).

Parchment (stained). 1 folio. 210 x 145 mm (written space 150 x 105 mm). 1 column. 13 lines. No visible ruling.

Written in Caroline minuscule, which Bernhard Bischoff dated to the first third of the ninth century (letter of 9 December 1985). The letters have been almost entirely retraced due to water damage, perhaps in the eleventh century when the antiphons and responses were added in the margins (another early manuscript from

Lambach with extensive water damage and retracing is Beinecke MS 481.21). 2-line initials are in brown uncials, some highlighted with red, and are set apart from the text. There are traces of red ink in the space between the two sermons, suggesting that there was once a rubric there. Punctuation consists of the punctus, punctus versus, and punctus elevatus.

A bifolium from the same manuscript is now in the collection of Martin Schøyen, London and Oslo (Bernard Quaritch, Ltd., *Bookhands of the Middle Ages: Part V* [London], catalogue 1147, item 73, pp. 60-62, with plate). The Schøyen bifolium contains the leaf preceding the Beinecke fragment and an earlier leaf with Pseudo-Augustine's Sermon 193 (On the feast of the Holy Innocents; Inc: "Tempore quo Dominus . . . "; Mai, 1:450–51).

The leaf was formerly used in the binding of a volume from the Lambach Stiftsbibliothek with the shelf number 312 (number "312" on recto). Although the measurements of MS 481.8 correspond with those of Lambach Ccl 312 (220 x 145 mm), Holter (1989), 213, cat. no. IX.17, notes that the flyleaf of Ccl 312 is from a Hebrew manuscript. The number "312" on MS 481.8 may therefore be an older Lambach number.

Zinniker 229.

Bibliography:
Babcock, *Reconstructing a Medieval Library*, 88 and 92, fig. 19.

MS 481.9   Southern France, s. IX^{ex}
Smaragdus, *Expositio in Regulam S. Benedicti*   Pl. 9

f. 1   //inuicem praeuenientes. spiritui feruentes . . . ut maiora praecepta patrum
            per omnia conseruetis.//

            Smaragdus, *Expositio in Regulam S. Benedicti*, chaps. 72–73; A. Spannagel,
            ed., Corpus Consuetudinum Monasticarum 8 (Siegburg, 1974), 334–36;
            PL 102.929–31.

Parchment (several holes and other imperfections which the scribe has written around). 1 folio. 260 x 165 mm (written space 223 x 125 mm). 1 column. 34 lines. Dry-point ruling on the hair side; double vertical and single horizontal bounding lines.

Written in Caroline minuscule, which Bernhard Bischoff has dated to the end of the ninth century (letter of 9 December 1985). 1-line capitals are in brown uncials, with occasional rustic capital forms, and are occasionally set apart from the text. The rubric of chap. 73 is written in bright orange rustic capitals with round *D*

and E. Quotations from the *Regula S. Benedicti* are written in bright orange minuscule. Punctuation consists of the punctus for minor pauses, punctus elevatus for
major pauses, punctus versus for completion of sententiae, and a set of three punctus, sometimes with a comma, to indicate the end of a section. Accents added by
a later hand. A sixteenth-century cursive hand has added biblical references in the
margins.

A modern hand has written the number "XII" in pencil in the upper margin of
the recto.

Zinniker 212. The number "11" is written in ink in the upper margin of the
recto.

MS 481.10   France, s. X[1]
Augustine, *In Iohannis Evangelium Tractatus cxxiv*   Pl. 10

The numbers given to the tractates in this manuscript are one less than those given
in the edition. This could be the result of error on the part of the scribe, but it
could also reflect the contents of the manuscript. Several manuscripts of the text
include Augustine's so-called Sermon 125 after Tractatus 17, and a number of
these omit Tractatus 18 and 19. The result of these changes would give the numbering found here; however, the manuscripts that include Sermon 125 almost
always include it as part of Tractatus 17, that is, without an extra number. See
David F. Wright, "The Manuscripts of St. Augustine's *Tractatus in Euangelium Iohannis*: A Preliminary Survey and Check-List," *Recherches augustiniennes* 8 (1972):
55–143. This fragment is not listed by Wright.

f. 1r–v   [Inc: De uerbis domini nostri iesu christi ubi ait . . .] //diei. propter
           infirmitatem nostram . . . sed cum ab inuicem recedimus. ab illo non
           recedamus;
           Explicit xxxiiii omelia

           Augustine, *In Iohannis Evangelium Tractatus cxxiv*, Tractatus 35.8–9 (on
           John 8.13–14); R. Willems, ed., CCSL 36 (1954), 321–23; PL 35.1661–
           62. CPL 278.

f. 1v   *Incipit xxxv^{ta}.*
           Ab eo quod dictum est, uos secundum carnem . . . qui misit me pater.
           Omelia
           In quatuor euangelii uel potius quatuor libris . . . in terra ambulabant;//

           Tractatus 36.1 (on John 8.15–18); Willems, 323; PL 35.1662.

Parchment. 1 folio. 355 x 255 mm (written space 275 x 200 mm). 2 columns. 33 lines. Dry-point ruling on the hair side; single vertical and double horizontal bounding lines. Additional vertical ruling between columns. Prickings in outer margins.

Written in Caroline minuscule, which Bernhard Bischoff has dated to the first half of the tenth century (letter of 9 December 1985). Tractatus 36 begins with a 4-line initial "I", written on the vertical bounding line, in orange with simple foliate ornamentation; the interior of the shaft is hollow and is decorated with a geometric pattern in orange. The 2-line initial "A" of the lesson is in a similar style and is not set apart from the text. 1-line initials are in brown uncials, with minuscule n, and are written within the text; one is highlighted with orange. The rubrics are written in orange rustic capitals; the first line of Tractatus 36 is written in brown rustic capitals with minuscule e, highlighted in red. Punctuation consists of the punctus for a minor pause, punctus elevatus for a major pause, punctus versus for completion of sententiae, and the punctus interrogativus. The punctus flexus is also used to separate parallel phrases, usually within a question (Parkes, 36, notes that this form first appears in French manuscripts of the tenth century).

The notation "IV 123" is written in black ink in a modern hand in the lower margin of the verso. A modern hand has identified the text in pencil.

Zinniker 204. The number "4" is written in ink in the upper margin of the recto.

MS 481.11   Italy, s. XI[1]
Gregory the Great, *Moralia in Iob*   Pl. 11

f. 1r   //mentes cum bona de aliis . . . postmodum in ortu atque//

         Gregory, *Moralia in Iob*, chap. 22.7.17–7.68; M. Adriaen, ed., CCSL 143A (1979), 1103–4. Only the inner column of the leaf survives. Torn on upper left corner with loss of text in first six lines.

f. 1v   //et in fornace aurum . . . sed ad auctoris laudem//

         Moralia in Iob, chap. 22.8.48–9.28; Adriaen, 1106–8. Only the inner column of the leaf survives.

ff. 2–3   [lon]//ge quippe praenotat ex unaquaque re . . . habitabit monumenta saxorum s//[ublimata]

         Moralia in Iob, chaps. 31.43.14–51.27; M. Adriaen, ed., CCSL 143B (1985), 1608–20. The upper margin of fol. 2 has been trimmed with loss of the first four lines of text; the current top line is mostly illegible. The outer margin of fol. 3 is damaged from use in a binding, with some loss of text.

Parchment (badly stained and damaged from binding use). 3 folios. Fol. 1 measures 455 x 155 mm; fol. 2 measures 410 x 290 mm; fol. 3 measures 455 x 320 mm, probably the size of the original leaf (written space 380 x 235 mm). 2 columns. 55 lines. Dry-point ruling.

Written in Caroline minuscule. 1- and 2-line initials are in brown uncials and are set apart from the text when they occur at the beginning of a line. Punctuation consists of the punctus, punctus elevatus, and punctus interrogativus. Accents are in the same ink as the text. There is a marginal notation on fol. 1v by a contemporary hand, probably the text scribe.

The fragments were used in the binding of a volume measuring ca. 410 x 270 mm. Fols. 2 and 3 were outside covers; the shelf number "III 2 A 30" is written on fol. 2. Fol. 1 was used around the spine of the volume.

Fol. 1 was formerly Zinniker 198; fol. 2 was Beinecke MS 482.17, Zinniker 81; fol. 3 was Zinniker 199.

MS 481.12   Italy, s. X[1]
Alan of Farfa, Homiliary   Pl. 11

ff. 1–2r [Inc: Egreditur de Hiericho turbis eductis . . .] //uiculus erat et confessionis portabat . . . saluum faciet populum suum a peccatis eorum qui uiuit et regnat per omnia saecula saeculorum amen.

> Alan of Farfa, Homily I.87 (Vigil of Palm Sunday). The homily is a combination of Jerome, *Commentarium in Euangelium Matthei* (on Matthew 21), III.1176–1286 and Jerome, *Commentarium in Zachariam* (on Zachariah 9.10), II.9.209–20; D. Hurst and M. Adriaen, eds., CCSL 77 (1969), 182–86 and M. Adriaen, ed., CCSL 76A (1970), 829–30. See Grégoire, 158.

ff. 2r–4 *Incipit sermo in cena domini*
Pascha non sicut quidam estimant grecum nomen est . . . causa compellit. fieri sine ecclesię//

> Alan of Farfa, Homily I.88 (Maundy Thursday). The homily consists of extracts from Augustine, *In Iohannis Euangelium Tractatus cxxiv*, Tractatus 55–56, 58–59, 61–63 (here through 61.1.11); R. Willems, ed., CCSL 36 (1954), 463–88; CPL 278. For a description of this homily, see Grégoire,

158–60. A portion of the parchment on fol. 2 has been cut out with the loss of four lines of text (recto, from Homily I.87 [CCSL 76A, p. 829]: *phariseis* [undeciphered sign] *quur . . . iubila hierusalem*; verso, from Homily I.88 [CCSL 36, pp. 465–66]: pa]*ter in manus . . . tradendo faciebat*); these lines have been rewritten in the lower margins of the recto and verso by two different scribes, both apparently contemporary with the text scribe. Tie marks resembling a capital "Z" (fol. 2r) and a cross (fol. 2v) indicate where the passages are to be supplied in the text.

Parchment. 4 folios (fols. 1 and 4 and fols. 2 and 3 are bifolia: they formed the inner two bifolia of a quire). 415 x 308 mm (written space 298 x 230 mm). 2 columns. 33 lines. Dry-point ruling before folding; double outer and single inner vertical bounding lines. Single horizontal bounding lines. Remains of prickings in upper and lower margins.

Written in Caroline minuscule. On fol. 2r there is a four-line initial "P" ("Pascha") in brown and red. 1-line initials are in brown uncials written on the inner vertical bounding line when they occur at the beginning of a line. The rubric is written in red uncials. The first line of the homily is written in brown uncials. Punctuation consisting of punctus, punctus elevatus, punctus versus (with one or two points), and punctus interrogativus. Accents are in the same ink as the text. A contemporary hand has made corrections in dark ink (see above on the more extensive correction involving the excision of a section of parchment and the suppletion of the text in the lower margins). A modern hand has identified passages from the Bible and from Augustine's tractates in pencil.

Zinniker 208. The number "8" is written in ink in the upper margin of fol. 1r.

MS 481.13   Austria or Northern Italy, s. X²
Bede, Homily II.10 (from a Homiliary)   Pl. 12

f. 1ra   [Inc: Aperta nobis est fratres de resurrectione domini . . .] //angelicę presentię memores . . . stetisse perhibentur//

Bede, *Homiliarum evangelii libri II*, Homily II.10.110–15 (on Luke 24.1–9, after Easter); D. Hurst, ed., CCSL 122 (1955), 249. The upper portion of the leaf has been trimmed with loss of text.

f. 1rb   [p]//ontificem interpellare . . . qui ad uitam//

Homily II.10.124–30; Hurst, 249. The upper portion of the leaf and the inner margin of the column have been trimmed with loss of text.

f. 1va   //hominis fieri dignatus . . . dispensationis archana et//

Homily II.10.138–44; Hurst, 250. The upper portion of the leaf and the inner margin of the column have been trimmed with loss of text.

f. 1vb   //humana tenebatur obnoxia . . . uita illius. Sicut etiam//

Homily II.10.153–58; Hurst, 250. The upper portion of the leaf has been trimmed with loss of text.

Parchment. 1 folio (the upper one-half to two-thirds of the leaf has been trimmed off and the remaining portion cut vertically into two pieces). Each fragment measures 130 x 105 mm (width of written space of 1 column: 80 mm). 2 columns. 10–11 lines remaining. Dry-point ruling on the flesh side.

Written in Caroline minuscule. 1-line initials are in brown rustic capitals or uncials and are not set apart from the text. Punctuation consists of the punctus, punctus elevatus, punctus versus, and punctus interrogativus. Some of the punctuation may be by a hand later than the text. A contemporary hand has added corrections in a darker ink.

Both leaves have the notation "467P" written in pencil in the lower right corner, indicating that they were removed from the binding of Lambach, Stiftsbibliothek, Ccl 467. Ccl 467 still preserves binding stays from the same manuscript, containing portions of Alan of Farfa's Homily I.88 (In Cena Domini; Inc: "Pascha non sicut quidam . . ."), which is a compilation of Tractatus 56 and 58 of Augustine's *In Iohannis evangelium tractatus* (see Grégoire, 158–60).

Portions of columns A and B of another leaf from the same manuscript are preserved as flyleaves in the binding of Lambach Ccl 437. These fragments contain Augustine's Tractatus 31, for the thirteenth Sunday after Pentecost (Inc: "Meminet caritas uestra pristinis . . ."). Ccl 437 is described by Holter (1959), 263, with a brief notice of the fragment. Neither Bede's Homily II.10 nor Augustine's Tractatus 31 is found in Alan of Farfa's homiliary; we have not identified a collection containing all three of the homilies preserved on the surviving leaves of this manuscript.

The fragment preserving a portion of column A on the recto was formerly Zinniker 129; the other fragment was formerly Beinecke MS 482.7, Zinniker 40.2.

Bibliography:
Babcock, *Reconstructing a Medieval Library*, 92, figs. 11 and 49.

MS 481.14

Lectionary

f. 1r–v   //In diebus illis. Angelus domini locutus est … donec ueniret cęsaream nomen domini iesu christi.

Acts 8.26–40 (Feria V after Easter).

f. 1v   *Secundum iohannem.* In illo. Maria autem stabat … Dicit ei iesus;//

John 20.11–17 (Feria V after Easter).

f. 2r–v   //Et hoc cum dixisset … uitam habeatis in nomine eius.

John 20.20–31 (Octave of Easter).

f. 2v   *Feria iiii. Lectio epistolae beati pauli apostoli ad corinthios* [sic]. Fratres. Oboedite prepositis uestris … gloria in saecula saeculorum.

Hebrews 13.17–21 (Feria IV of the second week after Easter).

f. 2v   *Sequentia sancti euangelii secundum marcum.* In illo tempore. Surgens autem iesus mane … ex his ambulantibus//

Mark 16.9–12 (Feria IV of the second week after Easter).

Parchment. 2 folios (foliated "ciii" and "cvi" in the upper center of the recto by a later hand). Fol. 1 measures 202 x 152 mm; fol. 2 measures 209 x 169 mm (written space 170 x 135 mm). 1 column. 23 lines. Dry-point ruling on the hair side.

Written in Caroline minuscule, which according to Prof. Hartmut Hoffmann is similar to that written in Freising in the middle of the tenth century (letter of 16 October 1992); cf. N. Daniel, *Handschriften des zehnten Jahrhunderts aus der Freisinger Dombibliothek* (Munich, 1973), pls. 7 and 8. 2-line initials are written in dark red uncials and are set apart from the text. 1-line initials are in brown uncials with occasional square capital forms and are frequently filled with dark red; they are set apart from the text when they occur at the beginning of a line. Rubrics are written in dark red square capitals mixed with uncial and minuscule forms. Punctuation consists of the punctus, punctus elevatus, punctus versus, and punctus interrogativus, sometimes highlighted with dark red ink. Accents are in the same ink as the text.

The pencil notation "249P" is written in the lower margin of both leaves, indicating that the leaves were used in the binding of Lambach, Stiftsbibliothek, Ccl

249. These leaves match the descriptions of the flyleaves in Ccl 249 made by H. Gerstinger in 1923–25. Gerstinger's notes on the Lambach library are in Vienna, Österreichische Nationalbibliothek, s.n. 9713.

A modern hand has written in pencil the number "47" in the lower right corner of fol. 1r and "46" in the lower right corner of fol. 2r.

Fol. 1 was formerly Beinecke MS 482.10, Zinniker 75; fol. 2 was formerly Zinniker 255.

Bibliography:
Babcock, *Reconstructing a Medieval Library*, 88 and fig. 47.

MS 481.15   Italy, s. XII^{in}
Paul the Deacon, *Vita S. Gregorii Magni*   Pl. 13

f. 1   [Inc: Gregorius hac urbe romana patre giordano . . .] //succensus. Tunc ab
           eisdem fratribus . . . gerebat. Et uniuersis//

           Paul the Deacon, *Vita S. Gregorii Magni*; BHL 3640; PL 75.45–49. The
           outer margin has been trimmed with loss of text.

Parchment. 1 folio. 505 x 270 mm (written space 425 x ca. 270 mm). 2 columns. 52 lines. Dry-point ruling on the hair side; double outer and single inner vertical bounding lines.

Written in Caroline minuscule. 1-line initials are written in brown uncials and are not set apart from the text. Punctuation consists of the punctus.

The fragment was once used as the wrapper of a volume measuring ca. 270 x 200 mm. The leaf was wrapped lengthwise around the volume and secured with a toggle and loop. The toggle still remains.

Zinniker 224.

MS 481.16   Italy, s. XI$^{4/4}$
Passionary   Pl. 14

f. 1r–v   [Inc: Tempore quo Dioclitianus perrexit Panoniis . . .] //humanum sibi hu-
           miliari. Dioclitianus augustus . . . recoleretur dies eorum. Regnante domi-
           no et saluatore nostro iesu christo. cui est honor et gloria in saecula
           saeculorum. Amen.

Passion of the Four Crowned Martyrs (8 November); BHL 1837; *Acta Sanctorum, Nov.* 3:775–79.

f. 1v   *Incipit passio sancti theodoli* [sic] *martyris V idus novembri*
          Temporibus suis maximianus et maximus imperatores. miserunt per om-
          nem terram ... ad regem æternum atque cęlestem. ut ipsi efficia//[mini]

          Passion of St. Theodore (9 November); BHL 8077; *Acta Sanctorum, Nov.*
          4:29–31.

f. 2r   [Inc: In insula quae nautae ...] //sus sanctum eugenium, adhuc in isto
          saeculo infelix ... residens uicus uadensis ligurię, in saecula saeculorum.
          Amen.

          Life of St. Eugenius (13 November); BHL 2681c.

f. 2v   *III idus novembri natali sancti mennę martyris eodem die sancti martini epis-
          copi* [Inc: Anno secundo imperii sui Diocletianus augustus ...] //uel reli-
          gionis. cuncti ... esse christianum. Itaque//

          Passion of St. Mennas (11 November); BHL 5921; R. Miedema, *De heilige
          Menas* (Rotterdam, 1913), 106–10. The initial has been cut out with the
          loss of the beginning of the text.

Parchment (both leaves torn from binding use; fol. 1r is badly stained). 2 folios. 470
x 305 mm (written space 377 x 221 mm). 2 columns. 53 lines. Dry-point ruling on
the hair side; double outer and single inner vertical bounding lines. Additional
vertical ruling between columns. Double upper and triple lower horizontal bounding lines. Prickings in upper and outer margins.
     Written in Caroline minuscule. The Passion of St. Theodore begins with an
11-line initial "T" ("Temporibus"). The crossbar of the letter contains three panels,
the outer two of which are filled with square-shaped fan-leaves colored purple and
decorated with white dots. The inner panel is filled with a green geometrical design, colored with white dots, like that in K. Berg, *Studies in Tuscan Twelfth-Century
Illumination* (Oslo, 1968), pl. 25 (of a Tuscan manuscript of the fourth quarter of
the eleventh century). The shaft of the "T" has the purple fan-leaf design in the
bottom panel and the geometrical design in the top. The initial is outlined in red,
with yellow wash filling the space between the outline and the panels. This initial
is in the "early geometric style" practiced in central and northern Italy in the late
eleventh and early twelfth century (see Berg, pls. 18, 20, 23, and 24 of several
Tuscan manuscripts of the fourth quarter of the eleventh century; and E. B. Gar-
rison, "Twelfth-Century Initial Styles of Central Italy," in *Studies in the History of*

Mediaeval Italian Painting, 4 vols. [Florence, 1953–63], esp. 1:37–67). The initial
that began the Life of St. Mennas on fol. 2v has been cut out, with corresponding
loss of text. A small portion of it remains suggesting that it had a foliate motif at
the base of its shaft, as in Berg, pls. 21 and 25. 1-line initials are in brown and are
a mixture of uncial and rustic capital forms; they are written between the double
vertical bounding lines when they occur at the beginning of a line. Rubrics are
written in red majuscules written between two lines, with space between the lines.
Punctuation consists of the punctus and the punctus interrogativus. A hand in
lighter ink has made several corrections and altered some of the punctus to punctus
elevati. Accents were added by a later hand.

These two leaves were formerly sewn together and formed the wrapper of a
volume measuring ca. 305 x 215 mm. The outside of the cover (fol. 1r) bears a
mostly illegible inscription which reads "Liber reno[. . .] tempore [. . .] in isto libro
[. . .]." The inner cover (fol. 2r) has several calculations and a list, perhaps of
names.

Zinniker 196, 197.

MS 481.17   Southern Germany, s. X[1]
Sedulius, *Opus Paschale*   Pl. 14

f. 1   //lętitia quis ille nitor effulsit . . . domino fabricante plasmati//

              Sedulius, *Opus Paschale*, II.4–6; J. Huemer, ed., CSEL 10 (1885), 200–2.

f. 2r–v   //sed abhorrens diuinis . . . carpere iam securam.
              Explicit liber sedulii noui testamenti secundus.

              Opus Paschale, II.17; Huemer, 229–31.

ff. 2v–5   *Incipit tertius ubi aquam in uinum conuertit.*
              Prima dominus nuptiis interesse . . . Preces sępius sine corde//

              Opus Paschale, III.1–10; Huemer, 232–40.

Parchment. 5 folios (fols. 2 and 5 form a bifolium; fols. 3 and 4, originally a bifolium, are now separated; the bifolia 2/5 and 3/4 formed the inner two bifolia of a
quire). Fol. 1 measures 215 x 153 mm; fols. 2–5 measure 215 x 145 mm (written
space 150 x 105 mm). 1 column. 21 lines. Fols. 2–5 were ruled in dry-point on the
flesh side as conjugate leaves before folding. The quire is arranged so that the hair
side of a leaf faces the flesh side of the following leaf.

Written in Caroline minuscule, which Prof. Hartmut Hoffmann dated to the first half of the tenth century (letter of 16 October 1992). 2-line initials are in brown uncials and are written between the double bounding lines. 1-line initials are in brown uncials and are not set apart from the text. Incipits, explicits, and chapter titles are written in orange-red rustic capitals. Punctuation consists of the punctus for major and minor pauses and the punctus versus for the end of sections. A contemporary or slightly later hand has made corrections and marginal notes.

The bifolium 2/5 and fols. 3 and 4, which were originally a bifolium, were used as flyleaves in the binding of Lambach, Stiftsbibliothek, Ccl 245. The shelf number "245" is written in ink on fol. 3v.

A modern hand has written in pencil the number "35" on fol. 1, "33" on fol. 3 and "36" on fol. 4. Another modern hand has identified the text in pencil.

Fol. 1 was formerly Beinecke MS 482.6A, Zinniker 122; the bifolium 2/5 was formerly Beinecke MS 481.17A, Zinniker 256; fol. 3 was formerly Beinecke MS 481.17B, Zinniker 257; fol. 4 was formerly Beinecke MS 482.6B, Zinniker 141.

Bibliography:
Babcock, *Reconstructing a Medieval Library*, 92–93 and fig. 26.

MS 481.18   Austria (Lambach?), s. XII^{med}
Antiphonary   Pl. 15

f. 1   //A. Veritas de terra. *Ps.* Benedixisti. A. Homo natus est. *Ps.* Fundamus.
         A. Ipse inuocauit. *Ps.* Misericordias. A. Exultabunt omnia ligna … *Ps.*
         Cantate domino. A. Notum fecit. *Ps.* Cantate domino. *v.* Speciosus forma.
         R. Beata dei genetrix. *V.* Beata quę credidit. R. Sancta et immaculata. V.
         Exultent. R. Beata et uenerabilis … V. Qui femineo dignatus … R. De-
         scendit de cęlis. V. Tamquam sponsus. *Super C.* Virgo hodie. *v.* Diffusa est
         gratia. R. Nesciens mater. V. Celestis. R. Confirmatum. V. Ipsa enim. R.
         O regem cęli. V. Vilibus. R. Verbum caro. V. In principio erat uerbum. *In
         matut. laud. Ant.* O admirabile commercium … A. Quando natus est …
         A. Rubum quem uiderat … A. Germinauit radix iesse … A. Ecce maria
         genuit … R. Benedictus qui uenit. V. Verbum caro. *Super Bened.* A. Mag-
         num hereditatis misterium … *Ad proced.* A. Qui de terra est. *Ad horas* A.
         O admirabile. *Per ordinem. In ii^a uespera.* A. Tecum principium. *Per ordi-
         nem.* R. Verbum caro factum est. V. Benedictus qui. *Super Magn.* A. Mira-
         bile misterium de … passus neque diuisionem. *Ad proced.*//

         Circumcision (1 January), from the second nocturn of matins through
         second vespers.

f. 2r   [A. Fili quid fecisti . . .] //dolentes querebamus . . . *Dominica ii̯ᵃ.* A. Deficiente uino iussit . . . *Alia.* Nuptiẹ factẹ sunt . . . *Dominica iii̯ᵃ.* A. Cum
autem descendisset . . . *Alia.* Domine puer meus. *Dominica iiii̯ᵃ.* A. Descendente iesu in . . . salua nos perimus.

Antiphons for the Benedictus and Magnificat for Sundays I, II, III and IV
after Epiphany.

f. 2r–v   *Sabbato ad v.* A. Regnum tuum domine . . . A. Alleluia [4x] . . . Ps. Con-
fiteantur. A. Laudabo deum meum . . . Ps. Lauda anima. A. Deo nostro
iocunda . . . Ps. Laudate dominum . . . A. Lauda hierusalem . . . Ps. Lauda
hierusalem. R. Deus qui sedes. V. Tibi enim. *Siue* Quam magnificata . . .
V. Omnia in sapientia . . . *v.* Vespertina oratio . . . *Super Magn.* Puer iesus.
Siue Fili quid fecisti. *Siue* Deficiente uino. *Siue* Nuptiẹ facte sunt. *Siue*
Cum autem descendisset. *Inuitator.* Preoccupemus faciem . . . Ps. Venite.
In i. noct. A. Domine in uirtute . . . Al. Alleluia [3x]. Ps. Domine in uirtute. A. Misericordia tua subsequatur . . . Ps. Dominus regit me. A. Oculi
mei semper . . . Ps. Ad te domine leuaui. *v.* Memor fui nocte . . . R. Domine ne mira . . . V. Sana me domine . . . R. Deus qui sedes . . . V. Tibi
enim dere//[lictus]

Saturday throughout the year, vespers to the first nocturn of matins.

Parchment. 2 folios (1 bifolium). Fol. 1 measures 308 x 216 mm; fol. 2 measures
308 x 175 mm (written space 230 x 150 mm). 1 column. 18 lines. Apparently due
to insufficiently deep dry-point ruling, both sides have been scored. It seems impossible to determine which side was scored first. Single vertical bounding lines.
Prickings in upper and lower margins.

    Written in late Caroline minuscule. 2-line initials are in red capitals and are set
apart from the text. 1-line initials are in brown square capitals, with uncial M, and
are not set apart from the text. Rubrics are written in red minuscule. Interlinear
neumes in the St. Gall style. Neumed differentiae (evovae) are provided in the
outer margins for antiphons with full text. Punctuation consists of the punctus,
placed on the base line.

    Other leaves from the same antiphonary are preserved in the bindings of
Lambach, Stiftsbibliothek, Cml XVI (2 leaves) and Cml LXXIII (the Lambach
Rituale, 1 leaf). Both volumes are still at Lambach and are briefly described in Holter (1959), 235 (Cml XVI) and 242 (Cml LXXIII, with a mention of its binding
leaf), and in Holter (1989), 144, cat. no. I.21 and 209, VIII.33.

    The leaf was used as a flyleaf in the binding of a volume measuring ca. 395 x 290
mm. There are several inscriptions in a fifteenth-century cursive hand, one of
which is the name "Jacob Poseil(?)" on fol. 1v.

Zinniker 219.

Bibliography:
Babcock, *Reconstructing a Medieval Library*, 108 and fig. 58.

MS 481.19   Southern Germany or Austria, s. XII[1]
Antiphonary   Pl. 15

f. 1r   [A. Tolle] //quod tuum est ... A. Dixit autem pater ... A. Tolle quod
             tuum est ... A. Non licet michi ...[*entered with a tie-mark in the lower
             margin:* A. Erunt primi nouissimi ...] A. Sic erunt nouissimi ... A. Multi
             enim sunt ... electi dicit dominus.

             Antiphons for the week of Septuagesima.

f. 1r–v   *Dominica ii. in quadragesimam. Ad. v. R.* Formauit. *ym. Dies absoluti. In evg.*
             A. Plantauerat autem dominus ... *Invit.* Adoremus deum. *Historia in prin-
             cipio sicut in precedenti dominica per totum canitur. In matut. laud.* A.
             Miserere mei. *cum reliquis.* A. Cum turba plurima ... *Ad primam.* A. Exiit
             qui seminat ... *Ad iii.* A. Semen cecidit in terram ... *Ad vi.* A. Semen
             cecidit in terram ... *Ad viiii.* A. Hiesus hęc dicens ... *In ii. vespera.* A.
             Uobis datum est ... A. Qui uerbum dei ... A. Quod autem cecidit ... A.
             Si uere fratres ... A. Si culmen ueri ... quantocius properate.

             Sexagesima, first vespers to second vespers.

f. 1v   *Dominica iii. in lxam. Ad. v. R.* Angelus domini. *ymnus. Dies absoluti. v.*
             Uespertina ... *In evg.* A. Quod autem cecidit. *Invit.* Adoremus deum ...
             [R.] Quadraginta dies et noctes ... V. Noe uero et uxor ... R. Ponam
             arcum meum ... ad noe et recorda//[bor]

             Quinquagesima, from vespers to the first nocturn of matins.

Parchment. 1 folio. 348 x 238 mm (written space 260 x 170 mm). 1 column. 21
lines. Dry-point ruling on the hair side. Single vertical bounding lines, with an extra
vertical line further out in the margin on which the tonary letters are written.
       Written in late Caroline minuscule. 2-line initial "Q" ("Quadraginta") on fol. 1v
is in red and is not set apart from the text. 1-line initials are in brown capitals with
uncial M and an enlarged minuscule *e* and are not set apart from the text. The
rubrics are written in red minuscule, with occasional use of uncial M. The anti-

phons have interlinear neumes in the St. Gall style. Neumed differentiae and modal notations are provided in the outer margins for the antiphons. Punctuation consists of the punctus, placed on the base line. Cross-shaped ("+") tie mark is in brown ink on fol. 1r.

The fragment was used as the pastedown in the binding of a volume measuring ca. 309 x 196 mm over pages from an early printed book, remnants of which remain glued to the fragment.

Zinniker 159.

MS 481.20   Southern Germany, s. X^2
Augustine, *De trinitate*   Pl. 16

f. 1r–v   *Incipit epistola sancti augustini ad papam aurelium*
        Domino beatissimo et sincerissima karitate uenerando sancto fratri . . . iu-
        beas anteponi. ora pro nobis.
        Explicit epistola sancti augustini ad papam aurelium [erased: *episcopum char-taginis*]

        Augustine, *De trinitate*, prologue; W. J. Mountain, ed., CCSL 50 (1968), 25–26; CPL 329.

f. 1v   *Incipiunt libri trinitatis eiusdem ad eundem.*
        Lecturus hẹc quẹ de trinitate disserimus. prius oportet . . . Quorum nonnulli//

        De trinitate, Book I.i.1; Mountain, 27. A later hand has added "Incipiunt" to the end of the heading.

f. 2   //non esse deum aut non uerum deum . . . separauit a se//

        De trinitate, Book I.vi.9–10; Mountain, 37–39.

f. 3   [fac]//ta sunt etiam corpus . . . nisi ab eo qui//

        De trinitate, Book IV.i.3–ii.4; Mountain, 162–64. The outer margin has been trimmed with loss of text.

Parchment. 3 folios. Fols. 1 and 2 measure 210 x 170 mm (written space 175 x 125 mm); fol. 3 measures 225 x 154 mm (written space originally 181 x ca. 125 mm). 1 column. 20 lines. Dry-point ruling on the hair side; double vertical and single horizontal bounding lines.

Written by three scribes in Caroline minuscule, dated by Bernhard Bischoff to the second half of the tenth century (letter of 13 March 1991). A crude 6-line initial "D" ("Domino"; fol. 1r) and 5-line initial "L" ("Lecturus"; fol. 1v) are in brown and orange-red ink; these may be later additions, although the ink colors are the same as those of the text hand. The "L" terminates in a bird's head. 1-line initials are in brown uncials with an enlarged minuscule *e*, and on fol. 1r are frequently touched with red. Incipits and explicits are in brown rustic capitals, and the word "explicit" is traced with red. The first line of the epistola is in brown square capitals. Punctuation consists primarily of the punctus. The first scribe occasionally uses the punctus elevatus and the punctus versus. There are contemporary corrections in a lighter ink.

In the lower right corner of fol. 1v there is a faint notation in pencil "289," indicating that this leaf was formerly in the binding of Lambach, Stiftsbibliothek, Ccl 289. A similar "284" is written in pencil in the lower right corner of fol. 2r; the number "284" is also written in ink at the top of fol. 2r, indicating that this leaf was the front flyleaf in Lambach Ccl 284 (the crossed-out number "70", which is next to "284", is the old number of Ccl 284). These leaves were briefly described by Holter (1957), 441, no. 3, who saw them while they were still at Lambach. Holter also suggests that a leaf from the binding of Ccl 311 belonged to the Augustine manuscript (Holter [1957], no. 7), but his description of that leaf does not correspond to any of the Beinecke fragments. Another leaf of this manuscript, preserving Book IV.iv–vi, is now preserved as Lambach Fragment 8/11. According to Prof. Hartmut Hoffmann, letter of 8 November 1996, the front and back inside boards of Berlin, Staatsbibliothek zu Berlin Preussischer Kulturbesitz, theol. lat. qu. 140 (from Lambach) have offset images from leaves of this manuscript, containing Book IV.i and IV.5–6, corresponding, at least in part, to Lambach Fragment 8/11.

The Lambach library catalogue in Lambach Cml XIX includes a copy of Augustine's "De sancta trinitate," which may refer to the volume preserved in these leaves. See Holter (1956), 273, no. 71 and *MBKÖ*, 5:57.

A later hand has written "Domino B" in ink in the lower margin of fol. 1r. An unidentified notation "N. 13" is written in a modern hand in ink on fol. 3v. Another modern hand, writing in pencil in the lower right corner of the leaves, has written the number "64" on fol. 1, "30" on fol. 2, and "29" on fol. 3. Textual identifications are written in pencil in a modern hand.

Fol. 1 was formerly Zinniker 249; fol. 2 was formerly Zinniker 258; fol. 3 was formerly Beinecke MS 482.9, Zinniker 59.2.

Bibliography:
Babcock, *Reconstructing a Medieval Library*, 95 and figs. 20 and 50.

MS 481.21
Bible, 1 Kings

Germany, s. X^{ex}
Pl. 16

f. 1   //dolores subita . . . et quinque mures//

   1 Kings 4.19–6.5. The outer margin has been trimmed with loss of text.

f. 2   //populi in omnibus . . . propheta dicitur//

   1 Kings 8.7–9.9. The outer margin has been trimmed with loss of text.

f. 3   [perse]//ueraueritis in malicia . . . Descendebat ergo omnis//

   1 Kings 12.25–13.20. The outer margin has been trimmed with loss of text.

f. 4   [pecca]//tum hoc hodie . . . saul amalech ab//

   1 Kings 14.38–15.7. The outer margin has been trimmed with loss of text.

Parchment (with many worm holes). 4 folios (2 bifolia: fols. 1 and 2 form a bifolium that once comprised the third and sixth leaves of a quire of eight; fols. 3 and 4 form a bifolium that had the same position in the following quire). Fols. 1 and 2 measure 210 x 148 mm; fols. 3 and 4 measure 213 x 139 mm (written space originally ca. 175 x 130 mm). 1 column. 22 lines. Dry-point ruling on the hair side; double vertical and single horizontal bounding lines.

Written in Caroline minuscule, dated by Bernhard Bischoff to the end of the tenth century (letter of 13 March 1991). The letters in these leaves have been retraced over earlier letters (s. IX or X) which were presumably damaged by water (another early manuscript from Lambach with similar water damage is Beinecke MS 481.8). Large 1-line initials are in brown square capitals, with the round form of *E*, and are usually set apart from the text. Smaller 1-line initials are written in brown rustic capitals, with an enlarged minuscule *e*, and are set apart from the text when they occur at the beginning of a line. Punctuation consists of the punctus, punctus versus, and punctus interrogativus. Accents were added by a later hand. A hand using darker ink has altered the punctuation and made several corrections. Another hand of the tenth or eleventh century has added a word on fol. 3r; this hand is similar to the hand that made an addition on fol. 46v of a ninth-century manuscript containing works by Augustine and the epistles that was once at Lambach (Sotheby's Sale Catalogue, 11–14 November 1929, lot 386, with plate). Chapter numbers and paragraph marks were added by a hand of the fourteenth or fifteenth century in dark red. In the upper margin of fol. 1r the same hand, writing in an upright gothic bastarda in black ink, added verses (1 Kings 4.21–22) that had been omitted by the text scribe.

The inscription "Missal[e] Ordinis Benedicti 316" is written on fol. 2r; the fragments were used in the binding of Lambach, Stiftsbibliothek, Ccl 316 (the fragments were seen by Holter when they were still in Lambach; see Holter [1957], 441, no. 5). Ccl 316 is briefly described by Holter (1959), 262, but he does not mention the fragments.

The Lambach library catalogue in Cml XIX contains the item "Liber regum," which Holter identifies as "Fragm. s. IX" (Holter [1956], 275, no. 123 and MBKÖ, 5:58); these are now the Beinecke fragments.

A modern hand has added the following numbers in pencil in the lower right corner of the leaves: fol. 1, "66"; fol. 2, "65"; fol. 3, "68"; and fol. 4, "67".

The bifolium 1/2 was formerly Zinniker 176; the bifolium 3/4 was formerly Beinecke MS 482.11, Zinniker 33.

Bibliography:
Babcock, *Reconstructing a Medieval Library*, 88 and fig. 46.

MS 481.22   Lothringia, s. XI[2]
Bible, Ezechiel   Pl. 17

f. 1ra   [ab]//hominationes quas operari . . . moriemini domus//

            Ezechiel 18.24–31. The inner margin and bottom half of the leaf have been trimmed with loss of text.

f. 1rb   //eius inter frondes . . . lacte et melle//

            Ezechiel 19.11–20.6. The bottom half of the leaf has been trimmed with loss of text.

f. 1va   //eis fluentem lacte . . . reprobassent et sabbata//

            Ezechiel 20.15–24. The bottom half of the leaf has been trimmed with loss of text.

f. 1vb   //fiet dicentium erimus . . . in odorem suauitatis//

            Ezechiel 20.32–41. The inner margin and bottom half of the leaf have been trimmed with loss of text.

Parchment (stained from use in a binding). 1 folio. 205 x 266 mm (the folio originally measured ca. 410 x 300 mm; written space originally ca. 374 x 260 mm). 2
columns. 26 lines remaining of an original ca. 52. Dry-point ruling; double outer
and single inner vertical bounding lines with additional ruling in space between columns. Prickings in upper margin.

Written in Caroline minuscule. The attribution to Lothringia and the dating
("kaum vor der Mitte des 11. Jahrhunderts") were made by Prof. Hartmut Hoff-
man, letter of 8 November 1996. 2-line initials are in brown rustic capitals and are
set apart from the text. 1-line initials are in brown rustic capitals and are not set
apart from the text. There is a portion of a running head in red in the upper margin
of the verso. Punctuation consists of the punctus, punctus elevatus, punctus versus,
and punctus interrogativus. A contemporary hand has made some corrections and
added a paraph (//) at the beginning of chapter 20 (fol. 1rb).

The fragment was once used as a pastedown in the binding of a volume measuring ca. 266 x 205 mm.

A modern hand has identified the text in the upper margins in pencil.
Zinniker 175.

MS 481.23   Southern Germany (Augsburg?), s. XI^{med}
Noted Breviary (Nocturnale)   Pl. 17

This breviary contains the offices of vespers and matins. The manuscript seems to
have contained only the offices for select saints, with the offices of Sts. Ulric, Afra,
and Gall contained in a single quire (fols. 2–4 and the two Vienna leaves; see
below). Ulric and Afra are the patron saints of Augsburg. The *Vita* of Ulric and the
chants for his office preserved here were composed by Bern of Reichenau (d. 1048)
between 1020 and 1030 (see N. Hörberg, *Libri Sanctae Afrae: St. Ulrich und Afra zu
Augsburg im 11. und 12. Jahrhundert nach Zeugnissen der Klosterbibliothek* [Göttingen,
1983], 224–25 and R. Schmidt, "Reichenau und St. Gallen: Ihre literarische Überlieferung zur Zeit des Klosterhumanismus," in *St. Ulrich und Afra zu Augsburg um
1500*, Vorträge und Forschungen 33 [Sigmaringen, 1985], 86–89). This manuscript
was written soon afterwards, perhaps in Augsburg.

f. 1r   //errore domino . . . digneris transformare.

           Portion of a chant for an unidentified office. The upper half of the leaf is
           missing and mutilated with loss of text.

f. 1r   *In natali sancti nicolai episcopi.* O pastor ęternę o clemens . . . *Inuit. Ant.*
           Confessorum regem adoremus . . . A. Nobilissimis siquidem natalibus . . .

A. Postquam domi puerilem . . . prebuit auditum.//

St. Nicholas (6 December), from vespers to the first nocturn of matins.

f. 1v   [R. Confessor dei nicholaus . . .] //secutus dominum . . . [L.] Qua uidelicet
urbe . . . ¶R. Operibus sanctis nicolao . . . [L.] Reuera enim cum essent
. . . continentium se lege//

St. Nicholas, the first nocturn of matins; the lessons are from John the
Deacon's *Vita S. Nicolai* (Mombritius, 297.15–20; BHL 6104–13). The upper half of the leaf is missing with loss of text.

f. 2   *In natali sancti vodalrici confessoris. An.* Venerandi patris vodalrici . . . [A.]
Lętetur tellus tali . . . [A.] Exultet polus tanto . . . [A.] Solus demon inge-
mat . . . [A.] Aue nunc corona . . . [A.] Salue gloria confessorum . . . [A.]
Nos christo commenda . . . *Inv.* Adoremus regem christum . . . A. Beatus
vodalricus ex nobilibus . . . [Ps.] Beatus vir qui. A. Hunc religiosi parentes
. . . [Ps.] Quare fremuerunt. A. Qui inter egregios . . . [Ps.] Domine quod.
[L.] Egregius christi confessor vodalricus . . . R. Beatissimi pontifici vodalrici . . . V. Qui inter cetera . . . [L.] Qui tantę prolis . . . R. Puer dei inclitus
vodalricus . . . [L.] Qua ex causa . . . ¶R. Cum transacto infantię . . . galli
cenobium est commendatus//

Office of St. Ulric (4 July), from vespers to the first nocturn of matins.
The chants are edited in M. Gerbert, *Scriptores ecclesiastici de musica sacra
potissimum*, 2 vols. (St. Blasien, 1784), 2:117–18 (also PL 135.1075–7).
The lessons are from Bern of Reichenau's *Vita S. Vodalrici* (Inc: Egregius
christi confessor uodalricus . . .; PL 142.1185).

f. 3   //A. Cum sub diocletiano tiranno . . . [Ps.] Beatus vir. [A.] In qua civitate
. . . [Ps.] Quare fremuerunt. A. Cuius prostibulum . . . [Ps.] Domine quid
multiplicati. [L.] Apud prouinciam retiam in ciuitate . . . ¶R. Beatus pontifex narcissus . . . [V.] Domino pro ipsis supplicans . . . [L.] Quo cum iudici
. . . ¶R. Sancto presule precibus . . . V. Mundi cordis amatorem . . . [L.]
Gaius iudex dixit . . . ¶R. Hostis antiquus caelesti . . . V. Coactus a sancto
pontifice . . . A. Cum psalmis deo . . . [Ps.] Cum inuocarem. A. Audiens
uero beatum . . . [Ps.] Verba mea. A. Quam uir sanctus . . . [Ps.] Domine
dominus noster. [L.] Iudex gaius dixit . . . descendisse de cęlo. nam//

Office of St. Afra (9 August), from the first to the the second nocturn of
matins. The lessons are from the *Vita S. Afrae* (Inc: "Apud prouinciam retiam in ciuitate augusta . . ."; MGH Script. Rer. Merov. 3, pp. 61–62). An

eleventh-century hand has written "Tu autem domine; miserere nobis" in the upper margin of the recto.

f. 4 //curam ammistraret cellarii antiquo ... A. Nam ipsius ad uocem ... [L.] O [...] inuenerunt capturam piscium ... [...] post beati galli sepulturam ... [L.] At [...]tus. nouerat sibi passim ... R. Ueniens uir dei brigantium ... V. Orationem ... [L.] Quem uir ... R. Cum campidonam sanctus ue- nisset ... Gloria patri et filio et spiritui sancto.

Office of St. Gall (16 October), third nocturn of matins. The lessons are from a *Vita S. Galli* that is apparently not one of those listed in BHL. It includes here a portion describing St. Gall catching fish for St. Columban, including the phrase *in amne quę vocatur lignona*, which is similar to a passage in the *Vita S. Columbani* (MGH Script. Rer. Merov. 4, p. 77). A contemporary hand has added an antiphon for St. Gall in the upper margin of fol. 4r, with neumes, and has provided neumes for several of the original antiphons. The bottom half of fol. 4v was left blank and a slightly later hand has added there a chant with neumes. The outer margin is trimmed with loss of text.

Parchment. 4 folios (fols. 2 and 4 form a bifolium; fols. 1 and 3 are loose leaves; fols. 2 and 4 were the outer bifolium and fol. 3 was the third leaf of a quire). Fol. 1 measures 121 x 146 mm; fol. 2, 210 x 169 mm; fol. 3, 209 x 152 mm; and fol. 4, 208 x 92 mm (written space 170 x 130 mm). 1 column. 20 lines. Dry-point ruling on the hair side before folding. Double vertical and single horizontal bounding lines. Prickings in upper, lower, and outer margins.

Written in Caroline minuscule in two sizes, with a smaller script for the chants and a larger script for the lessons. In the upper margin of fol. 2r there is a drawing of a face with the words "Vita S. Uodalrici episcopi et confessoris" in brown ink. The 2-line initial "V" ("Venerandi") at the beginning of the office on fol. 2r is a red square capital and is written between the double bounding lines. 1- and 2-line in- itials of lessons are in red uncials or square capitals and are written between the double bounding lines when they occur at the beginning of a line. 1-line chant initials are in brown uncials or square capitals, with occasional use of an enlarged minuscule *a*. Rubrics are written in red capitals. Punctuation consists of the punc- tus for the end of chants and the punctus and punctus elevatus for lessons. The antiphons and responses have interlinear neumes in the St. Gall style, except for those for the office of St. Gall, which were originally left blank; a later eleventh- century hand has added St. Gall neumes to the antiphons on fol. 4r. In the blank portion of fol. 4v there is a circular, geometric design in dry-point.

Two other leaves from this manuscript are preserved as pastedowns in Vienna, Österreichische Nationalbibliothek, s.n. 4635, which formerly belonged to the

Lambach Stiftsbibliothek. The visible portions of these leaves (the verso of the front pastedown and the recto of the back one are exposed) contain the end of the lessons and responses for the second nocturn of St. Afra, and the beginning of the third nocturn, with lessons from a homily on Luke 15.1 (Inc: "Audistis in lectione euangelica fratres karissimi . . ."; see Barré, "Mondsee," at 93, no. 82). Thus, they are consecutive and originally followed Beinecke fol. 3; they must once have formed the inner bifolium of a quire of which Beinecke fols. 2 and 4 formed the outer bifolium. One leaf, which contained the end of the office of St. Ulric and the beginning of the office of St. Afra, is missing between Beinecke fols. 2 and 3. Two leaves are missing between the second pastedown in the Vienna binding and Beinecke fol. 4; these leaves would have contained the end of the office of St. Afra and the beginning of the office of St. Gall. The attribution to Augsburg was suggested by Prof. Hartmut Hoffmann, letter of 8 November 1996, noting that the scribe of MS 481.23 also appears in Vatican City, Pal. lat. 274, a manuscript whose provenance is Sts. Ulric and Afra, and which was also probably written there.

Fol. 1 was formerly Beinecke MS 482.15, Zinniker 140.2; the bifolium 2/4 was formerly Zinniker 195; fol. 3 was formerly Zinniker 194.

Bibliography:
Babcock, *Reconstructing a Medieval Library*, 95 and fig. 51.

MS 481.24   Southern Germany, s. XI
Noted Breviary   Pl. 18

f. 1   [*Hymnus.* Iesu nostra redemptio . . . c]//laustra penetrans tuos captiuos
            . . . A. Ascendit deus in iubilatione . . . [*In ev.* A. Pater ma]nifestaui
            nomen tuum . . . [*Or.* Adesto] domine supplicationibus nostris . . . *Inuita-*
            torium. [Alleluia] regem ascendentem . . . [Ps.] Venite. [A. Elevata est]
            magnificentia . . . Ps. Domine dominus noster. [A. Dominus] in templo
            sancto . . . Ps. In domino confido. [A. A summo] cẹlo . . . Ps. Cẹli enar-
            rant. [L. Post b]eatam et gloriosam resurrec[tionem] . . . R. Post passio-
            nem suam . . . V. Et conuescens prẹcepit . . . [L.] Nam cum sanctẹ mulieris
            . . . R. Omnis pulcritudo domini . . . V. Nisi ego abiero . . . [L.] Gratias
            agamus diuinẹ dispensationi . . . In his p[er]insufflat//

            Ascension, from vespers to the first nocturn of matins. The hymn (Schal-
            ler-Könsgen 7657) is printed in AH 51.89. The lessons are from Leo
            Magnus, *Tractatus septem et nonaginta*, Tractatus 73; A. Chavasse, ed.,
            CCSL 138A (1973), 450–51. The inner and lower margins have been
            trimmed with loss of text.

Parchment. 1 folio. 290 x 208 mm (written space originally ca. 220 x 190 mm). 1 column. 25 lines remaining of original 26. Dry-point ruling on the hair side; triple vertical bounding lines.

Written in Caroline minuscule in two sizes, a smaller module for the chants and a larger one for the lessons. 2-line initials are in red square capitals and are written between the inner two bounding lines. 1-line initials within the text are in brown square capitals. Rubrics are written in red minuscule and when they occur at the beginning of a line begin between the outer two vertical bounding lines. Punctuation consists of the punctus within chants and the punctus, punctus elevatus and punctus versus within the lessons. Accents are in the same ink as the text. Interlinear neumes in the St. Gall style. The lessons are numbered "I" through "[III]I" in the margins in brown ink.

Zinniker 190.

MS 481.25   Southern Germany, s. XI^2
Noted Breviary   Pl. 18

This breviary (perhaps more correctly, nocturnale or matutinale) includes the offices of vespers, matins, lauds and second vespers. Many of the homilies are from a homiliary that was compiled in Bavaria, perhaps at Augsburg or Salzburg, in the second quarter of the ninth century and that was based partly on the Homiliary of Mondsee (see Barré, *Homéliaires*, 26–27 and Barré, "Mondsee," at 85–91). Other homilies are taken from the homiliaries of Paul the Deacon and Alan of Farfa.

f. 1r   [V.] //Et dominabitur a mari . . . [L.] Sed [cum] ex lectione alia redemptoris . . . R. Nascetur nobis paruulus . . . V. Ecce aduenit dominator . . . *In mat. la*[*ud. A.*] Canite tuba in syon quia . . . domini ecce//

           Fourth Sunday of Advent, from the third nocturn of matins to lauds. The lesson is from Gregory, *Homiliae xl in evangelia*, I.7 (Inc: "Ex huius nobis lectionis uerbis . . ."; PL 76.1099; R. Étaix, ed., CCSL 141 [1999], 46) = Bavarian Homiliary B.II.77 (see Barré, *Homéliaires*, 26–27 and 301) = Paul the Deacon's Homiliary, I.8 (see Grégoire, 431). The bottom half of the recto and the entire verso have been erased.

f. 2r–v   [*first four lines erased*] //horam quando ueniet dominus. *Liber Luc.* In illo tempore. Missus est gabrihel . . . *Omelia lectionis eiusdem.* Exordium nostrę redemptionis hodierna . . . R. Missus est gabriel. [L.] Si ergo primordium . . . [R.] Aue maria gratia. [L.] Aptum profecto . . . [R.] Suscipe uerbum. *In mat. laud.* [*remaining chants on fol. 2r erased*] sui et regnauit in ęternum.

A. Ecce ueniet dominus ut ... A. Spiritus sanctus. A. Ecce ancilla. A. Quomodo fiet istud ... obumbrauit tibi.

Feria IV before Christmas, from the third nocturn of matins to lauds. The lessons are from Bede's Homily I.3 on Luke 1.26 (D. Hurst, ed., CCSL 122 [1955], 14) = Bavarian Homiliary B.II.74 (see Barré, *Homéliaires*, 26–27 and 302). The first four lines of fol. 2r and the antiphons for lauds at the bottom of fol. 2r have been erased.

f. 2v   *Feria v.* R. Emitte agnum domine ... V. Ex syon species ... R. Rorate celi desuper ... V. Emitte agnum domine ... R. Germinauerunt campi heremi ... V. Ecce dominator dominus ... [A.] De syon ueniet dominus ... A. Conuertere domine ... A. De syon ueniet qui ... A. Ecce deus meus ... A. Dominus legifer noster ... A. Intuemini quantus sit.

Feria V before Christmas, matins responses and lauds.

f. 2v   [*Invit.*] Uigilate animo. *Lectio sanctio evangelii secundum lucam.* In illo tempore. Exsurgens maria abiit in montana ... *Omelia lectionis eiusdem.* In lectione euangelica audiuimus fratres karissimi. quia beatissima uirgo maria ... memor scripture praecipientis. quanto magnus [...]//

Feria VI before Christmas, matins; the lesson is from Bavarian Homiliary B.II.75 (on Luke 1.39; see Barré, *Homéliaires*, 26–27 and 284).

f. 3r–v   [L.] //de [...] passionis domini sibi dixisse ... R. Uir israhelita gaude ... V. Ut precibus tuis ... [L.] Discipulus autem ille ... R. Apparuit caro suo ... V. Cumque complesset apostolus ... *In matut. laud.* A. Ecce puer meus ... A. Hic est discipulus meus sic ... A. Sic eum uolo ... A. Sunt de hic stantibus ... A. Hic est discipulus ille ... A. In medio ecclesiae aperuit dominus ... A. Qui uicerit faciam illum ... [...] nam et nomine ... *Ad vesp.* A. Iurauit dominus. [Ps]. Beatus uir. [A.] Collocere eum dominus. [Ps.] Laudate pueri dominum. A. Disrupisti domine. [Ps.] Credidi propter. A. Confortatus est. A. Domine probasti me. A. Iste est discipulus ... in principio apud deum.

John the Evangelist (27 December), from the third nocturn of matins to second vespers. The lessons are from an unidentified homily, possibly Bavarian Homily B.I.6 (Inc: "Sanctus Ioannes apostolus et evangelista cuius hodie natalitia celebramus ..."; see Barré, *Homéliaires*, 26–27 and 325). The upper margin has been trimmed with the loss of the first few lines of text.

f. 3v   *In natali innocentum.* Istorum est enim regnum . . . *Inv.* Adoremus salua-
         toris uenerantes . . . [*Inv.*] Regem regum dominum . . . *In i. n.* Secus de-
         cursus aquarum . . . [*Ps.*] Beatus uir qui. A. Predicantes preceptum domini
         . . . *Ps.* Quare fremuerunt. A. Filii hominum scitote . . . *Ps.* Cum inuo-
         carem. A. Scuto bone uoluntatis . . . *Ps.* Uerba mea. A. In uniuersa terra
         . . . *Ps.* Domine dominus noster. A. Habitabunt in tabernaculo . . . *Ps.* Do-
         mine quis habitabit. [*L.*] Dedicatur nouus infantibus sermo sanctis laudi-
         bus . . . R. Sub altare dei . . . et acceperunt di//[uinum]

         Holy Innocents (28 December), from vespers to the first nocturn of
         matins. The lesson is from Chrysostomus latinus, Sermon 5 = Paul the
         Deacon's Homiliary I.35 (PL 95.1176; see Grégoire, 436).

f. 4   [R.] //O magnum mysterium. [L.] Ingreditur [ergo haec] mundi infima
         filius . . . R. Sancta et immaculata. [L.] Incomprehensibilis uoluit . . . R.
         Ecce agnus dei. [L.] Inpassibilis deus non . . . R. Congratulamini. [L.] Ha-
         bentes ergo tante fidei . . . R. Benedictus. [L.] Nolite despicere fratres . . .
         [lines missing: *Lectio secundum lucam.* In illo tempore.] Erat [pater eius et]
         mater iesu mirantes . . . *Omelia l[ectionis eiusdem.*] Lectio sancti euangelii
         quę nunc lecta est . . . R. Nesciens mater. [L.] Quamuis lucas euangelista
         . . . R. Continet in gremio. [L.] Mirabantur autem de eo . . . [R.] O regem
         cęli. [L.] Adducentes autem puerum . . . R. In principio erat uerbum . . . V.
         Quod factum est . . . hominum Omnia//

         Sunday after Christmas, from the second to the third nocturn of matins.
         The lessons for the second nocturn are from a homily similar to Leo,
         Tractatus septem et nonaginta, Tractatus 22, recension α (Inc: "Exultemus
         in domino dilectissimi et spirituali iocunditate . . .", A. Chavasse, ed.,
         CCSL 138, pp. 90–101) = Alan of Farfa, Homily I.11 = Paul the Deacon,
         Homily I.18 (see Grégoire, 143 and 433); the lessons for the third nocturn
         are from Bavarian Homiliary B.I.8 (on Luke 2.33; see Barré, *Homéliaires,*
         26–27 and 278). The upper margin has been trimmed with the loss of the
         first two to four lines of text.

f. 5   //coram deo et [. . . *In octauam*] domini. [A.] Qui de terra est . . . [*Inv.*]
         Christus natus est. A. Dominus dixit ad me. *Ps.* Quare fremuerunt. A. In
         sole posuit . . . [*Ps.*] Cęli. A. Eleuamini porte eternales . . . [*Ps.*] Domini
         est terra. A. Speciosus forma . . . [*Ps.*] Eructauit. A. Rex omnis terrę. *Ps.*
         Omnes gentes. A. Suscepimus deus. [*Ps.*] Magnus deus. *v.* Dominus dixit
         ad me. [*L.*] Saluator noster karissimi fratres pro redemptione humani ge-
         neris . . . *In ii. n.* [A.] Orietur diebus. *Ps.* Deus iudicium. A. Ueritas de
         terra. *Ps.* Benedixisti. A. Homo natus. *Ps.* Fundamenta eius. [A.] Ipse

inuocabit. *Ps*. Misericordia domini. *A*. Exultabunt omnia ligna . . . *Ps*.
Cantate. [*A*.] Notum fecit. [*Ps*.] Cantate. [*L*.] Sicut ergo sum mortui sumus . . . super omne nomen. *Secundum lucam*//

Octave of Christmas (Circumcision; 1 January), from vespers to the
second nocturn of matins. The lessons are from Caesarius, *Sermo* 191, although a portion of the incipit has been omitted (Inc: "Salvator noster
karissimi fratres [natus de patre ante omnia . . .] pro redemptione . . ."; G.
Morin, ed., CCSL 104.778). The upper margin has been trimmed with the
loss of the first few lines of text.

f. 6   [*L*.] //Nuper c[elebrauimus diem fratres karissimi quo dominus et saluator
noster in carne natus est; ho]die celebramus quo a gentibus adoratus est
. . . *R*. Magi ueniunt ab oriente . . . *V*. Magi uenient [*corr. to*: ueniunt] ab
. . . [*L*.] Christus enim est . . . *R*. Interro[gabat] magos Herodes . . . *V*.
Uidimus enim stellam . . . [*L*.] Hodie ergo de istis . . . [*responsory and verse
erased*: Stella quam uiderunt . . . *V*. Et intrantes domum . . . *L*.] Nonne alii
reges iudeorum . . . *R*. Uidentes stellam magi . . . *V*. Stella quam uiderant
. . . *A*. Christo datus est . . . *Lectio sancti evangelii secundum matheum*. [Cum
ergo] natus esset iesus . . . *Omelia lectionis eiusdem*. [Sicut e]x lectione
euangelica fratres [audi]stis cęli rege nato . . . *R*. Dies sanctificatus . . . [*V*.]
Uenite adoremus eum . . . [*L*.] Sed querendum nobis est . . . *R*. Reges
tharsis et . . . *V*. Omnes de saba . . . [*L*. Quia iudae]is uero tamquam ra-
tione . . . id est angelus praedicare debuit gentiles uero//

Epiphany (6 January), from the second to the third nocturn of matins.
The lessons for the second nocturn are from a homily on Matthew 2.1 (=
Bavarian Homiliary B.I.12; see Barré, *Homéliaires*, 26–27 and 264), and
the lessons for the third nocturn are from Gregory, *Homiliae xl in evangelia*,
Homily I.10 (PL 76.1110; R. Étaix, ed., CCSL 141 [1999], 66) = Paul the
Deacon's Homiliary, Homily I.48 (see Grégoire, 439). The upper margin
has been trimmed with the loss of the first few lines of text.

f. 7r   [*A*. Baptizat miles regem] //seruus dominum suum . . . [*A*.] Aqua comburit
peccatum . . . diuinitatis ope.

Octave of Epiphany, second vespers.

ff. 7r–8r   *Dominica i*. [*L*.] Epiphaniam id est apparitione[m] domini saluatoris . . . *R*.
Omnes de saba. [*L*.] Hęc stella pulchrior . . . auariciam largitate delete.
Secundum lucam. Cum factus esset [*supr*: iesus] annorum duodecim . . .
[*Omelia*] Lectio sancti euangelii quę modo lecta est fratres mei infantiam

domini saluatoris . . . frequentare muneribus. A. Fili quid fecisti nobis sic ego . . . A. Quid est quod me . . . A. Puer iesus proficiebat . . . *In mat. laud.* A. Veterem hominem renouans . . . A. Te qui in spiritu . . . A. Baptista contremuit et . . . A. Caput draconis saluator . . . A. Magnum misterium declaratur . . . A. Praecursor iohannes exsultat . . . A. Iohannes quidem clamabat . . . omnem iusticiam alleluia.

First Sunday after Epiphany, matins through lauds. The lessons for the first and second nocturns of matins are from Pseudo-Augustine, Sermon 140 (Mai, 1:329); the lessons for the third nocturn are from Bavarian Homiliary B.I.13 (on Luke 2.42; see Barré, *Homéliaires*, 26–27 and 262). The upper margin of fol. 8 has been trimmed with the loss of one line of text.

ff. 8r–10v   *In natali sancti sebastiani.* A. Elegit dominus uirum . . . *In i. noct.* [A.] Sebastianus mediolanensium partium . . . *Ps.* Beatus uir. A. Sebastianus uir christianissimus . . . *Ps.* Quare fremuerunt. A. Erat enim in sermone . . . *Ps.* Cum inuocarem. A. Sebastianus dei cultor . . . *Ps.* Uerba. A. Sebastianus dixit ad nicostratum . . . *Ps.* Domine dominus noster. A. Sebastianus dixit marcelliano . . . *Ps.* Domine quis habitabit. *v.* Letamini in domino. [*L.*] Sebastianus uir christianus mediolanensium . . . *R.* Sebastianus dei cultor . . . *V.* Erat enim in sermone . . . [*L.*] Erat autem uir tocius prudentię . . . *R.* Sebastianus uir christianissimus . . . *V.* Quem perfuderat deus . . . [*L.*] Hunc milites acsi . . . *R.* In isto loco promissio . . . *V.* Nolite timere . . . [*L.*] Christo igitur cottidie . . . *R.* Erat namque in sermone . . . *V.* In commisso quoque . . . A. Ut uidit beatus sebastianus . . . *Ps.* Conserua. A. Chr[isto cot]tidie sedulum . . . *Ps.* Domini est terra. A. Zoe uxor nicostrati . . . *Ps.* Beati qui. A. Polycarpus pre[sbyter] dixit . . . *Ps.* Benedicam. A. Nos famuli domini . . . *Ps.* Te decet. A. Beatus calistus dedit . . . *Ps.* Deus uenerunt. [*L.*] Ad hoc tantum sub clamide . . . *R.* Christo cottidie sedulum . . . *V.* Ad hoc tantum . . . [. . . *L.* Qui cum beatissimis . . . carni]ficum animo perseueranti . . . *R.* Ad hoc tantum . . . *V.* Sebastianus uir christianissimus . . . [*L.*] Clarissimis igitur uiris . . . *R.* Clarissimis cottidie uiris . . . *V.* Beatus sebastianus suadebat . . . [*L.*] Erant enim non solum . . . *R.* Nolite timere non . . . *V.* Quas meruit christi martyr . . . *Ad cant.* Multitudo languentium . . . *Evangelium descendens iesus de monte cum omelia require in natali plurimorum martirum.* [. . . *R.* Zoe uxor nicostrati . . .] et benedictus sermo oris . . . [. . . *V.* Benedicti] qui in omnibus . . . *R.* Beatus es tu et bene . . . *V.* Beatus es christi martyr . . . *R.* Elegit dominus uirum . . . *V.* Beatus es et bene . . . *In mat. l.* A. Ad hoc tantum sub clamide . . . A. Clarissimis cottidie uiris . . . A. Si ego uerus . . . A. Ad hanc uocem . . . A. Nolite timere non . . . A. Beatus es et bene . . . A. Ad hoc

tantum. *Ps.* Confitebor. *Ps.* Credidi. *Ps.* In conuertendo. *Ps.* Eripe me. A.
Egregie dei martyr . . . non derelinquetur in secula.

St. Sebastian (20 January), from first vespers to second vespers. The lessons for the first and second nocturns of matins are from the *Vita S.*
Sebastiani (BHL 7543; *Acta Sanctorum, Jan.* II, p. 265). The upper margins
of fols. 8, 9, and 10 have been trimmed with the loss of the first line of
text.

ff. 10v–12r   *In natali sancte agnetis uirginis.* [A.] Christi uirgo nec terrore . . . [*Inv.*]
Regem uirginum. A. Discede a me pabulum . . . *Ps.* Beatus. A. Dextram
meam et collum . . . *Ps.* Celi enarrant. A. Posuit signum in faciem . . . *Ps.*
Domini est terra. A. Specie tua. *Ps.* Eructauit. A. Adiuuabit. *Ps.* Deus
noster. A. O quam pulchra. *Ps.* Magnus deus. *v.* Diffusa est gratia. [L.]
Ambrosius seruus christi uirginibus sacris . . . R. Diem festum sacratissime
uirginis . . . V. Ingressa agnes turpitudinis . . . [L.] Omnes enim gratulemur
. . . R. Dextram meam et collum . . . V. Induit me dominus . . . [L.] Infan-
tia computabatur . . . [R.] Ueni sponsa. [L.] Cum ab scolis reuertitur [*corr.*
to: reuerteretur] . . . R. Amo christum in cuius . . . V. Mel et lac . . . *In ii.* A.
Christus circumdedit me . . . [Ps.] Benedixisti. A. Induit me dominus
cyclade . . . [Ps.] Fundamenta. A. Mel et lac . . . [Ps.] Cantate. A. Ipsi sum
desponsata . . . [Ps.] Dominus regnabit. A. Cuius pulchritudinem sol . . .
Ps. Cantate. A. Ipsi soli seruo . . . [Ps.] Dominus regnabit. [L.] Denique
detulit secum . . . R. Ipsi sum desponsata . . . V. Propter ueritatem et . . .
[L.] Vnde factum est ut . . . [. . . R. Induit me dominus] uestimento salutis
. . . V. Induit me dominus cyclade . . . [L.] Ad hęc beata agnes . . . [R.]
Hec est uirgo sapiens. [L.] Anulo fidei suę . . . R. Mel et lac . . . V. Cuius
pulchritudinem sol . . . *Ad c.* A. Ecce quod cupiui iam . . . *Euangelium cum*
omelia require in natali uirginum. R. Iam corpus eius . . . V. Ipsi sum
desponsata . . . R. Ueni electa mea. V. Specie. R. Pulchra facie sed . . . V.
Specie. R. Omnipotens adorande . . . [V.] Ingressa agnes turpitudinis . . .
In mat. l[aud. A.] Ingressa agnes turpitudinis . . . A. Mecum enim habeo
. . . A. Anulo suo subarrauit . . . A. Benedico te pater . . . A. Congaudete
mecum et . . . A. Stans beata agnes . . . *Ad v.* A. Ingressa agnes. *Ps.* Dixit
dominus. *Ps.* Letatus. *Ps.* Ni[si dominus]. *Ps.* Memento. A. Beata agnes in
medio . . . R. Obtulerunt. V. Postquam impleti.

St. Agnes (21 January), from first vespers to second vespers. The lessons
for the first two nocturns of matins are from the *Vita S. Agnetis* (BHL 156;
Acta Sanctorum, Jan. II, p. 351). The upper margins of fols. 10 and 11
have been trimmed with loss of the first line of text.

f. 12r–v *In purificatione sancte ma[riae A.]* Adorna thalamum tuum sion . . . *Invit.*
Ecce uenit ad templum . . . *A.* Benedicta tu in mulieribus . . . *A.* Sicut
myrra electa odorem . . . *A.* Ante thorum huius uirginis . . . *Ps.* Domini est
terra. *A.* Specie. *Ps.* Eructauit. *A.* Adiuuabit. *Ps.* Deus noster. *A.* O quam
pulchra. *Ps.* Magnus. [*L.*] Hodiernus dies magnum nobis contulit gaudium
. . . [*R.* A]dorna thalamum tuum . . . *V.* Accipiens symeon puerum . . . [*L.*]
Exultent uiduę infantem christum . . . *R.* Senex puerum portabat . . . *V.*
Accipiens symeon. [*L. N*]umquid enim sole uirgines . . . *R.* Obtulerunt pro
eo . . . *V.* Postquam impleti sunt . . . [*L.*] Octoginta namque gerens annos
. . . *R.* Postquam impleti sunt . . . in lege domini quia//

Purification of Mary (2 February), from first vespers to the first nocturn of
matins. The lessons are from Alan of Farfa's Homiliary, Homily I.48 (PL
95.1461; see Grégoire, 151–52).

f. 13 [*L.* Licet nobis dilectissimi adpropinquante festiuitate paschali . . .] //dic-
tum poscat augeri. nemo est ut confido . . . *R.* In omnibus exhibeamus . . .
V. Ecce nunc tempus . . . [*L.*] Quia ergo nemo nostrum . . . *R.* Paradysi
portas aperiat . . . *V.* Ecce nunc tempus . . . [*L.*] Parum enim religiosus
. . . *R.* Emendemus in melius . . . *V.* Peccauimus cum patribus . . . *A.*
Commendemus nosmetipsos in . . . [*L.*] Quid enim acceptius . . . *R.* In
ieiunio et . . . *V.* Inter uestibulum et . . . [*L.*] Nunc enim in toto . . . *R.* Derelinquat impius uiam . . . *V.* Non uult mortem . . . [*L.*] Nunc quoque
renuntiatur . . . *R.* Frange esurienti panem . . . *V.* Cum uideris nudum . . .
[*L.*] Semper quidem tibi . . . *R.* Tribularer si nescirem . . . sed ut conuer//
[tatur]

First Sunday of Quadragesima, from the first to the second nocturn of
matins. The lessons are from Leo, *Tractatus septem et nonaginta*, Tractatus
40.7–31 = Alan of Farfa's Homiliary, I.63 = Paul the Deacon's Homiliary, I.74 (see Grégoire, 154 and 443).

ff. 14–15r [*L.* . . . uel]//le patrem illius. et uestibus esau . . . *R.* Si dominus deus
. . . *V.* Uere dominus. Erit. [*L.*] Pulmentum autem et . . . *R.* Erit mihi
dominus . . . *V.* Si dominus deus . . . [*L.*] Dixit isaac. Accede huc . . . *R.*
Minor sum cunctis . . . *V.* Deus in cuius . . . *Ad cant.* [*A.*] Missus sum ad
oues . . . *Secundum matheum* . . . In illo tempore. Egressus iesus secessit
. . . *Omelia.* In lectione euangelica audiuimus fratres karissimi magnam
mulieris constantiam . . . *R.* Orauit iacob et . . . *V.* Deus in cuius conspectu. [*L.*] Cum enim eundem . . . *R.* Dicit angelus ad iacob . . . *V.* Benedicens benedicam tibi . . . [*L.*] Hęc autem mulier . . . *R.* Uidi dominum
facie . . . *V.* Et dixit [*added supr*: mihi] nequaquam . . . [*L.*] Sicut ergo

mulierem ... R. Pater [peccaui in] ... V. [Quanti mer]cennarii in ... [*Ad laud.*] A. Domine labia mea ... A. Dextera deum fecit ... A. Factus es adiutor ... A. Statuit ea in ... R. Participem me fac ... V. Aspice in me ... A. Egressus iesus secessit ... A. Missus sum. [A.] O mulier [magna. *Ad ii. vesp.*] R. Bonum mihi domine ... V. [Manus tuae] domine ... A. Dixit dominus [mulieri] ... fiat tibi sicut petisti.

Second Sunday of Quadragesima, from the second nocturn to second vespers. The lessons for the second nocturn are from Genesis 27.14–23; the lessons for the third nocturn are from Bede, Homily on Matthew 15.21 (*Homiliae in evangelia*, Homily I.22; D. Hurst, ed., CCSL 122, p. 157); cf. Bavarian Homily B.I.39 (see Barré, *Homéliaires*, 26–27 and 275). The outer margin of fol. 15 has been trimmed with loss of text.

f. 15r   [*Feria ii.*] A. Ego principium qui ... A. Qui [me misit] ... quia que placita//

Feria II of the second week of Quadragesima, antiphons. The outer margin has been trimmed with loss of text.

f. 15v   *Feria.* [*iii.* A. Unus est enim] magister ... [A. Omnes autem uo]s fratres ... [A.] Qui maior est ... humiliabatur [dicit dominus].

Feria III of the second week of Quadragesima, antiphons. The outer margin has been trimmed with loss of text.

f. 15v   *Feria iiii.* [A.] Ecce ascendimus hierosolimam ... A. Tradetur enim [gentibus] ... A. Sedere autem mecum ... a patre meo.

Feria IV of the second week of Quadragesima, antiphons. The outer margin has been trimmed with loss of text.

f. 15v   [*Feria v.* A. Factum est autem] ut moreretur ... A. Pater abraham miserere ... A. Diues ille guttam ... [A. Rogo te] pater ut ... [A. ...] ait illi abraham ... moysen et prophetas//

Feria V of the second week of Quadragesima, antiphons. The outer margin has been trimmed with loss of text.

f. 15v   *Feria vi.* [A.] Malos male perdet ... [A.] Querentes iesum tenere ... [A.] Malos male perdet ... fructum [temporibus su]is.

Feria VI of the second week of Quadragesima, antiphons. The outer margin has been trimmed with loss of text.

f. 15v   *Sab.* Uado ad patrem . . . [A. Dixit autem pa]ter . . . [A.] Oportet te fili. [A.] Fili tu semper . . . mecum.

Saturday of the second week of Quadragesima, antiphons. The outer margin has been trimmed with loss of text.

f. 15v   *Dominica.* [R. Uidens iaco]b uestimenta. [A. Fili tu semper] mecum es . . . et inuentus est dixit dominus//

Third Sunday of Quadragesima, vespers. The outer margin has been trimmed with loss of text.

f. 16   [V. Tres enim adhuc . . .] //quos recordabitur pharao . . . [L.] Fecerunt ut dixerat et locum . . . R. Tollite hinc uobiscum . . . V. Tollite de fructibus . . . [L.] Nesciebat autem quod . . . R. Iste est frater . . . V. Adtollens aut ioseph . . . [L. At illi] portantes frumenta . . . [R. Dixit] ruben fratribus . . . [V.] Merito hẹc patimur . . . [L. In illo tempore.] Erat iesus eiciens . . . *Omelia.* [Daemonia]cus iste apud matheum non solum mutus . . . [R.] Merito hẹc patimur . . . [V. D]ixit ruben fratribus . . . uobis nolite//

Third Sunday of Quadragesima, second and third nocturns of matins. The lessons for the second nocturn are from Genesis 42.20–30; the lessons for the third nocturn are from Bede's Homily 3.49 and 3.58 on Luke 11.14 from his *Expositio in lucam* (PL 92.475; D. Hurst, ed., CCSL 120 [1960], 231) = Paul the Deacon's Homiliary, Homily I.90 (see Grégoire, 446). The outer margin has been trimmed with loss of text.

f. 17r–v   [L.] //Cum diuersis signis et miraculis diuinitatis . . . R. Dulce lig[num]. [L.] Multotiens enim desiderabat . . . [R.] Hoc signum. [L.] Necdum enim cor . . . [R.] O crux benedicta. [L.] Per diem semper . . . *In mat. l[aud. A.]* O magnum pietatis . . . A. Salua nos christe . . . A. O crux ammirabilis . . . A. Nos autem gloriari . . . A. Crux benedicta nitet . . . A. Adoramus te christe . . . A. Super omnia ligna . . . mors mortem superauit. alleluia.

Exaltation of the Cross (14 September), from the third nocturn of matins to lauds. The lessons are from Bavarian Homily B.II.9 (on John 3.1; see Barré, *Homéliaires*, 26–27 and 277).

ff. 17v–18v   *In natali sanctẹ mathẹ.* [A.] Sancta matheae dei euangelista . . .

[*Invit.*] Uenite adoremus. *In i. noct. A.* In omnem terram exiuit. [*L.* Q]uoniam deo cura est de hominibus ut plus animarum eorum curam gerat quam corporum . . . [*R.*] Ecce ego mitto. [*L.*] Et ideo dixi dominum . . . [*R.*] Tollite iugum. [*L.*] Cura ergo ut inchoauimus . . . *R.* Dum steteritis. [*L.*] Erant itaque duo magi Zaroes et Arfaxar [*sic*] . . . *R.* Uidi coniunctos uiros habentes. [*L.*] Hunc itaque ludificabant . . . [. . .] adorans et dicens . . . *R.* Nimis honorati. [*L.*] E[t susce]pit eum in domum . . . *R.* Non sunt loquele. [*L.* Post] hęc cum a nobis pauor . . . *R.* Constitues eos. [*In iii. noct.*] *A.* Estote fortes. [*L.*] In illo tempore. Uidit iesus hominem seden[tem] . . . *Omelia.* Ex lectione euangelica fratres karissimi [audiuimus quia] uidit iesus . . . [. . . *R.* . . . *L.*] Ideo enim peccatorem . . . *R.* Isti sunt uiri sancti. [*L.*] Matheus enim he// [. . .] donis spiritalibus . . . *In m. l.* Hoc est praeceptum.

St. Matthew (21 September), from first vespers to lauds. The lessons for first and second nocturns are from the *Vita S. Matthei* (BHL 5690; Mombritius, 257.35–258.35). The lessons for the third nocturn are from Bavarian Homily B.II.56 (on Matthew 9.9). The homily is based on Jerome, *In Mattheum* 9.9, with extracts from Bede, Homily II.22 (see Barré, *Homéliaires*, 26–27 and 342 and Barré, "Mondsee," 103). The upper margin of fol. 18 has been trimmed with loss of the first two lines of text. The outer margin of fol. 18 has been torn with loss of text.

f. 18v   *In natali sancti mauricii* [*A.* O uere sa]ncti milites thebei . . . [*L.*] Diocletianus [quondam romanae] rei publice princeps . . . [*R.* Martyres thebei bea]ti nobiles . . . [*V.* Erat eodem tempore] in exercitu . . . [*L.*] Illum namque contra amandum . . . *R.* Sanctus mauricius legionem . . . miles candidus et uictor//

St. Maurice (22 September), from first vespers to the first nocturn of matins. The lessons are from the *Vita Sancti Mauricii* (BHL 5741; *Acta Sanctorum, Sept.* VI, p. 345). The outer margin has been torn with loss of text.

f. 19r   [*A.* Archangele christi per gratiam . . .] //per unigenitum dominum . . . de laqueo mortis. alleluia.

St. Michael (29 September), portion of antiphon for second vespers. The upper margin has been trimmed with the loss of the top two lines of text.

f. 19r–v *In natali sancti dionisii. A.* Et facta est comes . . . *R.* Beatissimus dionisius christi . . . *V.* Et parisius domino . . . *R.* In hoc ergo loco . . . *V.* Hunc ergo

locum ... R. Hi sancti uiri ... V. Terrore subiecto multisque ... In mat.
laudes. A. Hi sancti uiri ... A. In hac ergo fidei ... A. Tali namque ad
dominum ... A. Beata nimium et ... [... A. In hoc ergo loco ...] quan‐
tum dei famulus ... recipere merentur auditum.

St. Dionysius (9 October), matins through second vespers. The upper
margin has been trimmed with the loss of the top two lines of text.

ff. 19v–20v In natali sancti [gal]li. [A.] Uenerabilis [gallus] diaconum ... Invita.
Confessorum regem adoremus ... In i. n. A. Parentes uero beati g[a]lli
... Ps. Beatus uir. A. Cumque bone indolis uir ... Ps. Quare. A. Cum
proficiscendi tempus ... Ps. Cum inuocarem. A. Pedibus uero sui ... Ps.
Uerba. A. O febrem omni ... Ps. Domine deus. A. Pro nobis [gallus] do‐
luit ... Ps. In domino confido. [L.] Cum praeclara sanctissimi uiri colum‐
bani qui et columba ... R. Parentes uero beati [gal]li ... V. Erant enim
religiosi ... [L.] Inter ceteros quos fama ... R. Beatus [gal]lus zelo pietatis
... V. In conspectu omnium ... [L.] Cumque bone indolis uir ... R. Co‐
lumbanus itaque beato gallo ... V. Cum ad horam ... [L.] Obscura autem
scripturarum ... R. Beatus [gall]us cum orandi ... V. Hoc uidens dia‐
conus ... In ii. noc. A. Inter prandendum diaconus ... Ps. Domine quis. A.
Uidentibus qui aderant [ad supr.] uiri ... Ps. Domine in uirtute. A. Cum
artifices de paruitate ... Ps. Domini est terra. A. Coeperunt omnes clerici
... Ps. Exaudi orationem. A. Sanctus pater respondit ... Ps. Te decet
ymnus. A. Ecclesie pastores audientes ... Ps. Bonum est confiteri. [L.]
Qua sapientię maturitate ... R. Domine iesu christe ... V. Qui de uirgine
nasci ... [L.] Ergo dum sacris instaret ... R. Electus dei [gallus] pariter
... et huiusmodi preces ef//[fudit]

St. Gall (16 October), from vespers to the second nocturn of matins. The
lessons are from Walahfrid Strabo's Vita S. Galli (BHL 3247; MGH Scrip‐
tores Rerum Merovingicarum 4, p. 285). The name of St. Gall has been
erased from the rubric and all the chants, but not from the lessons.

f. 21r [R. Fuerunt sine querela...] //calicem domum ... V. Tradiderunt corpora
sua ... In mat. l. [A.] Hoc est preceptum ... A. Maiorem caritatem nemo
... A. Uos amici mei ... A. Beati mundo corde ... A. Beati qui per‐
secutionem ... A. Tradent enim uos ... A. Dum steteritis ante reges ...
A. Uos autem dixi ... A. Non uos me elegistis ... A. Beati pacifici beati
... Ad vesp. A. Iurauit dominus. Ps. Dixit dominus. A. Collocet eum. Ps.
Laudate. A. Disrupisti. Ps. Credidi propter. A. Confortatus. Ps. Domine
probasti. A. Beati eritis cum uos ... A. Isti sunt triumphatores ... et acci‐
piunt palmam.

Common of Apostles, from the third nocturn of matins to second vespers.

ff. 21r–22   *Plurimorum sanctorum.* A. Absterget deus omnem . . . [*Invit.*] Regem martyrum. A. Secus decursus. *Ps.* Beatus uir. A. Predicantes. *Ps.* Quare fremuerunt. A. Filii hominum. *Ps.* Cum inuocarem. A. Scuto bonae. *Ps.* Uerba. A. In uniuersa. *Ps.* Domine dominus noster. A. Habitabunt. *Ps.* Domine quis habitabit. *v.* Letamini in domino. [*L.*] Quotiescumque fratres karissimi sanctorum martyrum sollempnia celebramus . . . R. Absterget deus omnem lacrimam . . . V. Iustorum autem anime . . . [*L.*] Ab eis enim sanctorum martyrorum . . . R. Uiri sancti gloriosum . . . V. Unus spiritus et . . . [*L.*] Imitari nos non pigeat . . . R. Tradiderunt corpora sua . . . V. Isti sunt qui . . . [*L.*] Sic et apostolus paulus . . . R. Sancti tui domine mirabile . . . V. Quoniam percussit petram . . . A. Sanctis qui in terra. [. . .] A. Hec est generatio. *Ps.* Domini est terra. A. Letamini. *Ps.* Beati qui. A. Clamau[erunt] A. Beati quos elegisti. *Ps.* Te decet. A. Vindica. *Ps.* Deus uenerunt. *v.* Ex[sultent iusti. *L.*] Sed dicit aliquis . . . R. Verbera carnificum non . . . V. Tradiderunt corpora sua . . . [*L.*] Audi non me . . . R. Propter testamentum domini . . . V. Ecce quam bonum. [*L.*] Ecce christus d[. . .] a me . . . R. In circuitu tuo domine . . . V. Magnus dominus et . . . [*L.*] Et lice[t . . .] ta in quibus . . . R. Cert[amen magnum habuerunt] sancti dei . . . V. Isti sunt sancti . . . [A. Dabo sanctis] meis locum . . . *v.* Mirabilis. *Lectio sancti evangelii secundum lucam.* [In illo tempore. D]escendens iesus de monte . . . [*Omelia.* Audisti]s ex lectione euangelica fratres karissimi exhortan[tem] . . . [R.] Hec est uera fratre[nitas] . . . V. Ecce quam bonum . . . [*L.* . . .] suum ad quod missus . . . R. Sancti mei qui . . . [V. Uenite bene]dicti patris . . . [*L.*] Quoniam uestrum est . . . [R. Exsultabunt] sancti in gloria . . . [V.] Epulen[tur et exsult]ent . . . [*L.* . . .]unc esuritis. quia . . . Qui enim iusticiam//

Common of Martyrs, from vespers to the third nocturn of matins. The lessons for the first two nocturns are from Caesarius, *Sermo* 223 (G. Morin, ed., CCSL 104 [1953], 882) = Alan of Farfa's Homiliary II.94 (see Grégoire, 185); the lessons for the third nocturn are from Bavarian Homily B.I.20 (on Luke 6.17; see Barré, *Homéliaires*, 26–27 and 267). The outer margin of fol. 22 has been trimmed with loss of text.

Parchment. 22 folios (11 bifolia from 6 quires of eight leaves each): the bifolium 1/2 formed the third and sixth leaves of Quire I; the bifolium 3/6 formed the second and seventh leaves, and the bifolium 4/5 formed the fourth and fifth leaves of Quire II; the bifolium 7/12 formed the second and seventh leaves, the bifolium 8/11 formed the third and sixth leaves, and the bifolium 9/10 formed the fourth and fifth leaves of Quire III; the bifolium 13/16 formed the second and seventh leaves and the bifolium 14/15 formed the fourth and fifth leaves of Quire IV; the bifolium 17/20 formed the second and seventh leaves and the bifolium 18/19 formed the third and sixth leaves of Quire V; the bifolium 21/22 formed the fourth and fifth leaves of Quire VI. The measurements of the fragments are as follows: fol. 1, 164 x 94 mm; fol. 2, 164 x 126 mm; fol. 3, 159 x 118 mm; fol. 4, 153 x 112 mm; fol. 5, 152 x 108 mm; fol. 6, 155 x 98 mm; fol. 7, 168 x 112 mm; fol. 8, 158 x 120 mm; fol. 9, 145 x 113 mm; fol. 10, 145 x 128 mm; fol. 11, 157 x 126 mm; fol. 12, 167 x 104 mm; fol. 13, 170 x 123 mm; fol. 14, 167 x 125 mm; fol. 15, 165 x 88 mm; fol. 16, 168 x 94 mm; fol. 17, 165 x 98 mm; fol. 18, 136 x 96 mm; fol. 19, 137 x 124 mm; fol. 20, 167 x 110 mm; fol. 21, 150 x 126 mm; fol. 22, 150 x 92 mm (written space 133 x 90 mm). 1 column. 27–29 lines. Dry-point ruling on the hair side before folding; double vertical and single horizontal bounding lines.

Written in two sizes of Caroline minuscule, with a smaller script for the chants and a larger script for the lessons. According to Prof. Hartmut Hoffmann, the script is similar to the style of Otloh of St. Emmeram and was perhaps written in Tegernsee or Regensburg (letter of 7 October 1993), perhaps in the circle of Otloh. Hoffmann further reports (letter of 8 November 1996) that there is a bifolium from the same manuscript among Bernhard Bischoff's papers now in Leipzig, Universitätsbibliothek, Nachlass Bischoff, s.n., and that Bischoff had also drawn a connection between the manuscript and Otloh. According to David Brafman of H. P. Kraus, Inc., the bifolium in Bischoff's collection was given to him by H. P. Kraus at the time that he wrote the expertise of the Zinniker collection, so it has the same provenance as the leaves now at Yale. 2-line initials at the beginning of offices and lessons are in red square capitals and are written between the vertical bounding lines. 1-line initials at the beginning of lessons are in red square capitals, with use of round E, and are written between the vertical bounding lines when they occur at the beginning of a line. 1-line initials at the beginning of chants are in brown square capitals with occasional use of uncial M and round E or an enlarged minuscule m. Rubrics are written in red rustic capitals. Rubric letters for chants are frequently written in the left margins. Liturgical directions are written in brown rustic capitals touched with red. Punctuation consists of the punctus for the end of chants, and the punctus, punctus versus, and punctus interrogativus for the lessons. The chants have interlinear neumes in the St. Gall style.

The manuscript formerly belonged to the Lambach library. The bifolium 21/22 was used in the binding of Lambach, Stiftsbibliothek, Ccl 261 (shelfmark on fol. 21v; the number "261P" is also written in the lower right corner of fol. 21r). Another bifolium from this manuscript is preserved as a flyleaf in the binding of Cologny, Bodmer Library, Codex 161 (formerly Lambach Cml VII). This bifolium contains the offices of St. Thomas and the fourth Sunday of Advent (fol. 1) and Christmas Eve (fol. 2) and would have been the outer bifolium of Quire I. These fragments are described by E. Pellegrin, *Manuscrits latins de la Bodmeriana* (Cologny-Geneva, 1982), 374–78. There are brief descriptions of both Cml VII and Ccl 261 in Holter (1959), 234 and 262 and Holter (1989), 220, cat. no. X.15 (Ccl 261). See above on the bifolium now in Leipzig.

A modern hand has added the following numbers in pencil in the lower right corner of several of the leaves: fol. 1, "133"; fol. 2, "132"; fol. 7, "122"; fol. 8, "136"; fol. 9, "120"; fol. 10, "121"; fol. 11, "137"; fol. 12, "123"; fol. 13, "130"; fol. 14, "135"; fol. 15, "134"; fol. 16, "131"; fol. 21, "128". It is possible that similar numbers once existed on the other folios but have since faded or been erased.

The bifolia 7/12 and 9/10 were formerly Beinecke MS 482.21 B and A. The Zinniker numbers for the bifolia are: fols. 1/2, Zinniker 232b; fols. 3/6, Zinniker 184a; fols. 4/5, Zinniker 184b; fols. 7/12, Zinniker 24.2; fols. 8/11, Zinniker 233b; fols. 9/10, Zinniker 24.1; fols. 13/16, Zinniker 233a; fols. 14/15, Zinniker 232a, fols. 17/20, Zinniker 183a; fol. 18/19, Zinniker 183b; fols. 21/22, Zinniker 231.

Bibliography:

Babcock, *Reconstructing a Medieval Library*, 95, 99, and figs. 23 and 52 (where the MS is incorrectly attributed to St. Gall).

MS 481.26   Southern Germany, s. XI/XII
Noted Breviary (Office of the Dead)   Pl. 19

ff. 1–3   //feruntur. pro ualde bonis gratiarum actiones sunt . . . Post resurrectionem uero facto . . . Quia sunt nonnulli qui de resurrectione . . . Multi enim sunt sicut et nos aliquando . . . Sicque apud se quasi ratio . . . Mirabilius namque est cælum . . . *De celebratione defunctorum atque resurrectione mortuorum lectio*. Quando cælebramus dies fratrum defunctorum in mente habere debemus . . . R. Scio enim quod redemptor . . . V. Surgunt mortui et resurgunt . . . [L.] In hac autem uita . . . R. Manus tuæ domine fecerunt . . . V. Dum ueneris iudicare . . . [L.] Qui credit in me . . . [R.] Memento queso domine quod . . . [. . . V. Uitam et misericordiam . . . L. Est autem fides . . .] hanc enim omnino . . . R. Si facta mea recompensare uolueris . . . [L.] Consolemur nos ergo inuicem . . . [. . . R. . . .]rum tabernaculum . . . V. Quando consumpseris uiuere . . . [L.] Si enim non praecessit peccatum . . . [. . . L. Si enim ergo nulla . . .] Omnia membrorum officia. R. Domine qui plasmasti me . . . V. Domine quicquid . . . [L.] Nonne ista est do//[mus]

Office of the Dead. The lessons are from Augustine, Sermon 173 (PL 38.937–39). The lessons are arranged in the same manner as they appear in twelfth-century sources from the diocese of Würzburg (see K. Ottosen, *The Responsories and Versicles of the Latin Office of the Dead* [Aarhus,

1993], 87; they correspond to his Group 10); Adalbero, bishop of Würzburg, founded Lambach in 1056. The responses, however, do not correspond to any of the sources examined by Ottosen. The lower margins of
fols. 1 and 2 have been trimmed with loss of text; the bottom two-thirds
of fol. 3 has been trimmed off.

Parchment. 3 folios. Fol. 1 measures 207 x 165 mm; fol. 2 measures 205 x 155 mm;
fol. 3 measures 97 x 207 mm (written space originally ca. 220 x 140 mm). 1 column. Fol. 1 preserves 24 lines, fol. 2 preserves 23 lines, and fol. 3 preserves 10 lines
of an original ca. 28. Dry-point ruling on the hair side. Double vertical and single
horizontal bounding lines. Prickings for horizontal rulings are on the inner vertical
bounding lines of the outer margin; prickings for the vertical lines are on the upper
and lower horizontal bounding lines.

Written in two sizes of Caroline minuscule, with a smaller script for the chants
and a larger one for the lessons, by the same scribe who copied the psalter preserved in Beinecke MS 481.46. Prof. Hartmut Hoffmann, letter of 8 November
1996, suggested the date, comparing the hand to that of Vienna, ÖNB, ser. n.
4236. On fol. 1v there is a 3-line initial "Q" in orange that has been filled, perhaps
at a later time, with crude brown cross-hatching. 2-line initials at the beginning of
lessons are in orange square capitals and are set apart from the text between the
double vertical bounding lines. 1-line initials are in brown rustic capitals, with use
of minuscule m and uncial M and round D, and are written between the double
bounding lines when they occur at the beginning of the line. The rubrics are
written in orange minuscules with rustic capital forms. Punctuation consists of the
punctus within chants, and the punctus and punctus elevatus within lessons. The
chants have interlinear neumes in the St. Gall style. A contemporary hand has
added marginal notation on fol. 3r.

These leaves were formerly used in the binding of Lambach, Stiftsbibliothek, Ccl
320 (shelf number "320" on fol. 2r; the number "106" that has been crossed out is
the old number of Ccl 320).

A modern hand has added in pencil in the lower right corner the number "111"
on fol. 1, "112" on fol. 2, and "113" on fol. 3.

Fol. 1 was formerly Beinecke MS 482.24B, Zinniker 42; fol. 2 was Zinniker
252A; fol. 3 was Zinniker 252B.

Bibliography:
Babcock, *Reconstructing a Medieval Library*, 99 and fig. 13.

MS 481.27   Southern Germany or Austria. s. XII
Noted Breviary   Pl. 19

f. 1   [Inc: Lectio sancti euangelii quam modo fratres audiuimus magnum
         nob]//is et in domino et in seruo . . . R. Dies sanctificatus illuxit nobis . . .
         V. Venite adoremus deum . . . [L.] Sed quia [omnis qui se hu]miliat . . . R.
         Videntes stellam magi . . . [. . . neces]sitate abluendi alicuius peccati . . . R.
         In [. . .] *Antip.* A. Magi uidentes stellam . . . A. Uidimus stellam eius . . . A.
         Vid[entes stellam] magi gauisi sunt . . . A. Cęli a[perti sunt super] eum
         . . . A. Aqua [comburit pec]catum hodie . . . A. Pater de cęlis fi[lium] . . .
         A. Baptizatur xpyctu[s et sanctificatur] omnis mundus et tribuens nobis
         remiss//[ionem]

         Epiphany (6 January), from the third nocturn of matins to lauds. The les-
         sons are from Bede, Homily I.12.2–27 (D. Hurst, ed., CCSL 122, pp. 80–
         81) = Paul the Deacon's Homiliary, Homily I.58 (see Grégoire, 440). In
         the margin of the verso a fifteenth-century hand has added neumed dif-
         ferentiae (evovae) and modal notations in roman numerals for the lauds
         antiphons. The inner and lower margins have been trimmed with loss of
         text.

f. 2   [R. Videte miraculum matris domini] //concepit uirgo uirile . . . V. Uirgo
         concepit et uirgo . . . [L.] Exultent uirgines; virgo maria . . . quę auditis et
         non audier[unt.] R. Gaude maria uirgo cunctas . . . V. Gabrielem arch-
         angelum credimus diuinitus t//[e]

         Purification of Mary (2 February), third nocturn of matins. The lessons
         are from Pseudo-Augustine, Sermon 370 (Inc: "Hodiernus dies ad ha-
         bendam spem . . ."; PL 39.1657–58); cf. also Alan of Farfa's Homiliary,
         Homily I.48 and Paul the Deacon's Homiliary, Homily I.65 (see Grégoire,
         151–52 and 442). A chant was added by a fifteenth-century hand next to
         the response "Gaude maria" in the lower margin of the verso. The lower
         margin has been trimmed with loss of text.

Parchment. 2 folios. 205 x 143 mm (written space originally ca. 217 x 130 mm). 1
column. 21 lines remaining of original ca. 24. Dry-point ruling on the hairside;
double vertical and single horizontal bounding lines. Prickings in outer margin.
    Written in two sizes of Caroline minuscule, with a smaller script for the chants
and a larger script for the lessons. 1-line initials at beginning of lessons and of lauds
are in orange square capitals or uncials and are not set apart from the text. Other
1-line initials are in brown rustic capitals with an enlarged minuscule *e* and are
occasionally highlighted with orange; they are written between vertical boundary

lines when they occur at the beginning of a line. The initials of the responses are ornamented with orange dots. Rubrics are written in orange capitals. Punctuation consists of the punctus within chants, and the punctus, punctus versus, and punctus interrogativus within lessons. Hyphenation is in the same ink as the text. The antiphons and responses have interlinear neumes in the St. Gall style. These are in a lighter shade of ink and may have been added by another hand.

Zinniker 223 A–B.

MS 481.28   France (?), s. XII^{med}
Pseudo-Clemens Romanus, *Recognitiones*   Pl. 20

ff. 1–2   //multitudine sequi eum cępi. et audire quę diceret . . . Vide inquit de reliquo. et interesto tractatibus meis.//

Pseudo-Clemens Romanus, *Recognitiones*, trans. into Latin by Rufinus of Aquileia, I.7–16; B. Rehm, ed., *Die Pseudo-Klementinen*, vol. 2, *Rekognitionen in Rufins Übersetzung*, Die Griechischen Christlichen Schriftsteller der ersten Jahrhunderte 51 (Berlin, 1965), 10.9–16.27.

Parchment. 2 folios (1 bifolium; the leaves formed the inner bifolium of the first quire of the manuscript). 270 x 240 mm (written space 235 x 172 mm). 2 columns. 36 lines. Ruled in lead. Prickings in upper and outer margin.

Written in late Caroline minuscule. 1-line initials are in a mixture of uncials and square capitals, mostly in black but occasionally in red, some of which seems to have oxidized to a silver color; they are not set apart from the text. Punctuation consists primarily of the punctus; there is occasional use of the punctus elevatus and the punctus versus, but these may be later alterations of the original punctus. Hyphenation is in the same ink as the text.

Zinniker 211. The number "10" is written in ink in the upper margin of fol. 1r.

MS 481.29   France or Italy, s. X/XI
Commentary on Galatians   Pl. 20

f. 1   //per repromissionem; Ismahel ex ancilla . . . caueat se de futuro et audiat quod sequitur//

Unidentified commentary on Galatians 4.23–29.

Parchment. 1 folio (a later hand has added the foliation "cxl" in the upper margin of the recto). 330 x 237 mm (written space 230 x 180 mm). 2 columns. 31 lines. Dry-point ruling on the hair side. Double outer and single inner vertical bounding lines; double horizontal bounding lines. Prickings in outer, upper, and lower margins.

Written in Caroline minuscule with archaic features such as half-uncial *g*, the *rt*-ligature, and occasionally half-uncial *a*. 1-line initials are in brown uncials, with an enlarged minuscule *e*. Punctuation consists of the punctus for major pauses and the punctus elevatus for minor pauses.

The fragment was used as the wrapper for a volume of an archival register measuring ca. 330 x 118 mm, when an inscription was added: "1670, 1671, 1672, et 1673, Second de la Cotte Deux, 3ᵉ Registre." There are also a number of pen trials in French on the verso.

Zinniker 207. The number "7" is written in ink in the upper margin of the recto.

MS 481.30   Southern Germany, s. XII
Gregory the Great, *Homeliae in Ezechielem*   Pl. 21

f. 1   [Inc: Uir cuius calamus mensurae in manu eius ecce describitur . . .]
            //nocte ac die et semen germinet . . . Et thalamum uno calamo in longum//

            Gregory, *Homeliae in Ezechielem*, Homily II.3.5-7; M. Adriaen, ed., CCSL
            142 (1971), 239–42; PL 76.960–62.

Parchment (recto is very faded). 1 folio. 320 x 200 mm (written space 240 x 135 mm). 1 column. 28 lines. Ruling is very faint, perhaps lead.

Written in late Caroline minuscule. 1-line initials are in brown in a mixture of uncial, rustic capital, and enlarged minuscule forms. Running titles are written in red rustic capitals in the upper margin (recto: "In ezechielem ult[imum(?)]" [very faint]; verso: "Omelia Gregorii III"). Punctuation consists of the punctus, punctus elevatus, punctus versus, and punctus interrogativus. Hyphenation is in the same ink as the text.

This folio was used as a pastedown in a binding. A modern hand has written the number "11" in pencil in the lower margin.

Zinniker 206. The number "6" is written in ink in the upper margin of the verso.

MS 481.31
Gradual

Southern Germany, s. XII[1]
Pl. 21

f. 1r   [V.]//Ad te domine clamaui . . . [Of.] Ad te domine. Co. Iustus dominus et . . . uidit uultus eius.

Feria IV of the second week of Quadragesima (from verse of graduale). The upper part has been trimmed with the loss of the top four lines of text.

f. 1r–v   *Feria quinta.* Deus in adiutorium meum . . . [Ps.] Auertantur retrorsum et . . . [Gr.] Propitius esto domine . . . Of. Precatus est moyses . . . V. Dixit dominus ad moysen . . . V. Dixit moyses et aaron . . . Co. Qui manducat carnem . . . in eo dicit dominus.

Feria V of the second week of Quadragesima. The upper part has been trimmed with the loss of the top four lines of text.

f. 1v   *Feria sexta.* Ego autem cum iusticia . . . Ps. Exaudi domine iusticiam meam. Gr. Ad dominum cum tribu//[larer]

Feria VI of the second week of Quadragesima.

f. 2r   [V. Quoniam do]//minus summus terribilis . . . V. Subiecit populos nobis . . . Co. Psallite domino qui . . . ad orientem alleluia.

Ascension. The upper part has been trimmed with the loss of the top four lines of text.

f. 2r   *Dominica.* Exaudi domine uocem meam . . . Ps. Dominus illuminatio mea. All. Ascendit deus. alleluia. [All.] Dominus in syna . . . Of. Viri galilei. Co. Pater cum essem cum eis.

Sunday after Ascension. The upper part has been trimmed with the loss of the top four lines of text. The last three lines are ruled but have been left blank. A fourteenth-century hand has added in those spaces and in the lower margin the following prayers for the mass of the "xi milium virginum" (21 October): *Coll.* Deus qui sanctam nobis huius diei sollempnitatem . . . *Secr.* Presentia munera quaesumus domine ita serena pietate . . . *Compl.* Sumpsimus domine sanctarum virginum . . . consequamur. Per D.

f. 2v   [*Off.* Emitte spiritum . . . fa]//ciem terrę sit gloria . . . *V.* Benedic anima
         mea . . . *V.* Confessionem et decorem induisti . . . *V.* Extendens cęlum
         sicut . . . *Co.* Ultimo festiuitatis die . . . credentes in eum alleluia. alleluia.

         Vigil of Pentecost. The upper part has been trimmed with the loss of the
         top four lines of text. The last four lines are ruled but have been left
         blank. A different fourteenth-century hand from that on fol. 2r has added
         in those spaces and in the lower margin the following prayers for the mass
         of St. Catharine of Alexandria (25 November): *Coll. de Sancta Katerina.*
         Deus qui moysi famulo tuo in monte syna . . . Munera nostra domine
         sacrificii praesentis que tibi offerimus . . . *Complendum.* Sumptis domine
         salutis nostre subsidiis suppliciter deprecamur . . . expellat. Per dom.

f. 3r   [*Co.* Uouete et red]//dite domino deo . . . principium terrib//[ili]

         Seventeenth Sunday after Pentecost. The upper margin has been trimmed
         with the loss of the top four lines of text. The outer margin has also been
         trimmed with loss of text.

f. 3r   *Feria iiii* Me[*nsis vii ad sanctam mariam.*] Exultate deo adiutori nostri . . .
         Gr. Quis sicut dominus deus . . . *V.* Su[scitans] a terra . . . *Of.* Meditabar
         in mandatis. *Co.* Comedite pingui[a et] . . . etenim [domini est for]titudo
         nostra.

         Feria IV after the seventeenth Sunday after Pentecost. The outer margin
         has been trimmed with loss of text.

f. 3r   *Feria Sexta.* Letetur cor querentium. *Gr.* Conuer[tere domine.] *Of.* Bene-
         dic anima mea. *Co.* Aufer a me obprob[rium et contemp]tum . . . exquisiui
         domine na//[m]

         Feria VI after seventeenth Sunday after Pentecost. The outer margin has
         been trimmed with loss of text.

f. 3v   [*Sabbato.* Uenite adoremus deum . . . no]//ster. *Ps.* Ipsum. *Gr.* Protector
         noster. *Gr.* Dirigatur. [*Gr.* Saluum fac. G]*r.* Conuertere. *Ymnus.* Bene-
         dictus es domine. [*Tract.* Laudate dominum.] *Of.* Domine deus salutis
         męę. *Co.* Mense septi[mo festa celebrabi]tis . . . dominus deus uester.

         Saturday after the seventeenth Sunday after Pentecost. The outer margin
         has been trimmed with loss of text.

f. 3v   *Dominica xviii.* [Da pa]cem domine sustinen[tibus] ... *Ps.* Letatus sum.
        [*All* ...] alleluia. *Of.* Sanctificauit moyses ... [*V.* Locutus est do]minus ad
        moysen dicens ascen//[de]

        Eighteenth Sunday after Pentecost. The outer margin has been trimmed
        with loss of text.

Parchment (fol. 1v damaged by glue from use in a binding). 3 folios (fols. 2 and 3
are a bifolium). Fol. 1 measures 220 x 157 mm; fol. 2, 210 x 116 mm; fol. 3, 210 x
188 mm (written space originally ca. 195 x 115 mm). 1 column. 16 of ca. 20 lines
remaining. Dry-point ruling on the hair side. Double vertical and horizontal bounding lines. Prickings in lower margin.

Written in Caroline minuscule. 3-line initials are in red, *D* in square capital and
E in uncial, and are not set apart from the text. 1-line initials are either red square
capitals or brown rustic capitals. Rubrics are written in red usually as rustic capitals,
but once as minuscules; rubrics are set apart from the text between the double
bounding lines when they occur at the beginning of a line. Punctuation consists of
the punctus, placed on the bottom line, at the end of chants. Interlinear neumes
are in the St. Gall style. Numbered cues have been added in red above all abbreviated chants, perhaps by one of the hands who added prayers at the bottom of
fols. 2r and 2v. The initials of the two added collects are also in red, and the rubrics
are written in red minuscule.

Fol. 1 was used as a pastedown in a binding. The bifolium was used as a wrapper
for the binding of a volume measuring ca. 210 x 150 mm, perhaps owned by "Frater
Fridericus Flokch," whose name is written on fol. 3r in a fifteenth-century German
hand. He is apparently identical to the man mentioned as a *plebanus* in the inscription dated 1472 in a book sold by Christie's (New York, 17 April 2000) lot 43,
perhaps from Scheyern. A modern hand has added in pencil in the lower right corner the number "115" on fol. 2 and "116" on fol. 3. A different hand has written
the number "118" in pencil in the upper left corner of fol. 1v.

Fol. 1 was formerly Beinecke MS 482.16, Zinniker 39; the bifolium 2/3 was formerly Zinniker 236.

MS 481.32   Italy, s. XI²
Pseudo-Haimo of Halberstadt, *Comm. in Epistolam ad Hebraeos*   Pl. 22

f. 1   //moysen. uel per angelum data sunt ... Et hospitalitem. nolite obliuisci.//

        Pseudo-Haimo of Halberstadt, *Commentarium in Epistolam ad Hebraeos*,
        chaps. 12–13; PL 117.927–29; Stegmüller 3114.

f. 2   //Quia ergo inter illos erant ... et feruore sancti spiritus accensi. con-
          sumunt//

          Commentarium in Epistolam ad Hebraeos, chap. 13; PL 117.932–33.

Parchment (fols. 1r and 2v are stained with glue from use in a binding). 2 folios
(probably formed the third bifolium of a quire, with two leaves missing in between).
325 x 232 mm (written space 255 x 150 mm). 1 column. 35 lines. Dry-point ruling
on the hair side; double vertical bounding lines. Prickings in upper and lower
margins.
      Written in Caroline minuscule. 1-line initials are in brown rustic capitals with
occasional use of an enlarged minuscule *e*; the initials are set apart from the text
between double bounding lines when they occur at the beginning of a line.
Punctuation consists of the punctus and punctus interrogativus. A contemporary
hand has made corrections and altered punctuation in a somewhat lighter ink.
      Both leaves, which were originally a bifolium, were once used as pastedowns in
a binding. A modern hand has written the number "XI" in pencil in the upper
margin of both leaves.
      Zinniker 209, 210. The numbers "9" and "9 bis" are written in ink in the upper
margin of the recto of fols. 1 and 2.

MS 481.33   Southern Germany or Austria, s. XII^{med}
Breviary   Pl. 22

f. 1r   In illo tempore. Factum est in una dierum; ... erat ad sanandum eos. Et
          reliqua. *Omelia lectionis ei[usdem.]* Dominus ac redemptor noster fratres
          dilectissimi. multis signis ... [L.] Curatio paralytici huius saluationem ...
          [L.] Qui bene marco narrante ... omnia uicia curantur.

          Feria VI after Pentecost. The lessons are from the Homiliary of Mondsee,
          Homily 77 (see Barré, "Mondsee," at 92). The outer margin has been
          trimmed with loss of text.

f. 1r–v   S[abbato.] Secundum Lu[cam.] In illo tempore. Surgens iesus de synagoga;
          ... tenebatur magnis febribus. Et reliqua. O[melia.] Quia ergo dominus et
          saluator noster ad liberandum ... [L.] Primo lingua ... animę quam
          prauitate peccauerat.

          Saturday after Pentecost. The lessons are from the Homiliary of Mondsee,
          Homily 78 (see Barré, "Mondsee," 92). The lower and outer margins have
          been trimmed with loss of text.

f. 1v   *In octaua pentecosten. Secundum Iohannem.* [In] illo tempore. Erat homo ex
         pharis nichodemus . . . a deo uenisti magister. Et reliqua. [*Omelia.* Si]cut
         ex lectione sancti ęuangelii fratres karissimi audistis . . . R. Benedicat nos
         deus. [L. Ra]bbi inquit. scimus quia a deo . . . R. Benedictus. [L. Res]-
         pondit enim iesus . . . Or. Gracias agimus deo qui . . . de potestate tene-
         brarum. et transtu//[lit]

         Octave of Pentecost. The lessons are from Bede, Homily II.18 (D. Hurst,
         ed., CCSL 122 [1955], 311) = Paul the Deacon's Homiliary, Homily II.16
         (see Grégoire, 456). The lower and outer margins have been trimmed with
         loss of text.

Parchment. 1 folio. 270 x 205 mm (original written space uncertain; width of
written space originally ca. 205 mm). 1 column. 28 lines remaining. Dry-point
ruling on the hair side. Double vertical bounding lines.

Written in two sizes of late Caroline minuscule, with a smaller script for the
responses and a larger script for the lessons. 2-line initials are in orange-red square
capitals and are set apart from the text between double bounding lines. 1-line initials are in orange-red square capitals and are set apart from the text between the
double bounding lines when they occur at the beginning of a line. Other 1-line
initials are in brown rustic capitals and are not set apart from the text. Rubrics are
written in orange-red, which in places has oxidized into a silver color. Punctuation
consists of the punctus and the punctus elevatus. Hyphenation is in the same ink
as the text.
Zinniker 187.

MS 481.34   Italy, s. XII[1]
Homiliary   Pl. 23

We have not identified a homiliary containing all five of these homilies. The manuscript seems to contain a compilation of several homiliaries, including those of Paul
the Deacon and Alan of Farfa (cf. Beinecke 481.13).

ff. 1–2r   [Inc: Congregemus in unum ea quae in ortu iesu dicta . . . re]//dimeret a
           peccatis. et daret nobis spem . . . quam lucas sapientię nomine com-
           mendans. Praestante domino nostro iesu christo qui cum patre et spiritu
           sancto uiuit et regnat deus. per omnia saecula saeculorum. Amen.

           Paul the Deacon's Homiliary, Homily I.41 (Sunday after Christmas); PL
           95.1183–85. This homily combines material from Origen and Bede on

Luke 2.33 (see Grégoire, 438). Grégoire omits from his description the first of the excerpts from Bede that is found in the fragment ("nulla docet ... mentis intelligitur," from Bede, *In Lucae evangelium expositio*, I.2.1941–51; D. Hurst, ed., CCSL 120 [1960], 68). The upper margin has been trimmed with the loss of the first line of text.

f. 2r–v   *Sermo sancti augustini Infra O[ctava] d[omini]* Predicamus uobis fratres karissimi saluatorem nuper de uirgine natum ... Probat uirtutem domini ordo nascendi.//

Pseudo-Augustine, Sermon 121 (Octave of Christmas); PL 39.1987–88 and PLS 3.180–81 = Alan of Farfa, Homiliary, Homily I.2e (see Grégoire, 139–40); on this homily see H. Barré, "Le sermon pseudo-augustinien *App. 121*," *Revue des Études Augustiniennes* 9 (1963): 111–37, esp. 129–36. The upper margin has been trimmed with the loss of the first line of text.

f. 3r   [Inc: Christus nascitur exultat mens hominum ...] //quam suauis est dominus ... ut nemo de ipsius deitate dubitet nunciatur.

Pseudo-Augustine, Sermon 177 (Octave of Christmas); Mai, 1:399; PLS 2.1275–76. CPL 372.

f. 3r–v   *In octaua domini lectio.*
Primo tempore. Et consolamini. Et consurge. Require retro in natiuitate domini. *Sermo Sancti augustini episcopi.*
Audistis fratres karissimi quemadmodum nobis beatus euangelista ... merito hodie locuti sunt celi//

Pseudo-Augustine, Sermon 128 (Octave of Christmas; on Isaiah 9.1; 40.1; 52.1); PL 39.1997–98 (incipit given in note b) = Alan of Farfa, Homiliary, Homily I.2a; PL 39.1997–98 (see Grégoire, 139). CPL 368.

f. 4r–v   [Inc: Fateor sanctitate uestrae timueram ne frigus ...] //pater in uoce. et filius in homine ... Ipse uos baptizabit in spiritu sancto et igni.

Augustine, *In evangelium Iohannis tractatus* 6.5.11–7.23 (on John 1.32–33; Feria VI of the fourth week of Quadragesima); R. Willems, ed., CCSL 36 (1954), 56–57. CPL 278.

f. 4v   *Lectio sancti euangelii secundum matheum.*
In illo tempore. Venit iesus a galilea ... baptizaretur ab eo. Et reliqua.
Omelia beati hieronomi presbyteri.

Triplicem ob causam saluator a iohanne . . . ne quis putaret//

Jerome, *Commentariorum in Mattheum libri IV*, I.277–303 (on Matthew 3.13); D. Hurst and M. Adriaen, ed., CCSL 77 (1969), 18–19.

Parchment. 4 folios (fols. 1 and 2 are a bifolium). Fols. 1 and 2 measure 330 x 210 mm; fols. 3 and 4 measure 315 x 240 mm (written space 265 x 180 mm). 2 columns. 31 lines. Dry-point ruling on the hair side before folding. Double vertical and triple horizontal bounding lines.

Written in Caroline minuscule. 1-, 3-, and 4-line homily initials and lesson initials are in red square capitals and are set apart from the text between double bounding lines. 1-line initials are in brown rustic capitals with enlarged minuscule forms of *e*, *h*, and *n*; they are set apart from the text between double bounding lines when they occur at the beginning of a line. Rubrics are written in red minuscule. The first word of the sermon on fol. 3r ("Audistis") is written in brown rustic capitals highlighted with red. The first letter after the initials of other sermons and of lessons is in brown rustic capitals. Punctuation consists primarily of the punctus, with rare use of the punctus elevatus. The punctus interrogativus is also used. Accents and hyphenation are in the same ink as the text.

The bifolium was used as a wrapper for an archival register measuring ca. 330 x 210 mm. The date "1603" is written on the spine, and on fol. 2v it has the following title, "Colligenda des Zinns und Gülltten von Sanct Arbogast, Geföllen de Anno 1603." Fols. 2 and 3 were each used as wrappers for volumes measuring ca. 315 x 112 mm. A modern hand has written in pencil the number "XII" in the upper margins of fols. 3r and 4v (erased). The number "XII" is written in pencil in the upper margins of fol. 3.

Zinniker 213, 214, 215. The numbers "12," "12a" and "12b" are written in ink in the upper margins.

MS 481.35   Italy, s. XII^{in}
Homiliary   Pl. 23

f. 1r   [Inc: Post illum sacrosanctum domini diem . . .] //a delectationibus et mollissimis suauitatibus . . . et ea ieiuniis atque elemosinis redimendo. Ipso adiuuante qui cum patre et spiritu sancto uiuit et regnat in saecula saeculorum.

Pseudo-Augustine, Sermon 196 (John the Baptist; 24 June); PL 39.2112–13; CPL 368.

f. 1r   *Lectio sancti euangelii secundum lucam.*
          In illo tempore. Dixit Zacharias ad angelum Unde hoc sciam . . . quae
          implebuntur in tempore suo. Et reliqua.
          Omelia beati ambrosii episcopi lectionis eiusdem.
          Condempnatur silentio incredulitas sacerdotis . . . et ideo ubi desiuit//

          Ambrose, *Expositio evangelii secundum Lucam*, I.593–613 (on Luke 1.18–
          20; John the Baptist, 24 June); M. Adriaen, ed., CCSL 14 (1957), 26;
          CPL 143.

f. 2v   [Inc: Quia longius ab urbe digressi sumus . . .] //prelia et seditiones nolite
          terreri . . . Et quidem si inimicus meus male//[dixisset]

          Gregory the Great, *Homiliae xl in evangelia*, Homily II.35 (St. Mennas; 11
          November); PL 76.1259–61. The "Quia" of the incipit is visible on the
          recto, which has been otherwise erased.

Parchment (fols. 1v and 2r have been completely erased except for a large initial
"Q" on fol. 2r). 2 folios (a later hand has added the folio number "ccxliii" in the
center of the upper margin of fol. 1r; the foliation on fol. 2r is illegible). Fol. 1
measures 455 x 316 mm; fol. 2 measures 513 x 330 mm (written space 381 x 255
mm). 2 columns. 52 lines. Dry-point ruling. Single vertical bounding lines.

Written in Caroline minuscule. Two 7-line initials in yellow on a square ground,
colored with blue, red, dark red, and green and decorated with white interlacing
foliage, not set apart from the text (cf. O. Pächt and J. J. G. Alexander, *Illuminated
Manuscripts in the Bodleian Library* [Oxford, 1966–73], vol. 2, pl. IV.36, a manuscript of the first half of the twelfth century from northern Italy). 2-line initials at
the beginning of lessons are in red square capitals, set apart from the text. 1-line
initials are in brown uncials and are not set apart from the text. The rubrics are
written in red uncials with rustic capital D. The first word of the homily, the phrase
"[I]n illo tempore" and the first initial of the biblical text are written in brown
uncials with rustic capital D filled with red. Punctuation consists of the punctus,
punctus elevatus, and punctus interrogativus.

The fragments were used as outer wrappers for a volume measuring ca. 420 x
290 mm. On fol. 2r a sixteenth-century hand has written "Bal: super .i. pars ue-
teri:", referring to Baldus de Ubaldis, *Super I parte Digesti veteris*, which was published in several fifteenth- and sixteenth-century editions.

Fol. 1 was formerly Zinniker 180; fol. 2 was formerly Beinecke MS 482.50, Zinniker 80.

MS 481.36   Münster-Schwarzach or Lambach, s. XI^{med}
Hymnal   Pl. 24

It is likely that this hymnal once formed a companion volume to several other manuscripts from Lambach. These include a sequentiary (now Beinecke 481.39; see below), a troper (Lambach Fragment 1), an Easter table (Lambach Fragment 2) and a calendar (Lambach Fragment 4). All were written in the same scriptorium and are of similar, if not exact, format. Collections of such volumes were common in this period; see Heinrich Husmann, *Tropen- und Sequenzen-handschriften* (Munich, 1964), esp. 35–46, on St. Gall MSS 378, 380, 381, and 382.

f. 1r   Illuminans altissimus micantium . . . subrepunt uiris. Gloria tibi domine.

           Ambrose, hymn 7 (Epiphany, 6 January); AH 50.10; Schaller-Könsgen 7737.

f. 1r–v   *In natali Sancti Benedicti.* Christe sanctorum decus atque uirtus vita . . . creator spiritus regnat. Amen.

           Anon., s. IX (St. Benedict, 21 March); AH 2.31; Schaller-Könsgen, 2246. Two lines of text have been erased and then rewritten by a late twelfth-century hand.

f. 1v   *In lxxma.* Alleluia dulce carmen . . . laudaturi perpetim. Amen.

           Anon., s. IX (Septuagesima); AH 51.53; Schaller-Könsgen 559.

ff. 1v–2r *In xlma.* Clarum decus ieiunii . . . auge mentium dans spiritale gaudium. Preces pater.//

           Anon., s. VII? (Quadragesima); AH 51.57; Schaller-Könsgen 2365. A late twelfth-century hand has made some additions to the text.

f. 2r   *Item alia.* Nunc tempus acceptabile . . . perenne pascha transitu. Preces beata trinitas.

           Anon., s. X? (Quadragesima); AH 51.56; Schaller-Könsgen 10773.

f. 2r–v   *De ascensione domini.* Hymnum canamus glorię . . . et paraclito in sęculorum sęcula. Amen.

           Bede, Carm. 6 (Ascension); AH 50.82; Schaller-Könsgen 7438.

f. 2v   *De sanctis petro et paulo*. Apostolorum passio diem . . . caput sedes magistri
           gentium. Deo patri.

           Ambrose, hymn 12 (Sts. Peter and Paul, 29 June); AH 50.15; Schaller-
           Könsgen 940.

f. 2v   Petre pontifex inclite . . . disrumpe crimina//

           Anon., s. X? (St. Peter the Apostle, 29 June); AH 51.190; Schaller-
           Könsgen 11949.

Parchment. 2 folios. Fol. 1 measures 283 x 212 mm (written space 222 x 145 mm);
fol. 2 measures 243 x 203 mm (written space 215 x 145 mm). 1 column. 23 lines.
Dry-point ruling on the hair side. Double vertical and single horizontal bounding
lines. Prickings in outer margins.

Written in an elegant Caroline minuscule in the same style and presumably in
the same scriptorium as Beinecke MS 481.39 (a sequentiary) and several other
fragments still in Lambach: Lambach Fragment 1, preserving portions of a troper
that include the Lambach Magi play (see K. F. Lerner, "Zum Lambacher Dreikön-
igspiel, einer liturgischen Dreikönigsfeier des 11. Jahrhunderts aus Schwarzach am
Main. Eine Neumenfragmentstudie" [Diss., Hochschule für Musik, Munich,
1957]); Lambach Fragment 4, a calendar with necrological entries preserving entries for July and August (see MGH *Necrologia Germaniae* [Berlin, 1920], 4:404–16;
and Elmar Hochholzer, "Ein Lambacher Kalendar-Nekrologfragment [11. Jahr-
hundert] aus Münsterschwarzach?," *Frühmittelalterliche Studien* 29 [1995]: 226–72);
and Lambach Fragment 2, a computistical fragment containing an Easter table. The
localization of these fragments to Münster-Schwarzach or Lambach is related to the
question of their date, specifically whether they were copied before or after 1056,
the year that Bishop Adalbero of Würzburg sent monks from Münster-Schwarzach
to found Lambach. The dating of the leaves is complicated by the absence of iden-
tifiable samples from the eleventh-century scriptorium of Münster-Schwarzach.
Believing the Magi play to have been written for use at Münster-Schwarzach before
the founding of Lambach, Bernhard Bischoff dated the troper fragments (Lambach
Fragment 1) to the end of the tenth or the beginning of the eleventh century (cited
by Lerner, 8 and by Gamber, CLLA, 557, probably repeating Lerner); however,
when he examined the leaves of Beinecke 481.39, which are in better condition
than the leaves still at Lambach (and thus should provide a better basis for paleographical dating), and not knowing their connection to the Lambach fragments,
Bischoff assigned them a date at the end of the eleventh or beginning of the twelfth
century (*Monumenta Palaeographica* [unpublished typescript at the Beinecke Rare
Book and Manuscript Library], 11).

Further evidence on the date of the fragments is supplied by the deaths noted in the calendar in Lambach Fragment 4 (see Lerner, 49–58; Hochholzer, 258 ff.). An edition of the calendar fragment and discussion of the dating and localization of the manuscript is provided by Hochholzer, who favors the attribution to Münster-Schwarzach.

The 2-line initials at the beginning of hymns and the 1-line initials at the beginning of verses are set apart from the text between the vertical bounding lines and are written in orange uncials. The rubrics are written in orange rustic capitals. The first 1 to 4 words of each hymn are written in brown rustic capitals. There is space for neumes in the outer margins, but they have not been added, nor are the margins ruled for them (cf. MS 481.39). Punctuation consists of the punctus.

In addition to Beinecke 481.39 and Lambach Fragments 1, 2, and 4, other fragments related to this manuscript are preserved in the fifteenth-century binding of Lambach Ccl 314 (see Holter [1959], 262 and "Mittelalterliche Buchkunst," cat. no. X.07). The pastedown on the front cover preserves portions of the sequences "[Hanc concordi famulatu]" (for St. Stephen, 26 December; AH 53.215; von den Steinen, 14; Schaller-Könsgen 6070) and "Christi domini militis" (for St. Stephen; AH 53.216; von den Steinen, 95; Schaller-Könsgen 2259); the pastedown on the back cover preserves "Christe cunctorum dominator" (Schaller-Könsgen 2167). There are also strips from the manuscript sewn around each quire. The texts on the front pastedown, both of which are sequences from the St. Gall Hymnal, suggest that they were taken from the same manuscript as Beinecke MS 481.39. The back pastedown, however, may belong to the same hymnal as MS 481.36, since it contains a hymn not found in the St. Gall Hymnal. Furthermore, like MS 481.36, it has no neumes in its outer margin. The margin of the front pastedown, which would have contained neumes if it had the same format as MS 481.39, has been trimmed off. The use of these two pastedowns in the same binding strongly suggests that the hymnal and the sequentiary were bound together as part of the same volume, at least in the fifteenth century.

A modern hand has written the number "37" in pencil in the lower right corner of fol. 1 and "38" in the lower right corner of fol. 2.

Fol. 1 was formerly Zinniker 254; fol. 2 was formerly Beinecke MS 482.18, Zinniker 9.

Bibliography:
Babcock, *Reconstructing a Medieval Library*, 100 and fig. 54.

MS 481.37   Germany, s. XI^2
Noted Missal   Pl. 24

f. 1r   //*Ad co.* Praesta quaesumus omnipotens deus ut sanctorum tuorum . . . *Co.*

Iustorum animę in manu.

Sts. Felix, Simplicius, Faustinus, and Beatrice (29 July).

f. 1r   *Eodem die. sancti felicis.* Sancti felicis domine ... *Secretum.* Hostias tibi
         domine pro commemoratione ... *Ad co.* Repleti cibo potuque ... et
         precibus. Per.

St. Felix II, Antipope (29 July).

f. 1r–v *III kalendas augusti. natalis sanctorum abdon et sennes.* Ant. Intret in con-
         spectu ... *Ps.* Deus uenerunt gentes. *Or.* Deus qui sanctis tuis abdon et
         sennen ... *Lectio epistulae beati [pauli] ad corinthios.* Fratres. Spectaculum
         facti sumus ... *Gr.* Gloriosus deus in ... *G.* Te martirum candidatus.
         Evang. Hoc est praeceptum meum. *require in natali sancti marci euan-
         gelistae; id est in .vii. kalendis maii. Of.* Mirabilis deus in ... *Secretum.* Hostia
         hęc quaesumus domine. *Co.* Posuerunt mortalia seruorum tuorum do-
         mine. *Ad co.* Per huius domine operationem ... compleantur. Per.

Sts. Abdon and Senan (30 July). The lesson is from 1 Corinthians 4.9–12.
The lower margin has been trimmed with loss of text.

f. 1v   *Kalendae augusti uincula sancti petri.* Ant. Nunc scio uere quia misit domi-
         nus. [*Or.*] Deus qui beatum petrum ... exclude. Per.

Chains of St. Peter (1 August).

f. 1v   *Natalis vii. fratrum.* Fraterna nos domine ... *Lectio libri sapientiae.* Mulie-
         rem fortem quis ... surrexit. d//[editque]

Seven Maccabean Brothers (1 August). The lesson is from Proverbs
31.10–15. The lower margin has been trimmed with loss of text.

Parchment. 1 folio. 208 x 190 mm (written space originally ca. 223 x 148 mm). 1
column. 21 lines remaining of an original ca. 24 lines. Dry-point ruling on the hair
side. Double vertical and upper horizontal bounding lines. Prickings in upper
margin.
    Written in two sizes of Caroline minuscule, with a larger script for the lessons
and prayers and a smaller script for the chants. 2-line initials are in orange square
capitals, but with round *D*, and are set apart from the text between double bounding lines. 1-line initials are in brown rustic capitals, frequently filled with orange,
and are not set apart from the text. Rubrics are written in orange minuscule with

uncial M and occasional rustic capital forms. Punctuation consists of the punctus and the punctus elevatus. Chants on the recto have interlinear neumes in the St. Gall style.

In the lower margin of fol. 1r a modern hand has written the number "110" in pencil.

Zinniker 237.

MS 481.38
Paul the Deacon, Homiliary

Germany, s. X/XI
Pl. 25

f. 1r–v [Inc: Iohannes baptista et praecursor domini . . .] //attestante qui ait . . . reconciliaret nos deo patri cum quo uiuit et regnat deus in unitate spiritus sancti per omnia saecula saeculorum. Amen.

Paul the Deacon, Homily I.49 (Feria IV after Epiphany) = Bede, Homily I.15; D. Hurst, ed., CCSL 122 (1955), 109–10. See Grégoire, 439.

f. 1v *Item sermo beati maximi episcopi de eodem epiphaniorum die.*
Quamuis dilectissimi fratres christus salutis . . . dedit eam//

Paul the Deacon, Homily I.50 (Within the Octave of Epiphany) = Pseudo-Maximus Taurinensis, Homily 26; PL 57.281. See Grégoire, 439. CPL 220.

Parchment (badly stained on both recto and verso and areas cut out for use in binding). 1 folio, cut in half (the quire mark "xvi" is in the center of the lower margin on the verso). 397 x 315 mm (written space 313 x 220 mm). 2 columns. 32 lines. Dry-point ruling. Double vertical bounding lines. Pricking close to text in outer margin.

Written in Caroline minuscule. According to Prof. Hartmut Hoffmann, letter of 8 November 1996, the manuscript was written "ca. 1000" and "das x hat eine Form, die vor allem am Niederrhein zu finden ist." 3-line square capital "Q" ("Quamuis") is orange and extends partially into the margins across the double bounding lines. The next three letters of the word are in brown square capitals and are written inside the bowl of the "Q". The remainder of the first line is written in brown rustic capitals. 1-line initials are in brown uncials and are not set apart from the text. The rubric is written in orange rustic capitals. The first line of the sermon is in brown rustic capitals. Punctuation consists of the punctus.

This leaf has been cut in half horizontally and used in the binding of two volumes, one measuring ca. 165 x 105 mm and the other ca. 170 x 110 mm. A modern hand has written textual identifications and the date "saec. X" one the upper portion of fol 1v. Another modern hand has written a partially illegible notation ". . . 10269" on fol. 1v.

    Zinniker 186 A, B.

MS 481.39   Münster-Schwarzach or Lambach, s. XI^med

Sequentiary   Pl. 26

f. 1r   [Inc: Festa Christi omnis . . .] //nobis baptisma . . . populi preceptori.

        Notker Balbulus (Epiphany, 6 January); AH 53.29; von den Steinen, 22; Schaller-Könsgen 5069. The inner margin has been trimmed with loss of text.

f. 1r   *De una uirgine. filia matris.*
        [Uirgi]nis uenerande [de num]ero . . . [co]nsolationem precando.

        Anon., Hymn. Sangall. (Agnes, 21 January); AH 53.246; von den Steinen, 105; Schaller-Könsgen 17306. The words "uel socii" have been added, perhaps by the text scribe, above the name of Agnes in the text. The inner margin has been trimmed with loss of text.

f. 1r–v   *Symphonia. in purificationem sancte marie.*
        [Conc]entu parili hic . . . spiritui sit per euum.

        Notker Balbulus (Purification of Mary; 2 February); AH 53.99; von den Steinen, 24; Schaller-Könsgen 2505. A supplementary stanza ("[Sanc]tissima corpore . . . virginum") has been added by a contemporary hand in the lower margin of fol. 1r. The inner margin has been trimmed with loss of text. The last five lines of the verso are blank.

f. 2r–v   *In die sancto pasche. Fricdola.*
        Laudes saluatori uoce . . . spiritales chori trinitati.

        Notker Balbulus (Easter); AH 53.36; von den Steinen, 28; Schaller-Könsgen 8759. The bottom seven lines of the leaf have been trimmed off.

f. 2v   *Feria II.*
        Laudes Christo redempti . . . adunate gaudia//

Anon., Hymn. Sangall. (Feria II after Easter); AH 53.45; von den Steinen, 109; Schaller-Könsgen 8742. The bottom seven lines of the leaf have
been trimmed off.

f. 3r   [Inc: Summi triumphum regis . . .] //nubes polosque cursu . . . semper sit
nobiscum.

Notker Balbulus (Ascension); AH 53.67; von den Steinen, 50; Schaller-
Könsgen 15834.

f. 3r   *Alia unde supra. dominus in syna.*
Christus hunc diem . . . tu dignare custodire.

Notker Balbulus (Ascension); AH 53.68; von den Steinen, 52; Schaller-
Könsgen 2292.

f. 3r–v   *In Pentecosten. occidentana.*
Sancti spiritus assit . . . diem gloriosum fecisti.

Notker Balbulus (Pentecost); AH 53.70; von den Steinen, 54; Schaller-
Könsgen 14655.

f. 3v   *Alia.*
Ueni spiritus ęternorum . . . munus esse crederis.//

Anon., s. X/XI (Pentecost); AH 53.71; Schaller-Könsgen 17050.

Parchment. 3 folios. Fol. 1 measures 262 x 185 mm; fol. 2 measures 190 x 208 mm;
fol. 3 measures 270 x 230 mm (written space 220 x 145 mm). 1 column. 28 lines.
Dry-point ruling on the hair side. Horizontal text rulings extend into outer margins
to accommodate neumes. Double vertical bounding lines.
    Written in Caroline minuscule in the same style and apparently in the same
scriptorium as the hymnal Beinecke MS 481.36. On the dating and localization of
these leaves see the description of MS 481.36. 1- and 2-line initials are a mixture
of orange uncials and square capitals and are set apart from the text between
double bounding lines. Rubrics are written in orange rustic capitals. The first 2 to
4 words of each sequence are written in a mixture of brown uncials and square
capitals. Punctuation consists of the punctus. Neumes in the St. Gall style are in
the outer margins. The phrase "alleluia" is written with neumes in the margins in
orange rustic capitals (fol. 1) or orange uncials (fols. 2 and 3) next to the first line
of each sequence.
    The inscription "Stift Lambach," visible under ultraviolet light, is written in the

upper margin of fol. 3r. For other manuscripts by the same scribe see the description of MS 481.36. All three leaves have remnants of paper glued to them from their use in a binding; on one of the paper fragments there is writing in a fifteenth-century German cursive gothic hand.

A modern hand has written "N^{ro} I" in ink in the upper margin of fol. 1r and "N. II" in the upper margin of fol. 3r.

Fols. 1 and 2 were formerly Beinecke MS 482.22 A and B, Zinniker 11 and 54; fol. 3 was formerly Zinniker 220.

Bibliography:
Babcock, *Reconstructing a Medieval Library*, 99–100 and fig. 21.
Hochholzer, Elmar, "Ein Lambacher Kalendar-Nekrologfragment (11. Jahrhundert) aus Münsterschwarzach?," *Frühmittelalterliche Studien* 29 (1995): 226–72.

MS 481.40   Kremsmünster, Austria, s. XII$^{3/4}$
Sequentiary   Pl. 27

f. 1r   [Caeli enarrant gloriam . . .] //non ab uno . . . rex in cęlis.

         Gottschalk (In diuisione apostolorum); AH 50.267; RH 3488.

f. 1r–v *In nataliciis martyrum.*
         Agone triumphali militum regis . . . commendare curate.

         Notker Balbulus (Common of Martyrs); AH 53.229; von den Steinen, 82;
         Schaller-Könsgen 499.

f. 1v   *De uno martyre.*
         Quid tu uirgo mater . . . apud deum auxilietur.

         Notker Balbulus (Common of a Martyr); AH 53.239; von den Steinen,
         86; Schaller-Könsgen 13573.

ff. 1v–2r *Unde supra.*
         Martyr beate tuum colentes . . . fore regi christo.

         Anon. (Common of a Martyr); AH 53.238; RH 11215.

f. 2r   *De confessoribus.*
         Rex regum deus noster colendę . . . O miles dei precelse.

Notker Balbulus (Common of Confessors); AH 53.243; von den Steinen, 88; Schaller-Könsgen 14301.

f. 2r   *De uirginibus.*
Uirginis uenerand̨e de numero . . . consolationem praecando.

Anon., Hymn. Sangall. (Common of Virgins); AH 53.246; von den Steinen, 105; Schaller-Könsgen 17306.

f. 2r–v *Ut supra.*
Exultent filįe syon in rege . . . tu nos tuere.

Gottschalk (Common of Virgins); AH 50.271; RH 5780.

f. 2v   *In conuersione sancti Pauli.*
Dixit dominus ex basan . . . rediens ad te deus.//

Gottschalk (Conversion of St. Paul); AH 50.269; RH 4786.

Parchment. 2 folios. Fol. 1 measures 295 x 195 mm; fol. 2 measures 306 x 193 mm (written space 245 x 152 mm). 2 columns. 24 lines. Ruled in lead. Double outer and single inner vertical bounding lines.

Written in Caroline minuscule. 3-line initials at the beginning of each sequence are written in a mixture of orange square capitals and uncials and are not set apart from the text. 1-line initials at the beginning of verses are in a mixture of orange square capitals and uncials, and are set apart from the text when they occur at the beginning of a line. Rubrics are written in orange minuscule. The first line of each sequence is written in brown rustic capitals. Punctuation consists of the punctus. The sequence "Exultent filie syon" has interlinear neumes.

Portions of three other leaves from this sequentiary are preserved in the binding of Melk, Stiftsbibliothek, Cod. 746 (fols. I and 212) and Cod. 1942 (fol. 136). This sequentiary was part of a missal made for the Benedictine abbey of Kremsmünster, also originally containing a calendar, gradual, sacramentary, and lectionary. See Christine Glassner and Alois Haidinger, *Die Anfänge der Melker Bibliothek* (Melk, 1996), 89–97, pls. 62–69 (the sequentiary fragment is illustrated in pl. 64). Two more fragments of the sacramentary illustrated in pl. 65 are now Beinecke MS 785.1 (the artist of the 1- and 2-line initials and the rubrication in these fragments is the same as the artist of the initials and rubrication in the sequentiary, but the text hand is different). The scribe of the sequentiary also wrote the gradual. According to Haidinger, the missal was in use at Melk from at least the late thirteenth century until the first third of the fifteenth, when it was broken up for use in bindings.

The fragments were used as pastedowns in a chain binding. Both leaves have rust holes in the corners from the bosses of the binding; fol. 1, the front pastedown, also has two rust stains from the hardware which held the clasps for the binding straps, and fol. 2, the back pastedown, has two sets of five rust holes from the nails holding the binding straps, as well as a hole cut in the lower margin where the chain was attached to the board.

Fol. 1 was formerly Beinecke MS 482.61, Zinniker 22; fol. 2 was formerly Zinniker 167.

MS 481.41   Southern Germany, s. XII[1]
Ordinal   Pl. 27

f. 1r   //V. Unus autem. Quo finito. Ne forte chorus prosequatur. Deinde legatur euangelium secundum marcum. Cum appropinquasset . . . *In ii. vespera. A.* Scriptum est enim. Si aliquod festum in ii. feria uel iii. uel iiii. occurrerit. Regula et Matutinalis lectio illi feriȩ ascripta in praecedenti ebdomada in eadem feria praeoccupantur cum A. eadem die ad horas.

Liturgical directions for the mass and office of Palm Sunday. In the right margin of the recto another antiphon for Palm Sunday ("Scriptum est enim percutiam pastorem") is added in a fourteenth-century hand.

f. 1r–v   *Feria ii. Inuit.* Quibus iuraui, quod in iii. et iiii. feria canitur . . . *Ad vesperam. A.* Recordare mei domine.

Feria II before Easter.

f. 1v   *Feria iii. R. R.* [sic] Contumelias. *V.* Omnes inimici . . . *Ad vesperam. A.* Non sis mihi.

Feria III before Easter.

f. 1v   *Feria iiii. R.* Amicus meus osculi. *V.* Melius illi . . . *In ev. A.* Cottidie apud. Preces tamen sicut in priuatis diebus dicimus. Cetera omnia praeter regularem cursum sicut in summis festiuitatibus omittimus. Completorium solito more canimus. et .xx.iiii. candelȩ in sanctuario ordinantur quae ad nocturnos ante populi accenduntur ingressum.

Feria IV before Easter.

f. 1v   *In cena domini.* Ad matutinas non dicatur. Domine labia mea nec deus in adiutorium nec uenite ... Tres sequentes de tractatu sancti augustini super psalmis. Exaudi deus orationem meam cum deprecor tres nouissimas in hac nocte de apostolo//

Feria V before Easter (Maundy Thursday).

Parchment. 1 folio. 205 x 136 mm (written space 164 x 100 mm). 1 column. 30 lines. Dry-point ruling on the hair side. Double vertical and single horizontal bounding lines.

Written in late Caroline minuscule. 1-line square capital "A" ("Ad matutinas") is in orange and partially set apart from the text. Smaller 1-line initials are a mixture of square capitals, uncials, and rustic capitals and are in brown, sometimes dotted with red. Rubrics are written in orange minuscule and are set apart from the text when they occur at the beginning of a line. Punctuation consists of the punctus.

Zinniker 216. The number "13" is written in ink in the upper margin of the recto.

MS 481.42   Italy, s. XI²
Conversio S. Justinae (from a Homiliary?)   Pl. 28

f. 1   [Inc: Illuminatio domini nostri iesu christi saluatoris de celo facta est . . .] //Cuius pater erat edusius hoc in ciuitate antiochia ... crescite et multiplicamin[i et replete] terram. Puto enim si in//

Conversio Sanctae Justinae virginis et Sancti Cypriani episcopi (Sts. Cyprian and Justina, 26 September); BHL 2047; *Acta Sanctorum, Sept.* 7:217–19. The upper and lower margins have been trimmed with loss of text.

Parchment. 1 folio. 295 x 270 mm (written space originally ca. 365 x 240 mm). 2 columns. 37 lines remaining of original ca. 45. Dry-point ruling; single vertical bounding line.

Written in Caroline minuscule. Only six lines of the homily initial "I" ("Illuminatio") are preserved; the shaft of the letter is half red and half yellow on a geometric ground of blue and pale purple, with vine-stem decoration in red; it is written on the vertical bounding line. 1-line initials are in brown uncials, with occasional rustic capital forms (D, Q, M) and enlarged minuscule forms (n), and are not set apart from the text. Punctuation consists of the punctus and the punctus interrogativus.

The fragment was used as a wrapper for a volume measuring ca. 270 x 200 mm. The notation "46" in ink on the verso has been written over in pencil with the number "70."
Zinniker 188.

MS 481.43   Italy, s. XI^{ex}
Homiliary   Pl. 28

f. 1r   [Inc: Si diligenter audistis euangelicam lectionem . . .] //uersatur. Nature quidem uinculis alligatus . . . iudicandi saeculi fluctibus demergatur.

          Maximus Taurinensis, Sermon 48.83–102 (on Matthew 18.1; St. Michael, 29 September); A. Mutzenbecher, ed., CCSL 23 (1962), 189–90; PL 57.448–50. See Grégoire, 469.

f. 1r–v   *Passio sancti cypriani episcopi et martyri et iustine uirginis.*
          Illuminatio domini nostri iesu christi saluatoris de celo facta est . . . serpentis obedientis. et morti traditis//

          Conversio Sanctae Justinae virginis et Sancti Cypriani episcopi (Sts. Cyprian and Justina, 26 Sept.); BHL 2047; *Acta Sanctorum, Sept.* 7:217–19. The lower margin has been trimmed with loss of text.

Parchment (stained from use in a binding). 1 folio. 322 x 247 mm (written space originally ca. 335 x 225 mm). 2 columns. 34 lines remaining of original ca. 39. Dry-point ruling; double horizontal bounding lines.
    Written in Caroline minuscule. Only the upper eight lines of the homily initial "I" ("Illuminatio") are preserved; the initial is yellow on a red, blue, purple, and green ground and is written on the vertical bounding line. 1-line initials are a mixture of brown rustic capital and uncial forms with occasional use of an enlarged minuscule *e*. The rubric is written in red minuscule. The first word of the sermon is in brown square capitals traced with red. Punctuation consists of the punctus, punctus elevatus, and punctus interrogativus. Hyphenation and diacritical marks over double *i* are in the same ink as the text.
    The fragment was used as a pastedown in the binding of a volume measuring ca. 322 x 229 mm.
    Zinniker 193.

MS 481.44
Priscian, *Institutio Grammatica*

Western Germany, s. XI²
Pl. 29

f. 1r   //itane est madida . . . sine ulla causa//

Priscian, *Institutio grammatica*, Book VII.78–79; Keil, 2:354.12–355.9. The upper margin has been trimmed with loss of text. Some letters have also been trimmed off in the inner and outer margins.

f. 1v   //ducum a patre . . . huius hominis his//

Institutio grammatica, Book VII.80–82; Keil, 2:355.23–356.22. The upper margin has been trimmed with loss of text. Some letters have also been trimmed off in the inner and outer margins.

f. 2r   [passiu]//as quoque pro actiuis . . . se pati demonstrant; [. . .] multos domina//[ta]

Institutio grammatica, Book VIII.26; Keil, 2:393.10–394.7. The inner and lower margins have been trimmed with loss of text.

f. 2v   //quod et quo itur . . . numero et numeror. m[ino] et minor. meridi//[o]

Institutio grammatica, Book VIII.28–29; Keil, 2:395.8–396.11. The inner and lower margins have been trimmed with loss of text.

Parchment (three original holes on fol. 2). 2 folios. 195 x 147 mm (written space originally ca. 245 x 145 mm). 1 column. Fol. 1 has 17 and fol. 2 has 15 lines of an original 30 lines. Dry-point ruling on the flesh side. Double vertical bounding lines.

Written in Caroline minuscule. 2-line initial "S" ("Sunt") in brown is set apart from the text between double vertical bounding lines. 1-line initials are in brown rustic capitals with occasional use of an enlarged minuscule *n* and *m*. One "L" ("Lucanus") has a hollow shaft that is filled with brown cross strokes. Punctuation consists of the punctus, punctus elevatus, and punctus versus.

Three other leaves from the same manuscript are preserved as Lambach, Stiftsbibliothek, Fragment 12 (see Holter [1989], 212, cat. no. IX.11). These leaves measure ca. 310 x 210 mm and preserve text from Book VII.35–39 and VII.51–55. The Beinecke leaves were used in the binding of a volume measuring ca. 195 x 138 mm. The Beinecke fragments and the related leaves in Lambach are not listed in M. Gibson, "Priscian, 'Institutiones grammaticae': A Handlist of Manuscripts," *Scriptorium* 26 (1972): 105–24 nor in M. Passalacqua, *I codici di Prisciano* (Rome, 1978).

A modern hand has written in pencil in the lower right corner the number "62" on fol. 1r and "63" on fol. 2r. Another modern hand has identified the text as "Grammatik" in pencil on the recto of both leaves.

Fol. 1 was formerly Beinecke MS 482.62, Zinniker 59.1; fol. 2 was Zinniker 230.

Bibliography:
Babcock, *Reconstructing a Medieval Library*, 100 and fig. 25.

MS 481.45   Fulda, Germany, s. XI$^{2/3}$
Psalter   Pl. 29

f. 1r   //terra et deglutiuit . . . comederunt [sacrifici]a mortuorum.//

            Psalm 105.17–28. The inner margin has been trimmed with loss of text.

f. 1v   //et reputatum est . . . inimici eorum. et//

            Psalm 105.31–42. The inner margin has been trimmed with loss of text.

f. 2r   //Confitemini domino quo . . . diuisiones. [Et eduxit] israhel per medium
            eius.//

            Psalm 135.1–14. The refrain "quoniam in aeternum misericordia eius"
            (here abbreviated "Quo" or "Qm") is written between the vertical bound-
            ing lines. The bottom half of the leaf has been trimmed with loss of text.

f. 2v   //Quia in humilitate nostra . . . Adhęreat lingua mea faucibus//

            Psalms 135.23–136.6. The bottom half of the leaf has been trimmed with
            loss of text.

f. 3r   //absorti sunt iuncti petrę . . . orationem meam. tribulatio//[nem]

            Psalms 140.6–141.3. The bottom half of the leaf has been trimmed with
            loss of text.

f. 3v   //Libera me . . . turbatum est cor//

            Psalms 141.7–142.4. The bottom half of the leaf has been trimmed with
            loss of text.

Parchment. 3 folios. 210 x 155 mm (written space originally ca. 211 x 140 mm). 1 column. Fol. 1 preserves 20 lines, fol. 2 preserves 15 lines, and fol. 3 preserves 14 lines of an original ca. 22 lines. Dry-point ruling on the hair side. Double vertical and single horizontal bounding lines. Prickings in upper margin.

Written in Caroline minuscule at Fulda in the second third of the eleventh century. The Psalms begin with 4-line initials in brown ink, with vine-stem decoration, partially outlined in orange; they are not set apart from the text. 1-line initials at the beginning of verses are in orange and set apart from the text between vertical bounding lines. 1-line initial "Q" ("Quoniam") on fol. 2r in black dotted with red. Rubrics are written in orange uncials. The first line of each Psalm is written in brown uncials with long ticks descending from each letter. Punctuation consists of the punctus.

Several other fragments from the same Psalter survive. Beinecke MS 712.22 preserves a portion of one leaf containing Psalms 38.10–14 and 39.6–11 (see Bernard Quaritch, Ltd., *Bookhands of the Middle Ages: Part V* [London], catalogue 1147, item 8, p. 16, with plate). Lambach Fragment 15 contains two leaves preserving Psalms 118.73–100 and 118.160–119.8 (see K. Holter, "Beiträge zur Geschichte der Stiftsbibliothek Lambach," in *15. Jahrbuch des Musealvereines Wels* [1968/69]: 101 and Holter [1989], 212, cat no. IX.08). Another fragment is in the binding of Lambach Ccl 477a (see Holter [1989], 212, cat no. IX.09; Ccl 477a is briefly described in Holter [1959], 264, with a notice of the fragment). Other binding fragments are in two incunabula, formerly Lambach Ink. 37 and 53; others were once in the binding of Lambach Ink. II.16, but they have since been removed (see Holter [1968/69], 101).

Fragments of a hymnal written by the same scribe are preserved in the binding of Vienna, Österreichische Nationalbibliothek, s.n. 3622 (formerly Lambach Ccl 462) and as Lambach Fragment 13d–f. Prof. Hartmut Hoffmann has ascribed the Vienna fragment to Fulda in the second third of the eleventh century (see idem, *Buchkunst und Königtum*, 1:175).

Fol. 2 was a flyleaf in the binding of Lambach Ccl 223 (shelf number "223" written twice on fol. 2r). Ccl 223 is briefly described by Holter (1959), 261, who mentions that the manuscript once had flyleaves from a Psalter. The other flyleaf was probably MS 481.45, fol. 3, since in the lower corner of the recto there is a pencilled notation that is very faint but seems to read "223P". A notation in the lower corner of fol. 1r is also very faint but may read "P477"; although Lambach Ccl 477a contains a leaf from this Psalter, the Beinecke leaf could not have been used in its binding since the volume measures only 150 x 110 mm.

In the lower corners of the leaves a modern hand has written in pencil the number "48" on fol. 1r, "39" on fol. 2r, and "40" on fol. 3r.

Fol. 1 was formerly Zinniker 263; fols. 2 and 3 were formerly Beinecke MS 482.23 A and B, Zinniker 94, 95.

Bibliography:
Babcock, *Reconstructing a Medieval Library*, 100 and fig. 22.

MS 481.46   Southern Germany, s. XI/XII
Psalter   Pl. 30

f. 1   //meus inebrians quam preclarus . . . Quia unicus//

            Psalms 22.5–24.16.

f. 2   //et in umbra mortis . . . uultus tui ambulabunt//

            Psalms 87.7–88.16.

f. 3   [exarde]//scet sicut ignis . . . sperabo in eum//

            Psalms 88.47–90.2.

Parchment. 3 folios. Fol. 1 measures 305 x 203 mm; fol. 2 measures 289 x 202 mm;
fol. 3 measures 289 x 193 mm (written space 230 x 140 mm). 1 column. 28 lines.
Dry-point ruling on the hair side. Double vertical and single horizontal bounding
lines. Prickings for horizontal rulings on inner vertical bounding line of outer
margin; prickings for vertical lines on horizontal bounding lines.

Written in Caroline minuscule. The beginning of each Psalm has a 4-line initial
in orange or brown square capitals with a single round form of D, occasionally filled
with yellow and green wash; they are not set apart from the text. 1-line initials at
the beginning of verses alternate in brown and orange filled with yellow wash and
are set apart from the text between double bounding lines. Other 1-line initials are
in brown rustic capitals and uncials. Rubrics are written in orange minuscule except
for the phrases "Psalmus David" and "Christi Regnum", which are written in rustic
capitals. Punctuation consists of the punctus, the punctus elevatus, and the punctus interrogativus.

This Psalter was written by the same scribe who wrote the breviary preserved in
Beinecke MS 481.26 and may have formed part of the same volume; both
fragments have the same style of pricking and almost the same measurements. Fol.
1 has been cut in half horizontally, each piece measuring 205 x 150 mm. This size
corresponds to that of the breviary fragments in MS 481.26, which were used in the
binding of Lambach, Stiftsbibliothek, Ccl 320. Another leaf of the Psalter is still in
the binding of Lambach Ccl 315.

Fol. 1 was formerly Beinecke MS 482.24A, Zinniker 72; fol. 2 was formerly Zinniker 253; fol. 3 was Beinecke 481.89, Zinniker 266.

Bibliography:
Babcock, *Reconstructing a Medieval Library*, 99 and fig. 12.

MS 481.47   Melk, Austria, s. XIII[1]
Antiphonary   Pl. 30

f. 1   [R. Ista est speciosa ...] //cubilibus et in hortis ... [V.] Specie tua et
       pulchritudine ... R. Salue nobilis uirga ... V. Odor tuus super ... *Ad cant.*
       A. Maria uirgo semper ... R. Super salutem et omnem ... V. Paradysi
       porte per euam ... R. Beata es uirgo maria ... V. Aue maria. R. Beata es
       maria que ... V. Aue maria. R. Felix namque es ... V. Ora pro populo. *Ad*
       laud. A. Assumpta est maria ... A. Maria uirgo assumpta est ... A. Bene-
       dicta filia tu ... A. Pulchra es et decora ... *In evg.* A. Que est ista que ...
       i^a. A. Oculi tui sancta dei ... iii^a. A. Dilecte mi apprehendam te ... vi^a. A.
       Quam pulchra es ... viiii^a. A. Ista est speciosa. *In* ii^a *vespera.* Assumpta est
       maria.//

       Assumption of Mary (15 August), second nocturn of matins through
       second vespers. The last line and a half on the verso were originally left
       blank. A fifteenth-century hand has added psalms and chants for Mary
       (*Ps.* Dixit dominus. *A.* Maria virgo. *Ps.* Letatus. *An.* In odore. *Ps.* Nisi do-
       minus. *A.* Pulchra es. *Ps.* Memento. *R.* Adiuua nos.).

Parchment. 1 folio. 298 x 223 mm (written space 230 x 160 mm). 1 column. 21
lines. Ruled in lead (very faint). Double vertical and single horizontal bounding
lines.
     Written in early Gothic script. Initials of the first antiphons of lauds and of
second vespers are 1-line red capitals and are set apart from the text. Other 1-line
initials are in brown rustic capitals and are not set apart from the text; those for the
antiphons and responses of matins are dotted or traced with red. Rubrics are
written in red rustic capitals with frequent minuscule forms such as *a* and *t* and are
set apart from the text when they occur at the beginning of a line. The name
"maria" is sometimes written with uncial M and mostly with a capital R. Punctuation consists of the punctus. Chants and marginal tonary letters have neumes in
the St. Gall style.
     This leaf was folded in half and used as the pastedown and flyleaf in the binding
of a volume measuring ca. 223 x 150 mm. According to Alois Haidinger, the same

scribe also wrote an antiphonary for the monastery of Melk, of which only fragments are extant (letter of 23 December 1996); the Melk fragments are described
by Ewald Höchtl, "Die adiastematisch notierten Fragmente aus den Handschriften
der Stiftsbibliothek Melk. Versuch einer Bestandsaufnahme" (Diss., Universität
Wien, 1990), 235–44.
    Zinniker 238.

MS 481.48   Lambach, Austria, s. XII^ex
Gradual   Pl. 31

f. 1r–v   *Dominica priama* [sic] *in aduentu domini.* Ad te leuaui . . . *Ps.* Uias tuas do-
          mine . . . *Gr.* Uniuersi qui te . . . *V.* Uias tuas domine . . . Alleluia. Ostende
          nobis domine . . . [*Off.*] Ad te domine leuaui . . . *V.* Dirige me in ueritate
          . . . [*V.*] Respice in me . . . *Co.* Dominus dabit benignitatem . . . fructum
          suum.

          First Sunday of Advent.

f. 1v   *Dominica secunda.* Populus syon ecce dominus . . . *Ps.* Qui regis israhel . . .
          Gr. Ex syon species . . . *V.* Congregati illi sancto . . . Alleluia. Letatus sum
          in his . . . *V.* Stantes erant pedes . . . *Off.* Deus tu conuersus//

          Second Sunday of Advent.

f. 2r   [Alleluia. Hic est discipulus . . .] //est testimonium eius. *Of.* Iustus ut
          p[al]ma . . . *V.* Bonum est confiteri . . . *V.* Ad annuntia[ndum] mane . . .
          V. Plantatus in domo . . . *Co.* Exiit sermo in[ter] fratres . . . manere do-
          n[ec] ueniam.

          St. John the Evangelist (27 December). The outer margin has been
          trimmed with loss of text.

f. 2r–v   *De innocentibus.* Ex ore infantium . . . *Ps.* Domine dominus noster . . . *Gr.*
          Anima nostra sicut . . . *V.* Laqueus contritus est . . . Laus tibi christe . . .
          Of. Anima nos[tr]a sicut . . . *V.* Nisi quod dominus . . . *V.* Tor[re]ntem
          pertransiuit anima . . . *Co.* Uox in rama . . . quia non sunt.

          Holy Innocents (28 December). The outer margin has been trimmed with
          loss of text.

f. 2v   *Sylvestri papae.* Sacerdotes tui domine . . . *Ps.* Me[me]nto domine dauid
         . . . *Gr.* Ecce sacerdos [mag]nus . . . *V.* Non est inuentus . . . Alleluia Iurauit
         dominus. [*Off.* Inue]ni dauid seruum . . . *V.* Potens es do[min]e . . . [*V.* Et
         ponam in saeculum saeculi sedem eius] et tronum e[i]us sicut dies celi//

         St. Silvester (31 December), to second verse of offertory. The outer mar-
         gin has been trimmed with loss of text.

f. 3r   [*Tract.* Iubilate domino omnis terra . . .] //nos nos autem populus eius . . .
         Of. Benedictus es domine doce me . . . *V.* Beati inmaculati in uia . . . *V.*
         Aufer a plebe . . . *V.* In uia testimoniorum . . . *V.* Uiam iniquitatis domine
         . . . *Co.* Manducauerunt et saturati . . . a desiderio suo.

         Sunday of Quinquagesima.

ff. 3r–4r *Feria iiii^a In Capite Ieiunii.* Exaudi nos domine . . . *Ps.* Saluum me fac . . . *A.*
         Inmutemur habitu in cinere . . . *Ps.* Deus misereatur nostri . . . *Ad missam.*
         Misereris omnium domine . . . *Ps.* Miserere mei deus . . . *Gr.* Miserere mei
         deus . . . *V.* Misit de celo . . . *Tr.* Domine non secundum peccata . . . *V.*
         Domine ne memineris iniquitatum . . . *V.* Adiuua nos deus . . . *Of.* Exal-
         tabo te domine . . . *V.* Domine abstraxisti ab inferis . . . *V.* Ego autem dixi
         . . . *Co.* Qui meditabitur in lege . . . in tempore suo.

         Feria IV of Quinquagesima (*In Capite Ieiunii*) (Ash Wednesday).

f. 4r   *Feria v^a.* Dum clamarem ad dominum . . . *Ps.* Exaudi deus orationem . . .
         Gr. Iacta cogitatum tuum . . . *V.* Dum clamarem ad dominum . . . *Off.* Ad
         te domine leuaui. [C]*o.* Acceptabis sacrificium iusticie . . . super altare
         tuum domine.

         Feria V of Quinquagesima.

f. 4r–v *Feria vi^a.* Audiuit dominus et misertus est . . . *Ps.* Exaltabo te domine . . .
         Gr. Unam petii a domino . . . *V.* Ut uideam uoluntatem . . . *Of.* Domine
         uiuifica me . . . *V.* Fac cum seruo tuo . . . *V.* Da michi intellectum . . . Co.
         Seruite domino in timore . . . de uia iusta.

         Feria VI of Quinquagesima.

f. 4v   *Sabbato.* Esto mihi in deum per totum.

         Saturday of Quinquagesima.

f. 4v   *Dominica prima in xl^a. Statio ad sanctum petrum.* Inuocauit me et ego . . . *Ps.*
    Qui habitat in adiutorio . . . *Gr.* Angelis suis mandauit . . . *V.* In manibus
    portabunt . . . *Tr.* Qui habitat in adiutorio . . . *V.* Dicet domino susceptor
    . . . *V.* Quoniam ipse libera//[uit]

    First Sunday of Quadragesima. The rubric *Statio ad sanctum Petrum* is writ-
    ten in the left margin.

f. 5r   [*V.* Veniat super me . . . medita]//tio mea est et consolatio . . . *Co.* Uoce
    mea ad dominum . . . populi circumdantis me.

    Feria II of the first week of Quadragesima.

f. 5r   *Feria tercia.* Domine refugium factus es . . . *Ps.* Priusquam montes fierent
    . . . *Gr.* Dirigatur oratio mea . . . *V.* Eleuatio manuum mearum . . . *Of.* In
    te speraui . . . *V.* Illumina faciem tuam . . . *V.* Quam magna multitudo . . .
    Co. Cum inuocarem te . . . exaudi orationem meam.

    Feria III of the first week of Quadragesima.

f. 5r–v   *Feria iiii^a.* Reminiscere miserationum tuarum . . . *Ps.* Ad te domine leuaui
    . . . *Gr.* Tribulationes cordis mei . . . *V.* Uide humilitatem meam . . . *Tr.* De
    necessitatibus meis eripe . . . *V.* Ad te domine leuaui . . . *V.* Etenim
    uniuersi qui . . . *Of.* Meditabar in mandatis tuis . . . *V.* Pars mea domine
    . . . *V.* Miserere mei secundum eloquium . . . *Co.* Intellege clamorem
    meum in//[tende]

    Feria IV of the first week of Quadragesima.

f. 6r   [*Co.* Qui manducat carnem meam et bibat sanguinem me]//um in me ma-
    net . . . dicit dominus.

    Feria V of the second week of Quadragesima.

f. 6r   *Feria sexta.* Ego autem cum iusticia . . .*Ps.* Exaudi domine iusticiam . . . *Gr.*
    Ad dominum cum tribularer . . . *V.* Domine libera animam meam . . . *Of.*
    Domine in auxilium meum . . . *V.* Auertantur retrorsum et . . . *V.* Expec-
    tans expectaui dominum . . . *Co.* Tu domine seruabis . . . in eternum.

    Feria VI of the second week of Quadragesima.

f. 6r–v   *Sabbato.* Lex domini inreprehensibilis . . . *Ps.* Celi enarrant gloriam . . . *Gr.*

Bonum est confiteri . . . V. Ad annuntiandum mane . . . Of. Illumina oculos meos . . . V. Usquequo domine . . . V. Respice in me . . . Co. Oportet te
fili . . . et inuentus est.

Saturday of the second week of Quadragesima.

f. 6v   *Statio ad sanctum laurentium. Dominica iiiᵃ.* Oculi mei semper . . . Ps. Ad te
domine leuaui . . . Gr. Exurge domine non preualeat . . . V. In conuertendo inimicum . . . Tr. Ad te leuaui . . . V. Eccce [sic] sicut oculi . . . V. Et
sicut oculi ancille in manibus//

Third Sunday of Quadragesima. The rubric *Dominica iiiᵃ* is written in the
left margin.

f. 7r   //Alleluia. Benedictus es dei filius . . . Alleluia. Obtulerunt discipuli . . .
fauum mellis.

First Sunday after Easter.

f. 7r   *Dominica secunda.* Misericordia domini plena est . . . Ps. Exultate iusti in
domino . . . Alleluia. In die resurrectionis. Alleluia. Surrexit pastor bonus
. . . Of. Deus deus meus . . . V. Sitiunt in te . . . V. In matutinis meditabor
. . . Co. Ego sum pastor . . . cognoscunt me mee. alleluia. alleluia.

Second Sunday after Easter.

f. 7r–v *Dominica tercia.* Iubilate deo omnis terra . . . Ps. Dicite deo quam . . .
Alleluia. In die resurrectionis. Alleluia. Nonne cor nostrum . . . Of. Lauda
anima mea . . . V. Qui custodit ueritatem . . . V. Dominus erigit elisos . . .
Co. Modicum et non uidebitis . . . ad patrem alleluia alleluia.

Third Sunday after Easter.

f. 7v   *Dominica iiiiᵃ.* Cantate domino canticum . . . Ps. Saluauit sibi dextera . . .
Alleluia. In die resurrectionis. Alleluia. Christus resurgens ex mortuis//

Fourth Sunday after Easter.

f. 8r   //pelle atque ad protegendum . . . V. Qui pro mundi salute . . . V. Te sancta crux . . . Co. Nos autem gloriari . . . christi. alleluia.

Invention of the Cross (3 May).

f. 8r   *Gordiani et Epymachi.* Sancti tu[i] domine. Alleluia. Gaudete. *Of.* Mirabilis
            deus in sanctis . . . *V.* Exsurgat et dissipentur . . . *V.* Pereant peccatores a
            facie . . . *Co.* Iustorum anime.

            Sts. Gordian and Epimachus (10 May).

f. 8r–v   *Pancratii. Nerei et Achillei.* Ecce oculi domini . . . *Ps.* Exultate iusti in
            domino . . . Alleluia. Gaudete. *Of.* Confitebuntur celi. *Co.* Gaudete iusti.

            Sts. Pancras, Nereus, and Achilleus (12 May).

f. 8v   *Uigilia ascensionis.* Uocem iocunditatis. Alleluia Omnes gentes. *Of.* Uiri
            galylei quid . . . *V.* Cumque intuerentur in celum . . . *Co.* Pater cum essem
            . . . a malo alleluia alleluia.

            Vigil of the Ascension. A later hand has added "R. in dominica. Dominus
            forti" above "Alleluia Omnes gentes."

f. 8v   *In die sancto.* Uiri galylei quid . . . *Ps.* Omnes gentes plaudite . . . Alleluia
            Ascendit deus . . . Alleluia. Dominus in syna in sancto ascendens//

            Ascension.

Parchment. 8 folios (fols. 1 and 2 are a bifolium: fols. 3–8 are single leaves). The
measurements of the folios are as follows: fol. 1, 310 x 180 mm; fol. 2, 308 x 165
mm; fol. 3, 290 x 210 mm; fol. 4, 296 x 207 mm; fol. 5, 293 x 215 mm; fol. 6, 290
x 210 mm; fol. 7, 287 x 210 mm; fol. 8, 284 x 213 mm (written space 230 x 150
mm). 1 column. 27 lines. Dry-point ruling (very faint). Double vertical and horizontal bounding lines; prickings in the outer margins.

Written in Caroline minuscule by the same scribe who copied the antiphonary
now preserved as flyleaves in Vienna, Österreichische Nationalbibliothek, s.n. 3619
(formerly Lambach, Stiftsbibliothek, Ccl 454; 2 folios) and s.n. 3620 (formerly
Lambach Ccl 436; 2 folios). See Holter (1989), 215, cat. no. IX.24. According to
A. Haidinger, fragments in a very similar hand are preserved in Kremsmünster:
Fragments V/191 and V/192.

Three-quarter page initial "A" on green, red, and pale yellow ground with vine-
stem decoration (fol. 1); 5-line initial "O" with a face (fol. 6); 4-line initial "C" with
a face (fol. 7); 5-line initial "U" with portrait of Christ on a red and green ground
with modest foliate appendages (fol. 8). Other 3- and 4-line initials, some with
herringbone patterns, in red. Rubrics are written in a mixture of red capitals and
minuscule. The initials and rubrication are by the same artist as those in Beinecke
481.52 and the Lambach Rituale (Lambach Cml LXXIII, described by Holter

[1989], 209, cat. no. VIII.33 with plate of initial "A"; see also Davis, *Epiphany*, 186–87). Punctuation consists of the punctus. Interlinear neumes in the St. Gall style.

The bifolium (fols. 1/2) was formerly Beinecke MS 481.50, Zinniker 165; fols. 3 and 6 were formerly Zinniker 240 and 239; fols. 4, 5, 7, and 8 were formerly Beinecke MS 482.49 (B, D, A, and C) and Zinniker 20, 97, 5, and 21.

Bibliography:
  Babcock, *Reconstructing a Medieval Library*, 108 and fig. 24.
  Holter, K., "Initialen aus einer Lambacher Handschrift des 12. Jahrhunderts," *Wiener Jahrbuch für Kunstgeschichte* 46/47 (1994): 260n; reprinted in idem, *Buchkunst, Handschriften, Bibliotheken*, ed. G. Heilingsetzer and W. Stetzer, Schriftenreihe des Oberösterreichischer Musealvereins, Gesellschaft für Landeskunde vol. 16 (Linz, 1996), 1196n.

MS 481.49   Melk, Austria, s. XII
Antiphonary   Pl. 32

f. 1r–v   //R. Induit me dominus uestimento … V. Induit me dominus ciclade … A. Cuius pulchritudinem sol … Ps. Cantate. A. Christus circumdedit me … Ps. Dominus regnauit. A. Ipsi sum desponsata … Ps. Cantate. *v.* Adiuuabit eam deus. R. Iam corpus eius … V. Ipsi sum desponsata … R. Pulchra faciem [sic] sed … V. Specie tua et pulchritudine … R. Mel et lac … V. Cuius pulchritudinem sol … [A.] Ingressa agnes turpitudinis .. Ps. Dominus regnauit. A. Mecum enim abeo [sic] … Ps. Iubilate. A. Anulo suo subarauit … Ps. Deus deus. A. Benedico te pater … Ps. Benedictus. [A. Con]gaudete mecum et … [Ps. Laudate.] A. Stans beata agnes … Ps. Benedictus. Ad *i̇ᵃ*. Ad *ii̇ᵃ*. Ad *vi̇ᵃ*. Ad *viii̇ᵃ*. Ad *vesper. ii.* A. Ingressa agnes. Ps. Dixit dominus. A. Mecum enim. Ps. Laudate. A. Anulo suo. Ps. Letatus. A. Benedico. Ps. Nisi dominus. A. Congaudete. Ps. Memento. R. Mel et lac. *ymnus.* Virginis proles. *v.* Specie tua. A. Beata agnes in medio … Ps. Magnificat.

St. Agnes (21 January), from the second nocturn of matins to second vespers. The lower margin has been trimmed with the loss of one line of text.

f. 1v   *Sancte* [sic] *vincencii martyris.* R. Desiderium anime. *ymnus.* Deus tuorum. *v.* Gloria et honore. A. Sacram huius diei … Ps. Magnificat. *vit.* Regem uenturum. [Ps.] Venite. A. In lege domini. Ps. Beatus uir. A. Predicans. Ps. Quare fremuerunt. A. Voce mea. Ps. Domine quid. *v.* Gloria et honore. *R*. Iste sanctus. *R*. Iustus germinabit. *R*. Desiderium. *ymnus*. Qui me c. *Ps*. Dominus regnauit. *ymnus*. Martir dei qui. *v*. Magna est gloria. *A*. Hic uir despiciens. *Ps*. Benedictus.

St. Vincent (22 January).

f. 1v   *Conuersio sancte* [sic] *pauli apostoli*. Excelsus super. *Ps*. Laudate. *Ps* Laudate. *Ps* Laudate. *Ps* Laudate. *Ps* Laudate. *R*. Magnus sanctus paulus. *ymnus*. Doctor egregie. *v*. In omnem terram exiuit. *A*. Cum autem complacui ... *Ps*. Magnificat. *viter*.[sic] Laudemus deum nostrum ... [*Ps*.] Venite. *A*. Hodie electorum omnium caput et sponsus ecclesie christus sa//[ulum]

Conversion of St. Paul (25 January). The lower margin has been trimmed with the loss of one line of text.

f. 2r–v   [*R*. Qui me dignatus est] //ab omni plaga ... *V*. Medicinam carnalem corpori ... [*R*. Be]ata agathes ingressa ... *V*. Agathes ingressa [ca]rcerem ... *R*. Gaudeamus [o]mnes in domino ... *V*. Inmaculatus dominus inmaculatam ... *Mat*. Quis es tu ... *Ps*. Dominus. *A*. Medicinam carnalem corpori ... *Ps*. Iubilate. *A*. Gracias tibi ago ... *Ps*. Deus deus. *A*. Benedicite pater domini ... *Ps*. Benedictus. *A*. Qui me dignatus ... *Ps*. Laudate. *ymnus*. Iesu corona uir. *v*. Audi filia et uide. *A*. Paganorum multitudo fugiens ... *Ps*. Benedictus. *Ad i*ᵃ. Quis es tu. *Ps*. Deus in nomine. *Ad iii*ᵃ. Medicinam. *Ps*. Legem pone. *Ad vi*ᵃ. Gracias tibi. *Ps*. Defecit. *viii*ᵃ. Benedicite. *Ps*. Mirabilis. *vespera*. Qui [...] *v*. Specie tua et pulchritudine. *A*. Beata agathes ingressa ... *Ps*. Magnificat.

St. Agatha (5 February). from third nocturn to second vespers. The lower margin has been trimmed with the loss of one line of text.

f. 2v   *Scolastica virgo*. *A*. Sanctimonialis. *Ps*. Magnificat. *vit*. Regem virginum. [*Ps*.] Venite. *A*. Veni sponsa. *Ps*. Domine deus. *A*. O quam. *Ps*. Celi enarrant. *A*. Ante thorum. *Ps*. Domini est. *v*. Specie tua. *R*. Hec est uirgo. *R*. Concupiuit. *R*. Ven[i electa]. *A*. Hec est uirgo. *Ps*. Dominus regnauit. *per totum*. *ymnus*. Iesu corona. *v*. Audi filia. *A*. Simile est. [*Ps*.] Benedictus.

St. Scholastica (10 February).

f. 2v   *Vitalis* [sic] *martyr*. *R*. Desiderium anime. *ymnus*. Deus tuorum. *v*. Gloria et honore. *A*. Beatus uir. *Ps*. Magnificat. *R*. Absterge deus. *vit*. Regem martyr. [*Ps*.] Venite. *A*. In lege domini. *Ps*. Beatus uir. *A*. Predican[s.] *Ps*.

Quare fremuerunt. A. Voce mea. Ps. Domine quid. v. Gloria et honore. R.
Hic est uere martyr. R. Posui adiuto. R. Gloria et honore. ymnus. Qui me
con. Ps. Dominus regnauit. ymnus. Martir dei qui. v. Magna est gloria. A.
Hic uir despiciens. Ps. Benedictus.

St. Valentine (14 February).

Kathedra sancti petre. [sic] A. Solue iubente deo . . . Ps. Laudate pueri. R.
Petre amas me. [*ymnus.*] Iam bone pastor . . . A. Quodcumque ligaueris.
Ps. Magnificat. A. O princeps apostolorum . . . Ps. Magnificat. *viter.* [sic]
Tu es pastor ouium . . . [Ps.] Venite. A. Beatus uir. Ps. Ipsum. A. Beatus
iste. Ps. Quare fremuerunt. A. Tu es gloria. A. Domine quid. v. Amauit
eum. R. Euge serue. R. Ecce sacerdos. R. Iurauit d. A. Inuocantem. Ps.
Cum inuocarem. A. Letentur. Ps. Verba mea. A. Domine dominus. Ps. Ip-
sum. v. Iustum deduxit. R. Posui ad. R. Amauit eum. R. Inueni dauid. A.
Domine iste. Ps. Domine quis. A. Vitam peciit. A. Hic accipiet. Ps. Do-
mini est terra. y. Iustus ut. R. Iste homo. R. Iste est qui. R. Iste homo. Mat.
Ecce sacerdos. Ps. Dominus regnauit. A. Non est. Ps. Iubilate. A. Ideo. Ps.
Deus deus. A. Benedictus. A. Statuit. Ps. Laudate. ymnus. Iam bone. v.
Non est in. A. Quem dicunt. Ps. Benedictus. *i͞* A. Ecce sacerdos. Ps. Deus
in.//

Chair of St. Peter (22 February), from vespers to prime. The lower margin
has been trimmed with the loss of two lines of text.

Parchment. 2 folios. Fol. 1 measures 246 x 193 mm; fol. 2 measures 239 x 170 mm
(written space originally ca. 240 x 155 mm). 1 column. Fol. 1 preserves 25 lines and
fol. 2 preserves 24 lines of an original 26. Dry-point ruling on the hair side (very
faint). Double vertical bounding lines. Pricking in outer margin.
    Written in early Gothic script (littera textualis). Initials of the first antiphon for
lauds and for several hymns are 1- or 2-line square capitals in red and are not set
apart from the text. Other initials are 1-line brown rustic capitals highlighted with
red and not set apart from the text. Rubrics are written in red minuscule. Abbreviations for the invitatory are either *vit.* or *viter.* Minor initials in black highlighted
with red. Punctuation consists of the punctus. Interlinear neumes in the St. Gall
style have been added by several hands for the chants with full text.
    These leaves were used in the binding of Lambach, Stiftsbibliothek, Ccl 163
(shelf number "163" on fol. 1r; the leaves have the characteristic rust stains, one in
each corner and one in the center, from the five nails used for the bosses on
Lambach bindings). According to Alois Haidinger, a series of fragments from this
manuscript are now in the library of Melk, suggesting that Lambach Ccl 163 was
originally a Melk manuscript (letter of 7 November 1995).

Along the left margin of fol. 2v a fifteenth-century hand has written, "Dem erbg[ut?] mang(?) cumbe(?) ich Jans rōllzz mein diunst(?) und." A modern hand has written in pencil in the lower right corners the number "106" on fol. 1r and "107" on fol. 2v.

Fol. 1 was formerly Zinniker 241; fol. 2 was formerly Beinecke MS 482.30, Zinniker 43.

Bibliography:
Babcock, *Reconstructing a Medieval Library*, 111, 114, and fig. 62

MS 481.50

transferred to Beinecke MS 481.48

MS 481.51   Lambach, Austria, s. XII[ex]
Gottschalk Antiphonary   Pl. 33

f. 1r–v   [R.] //Canite tuba in syon uocate gentes . . . V. Annunciate in finibus terre . . . [R.] Uicesima quarta die . . . V. Ego sum dominus . . . R. Non auferetur sceptrum . . . V. Pulchriores sunt oculi . . . R. Me oportet minui . . . V. Hoc est testimonium . . . In ii° n°. A. Bethlehem non. [R.] Ecce iam ueniet . . . V. Prope est ut ueniat . . . R. Uirgo israhel reuertere . . . V. A solis ortu. R. Iuraui dicit dominus . . . V. Iuxta est salus . . . V. A solis ortu. R. Non discedimus a te . . . V. Domine deus uirtutum . . . *Ad cantica.* A. Ecce in nubibus celi . . . R. Intuemini quantus sit . . . V. Et dominabitur a mari . . . R. Radix iesse qui exurget . . . V. Deus a lybano. R. Egredietur uirga de radice . . . V. Et requiescet super eum . . . R. Nascetur nobis paruulus . . . V. Ecce aduenit dominator . . . *Ad laud.* A. Canite tuba in syon quia . . . A. Ecce ueniet desideratus . . . A. Erunt praua in directa . . . A. Dominus ueniet occurrite . . . A. Omnipotens sermo tuus . . . R. Ostende nobis. *In ev.* A. Dixerunt pharisei ad iohannem . . . i[a]. A. Canite tuba. iii[a]. A. Ecce ueniet. vi[a]. A. Erunt praua. viiii[a]. A. Omnipotens sermo. *Vesper.* R. Tu exurgens. *In ev.* A. O[riens splendor?].

Fourth Sunday of Advent, from matins to second vespers.

ff. 1v–2r   *Invit.* Surgite uigilemus quia . . . R. Clama in fortitudine qui . . . V. Super montem excelsum . . . [R.] Orietur stella ex iacob . . . V. A solis ortu. [R.]

Modo ueniet dominator . . . V. Ecce dominator. R. Egredietur dominus et
. . . V. Ex syon species. R. Precursor pro nobis . . . V. Ecce dominator.
Pontifex. R. Uidebunt gentes iustum . . . V. Et eris corona . . . R. Emitte
agnum domine . . . V. Ex syon species. R. Rorate celi desuper . . . V. Emitte
agnum domine . . . R. Germinauerunt campi heremi . . . V. Ecce dominator. R. Radix iesse. R. Egredietur uirga. R. Annunciatum est.

Week after the fourth Sunday of Advent, responses and verses of matins.

f. 2r   *Feria ii^a. Invit.* Prope est iam dominus . . . *Ad laud.* [A.] Ecce ueniet
dominus princeps . . . A. Dum uenerit filius . . . A. Ecce iam ueniet . . . A.
Haurietis aquas in gaudio . . . A. Egredietur dominus de loco . . . *In ev.* [A.]
Egredietur uirga de radice . . . caro salutare dei.

Feria II after the fourth Sunday of Advent, diurnal antiphons.

f. 2r–v *Feria iii^a.* A. Rorate celi desuper . . . A. Emitte agnum Domine . . . A. Ut
cognoscamus domine . . . A. Da mercedem domine . . . *In evangelio.* A. Lex
per moysen . . . A. Tu bethlem terra . . . populum meum israhel.

Feria III after the fourth Sunday of Advent, diurnal antiphons.

f. 2v   *Feria iiii^a.* A. Prophete predicauerunt nasci . . . A. Spiritus domini super
. . . A. Annunciate populis et dicite . . . A. Ecce ueniet dominus ut . . . A.
Propter syon non . . . *In evg.* A. Quomodo fiet istud angele . . . *i^a.* A. Missus
est gabriel. *iii^a.* A. Aue maria gratia plena . . . *vi^a.* A. Dabit illi dominus . . .
viiii^a. A. Ecce ancilla domini . . . secundum uerbum tuum.

Feria IV after the fourth Sunday of Advent, diurnal antiphons.

f. 2v   *Feria quinta.* A. De syon ueniet dominus . . . A. De syon ueniet qui . . . A.
Conuertere domine aliquantulum . . . A. Ecce deus meus . . . A. Dominus
legifer noster . . . *In evg.* A. Intuemini quantus sit . . . *Alia.* A. Uigilate animo in . . . dominus deus noster.

Feria V after the fourth Sunday of Advent, diurnal antiphons.

f. 2v   *Feria vi^a.* A. Constantes estote uidebitis . . . A. Ecce rex ueniet dominus
. . . A. Ueni Domine et noli . . . A. Deus a lybano . . . et splendor//

Feria VI after the fourth Sunday of Advent, diurnal antiphons.

f. 3   //A. Adorate dominum alleluia in aula . . . Ps. Cantate domino. A. Adorate dominum alleluia omnes . . . Ps. Dominus regnabit exultet. A. Notum
fecit dominus . . . Ps. Cantate domino. A. Ecce aduenit dominator. Ps. Dominus regnabit irascantur. v. Omnes gentes quascumque . . . R. Magi ueniunt ab oriente . . . V. Uidimus enim stellam . . . R. Interrogabat magos
herodes . . . V. Magi ueniunt ab oriente . . . R. Stella quam uiderunt . . . V.
Et intrantes domum . . . R. Uidentes stellam magi . . . V. Reges tharsis et
insulę . . . Ad cant. A. Tria sunt munera . . . Cant. Populus qui ambulabat.
v. Adorate dominum . . . R. Tria sunt munera preciosa . . . V. Reges tharsis
et . . . R. Dies sanctificatus illuxit . . . V. Uenite adoremus eum . . . R. Hic
est dies praeclarus . . . V. Et intrantes domum . . . R. In columbe specie
. . . V. Celi aperti sunt . . . V. Gloria patri. [Prosula.] Quem non preualent
. . . Ad laudes. A. Ante luciferum genitus . . . A. Uenit lumen tuum . . . A.
Apertis thesauris suis . . . A. Maria et flumina . . . A. Magi uidentes
stellam//

Epiphany (6 January), from the second nocturn of matins to lauds.

f. 4r   //A. Adiuua me et . . . Ps. Lucerna pedibus. Ps. Iniquos odio. Ps. Feci iudicium. v. Adiutor meus esto . . . vi^a. A. Aspice in me . . . Ps. Mirabilia
testimonia. Ps. Iustus es domine. Ps. Clamaui in toto. v. Dominus regit me
. . . Ad viiii^a. A. Uide humilitatem meam . . . Ps. Ipsum. Ps. Principes
persecuti. Ps. Appropinquet deprecatio. v. Ab occultis meis . . . Ad vesper.
A. Domus iacob de populo . . . Ps. In exitu Israhel. A. Inclinavit dominus
aurem . . . Ps. Dilexi quoniam. A. Laudate dominum omnes . . . Ps. Credidi
propter. Ps. Laudate dominum omnes gentes. A. Benediximus uobis in
nomine . . . Ps. Sepe expugnauerunt. R. Adiutorium nostrum in . . . V. Qui
fecit celum et terram. v. Dirigatur domine oratio. In ev. A. Magnificat anima mea dominum. Ps. Ipsum.

Feria II throughout the year, from terce to second vespers. Two small
scraps of inscribed parchment, one from the eleventh (?) century, the
other from the fourteenth (?), are pasted to the lower margin of fol. 4r to
repair early tears in the parchment. The text of the scraps has not been
identified.

f. 4r–v   Feria iii^a. Invit. Iubilemus deo . . . Ps. Venite exultemus. i^o n^o. A. Adiutor in
tribulationibus. Ps. Deus nostrum refugium. Ps. Omnes gentes. A. Magnus
dominus et . . . Ps. Ipsum. Ps. Audite hęc. A. Deus deorum dominus . . .
Ps. Ipsum. Ps. Quid gloriaris. v. Immola deo . . . R. Ne perdideris me . . . V.
Miserere mei deus miserere . . . R. Paratum cor meum . . . V. Exurge gloria
mea . . . R. Adiutor meus tibi . . . V. Eripe me de inimicis . . . In estate.

Dominus sapientia fundauit terram . . . concrescunt. *R*. Deus in nomine
tuo . . . *V*. Et in uirtute tua . . . *V*. Gloria patri. *In ii° n°*. *A*. Alleluia [3x] *ut*
A. Iuste iudicate. *A*. Auertit dominus captiuitatem . . . *Ps*. Dixit insipiens.
A. Intende in me . . . *Ps*. Exaudi deus deprecationem. *Ps*. Miserere mei
deus qui. *A*. Iuste iudicate filii . . . *Ps*. Si uere utique. *Ps*. Eripe me de inimicis. *v*. Deus uitam meam . . . *Ad laud*. *A*. Secundum magnam misericordiam . . . *Ps*. Miserere. *A*. Salutare uultus mei . . . *Ps*. Iudica me deus.
A. Quoniam in te . . . *Ps*. Miserere mei deus miserere. *A*. Cunctis diebus
uitae . . . *Ps*. Ego dixi in. *A*. Omnes angeli eius . . . *Ps*. Laudate dominum
de. *R*. Miserere mei deus . . . *V*. Quoniam in te . . . *v*. In matutinis domine
. . . *In ev*. *A*. Erexit dominus nobis . . . *Ps*. Benedictus dominus. *Ad iᵃ*. *A*.
Domine deus meus . . . *Ps*. Ipsum. *Ps*. Domine dominus noster. *Ps*. Confitebor. *Ps*. Quicumque uult. *Ad iiiᵃ*. *A*. Clamaui et exaudiuit . . . *Ps*. Ad
dominum cum tribularer. *Ps*. Leuaui oculos. *Ps*. Letatus sum. *Ad viᵃ*. *A*.
Qui habitas in celis . . . *Ps*. Ad te leuaui. *Ps*. Nisi quia dominus. *Ps*. Qui
confidunt. *Ad viiiᵃ*. *A*. Facti sumus sicut . . . *Ps*. In conuertendo. *Ps*. Nisi
dominus edificauerit. *Ps*. Beati omnes qui. *Ad vesperam*. *A*. De profundis
clamaui . . . *Ps*. Ipsum. *A*. Speret israhel in . . . *Ps*. Domine non est. *A*. Et
omnis mansuetudinis . . . *Ps*. Memento domine. *A*. Ecce quam bonum . . .
Ps. Ipsum. *R. et uersum. per totam ebdomadam ut in priori die. In ev*. *A*. Quia
fecit mihi . . . sanctum nomen eius.

Feria III throughout the year, from matins to second vespers. The capitulum is from Proverbs 3.19–20.

f. 4v   *Feria quarta. Invit*. In manu tua . . . *In i° n°*. *A*. Da nobis domine . . . *Ps*.
Deus repulisti. *Ps*. Exaudi deus deprecationem. *A*. Benedicite gentes deo
. . . *Ps*. Nonne deo subdita. *Ps*. Iubilate deo. *A*. In ecclesiis benedicite . . .
Ps. Exurgat deus. *Ps*. Benedictus dominus die. *v*. Benedicite gentes deo
. . . *R*. Exaudi deus deprecationem . . . *V*. Dum anxiaretur cor . . . *R*. Deus
in te speraui . . . *V*. Esto mihi domine . . . facias. In tua iust//[itia]

Feria IV throughout the year, first nocturn of matins.

ff. 5–6r   [*R*. Dum ingrederetur beata agathes . . .] //iudicem impie crudelis . . . *V*.
Ego autem habeo . . . *R*. Uidisti domine et . . . *V*. Propter ueritatem et . . .
R. Quis es tu . . . *V*. Nam et ego . . . *R*. Medicinam carnalem corpori . . . *V*.
Ego autem adiuta . . . *In ii° n°*. *A*. Nisi diligenter perfeceris . . . *A*. Mens
mea solidata . . . *A*. Ego christum confiteor . . . *A*. Beata agathes ingressa
. . . *A*. Uidisti domine agonem . . . *A*. Propter fidem castitatis . . . *v*. Specie
tua. *R*. Ipse me coronauit . . . *V*. Uidisti domine agonem . . . *R*. Agathes
letissima et . . . *V*. Beata agathes ingressa . . . *R*. Propter ueritatem. *V*.

Dilexisti iusticiam et . . . *R*. Ego autem adiuta . . . *V*. Medicinam carnalem corpori . . . *Ad cant*. *A*. Mentem sanctam spontaneam . . . *R*. Induit me dominus. *R*. Qui me dignatus . . . *V*. Medicinam carnalem corpori . . . *R*. Beata agathes ingressa . . . *V*. Agathes ingressa carcerem . . . *R*. Gaudeamus omnes in . . . *V*. Immaculatus dominus . . . *Ad laud*. *A*. Quis es tu . . . *A*. Medicinam carnalem corpori . . . *A*. Gratias tibi ago . . . *A*. Benedico te pater . . . *A*. Qui me dignatus . . . *R*. Specie tua et pulchritudine. *v*. Audi filia et uide. *In ev*. *A*. Paganorum multitudo fugiens . . . *Ad i͡ᵃ*. *A*. Agatha sancta dixit. *iii͡ᵃ*. *A*. Agathes lᶒtissima. *vi͡ᵃ*. *A*. Beata agathes. *viii͡ᵃ*. *A*. Mentem sanctam. *In ii͡ᵃ vespera*. *A*. Quis es tu qui uenisti. *Ps*. Dixit dominus. *A*. Medicinam carnalem. *Ps*. Laudate pueri. *A*. Gratias tibi ago. *Ps*. Letatus sum. *A*. Qui me dignatus. *Ps*. Nisi dominus edificauerit. *In ev*. *A*. Beata agathes ingressa . . . ad tuam misericordiam peruenire.

St. Agatha (5 February), from the first nocturn of matins to second vespers.

f. 6r   *De sancta scolastica. Ad ves*. *R*. Benedictus quam deuotas . . . *In ev*. *A*. Sanctimonialis autem femina . . . *Invit*. Regem virginum. *Et cᶒtera omnia ut de virginibus*. *A*. Ueni sponsa. *non canitur*.

St. Scholastica (10 February), vespers, invitatory, and a cross-reference to the common of virgins. A fourteenth-century hand has added the following chants in the lower margin of fol. 6r: *De sancta Scolastica. Ad vesp*. *R*. Benedictus. *V*. Uterque. *sequitur*. Gloria patri.

f. 6r–v   *In kathedra sancti petri*. *R*. Tu es petrus. *v*. Annunciauerunt opera dei. *In ev*. *A*. Tu es pastor ouium . . . *Invit*. Tu es pastor ovium . . . *Ps*. Venite. *In i° n°*. *A*. In omnem terram. *Cum reliquis*. *v*. In omnem terram. *R*. Symon petre. *R*. Si diligis me. *R*. Tu es petrus. *R*. Quodcumque ligaueris. *In ii° n°*. *A*. Exaltabuntur cornua. *Ps*. Confitebimus. *Cum reliquis*. *A*. Tollite iugum. *A*. Qui diligitis dominum . . . *Ps*. Dominus regnauit. *A*. Iugum enim. *A*. Custodiebant. *A*. Manete. *v*. Constitues eos principes. *R*. Posui adiutorium. *R*. Ecce uere israhelita. *R*. Solue iubente. *R*. Tu es pastor ouium. *Ad cant*. *A*. Solue iubente. *R*. Quem dicunt. *R*. Qui regni claues. *R*. Ego pro te rogaui. *R*. Petre amas. *Ad laud*. *A*. Petre amas me. *Cum reliquis*. *R*. Exaltent eum in ecclesia . . . *V*. Et in cathedra seniorum . . . *v*. Annunciauerunt opera dei. *In ev*. *A*. Quodcumque ligaueris super . . . *Ad i͡ᵃ*. *A*. Petre amas. *iii͡ᵃ*. *A*. Tu es pastor ouium. *vi͡ᵃ*. *A*. Tu es petrus et. *Ad viii͡ᵃ*. *A*. Solue iubente. *In ii͡ᵃ vesper*. *A*. Iurauit dominus. *Ps*. Potens in terra. *A*. Collocet eum. *A*. Confortatus. *ymnus*. Iam bone pater. sit trinitati. *v*. Annunciauerunt opera dei. *In ev*. *A*. Simon bar iona. *v*. Parce tuis ouibus . . . *A*. Simon bar iona . . . dimitte septuagies septies.

Chair of St. Peter (22 February), from first to second vespers.

f. 6v   *Gregorii papae. R.* O pastor apostolice. *In ev. A.* Gloriosa sanctissimi sollempnia gregorii ... *Invit.* Ad dominum uigiles ... *Ps.* Venite. *In i° n°. A.*
Gregorius ortus rome ... *Ps.* Beatus uir. *Cum reliquis. A.* Lineam sui
generis ... *A.* Adherebat moralibus seniorum ... *A.* Gregorius ut creditur
... *A.* Studiis liberalibus nulli ... *A.* Hic ab adolescentia ... *Ps.* In domino
confido. *v.* Iustum deduxit dominus ... *R.* Fulgebat in uenerando ... *V.*
Beatus uir qui ... *R.* Uidens rome vir beatus ... *V.* Quoniam domini est//

St. Gregory (12 March), from first vespers to the first nocturn of matins.
A fourteenth-century hand, different from the one on fol. 6r, has added a
hymn incipit ("Confessor dei") over the invitatory Psalm.

f. 7   //*V.* Aue maria gratia plena ... *R.* Maria ut audiuit ...*V.* Quomodo fiet
istud ... *R.* Posuit moyses bis senas ... *V.* Scientes hoc signum ... *V.* Glo-
ria patri et ... *In ii° n°. A.* Hec est qu[e]. *A.* Dixit autem maria ... *A.* Ideo-
que et quod ... *A.* Dixit autem maria ... *A.* Post abscessum angeli ... *A.*
Spiritu sancto reple[ta] ... *A.* Beata que credidit ... *R.* Dixit angelus ad
... *V.* Ecce concipies et ... *R.* Ecce concipies et ... *V.* Hic erit magnus
... *R.* Dabit illi dominus ... *V.* Et regni eius ... *R.* Salue nobilis uirga ...
V. Odor tuus super ... *V.* Gloria patri [parilique proli] et ... *Ad cant.* [*A.*
O gloriosa fe]mina ... *siue A.* Dabit illi dominus. *Cant.* Audite me. *v.* Spe-
ciosa facta es et suauis. [*R.* Quomodo] fiet istud respondens ... *V.*
Ideoque et quod ... [*R.* Conuersus e]zechiel ad ... *V.* Hinc euidenter os-
tensum ... [*R.* Dixit aut]em maria ... *V.* Spiritus sanctus superueniet
... [*R.* Christi uirg]o dilectissima ... [*V.*] Quoniam peccatorum ... *V.*
Gloria patri et ... *Ad laud.* [*A.* Missus est g]abriel. *A.* Aue maria gratia. *A.*
Spiritus sanctus. [*A.* Ne timeas m]aria inuenisti. *A.* Ecce ancilla domini
fiat mihi. *Ad laudes alię.* [*A.* Quando u]enit ergo ... *A.* Uerbum supernum
a patre ... *A.* Beatus auctor [seculi] ... *A.* Clausa parentis uiscera ...
gratia uenter//

Annunciation (25 March), from the first nocturn of matins to lauds. The
outer margin has been trimmed with loss of text.

f. 8r   [*Ad i°. A.* Exiit qui seminat ...] //suum et dum seminat ... *Ad iii°. A.* Iesus
hęc dicens. *vi°. A.* Si uere fratres ... *Ad viii°.* Si culmen ueri ... *Ad vesper.*
R. Spes mea domine. *In ev. A.* Uobis datum est ... iesus discipulis suis.

Sunday of Sexagesima, from prime to second vespers. The upper margin
has been trimmed with the loss of the first three lines of text.

f. 8r   *Unde supra.* A. Exiit qui seminat. A. Iesus hęc dicens. A. Semen cecidit in terram . . . A. Semen cecidit in terram . . . A. Si uere fratres. A. Si culmen. A. Si gloriam dignitatum . . . A. Qui uerbum dei . . . fructum afferunt inpatentia.

        Diurnal antiphons for the week of Sexagesima.

f. 8r–v   *Dominica in l*^{ma}. *Ad vesp.* A. Angelus domini. *v.* Uespertina oratio. *In ev.* A. Quod autem cecidit . . . *Invit.* Adoremus deum quia . . . *Ps.* Venite. *In i̊ n̊.* A. Domine in uirtute. R. Quadraginta dies et noctes . . . V. Noe uero et uxor . . . R. Ponam arcum meum . . . V. Cumque obduxero nubibus . . . R. Per memetipsum iuraui . . . V. Ponam arcum meum . . . R. Locutus est dominus . . . V. Benedicens benedicam tibi . . . R. Dum staret abraham . . . V. Dixit dominus ad . . . R. Temptauit deus abraham . . . V. Immola deo sacrificium . . . R. Angelus domini vocauit . . . V. Et benedicentur in te . . . *Ad cant.* A. Miserere mei fili . . . *Ps.* Domine miserere. R. Uocauit angelus domini . . . V. Et benedicentur in te . . . R. Deus domini mei . . . V. Obsecro domine fac . . . V. Deus in cuius conspectu . . . R. Ueni hodie ad fontem . . . V. Igitur puella cui . . . R. Cecus sedebat secus . . . exclamauit ad//

        Sunday of Quinquagesima, from first vespers to the third nocturn of matins. The upper margin has been trimmed with the loss of the first three lines of text.

f. 9r   [A.] //Dixit dominus. R. Bonum michi domine . . . V. Manus tue domine . . . *In ev.* A. Non in solo pane . . . in omni uerbo dei.

        First Sunday of Quadragesima, second vespers.

f. 9r–v   *Feria ii̊.* *Invit.* Non sit uobis uanam . . . *Ps.* Venite. *In i̊ n̊.* A. Rectos decet. *Ad laud.* A. Miserere mei deus. *Cum reliquis.* R. Participem me. *In ev.* A. Cum uenerit filius . . . *Ad i̊.* A. Uenite benedicti patris . . . *Priuatis diebus ad i̊ cum non est propria.* A. Uiuo ego dicit . . . *iii̊.* A. Aduenerunt nobis dies . . . *Ad vi̊.* A. Commendemus nosmetipsos in . . . *Ad viii̊.* A. Per arma iusticie . . . *Ad vesperam.* A. Quod uni ex minimis . . . *Feria iii.* A. Domus mea domus . . . *i̊.* A. Osanna filio dauid . . . *Vesper.* A. Scriptum est enim . . . *Feria iiii̊.* A. Generatio hec praua . . . *Ad i̊.* A. Sicut fuit ionas . . . *iii̊.* A. Si quis fecerit . . . *Ad vesp.* A. Dixit quidam ad iesum . . . *Feria v̊.* A. Si manseritis in sermone . . . *Feria v[i̊.]* A. Si ueritatem dico . . . [*Ad i̊.*] A. Angelus domini descendebat . . . [*Ad iii̊.*] A. Domine non habeo . . . [*Ad vi̊.*] A. Qui me sanum fecit . . . [*Ad viiii̊.*] A. Uade iam et noli . . .

Sabbato. A. Assumpsit iesus discipulos . . . [*Ad iᵃ.*] A. Domine bonum est
. . . *iiiᵃ.* A. Faciamus hic tria . . . *viᵃ.* A. Descendentibus illis de monte . . .
viiiᵃ. A. Uisionem quam uidistis . . . resurgat filius hominis.

Feriae II, III, IV, V, VI, and Saturday of the first week of Quadragesima.

f. 9v   *Dominica iiᵃ in xlma.* R. [erased]. *In ev.* A. Nemini dixeritis uisionem . . .
Invit. Quoniam deus magnus . . . *Ps.* Venite. exultemus. *In iᵒ nᵒ.* A. Aduenerunt nobis. *ut supra.* R. Tolle arma tua pharetram . . . V. Cumque
uenatu aliquid . . . R. Ecce odor filii . . . V. Qui maledixerit tibi . . . R. Det
tibi deus . . . V. Et incuruentur ante . . . R. Quis igitur ille . . . attulit mihi et//

Second Sunday of Quadragesima, from first vespers to the first nocturn of
matins. The inner margin has been trimmed with slight loss of text.

f. 10r   [*Feria iiᵃ* . . . *Ad vesp.* A. Qui me misit . . .] //non reliquit me . . . [*Feria iiiᵃ.*]
A. Unus est enim magister . . . [*Ad vesp.* A. Qui maior] est uestrum erit ..
[*Feria ivᵃ.*] A. Ecce ascendimus ierosolimam . . . *Ad iᵃ.* A. Tradetur enim
gentibus . . . *Ad vesp.* A. Sedere autem mecu[m] . . . *Feria vᵃ.* A. Non [pos-
sum ego] . . . [A. Quia non quaero] uoluntatem meam sed . . . [A. Ego
ueni in nomi]ne . . . *siue* A. Pater abraham. A. Fili recor[dare. A. Diues illi
(?). *Feria vi.*] A. Malos male perdet . . . *Ad iᵃ.* A. Malos male perdet . . . [A.
Quaerentes eum] tenere timuerunt . . . R. Pater peccaui in celum . . . V.
Quanti mercennarii in domo . . . [*Sabbato.*] A. Uado ad patrem . . . *Ad iᵃ.*
A. Dixit autem [pater] . . . *Ad iiiᵃ.* A. Fili tu sem[per] . . . tua sunt.

Feria II, III, IV, V, VI, and Saturday of the second week of Quadragesima.
The upper margin, including the top three lines, and the outer half of the
leaf have been trimmed with loss of text.

f. 10r–v   *Dominica. iiiᵃ in xl. Ad vesp.* R. Igitur i[oseph ductus est] . . . [A. Fili tu
semper . . .] mea tua sunt . . . [*Invit.* Deus ma]gnus dominus et . . . [R. Ui-
dentes] ioseph a longe . . . [V. Cumque uidissent ioseph . . .] sui quod . . .
[R. Dixit iudas fratribus su]is ecce . . . [V. Cumque abisset ruben . . .] et
non . . . [R. Uidens iacob uestimenta io]seph . . . V. Uide [si tunica] . . .
[R. Ioseph dum] intraret . . . V. Diuertit ab oneribus . . . [R. Memento mei
dum bene] tibi fuerit . . . V. Tres enim adhuc . . . memento mei. Ut
suggeras//

Third Sunday of Quadragesima, from first vespers to the second nocturn
of matins. The upper margin, including the top three lines, and the outer
margin of the leaf have been trimmed with loss of text.

f. 11r //v. Custodi nos domine. Pater noster. v. In pace in idipsum ... *Preces.*
        Benedictus es domine ... *Cum reliquis. Ps.* Miserere mei. *Or.* Visit//[a
        quaesumus domine.]

Maundy Thursday, compline. The outer margin of the leaf has been
trimmed with loss of text. When this leaf was a flyleaf, a sixteenth-century
cursive hand added marginalia on both sides of the leaf, including a quotation from Aristotle's *Ethics* and two misogynist statements: "Uxor autem
est perpetuum tormentum" and "Mulieris est obliuio rationis."

f. 11r–v *Feria vi^a. In pa*[rasceve. in i^o n^o.] A. Astiterunt reges terre ... A. Diuiserunt
          sibi uestimenta ... A. Insurrexerunt in me ... v. Diuiserunt sibi uesti-
          menta ... R. Omnes amici mei ... [V. Et dederunt in escam] mea[m] ...
          R. Uelum templi scissum ... V. Amen dico tibi ... R. Uinea mea electa
          ... V. Ego q[uidem plantaui] ... [in ii^o n^o.] A. Uim faciebant qui ... Ps.
          Domine ne [in furore. A. Confundantur] et reuereantur ... A. Alieni in-
          surrexerunt in me ... v. Insurrexerunt in me ... R. Tamquam ad latronem
          ... V. Filius quidem hominis ... R. Tenebre facte sunt ... V. Et uelum
          templi ... [R. Barabbas latro di]mittitur ... V. Uerax datur fallacibus ...
          In iii^o n^o. [A. Ab insurgentibus in] me ... [A. Lo]nge fecisti notos ... [A.
          Captab]ant in animam iusti ... [v. Locuti] sunt aduersum me ... [R. Tra-
          diderunt me in] manus ... V. Asstiterunt [reges terre] ... [R. Iesum tradi-
          dit] impius ... V. Et ingressus petrus ... [R. Caligauerunt ocul]i mei ...
          [V. O uos] omnes ... *Ad laudes.* [A. Proprio filio suo] non ... Ps. Mise-
          rere. [A. Anxiatus est in m]e spiritus ... Ps. Domine exaudi. [A. Ait latro
          ad latrone]m nos ... Ps. Deus deus meus. Ps. Deus misereatur. [A. Dum
          conturbata fuer]it anima ... Ps. Domine audiui. [A. Memento mei domi]-
          ne deus ... Ps. Laudate dominum de cęlis. v. Proprio filio suo non pe]-
          percit ... *In ev.* A. Posuerunt super//

Good Friday, from first vespers to lauds. The outer margin has been
trimmed with loss of text.

f. 12r–v //alleluia. Ps. Benedictus dominus. *De sancta cruce.* A. Crucem sanctam
          subiit ... *De sancta maria.* Alleluia sancta dei genitrix ... *De sancto kyli-
          ano.* Fulgebunt iusti sicut. *Ad vesp.* A. In tabernaculis iustorum. *Suffragia
          sanctorum et de omnibus sanctis ut in breuiario scriptum est. Ad i^a.* A. Surgens
          iesus mane ... *iii^a.* A. Et dicebant ad inuicem ... v. Hec est dies quam ...
          *iste uersus per omnes horas dicendus est nisi tantum completorium et ad ma-
          tutines. siue v.* In resurrectione tua ... *Ad vi^a.* A. Et respicientes uiderunt
          ... v. Surrexit dominus uere. *Ad viiii^a.* A. Nolite expauescere iesum ... v.
          Surrexit dominus de ... *In ii^a vespera.* alleluia [6x] *ut* A. Crucifixus

resurrexit. *Ps.* Laudate pueri. *Ps.* Laudate dominum omnes gentes. *Ps.*
Laudate dominum quoniam bonus psalmus. *Ps.* Lauda ierusalem. *Et ita*
dicantur usque ad sabbatum. R. Surrexit dominus de . . . *V.* Qui pro nobis
pependit . . . *V.* Gloria patri et . . . *v.* Gauisi sunt discipuli . . . *In evg. A.*
Surrexit enim sicut . . . *De sancta cruce. A.* Crucem sanctam subiit. *Ad*
processionem. A. Christus resurgens ex mortuis . . . *item. A.* Dicant nunc
iudei . . . *Antiphona de resurrectione domini in evangelio ad laudes. A.* Post
passionem domini . . . A. Surgens iesus. A. Nolite expauescere. A. Scio
quod iesum . . . A. Iesum qui crucifixus . . . A. Cito euntes dicite . . . A. Et
recordate sunt . . . A. Oportebat pati christum . . . A. Nonne cor nostrum
. . . A. Cognouerunt discipuli dominum . . . A. Inclinauit se maria . . . A.
Ardens est cor . . . A. Ite nunciate fratribus . . . A. In galylea iesum . . . A.
Alleluia resurrexit dominus . . . A. Alleluia quem quaeris mulier. *R. in*
sancta nocte ad completorium. A. Alleluia noli flere . . . A. Ego sum alpha
. . . A. Surrexit dominus de . . . A. Surrexit dominus de . . . A. Surrexit
christus et . . . A. Crucifixus surrexit a mortuis . . . A. Crucem sanctam
subiit. A. Iesum quem quaeritis . . . A. Crucifixus resurrexit alleluia.

Easter, from lauds to second vespers, including antiphons to be said at
lauds during the Easter season. When this leaf was a flyleaf, several sixteenth-century hands added marginalia on the recto and verso, including
quotations from Seneca, Ovid, and Bernard of Clairvaux.

f. 12v   *Feria secunda. Invitatorium.* Surrexit dominus uere . . . *Ps.* Venite. *In $\overset{o}{i}$ n^o.*
           A. Nolite expa//[uescere]

           Feria II after Easter, matins.

f. 13r   //*Ps.* Beatus uir qui non . . . *Ps.* Quare fremuerunt. *Ps.* Cum inuocarem. *Ps.*
           Uerba mea. *Ps.* Domine dominus noster. *Ps.* In domino confido. *In $\overset{o}{i}$ n^o. v.*
           Resurrexit dominus. sicut dixit. *In $\overset{o}{ii}$ n^o. v.* Surrexit dominus uere . . . *In $\overset{o}{iii}$*
           n^o. v. Surrexit dominus de sepulchro . . . *Ad laud. v.* Surrexit christus . . .
           Ad vesperas. v. Gauisi sunt discipuli . . . *Aliter in $\overset{o}{i}$ n^o. v.* Quem quaeris
           mulier. Uiuentem. *$\overset{o}{ii}$ n^o. v.* Tulerunt dominum meum . . . *$\overset{o}{iii}$ n^o. v.* Noli
           flere maria . . . *Ad laud. v.* Resurrexit dominus. sicut dixit. *Ad vesper. v.*
           Gauisi sunt discipuli.

           Saturday after Easter, versicles for matins, lauds, and second vespers.
           When this leaf was a flyleaf, two sixteenth-century hands added margi-
           nalia in the upper margins of both recto and verso.

f. 13r–v   *R.* Maria magdalena et altera . . . *V.* Cito euntes dicite . . . *R.* Surgens iesus dominus ... *V.* Surrexit dominus de ... *R.* Congratulamini mihi omnes ... *V.* Tulerunt dominum meum ... *In ii⁰ n⁰.* A. Scio quod iesum quaeritis. *Ps.* Saluum me fac domine quoniam defecit. *Ps.* Usquequo. *Ps.* Dixit insipiens. *Ps.* Domine quis habitabit. *Ps.* Conserua me domine. *Ps.* Exaudi domine iusticiam. *Ad laud. A.* Angelus autem domini. *R.* Surrexit dominus uere. *In ev. A.* Iesus iunxit se ... *Ad i^a. A.* Tu solus peregrinus ... *iii^a. A.* Nonne sic oportuit ... *v.* In resurrectione tua christe ... *vi^a. A.* Et incipiens a moyse ... *v.* Surrexit dominus uere. *viiii^a. A.* Et coegerunt illum ... *v.* Surrexit dominus de sepulchro. *Ad vesp.* Alleluia [8x] *ut A.* Surrexit. *Ps.* Laudate pueri *ut supra. R.* Surrexit dominus de ... *V.* Qui pro nobis ... *V.* Gloria patri et ... *Priuatis diebus. R.* Surrexit dominus de ... *V.* Qui pro nobis ... *In ev. A.* Qui sunt hi ... alleluia.

Feria II after Easter, from matins to second vespers.

f. 13v   *Feria iii^a Inv.* Surrexit dominus uere ... *In i⁰ n⁰.* A. Iesum qui crucifixus est. *Ps.* Domine dominus noster. *Ps.* Domine quis habitabit. *Ps.* Celi enarrant. *Ps.* Exaudiat te dominus. *Ps.* Domine in uirtute. *Ps.* Dominus regit me. *v.* Resurrexit dominus ... *R.* Uirtute magna reddebant ... *V.* In omnem terram ... *R.* Tulerunt dominum meum ... *V.* Cito euntes dicite ... *R.* Expurgate uetus fermentum ... *V.* Non in fermento ... *In ii⁰ n⁰.* A. Uenite et uidete. *Ps.* Domini est terra. *Ps.* Iudica me domine. *Ps.* Ad te domine clamabo. *Ps.* Afferte domino. *Ps.* Exaltabo te domine. *Ps.* Exultate iusticiam. *Ad laudes. A.* Et ecce terre motus. *R.* Surrexit dominus uere ... *V.* Et apparuit symoni ... *In ev. A.* Stetit iesus in medio ... pax uobis alleluia alleluia//

Feria III after Easter, from matins to lauds.

f. 14r   [*A.* Modicum et non ...] //me quia uado ... *A.* Quid est hoc quod ... *A.* Amen amen dico uobis ... *A.* Mulier cum parit ... *A.* Tristitia implebit cor ... *A.* Tristitia uestra alleluia ... *A.* Iterum autem uidebo ... *A.* Iterum autem uidebo ... a uobis alleluia.

Sunday III after Easter, lauds. When this leaf was a flyleaf, several sixteenth-century hands added marginal quotations from Chrysostom, Augustine, Ambrose, Bernard of Clairvaux, Gregory, Seneca, and the Bible.

f. 14r   Uado ad eum qui ... *A.* Ego ueritatem dico ... *A.* Dum uenerit paraclytus ... *A.* Adhuc multa habeo ... *A.* Cum autem uenerit ... *A.* Non enim loquetur ... *A.* Ille me clarificabit ... annunciabit uobis alleluia.

Sunday IV after Easter, lauds.

f. 14r–v *Dominica quinta.* A. Usque modo non petistis . . . A. Petite et accipietis
. . . A. Exiui a patre et . . . A. Exivi a patre meo . . . A. Ecce nunc palam
. . . *In rogationibus.* A. Petite et dabitur . . . A. Omnis qui petit . . . A. Si
ergo uos . . . petentibus se alleluia.

Sunday V after Easter, lauds, including antiphons for rogation.

f. 14v *Dominica. prima post octavam pasche. Ad vesp.* R. Audiui uoces in celo . . .
Inv. Alleluia alleluia. *Ps.* Venite exultemus. R. Dignus es domine . . . V.
Parce domine parce . . . R. Ego sicut uitis . . . V. Ego diligentes me . . . R.
Audiui uocem de celo . . . V. Uidi angelum dei . . . R. Resurrexit dominus
alleluia . . . V. Sicut dixit uobis . . . R. Locutus est ad me . . . V. Et sustulit
me . . . V. Ego diligentes. R. Audiui uoces in celo . . . V. Uidi angelum dei
. . . R. Decantabat populus in . . . V. Moyses et aaron . . . inter eos. Et
dauid//

First Sunday after the Octave of Easter, from first vespers to matins.

f. 15r–v //V. Natiuitatem hodierna perpetue . . . R. Corde et animo . . . V. Cum io-
cunditate natiuitatem . . . R. Regali ex progenie . . . V. Corde et animo
. . . R. Stirps iesse uirgam . . . V. Uirgo dei genitrix . . . V. Gloria patri et
. . . *Ad cant.* A. Beatissime uirginis marie . . . *Cant.* Audite me. *v.* Speciosa
facta es . . . R. Natiuitas tua dei . . . V. Aue maria gratia . . . R. Natiuitas
gloriose uirginis . . . V. Gloriose uirginis marie . . . R. Felix namque es. V.
Ora pro populo . . . R. Ad nutum domini . . . V. Ut uicium uirtus . . . V.
Gloria patri et . . . *Ad laud.* A. Natiuitas gloriose uirginis . . . A. Natiuitas
est hodie . . . A. Regali ex progenie . . . A. Corde et animo . . . A. Cum iocunditate natiuitatem . . . R. Adiuua nos tuis . . . V. Oraculum eterne uite
. . . V. Gloria patri et . . . *v.* Egredietur uirga . . . *In ev.* A. Natiuitatem
hodiernam perpetue . . . *Ad i̅ᵃ.* A. Natiuitas gloriose. *alia.* A. Hodie nata est
. . . *Ad iii̅ᵃ.* A. Adest namque. *vi̅ᵃ.* A. Regali ex progenie. *viii̅ᵃ.* A. Beatissime uirginis. *In ii̅ᵃ vespera.* A. Natiuitas est hodie. *cum reliquis.* *Ps.* Dixit
dominus. *Ps.* Letatus sum. *Ps.* Nisi dominus. *Ps.* Memento. R. Adiuua nos
tuis. *v.* Egredietur uirga. *In ev.* A. Quando nata est benedictus fructus eius.

Nativity of the Virgin Mary (8 September), from the second nocturn of
matins to second vespers.

f. 15v *In exaltatione sanctae crucis. Ad vesper.* R. Hoc signum crucis. *v.* Adoramus
te christe . . . *In ev.* A. Sanctifica nos domine . . . *De sanctis.* A. Isti sunt

sancti qui . . . *Invit.* Adoremus regem. C*ætera ut de martyribus. Ad cant. A.*
Dulce lignum. *R. in inuentione. Cantica.* Domine audiui. *C.* Numquid in
flumen. *C.* Egressus es in salutem. *v.* Salua nos christe . . . *R.* Dulce lignum. *R.* Hoc signum crucis. *R.* O crux gloriosa. *R.* O crux benedicta. *R. in
inuentione. Ad laudes. A.* O magnum pietatis . . . *A.* Salua nos christe . . . *A.*
O crux ammirabilis . . . *A.* Nos autem gloriari . . . *A.* Crux benedicta nitet
. . . *R.* Hoc signum crucis . . . *V.* Cum dominus ad . . . *v.* Adoramus te
christe . . . *In ev. A.* Super omnia ligna . . . *Ad i^a. A.* Nos autem gloriari. *iii^a.*
A. Lignum uite. *R. in inuentione. v.* Hoc signum crucis. *Ad vi^a. A.* Saluator
mundi salua. *v.* Per signum crucis. *Ad viiii^a. A.* Dulce lignum. *v.* Salua nos
christe saluator. *In ii^a vespera. A.* O magnum pietatis. *Ps.* Dixit dominus.
A. Salua nos christe//

Exaltation of the Cross (14 September), from first vespers to second
vespers.

f. 16   [*R.* Dum deambularet dominus . . .] //et andream retia . . . *V.* Erant enim
piscatores . . . *R.* Uenite post me . . . *V.* Dum deambularet dominus . . . *R.*
Mox ut uocem . . . *V.* Ad unius iussionis . . . *R.* Homo dei ducebatur . . . *V.*
Cumque carnifices ducerent . . . *In ii^o n^o. A.* Salue crux que . . . *A.* Recipe
me ab . . . *A.* Biduo uiuens pendebat . . . *A.* Andreas christi famulus . . . *A.*
Dignum sibi dominus . . . *A.* Dilexit andream dominus . . . *R.* Cum uidisset
beatus . . . *V.* Exspecta me sancta . . . *R.* Salue crux que . . . *V.* O bona
crux . . . *R.* O bona crux . . . *V.* Salue crux que . . . *R.* Doctor bonus et . . .
V. Salue crux que . . . *V.* Cum uero peruenisset . . . *Ad cant. A.* Concede
nobis hominem . . . *Cant.* Uos sancti domini. *R.* Orauit sanctus Andreas
. . . *V.* Tu es magister . . . *R.* Expandi manus meas . . . *V.* Deus ultionum dominus . . . *R.* Uir iste in populo . . . *V.* Pro eo ut me . . . *R.* Dilexit andream
dominus . . . *V.* Elegit eum dominus . . . *Ad laudes. A.* Salue crux preciosa
. . . *A.* Non me permittas . . . *A.* Beatus andreas orabat . . . *A.* Qui perse-
quebatur iustum . . . *A.* Maximilla christo amabilis . . . optimo loco cum//

St. Andrew (30 November), from the first nocturn of matins to lauds.

f. 17r   [*R.* Grata facta est . . . ho]//mines glorificata est . . . *V.* Adiuuabit eam deus
. . . *Ad laudes. A.* Orante sancta lucia . . . *A.* Lucia uirgo quid . . . *A.* Per te
lucia . . . *A.* Benedico te pater . . . *A.* Tanto pondere eam . . . *In ev. A.* Co-
lumna es immobilis . . . *Ad horas. A.* Orante sancta lucia. *A.* Lucia uirgo.
A. Per te lucia uirgo. *A.* Tanto pondere. *In ii^a vespera. A.* Uidi speciosam.
Ps. Dixit dominus. *A.* Ueni electa. *Ps.* Laudate pueri. *A.* Ista est speciosa.
Ps. Lętatus. *A.* Ornatam. *Ps.* Nisi dominus ędificauerit. *In ev. A.* In tua patientia . . . inimicum subisti.

St. Lucy (13 December), from the third nocturn of matins to second vespers.

f. 17r   *Hic incipiatur. A. O* sapientia.

"O" antiphons.

f. 17r   *De sancto thoma apostolo. Ad vesperam. A. in evangelio. A. O* thoma didime
         ... Cǫtera omnia pleniter sicut de apostolis. Ad laudes. In ev. A. Thomas qui
         dicitur. *Post benedicamus domino canitur. A.* Nolite timere quinta. *In iĩ ves-
         per. in ev. A.* Quia uidisti me.

St. Thomas (21 December), from first to second vespers.

f. 17r   *De evangelistis. R.* Qui sunt hii ... *V.* Dorsa eorum plena ... *V.* Gloria patri
         et ... *In ev. A.* Ecce ego iohannes ... in secula seculorum.

Common of Evangelists, vespers only.

f. 17r–v *De apostolis in ĩ vesp. R.* In omnem terram. *uel R.* Tollite iugum. *v.* An-
          nuntiauerunt opera dei. *uel v.* Nimis honorati sunt. *In ev. A.* Isti sunt uiri
          ... *A.* Ecce ego mitto ... *A.* Dum steteritis ante ... *Invit.* Regem apos-
          tolorum dominum ... *Ps.* Venite. *uel.* Regem apostolorum dominum ...
          Ps. Venite. *In ĩ n°. A.* In omnem terram ... *Ps.* Cǫli enarrant. *A.*
          Clamauerunt iusti et ... *Ps.* Benedicam. *A.* Constitues eos principes ...
          Ps. Eructauit. *A.* Principes populorum congregati ... *Ps.* Omnes gentes. *A.*
          Dedisti hereditatem timentibus ... *Ps.* Exaudi deus deprecationem. *A.*
          Annunciauerunt opera dei ... *Ps.* Exaudi deus orationem meam. *Alia A.*
          In omnem terram. *A.* Hec est generatio ... *Ps.* Domini est terra. *A.*
          Exsultate iusti in ... *Ps.* Ipsum. *A.* Clamauerunt iusti. *A.* Constitues eos
          principes. *A.* Principes populorum. *Responsorium.* Ecce ego mitto ... *V.*
          Dum lucem habetis ... *uel V.* Ut filii lucis ... *R.* Tollite iugum meum ...
          V. Et inuenietis requiem ... *R.* Dum steteritis ante ... *V.* Non enim uos
          ... *R.* In omnem terram ... *V.* Non sunt loquele neque ser//[mones]

Common of Apostles, from first vespers to the first nocturn of matins. An early fifteenth-century hand has added Psalm incipits in the bottom margin.

Parchment. 17 folios (fols. 3 and 4, fols. 5 and 7, and fols. 8 and 10 are bifolia). The measurements of the leaves are as follows: fols. 1–2, 310 x 213 mm; fols. 3–4, 320 x 240 mm; fol. 5, 264 x 243 mm; fol. 6, 290 x 215 mm (plus strip from conjoint leaf); fol. 7, 272 x 167 mm; fol. 8, 258 x 243 mm; fol. 9, 310 x 205 mm; fol. 10, 258 x 129 mm; fol. 11, 312 x 157 mm; fol. 12, 308 x 227 mm; fol. 13, 310 x 233 mm; fol. 14, 313 x 230 mm; fol. 15, 310 x 228 mm; fol. 16, 281 x 223 mm; fol. 17, 290 x 210 mm (written space 240 x 186 mm). 1 column. 26 lines. Dry-point or lead ruling. Double vertical bounding lines; additional vertical bounding line in outer margin to accomodate marginal tonary letters. Horizontal rulings extend into outer margin. Prickings in upper margin.

Written in late Caroline minuscule by Gottschalk, a scribe at Lambach in the twelfth and early thirteenth century (see Davis, *Epiphany, passim*, and Holter [1959], 216–19). His hand also appears in the following manuscripts: Beinecke 481.93; Berlin, Preussische Staatsbibliothek, Theo.Lat.Qu. 140 (formerly Lambach Cml XCIII); Kremsmünster, Stiftsbibliothek, CC 35; Lambach, Stiftsbibliothek, Cml L, LIV, CXL, and Fragment 2; Princeton, University Library, MS 51 (formerly Lambach Cml CXLIII; listed in K. Holter, "Neue Beiträge zur Geschichte der Stiftsbibliothek von Lambach im hohen Mittelalter," in *Kunstgeschichtsforschung und Denkmalpflege: Festschrift für Norbert Wibiral zum 65. Geburtstag*, ed. G. Heilingsetzer [Linz, 1986], 85–89, here 86 as Princeton, Nr. 215 C); Vienna, Österreichische Nationalbibliothek, Cvp 373 (see Davis, *Epiphany*, 173–78, and Holter [1989], cat. nos. II.02, VIII.14, 17, 19, 25, and IX.14). Initials by him appear in Cml LXXIIIa (the Lambach Rituale) and in fragments of a missal preserved in Lambach Ccl 308 and Göttweig, Stiftsbibliothek, 1117. There are brief descriptions and some plates of the Cml volumes and of Ccl 308 in Holter (1959), 240, 242–43, 245–46, 249–50, and 262.

The responsorial liturgy of most feasts begins with a 3- to 5-line initial in red, written on the vertical bounding lines, with red vine-stem decoration and violet bands and foliage, drawn by Gottschalk. These occur on fols. 1r, 1v, 6v, 8r, 9v, 11r, 13r, 13v, 14v, and 17r. Three of these are historiated initials: fol. 1r, trumpeter (fourth Sunday of Advent); fol. 1v, Prophet Isaiah (feria VI), and fol. 6v, Gregory the Great (see Babcock, *Reconstructing a Medieval Library*, figs. 1 and 56; initials by Gottschalk in other manuscripts are in Babcock, *Reconstructing a Medieval Library*, fig. 2 and Holter [1959], pl. 237). The initials of the first antiphons for the feriae of the fourth Sunday of Advent, for vespers of Good Friday, and for most of the antiphons for Easter are plain red 1-line capitals. 1-line initials of responses and Benedictus or Magnificat antiphons are in thick brown uncials, traced or dotted with red. Other 1-line initials are brown rustic capitals sometimes traced with red. All 1-line initials are set apart from the text between double bounding lines when they occur at the beginning of the line. Rubrics are written in red rustic capitals; liturgical directions are written in brown minuscule traced with red. The first 1 to 4 words after major initials and the names of major saints (Peter, Mary) are written in brown rustic capitals frequently traced with red. The names of other saints are written in brown minuscule and are occasionally traced with red. Punctuation consists of the punctus. Interlinear neumes in the St. Gall style. Tonary letters, indicating mode and differentia of antiphons, responsories and invitatories, are written

in the outer margin of each folio, drawn on tiers of a column resembling an archi-
tectural support.

Other leaves of the Gottschalk Antiphonary are preserved in Cambridge, Mass.,
Harvard University, Houghton Library, Pf. MS Typ 705, fols. 5–6 (2 leaves);
Lambach, Stiftsbibliothek, Ink. I.95 (strips from the upper margins of 2 bifolia, one
of which is Beinecke fols. 8 and 10; the other strip comes between these leaves);
Ink. II.1.i (4 leaves in the binding); Ink. II.36 (strips from the side margins of 2
leaves); St. Louis, Public Library, Rare Books and Special Collections, Grolier #44
(identified by Karen Gould); St. Paul-im-Lavanttal, Stiftsbibliothek, Fragment 54/8,
fol. 1–2 (2 leaves); and a private Austrian collection (1 leaf).

These leaves preserve portions of twelve quires: QI: Beinecke fols. 1 and 2 (consecutive); QII: St. Paul-im-Lavanttal, fols. 1 and 2; QIII: Beinecke fol. 3, 4 leaves
from Lambach, Ink. II.1.i, Beinecke fol. 4 (fols. 2–7 of quire); QIV: Beinecke fols.
5, 6, [1 leaf missing], Private Coll., Harvard fol. 5, Beinecke fol. 7 (fols. 2–7 of
quire); QV: Beinecke fol. 8 (+ strip), strip from Lambach Ink. I.95, [1 leaf miss-
ing], Beinecke fol. 9, strip from Ink. I.95, Beinecke fol. 10 (fols. 2–7 of quire); QVI:
Beinecke fol. 11; QVII: fol. 12, [four leaves missing], fol. 13 (fols. 2 and 7 of quire);
QVIII: fol. 14; QIX: St. Louis leaf, strip from Ink. II.36, Beinecke fol. 15 (fols. 1, 7
and 8 of quire); QX: fol. 16; QXI: fol. 17; QXII: Harvard fol. 6. See Davis, *Epiphany*, 292.

Fol. 1 was formerly Zinniker 145A; fol. 2, Zinniker 145B; the bifolium 3/4, Zinniker 147; the bifolium 5/7, Zinniker 146A; fol. 6, Zinniker 146B; the bifolium
8/10, Zinniker 153; fol. 9, Zinniker 152; fol. 11, Zinniker 150; fol. 12, Zinniker
144B; fol. 13, Zinniker 144A; fol. 14, Zinniker 151; fol. 15, Zinniker 149; fol. 16,
Beinecke MS 482.29, Zinniker 118; and fol. 17, Zinniker 148.

Bibliography:
Babcock, *Reconstructing a Medieval Library*, 104 and figs. 1 and 56.
Babcock, R. G. and L. F. Davis, "Two Romanesque Manuscripts from Lam-
bach," *Codices Manuscripti* 15 (1990): 137–47.
Davis, L. F., "Two Leaves of the Gottschalk Antiphonary," *Harvard Library
Bulletin*, n.s. 5 (1994): 38–44.

MS 481.52   Lambach, Austria, s. XII^2
Antiphonary   Pl. 34

It is possible that not all these leaves come from the same manuscript. They were
written by several scribes, and the written space varies.

f. 1r   [A. Iucundare filia sion exsulta] //satis filia hierusalem alleluia. A. Ecce

dominus ueniet . . . A. Omnes sitientes uenite . . . A. Ecce ueniet propheta
. . . [A.] Super te hierusalem . . . *v*. Et gloria eius . . . *v*. Gloria patri . . . *In
evg*. A. Spiritus sanctus in te . . . *De sancta maria*. A. Angelus domini. *Ad
prima*. A. In illa die. *iii*ᵃ. A. Iocundare. *Ad sexta*. A. Omnes sicientes. *Ad
nona*. A. Ecce ueniet. *In secunda vespera*. *Ps*. Dixit dominus. *Cap*. Ecce
dies. R. Ueni ad liberandum . . . V. Et ostende faciem . . . [*v*.] Gloria patri
et filio. *ymnus*. Conditor alme. *v*. Rorate celi desuper. *In evg*. A. Ne timeas
maria . . . *De sancta maria*. Missus est gabriel.

First Sunday of Advent, from lauds to second vespers.

f. 1r–v   *Feria ii*ᵃ. *Invit*. Regem uenturum . . . *Ps*. Venite ex. *ymnus*. Uerbum super.
In *i*° *n*°. A. Rectos decet cum . . . *Uersus ut supra*. R. Aspiciebam. *cum
reliqua*. R. Ecce dies *non canitur per ebdomadam*. R. Super te hierusalem.
ymnus. Uox clara. *In evg*. A. Angelus domini nuntiauit . . . *De sancta maria*.
Missus est gabriel. *Aliis autem diebus*. A. Angelus domini. *Ad prima*. A. Qui
uenturus est . . . *Ad iii*ᵃ. A. Ueni et libera . . . *v*. Timebunt gentes. *Ad sexta*.
A. Tuam domine excita . . . *v*. Memento nostri domine. *Ad nona*. A. In
tuo aduentu . . . *v*. Domine deus uirtutum . . . *Ad Uesper*. R. Ueni ad
liberandum. R. Super te hierusalem. *Que duo per duas ebdomadas canuntur*.
In e. A. Hierusalem respice ad . . . *De sancta maria*. A. Missus est gabriel.

Feria II of the first week of Advent, from matins to second vespers.

f. 1v   *Feria iii*ᵃ. A. Ante quem conuenirent . . . A. Querite dominum dum . . .
prope est alleluia.

Feria III of the first week of Advent.

f. 1v   *Feria iiii*ᵃ. A. De syon exibit . . . A. Veniet fortior me . . . non sum dignus//

Feria IV of the first week of Advent.

f. 2   [R. Ecce apparebit dominus . . . mil]//lia et habet . . . V. Ecce dominator
[*supr*.: dominus] . . . R. Betheem [*sic*] ciuitas dei . . . V. Deus a lybano . . .
R. Qui uenturus est . . . V. Ex syon species . . . R. Suscipe uerbum uirgo
. . . V. Aue maria gratia . . . *In ii*° *n*°. Betlehem [*corr. ex*. Bethehem] non es
minima . . . R. Egypte noli flere . . . R. Ecce dominator dominus . . . R.
Prope est ut . . . V. Qui uenturus est . . . R. Descendet dominus sicut . . . V.
A solis ortu . . . R. Adnuntiatum est gabrihelem . . . V. Aue maria. *In iii*° *n*°.
A. Ite dicite iohanni . . . *Cant*. Confortate. [R.] Veni domine et . . . faci-
nora ple//[bis]

Third Sunday of Advent, first through third nocturns of matins.

f. 3r   //A. O rex gentium et desideratus ... A. O emmanuel rex ... A. O uirgo
uirginum ... A. O gabrihel nuntius ... A. O rex pacifice ... A. O hierusalem ciuitas dei ... A. O mundi domina ... et sidera regit.

"O" antiphons.

f. 3r–v *In vigilia natalis domini. Cap.* Gaudete in domino. *R.* De illa occulta. *ymnus.*
Conditor. *In evg.* O hierusalem. *Preces.* Ego dixi. *Ps.* Miserere *solus. In-
vitatorium.* Hodie scietis quia ... *Ps.* Uenite. *In i° n°. A.* Veni domine. *A.*
Paratus esto israhel ... *A.* Ecce deus noster ... *uel sola hec* Paratus e. *v.*
Crastina die delebitur. *R.* Sanctificamini hodie et ... *V.* Hodie scietis quia
... *R.* Constantes estote uidebitis ... *V.* Uos qui in puluere ... *R.* Sanc-
tificamini filii israhel ... *V.* Ecce dominus ueniet ut sal//[uos]

Christmas Eve (24 December), from vespers to the first nocturn of matins.

f. 4r   [A. Nesciens mater virgo ...] //peperit sine dolore ... A. Continet in gremio ... A. Beatus uenter qui ... A. Virgo dei genitrix ... A. Virgo uerbo
concepit ... omnium regum.

Christmas, second vespers.

f. 4r–v *In natale sancti stephani. R.* Lapides torrentis. *V.* Mortem enim. Gloria
patri. *V.* Magna est gloria ... *In evangelio. A.* Intuens in celum ... *Invitat.*
Regem protomartiris stephani ... *Ps.* Uenite ex. *ymnus.* Martyr dei. *In i° n°.*
R. Beatus stephanus iugi ... *Ps.* Beatus uir. *A.* Constitutus a deo ... *Ps.*
Quare fremuerunt. *A.* In tribulatione lapidum ... *Ps.* Domine quid
multiplicati. *A.* Lumine uultus tu[i] ... *Ps.* Cum inuocarem. *A.* Benedic-
tionis tue domine ... *Ps.* Verba mea. *A.* O quam admirabile ... *R.* Domine deus noster. *In Oct.* Stephanus seruus dei ... iudei uidit ce//los]

St. Stephen (26 December), first vespers through the first nocturn of
matins.

f. 5   //R. Ecce agnus dei qui tollit peccata ... V. Hoc est testimonium ... R.
Continet in gremio ... V. Domus pudici pectoris ... R. Benedictus qui.
[V.] Lapidem. *In ii° n°.* Verbum caro factum ... *v.* Ipse inuocabit me. *Ad
laud.* Quem uidistis. *R.* Benedictus qui uenit. *V.* Verbum caro. *In evg. A.*
Angelus ad pastores. *De sancta maria.* Sancta et inmaculata. *iii. A.* Natus
est nobis saluator. *A.* Ecce agnus dei. *vi. A.* Ecce de quo. *nona. A.* In

principio. *In ii^a vespera.* Tecum principium. R. Notum fecit dominus. V.
Tecum principium. *In e.* A. Gaudeamus omnes. *De sancta maria.* Beatus
uenter. *Altera die invitat.* Christus natus est. *In primo n°. si antiphona non
habetur* [one word illegible] *dicatur haec antiphona.* Nato domino. *v.* Ipse
inuocabit me . . . R. Congratulamini mihi omnes . . . V. Beatam me dicent
. . . V. Casta parentis uiscera . . . R. Hic qui aduenit . . . V. Ecce aduenit
dominator . . . R. O regem caeli . . . V. Domine audiui auditum . . . *In ii° n°.*
A. Ecce de quo. *v.* Benedictus qui uenit. *Ad laud.* A. Genuit puerpera. R.
Benedictus. V. Uerbum caro factum est. *In e.* A. Pastores loquebantur. *De
sancta maria.* Sancta et inmaculata. *Ad horas ut pridie. Ad Uesper.* Tecum
principium.

Within the Octave of Christmas, matins through second vespers.

f. 5v   *De sancto syluestro.* R. Iurauit. *In e.* A. Sacerdos et pontifex. *De nat.* O
regem. *De sancta maria.* Uirgo uerbum. *Et cetera omnia nocte dieque sicut de
uno confessore qui fuit episcopus. Ad laud. In e.* A. Qui dum esset. *Nat.* A.
Uerbum caro. *De sancta maria.* Sancta et inmaculata. *In ii^a v(esp).* A.
Iurauit.

St. Silvester (31 December), from first to second vespers.

f. 5v   *De octaua domini.* R. Sancta et inmaculata. V. Tecum principium. *In e.* A.
Qui de terra . . . eius testimonium//

Octave of Christmas, vespers.

f. 6r–v //A. Stella nobis uisa . . . A. Venient ad te . . . A. Videntes stellam magi
. . . *Ad Uesper. et Laud.* A. Uox de celis . . . A. Celi aperti sunt . . . A.
Iohannes quidem clamabat . . . A. Aqua comburit peccatum . . . A. Pater
de celis . . . A. Baptizatur christus et . . . A. Super ripam iordanis . . . A.
Baptizat miles regem . . . *Ad laud.* A. Ante luciferum. *Singulis nocte una* A.
Maria et flumina *non canitur.* R. Reges tharsys et . . . V. Reges arabum . . .
V. Omnes de saba uenient. *A(d) uesper.* A. Uox de celis. *cum reliqua. Ad
horas et uespera ut in die sancto.*

Within the Octave of Epiphany, vespers and lauds.

ff. 6v–7r *Dominica infra octava.* A. Tecum principium. R. Omnes de saba. *In e.* A.
Ab oriente uenerunt . . . *Post benedicamus non canitur de epiphania. Invit.*
Christus apparuit. *In i° n°.* A. Stella nobis. *v.* Omnis terra . . . R. Hodie in
iordane. *cum reliqua. In ii° n°.* A. Afferte domino. *Ad laud.* A. Ante luci-

ferum. R. Reges tharsys. R. Omnes de saba uenient. *In evangelio* A. Cum factus esset . . . *De epyphania.* Vidimus stellam *ad horas ut in die sancto. In ii^a v(esp).* A. Tecum principium. *In e.* A. Fili quod fecisti . . . *De epyphania.* Uidentes stellam. A. Quid est quod . . . me esse alleluia.

Sunday within the Octave of Epiphany, from first to second vespers.

f. 7r–v   *Octava epyphaniae.* Tecum principium. R. Omnes de saba. V. Reges tharsys et insula. *In e.* A. Fontes aquarum sanctificati . . . *De sancto ylario.* A. Sacerdos et pontifex. *Invit..* Christus apparuit. *Et cetera omnia ut in die sancto. Ad cant.* In columbe specie . . . *Ps.* Populus qui. *v.* Adorate. *Ad laud.* A. Ueterem hominem renouans . . . A. Te qui in spiritu . . . A. Baptista contremuit et . . . A. Caput draconis saluator . . . A. Magnum mysterium declaratur . . . R. Uox domini super . . . V. Intonuit dominus super . . . *In evangelio.* Precursor iohannes exultat . . . *Ad laud.* A. Euge serue. *Ad hor.* Laudes. *Ad v(esp).* A. Tecum principium. *v.* Omnes de saba . . . *v.* Reges tharsys . . . [A]. Christo datus est . . . in eternum alleluia.

Octave of Epiphany, from first to second vespers.

f. 7v   *Dominica i^a post octavam epiphaniae.* A. Nuptie facte sunt . . . A. Qui michi et tibi . . . A. Deficiente uino iussit . . . conuerse sunt alleluia.//

Second Sunday after Epiphany, vespers.

ff. 8–9v   [A. Christi virgo nec . . .] //blandimento seducitur . . . *In i^o n^o.* A. Discede a me pabulum . . . *Ps.* Domine dominus. A. Dextram meam et collum . . . A. Posuit signum in faciem . . . A. Induit me dominus cyclade . . . A. Mel et lac . . . A. Ipsi soli seruo . . . [R.] Diem festum sacratissime . . . V. Ingressa agnes turpitudinis . . . R. Dextram meam et collum . . . V. Induit me dominus cyclade . . . R. Diffusa est gratia. R. Amo christum in . . . V. Mel et lac . . . *In ii^o n^o.* A. Cuius pulchritudinem sol . . . A. Christe circumdedit me . . . A. Ipsi sum desponsata . . . A. Iam corpus eius . . . A. Leua eius sub capite . . . A. Ecce quod cupiui . . . R. Omnipotens adorande colende . . . V. Te confiteor labiis . . . R. Ipsi sum desponsata . . . V. Propter ueritatem et . . . R. Concupiuit rex. R. Induit me dominus uestimento . . . V. Induit me dominus cyclade . . . *Ad cant.* A. Stat a dextris . . . R. Iam corpus eius . . . V. Ipsi sum desponsata . . . R. Veni electa. V. Audi filia. R. Pulcra facie sed . . . V. Specie tua et . . . R. Mel et lac . . . V. Cuius pulcritudinem sol . . . *Laudes.* A. Ingressa agnes turpitudinis . . . A. Mecum enim habeo . . . A. Anulo suo subarrauit . . . A. Benedico te pater . . . A. Congaudete mecum et . . . *In evangelio.* A. Beata agnes in medio . . . *Ad horas.* A. Induit me. A. Christe circumdedit. A. Ipsi sum. A. Ecce. In ii^a v. A. Ingressa agnes. Ps. Dixit dominus. A. Mel et lac. Ps. Laudate pueri. A. Anulo suo. Ps. Letatus sum. A. Congaudete. Ps. Nisi dominus. In evangelio. A. Stans beata agnes ... nomen tuum in eternum.

St. Agnes (21 January), from first to second vespers.

ff. 9v–10r   In conuersione sancti pauli. R. Tu es uas electionis. ymnus. Doctor egregie. v. Sit tibi. v. Annuntiauerit opera dei ... A. O gloriosum lumen ... Ad processionem. Magnus sanctus paulus. Invitatorium. Regem aposto- lorum. In i^o n^o. A. Qui operatus est ... In evangelio. A. Hodie electorum omnium ... In ii^a vsp. e. A. Iste est qui ... pro peccatis omnium populorum.

Conversion of St. Paul (25 January), from first to second vespers.

f. 10r–v   In purificatione mariɇ. A. O admirabile commercium. Ps. Dixit dominus. A. Quando nata. Ps. Confitebor. A. Rubum quem uiderat. Ps. Beatus. A. Germinauit. Ps. Memento. R. Postquam impleti. V. Responsum accepit symeon. In evg. A. Senex puerum portabat ... Invit. Ecce uenit ad templum ... ymnus. Fit porta. In i^o n^o. A. Benedicta tu in mulieribus ... Ps. De uirginibus. A. Speciosa facta es ... A. Sicut myrra electa ... A. Ante thorum huius ... A. Super salutem et omnem ... A. Optimam partem ele- git ... v. Accipiens symeon ... R. Adorna thalamum tuum ... V. Acci- piens symeon puerum ... R. Senex puerum portabat ... V. Accipiens. R. Symeon iustus et ... V. Responsum acceperat symeon ... R. Responsum acceperat symeon ... domini. et bene//[dixit]

Purification of the Virgin (2 February), first vespers to first nocturn.

f. 11r   [A. Et intrauit cum illis ...] //et benedixit. fregit. ac porrigebat illis alleluia.

Feria II after Easter, second vespers.

f. 11r–v Feria iii^a. Invit. Surrexit dominus uere. In i^o n^o. A. Iesum qui crucifixus. vel. Et intrauit cum illis. Ps. Domine deus noster. Ps. Domine quis habitabit. Ps. Celi enarrant. Ps. Exaudiat te. Ps. Domine in virtute. Ps. Dominus regit. R. Uirtute magna reddebant ... V. In omnem terram ... R. Tulerunt dominum meum ... V. Cito euntes dicite ... R. Expurgate uetus fer- mentum ... V. Non in fermento ... In ii^o no. A. Uenite et uidete. uel Nonne cor nostrum. Ps. Domini est terra. Ps. Iudica me domine quoniam. Ps. Ad te domine clamabo. Ps. Afferte. Ps. Exaltabo. Ps. Exultate iusti.

Laud. A. Et ecce terre motus. R. Surrexit dominus uere. *In evangelio.* A. Stetit iesus in medio … *Ad i*ᵃ. A. Pax uobis ego … *Ad iii*ᵃ. A. Videte manus meas … *Ad vi*ᵃ. A. Spiritus carnem et ossa … *Ad nona.* A. Obtulerunt discipuli domino … *Ad uesper.* A. Alleluia. *ut* A. Crucis. R. Surrexit dominus. *In evg.* A. Isti sunt sermones … sum essem uobiscum alleluia alleluia.

Feria III after Easter, first to second vespers.

f. 11v   *Feria iiii*ᵃ. *Invit.* Surrexit dominus. *In i*° *n*°. A. Cito euntes. *vel* A. Pax uobis ego … *Ps.* Celi enarrant. *Ps.* Domine in uirtute. *Ps.* Domini est terra. *Ps.* Exultate iusti. *Ps.* Benedicam dominum. *Ps.* Dixit iniustus. R. Ecce vicit leo … V. Et unus de senioribus … R. Isti sunt agni … alleluia. modo uenerunt//

Feria IV after Easter, first nocturn of matins.

Parchment. 11 folios. The measurements of the fragments are as follows: fol. 1, 253 x 168 mm; fol. 2, 247 x 167 mm; fol. 3, 226 x 157 mm; fol. 4, 228 x 152 mm; fol. 5, 227 x 155 mm; fol. 6, 227 x 155 mm; fol. 7, 219 x 153 mm; fol. 8, 257 x 175 mm; fol. 9, 227 x 182 mm; fol. 10, 226 x 178 mm; fol. 11, 206 x 151 mm (written space 187 x 125 mm; fol. 2's written space is 203 x 125 mm). 1 column. 20 lines (fol. 1 has 19 lines and fol. 2 has 21 lines). Dry-point ruling.

Written in late Caroline minuscule by several scribes. 7-line responsory initial "D" ("Diem", fol. 8r) is a red uncial, not set apart from the text, with red and black penwork and a portrait of St. Agnes. 4-line responsory initial "A" ("Adorna", fol. 10v) in red with vine-stem decoration colored with pale yellow, on a green ground. Other 3- and 4-line initials at the beginning of responses are in red capitals, some with red and black penwork. 1-line initials of "O" antiphons, and occasionally other antiphons such as the first antiphon of lauds or vespers, are in red capitals and are set apart from the text when they occur at the beginning of a line. 1-line initials of other responses and Benedictus or Magnificat antiphons are in thick brown uncials, traced or dotted with red. Other 1-line initials are brown rustic capitals sometimes traced with red. Rubrics are written in red minuscule. The initials and rubrication are by the same artist who produced those in Beinecke MS 481.48, and in the Lambach Rituale (Lambach Stiftsbibliothek Cml LXXIII; see Davis, *Epiphany*, 186–87). Punctuation consists of the punctus. Interlinear neumes in the St. Gall style. There are tonary letters in the margins of fol. 1 (the other margins have been trimmed). These letters are similar to those found in the Gottschalk Antiphonary (see above, Beinecke MS 481.51).

These fragments were formerly used in the bindings of volumes from the Lambach Stiftsbibliothek, some of which are now in Vienna, Österreichische Nationalbibliothek. Fols. 1 and 8 were in Vienna s.n. 3599 (formerly Lambach Cml LXVII); fol. 2 was in Vienna s.n. 3604 (formerly Lambach Cml XCVI; the leaf that was bound in the front of this volume was removed and is now missing); fols. 9 and 10 were in Vienna s.n. 3607 (formerly Lambach Cml CVIII); fols. 3–6 were in Vienna s.n 3608 (formerly Lambach Cml CIX). See O. Mazal and F. Unterkircher, *Katalog der datierten Handschriften in lateinischer Schrift in Österreich* (Wien, 1969-88), 141, 149, 152, and 154. Other leaves from the antiphonary are in the binding of Lambach Cml V (2 bifolia) and of Leutkirch, Fürstlich Waldburg-Zeilsches Gesamtarchiv, ZMs.5 (formerly Lambach Cml XVII). These leaves are described by Holter (1959), cat. no. VIII.07 (Vienna s.n. 3608), VIII.20 (Waldburg-Zeilsches ZMs.5), and IX.12 (Cml V).

Before fols. 3 and 4 were used in the binding of Vienna s.n. 3608, they formed a bifolium and were used as a pastedown in a volume measuring ca. 315 x 225 mm. Fols. 5 and 6 also formed a bifolium.

Fol. 1 was formerly Zinniker 155; fol. 2 was Zinniker 156; fol. 3 was Beinecke MS 482.34, Zinniker 26; fol. 4 was Beinecke MS 482.34, Zinniker 18; fol. 5 was Beinecke MS 482.34, Zinniker 12; fol 6 was Zinniker 158B; fol. 7 was Beinecke MS 482.34, Zinniker 13; fol. 8 was Zinniker 157A; fol. 9 was Zinniker 157B; fol. 10 was Zinniker 158A; fol. 11 was Beinecke MS 482.34, Zinniker 10.

Bibliography:
Babcock, *Reconstructing a Medieval Library*, 104 and figs. 9, 10, and 57.

MS 481.53   Schaffhausen, Switzerland, ca. 1100
Augustine, *In Iohannis evangelium tractatus*   Pl. 34

f. 1r–v   //et uos uultis. Iam uideo sed non inuideo . . . sed ut saluetur mundus per
           ipsum.
           Explicit omelia xliiii.

           Augustine, *In Iohannis evangelium tractatus cxxiv*, Tractatus 44.11.14–
           17.27; R. Willems, ed., CCSL 36 (1954), 386–88. CPL 278.

f. 1v   *Incipit xlv ab eo quod scriptum est. Amen amen dico uobis qui non intrat per
           ostium in ouile ouium sed ascendit aliunde ille fur est et latro usque ad id quod
           scriptum est. Ego ueni ut uitam habeant et habundantius habeant.*
           De illuminato illo qui natus est cẹcus . . . nisi agnoscat uitam quod est
           christus et per//

           Tractatus 45.1.1–2.26; Willems, 388–89.

Parchment. 1 folio. 350 x 261 mm (written space 290 x 182 mm). 2 columns. 40 lines. Ruled in dry-point on the hair side. Double vertical and single horizontal bounding lines. Prickings in upper margin.

Written in late Caroline script, similar to that written at Schaffhausen in manuscripts dated around 1100 (see Albert Brückner, *Scriptoria Medii Aevi Helvetica* [Genf, 1935–78], vol. 4, pls. VII.c and d, IX, XXVII, and XXVIII; and R. Gamper, G. Knoch-Mund and M. Stähli, *Katalog der mittelalterlichen Handschriften der Ministerialbibliothek Schaffhausen* [Zürich, 1994], *passim*, for the dates of these manuscripts).

Inelegant 9-line initial "D" on the verso, in rough gold with silver bands, outlined in red and with red in the center; the initial is on an orange, green and blue ground. In the middle of the initial there is an an eagle in gold and silver, with red dots, which holds a vine with flowers in his beak. The gold and silver, which are corroded and oxidized, and the colors, which bleed considerably, may be later additions. 1-line initials are in brown rustic capitals and are not set apart from the text. The first two words of the sermon ("[D]e illuminato") are written in alternating lines of orange and black capitals by the artist of the initial. The scribal guidewords for the rubricator are preserved in the margin. The heading of Tractatus 45 is written in red minuscule. Punctuation consists of the punctus, punctus elevatus, and punctus interrogativus. Single quotation marks in the margins.

This fragment was used as a wrapper for a volume measuring ca. 318 x 125 mm. The letter "R" is written on the outside of the cover (the recto of the fragment).

Zinniker 226.

MS 481.54   Italy, s. XII[1]
Augustine, *In Iohannis evangelium tractatus*   Pl. 35

The text of the tractates in these leaves is abbreviated, and there is no separation between them, suggesting that this may be an epitome of the text or a homily.

f. 1ra   [u]//bi tecum habitabunt ... qui non recedis. Dicendum est etiam quomodo intelligi possunt ... An iste mansiones//

Augustine, *In Iohannis evangelium tractatus cxxiv*, Tractatus 67.4.5–7 and 68.1.2–13; R. Willems, ed., CCSL 36 (1954), 497; CPL 278. The upper, lower, and inner margins have been trimmed with loss of text.

f. 1rb   //sunt si ipse non fecit ea ... et si abiero inquit et preparauero uobis//

Tractatus 68.1.24–37; Willems, 498. The upper and lower margins have been trimmed with loss of text.

f. 1va   [con]//templando etiam patri suo . . . ut non solum regni//

Tractatus 68.2.10–22; Willems, 498. The upper and lower margins have
been trimmed with loss of text.

f. 1vb   //cum profecto nos ipsos . . . creditus ut desideretu[r ut desideratus
h]abeatur//

Tractatus 68.3.1–14; Willems, 498–99. The upper, lower, and inner margins have been trimmed with loss of text.

f. 2ra   [rece]//dis uadis latendo. uenis apparendo . . . ubi possimus manere per-
fruendo. Dixerat enim superius dominus . . . et si abiero et preparauero//

Tractatus 68.3.24–26 and 69.1.4–14; Willems, 499. The lower margin has
been trimmed with loss of text.

f. 2rb   //audiuimus et magistrum docentem . . . scire. et quo uadit et uiam.//

Tractatus 69.1.24–2.6; Willems, 500. The lower margin has been trimmed
with loss of text.

f. 2va   //uado. Sed hoc loco propter nos . . . qui posuit pro me suam. Dicam ego//

Tractatus 69.2.14–24; Willems, 500–1. The lower margin has been
trimmed with loss of text.

f. 2vb   //uadis ad te. Numquidnam ut ueniress . . . Aliud quippe uerbum dei est.
aliud homo//

Tractatus 69.3.7–19; Willems, 501. The lower margin has been trimmed
with loss of text.

Parchment (both leaves stained and torn from use in a binding). 2 folios. 206 x 160
mm (written space originally ca. 273 x 178 mm). 2 columns. 20 lines remaining of
original ca. 34. Dry-point ruling on the hair side. Single vertical bounding lines.

Written in Caroline minuscule. 1-line initials are in brown uncials, not set apart
from the text. Punctuation consists of the punctus, punctus elevatus, and punctus
interrogativus. Hyphenation by first hand.

Both fragments were used as pastedowns in the binding of a volume measuring
ca. 206 x 155 mm. The inscription "RH" is written on fol. 1r in purple ink.

Fol. 1 was formerly Zinniker 173B; fol. 2 was Beinecke MS 482.35, Zinniker 110.

MS 481.55
Bible, Genesis, with commentary

France, s. XIII[1]
Pl. 35

The commentary accompanying the text contains excerpts from Jerome, *Quaestiones hebraicae in Genesim* (CCSL 72), Augustine, *Quaestiones in Heptateuchum* (CCSL 33), Gregory, *Moralia in Iob*, books 21 and 24 (CCSL 143B), Walafrid Strabo, *Glossa Ordinaria* (PL 131.160), and Andrew of St. Victor, *Expositio in Heptateuchum* (CCCM 53).

f. 1   //peperit filiam nomine . . . spatium itineris//

            Gen. 30.21–36. The outer margin has been torn off with the loss of some of the commentary.

f. 2   [Pha]//nuel ipse uero claudicabat . . . ubi edificata do//[mo]

            Gen. 32.31–33.17. The outer margin has been torn off with the loss of some of the commentary.

Parchment (fol. 1r and 2v badly stained). 2 folios (1 bifolium). 314 x 258 mm (written space 237 x 135 mm; the width of the written space for the biblical text is either 40 mm, 82 mm, or 135 mm, with the commentary taking up the remainder). 25 lines per page for biblical text, 49 for commentary. Ruled in lead; single vertical bounding lines. There are 50 ruled lines per page that guide the writing of the commentary; for the biblical text only alternate lines are used. Additional ruling for running headlines.

Written in two sizes of gothic script (littera textualis), above the top line, with the script of the biblical text approximately twice as large as the script of the commentary. 1-line initials are in red with blue penwork. Smaller 1-line initials are in brown. Paragraph marks, letters of running titles ("GE"/"NE"), and the roman numerals which are in the margins to designate chapters alternate in red and blue. The biblical text is written in the inner column although on fol. 2r, commentary also appears to the left of the biblical passage. At the bottom of fol. 2v, the biblical text is written across the entire width of the written space. There is occasional interlinear glossing. Punctuation consists of the punctus. Hyphenation is in the same ink as the text.

The fragment was used as a binding for a volume measuring ca. 314 x 195 mm. Zinniker 117.

MS 481.56
Bible, 1 Kings

Italy, s. XII²
Pl. 36

f. 1   //et cuius erunt ... [cla]mauerunt ad dominum et dixerunt. Pec//
         [cauimus]

      1 Kings 9.20–12.10. Text from 11.14–12.1 has been rewritten over an
erasure on the verso. The inner margin has been trimmed with loss of
text.

Parchment. 1 folio. 433 x 335 mm (written space 395 x 235 mm). 2 columns. 48
lines. Dry-point ruling on the hair side.
      Written in a protogothic minuscule. 2-line initials alternate in red and blue. 1-
line initials are in brown and a mixture of uncials and rustic capitals; they are not
set apart from the text. Running titles (Liber/Regum) are written in black. Instructions for the rubricator (letter "a") and number "xi" are in brown in the outer
margin next to the beginning of Chap. 11. Punctuation consists of the punctus.
Hyphenation, accents, and diacritical marks over double *i* and double *a* were added
in lighter ink (by a later hand?).
      This fragment was used in the binding of a volume measuring ca. 398 x 259 mm.
Zinniker 174.

MS 481.57
Lectionary (lessons from Job)

Germany, s. XII
Pl. 36

f. 1ra   [o]//ssa mea perterrita sunt.

      Job 4.14.

f. 1ra   *Feria III.* Et cum spiritus me praesente ... qui terrenum habent//

      Job 4.15–19, for an unidentified Feria III. The lower half of the fragment
has been trimmed with loss of text.

f. 1rb   //uidi stultum firma radice ... et inscrutabilia. et mira//[bilia]

      Job 5.3–9. The lower half of the fragment has been trimmed with loss of
text.

f. 1va   //palpabunt in meridie ... A flagello linguę absconderis. et non//

Job 5.14–21. The lower half of the fragment has been trimmed with loss of text.

f. 1vb   [abundan]//tia sepulchrum. sicut infertur . . . quod auditum mente per-
tracta.

Job 5.26–27.

f. 1vb   *Feria IIII.* Respondens autem iob dixit . . . et terrores militant//

Job 6.1–4, for an unidentified Feria IV. The lower half of the fragment has been trimmed with loss of text.

Parchment (stained and cut from binding use). 1 folio. 195 x 311 mm (written space originally ca. 410 x 210 mm). 2 columns. 17 of ca. 31 lines remaining. Dry-point ruling on the hair side. Single vertical and horizontal bounding lines. Prick-ings in outer margin.

Written in late Caroline minuscule. 3- to 4-line initials are written in red uncials and are not set apart from the text. 1-line initials are written in brown rustic capitals with an enlarged minuscule *e*. Rubrics are written in red rustic capitals. Punctuation consists of the punctus and the punctus elevatus.

The fragment was used as the wrapper of a volume measuring ca. 168 x 102 mm. Zinniker 169.

MS 481.58   Southern Germany or Austria, s. XII[1]
Psalter   Pl. 37

f. 1   //Laudate eum sol et luna . . . multitudinem magnitudinis eius//

Psalms 148.3–150.2.

Parchment (recto stained from use in a binding). 1 folio. 200 x 138 mm (written space 165 x 95 mm). 1 column. 24 lines. Dry-point ruling on the hair side. Double vertical and single horizontal bounding lines. Portions of string from binding use remain in the gutter.

Written in late Caroline minuscule. 1-line verse initials are in red square capitals with round *E* and are set apart from the text between double vertical bounding lines. Punctuation consists of the punctus. The Psalms are written in verse, and there are no divisions between the Psalms.

The fragment was used as a pastedown in a binding. Zinniker 101.

MS 481.59   Germany, s. XII[2]
Psalter   Pl. 37

f. 1   //motus est pes meus . . . [praeuarica]tiones od[iui non adhesit mihi cor]
            prauum//

            Psalms 93.18–100.4. A contemporary hand has added Glorias with
            neumes to the ends of Psalms 93, 96, and 98. A later hand has added
            marginalia next to Psalms 96 and 97 in a fourteenth-century cursive goth-
            ic script. The inner column has been trimmed with loss of text.

Parchment (verso badly stained). 1 folio. 345 x 205 mm (written space originally
ca. 305 x 190 mm). 2 columns. 34 lines.
    Written in late Caroline minuscule. 2- to 4-line initials at the beginning of
Psalms are in red uncials or capitals and are not set apart from the text. 1-line
initials at the beginning of verses are in red and are not set apart from the text. The
first word of each Psalm is written in rustic capitals. Punctuation consists of the
punctus. The Psalms are not written in verse.
    The fragment was used as the cover on a binding measuring ca. 305 x 190 mm
and has an inscription (mostly illegible) with the years "1580," "1581," and "1582."
    Zinniker 179.

MS 481.60   Italy, s. XI[ex]
Bible, Wisdom Books   Pl. 38

f. 1ra   //q[uae omni]a extinguit plus ignis . . . nec siderum//

            Sap. 16.17–17.5. The upper margin has been trimmed with loss of text.

f. 1rb   [con]//scien[tia nihil enim est timor] . . . [absco]nse enim//

            Sap. 17.10–18.9. The upper and outer margins have been trimmed with
            loss of text.

f. 1va   [r]//egalibus sedibus durus de]bellator . . . [transi]ret illi a[utem nouam
            mortem inuenirent omni]s enim cre//[atura]

            Sap. 18.15–19.6. The upper and outer margins have been trimmed with
            loss of text.

f. 1vb   //uiderunt nouam creaturam . . . in omni loco assistens ei.
          Explicit liber sap v(ersus?) n(umero?) I DCC.

          Sap. 19.11–20 (end). Similar explicits containing *IDCC* are listed in the
          apparatus of *Biblia Sacra Iuxta Latinam Vulgatam Versionem*, vol. 12
          (Rome, 1964). The upper margin has been trimmed with loss of text.

f. 1vb   *Incipit prologus sancti ieronimi presbyteri in libro iesu filii syrach.*
          Multorum nobis et magnorum . . . magisque adtendant animo ad l[egi-
          timam uitam] et conferm//[entur]

          Prologue to Sirach, 1–20; Stegmüller 26.

Parchment (stained and damaged from binding use). 1 folio. 320 x 220 mm (written space originally ca. 420 x ca. 285 mm). 2 columns. 46 lines remaining (of original ca. 60). Dry-point ruling on the hair side. Single vertical bounding lines.
      Written in Caroline minuscule. 2-line initials are in red square capitals, filled
with yellow, and are written on the vertical bounding line. 1-line initials are in
brown rustic capitals. The incipit is written in red and the explicit in brown rustic
capitals. Punctuation consists of the punctus.
      The fragment was used as the binding of a volume measuring ca. 160 x 110 mm.
The name "Appollinare Matterozzi" is written on the verso in a seventeenth-
century hand.
      Zinniker 170.

MS 481.61   Germany, s. XII[1]
Bible, *Liber Iesu Filii Sirach*   Pl. 38

f. 1r   //colloquium enim illius . . . inicium superbie ho//[minis]

          Sir. 9.11–10.14. The upper and lower margins have been trimmed with
          loss of text.

f. 1v   //disperdidit illos cessare . . . marcidus egens re//[cuperatione]

          Sir. 10.20–11.12. The upper and lower margins have been trimmed with
          loss of text.

f. 2r   //parce agendo et . . . et malitia illi//[us]

Sir. 11.18–12.9. The upper and lower margins have been trimmed with loss of text.

f. 2v   [o]//mnibus qui appropiant . . . peccator iusto. Quę co//[mmunicatio]

Sir. 12.13–13.22. The upper and lower margins have been trimmed with loss of text.

Parchment (fols. 1v and 2r badly stained). 2 folios (the inner bifolium of a quire). Fol. 1 measures 267 x 165 mm; fol. 2 measures 267 x 223 mm (written space originally ca. 325 x 200 mm). 1 column. 33 lines of original ca. 39. Dry-point ruling. Prickings in outer margin of fol. 2 near written space.
    Written in late Caroline minuscule. There are three plain 2-line initials in red, not set apart from the text. 1-line initials are brown filled with red and a mixture of uncial and rustic capital forms. Punctuation consists of the punctus, punctus elevatus, and punctus interrogativus.
    This fragment was used as the binding of a volume measuring ca. 235 x 155 mm. Before this it seems to have been used as the pastedown for a volume measuring ca. 388 x 250 mm. There is an illegible notation in pencil in the lower right margin of fol. 1r.
    Zinniker 185.

MS 481.62   Southern Germany, s. XII
Bible, Isaiah and Galatians   Pl. 39

f. 1   //ascendet super omnes riuos eius . . . sed quadris lapidibus ędifica-bim//[us]

Is. 8.7–9.10. Inner margin cut irregularly with loss of text.

f. 2   [circumcisio]//nis qui enim operatus est . . . factus pro nobis maledic//[tum]

Gal. 2.8–3.13. Outer margin cut irregularly with loss of text.

Parchment (severely damaged from binding use). 2 folios. Fol. 1 measures 272 x 183 mm; fol. 2 measures 273 x 172 mm (written space 240 x 145 mm). 1 column. Fol. 1 has 28 lines, and fol. 2 has 25. Dry-point ruling. Double vertical and single horizontal bounding lines.
    Written in late Caroline minuscule. 1-line initials are in brown rustic capitals.

Punctuation consists of the punctus, punctus versus, and punctus interrogativus.

Both fragments were used as pastedowns in the binding of a volume measuring ca. 270 x 152 mm.

Zinniker 181, A and B.

MS 481.63   Italy, s. XII[1]
Bible, Acts of the Apostles   Pl. 39

The recto of fol. 1 and the verso of fol. 2 have been entirely erased. Each leaf has been cut in half horizontally, and several lines are lost from the middle of the leaf.

f. 1va   //ubique docens. insuper . . . contigit ut portaretur//

            Acts 21.28–35.

f. 1va–1vb   //paulus. Ecce homo quidem . . . Surgens uade damascum//

            Acts 21.39–22.10.

ff. 1vb–2ra   //preordinauit te ut cognosceres . . . romanus es [at] ille//

            Acts 22.14–27.

f. 2ra–2rb   //ex causa acc[usaretur a iudeis sol]uit eum . . . Constans esto pau[lus].
            Sicut enim//

            Acts 22.30–23.11.

f. 2rb   //nos nichil g[ustaturos do]nec occidamus . . . perducere ad te. habentem//

            Acts 23.14–18.

Parchment. 2 folios (four fragments). Fol. 1 (upper portion): 198 x 257 mm; fol. 1 (lower portion): 150 x 255 mm; fol. 2 (upper portion): 200 x 259 mm; fol. 2 (lower portion): 165 x 258 mm (written space originally ca. 420 x 245 mm). Fol. 1 has 41 lines remaining, and fol. 2 has 42 lines remaining of an original ca. 51. Dry-point ruling.

Written in Caroline minuscule. The hand is very similar to that in MS 482.12, and it is possible that these leaves are from the same original codex as MS 482.12. The script, decoration, and preservation of the leaves (same trim size, ca. 200 x 260 mm, and one side erased — suggesting they were both reused in the same later binding) is very similar. The leaves of MS 481.63 are ruled for the same width of columns as 482.12 (245 mm); no other original measurements of either can be determined. The number of lines originally on each leaf of MS 481.63 must have been about 51, whereas MS 482.12 had only about 48 lines. This difference is perhaps not inconsistent with the degree of variation possible within a single book, especially considering that MS 481.63 (from Acts) would fall later in the volume than MS 482.12 (Zacharias), and the number of written lines seems generally to increase further into a book. Two plain 2-line initials in red, set apart from the text. 1-line initials are in brown uncials and are not set apart from the text. Punctuation consists of the punctus, punctus elevatus, and punctus interrogativus.

These leaves were used in a binding where each leaf was cut in half.

Zinniker 191 A, B and 192 A, B.

MS 481.64   Germany, s. XIII[1]
Noted Breviary   Pl. 40

f. 1   [L.] //Alleuiata est terra zabulon . . . R. Hodie nobis celorum rex . . . V. Gloria in excelsis . . . [L.] Consolamini consolamini popule . . . R. Hodie nobis de celo . . . V. Gloria in excelsis. [L.] Consurge consurge induere . . . R. Descendit de celo . . . V. Tamquam sponsus dominus procedens de thalamo//

            Christmas (25 December), first nocturn of matins. A contemporary hand has added "Gloria patri . . ." (fol. 1r) and "Gloria in excelsis deo . . ." (fol. 1v) with neumes in the margin. The lower margin has been trimmed with the loss of four lines.

f. 2   [V. Stepha]//nus uidit celos apertos. [L.] Gloria in excelsis deo heri exultantes . . . R. Videbant omnes stephanum . . . V. Stephanus autem plenus . . . A. Omnes intendentes in eum. Ps. Cum invocarem. A. Eicientes eum extra . . . Ps. Verba. A. Stephanus autem plenus . . . [. . . L.] Heri praesepis angustia christum . . . R. Lapidabant iudei stephanum . . . V. Positis autem genibus . . . L. Neque enim parui pendenda est . . . R. Ste[phanus autem plenus] . . . V. Stephanus uidit celos . . . L. Usque adeo inter frementes . . . R. Inpii super iustum . . . R. Captabant in animam . . . A. Lapidauerunt stephanum . . . Ps. In domino. A. Lapides torrentes (sic) illi . . . Ps. Domine quis habitabit . . . A. Ecce uideo celos . . . Secundum matheum. In illo tempore. Dicebat iesus turbis iudeorum et principibus sacerdotum. Ecce mitto ad uos . . . Omelia lectionis eiusdem. Hoc quod antea dixerat dominus

uos inplete . . . R. Inpetum fecerunt unanimes . . . V. Positis autem genibus
. . . L. Simulque obserua iuxta//

St. Stephen (26 December), from the first nocturn to the third nocturn of
matins. The homily for the third nocturn is from Fulgentius, Sermon 3
(De S. Stephano protomartyre et conversione S. Pauli), J. Fraipont, ed.,
CCSL 91A (1968), 905–9. The lower margin has been trimmed with the
loss of four lines.

Parchment. 2 folios (1 bifolium). 265 x 248 mm (written space originally ca. 295 x
177 mm). 2 columns. 29 lines remaining of original ca. 33. Ruled in ink. Single vertical bounding lines. Two sets of prickings in outer margins.
   Written in two sizes of gothic script (littera textualis). 2- to 4-line initials in red,
set apart from the text. 1-line initials at the beginning of responses are in thick
brown ink, sometimes highlighted with red, and are written on the vertical bounding line when they occur at the beginning of a line. Smaller 1-line initials at the
beginnings of antiphons, psalms and verses are in brown, highlighted with red, and
are written on the vertical bounding line when they occur at the beginning of the
line. Rubrics are written in red in the same script as the text. Punctuation consists
of the punctus. The chants have interlinear neumes. Another hand has added interlinear hufnagel neumes over several of the lessons on fol. 1.
   A modern hand has added the number "50" in pencil in the lower right margin
of fol. 1r.
   Zinniker 154.

MS 481.65   Germany, s. XII^{2}
Noted Breviary   Pl. 40

f. 1   [L.] //et incircumcisorum defensor factus . . . R. Simon petre antequam
          . . . [V.] Quodcumque ligaueris super . . . [L.] Sed et si forte aliquam uult
          introducere nouam doctrinam . . . R. Si diligis me . . . V. Si oportuerit me
          . . . [L.] Et post multa infra altercantibus illis cum simone mago . . . qui ue-
          rus rex est et regni eius non erit finis//

          Sts. Peter and Paul (29 June), matins. The lesson is from a Passion of Sts.
          Peter and Paul. A thirteenth-century hand has added an unidentified
          (and mostly illegible) text in the margin of the verso.

Parchment. 1 folio. 316 x 214 mm (written space 290 x 162 mm). 1 column. 28
lines. Dry-point ruling; single vertical bounding lines.

Written in two sizes of late Caroline/early gothic script. Two 3-line initials are in red uncials and are set apart from the text. 1-line initials are in brown rustic capitals occasionally highlighted with red and are not set apart from the text. Rubrics are written in red capitals. Punctuation consists of the punctus for the chants, and the punctus, punctus elevatus, and punctus interrogativus for the lessons. Interlinear neumes in the St. Gall style. Accents are in the same ink as the text.

This fragment was used as a pastedown in the binding of a volume measuring ca. 315 x 207 mm. A fourteenth-century(?) hand has written "Cro sla werra guerra idem est" on the left-hand margin of fol. 1r. A sixteenth-century hand has written the name "Theodoricus Algesheim" in the upper margin of the same folio.

Zinniker 160.

MS 481.66   Lambach, Austria, s. XII[2]
Noted Breviary   Pl. 41

f. 1r   [A. Surge ergo et . . .] //iohanni episcopo ut . . . *Ev.* Ecce ego mitto ad uos.
             R. Vides o frater . . . *V.* Introgressus in ostium . . . *R.* Cum scirem ego . . .
             V. Auditor domini nichodemus . . . *R.* Sanctus iohannes episcopus . . . *V.*
             Qui primus apud . . . *In mat. l.* A. Regressus lucianus presbiter . . . A. Apparuit sanctus gamaliel . . . A. Ibi olim positi . . . A. Audiens ergo lucianus
             . . . A. Dum inuentum esset . . . *In ev.* A. Ex odoris mira . . . A. Hodie sanctus iohannes . . . pro nobis quesumus intercessio.

             Invention of St. Stephen (3 August), from the third nocturn of matins to lauds.

f. 1r–v   *In natali s. Xixti felicissimi et Agapiti.* Factum est ut decius cesar et ualerianus praefectus iuberent sibi beatum xixtum episcopum cum clero suo praesentari . . . sanctos uero felicissimum et agapitum sepelierunt in cimiterio praetextati.

             Sts. Sixtus, Felicissimus, and Agapitus (6 August), lessons of matins only.

ff. 1v–2   *In natali s. afrę martiris.* A. Gratias tibi domine . . . *R.* Martir sancta dei
             . . . [V.] Crescit ut in nobis . . . *Imnus.* Iesu christe auctori. *In ev.* A. Gloriosa et beatissima . . . *Inuit.* Vigili corde dominum . . . *In i. n.* A. Cum sub
             diocletiano tyranno . . . A. In qua ciuitate . . . A. Cuius prostibulum cum
             . . . [L.] Apud prouinciam recie in ciuitate augusta cum christianorum
             esset gloriosa persecutio . . . *R.* Beatus pontifex narcissus . . . *V.* Domino
             pro ipsis . . . [L.] Afra respondit. Capitolium meum . . . *R.* Sancto presule
             precibus . . . *V.* Mundi cordis amatorem . . . [L.] Gaius iudex dixit. Sac-

rifica ut diligaris . . . R. Hostis antiquus celesti . . . V. Coactus a sancto . . .
In ii. n. A. Cum psalmis deo . . . A. Audiens uero beatum . . . A. Quam vir
sanctus . . . [L.] Gaius iudex dixit. Vnde nosti quia . . . nam torqueri te fa-
cio et postea uiuam incendi praecipio. Afra//

St. Afra (9 August), from first vespers to the second nocturn of matins.
The lessons are from the *Vita S. Afrae* (MGH Script. Rer. Merov. 3, pp.
61–62).

ff. 3–4v   //disti mihi tentus est a militibus et traditus est parthemio tribuno . . . R.
Strinxerunt corporis menbra . . . V. Carnifices uero urgentes . . . *In ii. n.* A.
Beatus laurentius dixit . . . *v.* Quia accusatus non negaui . . . A. Dixit romanus ad beatum . . . *v.* Afferens autem urceum . . . A. Beatus laurentius
dixit . . . *v.* Quia ipse dominus . . . [L.] Erat autem ibi homo lucillus nomine . . . R. Quo progrederis sine . . . V. Quid in me . . . [L.] Ex mandato
autem adductus est beatus laurentius . . . R. Noli me derelinquere . . . V.
Nos quasi senes . . . [L.] Completis igitur tribus diebus praesentauit se ipse
salustiano . . . R. Beatus laurentius clamauit . . . V. Mea nox obscurum
. . . *In iii. n.* A. Strinxerunt corporis menbra . . . *v.* Carnifices uero urgentes
. . . A. Igne me examinasti . . . *v.* Probasti domine cor . . . *Ps.* Exaudi domine. A. Interrogatus te domine . . . *v.* Gratias tibi ago . . . *Secundum
iohannem.* In illo tempore. Dixit iesus discipulis suis. Amen amen dico
uobis. nisi granum frumenti cadens . . . *Omelia s. augustini episcopi.* Saluator
noster fratres karissimi ipse erat granum mortificandum et multiplicandum
. . . R. Beatus laurentius clamauit . . . V. Gratias tibi ago . . . [L.] Magna et
mira sententia; quem admodum sit . . . R. In craticula te . . . V. Probasti
domine cor . . . [L.] Si quis mihi ministrauerit; me sequatur . . . R. Beatus
uir laurentius . . . V. Qui potuit transgredi . . . *In mat. l.* Laurentius ingressus est martir . . . A. Laurentius bonum opus . . . A. Adhesit anima mea
. . . A. Misit dominus angelum . . . A. Beatus laurentius orabat . . . *Ymnus.*
Martir dei. *In ev.* A. In craticula te . . . *Ad i^a.* A. Leuita laurentius bonum
. . . *Ad iii.* Gratias tibi ago . . . *Ad vi.* Laurentius bonum opus. *Ad viiii.* Beatus laurentius orabat. *In ii. v.* A. Iocundus homo cum reliqua. *Ymnus* Martir dei. *In ev.* A. Beatus laurentius dum . . . manus pauperum deportauerunt.

St. Laurence (10 August), from the first nocturn of matins to second vespers. The lessons for the third nocturn are from Augustine, *In Johannis evangelium tractatus* LI, ch. 9; PL 35.1766; R. Willems, ed., CCSL (1954), 442.

f. 4v   *Tyburcii martiris.* A. Inclitus martir tyburcius . . . [L.] Rome natalis sancti
tyburcii martiris filii cromatii urbis praefecti . . . et principum decreta non
contempnas. Tyburcius respondit. Ego//

St. Tiburtius (11 August), first nocturn of matins.

Parchment. 4 folios (fols. 1 and 4 and fols. 2 and 3 form bifolia, probably the second and third of a quire of eight). Fol. 1 measures 292 x 195 mm; fol. 2, 295 x 193 mm; fol. 3, 283 x 213 mm; fol. 4, 292 x 210 mm (written space 250 x 155 mm). 1 column. 33 lines. Dry-point ruling. Double vertical and horizontal bounding lines. Additional vertical ruling in margins for differentiae and tonary letters.

Written in two sizes of late Caroline minuscule. 2- to 4-line initials at the beginning of feasts and lessons are written in red square capitals and are set apart from the text between double vertical bounding lines. 1-line initials at the beginning of lessons are written in red square capitals with round E and are set apart from the text when they occur at the beginning of a line. 1-line initials of responses and Benedictus and Magnificat antiphons are in thick brown uncials, not set apart from the text. 1-line initials for the other chants are in brown rustic capitals and are frequently traced or dotted with red. 1-line initials within lessons are in brown rustic capitals and are set apart from the text when they occur at the beginning of a line. Rubrics are written in red minuscule. Punctuation consists of the punctus for the chants, and the punctus, punctus elevatus, and punctus interrogativus for the lessons. Interlinear neumes in the St. Gall style. Neumed differentiae and tonary letters for antiphons are in the outer margins.

These bifolia were used as flyleaves in the binding of Lambach, Ink. 179 (the shelf number "179" is written in ink on fol. 1r), which measured ca. 406 x 285 mm.

The bifolium 1/4 was formerly Beinecke MS 482.42, Zinniker 67; the bifolium 2/3 was formerly Zinniker 172.

Bibliography:
Babcock, *Reconstructing a Medieval Library*, 108 and fig. 59.

MS 481.67   Southern Germany or Austria, s. XII^2
Noted Breviary   Pl. 41

f. 1   [A.] //Ante luciferum genitus ... A. Venit lumen tuum ... A. Ape[rtis]
        thesauris suis ... A. Maria et flumina ... A. Magi uidentes stellam ... C.
        Leua in circuitu [oculos] tuos et uide omnes ... *v.* Omnes de saba ueni-
        ent. A. Hodie cęlesti sponso ... *Or.* Deus qui hod[ier]na die unigenitum
        ... *Cap.* Tunc uidebis et afflues ... R. Omnis terra adoret ... V. Psalmum
        dicat ... V. Reges tharsis. [*Or.*] Praesta quaesumus omnipotens d[eus]
        saluatoris mundi stella ... Inundatio camelorum operiet te ... R. Reges
        tharsis et ... V. Reges arabu[m et] ... [*Or.*] Deus inlumin[ator] omnium
        gentium ... [*Or.* ...]r congregabitur tibi arietes ... R. Omnes [gent]es

quascumque ... *V*. Venient et adorabunt ... [*Or.*] Omnipotens semper
deus fideli[um] ... *In ii. Vesper. A.* Tecum principium. *Ps.* Dixit. [*L.*...]
terra profert germen suum ... *A.* Tribus miraculis [orna]tum ... [*Or.*
Co]ncede quaesumus omnipotens deus. ut salutare tuum ... *A.* Ab
oriente uenerunt ... *A.* Videntes [stella]m magi ... *A.* Uidimus stel[lam]
eius ... *A.* Uox de celis ... *A.* Stella [ista] sicut ... regum demonstrat
ma//[gi]

Epiphany (6 January), from lauds to second vespers. The outer margin has
been trimmed with loss of text.

f. 2r   //rint conualescant. Per dominum nostrum. *Alia.* Que tanta est in pectore
tuo mortifere obstina[tion]is ... Munera chaldei offerunt et adorant.
Unum ab illis deferunt ut regi aliud exhibetur ut deo.

Epiphany. The lessons are from Pseudo-Maximus Taurinensis, *Sermones*,
Homily 25 (Inc: [Audistis fratres lectionem evangelii salutari praesentis
diei ...]; PL 57.280; Paul the Deacon Homily I.49; see Grégoire, 439).
The upper and outer margins have been trimmed with loss of text.

f. 2r–v   *Octava Ep*[*ip*]*han*[*iae.*] Intelligere fratres karissimi possumus quantam
gratiam domino christo debeamus qui uota uotis accumulat ... dum
christum concepit. modo eum in gurgite circumfulsit. *Iohannem.* [I]n illo
tempore. Venit iesus a galilea in iordane ad iohannem ut baptizaretur ab
eo. Et reliqua. *Omelia.* Lectio sancti euangelii quam modo fratres karissimi
audiuimus magnum in nobis ... fidelissimus ille iohannis qui bap//

Octave of Epiphany, first through third nocturn of matins. The lessons for
the first and second nocturn are from Maximus Taurinensis, *Sermones*,
Sermon 13a (A. Mutzenbecher, ed., CCSL 23 [1962], 44–46; see Grégoire, 150. See also Pseudo-Augustine, Sermon 135 at PL 39.2011). The
lessons for the third nocturn are from Bede, Homily I.12 (D. Hurst, ed.,
CCSL 122 [1955], 80; Paul the Deacon, Homily I.58; see Grégoire, 440).
The upper and outer margins have been trimmed with loss of text.

f. 3r   [*A.* Baptizat] //miles regem seruus dominum ... hic est filius meus.

Octave of Epiphany, vespers. The upper margin has been trimmed with
loss of text.

f. 3r–v   *Dominica i.* Gaudete in domino dilectissimi. iterum dico gaudete; quoniam
breui interuallo temporis ... cum iudeorum infidelitas ueritatem ore

proferret. mendacium corde retineret. *Lucam*. [*lines cut out in upper margin*:
In illo tempore. Cum esset iesus annorum duodecim . . .] Et reliqua. *Omelia*. Aperta est nobis fratres karissimi sancti euangelii lectio recitata . . .
humiliter dicta sequamur. *Cap*. Fratres. Obsecro uos per misericordiam dei
. . . A. Fili quid nobis . . . A. Quid est quod me . . . A. Puer ihesus proficiebat . . . [*Or*.] Vota quaesumus domine supplicantis . . . prosequere. ut
quę//

Sunday I after Epiphany, matins through lauds. The lessons for the first
two nocturns are from Leo, *Tractatus septem et nonaginta*, Tractatus 32 (A.
Chavasse, ed., CCSL 138 [1973], 165–69; PL 54.237–40). The lessons for
the third nocturn are from Bede, Homily I.19 (D. Hurst, ed., CCSL 122
[1955], 134; Paul the Deacon I.59; see Grégoire, 441). The upper margin
has been trimmed with loss of text.

f. 4r–v   [*L*. . . .] //mentis oculis descendente super eum . . . *Mat. laus*. A. Ueterem
hominem renouans . . . A. Te qui in spiritu . . . A. Baptista contremuit et
. . . A. Caput draconis contriuit . . . A. Magnum mysterium declaratur . . .
C. Domine deus meus honorificabo . . . A. Precursor iohannes exultat . . .
A. Ordines angelorum uidentes . . . [. . . *Or*. Deus] cuius unigenitus in sub-
stantia . . . A. Puer iesus proficiebat.

Sunday I after Epiphany, lauds.

f. 4v   *Dominica .i.* [*Invit*.] Adoremus dominum qui fecit nos . . . A. Seruite domino in timore . . . *Ps*. Beatus uir. A. Exurge domine ut . . . *Ps*. Domine
deus meus. A. Cantabo domino qui . . . *Ps*. Saluum. *v*. Memor fui in nocte.
[*L*.] Paulus seruus christi iesu uocatus . . . [*R*.] Domine ne in ira . . . *V*.
Timor et tremor . . . [*L*.] Qui praedestinatus est filius dei . . . R. Deus qui
sedes . . . V. Tibi enim derelictus . . . [*L*.] Primum quidem gratias ago deo
. . . in uoluntate dei uenien//[di]

Sunday I per annum. Vespers to the first nocturn of matins. The lessons
are from Romans 1.1–10. The upper margin has been trimmed with the
loss of the top two lines of text.

Parchment (both leaves have stains and rust holes from use in binding). 4 folios (2
bifolia). 222 x 120–65 mm (written space originally ca. 190 x 112 mm). 1 column.
28–29 lines remaining of original 30. Ruled in dry-point. Prickings in outer margins.
    Written in two sizes of early gothic script (littera textualis). 1- to 3-line initials
at the beginning of lessons and prayers are in red square capitals and are not set
apart from the text. The responsorial liturgy on fol. 4v begins with a 2-line round

D ("Domine") in red; initials at the beginning of Benedictus and Magnificat antiphons are in 1-line red capitals. Other 1-line initials are in a mixture of brown uncials or rustic capitals, with initials of responses dotted with red. Rubrics are written in red in the same script as the text. Punctuation consists of the punctus for the chants, and the punctus, punctus elevatus, and punctus interrogativus for the lessons. Interlinear neumes in the St. Gall style. Hyphenation is in the same ink as the text.

These bifolia were formerly used as pastedowns in the binding of a volume measuring ca. 285 x 215 mm. A fifteenth-century inscription with an erased rubric on fol. 3v reads "Ista continentur in hoc uolumine. Augustini excerptum super psalterio applicabile in sermonibus declarandis ad populum. Sermones de corpore christi ante registrum, sermones de corpore christi post registrum. Sinonima Isiodori [sic], Isiodorus [sic] de summo bono."

The number "139" is written in pencil in the lower right corner of fol. 1r; the number "90" is written in a different hand in the lower right corner of fol. 2r, and "89" is written in the lower right corner of fol. 3r.

The bifolium 1/4 was formerly Beinecke MS 481.69, Zinniker 242; the bifolium 2/3 was Zinniker 228.

MS 481.68   Germany, s. XII^2
Office for the Virgin Mary, Canticles (Breviary or Psalter)   Pl. 42

f. 1   [R. Salue nobilis uirga] //flos campi maria . . . V. Odor tuus super . . . Vnde
          Gloria patri. Vnde. Te deum laudamus. v. Adiuuabit eam . . . Deus in
          adiutorium meum. A. Sub tuum praesidium. Ad laud. Ps. Dominus reg-
          nauit. Ps. Iubilate domino. Ps. Deus deus meus. Ps. Deus misereatur. Ps.
          Benedictus est. Ps. Laudate dominum. A. Sub tuum praesidium . . . Cap.
          Beata es maria quę dominum portasti . . . R. Elegit eam deus . . . V. Et in
          tabernaculo . . . Gloria patri. ymnus. Prefulgens sol iusticię . . . v. Speciosa
          facta es . . . A. O gloriosa dei . . . Ps. Benedictus dominus. Collecta. Famu-
          lorum tuorum domine delictis ignosce . . .In aduentum domini. A. Missus
          est gabriel . . . v. Benedicta tu in mulieribus . . . collecta. Deus qui de beate
          marię uirginis . . . In natiuitate domini. A. Virgo uerbo concepit . . . v. Post
          partum uirgo . . . Collecta. Deus qui salutis ęterne beate marię . . . In
          resurrectione domini. Alleluia sancta dei . . . v. Post partum uirgo . . . [col-
          lecta.] Gratiam tuam quaesumus domine mentibus . . . De sancto iohanne.
          Iohannes apostolus et . . . v. Verbum domini celi . . . collecta. Ecclesiam
          tuam domine benignus illustra . . . De s. laur//[entio.]

          Hours of the Virgin for the Assumption (15 August); Advent; Christmas
          (25 December); Easter; St. John the Evangelist (27 December).

f. 2   [Nunc dimittis seruum . . .]//Lumen ad reuelationem gentium; et gloriam
           plebis tuę israhel. *ymnus*. Te Deum laudamus . . . *Fides catholica*. Qui-
           cumque uult saluus esse . . . nec creatus nec genitus. Filius a patre//

           Ferial canticles: Nunc dimittis; Te Deum; Quicumque uult ("Fides ca-
           tholica").

Parchment. 2 folios (1 bifolium). 184 x 146 mm (written space 158 x 100 mm). 1
column. 24 lines. Ruled in lead. Single vertical bounding lines.
       Written in two sizes of late Caroline minuscule. 1- to 3-line initials alternate red
and green square capitals with round *E* and are written on the vertical bounding
line when they occur at the beginning of a line. 1-line initials of chants are written
in brown rustic capitals with an enlarged minuscule *e* and are frequently dotted
with red or green. Rubrics are written in red and green minuscule with uncial M.
Punctuation consists of the punctus and punctus elevatus. Hyphenation is in the
same ink as the text.
       The bifolium was once used as a pastedown in the binding of a volume meas-
uring ca. 288 x 185 mm. The number "M103" is written in pencil on fol. 1r in the
same hand that wrote the numbers "M105" on Beinecke 481.70 and "M106" on
Beinecke 481.106. The number "12" is written in pencil in the lower margin of
fol. 1r.
       Zinniker 177.

MS 481.69

transferred to Beinecke MS 481.67

MS 481.70   Germany, s. XIII[1]
Song of Moses (Psalter)   Pl. 42

f. 1   [Audite caeli quae loquor . . . inter]//roga patrem tuum et annuntiabit tibi
           . . . dereliquid de//[um]

           Canticle: Audite caeli.

Parchment. 1 folio. 198 x 170 mm (written space 160 x 105 mm). 1 column. 17
lines. Ruled in lead. Single vertical and double horizontal bounding lines. Prickings
in outer margin.
       Written in gothic script (littera textualis), below top line. 1-line initials alternate

red and blue and are written on the vertical bounding line when they occur at the beginning of the line. Punctuation consists of the punctus. Hyphenation is in the same ink as the text.

Unidentified number "M105" is written in pencil on fol. 1r, in the same hand that wrote "M103" on Beinecke 481.68 and "M106" on Beinecke 481.106. This fragment was used as the binding of a volume measuring ca. 132 x 75 mm. The shelf mark "B 11 25" (or "B 11 2S") is written on the verso where the spine of the volume would have been.

Zinniker 132.

MS 481.71   France, s. XI/XII
Gregory the Great, *Moralia in Iob*   Pl. 43

f. 1ra   //homo crederet; si nullum . . . dissolutam mentem corrup//[tori]

           Gregory the Great, *Moralia in Iob*, II.49.117–126; M. Adriaen, ed., CCSL 143 (1979), 108. Approximately the top half of the folio has been cut off, and the inner margin has been trimmed with loss of text.

f. 1rb   //oculos mentis aperimus . . . uittę sunt; quia//

           Moralia, II.51.10–52.6; Adriaen, 109. Approximately the top half of the folio has been cut off with loss of text.

f. 1va   [tan]//to deterius delinquitur . . . quasi in tyrannidem//

           Moralia, II.52.27–37; Adriaen, 110. Approximately the top half of the folio has been cut off with loss of text.

f. 1vb   //Et notandum quod . . . ut pulsatus uic//[iis]

           Moralia, II.52.56–53.6; Adriaen, 110–11. Approximately the top half of the folio has been cut off, and the inner margin has been trimmed with loss of text.

Parchment. Part of 1 folio. "C ii", perhaps referring to book 2, is in the center of the lower margin of both the recto and the verso. 215 x 150 mm (written space originally ca. 250 x ca. 190 mm). 2 columns. 14 lines remaining (of original ca. 40). Ruled in lead. Double outer and single inner vertical bounding lines, with additional ruling between columns.

Written in late Caroline minuscule. 1-line initials are in brown uncials, not set apart from the text, with occasional use of an enlarged minuscule *e*, *n*, or rustic capital *N*. Punctuation consists of the punctus, punctus elevatus, punctus versus, and punctus flexus. Double quotation marks are in the margin. Hyphenation is in the same ink as the text.

The fragment was used as the binding of a volume measuring ca. 130 x 80 mm. The shelf mark "F" was written in ink on the spine of the volume. The number "28" is written in ink in the margin of the recto.

Zinniker 109B.

MS 481.72   Southern Germany or Austria, s. XII[1]
Jerome, *Commentaria in Ezechielem*   Pl. 44

f. 1   //Et hi egressus ciuitatis . . . ad consummationem seculi. AMEN//

Jerome, *Commentaria in Ezechielem*, 14.1924–96 (Ezek. 48.30–35); F. Glorie, ed., CCSL 75 (1964), 741–43. The lower portion of the verso is blank.

Parchment. 1 folio. 315 x 228 mm (written space 260 x 170 mm). 1 column. 37 lines. Dry-point ruling on the hair side. Double vertical and horizontal bounding lines. Prickings in outer margin.

Written in late Caroline minuscule. 1-line initials are in brown rustic capitals, not set apart from the text. Two words in Greek majuscules, with a line drawn above them (see plate of recto in Robert G. Babcock and Mark L. Sosower, *Learning from the Greeks: An Exhibition Commemorating the Five-Hundredth Anniversary of the Founding of the Aldine Press* [New Haven, 1994], 13 and 15, item 10). Punctuation consists of the punctus and the punctus elevatus. Double quotation marks are in the outer margin of the recto. On the verso, the left and right margins of the written space taper as the text ends.

The fragment was used as a pastedown in the binding of a volume measuring ca. 315 x 230 mm. It was sold by E. von Scherling (Leiden), *Rotulus*, 4 (winter, 1937): 15, item 1855.

Zinniker 189.

MS 481.73   Germany, s. XII
Bede, Homily   Pl. 45

f. 1   [Inc: Potest mouere infirmos auditores quomodo in capite lectionis . . .]
         //gaudium a patre petite; cuius plenitudo . . . Vnde continuo responderunt.
         Ecce nunc palam//

         Bede, Homily II.12.72–177 (on John 16.23–30); D. Hurst, ed., CCSL 122
         (1955), 262–65. The upper and outer margins have been trimmed with
         loss of text.

Parchment (recto badly stained). 1 folio. 294 x 193 mm (written space originally ca.
290 x ca. 203 mm). 2 columns. 35 lines (of original 37). Ruled in lead.

Written in late Caroline minuscule. 1-line initials are in brown uncials with the
use of some rustic capital forms and of an enlarged minuscule *e*. Punctuation consists of the punctus, punctus versus, and punctus elevatus. Hyphenation is in the
same ink as the text.

The fragment was used as a pastedown in the binding of a volume measuring ca.
294 x 180 mm. The shelf number "D" / "L4NA" is written on the verso; it has been
crossed out. On the verso a fifteenth-century cursive hand has written "Generosus
est animus hominis et naturaliter contra potestatem recalcitrans facilius ducitur
quam trahatur Seneca." The statement is a partial paraphrase from Seneca, *Epistolae morales*, 102.21 ("magna et generosa res est humanus animus").

Zinniker 178.

MS 481.74   Germany, s. XII/XIII
Gregory the Great, *Homiliae in Evangelia*   Pl. 45

f. 1r   //uirtutum ita iam plana facta est . . . desideria in mente trucidemus [*corr.
         from* trucidamus].

         Gregory the Great, *Homiliae xl in evangelia*, Homily I.3; PL 76.1088–89; ed.
         Étaix, CCSL 141, 24–25..

f. 1r–v *Lectio sancti euangelii secundum matheum.*
         In illo tempore. Disit [*sic*] iesus duodecim discipulos suos. precipiens eis di-
         cens . . . ite ad oues quę perierunt domus israhel. Et reliqua. [Matt. 10.5–6]
         Constat omnibus fratres karissimi quod redemptor noster in mundum pro
         redemptione gentium uenit . . . facile ergo est nunc iam cum defacta//

         Homily I.4; PL 76.1089–90.

Parchment. 1 folio. 255 x 190 mm (written space 175 x 130 mm). 2 columns. 29 lines. Dry-point ruling on the hair side. Double outer and single inner vertical bounding lines; double horizontal bounding lines. Prickings in upper, lower, and outer margins.

Written in late Caroline minuscule. Two initials, "I" (4-line) and "C" (3-line), are in red and yellow. The red 1-line initial "D" ("Disit") beginning the lesson is round, highlighted with yellow. Other 1-line initials are in brown uncials, with some rustic capital and enlarged minuscule forms, usually highlighted with red, and are set apart from the text between the vertical bounding lines when they occur at the beginning of a line. The rubric is written in red minuscule highlighted with yellow. Punctuation consists of the punctus and punctus elevatus. Hyphenation is in the same ink as the text. The quire signature ".i." is in the center of the lower margin of the verso.

Zinniker 218. The number "15" is written in ink in the upper margin of the recto.

MS 481.75

Isidore, *Etymologiae*

Germany, s. XII^2

Pl. 46

f. 1   //In achaia. fluit e saxis. Stix appellata . . . unde et estuaria per quę//

Isidore, *Etymologiae*, Book 13.13.7–18.1; *Isidori Hispalensis episcopi Etymologiarum sive Originum Libri XX*, ed. W. M. Lindsay, 2 vols., OCT (Oxford, 1911).

f. 2   //frug[is rena]scantur. Zeugis. ubi cartago magna . . . adeo fęcundę copia metallorum; ut//

Etymologiae, Book 14.5.7–6.11; ed. Lindsay.

Parchment. 2 folios (1 bifolium, the outer of a quire; fol. 2v has the quire signature "xvi" in the center of the lower margin; the leaves are foliated "117" and "124" in the upper center of the recto in a fifteenth- or sixteenth-century hand). 340 x 265 mm (written space 283 x 195 mm). 2 columns. 38 lines. Dry-point ruling on the hair side. Single vertical and horizontal bounding lines. Prickings in upper, lower, and outer margins.

Written in late Caroline minuscule. 2- and 3-line initials are in red capitals, with an uncial M and round E, decorated with small round balls or with two or three cross-hatches; they are written on the vertical bounding line. 1-line initials are in brown and a mixture of rustic capitals, uncials, and enlarged minuscules. Rubrics are written in red minuscule with some capital forms. The first word after each red initial is written in brown capitals with some minuscule forms. Punctuation consists of the punctus, punctus elevatus, and, at the end of chapters, the punctus versus. Hyphenation is in the same ink as the text. Accents were added by a later hand.

The bifolium was used as a wrapper for a volume measuring ca. 300 x 210 mm. A modern hand has written the number "15" in pencil in the upper left corner of fol. 1r.

Zinniker 161.

MS 481.76   Southern Germany, s. XII²
Isidore, *Synonyma*   Pl. 46

ff. 1–2   //fontes lacrimarum. ubi . . . non ingruit//

Isidore, *Synonyma*, I.58–68; PL 83.840–43. The first line and half of the second leaf are obscured from the fragment's use in a binding.

Parchment (badly rubbed and stained). 2 folios (1 bifolium). 252 x 180 mm (written space 195 x 130 mm). 1 column. 23 lines. Dry-point ruling; single vertical bounding lines. Prickings preserved in outer margins.

Written in late Caroline minuscule. 1-line initials in brown square capitals (with uncial M) highlighted with red are written on the vertical bounding line. Other 1-line initials are in brown rustic capitals and are not set apart from the text. Rubrics are written in red minuscule. Punctuation consists of the punctus, punctus elevatus, and punctus interrogativus.

The bifolium was used as a wrapper for a volume measuring ca. 205 x 145 mm; two sets of leather ties are still present. "Decreta sacerdot[um] 14" is written on the spine. An unidentified notation "S 87" is in a different hand.

Zinniker 143.

MS 481.77   Judaea?, s. XII^{1/4}
Pilgrim's Guide to Jerusalem   Pl. 47

The text gives a reference to the capture of Jerusalem by the Frankish army on 15 July 1099. There is also a mention of the resting place outside of Jerusalem of Abraham, Isaac, and others, suggesting the text was written after 1113 when the tombs of the patriarchs were discovered in Hebron (see Davis, "A Twelfth-Century Pilgrim's Guide," 18). The text of the Guide shows some similarities with the

Ottobonian Guide which was probably written between 1103–13 (see Davis, "A Twelfth-Century Pilgrim's Guide," 15–18).

f. 1r–v   Ab occidente est introitus ierusalem per portam dauid intra citate [*sic; for* ciuitatem] est sepulchrum domini ... Idus iulii capta est ciuitas sancta ierusalem franci. Eodem die diuisio apostolorum.

Pilgrim's Guide to Jerusalem; The text is complete and is edited by Davis, "A Twelfth-Century Pilgrim's Guide," 14–15. The lower margin is torn with the loss of a portion of the bottom line of text on the recto.

f. 1v   Fur di valluntsuch — scribe an ain zedel.

Beginning of a charm for epilepsy in Middle High German. The rest of the text is missing.

Parchment. 1 folio. 118 x 184 mm. 1 column. 20 lines. Dry-point ruling; two full sets of text rulings, one horizontal (for this text) and the other vertical, suggesting that the parchment was originally intended for another purpose.

The Guide is written in late Caroline minuscule. At the beginning of the text is a cross with ornamentation in brown penwork. 2-line initial "A" in brown ink with the left shaft and crossbar hollow and the right shaft solid. 1-line initials are in brown rustic capitals. Punctuation consists of the punctus and punctus versus. The charm is written in a thirteenth-century gothic hand (littera textualis), evidently in Germany.

According to the description prepared by H. P. Kraus, Inc., Bernhard Bischoff considered the manuscript "a sort of amulet or souvenir written in the Holy Land, in the early decades of the Jerusalem Kingdom." We have no record of the document in which Bischoff made this attribution. The script resembles early twelfth-century Italian hands.

A modern hand has written the number "96" in the lower margin of the recto. Zinniker 264.

Bibliography:

Davis, L. F., "A Twelfth-Century Pilgrim's Guide to the Holy Land: Beinecke MS 481.77," *Yale University Library Gazette* 65 (1990): 11–19.

MS 481.78   Southern Germany or Austria, s. XII^{ex}
Homiliary   Pl. 47

f. 1r   //ergo dominus hodie resurrexit ... futurę resurrectionis speciem iam
         uidemus. et cetera.

         Unidentified sermon on the Resurrection.

f. 1r–v *Passio sancti iohannis baptistę.*
         Sancti precursoris domini iohannis baptistę natiuitatem quam hodie cęle-
         brat ... Et uxor Zacharię de filiabus aaron. cui nomen//

         Pseudo-Maximus Taurinensis, *Sermones*, Sermon 60, St. John the Baptist
         (24 June); PL 57.651–52. The lower margin has been trimmed with the
         loss of the bottom two lines of text.

f. 2r–v //cui adhuc odium uel inuidia manet ... Magna enim infidelitas. qui se
         tanta gloria et honore ęterni regni. sua prauitate priuatur.

         Unidentified sermon on confession.

f. 2v   Hortatur uos fratres sacra scriptura ad medicamenta animę uestrę per
         confessionem ... quia non est fructuosa confessio aput [words cut out] ibi
         salutem. Ecce//

         Sermon on confession based on Ps.-Augustine's Sermon 254; PL 39.2215.
         The lower margin has been trimmed with the loss of the bottom two lines
         of text.

Parchment. 2 folios. 188 x 147 mm (written space originally ca. 185 x 105 mm). 1
column. 22 lines remaining of original ca. 24. Ruled in lead. Single vertical and
double horizontal bounding lines. Pricking in outer margins.
    Written in late Caroline minuscule. 2-line initials at the beginning of sermons
are in red uncials. 1-line initials are in brown rustic capitals and uncials with an
enlarged minuscule m. Rubrics are written in red minuscule. Punctuation consists
of the punctus.
    These two fragments were once used as flyleaves in the binding of a volume
measuring ca. 188 x 130 mm. Another leaf of this manuscript, preserving portions
of the homily on John the Baptist, is now a flyleaf in Vienna, Österreichische Nationalbibliothek, s.n. 3602, originally Lambach, Stiftsbibliothek, Cml LXXXVI.
    Fol. 1. was formerly Zinniker 248; fol. 2. was Beinecke MS 482.43, Zinniker 3.

Bibliography:
Babcock, *Reconstructing a Medieval Library*, 102 and fig. 55.

MS 481.79   Germany, s. XII
Noted Missal   Pl. 48

f. 1r   [*Post co.* Auxilientur nobis domine letabitur . . . sem]//piterna protectione confirment. Per.

St. Agatha (5 February). The upper margin has been trimmed with the loss of the first three lines of text.

f. 1r–v   *Valen*[*tinus. Int.*] In virtute tua domine . . . *Ps.* Magna est gloria . . . *Collecta.* Praesta quesumus omnipotens deus. ut qui . . . *Lectio libri sapientię.* Beatus uir qui inuentus est sine mac[ula] et qui . . . *Gr.* Beatus uir qui timet . . . *Tr.* Desiderium anime eius . . . *V.* Posuisti super ca[pu]t . . . *Euangelium.* Si quis uult [po]st me uenire. *require in natali s. Blasii. Of.* In [uir]tute tua . . . *Complenda.* [Ob]latis quesumus domine placare muneribus . . . *Co.* Magna [est] gloria eius in salutari. *Complenda.* [S]it nobis domine reparatio . . . effectum. Per.

St. Valentine (14 February). The upper margin has been trimmed with the loss of the first three lines of text.

ff. 1v–2v   *In kathedra s. petri missa.* [*Int.*] Statuit ei dominus. *Collecta.* [. . . Deus qui beato petro . . . intercessio]nis eius auxilio . . . *Pauli apostoli ad hebreos.* Fratres. Omnis pontifex ex hominibus assumptus . . . *Gr.* Exaltent eum in ecclesia . . . *V.* Cantate domino canticum . . . [. . . *Tr.* Tu es petrus . . . *V.* Et porte inferi . . .] aduersus eam . . . *V.* Et quodcumque ligaueris . . . *V.* Et quodcumque solueris . . . *Secundum matheum.* In illo tempore. Venit iesus in partes cesarę . . . aduersus eam et tibi dabo cla//[ues]

Chair of St. Peter (22 February). The upper margin has been trimmed with the loss of the first three lines of text. A fifteenth- or sixteenth-century cursive hand has written "Temporibus nostris quicunque placere laborat / Det capiat quaerat plurima pauca nihil. 382." This verse proverb is found in a number of fourteenth- and fifteenth-century manuscripts (see Walther, *Sprichwörter*, 19162). In the inner margin, perpendicular to the text, a similar hand has written "Lautante [?] Reo et contumace existente, actor ex Iudicis decreto mittitur in possessionem: Sed Reus post annum reversus animo litem contestandi restituitur in integrum; sed actor potest caute agere, ut nempe reo contumace existente, offerat libellum et petat se ad eius probationem admitti, quo probato reus non restituitur post annum reversus; Et hoc semper facit actor si iustam causam foveat, alias non esset consultum."

Parchment. 2 folios (1 bifolium). 275 x 230 mm (written space originally ca. 270 x 165 mm). 1 column. 20 lines remaining of original ca. 23. Ruled in lead (very faint).

Written in two sizes of late Caroline minuscule, a larger module for the lessons and prayers and a smaller module for the chants. 2- and 3-line initials are in red square capitals, which in places has oxidized to a silver color, and are written on the vertical bounding line. 1-line initials are in brown rustic capitals and are not set apart from the text; those for the gradual and tract are dotted with red. Rubrics are written in red minuscule. Line fillers are in red. Punctuation consists of the punctus and punctus elevatus. The chants have interlinear neumes in the St. Gall style.

This fragment was used as a pastedown in the binding of a volume measuring ca. 410 x 275 mm.

Zinniker 162.

MS 481.80   Italy, s. XII^{med}
Sacramentary   Pl. 48

f. 1ra   [Perpetuum nobis domine tuae miserationis praesta . . .] //prestitisti suf-
          fragia non deesse. Per. *Sec.* [H]ostias tibi domine laudis offerimus . . . *Post*
          co. [R]epleti benedictione celesti suppliciter . . . *Missa ad gratiam spiritus*
          sancti adpostulandam. [D]eus cui omne cor patet et omis[sic] uoluntis[sic]
          loquitur//

          Votive masses.

f. 1rb   [Propitiare quaesumus domine nobis famulis tuis . . .] //requiescit ecclesia
          merita gloriosa . . . *Sec.* Suscipiat domine quaesumus clementiam tuam de
          manibus . . . *Post co.* Diuina libantes misteria que pro huiuus [sic] sancti
          confessoris . . . reficiamur. Per.//

          Votive masses. Several words of the text have been erased.

f. 1va   *Alia missa pro contra temptationem cogitationum. Or.* Omnipotens mitissime (*in ras.*) deus respice ... *Sec.* Has tibi domine offerimus oblationes ... *Post co.* Deus qui illuminas omnem ... *Missa de quacumque tribulatione*//

Votive masses.

f. 1vb   //habere fide dei. Amen dico uobis quia si quis dixerit huic monti ... peccata uestra. *Sec.* Quaesumus domine placare muneribus nostris quoniam tu eadem//

Votive masses, including lesson from Mark 11.22–25.

Parchment. 1 folio (partial; top half of leaf trimmed off). 243 x 170 mm (width of written space 196 mm). 2 columns. 20 lines remaining. Dry-point ruling on the hair side. Single vertical bounding lines.

   Written in late Caroline minuscule. 2-line initials are in red square capitals, with minuscule *h*, and are set apart from the text. 1-line capitals are in brown uncials. Rubrics are written in red uncials. Punctuation consists of the punctus and punctus elevatus. Hyphenation is in the same ink as the text. A thirteenth-century hand has added text in the margin. There are numerous erasures and corrections in the text.

   Zinniker 142.

MS 481.81   Southern Germany, s. XII^2
Sacramentary   Pl. 49

f. 1ra   [*Missa pro salute vivorum et mortuorum.* Sanctorum tuorum intercessionibus ... requiesc]//unt. uel quorum nomina ... [*Se*]*cr.* Propitiare domine [supplic]ationibus nostris et has [oblatio]nes quas ... *Comp.* Purifi[cet nos] quaesumus domine et diuini ... agimus. remissionem//

          Mass for the living and dead. All margins have been trimmed with loss of text; only a portion of the inner column remains.

f. 1vb   [*Missa pro defunctis episcopis.* ... *Secr.* Suscipe quaesumus domine pro anima ... offe]//rimus hostias. ut quibus [pontifi]cale donasti ... *Com.* [Propiti]are domine supplicati[onibus] nostris et animas fam[ulorum tuorum] N. episcoporum ... *Pro sacer*[*dote*]. Praesta quaesumus domine ut [anima] famuli tui N. [sacerdo]tis quem ... S[*ecr.* Pre]ces nostras quaesumus domine qua[s in famu]li tui N. sacerdotis ... *Com.* [Praesta quaesumus] omnipotens deus ut an[ima fa]muli tui N sacerdo[tis in] congregatione ius//[torum]

Masses for dead bishops and for a dead priest. All margins have been trimmed with loss of text; only a portion of the inner column remains.

Parchment. 1 folio. 200 x 64 mm (original dimensions uncertain; width of written space originally ca. 150 mm). 1 column remaining of original 2. 24 lines remaining. Ruling no longer visible.

Written in late Caroline minuscule. 4-line initial "P" ("Praesta") in red, partially set apart from the text. The initials of other prayers are in red, not set apart from the text. Rubrics are written in red minuscule. The rest of the word "praesta" after the initial and the letter "N" (for "nomen") are 1-line brown uncials. Punctuation consists of the punctus and punctus elevatus.

A strip of paper is glued to the recto with a note in ink on the script in a modern German hand. A modern hand has written the number "7" in pencil on the verso.

Zinniker 173A.

MS 481.82   Austria (Melk?), s. XIII[2]
Passionary   Pl. 49

f. 1ra   [Inc: Simon itaque Chananaeus et Iudas Zelotes apostoli . . .] //qui per sin-
           gulas mansiones sacrificantes . . . ut agnoscas errorem horum quos putas
           tibi//

           Sts. Simon and Jude (28 October); the text is an excerpt from the *Passio
           SS. Simonis et Iudae* (BHL 7750); Mombritius, 534.23–42. The leaf has
           been cut in half and one line is missing from the middle; only the inner
           column remains.

f. 1vb   [Inc: Apud prouinciam Retiam in ciuitate Augusta Narcissus episcopus
           . . . uulneri]//bus elefantie corpore toto plenus . . . princeps noster ab eo
           qui crucifixus//

           St. Narcissus (29 October); the text is an excerpt from the *Conversio et
           Passio S. Afrae* (BHL 108); MGH Script. Rer. Merov. III.58.8–24. The leaf
           has been cut in half and one line is missing from the middle; only the in-
           ner column remains.

Parchment. 1 folio. Each fragment measures 200 x 135 mm; the original leaf measured ca. 435 x ca. 260 mm (written space originally ca. 325 x 240 mm). 1 (inner)
of 2 columns remaining. 29 of 30 lines remaining. Ruled in ink; single vertical
bounding lines.

Written in late Caroline minuscule. 1-line initials in red are written on the vertical bounding line when they occur at the beginning of a line. Other 1-line initials are in brown and are not set apart from the text. Punctuation consists of the punctus, punctus elevatus, and punctus interrogativus. Hyphenation is in the same ink as the text.

The pieces were used as pastedowns in the binding of a volume measuring ca. 200 x 135 mm.

Zinniker 166A and 166B.

MS 481.83   Southern Germany, s. XII^2
Passio S. Margaritae   Pl. 50

f. 1   [Inc: Post resurrectionem domini nostri iesu christi et gloriosam ascensi-
         onem saluabantur . . .] //saluatoris. Ista uero spiritu . . . V. Olibrius immu-
         tauit habitum suum et iussit eam . . . VI. Secundo autem die uenit et sedit
         pro tribunali . . . autem deus meus adiut//[or]

         St. Margaret (20 July); *Passio S. Margaritae* (BHL 5303); Mombritius,
         190.38–191.46. In the outer margin of the recto there are two lines from
         an unidentified hymn, followed by a hymn for St. Margaret (Inc: Martyr
         insignis margareta . . . ; RH 11239) in an early thirteenth-century hand.
         The inner margin has been trimmed with loss of text.

Parchment (verso badly rubbed and stained). 1 folio. 335 x 235 mm (written space 300 x ca. 190 mm). 2 columns. 32 lines. Ruling very faint, perhaps lead. Single vertical bounding lines. Prickings in outer margin.

Written in late Caroline minuscule. 2-line initial "O" is in red, decorated with two small red dots protruding into the interior of the letter, and is not set apart from the text. 1-line initials are in a mixture of brown uncial and rustic capital forms, with an enlarged minuscule *e*. Punctuation consists of the punctus and punctus interrogativus. Lesson marks ("v" and "vi") are written in red in the margin. The marginal hymn has 1-line capitals, rubrics, and paragraph marks in brown highlighted with red, as well as interlinear neumes in the St. Gall style.

The fragment was used as the binding of a volume measuring ca. 196 x 151 mm.

Zinniker 235.

MS 481.84
Psalter

f. 1   //inimici uero domini mox honorificati fuerint . . . non est inuentus locus eius.//

      Psalm 36.20–36.

Parchment (tear in outer and lower margin repaired with gold and pale red thread). 1 folio. 330 x 213 mm (written space 255 x 140 mm). 1 column. 21 lines. Ruled in lead; double vertical bounding lines. Prickings in upper, lower, and outer margins.

      Written in large late Caroline minuscule. 1-line initials of each verse are in orange square capitals, with round forms of *D* and *E*, and are set apart from the text between the vertical bounding lines. Punctuation consists of the punctus and punctus elevatus.

      The leaf was used in the binding of a volume measuring ca. 330 x 203 mm. Zinniker 182.

MS 481.85
Psalter

ff. 1–2   //omnes tribus terrę omnes gentes magnificabunt . . . inuocabimus nomen tuum. Narrabimus//

      Psalms 71.17–74.2. The outer and upper margins of fol. 2 have been trimmed with loss of text.

ff. 3–4   //ceciderunt. et uiduę eorum . . . liberaui te et exaudiui//

      Psalms 77.64–80.8. The upper margin of fol. 3 and the outer margin of fol. 4 have been trimmed with loss of text.

Parchment. 4 folios (2 bifolia, 1/4 and 2/3, the first and second of a quire). 214 x 165 mm (written space 187 x 125 mm). 1 column. 20 lines (fols. 2 and 3 preserve 19 lines). Dry-point ruling on the hair side. Double vertical and horizontal bounding lines.

      Written in late Caroline minuscule. 2-line initials at the beginning of the Psalms are in red, which in places has oxidized into a silver color, and decorated with two or three small round red dots protruding into the interior of the letter, and are written on the inner vertical bounding line. 1-line initials at the beginning of verses

are in red uncials and square capitals. Rubrics are written in red capitals. Punctuation consists of the punctus and punctus elevatus. There are several antiphons in
the margins in a contemporary hand with interlinear neumes in the St. Gall style.

Both fragments were used as pastedowns in the binding of a volume measuring
ca. 292 x 214 mm.

The bifolium 1/4 was Zinniker 164; the bifolium 2/3 was Zinniker 163.

MS 481.86   Melk, Austria, s. XII/XIII
Psalter   Pl. 51

f. 1ra   //labiorum ipsorum. et comprehendantur ... spes mea. turris forti//
           [tudinis]

           Psalms 58.13–60.3. The outer and lower margins have been trimmed with
           the loss of the outer column and the bottom two lines of text.

f. 1vb   [t]//urbabuntur gentes et timebunt ... fecit animę mee//

           Psalms 64.8–65.16. The outer and lower margins have been trimmed with
           the loss of the outer column and the bottom two lines of text.

f. 2   //lingua mea ... pauper sum. deus ad//

           Psalms 65.17–69.6. The bottom two lines have been trimmed off. A con-
           temporary hand has added a verse which was omitted in the upper margin
           with a +-shaped tie-mark.

Parchment. 2 folios (1 bifolium; the inner bifolium of a quire). 288 x 260 mm
(written space originally ca. 275 x 187 mm). 2 columns. 36 lines remaining of original 38. Ruled in lead; double vertical bounding lines. Prickings in outer margin.

Written in late Caroline minuscule. Each Psalm begins with a plain 2- or 3-line
initial in red square capitals, with round E, written on the vertical bounding lines.
1-line initials at the beginning of verses are in red rustic capitals, with occasional
use of enlarged minuscule e and n and uncial M, and are set apart from the text
between the vertical bounding lines. Rubrics are written in red capitals. Verse
dividers are in red. The first words of each Psalm are written in brown rustic capitals. Punctuation consists of the punctus. There are several later marginal annota-
tions which are mostly illegible.

Other fragments of this Psalter are preserved in the bindings of Melk, Stiftsbibliothek, P 224 (fols. I and I*), P 229/3 (fols. I and I*), and P 260, which pre-

serves only an offprint from the front pastedown. P 224, fol. I preserves Psalms 51.10–58.13 and thus comes directly before Beinecke MS 481.86, fol. 1. The offprint from the pastedown in P 260 preserves Psalms 63.4–64.8 and is thus from the outer column of our fol. 1. These fragments are briefly described in Christine Glassner and Alois Haidinger, *Die Anfänge der Melker Bibliothek* (Melk, 1996), 109 (with several plates of manuscripts written by the same scribe, pls. 82–86; see also pp. 107–10).

The bifolium was once used as a pastedown in the binding of a volume measuring ca. 375 x 278 mm.

Zinniker 136.

MS 481.87   Germany, s. XIII[1]
Canticles (Psalter)   Pl. 52

f. 1r–v   //numerus. Te martyrum candidatus ... non confundar in eternum.

   Te Deum.

f. 1v   Benedictus dominus deus israhel ... parare uias eius. Ad dan//[dam]

   Canticle: Benedictus dominus deus.

Parchment (verso rubbed and stained). 1 folio. 205 x 150 mm (written space 140 x 95 mm). 1 column. 17 lines. Ruled in lead; double vertical and double upper horizontal bounding lines.

Written in gothic script (littera textualis), above top line. 3-line initial "B" ("Benedictus") is in red with blue and red penwork and is written on the inner vertical bounding line. 1-line initials at the beginning of verses are in red uncials and are not set apart from the text. Line dividers are in red. Punctuation consists of the punctus.

This fragment was used as a wrapper for a volume measuring ca. 123 x 72 mm. Zinniker 234.

MS 481.88   Lambach, Austria, s. XII[ex]
Psalter   Pl. 52

ff. 1–4   [partu]//rit iniusticiam. concepit dolorem ... subtus me et non sunt//

   Psalms 7.15–17.37. Liturgical antiphons with St. Gall neumes were added in the margins of fols. 1v (Psalm 9) and 2v (Psalm 12). These were later erased and rewritten with square notation on a 4-line staff.

Parchment. 4 folios. Fol. 1 measures 287 x 200 mm; fol. 2, 285 x 198 mm; fol. 3, 288 x 197 mm; fol. 4, 288 x 199 mm (written space 223 x 153 mm). 1 column. 28 lines. Dry-point ruling. Double vertical bounding lines.

Written in late Caroline minuscule. 3- and 4-line initials at the beginning of Psalms are in red and are not set apart from the text; some are decorated with two or three small round red dots protruding into the interior of the letter and/or with thin lines crossing the stem of the letter in a herringbone pattern. These initials are similar to, and may have been produced by, the artist of the initials in Beinecke MSS 481.48 and 481.52 and the Lambach Rituale (Cml LXXIII). 1-line initials at the beginning of verses are in red square capitals, with uncial M and round E, and are set apart from the text when they occur at the beginning of a line. Rubrics are written in red minuscule. The first few words of each Psalm are written in brown rustic capitals. Punctuation consists of the punctus and punctus elevatus.

Fols. 1 and 4, originally a bifolium, were used as the wrappers for a volume measuring ca. 215 x 155 mm. The number "211" (which has been crossed out) on fol. 1r was probably a shelf number in the Lambach Stiftsbibliothek, although the hand is different from the one that wrote other Lambach shelf numbers; a similar hand wrote the number "146" on Beinecke MS 482.84, perhaps referring to Lambach Cml CXLVI. Fol. 4 has string tied in a chain-link pattern in the outer margin, which was once used to close the volume.

Fols. 2 and 3, originally a bifolium, were used as the wrappers of a volume measuring ca. 220 mm in height. Strings on fol. 2r are perhaps remnants from sewing on the spine of the volume.

Fol. 1 was formerly Zinniker 268. Fol. 2 was formerly Beinecke 482.68, Zinniker 52; fol. 3 was Beinecke 482.68, Zinniker 25; fol. 4 was Beinecke 481.90, Zinniker 261.

Bibliography:
Babcock, *Reconstructing a Medieval Library*, 111 and fig. 60.

MS 481.89

transferred to Beinecke MS 481.46

MS 481.90

transferred to Beinecke MS 481.88

MS 481.91
Sacramentary

Southern Germany or Austria, s. XII²
Pl. 53

f. 1r   [*Super populum*. Tuere domine populum tu]//um et ab omnibus ... domi-
           netur iniquitas. Per.

           Feria VI of Quinquagesima.

f. 1r   *Sabbato.* [*Or.*] Preces nostras. *Super populum.* Adesto quaesumus domine
           supplicationibus nostris et in tua ... custodi. Per.

           Saturday of Quinquagesima.

f. 1r   *Dominica in xl.* [*Or.*] Deus qui ęcclesiam tuam annua quadragesimali ...
           Sec. [S]acrificium quadragesimalis initii ... *Co.* Tui nos domine sacra-
           menti libatio ... consortium. Per.

           First Sunday of Quadragesima.

f. 1r–v   *Feria ii.* [*Or.*] Conuerte nos deus salutaris noster ... *Sec.* [M]unera
           domine oblata sanctifica; nosque a peccatorum ... *Compl.* Salutaris tui
           domine munere saciati supplices ... *Super populum.* Absolue quaesumus
           domine nostrorum uincula peccatorum ... auerte. Per.

           Feria II of the first week of Quadragesima.

f. 1v   *Feria i[ii.]* [*Or.*] Respice domine familiam tuam ... *Sec.* Oblatis quaesu-
           mus domine placare muneribus ... *Compl.* Quaesumus omnipotens deus
           ut salutaris capiamus effectum ... *Super populum.* Ascendant ad te domine
           preces nostrae ... nequiciam. Per.

           Feria III of the first week of Quadragesima.

ff. 1v–2r *Feria iiii.* [*Or.*] Preces nostras quaesumus domine clementer exaudi ...
           Alia. Deuotionem populi tui quaesumus domine benignus intende ... *Sec.*
           Hostias tibi domine placationis offerimus ... *Compl.* Tui domine percep-
           tione sacramenti ... *Super populum.* Mentes nostras quaesumus domine
           lumine tuę ... ualeamus. Per.

           Feria IV of the first week of Quadragesima.

f. 2r   *Feria v.* [*Or.*] Deuotionem populi. *ut supra. Sec.* Sacrificia domine quae-

sumus propicius ista nos . . . Co. [T]uorum nos domine largitate donorum
. . . Super populum. Da quaesumus domine populis christianis . . . frequen-
tant. Per.

Feria V of the first week of Quadragesima.

f. 2r   Feria vi. [Or.] Esto domine propicius plebi tuę . . . Sec. Suscipe quaesumus
domine nostris oblata . . . Compl. Per huius domine operationem mysterii
. . . Super populum. Exaudi nos misericors deus . . . ostende. Per.

Feria VI of the first week of Quadragesima.

f. 2r–v   Sabbato. [Or.] Populum tuum quaesumus domine propicius respice . . .
Alia. Deus qui nos in tantis periculis . . . Al. Protector noster aspice deus
. . . A[lia.] Adesto quaesumus domine supplicationibus nostris . . . Alia.
Actiones nostra[s] quaesumus domine et aspirando . . . Ad missam. [Or.]
Deus qui tribus pueris mitigasti flammas . . . Sec. Presentibus sacrificiis
domine ieiunia nostra sanctifica . . . Compl. Sanctificationibus omnipotens
deus et uicia nostra curentur . . . Super populum. Da populo tuo quaesumus
domine spiritum ueritatis . . . sunt placita toto corde sectetur//

Saturday of the first week of Quadragesima.

Parchment. 2 folios. 305 x 204 mm (written space 210 x 150 mm). 1 column. 22
lines. Ruled in lead (very faint). Prickings in upper, lower, and outer margins.
    Written in late Caroline minuscule. 2- to 3-line initials at the beginning of each
Mass are in red square capitals, with round E, and are not set apart from the text.
1-line initials are in a mixture of red uncials and square capitals and are set apart
from the text when they occur at the beginning of a line. Rubrics are written in red
minuscule, with some rustic capital forms. The first word after the major initial is
frequently written in brown rustic capitals. Punctuation consists of the punctus and
punctus elevatus.
    Both leaves were used as pastedowns in a binding. In the lower margin of fol. 2r
is written "Peccatorum illecebra in hoc mundo . . . [rest illegible]" in a seventeenth-
century hand similar to the one that annotated an incunabulum from the Lambach
Stiftsbibliothek (now Beinecke Zi +2508).
    Fol. 1 was formerly Beinecke MS 482.69, Zinniker 4; fol. 2 was Zinniker 244.

Bibliography:
    Babcock, Reconstructing a Medieval Library, 111 and fig. 61.

MS 481.92   Southern Germany or Austria, s. XII^{med}
Sacramentary   Pl. 53

f. 1r   [*Co.* Sacro munere satiasti supplices te domine depre]//camur. ut quod
         ... augmentum. Per.

St. Sebastian (20 January).

f. 1r   [*Or.*] Omnipotens sempiterne deus qui infirma mundi ... [*Secr.*] Hostias
         domine quas tibi offerimus propicius ... [*Post Co.*] Refecti cibo potuque
         cęlesti deus noster ... precibus. Per.

St. Agnes (21 January).

f. 1r   [*Or.*] Adesto quaesumus domine supplicationibus nostris ut qui ex ini-
         quitate ... [*Secr.*] Muneribus nostris quaesumus domine precibusque ...
         [*Post Co.*] Quaesumus omnipotens deus ut qui cęlestia alimenta ... mu-
         niamur. Per.

St. Vincent (22 January).

f. 1r   [*Or.*] Deus qui uniuersum mundum beati Pauli apostoli praedicatione
         docuisti ... [*Secr.*] Apostoli tui Pauli precibus tua domine dona sanctifica
         ... [*Post Co.*] Satiasti nos domine salutari mysterio ... gubernari. Per.

Conversion of St. Paul (25 January).

f. 1r   *Preiecti martyris.* [*Or.*] Martyris tui Preiecti nos quaesumus domine ...
         [*Secr.*] Suscipe domine propicius orationem nostram cum oblationibus
         ... [*Post co.*] Votiua domine pro beati martyris tui preiecti passione ...
         praesiduum. Per.

St. Praejectus (25 January).

f. 1r   *Agne martyris.* [*Or.*] Deus qui nos annua beatę Agnę ... [*Secr.*] Super has
         quaesumus domine hostias benedictio copiosa ... [*Post Co.*] Sumpsimus
         domine cęlebritatis annue ... et ęterne. Per.

St. Agnes (28 January).

f. 1r–v *In* p[... *Or.*] Omnipotens sempiterne deus maiestatem tuam supplices
         ... [*Secr.*] Exaudi domine preces nostras et ut digna sint ... [*Pref.*] UD

ęternę deus. Quia per incarnati uerbi mysterium. [*Post Co.*] Quaesumus
domine deus noster ut sacrosancta mysteria . . . [*Sequitur*] Perfice in nobis
quaesumus domine gratiam tuam . . . ęternam. Per.

Missa ad S. Mariam maiorem.

f. 1v   [*Or.*] Sancti Blasii martyris tui atque pontificis nos quaesumus . . . [*Secr.*]
Suscipe domine propicius orationes nostras . . . [*Post co.*] Votiua domine
pro beati blasii martyris tui . . . subsidium. Per.

St. Blaise (3 February).

f. 1v   [*Or.*] Indulgentiam nobis domine beata Agatha martyr . . . [*Secr.*] Suscipe
domine munera quę in beatę Agathę . . . [*Post co.*] Praesta quaesumus omnipotens deus ut sanctę agathę . . . commendemur. Per.

St. Agatha (5 February).

f. 1v   [*Or.*] Beati ualentini martyris tui domine natalicia recensentes . . . [*Secr.*]
Sancti Valentini martyris tui domine merita uenerantes . . . [*Post co.*]
Concede quaesumus omnipotens deus ut pro sancti valentini martyris
. . . ascribendos. Per.

St. Valentine (14 February).

f. 1v   [*Or.*] Deus qui apostolo tuo Petro collatis clauibus . . . [*Secr.*] Ecclesię tuę
quaesumus domine preces et hostias beati Petri . . . [*Post Co.*] Sanctificet
nos domine tuum sacramentum ut sicut in apostolo tuo . . . largitatem.
Per.

Chair of St. Peter (22 February).

f. 1v   *Mathie apostoli.* [*Or.*] Deus qui beatum Mathiam apostolorum tuorum
collegio sociasti . . . [*Secr.*] Deus qui proditoris apostate ruinam . . . [*Post
co.*] Praesta quaesumus omnipotens et misericors deus ut per hęc . . .
gratiam. Per.

St. Matthias (24 February).

f. 1v–2r *Gregorii papae.* [*Or.*] Deus qui animę famuli tui Gregorii ęternę beatitudinis . . . [*Secr.*] Annue nobis domine ut animę famuli tui gregorii . . .
[*Post Co.*] Deus qui beatum gregorium pontificem . . . exempla. Per.

St. Gregory (12 March).

f. 2r   [*Or.*] Deus qui de beatę Marię uirginis utero uerbum . . . [*Secr.*] In mentibus nostris domine uere fidei sacramenta . . . [*Pref.*] UD ęternę deus. Per
christum dominum nostrum. Et te in annunciatione beatę marię . . . [*Post
Co.*] Gratiam tuam domine mentibus nostris infunde . . . perducamur. Per.

Annunciation of the Virgin Mary (25 March).

f. 2r   *Ambrosii.* [*Or.*] Sancti ambrosii nos domine iugiter prosequatur . . . [*Secr.*]
Hęc in nobis sacrificia deus antecedente [*corrected to or from:* inter-
cedente] beato confessore tuo . . . [*Post co.*] Hęc nos communio domine
purge [*sic*] a crimine . . . consortes. Per.

Deposition of St. Ambrose (5 April).

f. 2r   *Dominica infra* [. . . *Or.*] Omnipotens sempiterne deus dirige actus nostros
in beneplacito tuo . . . [*Secr.*] Concede quaesumus domine ut oculis tuę
maiestatis . . . [*Post co.*] Per huius domine operationem mysterii obtineat
. . . compleantur. Per.

Sunday II after Christmas.

f. 2r   *Dominica* [*i post epiphaniam. Or.*] Uota quaesumus domine supplicantis
populi . . . [*Secr.*] Oblatum tibi domine sacrificium nos semper . . . [*Post
Co.*] Supplices te rogamus omnipotens deus ut quos . . . concedas. Per.

Sunday I after Epiphany.

f. 2r   [*Or.*] Omnipotens sempiterne deus qui cęlestia simul . . . [*Secr.*] Oblata
domine munera sanctifica . . . [*Post Co.*] Augeatur in nobis quaesumus
domine tuę uirtutis . . . munere . . . Per.

Sunday II after Epiphany.

f. 2r   *Dominica ii*[*i. Or.*] Omnipotens sempiterne deus infirmitatem nostram
. . . [*Secr.*] Hęc hostia domine emundet nostra delicta . . . [*Post Co.*] Quos
tantis domine largiris uti mysteriis . . . digneris. Per.

Sunday III after Epiphany.

f. 2v   [*Or.*] Deus qui nos in tantis periculis . . . [*Secr.*] Concede quaesumus om-

nipotens deus ut huius sacrificii . . . [*Post Co.*] Munera tua nos deus a delectationibus . . . alimentis. Per.

Sunday IV after Epiphany.

f. 2v   [*Or.*] Familiam tuam quaesumus domine continua pietate . . . [*Secr.*]
             Hostias tibi domine placationis offerimus . . . [*Post Co.*] Quaesumus om-
             nipotens deus ut illius salutaris capiamus . . . accepimus. Per.

Sunday V after Epiphany.

f. 2v   [*Or.*] Conserva populum tuum deus et tuo nomini fac . . . [*Secr.*] Hec
             oblatio deus mundet quaesumus et renouet . . . [*Post co.*] Cẹlestibus do-
             mine pasti deliciis . . . appetamus. Per.

Sunday VI after Epiphany.

f. 2v   *Dominica in septuagesima.* [*Or.*] Preces populi tui quaesumus domine cle-
             menter . . . [*Secr.*] Muneribus nostris quaesumus domine precibusque . . .
             [*Post Co.*] Fideles tui deus per tua dona . . . percipiant. Per.

Sunday of Septuagesima.

f. 2v   *Dominica in lx.* [*Or.*] Deus qui conspicis quia ex nulla nostra actione . . .
             [*Secr.*] Intende quaesumus domine hostias familiẹ tue . . . [*Post co.*] Sit
             nobis quaesumus domine cibus . . . ẹternam. Per.

Sunday of Sexagesima.

f. 2v   *Dominica in l.* [*Or.*] Preces nostras quaesumus domine clementer exaudi
             . . . [*Secr.*] Concede nobis misericors deus digne tuis seruire altaribus . . .
             [*Post co.*] Repleti domine donorum participatione cẹlestium . . . ambiamus.
             Per.

Sunday of Quinquagesima.

f. 2v   *In cap*[*ite ieiunii.* *Or.*] Concede nobis domine praesidia militiẹ . . . [*Or.*]
             Praesta domine fidelibus tuis . . . [*Secr.*] Fac nos quaesumus domine his
             muneribus . . . [*Pref.*] UD ẹterne deus. Qui corporali ieiunio . . . [*Post co.*]
             Percepta nobis domine praebeant sacramenta . . . auxiliis. Per.

Feria IV of Quinquagesima.

f. 2v   *Feria v.* [*Or.*] Deus qui culpa offenderis ... [*Secr.*] Sacrificiis praesentibus
         quaesumus domine intende ... [*Post Co.*] Cęlestis doni benedictione per-
         cepta ... salutis. Per.

         Feria V of Quinquagesima.

f. 3r   [*Or.*] Deus qui per filium tuum angularem ... ualeamus. Per.

         Holy Saturday.

f. 3r   *Deinde hora iii. sonetur signum. ut omnes ueniant ... Et ita perficiatur missa
         pleniter in ordine suo.*

         Liturgical directions for Holy Saturday Mass.

f. 3r–v *Prefatio.* Et ideo cum angelis et archangelis ... *Praefatio.* UD equum et
         salutare. Te domine ... [*Pref.*] Per omnia saecula saeculorum ... [*Pref.*]
         UD ęquum et salutare. Nos tibi semper ... Osanna in excelsis.

         Prefaces and canon of the Mass. Only three lines of the verso are filled,
         and the rest of the page was originally left blank, presumably so that the
         Te igitur could begin with a full-page decorative format. Two different
         fourteenth-century gothic hands (littera textualis) have filled this space
         with Bible lessons (John 21.19–24 and Sirach 15.1–6).

f. 4r   //bene laudem tibi hostias immolamus. Per. [*Post co.*] Sacramenti tui
         domine munere uegetati ... ęternis. Per.

         Unidentified feast.

f. 4r   *In uigilia unius apostoli.* [*Or.* Co]ncede nobis quaesumus omnipotens deus
         uenturam ... [*Secr.*] Accepta tibi sit domine nostrae deuotionis ... [*Post
         co.*] Praesta nobis eterne felicitatis ... obsequio. Per.

         Vigil of the Common of an Apostle.

f. 4r   *In die sancto.* [*Or.* Beatus] apostolus tui *N.* domine quaesumus te ...
         [*Secr.*] Beati apostoli tui *N.* sollemnitates recensentes ... [*Post co.* Beati]
         apostoli tui *N.* quaesumus domine intercessione ... [*Post co.*] Perceptis
         domine. *Require in vigilia s. andreę.*

         Common of an Apostle.

f. 4r   [Or. Concede quaesumus] omnipotens. *Require in uigilia s. apostolorum sy-*
         monis et iude.

         Vigil of the Common of Apostles.

f. 4r   *In natale apostolorum.* [Or.] Exaudi [*corr. from:* Concede] nos deus salu-
         taris noster ... [*Secr.*] Respice domine munera quę in sanctorum ... [*Post
         co.*] Quaesumus domine salutaribus repleti ... *Alia. require in natale apos-*
         tolorum phylippi et iacobi.

         Common of Apostles.

f. 4r   *De uno martyre.* [Or. Sancti martyris] tui quaesumus domine ueneranda
         ... [*Secr.*] Praesta nobis quaesumus ... [*Post co.* Sumptis domine sacra-
         mentis] quaesumus intercedente ... *Alia. require in natale s. menne.*

         Common of a Martyr.

f. 4r   *De uno martyre qui fuit pontifex.* [Or.] ... omnipotens deus et quia ...
         [S]uscipe domine munera propitius oblata ... Beati N. martyris tui ...
         [intercessione] placatus praesta quaesumus ... Omnipotens sempiterne
         deus qui gloriosa ... Hęc hostia quaesumus domine sollemniter immo-
         landa ... [Quaesumus] omnipotens deus ... [...]a nos quaesumus do-
         mine tui commemorationis ... [*Secr.*] Hostias tibi domine pro ... salutem.
         Per. [*Post co.*] ... sacramenti domine perpetua nos tuitio ...

         Common of a Martyr Bishop.

f. 4r   *De uno confessore.* [Or.] Exaudi domine preces nostras quas in sancti ...
         [*Secr.*] Hostias [tibi domine] pro commemoratione sancti confessoris ...
         [*Post co.*] Refecti domine benedictione ... *Require in natale damasi papae.*
         Offerimus domine preces et munera ... Sumptum domine. *Item de sancto*
         damaso.

         Common of a Confessor.

f. 4r   *In natale unius confessoris* [...]. [Or.] Praesta quaesumus deus ut beati N.
         confessoris tui atque pontificis ... [*Secr.*] Sancti confessoris atque ponti-
         ficis quaesumus domine ueneranda ... [*Post co.*] Beati N. confessoris tui
         atque pontificis domine precibus ... capiamus. Per.

         Common of a Confessor Bishop.

f. 4r   *In natale plurimorum confessorum.* [*Or.*] Sanctorum confessorum N. nos
         quaesumus domine foueat ... [*Secr.*] Munera plebis tuae quaesumus
         domine sanctorum confessorum... [*Post co.*] Sumentes gaudia sempiterna
         de participatione ... ęternam. Per.

         Common of Confessors.

f. 4r–v *In natale unius uirginis et martyris.* [*Or.*] Deus qui nos beatae N. virginis ac
         martyris ... [*Secr.*] Hostias domine quas tibi offerimus propitius suscipe
         ... [*Post co.*] Auxilientur nobis domine sumpta ... confirment. Per.

         Common of a Virgin and Martyr.

f. 4v   *In natale virginis.* [*Or.*] Praesta quaesumus omnipotens deus ut qui beatae
         N. virginis ... [*Secr.*] Hostias domine quas tibi offerimus propitius suscipe
         ... [*Post co.*] Hęc in nobis quaesumus domine gratia tua semper exerceat
         ... lętificet. Per.

         Common of a Virgin.

f. 4v   *In natale plurimarum virginum.* [*Or.*] Da nobis quaesumus domine deus
         noster sanctarum martyrum tuarum... [*Secr.*] Suscipe quaesumus domine
         ob honorem sacrarum virginum ... [*Post co.*] Sacramentis quaesumus
         domine muniamur ... protegantur. Per.

         Common of Virgins.

f. 4v   *De anniuersario ecclesie.* [*Or.*] Deus qui inuisibiliter omnia ... [*Secr.*] Des-
         cendat quaesumus domine deus noster ... [*Post co.*] Multiplica quaesu-
         mus domine per haec diuina mysteria ...

         Anniversary of the dedication of a church.

f. 4v   *In dedicatione.* [*Or.*] Deus qui nos ad anniuersarium diem consecrationis
         huius ecclesie ... [*Secr.*] Praesta quaesumus domine ut munera quę sacris
         ... [*Post co.?*] Refecti celestis doni ... gloriemur. Per. *In dedicatione a[lta-
         ris?]* [*A.*] Dicit dominus si. *require de sancto clemente.* [*Post co.*] Quae-
         sumus omnipotens deus ut hoc in loco qui nomini tuo dedicatus est ...
         accomodes. Per. *L[ectio] ysaie.* Hęc dicit dominus. In die illa defertur
         domino exercituum munus ... Alleluia. Dextera domini uel Letatus.
         Matheum. In illo tempore. Dicit iesus discipulis suis. Si offers munus tuum
         ad altare ... [*Secr.*] Descendat quaesumus. *require s[upra]* Co. [*A.*] In-

troibo. [*Post co.*] Omnipotens sempiterne deus effunde super hunc ...
ostende. Per

On the dedication of a church (and an altar?). The readings are extracts
from Isaiah 18.7–19.22 and Matthew 5.23.

f. 4v   *Dominica i.* [*Or.*] Deus in te sperantium ... [*Secr.*] Hostias nostras quae-
            sumus domine tibi dicatas ... [*Post co.*] Tantis domine repleti muneribus
            ... cessemus. Per.

First Sunday after Pentecost.

f. 4v   *Dominica ii.* [*Or.*] Sancti nominis tui domine timorem ... [*Secr.*] Oblatio
            nos domine tuo nomini ... [*Post co.*] Sumptis muneribus quaesumus do-
            mine ut cum frequentatione ... effectus. Per.

Second Sunday after Pentecost.

f. 4v   *Dominica iii.* [*Or.*] Protector in te sperantium deus ... [*Secr.*] Respice do-
            mine munera supplicantis ęcclesię ... [*Post co.*] Sancta tua nos domine
            sumpta uiuificent ... expiatos. Per.

Third Sunday after Pentecost.

f. 4v   *Dominica iiii.* [*Or.*] Da nobis quaesumus domine ut et mundi ... [*Secr.*]
            Oblationibus quaesumus domine placare susceptis ... [*Post co.*] Mysteria
            nos domine sancta purificent ... tueantur. Per.

Fourth Sunday after Pentecost.

f. 4v   *Dominica v.* [*Or.*] Deus qui diligentibus te bona inuisibilia ... [*Secr.*] Pro-
            piciare domine supplicationibus nostris et has oblationes ... [*Post co.*]
            Quos cęlesti domine dono satiasti ... insidiis. Per.

Fifth Sunday after Pentecost.

f. 4v   *Dominica vi.* [*Or.*] Deus uirtutum cuius est totum ... [*Secr.*] Propiciare
            domine supplicationibus nostris et has populi ... [*Post co.* R]epleti domine
            muneribus tuis tribue ... auxilio. Per.

Sixth Sunday after Pentecost.

f. 4v   *Dominica vii.* [*Or.*] Deus cuius prouidentia in sui dispositione ... [*Secr.*]
         Deus qui legalium differentias ... singuli obtulerunt//

         Seventh Sunday after Pentecost.

f. 5r   *//Pro elemosina.* [*Or.* Deus qui] post baptismi sacramentum secundam abo-
         litionem ... [?] quos ... [*Secr.*] Hostias nostras clementissime ... [*Post
         co.*] Sumpsimus domine tua ... mentis et c. Per.

         Mass for almsgiving.

f. 5r   *Pro infirmis.* [*Or.*] Omnipotens sempiterne deus salus eterna ... [*Secr.*]
         Deus sub cuius nutibus uitẹ ... [*Post Co.*] Deus infirmitatis humane ...
         mereatur. Per.

         Mass for the sick.

f. 5r   *Contra mortalitatem.* [*Or.*] Omnipotens et misericors deus respice propitius
         ... [*Secr.*] Subueniat nobis domine sacrificii tui praesentis oblatio ... [*Post
         co.* N?]e perdideris nos domine cum iniquitatibus nostris ... periculo. Per.

         Mass against mortality.

f. 5r   *De tribulatione.* [*Or.*] Concede quaesumus omnipotens deus famulo tuo *N.*
         consolationis ... [*Secr.*] Quaesumus domine nostris placare muneribus et
         quicquid ... [*Post co.*] Sumpti sacrificii libamen domine quaesumus
         cẹlestis ... depellat. Per.

         Mass in tribulation.

f. 5r   *Contra temptationem.* [*Or.*] Omnipotens mitissime deus respice propitius
         preces nostras ... [*Secr.*] Has tibi domine deus offerimus oblationes ...
         [*Post co.*] Per hoc quaesumus domine sacrificium quod ... temptationibus.
         Per.

         Mass against temptation.

f. 5r   *Pro temptatione carnis.* [*Or.*] Ure igne quaesumus domine sancti spiritus
         ... [*Secr.*] Dirumpe domine uincula peccatorum ... [*Post co.*] Sancti spiri-
         tus gratia quaesumus domine corda nostra ... extinguat. per.

         Mass on the temptation of the flesh.

f. 5r   *Ad postulandas lacrimas.* [*Or.*] Omnipotens mitissime deus qui sitienti
         populo ... [*Secr.*] Hanc igitur oblationem quaesumus domine deus ...
         [*Post co.*] Sacramentum domine tuę largitatis quod sumpsimus ... sola-
         tium. Per.

         Mass to ask for tears.

f. 5r   *Pro confitentibus.* [*Or.*] Exaudi quaesumus domine supplicum ... [*Secr.*]
         Hostias tibi placationis offerimus ... [*Post co.*] Praesta nobis quaesumus
         eterne saluator ... peccata uitemus. Per.

         Mass for those who are confessing.

f. 5r   *Pro peccatis.* [*Or.*] Parce domine parce peccatis ... [*Secr.*] Sacrificia tibi
         domine cum ecclesia ... [*Post co.*] Vitia cordis humani hęc domine ...
         languores. Per.

         Mass for sins.

f. 5r   *Item pro peccatis.* [*Or.*] Ineffabilem misericordiam tuam domine ... [*Secr.*]
         Quaesumus domine nostris placare muneribus quos tu eadem ... [*Post
         Co.*] Praesta quaesumus domine ut terrenis ... tendamus. Per.

         Mass for sins.

f. 5r   *Pro tribulacione.* [*Or.*] Ne despicias omnipotens deus populum ... [*Secr.*]
         Munera domine tibi dicata ... [*Post co.*] Viuificet nos domine sacrę par-
         ticipationis ... defendat. Per.

         Mass in tribulation.

f. 5r   *Pro persecutione.* [*Or.*] Famulos tuos quaesumus domine ... [*Secr.*] Oblatis
         quaesumus domine placare muneribus et fideles ... [*Post co.*] Hęc nos
         quaesumus domine participatio diuini mysterii ... protegat. Per.

         Mass in persecution.

f. 5r   *Ad postulandam pluuiam.* [*Or.*] Deus in quo uiuimus ... [*Secr.*] Oblatis do-
         mine placare muneribus et oportunum ... [*Post co.*] Cęlestibus refecti
         sacramentis ... pluuiarum. Per.

         Mass to ask for rain.

f. 5r–v   *Pro serenitate.* [*Or.*] Ad te nos domine clamantes . . . [*Secr.*] Preueniat nos quaesumus domine gratia . . . [*Post Co.*] Quaesumus omnipotens deus per hanc sacram clementiam . . . digneris. Per.

Mass to ask for fair weather.

f. 5v   *Pro tribulacione.* [*Or.*] Deus qui contritorum [non despicis] gemitum . . . [*Secr.*] Deus qui tribulatos cor[de sanas] . . . [*Post Co.*] Dimitte nobis domine per hoc celeste mysterium . . . clementer exaudias. Per.

Mass in tribulation.

f. 5v   *Pro nauigantibus.* [*Or.*] Deus qui transtulisti patres nostros . . . [*Secr.*] Suscipe domine preces famulorum tuorum . . . [*Post Co.*] Sanctificati diuino mysterio maiestatem . . . eripias. Per.

Mass for sailors.

f. 5v   *Missa propria sacerdotis.* [*Or.*] Suppliciter te deus pater omnipotens qui es creator . . . [*Secr.*] Deus qui te praecipes a peccatoribus . . . [*Post co.*] Misericors et miserator domine qui parcendo . . . culparum. Per.

Proper Mass for priests.

f. 5v   *Item.* [*Or.*] Omnipotens et misericors deus qui subuenis in periculis . . . [*Secr.*] Sanctifica domine hec tibi sacrificia . . . [*Post co.*] Deus qui me indignum sacris mysteriis . . . sempiternam. Per.

Mass for priests.

f. 5v   *Pro salute uiuorum.* [*Or.*] Praetende domine fidelibus tuis . . . [*Secr.*] Propiciare domine supplicationibus nostris . . . [*Post Co.*] Da famulis et famulabus tuis . . . uellantur. Per.

Mass for the health of the living.

f. 5v   *Pro tribulacione et angustia.* [*Or.*] Deus sub cuius oculis . . . [*Or.*] Deus refugium pauperum spes . . . consolatos. Per.

Mass in tribulation.

Pro uiuis et defunctis. [*Or.*] Omnipotens sempiterne deus qui uiuorum do-

minaris . . . [*Secr.*] Deus cui soli cognitus est . . . [*Post Co.*] Purificent nos
quaesumus omnipotens et misericors deus . . . omnium delictorum. Per.

Mass for the living and dead.

f. 5v *Missa generalis.* [*Or.*] Pietate tua quaesumus domine nostrorum solue
uincula . . . omnesque affinitate et familiaritate nobis coniunctos et omnes
christianos a uiciis purga//

General Mass for the living and dead.

Parchment. 5 folios. Fol. 1 measures 191 x 153 mm; fol. 2, 193 x 152 mm; fol. 3,
206 x 154 mm; fol. 4, 184 x 155 mm; fol. 5, 185 x 154 mm (written space 155 x 120
mm). 1 column. 35 lines. Dry-point ruling. Double vertical bounding lines. Prickings in upper, lower, and outer margins.

Written in small late Caroline minuscule. Initials for masses on fols. 1–3 are 2-
to 5-line square capitals or uncials in red, written on the inner vertical bounding
line; on fols. 4–5 they are 1-line capitals in red. Other 1-line initials are in red and
are set apart from the text when they occur at the beginning of a line. The rubrics,
many rubbed and illegible, are written in red minuscule. Guide words for the rubricator are written in brown minuscule in the outer margins of fols. 4 and 5. Occasional chants have interlinear neumes in the St. Gall style. Punctuation consists
of the punctus and punctus elevatus.

A bifolium from this manuscript is now a flyleaf in the binding of Lambach,
Stiftsbibliothek, Cml XXXI. Fol. 1 of this bifolium is consecutive with Beinecke fol.
4, with the visible portion containing prayers for the ninth through the twenty-
third Sundays after Pentecost and votive masses. Fol. 2 contains a portion of the
common of saints. Further fragments from the same manuscript are preserved as
sewing supports in the binding of Burgess MS 25 in the University of Oregon Library, Eugene, Oregon. MS 25 comes from Lambach, cf. Faye and Bond, 431, item
1; and Sotheby's, *Catalogue of Important Literary and Mediaeval Manuscripts*, London, 12 November 1929, lot 387 (the fragments from the sacramentary are not
mentioned in the Sotheby's nor in the Faye and Bond description).

Fol. 1 was formerly Zinniker 245A; fol. 2 was Zinniker 245B; fol. 3 was Zinniker
246; fol. 4 was Beinecke 482.56A, Zinniker 34; and fol. 5 was Beinecke 482.56B,
Zinniker 37.

Bibliography:
Babcock, *Reconstructing a Medieval Library*, 92 and fig. 29.

MS 481.93
Lambach, Austria, s. XII^{ex}
Augustine, _Tractatus in Iohannis Evangelium ccxxiv_   Pl. 54

f. 1   [Inc: Non parua quaestio est cur apostolo petro . . . ac]//tio informata meę
          passionis exemplo . . . nec ille in principio uerbum domini apud deum et
          cetera de christi//

          Augustine, _Tractatus in Iohannis evangelium ccxxiv_, Tractatus 124.5.111–
          7.19; R. Willems, ed., CCSL 36 (1954), 686–87.

Parchment. 1 folio. 275 x 183 mm (written space 196 x 116 mm). 1 column. 31
lines. Dry-point ruling.

Written in late Caroline minuscule by Gottschalk, a monk from the abbey of
Lambach, Austria, whose hand appears in a number of other manuscripts, including Beinecke MS 481.51 (see the description of Beinecke MS 481.51 and Davis,
Epiphany, 173–78). In the upper left corner of the verso is a faint sketch of a cat (or
possibly a wolf or lion), probably contemporary with the manuscript (see Babcock,
fig. 27). 1-line initials are in brown rustic capitals. Punctuation consists of the
punctus and punctus elevatus.

The Lambach library catalogue in Cml XIX includes the item "Super Iohannem
duo vol"; Holter suggests that the first of these volumes is Lambach, Stiftsbibliothek, Cml L, which contains Tracts 1–45 (see Holter [1956], 273, nos. 68–69
and MBKÖ, 5:57; Cml L is briefly described by Holter [1959], 240). The Beinecke
leaf was the penultimate leaf of volume two, which contained the remaining Tracts,
46–124.

The leaf was used as the wrapper of a volume measuring ca. 135 x 93 mm.
Zinniker 171.

Bibliography:
Babcock, _Reconstructing a Medieval Library_, 102 and 104 and figs. 15 and 27.

MS 481.94
Germany, s. XII^{in}
Isidore's _Differentiae_, etc.   Pl. 54

ff. 1–2   //mouetur sed per tranquillitatis mansuetudinem . . . ista uero boni operis
          transituri merces est et requies.//

          Isidore, _Differentiae_, Book II.31.112–34.131; PL 83.87–90.

f. 3r   //humanę suspitionis sententiam proponit cum dicit . . . et hoc post modum ex spirituali ueritate diffiniuit.

        Gregory, *Dialogorum libri IV*, Book 4.4; PL 77.325.

f. 3r–v   [D]e duodecim lapidibus qui in rationali ponuntur . . . Et uos igitur onix esse potestis si studeatis habere//

        Unidentified commentary on Exodus 28.17–20 (On the Twelve Stones). The lower margin has been trimmed with loss of text.

f. 4r   Epistola [*illegible*: domini nostri iesu christi desc]endens de cęlo super altari sancti petri in ierusalem . . . resurrectio mea neque festiuitates sanctorum meorum.

        Letter Fallen From Heaven, added by a different hand of s. XII^2. The text does not end, but fol. 4v is blank. The Letter from Heaven was supposedly written by Christ and dropped on the altar of St. Peter's in Jerusalem. It concerns the proper observance of Easter. The version found here is very similar to the text found in a manuscript from Erfurt (A. Stumpf, "Historia Flagellantium, praecipue in Thuringia," *Neue Mittheilungen aus dem Gebiete historisch-antiquarischer Forschungen* 2 [1835]: 1–37, here 9–10; see also H. Delehaye, "Note sur la Légende de la Lettre du Christ tombée du ciel," *Bulletin de la Classe des Lettres de l'Académie royale de Belgique*, vol. 1 [1899]: 171–213, here 190).

Parchment. 4 folios (2 bifolia: 1/4 and 2/3). 175 x 125 mm (written space 150 x 100 mm). 1 column. 34 lines. Dry-point ruling on the hair side. Double vertical and single horizontal bounding lines. Prickings in upper, lower, and outer margins.

Written in late Caroline minuscule. The initials and the rubrics for the chapters have not been added; the initials would have been written between the vertical bounding lines. The first word following this initial is written in brown rustic capitals. Other 1-line initials are written in brown rustic capitals and are set apart from the text between the vertical bounding lines when they occur at the beginning of a line. Punctuation consists of the punctus. The Letter from Heaven was added to fol. 4r by a different hand later in the twelfth century.

The bifolia were used in the binding of a volume measuring ca. 235 x 164 mm.

A modern hand has written in pencil in the lower right corners the number "43" on fol. 1r, "44" on fol. 2r, "45" on fol. 3r, and "42" on fol. 4r.

Zinniker 259 A–B.

MS 481.95
Antiphonary

Germany, s. XIII
Pl. 55

f. 1r   //domini euouae. A. Corpora sanctorum in pace ... A. Martires domini
         dominum ... A. Martirum chorus laudate ... *v*. Mirabilis deus in. *Ad B.*
         A. Isti sunt sancti qui ... sanctorum qui assidue as//[sistunt]

Common of Martyrs, lauds.

f. 1v   [R. Laeta]//mini in domino et ... V. Et gloriamini omnes ... *Ad vi^a^. R.*
         Exultent iusti in conspectu ... V. Et delectentur in ... *Ad ix^a^. R.* Iusti
         autem imperpetuum [*sic*] ... V. Et apud dominum ... *Ad vesperas super ps.*
         ant. Iustorum autem anime. *Ps.* Dixit dominus. *Ps.* Laudate pueri. *Ps.*
         Credidi. *Ps.* In conuertendo. *Ps.* Eripe me. *v.* Letamini. *Ad Mag. ant.* [Ab-
         sterget deus omnem] lacrimam ... *Ca.* Magnificat. euouae. *In commune*
         unius confessoris extra tempus paschale ad vesperas v. Amauit eum dominus
         ... *Ad Mag. A.//*

Common of a Confessor, from terce to second vespers.

Parchment. 1 folio (small portion of conjugate leaf with some text is also preserved). 270 x 150 mm (width of written space 148 mm). 1 column. 7 lines remaining. Ruled in lead.
    Written in two sizes of gothic script (littera textualis). 1- and 2-line initials at
the beginning of chants are in brown highlighted with red. Rubrics are written in
red in the same script as the text. Square musical notation in black on four-line red
staff. The Psalms, versicles, and some rubrics are written in a smaller script in boxes
set apart from the staves. Punctuation consists of the punctus. Hyphenation is in
the same ink as the text.
    This fragment was once used as a wrapper for a volume measuring ca. 115 x 75
mm.
    Zinniker 267A.

MS 481.96
Bible commentary (in Latin and Middle High German)

Germany, s. XIII
Pl. 55

f. 1   //exorbitantes arcem et sensu hiberas uenias hyspanicas uanitates res ...
         adulteratur autem admixta resina siue gummi. Sed dinoscitur thus sua
         proprietate nam igni inponitum//

Commentary and glosses on the Prologue to the Pentateuch through Exodus 30.34. The commentary consists of lemmata from the Bible followed by explanations of the meaning and origin of the words, occasionally in Middle High German; many passages are taken from Isidore's *Etymologiae*. Upper margin trimmed with loss of text.

f. 2   [Malum punicum . . .] //corticis rotunditatem granorum in se contineat multitudinem . . . Iota unum aut unus apex. iota est graeca littera. Apex//

Commentary and glosses on Song of Songs 4.3 through Matt. 5.18. Upper margin trimmed with loss of text.

Parchment. 2 folios (1 bifolium). 180 x 132 mm (width of written space 130 mm). 2 columns. 51 lines remaining. Ruled unevenly in ink; single vertical bounding lines. Prickings in outer margin.

Written in a very small, heavily abbreviated gothic bookhand (littera textualis). 1-line initials are written in brown and are not set apart from the text. Punctuation consists of the punctus.

The bifolium was used in the binding of a volume measuring at least 285 x 180 mm. The number "1477" is written in ink in the lower margin of fol. 2r. The inscription "hic est solus liber" is written in the lower margin of fol. 2v. A modern hand has written in pencil in the lower right corners the number "77" on fol. 1r and "78" on fol. 2r.

Zinniker 270.

MS 481.97   Germany, s. XIII
Breviary   Pl. 56

f. 1r   *De sanctis post pascha tiburcii et valeriani.* Praesta quaesumus omnipotens ut qui sanctorum martyrum . . . imitemur.

Sts. Tiburtius and Valerian (14 April).

f. 1r   *Sotheri et Gaii.* Beatorum martyrum pariter . . . martyrum.

Sts. Soter and Caius (22 April).

f. 1r   *In festa sancti georgii martyris.* Deus qui nos beati georgii . . . *Lectio prima.* Cum primates multarum [sic; *for* militarium] gentium . . . celos fecit. *Lectio ii.* Quo audito iussit . . . in celis coronatus quiescit. . . .

St. George (23 April). The lessons are from a version of the *Passio S. Georgii* (cf. BHL 3383f).

f. 1r–v   *Marci ewangeliste*. Deus qui beatum marcum … [illegible: *Lectio prima* …] Sic ergo beatus marcus ewangelista primus martyr alexandrie ibidem quiescit in domino cui est honor et gloria in saecula saeculorum amen.

St. Mark (25 April). The lessons are similar to the latter half of the *Passio S. Marci*, ed. Mombritius, 174–75 (BHL 5276).

f. 1v   *Cleti*. Cletus natione romanus de regione uico patricii … cessauit episcopatus dies uiginti.

St. Cletus (26 April). The lesson is from the *Liber pontificalis*, ed. T. Mommsen, MGH *Gesta romanorum pontificum* (Berlin, 1898), 6.

f. 1v   *Vitalis martyris*. Praesta quaesumus omnipotens deus. ut intercedente beato uitale … *Lectio prima*. Aput Reuennam [*sic*] ciuitatem natale sancti uitalis martyris … quod arboris palme illic erant.

St. Vitalis (28 April). The lesson is from the Martyrology of Ado; J. Dubois, ed., *Le Martyrologe d'Adon* (Paris, 1984), 135–36.

f. 1v   *De sanctis a pasca usque pentecosten siue plures fuerint siue unus officium tali ordine celebretur*. Stabunt iusti in magna … *ymni qui competunt ad festum*. Rex gloriose. *v*. Sancti et iusti … *Ad m*. Lux perpetua lucebit. *oratio quae spectat ad diem dicatur. Inuitat*. Exultent in domino … *ymnus*. Eterna christi. *in i° n°*. Stabunt iusti in magna … [Ps.] Beatus uir. [Ps.] Quare. [Ps.] Domine qui. *v*. Sancti et iusti … *Sermo sancti ambrosii*. Dignum et congruum est fratres ut gaudia nostra … R. Beatus uir qui … V. Gloria et diuicie … L. *ii*. Qui enim socii sunt contumelie debent … R. Tristicia uestra alleluia … V. Mundus autem gaudebit … L. *iii*. Annuntiemus inquam cum sanctis martyribus … R. Priciosa [*sic*] in conspectu … V. Custodit dominus omnia … *In ii° n°*. Ecce quomodo conputati … [Ps.] Domine quis. [Ps.] Conserua. [Ps.] Domini est. *v*. Lux perpetua lucebit … [L.] … eadem resurrectio martires suscitat que et dominum suscitauit. Nam sicut uiam passionis eius experti sunt … De quibus sanctus ewangelista ait. Multorum sanctorum corpora surrexerunt cum eo. et introierunt//

Common of Saints. The lessons are from Pseudo-Ambrose, Sermon 61 (PL 17.728–29) = Pseudo-Maximus Taurinensis, *Sermones*, Sermon 86

(PL 57.703) = Alan of Farfa, Homily II. 97 (see Grégoire, 186); CPL 221. A later hand has added several antiphons for the common of saints in the lower margin of fol. 1v.

f. 2r   //ualde desidero martyres certantes. Festinans itaque ad locum beatissimos alium suspensum per pedes igne supposito . . . ista enim tormenta quae pro diuinitatis amore patimini temporalia sunt et quasi in momenta trans-euntia.

          Lesson for unidentified martyrs.

f. 2r   *Potentiane virginis*. Rome sancte potentiane virginis. Que illustrissimi generis pudentis discipuli sancti pauli apostoli filia . . . ad christum mi-grauerunt.

          St. Pudentiana (19 May). The lesson is from the Martyrology of Ado; ed. Dubois, 164–65.

f. 2r   *Urbani pape et martyris*. Da quaesumus omnipotens deus ut qui beati urbani . . . *L. i.* Urbanus natione romanus ex pontiano sedit . . . et cessauit episcopatus dies [xxx.]

          Pope Urban I (25 May). The lesson is from the *Liber pontificalis*, ed. Mommsen, 22–23.

f. 2r   *Eleutherii martyris*. Eleuterius natione grecus ex patre habundio de opido nicopolim . . . sepultus est iuxta corpus beati petri in uaticano vii. kal. iunii.

          St. Eleutherius (26 May). The lesson is from the *Liber pontificalis*, ed. Mommsen, 17.

f. 2r   *Iohannis pape*. Iohannes tuscus ex patre constantino sedit annos duos . . . uicarium beati petri apostoli suscepisse cum gaudio et gloria.

          Pope John I (27 May). The lesson is from the *Liber pontificalis*, ed. Mommsen, 133–34 (col. b).

f. 2r   *Felicis pape*. Felix natione romanus ex patre constantino sedit annos duos . . . et cessauit episcopatus dies quinque.

          Pope Felix I (30 May). The lesson is from the *Liber pontificalis*, ed. Mommsen, 37.

f. 2r–v   *Petronilla.* Petronillam bene nostis uoluntate petri apostoli . . . cuius corpus uia ardeatina sepultum.

St. Petronilla (31 May). The lesson is from the *Vita SS. Petronillae et Feliculae* (BHL 6061).

f. 2v   *Petri et marcellini.* Petrus exorcista pro nomine iesu multotiens . . . atque manibus angelorum susceptas ad celum ferri gaudentes ubi cum deo patre et filio et spiritu sancto uiuit et regnat. Per omnia.

Sts. Peter and Marcellinus (6 June).

ff. 2v–3r   *Primi et feliciani.* Temporibus diocleciani et maximiani inperatorum seua fuit . . . ab urbe miliariario [*sic*] tertiodecimo ibique passi sunt martyres christi. *Coll.* Deus qui nos annua beatorum marcellini et petri atque herasmi . . . *Collecta.* Fac nos quaesumus domine sanctorum tuorum primi et feliciani . . . sentiamus.

Sts. Primus and Felician (9 June), with a collect for Peter and Marcellinus. The lesson is from the *Passio SS. Primi et Feliciani* (BHL 6922); Mombritius, 411–14.

f. 3r   *Barnabe.* Deus qui nos beati apostoli tui Barnabe . . . consequamur.

St. Barnabas (11 June).

f. 3r   *Basilidis. cirini et.* Sanctorum martyrum tuorum. Basilidis. cirini. naboris. et nazari quaesumus . . . crescat. Per.

Sts. Basilides, Quirinius, Nabor, and Nazarius (12 June).

f. 3r   *Viti et modesti.* Da ecclesie tue quaesumus domine, sanctis tuis uito modesto . . . *L. i.* In prouincia lucana sub tempore diocletiani et maximiani imperatorum multas uirtutes operabatur . . . Quam dulcia faucibus meis eloquia tua domine super mel et fauum.

Sts. Vitus and Modestus (15 June). The lesson is from the *Passio SS. Viti et Modesti* (BHL 8713).

f. 3r   *Marci et marcelliani.* Praesta quaesumus omnipotens deus ut qui sanctorum tuorum marci et marcelliani . . . *L. i.* Ambrosius christi seruus fratribus per omnem ytaliam in domino eternam salutem. In diuinis uoluminibus reus ascribitur qui non studuerit . . . manibus extensis orantes.

Sts. Mark and Marcellian (18 June). The lesson is from Pseudo-Ambrose's *Passio SS. Gervasii et Prothasii* (Epistola 2; PL 17.743; BHL 3514); perhaps its placement with Mark and Marcellian is a mistake, since it is immediately followed by a prayer for Gervase and Protase.

f. 3r   *Geruasii.* Deus qui nos annua sanctorum martyrum tuorum geruasii et prothasii sollempnia . . . exemplis.

Sts. Gervase and Protase (19 June). See also the lesson for the previous feast.

f. 3r–v   *Iohannis baptiste.* [A.] Ipse precedet ante illum . . . [Ps.] Dixit dominus. [A.] Iohannes est nomen . . . [Ps.] Confitebor. A. Ex utero senectutis . . . [Ps.] Beatus uir. [A.] Iste puer magnus . . . [Ps.] Laudate pueri. [A.] Nazareus uocabitur puer . . . [Ps.] Laudate dominum. Audite insule et attendite populi . . . Vt queant. *v.* Fuit homo missus . . . *Ad m.* Ingresso zacharia . . . *coll.* Deus qui praesentem diem honorabilem in beati iohannis . . . *Inuit.* Regem praecursoris dominum . . . *Ant.* Priusquam te formarem . . . [Ps.] Beatus vir. [A.] Ad omnia quae mittam . . . [Ps.] Quare. [A.] Ne ti[meas] a facie . . . [Ps.] Dominus qui. *v.* Fuit homo. *L. i.* Post illum sacri [sic] domini natalem diem nullus [sic] hominis natiuitatem legimus celebrari nisi solam beati iohannis baptiste . . . *R.* Fuit homo missus . . . *V.* Erat iohannes in deserto . . . *L. ii.* In aliis consummata ultimi diei merita celebrantur . . . *R.* Elizabet zacharie magnum . . . *V.* Fuit homo missus . . . *L. iii.* Quod autem nondum natus de secreto . . . *R.* Priusquam te formarem . . . *V.* Vir dilectus a deo . . . *In ii^o n^o.* Misit deus manum . . . [Ps.] Verba. [A.] Dominus ab utero . . . [Ps.] Domine deus. [A.] Inter natos mulierum. *L. iiii.* Quod autem iohannes in carcere constitutus . . . *R.* Descendit angelus domini . . . *V.* Iste puer magnus . . . *L. v.* Quid est quod iohannes uocem esse dicit . . . *R.* Hic est praecursor . . . *V.* Ipse peribit ante illum . . . *L. vi.* Vides angelos que audierunt non que usurpauerunt . . . *R.* Innuebant patri eius . . . *V.* Apertum est os . . . *in iii^o n^o.* Posuit os meum . . . [Ps.] Domine quis. A. Formans me ex utero . . . [Ps.] Domine in uirtute. [A.] Reges uidebunt et consurgent . . . [Ps.] Benedicam. Elizabeth Zacharie. *Lectio sancti evangelii secundum lucam.* In illo. Elizabeth inpletum est tempus pariendi . . . *Ambrosii.* Peperit ergo filium helizabeth et congratulabantur . . . *R.* Praecursor domini uenit . . . *V.* Ipse enim propheta . . . *L. viii.* Pulchre autem tempore quo fuit in utero propheta . . . *R.* Gabriel angelus apparuit zacharie . . . *V.* Erit enim magnus . . . *L. viiii.* Et ideo in ewangelio nichil super eo legimus nisi ortum eius . . . Te deum uel *R.* Ecce constitui te . . . *V.* Tu puer propheta altissimi u[oca]beris praeibis enim//

St. John the Baptist (24 June), from vespers to the third nocturn of matins. The lessons for the first two nocturns are from Pseudo-Augustine, Sermon 196 (PL 39.2111–13) = Pseudo-Maximus Taurinensis, *Sermones*, Sermon 65 (PL 57.661) = Alan of Farfa, Homily II.37 (see Grégoire, 173; CPL 868). The lessons for the third nocturn are from a homily on Luke 1.57 from the *Lectionarium romanum*.

f. 4r   [A. Ego plantavi . . . incre]//m[entu]m dedit. [V.] Vnusquisque propriam mercedem . . . [A.] Libenter gloriabor in infirmitatibus . . . [V.] Quando autem infirmor . . . [A.] Gratia dei in me . . . [V.] Gratia dei sum . . . [A.] Damasci praepositus gentis . . . [V.] Deus et pater domini . . . [A.] Ter uirgis cesus . . . [V.] Nocte et die in profundum . . . [R.?] Bonum certamen. [A.] Tu es uas . . . [A.] Vos qui secuti . . . Deus qui multum(?). [A.] Bonum certamen. In omni terra. *vi.* Ne magnitudo tribulationum extollat me . . . *ad ix.* Ego sum minimus apostolorum . . . R.(?) Nimis honorati. Iurant [*sic*] dominus. Dixit dominus etc. Audite. *In octaua sancti iohannis ut supra.*

St. Paul (30 June), from lauds to nones.

f. 4r   Nuntiatum est paulino uiro clarissimo officiorum magistro. eo quod processus et martynianus christiani essent effecti . . . quem beatus petrus et paulus apostoli predicauerunt. *Col.* Deus qui nos sanctorum tuorum processi et martiniani . . . intercessione gaudere.

Sts. Processus and Martinian (2 July).

f. 4r   *Per octauam omnia de apostolis. Ew.* Hoc est praeceptum. R. Ecce ego mitto. *Ad laud.* Iam non estis. Exultet. *Ad B.* Petrus apostolus et paulus. *In uesperis.* Iurauit dominus. *An.* Gloriosi principes. *Lectio i[a].* Cum uenisset paulus romam, iudei accurrentes ut legem circumcisionis in qua natus fuit defenderent . . . Tunc nero dixit symoni. puto uicto sumus.

Octave of Sts. Peter and Paul. Fol. 4v is too stained to be read; it contains lessons for the feast of Sts. Felix and Philip (10 July).

Parchment (fols. 1r and 4v badly rubbed and stained). 4 folios (fols. 1 and 4 are a bifolium and fols. 2 and 3 are a bifolium; fols. 2 and 3 formed the inner bifolium of a quire). Fol. 1 measures 228 x 157 mm; fol. 2, 220 x 146 mm; fol. 3, 220 x 153 mm; fol. 4, 232 x 147 mm (written space 190 x 128 mm). 2 columns. 56 lines. Ruled in ink; single vertical bounding lines. Prickings in the outer and upper margins.

Written in two sizes of gothic script (littera textualis), below the top line. 1- to 5-line initials are in red and are written on the vertical bounding line when they occur at the beginning of a line. Other 1-line initials are in black highlighted with red. Rubrics are written in red in the same script as the text. Liturgical directions are written in brown minuscule, sometimes underlined with red. Psalm incipits are underlined with red. Punctuation consists of the punctus. Hyphenation is in the same ink as the text.

The bifolia were used in the binding of a volume measuring ca. 232 x 146 mm. Bifolium 1/4 was the outside wrapper.

Fols. 1/4 were formerly Zinniker 127B; fols. 2/3 were formerly Beinecke MS 482.87A, Zinniker 116.2.

MS 481.98   Southern Germany, s. XIII^2
Calendar   Pl. 56

f. 1   //K *Ianuarius habet xxxi. luna xxx* . . . C. *ii. k.* Constantini martyris//

            January; includes "Herhardi episcopi" (8 January); on 3 January a later hand has added "Albertus sacerdos obiit" and "R[. . .] miles ob[iit]" and on 19 January "Gedraut Valchenb( ) obiit."

f. 2   //K *Iunius habet dies xxx. luna xxviii* . . . F. *ii. k. Festum sancti Pauli*//

            June; on 13 June a later hand has added "Aniversarius Gotfridi sacerdotis."

Parchment (fol. 1r is badly stained from binding use). 2 folios. 204 x 149 mm (written space 160 x 120 mm). 16 lines. Ruled in ink.

Written in gothic script (littera textualis) in red and black ink. The first column consists of the letters A through G, representing the days of the week, written in black capitals except for the letter A in red. The next two columns specify the day of the month and are written in red minuscule. The last column contains the names of saints in black minuscule, with major saints in red minuscule.

These leaves were used as pastedowns in the binding of a volume measuring ca. 204 x 149 mm. A modern hand has written in pencil in the lower right corners the number "98" on fol. 1v and "97" on fol. 2r.

Fol. 1 was formerly Beinecke MS 482.89, Zinniker 91; fol. 2 was Zinniker 271.

MS 481.99
Casus Breves Decretalium Gregorii IX

Italy, s. XIII[2]
Pl. 57

The text appears to be closely related to Bernard of Parma's *Casus longi super quinque libros decretalium* (printed: Basel, Michael Wenssler, not after 1479=GKW 4093); the commentary paraphrases Bernard but is much abbreviated (see J. F. Schulte, *Die Geschichte der Quellen und Literatur des Canonischen Rechts*, vol. 2: *Von Gratian bis auf Papst Gregor* [Graz, 1877], 114–17 and 492–94).

ff. 1–2 //enim effectum hoc idem ut [some words trimmed] tota decinent arregando. Nota. quod ex libro sunt superflua resecanda sed decretales quae non tenent sunt superflue . . . Nota. quod postulatio soli gratie nitit etiamsi a toto .c. fuerit celebreta//

Unidentified epitome of the *Decretales* of Gregory IX, Prologue and Book I.1.1–I.3.18 (fol. 1), I.3.20–I.5.3 (fol. 2); E. Friedberg, ed., *Corpus iuris canonici*, vol. 2: *Collectiones decretalium* (Leipzig, 1922), coll. 5–24. The upper margin has been trimmed with loss of text.

ff. 3–4 //ut infra sequitur. Nota. quod sus cui datur eligendi potestas eligat . . . Significauit. Nota. eum puniri qui ut caste uiuere ualeat sibi facit uirilia amputari. Nota. eum re//

Epitome of *Decretales* I.3.20–I.5.3 (fol. 3); I.9.11–I.14.4 (fol. 4). The upper margin has been trimmed with loss of text.

f. 5 //ut lite pendente. Nota. quod sint pendente non est aliquis priuandus iure suo . . . Nota. quod si quis probauerit aliquos esse fratres et ego possum probare contrarium et adtestacionibus publicatis debet exaudire et//

Epitome of *Decretales* II.16.1–II.20.26. The lower margin has been trimmed with loss of text.

f. 6 //Ad uires. Nota. quod una ecclesia potest in alterius parrochia . . . contra alios quam eos contra quos conspirauerant (*con* add. man. alt.) ad testimonium admittuntur quod est bene notandum. Nota. quod dominus//

Epitome of *Decretales* II.26.6–II.27.22. The lower margin has been trimmed with loss of text.

Parchment. 6 folios (fols. 1 and 4, fols. 2 and 3, and fols. 5 and 6 form bifolia). Fol. 1 measures 203 x 119 mm; fol. 2, 251 x 170 mm; fol. 3, 225 x 173 mm; fol. 4, 203 x 173 mm; fol. 5, 189 x 104 mm; and fol. 6, 188 x 163 mm (written space originally ca. 215 x 135 mm). 2 columns. 46–49 lines remaining (portions of 55 lines on fol. 2). Ruled in lead.

Written in a small, highly abbreviated gothic script (littera textualis). There are guide letters and spaces for rubrics and initials, but none have been added. A fourteenth-century hand has added some rubrics in brown in a cursive gothic script. Punctuation consists of the punctus.

The bifolium 5/6 was used in the binding of Lambach Cml LXIV, now Beinecke MS 699 (see figs. 6–7 in Babcock, *Reconstructing a Medieval Library*); the shelf number "64" is marked on fol. 6v. Fragments of other leaves are still in the binding of MS 699. The bifolium 1/4 may have been taken from the binding of Lambach Cml LVII, which has the same measurements as the fragment (290 x 205 mm). The bifolium 2/3 was used as a flyleaf in a volume measuring ca. 345 x 225 mm. Another leaf from this manuscript, containing commentary on I.36.9–I.40.1, is now a flyleaf in Vienna, Österreichische Nationalbibliothek, s.n. 3610 (formerly Lambach Cml CXIII).

A modern hand has written in pencil in the lower right corners the number "82" on fol. 1r, "80" on fol. 2r, "79" on fol. 3r, "81" on fol. 4r, "84" on fol. 5r, and "86" on fol. 6r.

Fols. 1/4 were formerly Beinecke MS 482.90B, Zinniker 36; fols. 2/3 were Zinniker 273; fols. 5/6 were Beinecke 482.90A, Zinniker 30.

Bibliography:
Babcock, *Reconstructing a Medieval Library*, 114 and figs. 6–7.

MS 481.100   France (?), s. XIII
Commentary on Luke   Pl. 57

f. 1   //Lu. vi. Estote ergo misericordes sicut et pater uester misericors est. No-
         lite iudicare et non iudicabimini. Nolite condempnare et non condemp-
         nabimini. Dimittite et dimittetur uobis. date et dabitur uobis . . . uidimus
         eum percussum a deo et despectum qui leprosum terre et in//

         Unidentified commentary on Luke 6.36–38.

f. 2   //Sic contingit quod spiritualiter [*corr. from*: ad litteram] nouitii con-
         sumunt bona claustri dum alicui administrationi praefitiuntur . . . cum
         mansuetudine serua animam//

         Unidentified commentary on Luke 15.13–19.

Parchment. 2 folios. 289 x 215 mm (written space 230 x 170 mm). 2 columns. 51 (fol. 1) and 58 (fol. 2) lines. Ruled in lead (very faint). Single vertical and double horizontal bounding lines.

Written in a small, highly abbreviated gothic script (littera textualis currens). 1-line initials in black are not set apart from the text. Punctuation consists of the punctus. Accents added by a later hand.

These leaves were used as flyleaves in the binding of Lambach, Stiftsbibliothek, Ccl 48 (shelf number "48" on fol. 1r). A brief description of Lambach Ccl 48, with no mention of the fragments, is in Holter (1959), 255.

A modern hand has written in pencil in the lower right corner the number "85" on fol. 1r and "86" on fol. 2r.

Fol. 1 was formerly Zinniker 227; fol. 2 was Beinecke MS 482.85, Zinniker 15.

Bibliography:
Babcock, *Reconstructing a Medieval Library*, 114 and fig. 33.

MS 481.101   Germany, s. XIII/XIV
Gradual   Pl. 58

f. 1r   *//Siluestri sancti pape.* Sacerdotes tui domine induant . . . *Ps.* Memento domine dauid . . . *Gra.* Ecce sacerdos magnus . . . *V.* Non est inuentus . . . *Off.* Inueni dauid seruum . . . *Co.* Beatus seruus quem . . . eum.

St. Silvester (31 December).

f. 1r–v   *Mauri abbatis.* Os iusti meditabitur . . . *Ps.* Noli emulari in malignantibus . . . *Gra.* Iurauit dominus et . . . *V.* Dixit dominus domino . . . *Off.* Gloria et honore . . . *Co.* Posuisti domine in capite . . . precioso.

St. Maurus (15 January).

ff. 1v–2r   *Marcelli pape.* Statuit ei dominus . . . *Ps.* Misericordias domini in eternum . . . *Gra.* Inueni dauid seruum . . . *V.* Nichil proficiet inimicus . . . *Off.* Ueritas mea et . . . *Co.* Domine quinque talenta . . . tui.

St. Marcellus (16 January).

f. 2r–v   *Prisce uirginis.* Loquebar de testimoniis . . . *Ps.* Beati inmaculati in uia . . . *Gra.* Specie tua et . . . *Off.* Propter ueritatem. *Co.* Feci iudicium et . . . habui.

St. Prisca (18 January).

f. 2v   *Fabiani et sebastiani.* Intret in conspectu . . . *Ps.* Deus uenerunt gentes . . .
         Gra. Gloriosus deus in sanctis . . . *V.* Dextera tua domine . . . *Co.* Mul-
         titudo lang//[uentium]

         Sts. Fabian and Sebastian (20 January).

Parchment. 2 folios (1 bifolium). 245 x 195 mm (written space 225 x 151 mm). 1
column. 12 lines. Ruled in ink; double vertical bounding lines.
    Written in gothic script (littera textualis). 2- and 3-line initials at the beginning
of each feast are in blue with red penwork or red with blue penwork. 2-line chant
initials alternate red and blue. 2-line initials of gradual verses and of Psalms are in
brown highlighted in red. Rubrics are written in red minuscule. Punctuation consists of the punctus. Hyphenation is in the same ink as the text. Musical notation
on 4-line staves whose lines alternate yellow, green, red and green.
    The bifolium was used as a wrapper for a volume measuring ca. 213 x 170 mm.
Zinniker 118.

MS 481.102   Southern Germany or Austria, s. XIII^ex
Gradual   Pl. 58

f. 1r   //Ecce dominus ueniet . . . Benedictus es super thronum sanctum regni//

          Feria VI of the fourth week of Advent; Saturday of the fourth week of
          Advent. The page is mostly illegible because of stains from binding use.
          The bottom half of the leaf has been trimmed off with loss of text.

f. 1v   //Memento nostri domine in beneplacito populi . . . *Ps.* Peccauimus cum
          patribus . . . *Gr.* Prope est dominus. Alleluia. *V.* Ueni domine et noli
          tardare . . . *Off.* Aue maria gracia plena . . . *Co.* Ecce uirgo concipiet.

          Fourth Sunday of Advent.

f. 1v   *In uigilia natiuitatis domini.* Hodie scietis quia . . . *Ps.* Domini est terra . . .
          Gr. Hodie scietis quia . . . *V.* Qui regis israhel . . . *Off.* Tollite portas prin-
          cipes . . . *Co.* Reuelabitur gloria domini . . . dei nostri.

          Christmas Eve (24 December).

f. 1v   *In gallicantu officium.* Dominus dixit ad me ... *Ps.* Quare fremuerunt ...
            G. Tecum principium//

            Christmas (25 December). The bottom half of the leaf has been trimmed
            off with loss of text.

f. 2r   //*v.* Uenientes [*sic, for* uidentes] autem uenient ... *Off.* Offerentur. *Co.*
            Qui me dignatus ... deum uiuum.

            St. Agatha (5 February).

f. 2r   *Valentini martyris.* In uirtute tua ... *Ps.* Magna est gloria ... G. Beatus uir
            qui ... V. Potens in terra ... Alleluia. Beatus uir qui timet. *Tractus.* Desi-
            derium anime eius ... V. Quoniam preuenisti eum ... V. Posuisti super
            caput ... *Of.* In uirtute tua ... *Co.* Magna est gloria.

            St. Valentine (14 February).

f. 2r   *In kathedra sancti petri.* Statuit ei. G. Iurauit dominus. *Tractus.* Tu es pet-
            rus ... V. Et por[tae inferi non preualebunt] aduersus [eam] tibi dabo
            claues regni celorum//

            Chair of Peter (22 February). The bottom half of the leaf has been
            trimmed off with loss of text.

f. 2v   //Iustus ut palma. G. Os iusti. *Tractus.* Desiderium. *Of.* Posuisti. *Co.*
            Fidelis.

            Unidentified Mass.

f. 2v   *In annunciatione.* Rorate celi. G. A ssummo (*sic*) celo. *Tractus.* Audi filia.
            Of. Aue maria. *Co.* Ecce uirgo.

            Annunciation (25 March).

f. 2v   *Rudberti episcopi.* Statuit ei. Per totum. *Tractus.* Beatus uir qui timet.

            St. Rupert (27 March).

f. 2v   *Dominica i*^{a} *in lxx.* Circumdederunt me gemitus ... *Ps.* Diligam te domine
            ... *Gr.* Adiutor in oportunitatibus ... V. Quoniam non in finem ... *trac-*
            tus. De profundis clamaui ... V. Fiant aures tue ... V. Si iniquitates ... V.

Quia aput te ... *Off.* Bonum est confiteri ... *Co.* Illumina faciem tuam ... inuocaui te.

Septuagesima.

f. 2v   *Dominica in lx.* Exurge quare obdormis ... ne repellas in//

Sexagesima.

Parchment. 2 folios. Fol. 1 measures ca. 160 x 203 mm; fol. 2 measures 152 x 203 mm (written space originally ca. 235 x 167 mm). 1 column. 19 lines remaining of original ca. 30. Ruled in ink; single vertical bounding lines. Prickings in upper and outer margins.

Written in gothic script (littera textualis). 2-line initials of major feasts (and 1-line initials of abbreviated feasts on fol. 2v) are in red uncials and are not set apart from the text. 1-line chant initials are brown highlighted with red. Rubrics are written in red in the same script as the text. Punctuation consists of the punctus. Hyphenation is in the same ink as the rubrics. Interlinear neumes in the St. Gall style.

These fragments were used as a pastedown (fol. 1) and flyleaf (fol. 2) in the binding of Lambach, Stiftsbibliothek, Ccl 337. The shelf number "337" is marked on fol. 2r; both leaves have the pencil notations "337P", probably made when the leaves were removed from the binding. The inscription "Sermones ..." is written on fol. 1r. In the margin of fol. 2v, a thirteenth- or fourteenth-century hand has written "[Hunc] librum comparauit [...]us de Monte [Orate] pro eo."

The number "108" is written in pencil in a modern hand in the lower right corner of fol. 2r and the number "109" is in the lower right corner of fol. 1v.

Fol. 1 was formerly Zinniker 227; fol. 2 was Beinecke MS 482.93, Zinniker 46.

Bibliography:
Babcock, *Reconstructing a Medieval Library*, 114 and fig. 32.

MS 481.103   Perugia, Italy, 14 July 1235
Charter of Gregory IX   Pl. 59

Gregorius episcopus seruus seruorum dei. Venerabilibus fratribus archi-episcopis et episcopis et dilectis filiis abbatibus et aliis ecclesiarum prelatis ad quos littere iste peruenerint ... de ipsis habendo fiduciam quod cum spiritu uiuant, spiritu et ambulent, se operarios in uinea domini debeant inconfusibiles exhibere. Datum Perusii ii. Id. Iulii. pontificatus nostri anno nono.

Papal mandatum (*litterae cum filo canapis*) to archbishops, bishops, etc., commanding that Franciscan friars be received charitably. The docket on the verso reads "Gregorius 9 fratres undique benigne recipiant." We have not found the text in A. Potthast, *Regesta pontificum* (Berlin, 1874–75), nor in L. Auvray, *Les Régestes de Grégoire IX* (Paris, 1896–1955).

Parchment. 1 folio. 250 x 215 mm (written space 169 x 232 mm). 1 column. 13 lines. Ruled in dry-point on the flesh side.

Written in chancery script. Large initial "G" and 1-line capitals are in brown. Punctuation consists of the punctus. Hyphenation is in the same ink as the text. The rope for the seal is at the bottom of the document. There are no chancery marks or signatures under the fold.

A modern hand has written "Gregor IX 492981" on the verso in pencil. Zinniker 141.

MS 481.104   Italy, s. XIV
Canon law   Pl. 59

Based on rubrics and content, the text seems to be a commentary on chapters of either Innocent IV's third collection of Decretals from the first Council of Lyon in 1245 (cf. J. D. Mansi, *Sacrorum Conciliorum Nova et Amplissima Collectio*, vol. 23 [Venice, 1779], coll. 651–74); or the Sixth Book of Decretals of Pope Boniface VIII (cf. E. Friedberg, *Corpus Iuris Canonici*, vol. 2, *Collectiones decretalium* [Leipzig, 1922], coll. 933–1124). Rubrics of various medieval collections of canon law can be found in S. Kuttner, *Index Titulorum Decretalium ex Collectionibus tam Privatis quam Publicis Conscriptus*, Ius Romanum Medii Aevi, Subsidia 2 (Milan, 1977).

f. 1r   //litteras et tunc inpedit litis contestatio. verbi gratia aliquis litteras in-
         petrans ut reciperetur in canonicum et in fraternitatem alicuius ecclesie
         excipitur contra litteram . . . sic fiunt finis est iuramentum .i. de iii. et iii.
         etsi christus.

         Commentary on *De litis contestatione*, Innocent chap. 14 (Mansi, col. 655)
         or Boniface chap. 2.3 (Friedberg, coll. 997–98).

f. 1r–v *De testibus rubrica*. Presencium nomine suo. sed numquid est neccesarium
         quoddam si praelatus hoc iuramentum de ueritate dicenda exibeat . . . et
         hoc innuit iste textus. postmodum super quolibet articulo etc.

         Commentary on *De testibus*, Innocent chaps. 19–20 (Mansi, col. 656) or
         Boniface chap. 2.10 (Friedberg, coll. 1002–3).

f. 1v   *De exceptionibus rubrica.* Pia communibus actibus appellatione contrarium
         actiuum intelligo omnem actum ... et excommunicato non sit suarum
         administratio interdicta sine//

         Commentary on *De exceptionibus*, Innocent chap. 21 (Mansi, col. 658) or
         Boniface chap. 2.12 (Friedberg, coll. 1003–6).

Parchment. 1 folio. 405 x 256 mm (written space 342 x 200 mm). 2 columns. 73
lines. Ruled in lead (very faint).
    Written in gothic script (littera textualis) with frequent abbreviations. 2-line
chapter initials are in red and are written on the vertical bounding line. 1-line initials within text are in brown capitals. Rubrics are written in red minuscule. Guide
letters for the rubricator are in the margins. Punctuation consists of the punctus.
    A modern hand has written "saec. XIII" in pencil in the lower right corner of fol.
1r.
    Zinniker 131.

MS 481.105
Justinian, *Digesta*, with commentary

Italy, s. XIV
Pl. 60

f. 1   //decretum habuit; cessat edictum. nam statuit uerbum ... Idem. libro.
         Patris adoptiui parentes impune uocabit quoniam hi eius parentes//

         Justinian, *Digesta*, 2.2.1–4; edd. T. Mommsen and P. Krueger, *Corpus iuris
         civilis* (Berlin, 1928), 1:47–48 (42.32–43.29). The commentary surround-
         ing the text seems to be a compilation of the *Glossa ordinaria* of Accursius
         and other works.

Parchment (the verso is badly stained and damaged from use in a binding; there is
a large hole in the center of the leaf). 1 folio. 370 x 240 mm (written space of text
of *Digest* 180 x 115 mm; written space of surrounding commentary ca. 362 x 225
mm). 2 columns. 37 lines of text. 89 lines of commentary. Ruled in lead.
    Written in gothic script (littera textualis). 3- to 7-line initials of each chapter are
orange on a dark blue ground, decorated with light blue, white, and yellow, and are
not set apart from the text. 2- to 3-line initials of the names of the authorities are
blue highlighted with red and are set apart from the text. 1-line initials following
the authorities are red highlighted with blue. Other 1-line initials within text are
brown and are frequently distinguished by paragraph marks which alternate red and
blue. Rubrics are written in red minuscule. A running title "ii" is in red in the
center of the upper margin of the recto. Punctuation consists of the punctus and

punctus elevatus. The text is written in the center of the page and is surrounded by two columns of commentary in the same hand. Other hands have added notes on the text or commentary in the margins.

The fragment was used as a wrapper for a volume measuring ca. 205 x 145 mm. Zinniker 137.

MS 481.106   Southern Germany, s. XIII
Lectionary   Pl. 60

f. 1r   //uniuersas abhominationes . . . operati sunt. Hec dicit.

Ezechiel 33.29.

f. 1r–v   *Feria v^a*. Et factum est uerbum . . . pastores semet [ipsos] Hec dicit.

Ezechiel 34.1–10, for Feria V of an unidentified feast.

f. 1v   *Feria vi^a*. [. . . Vos autem greges . . .] Ecce ego iudicabo inter pecus et pecus . . . pro eo quod lateribus et hu//[meris]

Ezechiel 34.17–21, for Feria VI of an unidentified feast.

Parchment. 1 folio. 276 x 200 mm (written space originally ca. 300 x 208 mm). 2 columns. 21 lines remaining of original ca. 23. Ruled in lead; single vertical bounding lines.

Written in large gothic script (littera textualis). 1- and 2-line lesson initials are in red and are written on the vertical bounding line. 1-line initials within text are in black traced or dotted with red. Rubrics are written in red minuscule with capital R. Punctuation consists of the punctus and punctus elevatus. Hyphenation is in the same ink as the text.

The fragment was once used as a pastedown in the binding of a volume measuring ca. 276 x 190 mm. A seventeenth-century hand has added the inscriptions "B L3N.15" and "Johan hauman von [*word illegible*] Joh. Bapt." in the upper margin of the verso. Another hand has added the number "Lin 3 N97." Modern hands have added the numbers "54317" in pencil in the upper right corner of the verso and "M106" in the lower left corner of the verso. The last inscription is by the same hand that wrote "M103" on Beinecke MS 481.68 and "M105" on Beinecke 481.70.

Zinniker 138.

MS 481.107
Canticles (from a Breviary)

Germany, s. XIII
Pl. 61

f. 1r   //Calcaui eos in furore ... auxiliata est michi.

        Isaiah 63.3–5. Canticle for the Octave of Easter (?).

f. 1r   *Aliud.* Uenite et reuertamur ... plus quam holocaustum.

        Hosea 6.1–6. Canticle for the Octave of Easter (?).

f. 1r–v   *Item aliud.* Expecta me dicit ... qui exterreat.

        Zephaniah 3.8–13. Canticle for the Octave of Easter (?).

f. 1v   *De apostolis et martiribus.* Vos sancti domini uocabimini ... et odio habens rapi//

        Isaiah 61.6–8. Common of Apostles and Martyrs.

Parchment. 1 folio. 308 x 207 mm (written space 231 x 155 mm). 1 column. 25 lines. Ruled in ink; single vertical and double horizontal bounding lines. Additional vertical bounding line in outer margin.

    Written in large gothic script (littera textualis), above the top line. 3-line lesson initials are in red and are written on the vertical bounding line. 1-line verse initials are in red and are set apart from the text. Rubrics are written in red minuscule. Punctuation consists of the punctus and punctus elevatus. Hyphenation is in the same ink as the text. Line fillers following rubrics are in red.

    The fragment was used as a pastedown in a binding
Zinniker 103.

MS 481.108
Noted Missal (Sequentiary and Sacramentary)

Germany, s. XIII[1]
Pl. 61

f. 1r   [*Or.* Deus qui beatum matthiam ...inter]//uencione tue ... *Secr.* Deus qui prodi[to]ris ... C[*omplendum*]. Praesta quaesumus omnipotens et misericors deus; ut per haec ... pacem. Per.

        St. Matthias (24 February).

f. 1r–v   *Gregorii pape.* [*Or.*] Deus qui animę famuli tui Gregorii . . . [*Secr.*] Annue
           nobis domine ut animę . . . *Complendum.* Deus qui beatum Gregorium . . .
           exempla. per.

           St. Gregory (12 March).

f. 1v   *Benedicti abbatis.* [*Or.* I]ntercessio nos quaesumus domine beati Benedicti
           . . . *Sec.* [O]blatis domine beati Benedicti . . . *Compl.* [R]eceptis tui cor-
           poris et sanguinis domine . . . eternis. Per.

           St. Benedict (21 March).

ff. 1v–2r   *In annunciatione s. marie.* [*Or.*] Deus qui hodierna die uerbum tuum
           . . . *Secretum.* In mentibus nostris domine . . . *Comp.* Gratiam tuam domine
           mentibus nostris . . . perducamur. Per.

           Annunciation (25 March).

f. 2r   *In lxxm^a.* [*Or.*] Preces populi tui quaesumus domine clementer . . . *Se-
           cretum.* Muneribus nostris quaesumus domine precibusque . . . *Conpl.* Fi-
           deles tui deus per tua dona . . . percipiant. Per.

           Septuagesima Sunday.

f. 2r–v   *Dominica ii^a.* [*Or.*] Deus qui conspicis quia . . . *Secretum.* Oblatum tibi do-
           mine sacrificium . . . *Complendum.* Suplices [*sic*] te rogamus omnipotens
           . . . concedas. Per.

           Sexagesima Sunday.

f. 2v   *Dominica iii^a.* [*Or.*] Preces nostras quaesumus domine clementer . . . *Se-
           cretum.* Hęc hostia domine quaesumus emundet . . . *Complendum.* Quae-
           sumus omnipotens deus; ut qui cęlestia . . . muniamur. Per.

           Quinquagesima Sunday.

ff. 2v–3r   *In Capite Ieivnii.* [*Or.*] Praesta domine fidelibus tuis . . . *Secretum.* Fac
           nos quaesumus domine . . . *Prefacio. UD* eterne deus. Qui corporali te.
           Complendum. Percepta [nobis] domine praebeant . . . *Super populum.* In-
           clinant[es] domine maiestati tuę . . . auxiliis. Per.

           Ash Wednesday.

f. 3r–v   *Feria v*^{a}. [*Or.*] Deus qui culpa offenderis . . . *Se*[cr.] Sacrificiis presentibus
domine quaesumus intend[e pla]catus . . . [*Compl.*] Celestis doni bene-
dictione percepta . . . *Super Populum.* Parce domine parce populo tuo . . .
respirent. Per.

Feria V before Quadragesima.

f. 3v   *Feria vi*^{a}. [*Or.* In]choata [iei]unia quaesumus domine benigno fauore . . .
Se. [Sac]rificium domine obseruancie paschalis . . . *Complendum.* Spiritum
[nob]is domine tuę caritatis . . . *Super populum.* [Tu]ere domine populum
tuum . . . iniquitas. Per deum.

Feria VI before Quadragesima.

f. 3v   *Sabbato.* [*Or.* P]reces nostras. *ut supra. Super populum.* Adesto quaesumus
domine supplicacionibus . . . custodi. Per.

Saturday before Quadragesima.

f. 4r   *Dominica in xlma.* [*Or.*] Deus qui ęcclesiam tuam annua quadragesimali
obseruacione . . . *Secretum.* Sacrificium quadragesimalis inicii . . . *Complendum.* Tui nos domine sacramenti libacio . . . consorcium. Per.

First Sunday of Quadragesima.

f. 4r–v   *Feria ii*^{a}. [*Or.*] Converte nos deus salutaris noster . . . *Secretum.* Munera
domine oblata sanctifica . . . *Complendum.* Salutaris tui domine munere
. . . *Super populum.* Absolue quaesumus domine nostrorum uincula . . .
auerte. Per.

Feria II of the first week of Quadragesima.

f. 4v   *Feria iii*^{a}. [*Or.*] Respice domine familiam tuam et praesta . . . *Secretum.*
Oblatis nos domine placare muneribus . . . *Complendum.* Quaesumus omnipotens deus; ut illius salutaris . . . *Super populum.* Ascendant ad te domine . . . nequiciam. Per.

Feria III of the first week of Quadragesima.

f. 4v   *Feria iiii*^{a}. [*Or.*] Preces nostras quaesumus domine clementer . . . *Alia.*
Deuocionem populi tui . . . qui per absti//[nentiam]

Feria IV of the first week of Quadragesima.

f. 5r   //quod a stirpe dauid exit ... deo iunctus homini.

Sequentia de evangelistis; AH 55.6.

f. 5r–v   *De appostolis.* [H.] Clare sanctorum senatus apostolorum princeps ... su-
plex inpendit.

Common of Apostles; St. Gall Hymnal; von den Steinen, 80; AH 53.228;
Schaller-Könsgen 2352.

f. 5v–6r   *De martyribus.* [H.] Agone triumphali militum regis summi dies ... com-
mendare cu[rate.]

Common of Martyrs; St. Gall Hymnal; von den Steinen, 82; AH 53.229;
Schaller-Könsgen 499. The outer margin of fol. 6 has been trimmed with
loss of text. At the bottom of fol. 6r a cursive hand of the second half of
the thirteenth century has written a Latin sequence beginning "Digni
dignis fulgent signis ..." (= AH 55.14, verses 3, 5, 6, 7, 9, 10 on which
see Keith E. Mixter, "A Newly Discovered Medieval Polyphonic Sequence," *Musica Disciplina* 44 [1990]: 233–53). RH II.12670.

f. 6r–v   *De uirginibus.* [H.] Exultent filie syon in rege suo ... tu nos tuere.

Common of Virgins; AH 50.271; RH 5780. The outer margin has been
trimmed with loss of text.

f. 6v   *In dedicacione ecclesie.* [H. P]sallat ecclesia mater illibata et uirgo ... trinitati laus et glo[r]ia semper resultent.

Dedication of a church; St. Gall Hymnal; von den Steinen, 74; AH
53.247; Schaller-Könsgen 12723. The outer margin has been trimmed
with loss of text.

f. 7r–v   *De sancta maria.* [H.] Ave preclara maris stella ... ad te transire.

Mary; AH 50.241; RH 2045.

f. 7v–8r   *Alia.* Ave maria gratia plena ... collocet per secula.

Mary; AH 54.216; Schaller-Könsgen 1544. The outer margin of fol. 4 has
been trimmed with loss of text.

f. 8r–v   *De sancta mar[ia. H.]* Gaude mater luminis . . . in solio o maria.

Mary; AH 54.225; RH 6871. The outer margin has been trimmed with loss of text.

f. 8v   *Alia.* [H. G]aude maria templum summe . . . Ubi te sanc[torum] con-templantur populi [*sic*]. Alleluia Hec est speciosior sole et celo [. . .]ior o regina glorie audi [. . .]s ecclesie. *Alia.//*

Mary; AH 54.213; RH 6830. Most versions of this hymn end with "sanc-torum contemplantur oculi." The addition "Alleluia . . . ecclesie." appears to be unique. The outer margin has been trimmed with loss of text. In the lower margin of fol. 8v a hand writing in a cursive gothic script of the fourteenth century has written "virginis que nos lauit a labe omnis cele-bratur hodie."

Parchment. 8 folios (bifolia 1/4 and 2/3 form the inner two bifolia of a quire; bifolia 5/ 8 and 6/7 form the inner two bifolia of another quire). Fol. 1 measures 208 x 124 mm; fol. 2, 221 x 145 mm; fol. 3, 221 x 120 mm; fol. 4, 208 x 145 mm; fol. 5, 185 x 141 mm; fol. 6, 213 x 126 mm; fol. 7, 213 x 143 mm; fol. 8, 188 x 119 mm (writ-ten space 170 x 105 mm). 1 column. 19 lines. Ruled in lead (very faint).

Written in early gothic script (littera textualis). 4-line initial "D" ("Deus") for the Annunciation (fol. 1v) is outlined in red with an interlace pattern and filled with blue and red on a square ground outlined with red; it is not set apart from the text. The letters of the words following this initial alternate in red and brown un-cials, and the third word is written in brown rustic capitals traced with red. 3- to 6-line initials for other feasts and for hymns are in red with red penwork and are writ-ten on the vertical bounding line. The letters of the word after the initial and the first letter of the following word are written in brown rustic capitals traced with red. 1-line initials of prayers and of hymn verses are in red and are not set apart from the text. Other 1-line initials are in brown rustic capitals traced with red. The word "maria" is written with an uncial M and capital R. Rubrics are written in red in the same script as the text. Punctuation consists of the punctus and punctus elevatus. The alleluia and prosula hymn following the "Gaude maria templum" has inter-linear neumes in the St. Gall style.

Bifolia 1/4 and 2/3 were glued to each other and formed a flyleaf in a volume measuring ca. 385 x 270 mm; bifolia 5/8 and 6/7 were also formerly glued to each other and formed a single flyleaf in a volume measuring at least 355 x 270 mm.

The bifolium 1/4 was formerly Beinecke MS 482.73A, Zinniker 103–1. The bifolium 2/3 was formerly Zinniker 133A. The bifolium 5/8 was formerly Zinniker 133B. The bifolium 6/7 was formerly Beinecke MS 482.73B, Zinniker 103–2.

MS 481.109
Sacramentary

f. 1   [UD et iustum est equum et salutare. nos tibi semper et ubique … ym] //num glorie tue … dicentes. *Infra.* Communicantes et diem sacratissimum … Hanc igitur oblationem seruitutis nostre … *De apostolis p.* UD equum et salutare. Te domine suppliciter … *De i̊ a.* UD eterne deus. Qui ecclesiam tuam in apostolicis tribuisti … *De sancta trinitate prefatio.* UD eterne deus. Qui cum unigenito filio tuo … *De sancta cruce.* UD eterne deus. Qui salutem humani generis in ligno … *De sancta maria.* UD. eterne deus. Et te in ueneratione … *Coitidiana [sic].* Per omnia secula seculorum amen. Dominus uobiscum … *prefatio.* UD et iustum est equum et salutare. nos tibi semper et ubique … Sanctus sanctus sanctus. dominus deus sabaoth … osanna in excelsis.//

Prefaces (De apostolis, De sancta trinitate, De sancta cruce, De sancta Maria, Ordo missae). On the lower margin of the verso a thirteenth-century cursive hand has written the *Secretum* "Suscipe sancta trinitas …" (cf. *Missale Romanum* [1899], 201 with some variations).

f. 2r   [*Or.* Excita domine potentiam tuam et ueni et magna …] //nostra peccata praepediunt … acceleret. Qui tecum. *Sec.* Sacrificiis praesentibus domine quaesumus placatus intende; ut et deuotioni … *Com.* Sumptis muneribus domine quaesumus; ut cum … effectus. Per.

Fourth Sunday in Advent (Dominica vacat).

f. 2r   *Thome apostoli.* [*Or.*] Da nobis quaesumus domine beati apostoli tui thome … *Sec.* Debitum domine nostre [*supr:*] reddimus … *Con.* Conserua domine populum tuum; et quem sanctorum … remediis. Per.

St. Thomas (21 December).

f. 2r   *Vigilia natiuitatis dei.* [*Or.*] Deus qui nos redemptionis nostre … *Se.* Da nobis quaesumus omnipotens deus; ut sicut adoranda … *Co.* Da nobis domine quaesumus unigeniti filii tui … potamur. Qui tecum.

Christmas Eve (24 December).

f. 2r–v   *In sancta nocte.* [*Or.*] Deus qui hanc sacratissimam noctem … *Se.* Accepta tibi sit domine quaesumus hodierne festiuitatis oblatio … *praef.* Qui per incarnati. Communicantes. *Co.* Da nobis quaesumus domine deus noster; ut qui natiuitatem … consortium. Qui tecum.

Christmas morning (25 December).

f. 2v *In mane.* [*Or.*] Da quaesumus omnipotens deus; ut qui noua . . . *Anastasie.* [*Or.*] Da quaesumus omnipotens deus; ut qui beate anastasie . . . *Sec.* Munera nostra quaesumus domine natiuitatis . . . *Sec.* Accipe quaesumus domine munera dignanter . . . [*Praef.*] Quia per incarnati. Communicantes et diem. *Com.* Huius nos domine sacramenti semper . . . *Co.* Saciasti domine familiam tuam . . . celebramus. Per.

St. Anastasia (25 December).

f. 2v *In die sancto.* [*Or.*] Concede quaesumus omnipotens deus; ut nos unigeniti tui noua . . . iugo uetusta seruitus//

Christmas (25 December).

f. 3r [*Com.*] //Sacramentorum tuorum domine . . . confirmet. Per.

St. Hippolytus (13 August).

f. 3r *Eusebii confessoris.* [*Or.*] Deus qui nos beati eusebii . . . *Secr.* Laudis tue domine hostias immolamus . . . *Comp.* Refecti cibo potuque celesti deus noster . . . precibus. Per.

St. Eusebius (14 August).

f. 3r *Vigilia assumptionis.* [*Or.*] Deus qui uirginalem aulam beate marie . . . *Sec.* Munera nostra domine aput clementiam tuam . . . *Com.* Concede misericors deus fragilitati . . . resurgamus. Per.

Vigil of the Assumption of the Virgin (14 August).

f. 3r–v *In die sancto.* [*Or.*] Famulorum tuorum domine delictis . . . *Secr.* Subueniat domine plebi tue . . . *Com.* Mense celestis participes effecti . . . liberemur. Per eundem.

Assumption (15 August)

f. 3v *Agapiti martyris.* [*Or.*] Letetur ecclesia tua deus beati agapiti . . . *Secr.* Suscipe domine munera que . . . *Com.* Saciasti domine familiam tuam . . . celebramus. Per.

St. Agapitus (18 August).

f. 3v   *Tymothei apostoli.* [*Or.*] Auxilium tuum nobis quaesumus domine . . . *Secr.*
          Accepta sit tibi domine sacrate . . . *Comp.* Diuini muneris largitate satiati
          . . . uiuamus. Per.

St. Timothy (22 August).

f. 3v   *Bartholomei apostoli.* [*Or.*] Omnipotens sempiterne deus qui huius diei . . .
          bartholomei festiuitate//

St. Bartholomew (24 August).

f. 4r   [*Super populum.* Omnipotens sempiterne deus qui] //nos omnium sanc-
          torum tuorum multiplici . . . aspectu. Per.

All Saints' Day (1 November).

f. 4r   *Cesarii martyris.* [*Or.*] Deus qui nos beati Cesarii . . . *Secr.* Hostias tibi do-
          mine beati Cesarii . . . *Com.* Quaesumus omnipotens deus; ut qui celestia
          . . . muniamur. Per.

St. Caesarius, martyr (1 November).

f. 4r   *Quatuor coronatorum.* [*Or.*] Praesta quaesumus omnipotens deus; ut qui
          gloriosos . . . *Sec.* Benedictio tua domine larga descendat . . . *Com.* Ce-
          lestibus refecti sacramentis . . . auxiliis. Per.

Four Crowned Martyrs (8 November).

f. 4r–v   *Theodori martyris.* [*Or.*] Deus qui nos beati Theodori . . . *Sec.* Suscipe do-
          mine fidelium preces . . . [*Com.*] Praesta nobis quaesumus domine inter-
          cedente . . . capiamus. Per.

St. Theodore (9 November).

f. 4v   *Menne martyris.* [*Or.*] Praesta quaesumus deus. ut qui beati Menne . . .
          Secr. Accepta tibi sit domine quaesumus . . . *Com.* Da quaesumus domine
          deus; ut sicut tuorum . . . aspectu. Per.

St. Mennas (11 November).

f. 4v   *Martini episcopi.* [Or.] Deus qui conspicis quia ex nulla ... *Sec.* Da mi-
         sericors deus ut hec nos ... *Com.* Praesta quaesumus domine deus noster
         ... reddantur. Per.

         St. Martin (11 November).

f. 4v   *Cecilie virginis.* [Or.] Deus qui nos annua beate Cecilie ... *Sec.* Hec hostia
         quaesumus domine placationis ... cecilia martyre tua//

         St. Cecilia (22 November).

Parchment. 4 folios (fols. 3 and 4 form a bifolium). Fol. 1 measures 259 x 210 mm;
fol. 2, 270 x 211 mm; fol. 3, 299 x 214 mm; fol. 4, 297 x 214 mm (written space
220 x 155 mm). 1 column. 24 lines. Ruled in lead (very faint). Double vertical
bounding lines.
    Written in early gothic script (littera textualis), above the top line. 2- to 3-line
Mass initials and UD are in red with red penwork and are written on the inner vertical bounding line. Initials of prayers are 1-line red uncial or square capitals and
are set apart from the text when they occur at the beginning of a line. Other 1-line
initials are in brown highlighted with red. Rubrics are written in red in the same
script as the text; instructions to the rubricator are in the outer margins. The first
word of each Mass is written in a mixture of rustic capitals and minuscule in brown
highlighted with red. Punctuation consists of the punctus and punctus elevatus.
Hyphenation is in the same ink as the text.
    Fols. 1 and 2 were each used as pastedowns in the binding of a volume meas-
uring at least 270 x 185 mm; both preserve green stains from a metal binding clasp.
The bifolium was used as a pastedown in the binding of a volume measuring at least
397 x 273 mm.
    Fol. 1 was formerly Zinniker 168B and fol. 2 was Zinniker 168A. The bifolium
3/4 was formerly Beinecke MS 482.71, Zinniker 111.

MS 481.110   France, s. XIII
Stephen Langton, Sermons   Pl. 62

f. 1r   //habentem diuitias. sed nimis diligentem male lucratur qui temporalia
         uenatur ... quod nobis praestare dignetur idem deus et dominus noster
         iesus christus etc.

         Unidentified sermon on St. Paul.

f. 1r–v   *De sancto paulo.* Surge et ingredire ciuitatem et dicetur tibi quid te oporteat facere uerbum illud sapientes egregium admodum auditoribus uerbi dei ... quo audito paulus tremens et stupefactus propter peccata praeterita.//

Stephen Langton, Sermon on the Conversion of St. Paul (25 January); this sermon is either Roberts 103b (see P. B. Roberts, *Studies in the Sermons of Stephen Langton* [Toronto, 1968], 189) or Sermon 17 of A. Barratt, "The Sermons of Stephen Langton. A New Manuscript," *Recherches de Théologie ancienne et médiévale* 43 (1976): 111–20; the Beinecke sermon has *egregium* like Robert's Sermon 103b, instead of Barratt's *egregii*, but it also has *illud* between *uerbum* and *sapientes* like Barratt's Sermon 17.

f. 2r   //putabis quae magis infestat uincenda superbia restat ... ut ipsa sicut stella maris huius id est mundi ad portum salutis nos perducat. Qui cum patre et cetera.

Unidentified sermon on the Annunciation (March 25).

f. 2r–v   *In annuntiatione tractatus.* Aperi soror mea amica mea columba mea ... ut recte transeuntes de hostio ad hostium ad ueram hostiam uite perueniamus.

Unidentified sermon on the Annunciation (March 25).

f. 2v   *De sancto iohanne baptista.* Posuit me dominus sicut sagittam electam sanctissimus ille miles christi ... iste autem erat repletus spiritu sancto in utero matris unde idem nuntiauit angelus scilicet ga//[briel]

Stephen Langton, Sermon on John the Baptist (24 June); Roberts, Sermon 72b (Roberts, *Studies in the Sermons of Stephen Langton*, 182).

Parchment. 2 folios (1 bifolium; fol. 1 is paginated "134" and "135", and fol. 2 is paginated "145" and "146"). 263 x 182 mm (written space 195 x 135 mm). 2 columns. 65 lines. Ruled in lead; single vertical and double horizontal bounding lines. Prickings are preserved in the inner margins.

Written in small gothic script (littera textualis), above the top line. 2-line and 6-line sermon initials are in red, except for the initial on fol. 1r, which is a 1-line capital in brown ink ("Surge"). 1-line initials are brown and are not set apart from the text. Rubrics are written in red in the same script as the text. Punctuation consists of the punctus, punctus elevatus, and punctus interrogativus. Hyphenation is in the same ink as the text.

Zinniker 108.

MS 481.111   France, s. XIII[2]
Quodlibetical text   Pl. 63

This text is not found in P. Glorieux, *La Littérature Quodlibetique de 1260 à 1320* (Kain, 1925–1935). Professor Timothy Noone of Catholic University, Washington, D.C. (letter in correspondence file), has suggested that the text seems heavily influenced by the metaphysical views of Henry of Ghent (fl. 1276–92), and may have been written by one of his students. It is not among the known works of Richard of Conington, who was "a great defender of Henry of Ghent in the late thirteenth century."

f. 1   //distinctio personalitatis in diuinis.
            43. Utrum in patre sit potentia passiva generandi . . . 44. Utrum esse realis
            uel actualis existentie [*supr*: creature] sit idem . . . De 4 sciendum breuiter
            quod aliud potest participare alio dupliciter sed subiectiue. sicut dicimus
            quod superficies participat//

            Quaestio 42 (portion), 43, 44, and perhaps more of an unidentified Quod-
            libetical text. The outer margin has been trimmed with loss of text.

f. 2   //potest ferri super ens dimittendo increabilem et similiter ex alia parte
            . . . 48. Utrum aliqua creatura sit immutabilis sed se et . . . 49. Utrum parte
            [. . .] . . . prout [. . .] diuise ideo etc.//

Parchment (fols. 1r and 2v faded and obscured by wood and glue from use in a binding). 2 folios (originally 1 bifolium). Fol. 1 measures 285 x 228 mm; fol. 2 measures 285 x 187 mm (written space 240 x 170 mm). 2 columns. 57 lines. Ruled in ink; single vertical bounding lines.

Written in a small, highly abbreviated gothic script (littera textualis). 2-line initials alternate red and blue, occasionally with red penwork, and are not set apart from the text. 1-line initials are in brown capitals, frequently preceded by a paragraph mark which alternates red and blue. Rubrics are written in red in the same script as the text. Punctuation consists of the punctus and the virgule. There are marginal corrections written in a contemporary cursive hand as well as numerous corrections within the main body of the text.

The bifolium was used as a pastedown in a volume measuring ca. 415 x 285 mm. Fol. 1 was formerly Zinniker 111. Fol. 2 was Beinecke MS 482.80, Zinniker 113.

MS 481.112   Italy, s. XIII^{med}
Thomas Aquinas, *Summa Theologiae*   Pl. 63

f. 1   //quod per successiones temporum creuit diuinae cognicionis augmentum. ... ratio uero uniuersalium non omnem quod [sit alius appetitus] debetur sensui//

Thomas Aquinas, *Summa Theologiae*, I.57.5–I.59.1; Thomas Aquinas, *Omnia Opera*, ed. Leonine Commission (Rome, 1889), 5: 79–92.

Parchment. 1 folio. 288 x 207 mm (written space originally ca. 273 x 200 mm). 2 columns. 67 lines remaining of original ca. 74. Ruled in ink; double vertical bounding lines at the outer sides of the columns.

Written in two different small, highly abbreviated gothic scripts, below the top line. The first hand, on the first seven lines of the recto, is a littera textualis. The second is littera textualis currens with occasional use of cursive *d*, frequent abbreviations, and wide word spacing. There are spaces for 2-line initials and for paragraph marks, but they have not been added. 1-line initials within text are brown. Punctuation consists of the punctus.

Zinniker 247.

Bibliography:
Dondaine, H. F. and H. V. Schooner, eds., *Codices manuscripti operum Thomae de Aquino*, 3 vols. (Paris, 1967–85), 3: 33, item 1960b.

MS 481.113   Germany, s. XIII^{med}
Wirnt von Gravenberg, *Wigalois* (Middle High German poem)   Pl. 64

f. 1   //die mich minnen daz si mir gewinnen ... daz sin nimmen wrde gewar. inner des//

Wirnt von Gravenberg, *Wigalois*, ll. 5589–701; J. M. N. Kapteyn, ed., *Wigalois der Ritter mit dem Rede, von Wirnt von Gravenberc*, Rheinische Beiträge und Hülfsbücher zur germanischen Philologie und Volkskunde 9 (Bonn, 1926), 235–39. The text of these leaves is also printed by Christa

Bertelsmeier-Kierst, "Zur ältesten Überlieferung des 'Wigalois': I. Die Handschrift E," *Zeitschrift für deutsches Altertum und deutsche Literatur* 121 (1992): 275–90, here 287–88.

f. 2   //lit; noch uf dem velde unbegraben . . . unze si da lagen bi im//

Wigalois, ll. 9849–965; Kapteyn, 417–21; Bertelsmeier-Kierst, 289–90.

Parchment. 2 folios. 150 x 100 mm (written space of fol. 1, 135 x 85 mm; written space of fol. 2, 138 x 87 mm). 1 column. Fol. 1 has 31 lines and fol. 2 has 33 lines. Dry-point ruling. Single vertical bounding lines. Prickings preserved in outer margins.

Written in gothic script (littera textualis). 1-line initials are in red uncials and are not set apart from the text. Other 1-line initials are in black highlighted with red. Punctuation consists of the punctus and punctus elevatus. The text is not written according to lines of verse.

Other leaves from the same manuscript are preserved in Freiburg, Universitätsbibliothek, 445 (1 bifolium), and Vienna, Österreichische Nationalbibliothek, Cod. 14612 (3 bifolia). See Bertelsmeier-Kierst, "Zur ältesten Überlieferung des 'Wigalois'."

The leaves were used in a binding. The lower margin of fol. 1r has an illegible inscription in a fifteenth-century German cursive gothic hand.

Zinniker 140 A–B.

MS 481.114   Southern Germany or Austria, s. XIV[1]
Antiphonary   Pl. 64

f. 1   [*Ps.* Quare] //fremuerunt. A. Filii hominum scitote . . . *Ps.* Cum inuo-
          carem. *v.* Letamini. R. Absterget deus omnem lacrimam . . . V. Iustorum
          anime in manu . . . R. Uiri sancti gloriosum . . . V. Unus spiritus et . . . R.
          Tradiderunt corpora sua . . . V. Isti sunt qui uenerunt . . . *In ii° n°.* A. Scuto
          bone uoluntatis . . . *Ps.* Uerba mea. A. In uniuersa terra . . . *Ps.* Domine
          deus noster. A. Habitabunt in tabernaculo . . . *Ps.* Deus quis habitabit. *v.*
          Exultent iusti. R. Sancti tui domine . . . V. Quoniam percussit petram . . .
          R. Uerbera canificum [*sic*] non . . . pro christi nomine//

          Common of Martyrs.

Parchment. 1 folio (paginated "321" and "322" in black ink in the upper center of each page; foliated "147" in red ink in the center of the upper margin and in the upper right corner of the recto). 383 x 280 mm (written space 282 x 210 mm). 1 column. 10 lines.

Written in gothic script (littera textualis). 4-line initial "A" ("Absterget") in red and blue and ornamented with red and blue penwork. Chant initials alternate as 2-line blue initials and 1-line red initials. Other 1-line capitals are in black. Rubrics are written in red minuscule. Musical notation is in black on 4-line staves in red. Punctuation consists of the punctus.

Zinniker 116.

MS 481.115   Germany, s. XIV[1]
Breviary   Pl. 65

f. 1ra   [R. Philippe qui uidet] //me uidet. et patrem meum . . . V. Domine ostende nobis . . . La. A. Domine ostende nobis . . . A. Phylippe qui uidet . . . A.
Tanto tempore nobiscum . . . A. Si cognouissetis . . . A. Si diligeritis me
. . . B. A. Si manseritis in me . . . In ves. A. Domine ostende. M. A. Non
turbetur cor . . . in me cre//[dite]

Sts. Philip and James (1 May), third nocturn of matins to second vespers.
The outer margin has been trimmed with the loss of most of the text in
the outer column.

f. 1vb   [Ps.] //Domine dominus noster. Ps. Domine in uirtute. Ps. Domini est
terra. v. Hoc signum crucis. Crisostomus in omelia xiii^a. Lectio prima. Si
nosse de cruce desideras karissime crucis uirtutem. audi quanta dicere
possum . . . R. Dulce lignum dulces . . . V. Hoc signum crucis erit . . . L. ii^a.
C[ru]x est murus obsessorum spes desper//[antium?]

Invention of the Cross (3 May), first and second nocturn of matins. The
lessons are similar to portions of a sermon by Chrysostomus latinus (PG
50.819). The outer margin has been trimmed with the loss of most of the
text in the outer column.

f. 2r   //ut expedicio astasii ualidi . . . geruasius respondit. Victoriam de celo
debes . . . dum spiritum exalaret. Lec. vi^a. Prothasius post hec adductus
cum in illo flecti posset . . . in domo sua. Lec vii^a. Horum corpora beatus
ambrosius apparente sibi uisione primo secundo et tercio reperit . . . Lec.
viii^a. Sanctus [?] ambrosius omnibus . . . Lec. ix^a. [illeg.] quorum capita
libellum inuenit . . . carnale cupientes. Tu.//

Sts. Gervase and Protase (19 June). Portions of the lessons are similar to
Pseudo-Ambrosius's Inventio et Passio SS. Gervasii et Prothasii (PL 17.746;
BHL 3514).

f. 2r–v *In vigilia sancti iohannis baptiste. L. i^a uel vii^a. si dominica fuerit secundum lucam.* Fuit in diebus herodis regis iudee sacerdos nomine zacharias . . . *Omelia venerabilis bedę presbiteri.* Ex iustis parentibus iohannes est genitus ut eo confidentius . . . *Lec. viii^a.* Redemptor etenim noster in carne apparens sicut rex nobis . . . *Lec. ix^a.* Melchisedech quippe ut legimus sacerdos dei summi . . . sanguis in nouo testamento offerendum instituit.

Vigil of John the Baptist (23 June). The lessons are from Bede, Homily II.19 (on Luke 1.5; D. Hurst, ed., CCSL 122, pp. 318–19).

f. 2v *Sancti iohannis baptiste fr. p. A.* Ingresso zacharia templum . . . *Capitulum.* Priusquam te formarem . . . gentibus dedi te. *R.* Inter natos mulierum. *ymnus.* Ut queant laxis resonare fibris mira gestorum . . . organa uocis. Uentris//

John the Baptist (24 June). The capitulum is from Jeremiah 1.5. On the hymn, see Schaller-Könsgen 16894.

Parchment (both folios are badly stained and worn from use as a binding). 2 folios (1 bifolium). 170 x 139 mm (written space 130 x 95 mm). 2 columns. 27 lines. Ruled in ink. Single vertical and double horizontal bounding lines.

Written in gothic script (littera textualis). 2- to 7-line initials alternate red with blue penwork and blue with red penwork. 1-line initials in red or in black highlighted with red. Rubrics are written in red in the same script as the text. Punctuation consists of the punctus.

The bifolium was used as the wrapper for a volume measuring ca. 151 x 95 mm.

A modern hand has written the number "78" in pencil in the upper right corner of fol. 1r.

Zinniker 130.

MS 481.116   Germany, s. XIV
Breviary   Pl. 65

f. 1r //sigillum tertium. audiui tertium animalium dicentium . . . [L.] Et cum apperuisset sigillum quartum audiui . . . sequebatur eum.

Feria III of an unidentified feast. The lessons are from Apoc. 6.5–8.

f. 1r *Feria quarta. L. i^a.* Et data est illi potestas . . . [L.] Et clamabant uoce magna . . . [L.] Et date sunt illis singule . . . sicut et illi.

Feria IV of an unidentified feast. The lessons are from Apoc. 6.8–11.

f. 1r   *Feria v^a. L. i^a.* Et uidi cum apperuisset sigillum sextum . . . [L.] Et stelle celi ceciderunt super terram . . . [L.] Et reges terre et principes . . . et petris montium.

Feria V of an unidentified feast. The lessons are from Apoc. 6.12–15.

f. 1r–v *Feria sexta. L. i^a.* Et dixerunt montibus . . . *Lectio ii^a.* Post hec uidi quatuor angelos . . . *Lectio iii^a.* Et uidi alterum angelum . . . frontibus eorum.

Feria VI of an unidentified feast. The lessons are from Apoc. 6.16–7.3.

f. 1v   *Sabbato. L. i^a.* Et cum apperuisset sigillum septimum . . . [L.] Et data sunt illi incensa multa . . . [L.] Et facta sunt tonitrua . . . in sanguinem. et missum est in//

Saturday of an unidentified feast. The lessons are from Apoc. 8.1–7.

f. 2r   [Inc: Ex multis sancti euangelii locis inuenimus quia discipuli ante ad]// uentum sancti spiritus minus capaces erant ad intelligenda archana diuine . . . R. Ponis nubem. [L.] Sed eis adueniente spiritu . . . R. Pater cum essem. [L.] Unde illis dominica passione nunc dicitur . . . R. Tempus est. [L.] Notandum autem inprimis . . . R. Nimis exaltatus es alleluia. alleluia. V. Super omnes celorum. *Ad ben. An.* Dum uenerit paraclitus . . . *Post benedicamus de ascensione. Ad horas alleluia. ut in superioribus dominicis. versus ut die ascensionis. Ad vesper. An.* Illi autem.

Sunday after Ascension. The lessons are from Bede, Homily II.16 (D. Hurst, ed., CCSL 122, p. 290).

f. 2r–v *Feria ii^a. Lectio. i^a.* Potest ecclesia omnis creature nomine . . . *L. ii^a.* In uiam gentium . . . [L.] Sed cum discipulos ad praedicandum . . . recipiat in messe. Tu.

Feria II after the Sunday after Ascension. The lessons are from a homily based on Gregory, *Homiliae xl in evangelia*, Homily II.29 (PL 76.1214; Inc: Quod resurrectionem dominicam discipuli tarde crediderunt . . .); R. Étaix, ed., CCSL 141 (1999), 244–54.

f. 2v   *Feria iii^a. L. i^a.* Etenim uniuerso mundo non tam fidelium . . . [L.] Unusquisque enim apud semetipsum . . . [L.] Qui crediderit et baptizatus fuerit

... condempnabitur.

Feria III after the Sunday after Ascension. The lessons are from a homily based on Gregory, *Homiliae xl in evangelia*, Homily II.29 (PL 76.1214); Étaix, 246.

f. 2v   *Feria iiii^a. L. i^a.* Uera etenim fides est ... [L.] Hinc est quod de quibusdam falsis fidelibus ... [L.] Hinc etiam est quod ait iohannes ... operibus implemus.

Feria IV after the Sunday after Ascension. The lessons are from a homily based on Gregory, *Homiliae xl in evangelia*, Homily II.29 (PL 76.1214–15); Étaix, 246–47.

f. 2v   *Feria quinta.* [L.] In die namque baptismatis omnibus nos antiqui ... [L.] Itaque unusquisque uestrum ... [L.] Ecce promisit quod minime ... plangat quod errauit.

Feria V after the Sunday after Ascension. The lessons are from a homily based on Gregory, *Homiliae xl in evangelia*, Homily II.29 (PL 76.1215); Étaix, 247.

f. 2v   *Feria vi^a.* [L.] Apud misericordem namque iudicem ... etiam postquam mentitur.//

Feria VI after the Sunday after Ascension. The lessons are from a homily based on Gregory, *Homiliae xl in evangelia*, Homily II.29 (PL 76.1215); Étaix, 247.

Parchment (fols. 1v and 2r are badly stained and holes have been worn in the parchment from use in a binding). 2 folios (1 bifolium). 195 x 147 mm (written space 145 x 108 mm). 2 columns. 27 lines. Ruled in ink. Single vertical and double horizontal bounding lines. Prickings preserved in outer margins.

Written in gothic script (littera textualis). 2- to 3-line initials alternate in red and blue and are written on the vertical bounding line. 1-line initials are in brown highlighted with red. Rubrics are written in red minuscule. Punctuation consists of the punctus. The quire mark "xiii" is in the center of the lower margin of fol. 1r.

This fragment was once used as the wrapper of a volume measuring ca. 170 x 115 mm.

A modern hand has written the number "33" in pencil in the outer margin of fol. 2v.

Zinniker 127A.

MS 481.117
Eberhardus Bethuniensis, *Graecismus*

France, s. XIV[1]

Pl. 66

f. 1   //A sum composita praeter tria non retinent ens . . . Passum uel caritum cassum natum libitumque//

Eberhardus Bethuniensis, *Graecismus*, 26.98–145; J. Wrobel, ed., *Eberhardi Bethuniensis Graecismus* (Breslau, 1887), 238–40.

f. 2   //Lo sic sola l per ui dic si duplices li . . . [*faded*: Sed sextum proprie donant pronomina quinque]//

Graecismus, 26.237–27.9; pp. 244–47.

Parchment. 2 folios. 202 x 140 mm (written space 130 x 58 mm). 1 column. 22 lines. Ruled in lead (very faint); double vertical bounding lines.

Written in gothic script (littera textualis). 3-line initials at the top of each page in black decorated with black penwork and highlighted with red. 2-line initial "P" in red. 1-line verse initials are in black highlighted with red. The text is written in verse lines, and all initials are written between the double bounding lines. Red paragraph marks appear immediately to the left of some initials. Punctuation consists of the punctus and is very rare.

The leaves were used as flyleaves in a binding. On fol. 1v a fifteenth-century German hand in gothic cursive referred to a portion of the contents of the volume by "Item sermones in isto libro de dedicatione templi . . . ." A modern hand has written the number "6" in the lower margin of both leaves.

Zinniker 139.

MS 481.118
Noted Missal

Klosterneuburg, Austria, s. XV/XVI

Pl. 66

f. 1   [Vere quia dignum et iustum est ut inuisibilem deus omnipotentem patrem . . .] //agnus occiditur eiusque sanguine postes . . . *Hic imponatur incensum in modum crucis.* In huius igitur noctis gracia . . . oblatione sollemni per ministrorum manus//

Holy Saturday (Exultet; Benedictio cerei).

Parchment. 1 folio. 391 x 298 mm (written space 305 x 212 mm). 1 column. 10 lines. Ruled in orange ink. Double vertical and horizontal bounding lines.

Written in gothic script in red ink (littera textualis), at Klosterneuburg according to Alois Haidinger. 2-line initials of each verse are in green. The rubric is written in red minuscule. Each word is separated by a green line. Punctuation consists of the punctus. Musical notation in gold outlined in black on 4-line staves in orange ink. The upper and lower margins are decorated with green foliage and penwork; the side margins are decorated with brown foliage and penwork.

Four leaves from the same manuscript are preserved at Klosterneuburg, Frag. 326.

Zinniker 114.

MS 481.119   Germany, s. XIV
Hymnal   Pl. 67

f. 1r   //iugi luceat. Deo patri.

          Unidentified hymn.

f. 1r   *Ad nocturnum.* Christe redemptor omnium ex patre ... nouum concinimus. Gloria tibi.

          Anon., s. VI (Christmas); AH 51.50; Schaller-Könsgen 2220.

f. 1r–v   *Ad laudes.* Agnoscat omne seculum venisse ... maria protulit. Gloria tibi domine qui natus es de uirgine cum patre.

          Venantius Fortunatus (Christmas); AH 50.71; Schaller-Könsgen 492.

f. 1v   A solis ortus cardine ad usque ... gratia uenter puelle ba//[iulat]

          Sedulius, *A solis ortus cardine* (Christmas); CSEL 10, p. 163; AH 50.53; Schaller-Könsgen 33.

Parchment. 1 folio. 289 x 208 mm (written space 225 x 145 mm). 1 column. 21 lines. Ruled in ink. Double vertical and horizontal bounding lines.

Written in large gothic script (littera textualis). 2-line hymn initials alternate red and blue. 1-line verse initials are in red and are not set apart from the text. Rubrics are written in red in the same script as the text; guides to the rubricator are written in the outer margin of fol. 1r in a cursive hand. Punctuation consists of the punctus. Hyphenation is in the same ink as the text. In the outer margin of fol. 1r a

fifteenth-century hand (littera cursiva libraria) has added the incipit for the hymn "Agnoscat omne seculum" several lines above where the text of the hymn begins.
Zinniker 134.

MS 481.120   Germany, s. XIV
Missal   Pl. 67

f. 1r   //*Alia*. Hostias tibi domine beati cesarii martyris . . . *Co.* Amen dico uobis quod uni . . . *Conpl.* Da quaesumus domine fidelibus populis . . . *Alia*. Huius nos domine percepcio . . . perducat. Per.

St. Caesarius of Arles (27 August).

f. 1r–v   *Pro infirmis*. Omnipotens sempiterne deus salus eterna . . . *Secreta*. Deus sub cuius nutibus . . . *Conpl.* Deus infirmitatis humane . . . mereatur. Per.

Mass for the sick.

ff. 1v–2r   *Pro iter agentibus*. Adesto domine supplicationibus nostris . . . *Sec.* Propiciare domine supplicacionibus . . . *Conpl.* Deus infinite misericordie . . . effectu. Per.

Mass for travelers.

f. 2r–v   *Pro uiuis et mortuis*. Omnipotens sempiterne deus qui uiuorum . . . *Sec.* Deus cui soli cognitus est . . . *Conpl.* Purificent nos quaesumus domine sacramenta . . . delictorum. Per.

Mass for the living and dead.

f. 2v   *De sancta anna*. Deus qui beate anne tantam gratiam//

St. Anne (26 July).

Parchment. 2 folios (folio numbers "xlix" and "l" are written in black ink in the top center of the verso). 195 x 150 mm (written space 150 x 100 mm). 1 column. 20 lines. Ruled in lead. Single vertical and horizontal bounding lines.
     Written in gothic script (littera textualis). 2-line initials at the beginning of Masses and 1-line initials at the beginning of prayers are in red and are not set apart from text. Other 1-line initials are in black highlighted with red. Rubrics are

written in red in the same script as the text. Punctuation consists of the punctus. Hyphenation is in the same ink as the text.

These leaves were once used as pastedowns in the binding of a volume measuring ca. 195 x 140 mm.

Zinniker 128 A, B.

MS 481.121   Italy, s. XIV
Missal   Pl. 68

f. 1r   [*Communio*. Dico uobis gaudium . . .] //angelis dei super uno . . . *Postcommunio*. Sacrificia tua nos domine . . . expiatos. Per.

Third Sunday after Pentecost.

f. 1r–v   *Dominica iiii^a. post pentecosten. introitus*. Dominus illuminatio mea . . . *Ps*. Si consistant aduersum . . . *v*. Gloria. *Oratio*. Da nobis quaesumus domine. ut et mundi cursus . . . *Pauli ad romanos*. Fratres. Existimo enim quod non sunt condigne passiones . . . *Gr*. Propitius esto domine peccatis . . . *V*. Adiuua nos deus deus salutaris . . . *V*. Deus qui iudicas equitatem . . . *Secundum lucam*. In illo tempore. Cum turbe irruerent in ihesum . . . *Off*. Illumina oculos meos . . . *Secreta*. Oblationibus nostris quaesumus domine placare susceptis . . . *Co*. Dominus firmamentum et refugium . . . *Post com*. Mysteria nos tua domine quaesumus . . . tueantur. Per.

Fourth Sunday after Pentecost.

f. 1v   *Dominica v^a. post penthecosten. introitus*. Exaudi domine uocem . . . *Ps*. Dominus illuminatio mea . . . *v*. Gloria. *Or*. Deus qui diligentibus te . . . *Beati petri apostoli*. Karissimi. Omnes unanimes in oratione . . . estis; ut be// [nedictionem]

Fifth Sunday after Pentecost.

f. 2r–v   [*Dominica viii^a. post pentecosten. Introitus*.] //Suscepimus deus misericordiam . . . *Ps*. Magnus dominus et . . . *v*. Gloria patri. *Oratio*. Largire nobis quaesumus domine semper spiritum . . . *Ad ro*. Fratres. Debitores sumus non carni; ut secundum carnem . . . *Gr*. Esto mihi in deum . . . *V*. Deus in te speraui . . . *V*. Magnus dominus et . . . *Secundum lucam*. In illo tempore. Dixit iesus discipulis suis parabolam hanc. Homo quidam erat diues . . . *Off*. Populum humilem saluum . . . *Secreta*. Suscipe munera quaesumus

domine que tibi ... *Co.* Gustate et uidete ... *Postcommunio.* Sit nobis
quaesumus domine reparatio ... effectum. Per.

Eighth Sunday after Pentecost.

f. 2v   *Dominica ix post penthecosten. introitus.* Ecce deus adiuua me ... *Ps.* Deus
         in nomine ... *v.* Gloria. *Oratio.* Pateant aures misericordie tue ... *Ad Ro.*
         Fratres. Non sumus concupiscentes malorum ... murmuraueritis//

Ninth Sunday after Pentecost.

Parchment. 2 folios (1 bifolium; folio numbers "44" and "47" are written in the
upper center margins of the recto; the numbers "xxxxiiii" and "xxxxvii" are written
in the upper right corners of the recto). 245 x 160 mm (written space 190 x 124
mm). 2 columns. 30 lines. Ruled in lead. Single vertical and horizontal bounding
lines.

   Written in gothic script (littera textualis). 2-line initials alternate red and blue
and are not set apart from the text; they are written over guide letters in black ink.
1-line capitals, which include the first letter after the 2-line initials, are in black
filled with yellow. Rubrics are written in red in the same script as the text. Punctuation consists of the punctus and punctus elevatus. Hyphenation is in the same
ink as the text.

   The fragment was used in the binding of a volume measuring ca. 150 x 105 mm,
with the title "Caterino Compendio d'errori" and shelf number "B14" (or "Bi4")
written on the spine. The title refers to the *Compendio d'errori* by Ambrosius Catha-
rinus Politus. An edition of this work was published in 1544 in Rome (*In Roma ne
la Contrada del Pellegrinus per M. Girolama de Cartolari, a instantia di M. Michele
Tramezino. MDXLIIII*), with two other tracts by the same author, the *Resolutione
sommaria contra le conclusioni luterane* and the *Reprobatione de la dottrina di frate
Bernardino Ochino.* Because the measurements of the edition of these three works
correspond closely to those of the volume bound by the Beinecke fragment, it is
likely that the Beinecke fragment was used as a binding for a copy of this edition.
   Zinniker 104.

MS 481.122   Germany, s. XIV
Prayers for the Dead (Rituale?)   Pl. 68

ff. 1–2   //opera; da seruis tuis illam ... Omnipotens senpiterne deus edificator et
           custos ... Ineffabilem misericordiam tuam nobis ... Praesta domine

quaesumus; ut anima famuli tui cuius [*with plural forms written above*] ...
Deus cuius miseratione anime fidelium ... Inclina domine aurem tuam ad
preces ... Quesumus domine pro tua pietate ... restitue. Per christum
dominum.

Prayers for the dead. Another fourteenth-century hand has added prayers
to the bottom of fol. 1r. The lower half of fol. 2v is blank.

Parchment. 2 folios. 190 x 137 mm (written space 135 x 105 mm). 1 column. 11
lines. Ruled in lead. Double vertical bounding lines. Prickings on outer and lower
margins.
    Written in large gothic script (littera textualis formata). 2- and 3-line initials are
in black with black penwork, some filled with red, and are written on the vertical
bounding lines. Punctuation consists of the punctus, punctus elevatus, and punctus
flexus. Hyphenation is in the same ink as the text. Line fillers are in black. A line
divider on fol. 2r is in the shape of a square with four compartments like a coat of
arms. One of the compartments contains the picture of a face.
    Zinniker 217 A, B. The number "14" is written in ink in the upper margin of fol.
1r.

MS 481.123   Spain, s. XV[1]
Aristotle, *Nicomachean Ethics*   Pl. 69
(Latin trans. by Leonardo Bruni Aretino)

Bruni (1369–1444) completed this translation between March 1416 and March
1417 (see H. Baron, *Leonardo Bruni Aretino: humanistisch-philosophische Schriften mit
einer Chronologie seiner Werke und Briefe* [Leipzig, 1928], 164); this is a very early
manuscript of the translation. The manuscript has extensive rubrication that is not
found in the 1469 edition. The chapter divisions also differ somewhat from that
edition.

f. 1r   //uidetur particeps rationis ut diximus. itaque p[aret] rationi continentis
        ... laudamus et sapientem [secundum] habitum habituum uero; eos qui
        laudabiles sunt; u[irtu]tes appellamus. *Explicit primus liber Ethicor[orum.]*

        Aristotle, *Ethica Nicomachea*, I.xiii.17–20; Leonardo Bruni Aretino, trans.,
        [Strassburg, Johann Mentelin, before 10 April 1469] (GKW 2367), fol.
        [b$_1$] recto–verso.

f. 1r   [Inci]*pit secundus qui est de uirtute in communi et continet trac[tatus] tres
        quorum primus est de causis effectiuis uirtu[tis] Capitulum primum quod uirtus*

moralis causetur in n[obis] ex operibus et primo proponit uirtutem moralem e[.]
nobis ex consuetudine operationum intellectiuam uero ex [. . .] Cum uero duplex sit [uirtus] alia intellectiua alia moralis . . . numquam assuesceret sursum ferri. non si milies//

Ethica Nicomachea, II.i.1–2; fol. [b₁] verso.

f. 1v   [sun]//t aliter assuesceret [t *added by corr.*] neque natura ergo . . . illo mo-
           do statim ab adolescentia consuescere.

           Ethica Nicomachea, II.i.2–8.; fols. [b₁] verso–[b₂] recto.

f. 1v   *[Capit]ulum secundum libri secundi tractatus primi Ethicorum.* [C]um igitur
           presens opus non contemplacionis gratia fiat . . . de actibus uidere qualiter
           agere illos//

           Ethica Nicomachea, II.ii.1; fol. [b₂] recto.

f. 2r   //innominate. Conandum autem [*corr. to:* tamen] est ut aliis . . . et eodem
           mo[do] de rationabilibus uirtutibus.

           Ethica Nicomachea, II.vii.11–16; fols. [b₅] verso–[b₆] recto.

f. 2r   *Tractatus secundus libri secundi de opposicione uirtutis et suorum uiciorum.*
           Cap[itulum.] Sed cum tres sint disposiciones; due quide[m] uiciorum in
           excessu et in defectu una u[ir]tutis que mediocritas est . . . et illi que
           media est et sibi ipsis inter se contra//[rie]

           Ethica Nicomachea, II.viii.1; fol. [b₆] recto.

f. 2v   [ex]//cedunt excessibus autem deficiunt et in affectibus [et] in actibus
           . . . magis graciam dicimus ad quam inclinacio magis fit. et ob//

           Ethica Nicomachea, II.viii.2–8; fol. [b₆] recto–verso.

f. 3r   //mediocritas alterius secundum excessum alterius secundum def[ectum]
           . . . qui parum excedit in alterutram partem; non uituper//[at]

           Ethica Nicomachea, II..ix.1–8; fols. [b₆] verso–[b₇] recto.

f. 3v   [i]//n singulis iudicium est quod et in sensu. Illud dumtaxat . . . sic enim
           facillime medium adipiscemur. *Explicit liber secundus.*

Ethica Nicomachea, II.ix.8–9; fol. [b₇] recto.

f. 3v   *Incipit liber tertius qui est de qui[b]usdam principiis actuum uirtutis. Continet
           tractatus [t]res quorum primus est de uoluntario electione consilio et uoluntate.
           Capitulum primum de inuoluntario per uiolenciam [e]t primo ostendit per rati-
           ones duas quod ad praesentem doctrinam [con]tinet determinare de uoluntario
           et inuoluntario.* Igitur cum uirtus circa affectus et actus uersetur . . . etenim
           principium mouendi organicas//

           Ethica Nicomachea, III.i.1–6; fol. [b₇] recto–verso.

f. 4r   //est cum in eorum potestate fuerit ne ebrii fierent . . . enim diligentiam
           adhibere.

           Ethica Nicomachea, III.v.8–9; fol. [c₁] recto.

f. 4r   *Capitulum decimum libri tertii eth[icorum.]* Sed forsan talis quis ut diligens
           esse ne[que]at . . . in aliis quoque uicia que culpantur in nostra potestate.
           Capitulum undedecimum libri tertii ethico[rum.]

           Ethica Nicomachea, III.v.10–16; fol. [c₁] recto–verso.

f. 4v   //quis sui habitus quodam modo causa ipse sibi est . . . ex quo etiam illud
           apparebit quot [ui]rtutes sint. ac primo de fortudine dicere ordinamus//

           Ethica Nicomachea, III.v.17–vi.1; fols. [c₁] verso–[c₂] recto.

Parchment. 4 folios (perhaps originally 2 bifolia; fols. 1 and 4 would have formed
the other bifolium of a quire of eight, and fols. 2 and 3, which are consecutive,
would have formed the inner bifolium of the quire). 222 x 157 mm (written space
originally ca. 190 x 120 mm). 1 column. Fol. 1 preserves 39 lines, fol. 2 preserves
24–25 lines, fol. 3 perserves 24–25 lines, and fol. 4 preserves 38 lines of an original
41. Ruled in lead. Double vertical and single horizontal bounding lines.
     Written in hybrida libraria with notarial influence. 8-line initials at the be-
ginning of each book are in red and purple. 3-line initials at beginning of each
capitulum alternate red and purple. 1-line initials are in brown highlighted with
red. Rubrics are written in red in the same script as the text. The first line of each
book is written in larger minuscule. Paragraph marks alternate red and purple.
Running headlines are in red and purple. Punctuation consists of the punctus and,
for major pauses, the punctus versus. Another hand in black ink has made some
corrections and added punctuation, including the punctus elevatus and punctus
interrogativus. Hyphenation is in the same ink as the text.

The fragments were used in the binding of a volume measuring ca. 222 x 157 mm. Fols. 1 and 3 were flyleaves and fols. 2 and 4 were pastedowns. Five strips from an earlier manuscript, written in a thirteenth-century gothic hand, were wrapped around the spine of this volume and are partially preserved glued onto fols. 2 and 4. A seventeenth-century hand, writing in purple ink, has written the words "Padre nostro" twice on fol. 3r.

Zinniker 113 A–D.

MS 481.124   Germany, s. XIV/XV
Statuta antiqua ordinis cartusiensis in tribus   Pl. 69
partibus comprehensa

f. 1r   //diem intermittis Comemorationem uero de sancto i[ohanne et] de omni-
         bus sanctis usque ad uigiliam natalis dei ... in nulla sollem[nitate] pro-
         cessionem facimus; nec ullum festum trans//

         Statuta antiqua, Ch. II.3–16; [Basel, J. Amerbach, 1510], fols. a$_3$ verso–a$_4$
         recto. Facsimile in J. Hogg, ed., *The Evolution of the Carthusian Statutes
         from the Consuetudines Guigonis to the Tertia Compilatio*, vol. 1: *Consue-
         tudines Guigonis, Prima pars statutorum antiquorum*, Analecta Cartusiana
         99.1 (Salzburg, 1989), 62–123.

f. 1v   //tamen uel passio sancti cuius est festum; in eadem [l]egi poterit in
         refectorio ... Porro in aduentu quarta et sexta feria oratio de ieiunio
         mane; nisi festum beati//

         Statuta antiqua, Ch. II.18–III.4; fol. a$_4$ recto.

f. 2r   Expeditque sacerdotem ipsum egredi ad preparandum se laudate domi-
         num de celis inchoato ... Si autem praesens episcopus uel abbas celebret
         et prior ebdomadarius non sit;//

         Statuta antiqua, Ch. V.10–18; fols. a$_5$ verso–[a$_6$] recto.

f. 2v   //honestos et etiam laicos de familia nostra; ... In festo autem sancti ste-
         phani et//

         Statuta antiqua, Ch. V.21–31; fol. [a$_6$] recto–verso.

f. 3r   [ante]//cessoribus nostris; de quibus die sequenti ... ad vi exaudi. ad
         nonam protege dicimus.

Statuta antiqua, Ch. XXVIII.11–XXIX.3; fols. [d$_5$] verso–[d$_6$] recto.

f. 3v   //[*partially trimmed:* secundam] dicimus ad nonam Si uero ulla propria habeat . . . sed ad prima [antiphona] et tertiam quoque et sextam antiphone
uersiculi et orationes dicuntur//

        Statuta antiqua, Ch. XXIX.5–XXX.1; fol. [d$_6$] recto–verso.

f. 4r   //ordine superiores uel corpore debiliores. [O]mni sabbato missa beate
marie dicatur in conuentu . . . oratio concede nos famulos. cum suffragiis
infra ebdomadas//

        Statuta antiqua, Ch. XXXXV.30–XXXVI.5; fol. e$_5$ recto–verso.

f. 4v   [I]//nde usque ad penthecosten; secundum alleluia non uos reli[n]qua[m]
. . . in quadragesima post uesperas diei sunt dicende; sed numquam completorium Tempore autem//

        Statuta antiqua, Ch. XXXVI.5–16; fols. e$_5$ verso–[e$_6$] recto.

Parchment. 4 folios (2 bifolia; fols. 1 and 2 were probably the fourth and seventh
leaves of a quire of ten; and fols. 3 and 4 probably formed the outer bifolium of a
quire of ten). Fol. 1 measures 158 x 99 mm; fol. 2, 158 x 123 mm; fol. 3, 154 x 109
mm; fol. 4, 160 x 113 mm (written space originally ca. 141 x 98 mm). 1 column. 25
lines remaining of original ca. 30. Ruled in ink. Single vertical bounding lines.
    Written by two scribes in gothic script, one writing a littera hybrida script (fols.
1–2) and the other writing littera textualis (fols. 3–4). There are spaces for 2-line
initials and rubrics, but they have not been added. 1-line capitals within text are in
black. Punctuation consists of the punctus, punctus elevatus, and punctus flexus.
Hyphenation is in the same ink as the text.
    These fragments were used as pastedowns in the binding of a volume measuring
at least 221 x 148 mm.
    Zinniker 122 A–B.

MS 481.125   Germany, s. XV[1]
Hymnal   Pl. 70

f. 1r   [Sacerdotem christi martinum . . .] //uite pristine. Hic ritus sacrilogos . . .
supplicatu tuo semper infundas.

Notker, Hymn. Sangall. (St. Martin, 11 November); RH 17622; AH 53.181; von den Steinen, 125; Schaller-Könsgen 14443.

f. 1r   De sancta Elyzabeth. Gaude syon quod egressus . . . a portis eruamur inferi.

Anon. (St. Elizabeth, 19 November); RH 6958.

f. 1r–v   [De sanct]a katherina. Sanctissime uirginis uotiua festa recolamur . . . regens per secula.

Anon. (St. Catharine of Alexandria, 25 November); RH 18580.

f. 1v   De sancto andrea. Deus in tua virtute sanctus andreas . . . in eternum.

Anon., Hymn. Sangall. (St. Andrew, 30 November); RH 4449; AH 53.122; von den Steinen, 131; Schaller-Könsgen 3553.

f. 1v   De sancto nycolao. Congaudentes exultemus uocali concordia . . . per eius suffragia//

Anon., s. XI (St. Nicholas, 6 December); RH 3795; AH 54.66; Schaller-Könsgen 2597.

Parchment (stained and torn from use in a binding). 1 folio. 341 x 233 mm (written space 261 x 172 mm). 2 columns. 35 lines. Ruled in ink. Single vertical bounding lines.

Written in gothic script (littera textualis formata). 2-line initials at the beginning of hymns alternate red and blue and are not set apart from the text; the first letter following these initials is a brown capital highlighted with red. 1-line initials at the beginning of verses alternate red and blue. Rubrics are written in red in the same script as the text. Punctuation consists of the punctus. Hyphenation is in the same ink as the text.

The fragment was used as the wrapper of a volume measuring at least 208 x 155 mm. In the lower margin of the verso, which would have been the upper right corner of the volume, a sixteenth-century cursive hand has written the inscription "[erased] magnus in Bucheri. Anno domini 1585 comparavit hunc librum per [illegible]". In the erased portion another hand has written "Iacobus Rittri[illegible]" (or "Kittri. . ."?). The shelf number "No. 37" has been written below the inscription, and the same hand has written "37" on what would have been the center of the back cover of the volume.

Zinniker 112.

MS 481.126   Germany, s. XV[1]
Hymnal   Pl. 70

f. 1r   //inclita nostra deo ... gloria condecantemus alleluia.

           Unidentified hymn.

f. 1r   *Fidis virginis et martiris.* Sursum corda tendite fratres et impen//

           St. Faith (6 October); RH 19942.

f. 1v   //estis amministrancia deo ... centesimam uerbigena//

           Unidentified hymn.

Parchment (stained from use in a binding). 1 folio. 250 x 170 mm (width of written space 165 mm). 1 column. 4 lines remaining. Ruled in ink.
     Written in gothic script (littera textualis). One large hymn initial "S" ("Sursum") is in red with red penwork and is not set apart from the text. 1-line verse initials alternate red and blue. Rubrics are written in red in the same script as the text. There is no punctuation. Hyphenation is in the same ink as the text. Musical notation on 5-line staves.
     The fragment was used as the wrapper of a volume measuring ca. 140 x 70 mm. Zinniker 267B.

MS 481.127   Southern Germany, s. XV
Missal   Pl. 71

f. 1   [*Oratio.* Deus qui nos ad celebrandum pascale sacramentum ... expecta]//
          tio futurorum. Per. *Lectio quarta.* In diebus illis. Scripsit moyses canticum;
          et docuit filios israhel ... et ad finem usque compleuit. *tractus.* Attende
          celum et loquar et audiat ... V. Date magnificenciam deo nostro ... V.
          Deus fidelis in quo ... *Col.* Deus qui ecclesiam tuam ... *tract.* Sicut ce-
          ruus desiderat ad fontes ... V. Sitiuit anima mea ad deum ... V. Fuerunt
          michi lacrime ... *Collecta.* Concede quaesumus omnipotens deus; ut qui
          festa paschalia agimus ... *post hec benedicitur baptisma sicut in agenda con-
          tinetur. Deinde dicit sacerdos Confiteor solito more. Et de post incipitur missa
          hoc modo. Kyrieleison paschale cum gloria in excelsis. Collecta.* Deus qui hanc
          sacratissimam noctem ... *Ad collocenses.* Fratres. Si consurrexistis cum
          christo que sursum sunt querite ... in gloria. Alleluia. *v.* Confitemini

domino ... Alleluia *non repetitur*. *Tractus*. Laudate dominum omnes gentes ... V. Quoniam confirmata est super nos ... *Secundum matheum*.
Uespere autem sabbati que lucescit in prima sabbati ... surrexit enim
sicut di//[xit]

Holy Saturday. The lessons are from Deuteronomy 31.22–30, Colossians
3.1–4, and Matthew 28.1–6.

Parchment. 1 folio. 315 x 200 mm (written space 278 x 178 mm). 2 columns. 31
lines. Ruled in ink. Single vertical and horizontal bounding lines.
  Written in gothic script (littera textualis formata). 2-line initials alternate red
and blue and are not set apart from the text. 1-line initials are in black highlighted
with red. Rubrics are written in red in the same script as the text; the liturgical
directions are written in black and are underlined in red. Punctuation consists of
the punctus and punctus versus. Accents added by a later hand.
  Zinniker 110.

MS 481.128   Germany or Austria, s. XV[1]
Missal   Pl. 71

f. 1r–v   [Fratres. induite uos sicut electi ... mo]//destiam patentiam supportantes
           ... *Secundum matheum*. In illo tempore. Dixit iesus discipulis suis para-
           bolam hanc. Simile factum est regnum celorum ... *Sec*. Hostias tibi do-
           mine placationis offerimus ut et delicta ... *Compl*. Quaesumus omnipo-
           tens deus ut illius salutaris ... accepimus. Per.

           Fifth Sunday after Epiphany, with lessons from Colossians 3.12–17 and
           Matthew 13.24–30.

f. 1v   *Dominica in lxx*. Circumdederunt me gemitus mortis ... *Ps*. Diligam te
           domine ... *Oratio*. Preces populi tui quaesumus domine clementer exaudi
           ... *Ad corinth*. Fratres. Nescitis quod hii qui in stadio currunt ...
           comprehen//[datis]

           Sunday of Septuagesima.

Parchment (recto stained and worn from use in a binding). 1 folio. 322 x 245 mm
(written space 210 x 143 mm). 2 columns. 24 lines. Ruled in ink. Single vertical
and double horizontal bounding lines.
  Written in gothic script (littera textualis). 1-, 2-, and 3-line initials alternate in

blue and red and are not set apart from the text. Other 1-line initials are in black highlighted with red. Rubrics are written in red in the same script as the text. Punctuation consists of the punctus, punctus interrogativus, and punctus elevatus. Hyphenation is in the same ink as the text.

This fragment was once used as a wrapper for a volume measuring ca. 200 x 155 mm. The letters "PBR" are written in ink on the recto.

Zinniker 126.

MS 481.129   Germany, s. XV
Missal   Pl. 72

f. 1r   //[. . .] spiritu sancto et dixit. Confiteor . . . audierunt.

           Luke 10.21–24.

f. 1r   *Feria sexta Iacobi appostoli.* Karissimi. Quid proderit fratres mei . . . *Secundum lucam.* In illo tempore. Afferebant ad iesum infantes ut eos tangeret . . . intrabit in illud.

           Feria VI after the fifth Sunday after Pentecost, with lessons from James 14.17 and Luke 18.15–17.

f. 1r–v   *Dominica vi^a In.* Dominus fortitudo plebis sue . . . *v.* Ad te domine clamabo . . . *Oratio.* Deus uirtutum cuius . . . *Ad romanos.* Fratres quicumque baptisati sumus . . . *Gr.* Conuertere domine aliquantulum . . . *V.* Domine refugium factus . . . *V.* In te domine speraui . . . *Secundum matheum.* In illo tempore. Dixit iesus discipulis suis. Amen dico uobis. Nisi abundauerit iusticia . . . *Credo. Ofr.* Perfice gressus meos . . . *Sec.* Propiciare domine supplicationibus nostris . . . *Co.* Circumibo et immolabo . . . *Compl.* Repleti sumus domine muneribus . . . auxilio. Per.

           Sixth Sunday after Pentecost, with lessons from Romans 6.3–11 and Matthew 5.20–24.

f. 1v   *Feria quarta ad hebreos.* Fratres. Habemus gratiam per quam seruiamus placentes deo . . . *Secundum matheum.* [sic] In illo tempore. Proficiscente iesu de iericho et discipulis eius; et plurima multitudine . . . Et commina// [bantur]

           Feria IV after the sixth Sunday after Pentecost, with lessons from Hebrews 12.28–13.8 and Mark 10.46–48.

Parchment. 1 folio (foliated "7" in the upper center margin of the recto). 368 x 262 mm (written space 305 x 193 mm). 2 columns. 36 lines. Ruled in ink. Single vertical and horizontal bounding lines.

Written in gothic script (littera textualis). 2- to 5-line initials alternate red and blue and are not set apart from the text, except for the letter "I" ("In" twice). 1-line initials are in brown and are highlighted with red. Rubrics are written in red in the same script as the text. Punctuation consists of the punctus and punctus elevatus. Hyphenation is in the same ink as the text.

This fragment was once used as a cover for one board and the spine of a binding of a volume that measured ca. 315 x 190 mm.

Zinniker 125.

MS 481.130
Missal

Germany, s. XV^2
Pl. 72

f. 1   //aliquando angelorum filius meus es tu . . . et anni tui non deficient. Gr. Uiderunt omnes fines terre . . . V. Natum fecit dominus . . . V. Dies sanctificatus illuxit . . . *Seq.* Natus ante secula dei filius . . . *Inicium sancti euangelii secundum iohannem.* In principio erat uerbum . . . plenum gratia et ueritate. *Offertorium.* Tui sunt celi et tua est terra . . . praeparacio sedis tue. *Secr.*//

Christmas (Lessons from John 1.1).

Parchment. 1 folio (foliated "x" in the upper center margin of the recto). 301 x 237 mm (written space 220 x 165 mm). 2 columns. 28 lines. Ruled in ink. Single vertical bounding lines.

Written in two sizes of gothic script, the small a littera textualis and the large a textualis formata. 1 10-line initial "I" is in red and is set apart from the text. 1- and 2-line initials are in red and are not set apart from the text. Other 1-line initials are in black highlighted with red. Rubrics are written in red in the same script as the text. The first letter after the initial of the sequence and the lesson from John is a capital written in black and highlighted with red. The foliation is written in red. Punctuation consists of the punctus and punctus elevatus. Hyphenation is in the same ink as the text.

The fragment was used in the binding of a volume measuring at least 301 x 210 mm.

Zinniker 124.

MS 481.131   N. France?, s. XVI^{in}
Noted Missal   Pl. 73

f. 1   [ma]//rie genetricis eiusdem *ut in Canone. In quadragesima.* UD Eterne
deus. Qui corporali ieiunio . . . *De sancta cruce in dupl.* UD Eterne deus.
Qui salutem humani generis . . . *In die cene domini. in canone.* Communicantes et diem sacratissimum celebrantes quo dominus noster iesus . . . *ut
in canone.* Hanc igitur oblationem seruitutis nostre sed . . . Qui pridie
quam pro nostra om//[nium]

Prefaces of the Mass (includes Quadragesima, Holy Cross, and Maundy
Thursday).

Parchment. 1 folio. 387 x 281 mm (written space 272 x 186 mm). 2 columns. 21
lines. Ruled in red ink. Single vertical and horizontal bounding lines.
    Written in gothic script (littera textualis formata). Four 2-line initials in light
brown, outlined in black and highlighted with gold penwork, on square grounds of
blue, green, or red. The grounds are split diagonally with a dark shade of color on
one side and a lighter shade on the other; the edges of the side with the dark color
are outlined in gold, and the edges of the other side are outlined in black. One 2-
line initial of similar design in white on a gold ground. 1-line capitals are in black
and are highlighted in red. The rubrics are written in red in the same script as the
text; traces of guide letters for the rubricator are preserved in the margins. Punctuation consists of the punctus. Hyphenation is in the same ink as the text. The
prefaces (*uere dignum*) have musical notation in black ink on 3-line staves in red.
    Another leaf from the same manuscript is Beinecke MS 804.17.
    Zinniker 115.

MS 481.132   Germany, s. XV^2
Missal   Pl. 73

f. 1r   [L. Fratres. Libenter suffertis insipientes . . .] //tibi gratia mea. Nam uirtus
. . . uirtus christi. *Gr.* Sciant gentes quoniam nomen . . . *V.* Deus meus
pone . . . *Tr.* Cognouisti domine terram . . . *V.* Sana contriciones eius . . .
V. Ut fugiant a facie . . . *Secundum lucam.* In illo tempore. Cum turba plurima conueniret . . . in paciencia. *Off.* P[erfice] gressus meos . . . [*Sec.*]
Oblatum tibi domine sacr[ificium] uiuificet . . . *Co.* Introibo a[d altare] dei
. . . *Compl.* Supplices [te ro]gamus omnipotens deus . . . concedas. Per.

Sunday of Sexagesima, with lessons from 2 Corinthians 12.9 and Luke
8.4–15. The outer margin of fol. 1 is torn with loss of text.

f. 1r–v *Feria iiii^a* A[d] *hebreo*[s]. Fratres. Recogitate [enim] christum qualem
susti[nuit a peccat]oribus adversus … uiuemus. In christo iesu domino
nostro. *Secundum marcum.* [In illo] tempore. Exiens iesus de [. . .] uidit
turbam multam … abiit in montem orare.

Feria IV after Sexagesima, with lessons from Hebrews 12.3–9 and Mark
6.34–46. The outer margin of fol. 1 is torn with loss of text.

ff. 1v–2r *Feria vi^a Ad thessalonicenses.* Fratres. Nos desolati a uobis ad tempus ore
aspectus non corde … gaudium. In christo iesu domino nostro. *Secundum
matheum.* In illo tempore. Vespere autem facto accesserunt ad iesum discipuli eius … mulieribus et paruulis.

Feria VI after Sexagesima, with lessons from 1 Thessalonians 2.17 and
Matthew 14.15–21. The outer margin of fol. 1 is torn with loss of text.

f. 2r–v *Dominica in l^{ma}.* Esto michi in deum protectorem … *Ps.* In te domine speraui … *Oratio.* Preces nostras quaesumus domine clementer exaudi …
Ad corinthios. Fratres. Si linguis homi[num] loquar et angelorum … est
caritas. *Gr.* Tu es deus qui facis … *V.* Liberasti in brachio … *Tractus.* Iubilate deo omnis terra … *V.* Intrate in conspectu … *V.* Scitote quoniam
dominus … *V.* Ipse fecit nos … *V.* Nos autem populos … *Secundum lucam.* In illo tempore. Assumpsit iesus xii discipulos … laudem deo. *Off.*
Benedictus es domine … *Secret.* Hec hostia quaesumus domine emundet
… *Co.* Manducauerunt et saturati … a desiderio suo. *Complen.//*

Sunday of Quinquagesima, with lessons from 1 Corinthians 13.1–13 and
Luke 18.31–43.

Parchment. 2 folios (foliated "xxv" and "xxvi" in the top center of the recto). 321
x 255 mm (written space 262 x 195 mm). 2 columns. 35 lines. Ruled in ink. Single
vertical bounding lines.

Written in two sizes of gothic script (littera textualis), with a slightly smaller
script for chants; on fol. 1v there is a change of hands. 2-line initials at the beginning of Masses and lessons alternate red and blue and are not set apart from the
text. 1-line initials are in brown highlighted with red. Rubrics are written in red in
the same script as the text. Punctuation consists of the punctus. Hyphenation is in
the same ink as the text. The foliation is in red. Several small original holes in the
parchment are circled in red.

The fragment was once used as a wrapper for a volume measuring ca. 320 x 200
mm, which had the shelf number "78" (or "18"?) at the top of the spine.

Zinniker 105.

MS 481.133   Germany, s. XV
Missal   Pl. 74

f. 1ra   [*Grad.*] //Audi filia et uide . . . *V.* Specie tua et pulchritudine . . . *Grad.*
           Propter ueritatem et mansuetudines . . . *V.* Audi filia et uide . . . *V.*
           Adducentur regi uirgines . . . *V.* Diffusa est gracia . . . *V.* Specie tua et
           pulchritudine . . . *V.* Omnis gloria eius . . . *V.* Egregia sponsa christi . . . *V.*
           Audi filia et uide . . . *Tractus.* Audi filia et uide . . . *V.* Uultum meum de-
           precabuntur . . . *V.* Adducentur regi uirgines . . . *V.* Adducentur in leticia
           . . . *Alius* [*tractus*]. Qui seminant in lacrimis . . . *V.* Euntes ibant [et
           flebant] . . . *V.* V//[identes]

           Common of Virgins. The outer margin of the leaf has been trimmed with
           the loss of column b.

f. 1vb   //deum saluatorem meum. Confitebor . . . *Sapientie.* [D]omine deus meus
           exalta[sti] super terram habitationem.

           Common of Virgins. The lessons are from Sirach 51.1–8, 12 and Sirach
           51.13. The outer margin of the leaf has been trimmed with the loss of
           column a.

f. 2   //Post partum uirgo . . . *Offer.* Gloria et honore . . . *Offer.* In uirtute tua
           . . . *Offr.* Iustus ut palma . . . *Offr.* Posuisti domine in capite . . . *Offr.* De-
           siderium anime eius . . . *Offr.* Repleti sumus mane . . . *Con.* Qui uult
           uenire . . . *Con.* Magna est gloria . . . *Co.* Letabitur iustus in domino . . .
           Con. Ego sum uitis . . . *Con.* Qui michi ministrat . . . *Con.* Se[mel iuraui in
           sancto meo] . . . *Oratio.* Uotiuos nos quaesumus domine . . . *Secr.* Prae-
           sentia munera quaesumus domine ita serena . . . *Complen.* Sumpsimus
           domine martyris tui sollemnitate . . . *Lectio ysaie prophete.* Nunc dicit domi-
           nus deus. Creans iacob et formans te israhel . . . *Lectio libri sapiencie.* Iustus
           cor suum tradet ad uigilandum diluculo . . . *Lectio libri sapiencie.* Iustum de-
           duxit dominus per uias rectas . . . *Sapiencie.* Iustus si morte praeoccupatus
           fuerit . . . *Sapiencie.* Beatus uir qui in sapiencia morabitur . . . Cibauit illum
           pane uite et intellectus et//

           Common of a Martyr not a Bishop. The lessons are from Isaiah 43.1–5,
           Sirach 39.6–13, Wisdom 10.10–14, Wisdom 4.7–15, and Sirach 14.22,
           15.3.

Parchment. 2 folios (fol. 2 is foliated "ccxi" in the center of the upper margin of the
recto). 268 x 270 mm (written space originally ca. 245 x 176 mm). 2 columns. 32

lines remaining of an original ca. 34. Ruled in ink. Single vertical bounding lines.

Written in gothic script (littera textualis). 1- and 2-line initials alternate red and blue and are not set apart from the text. Other 1-line initials are in brown highlighted with red. Rubrics are written in red in the same script as the text. Foliation is written in red. Punctuation consists of the punctus. Hyphenation is in the same ink as the text.

The bifolium was used in the binding of a volume measuring ca. 215 x 150 mm. There are illegible traces of a title or shelf number from the spine of the binding. Zinniker 102.

MS 481.134
Missal

Germany, s. XV[1]

Pl. 74

f. 1   //qui fecit illas. Hic est deus noster . . . *Tractus.* Cantemus domino gloriose
. . . V. Hic deus meus . . . V. Dominus conterens bella . . . *Sequitur collecta.*
Deus incommutabilis uirtus . . . *Tractus.* Sicut ceruus desiderat . . . V.
Sitiuit anima mea . . . V. Fuerunt michi lacrime . . . *Oratio.* Concede quaesumus omnipotens deus. ut qui sollempnitatem . . . *Ad missam.* Praesta
quaesumus omnipotens deus. ut claritatis . . . *Ad corinth.* [sic] In diebus
illis. Cum appollo esset corinthi. et paulus peragratis . . . Alleluia. *v.* Con-
fitemini domino quoniam bonus . . . *tractus.* Laudate dominum omnes
gentes . . . V. Quoniam confirmata est . . . *Secundum iohannem.* In illo tempore. Dixit iesus discipulis suis. Si diligitis me mandata mea seruate . . .
Off. Emitte spiritum tuum . . . *Secr.* Munera quaesumus domine oblata
sanctifica . . . *Praefatio.* UD. Per christum dominum nostrum. Qui ascen-
dens. *Infra ac.* Communicantes et diem sacratissimum . . . *Item ut supra.*
Hanc igitur oblacionem seruitutis nostre sed . . . *Co.* Ultimo festiuitatis die
. . . *Compl.* Sancti spiritus domine corda . . . *Clauditur cum.* Benedicamus
domino alleluia alleluia alleluia. *In die sancto.*//

Vigil of Pentecost, with lessons from Baruch 3.35–38, Acts 19.1–8, and John 14.15–21.

Parchment. 1 folio (foliated "lxxi" in the center of the upper margin of the recto). 310 x 250 mm (written space 265 x 175 mm). 2 columns. 34 lines. Ruled in ink. Single vertical bounding lines. Prickings in outer margin.

Written in two sizes of gothic script (littera textualis), with a slightly smaller script for the chants than for the lessons. Two 10-line lesson initials "I" in red, one decorated with a face, set apart from the text. 1-, 2-, and 4-line initials are in red and are not set apart from the text. Other 1-line initials are in brown highlighted with red. Rubrics are written in red in the same script as the text. Foliation is written in red. Punctuation consists of the punctus and the comma. Hyphenation is in the same ink as the text.

The fragment was used as a pastedown in a binding.

Zinniker 123.

MS 481.135   England or France, s. XV
Missal   Pl. 75

f. 1r //*Epistola*. Apparuit benignitatis. R. Benedicta et venerabilis. Alleluia. Post
partum. *Euangelium*. Pastores. *Off*. Ffelix namque. *Co*. Beata uiscera.

Mass for Mary from the Nativity to the Purification, with lessons from Titus 3.4 and Luke 2.15.

f. 1r *De beata maria*. Salue sancta parens ... P. Post partum uirgo ... *Or*. Concede nos famulos tuos ... *Sapiencie*. Ab inicio et ante secula creata sum
... R. Benedicta et venerabilis ... V. Virgo dei genetrix ... V. Post partum
uirgo ... V. Ante thronum trinitatis ... *Secundum lucam*. In illo tempore.
Loquente iesu ad turbas; extollens vocem ... *Off*. Ffelix namque es ...
deus noster. alleluia.

Mass for Mary from the Purification to Easter, with lessons from Sirach 24.14–16 and Luke 11.27–28.

f. 1r–v *Tempore paschali missa ut supra*. Salue sancta. *siue* R. Alleluia. V. Post partum ... V. Angelus domini descendit ... *Secundum iohannem*. In illo
tempore. Stabant iuxta crucem iesu mater eius ... *Off*. Regina celi letare
... *Se*. Tua nos domine propiciacione ... *Co*. Beata uiscera marie ... *Post
co*. Sumptis domine salutis nostre ... maiestati. Per.

Mass for Mary from Easter to Pentecost, with lessons from John 19.25–27.

f. 1v *De sancto cuius ecclesia fuit. oratio*. Sit domine quesumus beatus N. confessor tuus atque pontifex ... *Secre*. Sacris altaribus hostias superpositas
... *Post co*. Existat quaesumus domine pro nobis beatissimus N. ...
preparacio salutaris. Per. *De sanctis quorum reliquie habentur in ecclesia*.

Mass for the patron saint of the church. Rubric for the Mass for saints whose reliquaries are in the church.

Parchment. 1 folio (foliated "xii^x xix" in the center of the upper margin of the recto). 345 x 260 mm (written space 225 x 168 mm). 2 columns. 28 lines. Ruled in red ink. Single vertical and double horizontal bounding lines. Prickings preserved in the outer and lower margin.

Written in two sizes of gothic script (littera textualis formata), with a slightly smaller script for the chants. 2- and 3-line initials are in gold on ground of blue and purple decorated with white penwork. 1-line capitals, including the first letter after the initials in gold, are in brown filled with yellow wash. Rubrics are written in red or in brown underlined with red and are in the same script as the text. Punctuation consists of the punctus, punctus elevatus, and punctus interrogativus. Hyphenation is in the same ink as the text. The use of "Ff" suggests England.

The inscription "50129 FN/FH" is written in pencil in a twentieth-century hand. Zinniker 135.

MS 481.136   Germany, s. XV
Breviary   Pl. 75

f. 1r   [am]//plexibus iungerentur . . . deinde [?]ter clematius co//

The Passion of St. Ursula is very similar to the version in *Liber revelationum seu imaginationum S. Elizabethae Schoenaugiensis de SS. Ursula et sociabus*, chap. 3.21 in *Acta Sanctorum*, Oct. 9:172.

f. 2r   //ad ihesum domine . . . *An.* Adhuc eos loquente . . . *Cap.* Saluatorem expectamus dominum . . . *Ymnus.* Nouum sydus exoritur christi pia clementia . . . *v.* Corona aurea. *Ad b. A.* Et ecce vox de nube . . . complacui//

St. Ursula (21 October); the capitulum is from Philippians 3.20–21; the hymn is printed in AH 52.20 (RH 12374).

Parchment (badly stained from use in a binding). 2 folios (originally 1 bifolium). Fol. 1 measures 195 x 117 mm; fol. 2 measures 197 x 130 mm (written space 125 x 85 mm). 2 columns. 20 lines. Ruled in ink. Single vertical and horizontal bounding lines.

Written in gothic script (littera textualis libraria with simple form of *a*). 1- and 2-line initials alternate red and blue. Other initials are in brown highlighted with red. Rubrics are written in red in the same script as the text. There is no punctuation. Hyphenation is in the same ink as the text.

These leaves, when they formed a bifolium, were used as wrappers for a volume measuring ca. 150 x 95 mm. The center of the bifolium, which would have covered the spine of the volume, is now missing.

Fol. 1 was formerly Zinniker 109A; fol. 2 was formerly Beinecke MS 482.119, Zinniker 82–1.

MS 481.137   Germany, s. XV
Psalter   Pl. 76

f. 1   [mon]//tem syon . . . deduxit. Gloria. Tu es deus . . . Propicius euouae. Deus uenerunt gentes . . . secundum//

Psalms 77.68–78.11.

f. 2   //Quam . . . sperat in te. Gloria patri et filio. Tu solus altissimus . . . Benedixisti. euouae. *Psa.* Benedixisti domine terram tuam . . . in eternum//

Psalms 83.2–84.6.

Parchment (stained from use in a binding). 2 folios (1 bifolium). 191 x 151 mm (written space 141 x 108 mm). 1 column. 19 lines. Ruled in ink. Single vertical and horizontal bounding lines.

Written in gothic script (littera textualis). 2- and 3-line initials at the beginning of Psalms alternate red and blue and are not set apart from the text. 3-line initials of the versicles are in black highlighted with red and are not set apart from the text. 1-line initials at the beginning of verses alternate red and blue. Punctuation consists of the punctus and punctus elevatus. Hyphenation was added by a later hand. The versicles at the end of each Psalm have musical notation in black on a 4-line staff in red.

This fragment was used as the wrapper of a volume measuring ca. 155 x 100 mm.

Zinniker 272.

MS 481.138   Southern Germany, s. XV
Sacramentary   Pl. 76

f. 1   //tionis illi commisse . . . *Post co.* Quos celesti recreas . . . *Per omni gradu ecclesie.* Exaudi quaesumus domine pro omni gradu ecclesie . . . *Sec.* Suscipe domine preces et hostias pro omni . . . *Post co.* Tua nos domine medicinalis operatio . . . *Missa pro pace.* Deus a quo sancta desideria . . . *Sec.*

Deus qui credentes in te ... *Post co.* Deus auctor pacis et amator ... *Pro concordia.* Deus largitor pacis et amator ... *Sec.* Hiis sacrificiis domine quaesumus concede placatus ... *Post co.* Spiritum nobis domine tue cari-tatis ... *Pro familiaribus.* Deus qui caritatis dona per gratiam ... *Secreta.* Miserere quaesumus domine famulis et famulabus tuis ... *Post com.* Diuina libantes misteria quaesumus domine ut hec salutaria ... *Missa pro iter agentibus.* Adesto domine supplicationibus nostris et uiam famulorum tuorum ... omnes uie et uite//

Votive Masses for all ranks within the church, for peace, for harmony, for households, for travelers.

Parchment. 1 folio (foliated "xxxii" in the center of the upper margin of the recto). 276 x 205 mm (written space 230 x 168 mm). 2 columns. 26 lines. Ruled in lead. Single vertical and horizontal bounding lines.

Written in gothic script (littera textualis). 2- and 3-line initials are in red and are not set apart from the text. 1-line initials are in black, sometimes highlighted with red. Rubrics are written in red in the same script as the text. The foliation is written in black. Punctuation consists of the punctus and punctus elevatus. Hy-phenation is in the same ink as the text.

The fragment was used as a pastedown in the binding of a volume measuring at least 276 x 191 mm. There is a large rust stain in the center of the upper margin.

Zinniker 106.

MS 481.139–142

Miscellaneous papyrus fragments; transferred to the papyrus collection and now num-bered PCt.YBR inv. 2329–2342.

MS 481.143   N. France or Germany, s. XIII
Babylonian Talmud, Tractate Pesaḥim (Aramaic and Hebrew)   Pl. 77

We thank Ivan Marcus for his assistance with this fragment.

f. 1   //le-eimurin ba^cei reishit ... kol ha-qorbanot//

Tractate Pesaḥim, fols. 71a–72b. The text begins with a discussion of the *hagigah* or sacrifice required on all festivals, and is mostly about the animal sacrifices required on the Passover festival.

Parchment. 1 folio. 294 x 226 mm (written space 254 x 195 mm). 2 columns. 40 lines. Dry-point ruling.

Written in Ashkenazic script.

This fragment was once used as a pastedown in the binding of Lambach, Stifts- bibliothek, Ccl 214. The notation "214P" appears in pencil in the lower right mar- gin of the recto.

Zinniker 305.

Bibliography:
Babcock, *Reconstructing a Medieval Library*, 116 and fig. 64.

MS 481.144   Italy, s. XIII
Babylonian Talmud, Tractate Ḥullin (Aramaic and Hebrew)   Pl. 77

We thank Ivan Marcus for his assistance with this fragment.

The text contains the last sections of the Mishnah and Talmud of Chapter I, in- cluding interpolations of the running commentary of Rashi (Rabbi Solomon Yitz- haqi of Troyes, ca. 1040–1105). It contains a discussion of various cases that illus- trate a common principle of mutual exclusion, whereby when one of two conditions is required, the other is excluded. The cases involve a father's responsibility for his minor daughter; levirate marriage obligations; when the ram's horn (shofar) is blown; and when the separation (*havdalah*) prayer is said at the end of a festival. The verso concludes with the beginning of Chapter II which resumes the main subject, the laws and principles of the ritual killing of animals for food.

f. 1   //kol maqom she-yesh mekher . . . rabbi yehudah ome//[r]

           Tractate Ḥullin, fols. 26b–27a.

Parchment. 1 folio. 285 x 236 mm (written space 197 x 155 mm). 1 column. 26 lines. Dry-point ruling.

Written in semi-cursive script.

This fragment was once used in a chain binding.

Zinniker 306.

MS 482.1   E. France or SW Germany, ca. 800
Bible, Judges (Vetus Latina)   Pl. 78

f. 1   //Et occiderunt in die illa ... Et reminiscemini [*corr. to*: reminiscimini]//

Judges 8.10–9.2.

Parchment (with worm holes and tears in the corners from use in a binding). 1
folio. 270 x 198 mm (written space 266 x 153 mm). 1 column. 34 lines. Dry-point
ruling on the hair side; double vertical bounding lines. Prickings for the horizontal
rulings are on the outer vertical bounding line, and prickings for the vertical ruling
are on the upper and lower horizontal bounding lines.

Written in pre-Caroline minuscule, which Bischoff has dated to around 800 and
attributed to southwestern Germany or eastern France (*Schreibschulen*, 2:43, incorrectly cited as MS 448). 1-line initials are in brown uncials and are written on
the inner vertical bounding line when they occur at the beginning of a line. Portions of a running title in brown uncials are preserved in the upper margins of both
sides. Punctuation consists of the punctus, punctus elevatus, punctus versus, and
punctus interrogativus. A contemporary hand using darker ink has made corrections and altered some of the punctuation.

This fragment was formerly part of a bifolium that was bound in the back of
Lambach, Stiftsbibliothek, Cml XXVII, where it was briefly described by Holter
(1957), 440, no. 1; the number "82" on the recto refers to its page number in this
volume (for a brief description of Cml XXVII, see Holter [1959], 237). The location of the other leaf of the bifolium (containing Judges 1.23–2.17) is currently
unknown, but the text of both leaves was published by H. Gerstinger, "Zwei Fragmente einer altlateinischen Übersetzung des Buches der Richter in einem Codex
der Bibliothek des Benediktinerklosters Lambach in Oberösterreich," *Mitteilungen
des Vereins klassischer Philologen in Wien* 6 (1929): 94–107 and pl. 2. Two other
leaves from the same manuscript survive as Lambach Fragment 9; they contain the
Vulgate translation of Numbers 30.4 and 31.2–12 (briefly described in Holter
[1989], 211, cat. no. IX.05).

A modern hand has written the number "6" in pencil in the lower right corner
of the recto. The number "3" is written in pencil in the lower right margin of the
verso. On the left side of the upper margin of the recto "96 R" is written in pencil,
and on the right side of the upper margin of the verso "96 V" is written in pencil.
The text is identified in pencil in the left margin of the verso.

MS 482.1 was formerly Beinecke MS 482.1B, Zinniker 60; Beinecke MS 482.1A
is now MS 481.4, fol. 2.

Bibliography:
Babcock, *Reconstructing a Medieval Library*, 87 and fig. 17.

MS 482.2   Southeastern Germany, s. IX$^{1/3}$
Homiliary   Pl. 79

f. 1r   Solemne tempus advenit, quod amplius quam per anni cetera spatia
          ...]//tanto acceptior est deo; quanto animus qui orat a carnali uoluptate
          suspenditur ... Sepius cogitemus quod scriptum est; Post concupis-
          cen//[tias]

          Sermon on Fasting and Almsgiving for Quadragesima based on Augustine,
          Sermon 210, chaps. 6–7; PL 38.1052.

f. 1v   //pauperum sane praecipue recordemur; et quod nobis partius uiuendo
          subtrahimus ... Det ueniam qui accipit iniuriam; Ut non possi//

          Cf. Augustine, Sermon 210, chap. 10; PL 38.1053.

f. 2r   [cura]//re possit elymosinas dando redimere; Bonum est ieiunium fratres
          mei sed melior est elymosina ... Aut de ligni penuria se excu//[sare]

          Sermon on Fasting and Almsgiving for Quadragesima based on Caesarius,
          Sermo 199.1–3; G. Morin, ed., CCSL 104 (1953), 804. Cf. also Rabanus
          Maurus, Sermon 10 (PL 110.22–23).

f. 2v   //inquid. et sine tecto. Induc in domum tu[um] ... Igitur ammonemus
          caritatem uestram//

          Cf. Caesarius, Sermo 199.3, 4 and 6; Morin, 804–6.

Parchment. 2 folios (both partial). Fol. 1 measures 145 x 121 mm; fol. 2 measures
145 x 127 mm (original dimensions and written space uncertain; width of written
space of 1 column: 115 mm). 1 column. 14 lines of original ca. 25 remaining. Dry-
point ruling; single vertical bounding lines.

Written in pre-Caroline minuscule, dated by Bernhard Bischoff to the first third
of the ninth century and attributed to southeastern Germany (letter of 5 October
1985). The Kraus description is uncharacteristically specific in ascribing these fragments to Salzburg, s. IX^{in} (description on file in library). This ascription may reflect
some information on provenance that is unknown to us. 1-line initials are in brown
uncials, with rustic capital E, and are not set apart from the text. Punctuation consists of the punctus, punctus versus, and punctus elevatus.

A fifteenth-century hand has added "Deus qui sedes super tronos" between the
second and third lines and "iusti erunt in memoria eterna angelorum sanctorum"
between the third and fourth lines of fol. 2r.

Zinniker 125–1, 125–2.

MS 482.3
Lectionary

Freising, Germany, s. IX$^{3/4}$

Pl. 79

f. 1r   //diebus excitabo illud. Dixerunt ergo iudaei . . . quid esset in homine.

John 2.19–25; Feria II of the fourth week of Quadragesima.

f. 1r–v   *Feria iii. Lectio libri exodi. In diebus illis.* ¶LXVII Loquutus est dominus ad moysen dicens . . . et misertus est populo suo dominus deus noster.

Exodus 32.7–14. Feria III of the fourth week of Quadragesima. The lower margin has been trimmed with the loss of one line of text.

f. 1v   *Secundum iohannem. In illo tempore.* Iam die festo mediante . . . Quomodo hic litteras cum didicertur [*sic*]//

John 7.14–16. Feria III of the fourth week of Quadragesima. The lower margin has been trimmed with the loss of one line of text. The bottom two lines remaining are very faded.

Parchment. 1 folio (partial). 208 x 166 mm (written space originally ca. 200 x 130 mm). 1 column. 22 of 23 lines remaining. Dry-point ruling. Double vertical and single horizontal bounding lines.

Written in Caroline minuscule, which Bischoff has dated to the third quarter of the ninth century and attributed to Freising (letter of 5 October 1985 and *Schreibschulen*, 2:219, under no. 103b). 4-line initials at the beginning of lessons are written in red square capitals. The rubrics are written in red rustic capitals. The first three words of each lesson ("In illis diebus" and "In illo tempore") are written in red minuscule. Punctuation consists of the punctus, punctus elevatus, and punctus interrogativus.

The fragment was once a pastedown in a volume measuring ca. 208 x 155 mm. According to Bischoff, the fragment is related either to a lectionary fragment preserved as Munich, Bayerische Staatsbibliothek, Clm 29303/11 (formerly Clm 29164, Kasten I, 1b) or to a similar fragment preserved as the back pastedown in Munich Clm 6406 (see *Schreibschulen*, 1:125–26, no. 103 and 2:219, no. 103b). Clm 29303/11 is from a lectionary written at Freising under Bishop Anno (854–875) and may be by the same scribe who copied Munich Clm 17011 and Clm 6215. In fact, all three of these fragments may be remnants from a single lectionary (Bischoff, letter of 5 October 1985). Between two lines of fol. 1v are remnants of a text in red ink from the fifteenth century.

Around 1955 the leaf was in the collection of Pfarrer Hüsler of Luzern (see Bischoff, *Schreibschulen*, 2:219).

A modern hand has written "R 2 5" in pencil in the upper right corner of the recto.

Zinniker 79–1.

Bibliography:
Babcock, *Reconstructing a Medieval Library*, 48, n. 20.
Shailor, *The Medieval Book*, 70, no. 72.

MS 482.4   Southern Germany or Northern Italy, s. IX$^{2/4}$
South German Homiliary   Pl. 80

f. 1r   [Inc: Dominus noster iesus christus fratres karissimi post redemptionem
          nostram . . .] //caro. deuoluat. sed secum potiu[s] . . . corpus sanctificatum
          anima iusta pe[rducat] Praestante domino nostro iesu christo cui [cum]
          patre et spiritu sancto laus et gloria in s[aeculo saeculorum.]

          South German Homiliary, Homily II.1 (Ascension) = Pseudo-Augustine,
          Sermon 157; Mai, 1:351; see G. Folliet, "Deux nouveaux témoins du Ser-
          monnaire carolingien récemment reconstitué," *Revue des études augus-
          tiniennes* 23 (1977): 155–98, here 190. The upper and outer margins have
          been trimmed with loss of four lines of text.

f. 1r–v   *ii. quot uicibus post re[surrectio]nem discipulis suis domin[us apparuit.]* Multis
          ergo modis dilectissimi [fratres dominus noster iesus christus] post resur-
          rectionem [suam discipulis sae]pius . . . uolumus adipisci. [. . . n]ostra
          curemus.//

          South German Homiliary, Homily II.2 (Resurrection) = Bede, Homily
          II.8; D. Hurst, ed., CCSL 122 [1955], 236–37. See Folliet, 190. The upper
          and outer margins have been trimmed with loss of four lines of text.

Parchment. 1 folio. 210 x 105 mm. 1 column. 21 lines. Dry-point ruling.

Written in Caroline minuscule, which Bischoff has dated to the second quarter
of the ninth century. There is some confusion concerning the relationship of 482.4
and the related leaves in Lambach, Fragment 8/1–8 to the leaves which Bischoff is
reported in Holter (1957), 441, no. 9, to have attributed to Italy. Bischoff, *Schreibschulen*, 2:42–43, later retracted the attribution, but it appears that his attribution
concerned only the leaves in the binding of Ccl 480, which are from a different
manuscript from MS 482.4. The text is divided by paragraphs into short sense
units, each beginning with a 1-line uncial in red that is set apart from the text

between the vertical bounding lines. Rubrics are written in red uncials. Punctuation consists of the punctus, punctus elevatus, and punctus versus.

Other leaves from this manuscript are preserved as Beinecke MS 484.2 (1 leaf), Lambach, Stiftsbibliothek, Fragment 8/1–8 (14 leaves), and in the bindings of Vienna, Österreichische Nationalbibliothek, s.n. 3620 (1 leaf and binding strips; formerly Lambach Ccl 436), s.n. 3622 (binding strips), and in the binding of a manuscript illustrated in Holter (1957), pl. 185, and given the shelfmark Ccl 480 (according to Holter [1989], cat. no. IX.02, this manuscript is now Kremsmünster CC 417). See Holter (1989), 210–11, cat. nos. IX.01–02, and Bischoff, *Schreibschulen*, 2:42–43, where MS 484.2 is misidentified as "MS 3."

Zinniker 40–1.

Bibliography:
Babcock, *Reconstructing a Medieval Library*, 92 and fig. 48.

MS 482.5

transferred to Beinecke MS 481.6, fols. 6, 9, 12, 14, and 15

MS 482.6

transferred to Beinecke MS 481.17, fols. 1 and 4

MS 482.7

transferred to Beinecke MS 481.13, fragment B

MS 482.8   Italy, s. X
Lectionary   Pl. 81

f. 1r–v   //melius fuit occisis [gladio] quam interfectis . . . discoperiet peccata tua. Oratio ieremię prophetę. Recordare domine et uide quit [sic] acciderit . . . nos uehementer.

Lamentations 4.9–5.22. The inner margin has been trimmed with loss of text.

f. 1v   VII. Quapropter inter[mitten]tes inchoationis ... Terra enim s[aepe
            ue]nientem. super se bib//[ens]

            Hebrews 6.1–7. The inner margin has been trimmed with loss of text.

Parchment. 1 folio. 275 x 208 mm (written space originally ca. 265 x 204 mm). 2
columns. 34 lines. Dry-point ruling on the hair side. Single vertical bounding lines.
     Written in Caroline minuscule. Two 3-line initials outlined in brown, written on
the single vertical bounding line. 1-line capitals are in brown rustic capitals. Hebrew words in Lamentations are written in rustic capitals. Interlinear neumes for
the lessons from Lamentations were added later. Punctuation consists of the punctus and punctus elevatus.
     According to Hartmut Hoffmann (letter of 12 October 1997), this leaf is by the
same hand that copied the Homiliary fragments preserved in Melk, Cod. 793 (fols.
I and 394), and in Kremsmünster, Fr. I/17. The fragment was used as a flyleaf in
the binding of a volume measuring ca. 275 x 193 mm.
     Zinniker 32.

MS 482.9

transferred to Beinecke MS 481.20, fol. 3

MS 482.10

transferred to Beinecke MS 481.14, fol. 1

MS 482.11

transferred to Beinecke MS 481.21, fols. 3 and 4

MS 482.12   Italy, s. XII[1]
Bible, Zacharias   Pl. 81

f. 1ra   //lucernis quę erant super caput illud ... uerbum domini ad me di//[cens]

            Zacharias 4.2–8. The upper portion of the leaf is missing with loss of text.

f. 1rb   [plum]//bi portabatur. Et ecce mulier ... de medio duorum montium; montes//

Zacharias 5.7–6.1. The upper portion of the leaf is missing with loss of text. The verso has been completely erased.

Parchment. 1 folio. 200 x 260 mm (written space originally ca. 386 x 245 mm). 2 columns. 14 lines remaining of original ca. 48. Ruled in dry-point on the hair side. Single vertical bounding lines.

Written in Caroline minuscule. The hand is very similar to that of MS 481.63, and it is possible that this leaf is from the same original codex as MS 481.63. The script, decoration, and preservation of the leaves (same trim size, ca. 200 x 260 mm, and one side erased — suggesting they were both reused in the same later binding) is very similar. The leaves of MS 481.63 are ruled for the same width of columns as 482.12 (245 mm); no other original measurements of either can be determined. The number of lines originally on each leaf of MS 481.63 must have been about 51 or 52, whereas MS 482.12 had only about 48 lines. This difference is perhaps not inconsistent with the degree of variation within a single book, especially considering that MS 481.63 (from Acts) would fall later in the volume than MS 482.12 (Zacharias), and the number of written lines seems generally to increase further into a book. 1-line initials are brown rustic capitals, with round E and minuscule h, and are not set apart from the text. Traces of an initial, ca. 2 lines high, set apart from where the text should be, in red ink, on verso. Punctuation consists of the punctus, punctus elevatus, and punctus interrogativus.

The number "xxxxv" is written in ink in the lower left corner of the recto. Zinniker 145–2.

MS 482.13   France or Italy, s. X[1]
Pseudo-Bede, *In Matthaei evangelium expositio*   Pl. 82

f. 1ra   //quæ crediderit domino. et ab eo curata sit ... et a marco spicatum asseritur//

Pseudo-Bede, *In Matthaei evangelium expositio*, chap. 26 (on Matt. 26.6–7); PL 92.110–11. Stegmüller 1678. The upper and lower margins have been trimmed with loss of text.

f. 1rb   //furandi consuetudinem uoluit intonare ... ad illam iungenda est; ubi superius consilium//

In Matthaei evangelium expositio, chap. 26 (on Matt. 26.9–14); PL 92.111. The upper and lower margins have been trimmed with loss of text.

f. 1va   //agnum occidere solebant appellat ... Aquæ baiulus. praeco est noue gratiae//

In Matthaei evangelium expositio, chap. 26 (on Matt. 26.17–18); PL 92.112. The upper and lower margins have been trimmed with loss of text.

f. 1vb   [poeni]//tentiam; Numquid ego sum domine? ... in quod cum magistro discipulus//

In Matthaei evangelium expositio, chap. 26 (on Matt. 26.22–23); PL 92.112. The upper and lower margins have been trimmed with loss of text.

Parchment. 1 folio. 240 x 148 mm (written space originally ca. 267 x 205 mm). 2 columns. 18 lines remaining of original ca. 33. Dry-point ruling on the hair side. Double outer vertical bounding lines and single bounding lines between columns.

Written in Caroline minuscule, with a mixture of pre-Caroline and Caroline forms of *a*. 1-line initials are in brown rustic capitals, with occasional use of uncial *m* and *e*, and are set apart from the text when they occur at the beginning of a line. Punctuation consists of the punctus, punctus elevatus, punctus versus, and punctus interrogativus.

The fragment was used as a pastedown in the binding of a volume measuring ca. 240 x 148 mm.

Zinniker 145–1.

MS 482.14   Southern Germany, s. XI/XII
Noted Breviary   Pl. 82

f. 1r   [*Oratio.* Deus qui uiuis et electis ...] //proficit spaciis; spiritualibus amplificetur augmentis. Per. *In ii uespera. A.* Vota mea domino ... *Ps.* Credidi. *A.* In domum domini. *Ps.* Letatus sum. *A.* Benefac domine. *Ps.* Qui confidunt. *A.* Nisi tu domine. *Ps.* Nisi dominus. *A.* Quoniam confortauit seras ... *Ps.* Lauda hierusalem. *Cap.* Menbra uestra templum ... *In eu. A.* Sanctificauit dominus tabernaculum ... *Orat.* Deus qui nos ad anniuersarium ... *A.* Zache festinans desende [*sic; for* descende] ... facta est alleluia.

Dedication of a church, second vespers.

f. 1r–v   *De sancta trinitate.* A. Gloria tibi trinitas . . . A. Laus et perennis gloria . . .
A. Gloria laudis resonet . . . A. Laus deo patri . . . A. Ex quo omnia . . .
Cap. Gratias agimus deo qui dignos fecit . . . *v.* Benedicamus patrem et
filium . . . *In eu.* A. Gracias tibi deus . . . *Oratio.* Concede quaesumus omnipotens et misericors deus. ut sicut in nomine patris . . . *Ad inuit.* Deum
uerum unum . . . *In i noct.* A. Adesto deus unus . . . *Ps.* Dominus deus noster. A. Te unum in substancia . . . *Ps.* Celi enarrant. A. Te semper idem
. . . *Ps.* Domini est terra. *v.* Benedictus. [L.] Credimus sanctam trinitatem.
id est patrem et filium . . . per quem omnia. a quo omnia. in//

Holy Trinity, from first vespers to the first nocturn of matins.

Parchment. 1 folio. 204 x 140 mm (written space 158 x 100 mm). 1 column. 22
lines. Ruled in dry-point on the hair side. Double vertical bounding lines. Prickings,
which are not original, are in the outer margins.

Written in two sizes of Caroline minuscule, with a larger script for the lessons
and prayers and a smaller script for the chants. 1-line lesson and oration initials are
in orange rustic capitals with uncial M and are written on the inner vertical bounding line. Smaller 1-line initials are in brown rustic capitals, several highlighted with
orange, and are not set apart from the text. Rubrics are written in a mixture of
orange minuscule or in rustic capitals. Punctuation consists of the punctus. Interlinear neumes are in the St. Gall style.

The fragment was used as a flyleaf in the binding of Lambach Ccl 285 (the number "285P" is written in the lower right corner of the verso in pencil in a modern
hand).

A modern hand has written the number "117" in pencil in the lower right corner
of the recto.

Zinniker 77.

Bibliography:
Babcock, *Reconstructing a Medieval Library*, 99 and fig. 53.

MS 482.15

transferred to Beinecke MS 481.23, fol. 1

MS 482.16

transferred to Beinecke MS 481.31, fol. 1

MS 482.17

transferred to Beinecke MS 481.11, fol. 2

MS 482.18

transferred to Beinecke MS 481.36, fol. 2

MS 482.19   Italy, s. XI²
Missal   Pl. 83

It is possible that these two bifolia are not from the same missal. Although the size
and layout are similar, the script and decoration are different.

f. 1ra   [*Lectio.* Cum factus esset iesus annorum duodecim . . .] //quia [in his quae
           patris mei sunt oportet] me ess[e? Et ipsi non intel]lexerunt uer[bum]
           . . . et homin[es]. [*Off.* Iubilate deo] omnis terra iu[bilate] . . . [*Secr.*] Ob-
           [latum tibi domine sacrificium] . . . *Co.* F//[ili]

           Sunday within the Octave of Epiphany. The lesson is from Luke 2.42–52.
           Only a small portion of the inner column remains; the rest has been torn
           away.

f. 1vb   [*Secr.* Hostias tibi domine beati felicis confessoris] //ad [perpetuum nobis
           tribue] peruenire [subsidium. *Co.*] Posuisti domine [in capite] . . . *Post co.*
           [Quaesumus domine salutaribus rep]leti [mysteriis ut cuius sol]emnia [ce-
           lebramus eius orat]ionibus ad[iuuemur. Per.]

           St. Felix *in Pincis* (14 January). Only a small portion of the inner column
           remains; the rest has been torn away.

f. 1vb   //k feb. sancti [marcelini pa]pe. [Statuit ei dominus testamentum paci]s et
           principem [fecit eum ut sit illi sacerdotii di]gnitas in eternum. [*Ps.* . . . ge]-
           neratione//

           St. Marcellus (16 January). Only a small portion of the inner column re-
           mains; the rest has been torn away.

f. 2ra　[*Off.*] //Veritas mea et misericordia . . . *Secr.* Suscipe quaesumus domine munera dignanter . . . *Co.* Domine quinque talenta . . . [*Post co*]. Satiasti domine familiam tuam . . . celebramus. Per.

St. Marcellus. The first ten lines of the inner column are missing.

f. 2ra–vb　*Dominica iiᵃ post epyphania.* Omnis terra adoret . . . *Ps.* Iubilate deo . . . *Or.* Omnipotens sempiterne deus [qui celestia] simul . . . *Lectio epistole beati pauli apostoli ad romanos.* Fratres. Habentes donationes secundum gratiam que data est . . . consentientes. *Gr.* Misit [dominus uerbum] suum et . . . *V.* Confitean[tur] domino misericordie . . . Alleluia. *V.* Omnis terra adoret . . . *Sequentia sancti evangelii secundum iohannem.* In illo tempore. Nuptię facte sunt in chana galylee . . . discipuli eius. *Of.* Iubilate deo uniuersa terra . . . *Secr.* Oblata domine munera sanctifica . . . *Co.* Dicit dominus implete ydras . . . *Post co.* Augeatur in nobis domine quaesumus . . . preparemur.

Second Sunday after Epiphany. The lessons are from Romans 12.6–16 and John 2.1–11. The first ten lines of the inner column on the verso are missing, with the loss of portions of the gospel lesson.

f. 2vb　*V kl Feb. Sancte prisce virginis.* Loquebar de testimoniis tuis . . . *Ps.* Beati in//[maculati]

St. Prisca (18 January).

f. 3ra　[*L.*] //Ego e[nim dabo uobis os] et sapientiam. cui non poterunt resistere . . . In patientia uestra possidebitis animas uestras. *Of.* Confitebuntur celi mirabilia . . . *Sec.* Tanto tibi placabile quaesumus domine nostrę sint hostiæ . . . *Co.* Lætabitur iustus in domino . . . *Post com.* Beati georgii martyris//

St. George (23 April). The lesson is from Luke 21.15–19. The upper margin has been torn away with the loss of the first eight lines of the inner column.

f. 3rb　//consecrasti [. . .] praesta quaesumus . . . *Sec.* Hanc in conspectu diuinę et tremende maiestatis . . . *Post co.* Inenarrabili sacramenti dulcedini suauitate . . . beati marci euangelistę tui moniti//

St. Mark (25 April). The upper margin has been torn away with the loss of the first ten lines of the column.

f. 3va   //*Ps.* Venite. *Or.* Mentem familiæ tuæ quaesumus domine intercedente
          beato laurentio . . . *Alleluia.* P[opu]lus [syon.] Domine deus noster qui
          cum patribus . . . *Al.* Ego sum deus . . . *Or. ad s. valentinum.* Deus qui culpas
          delinquentiu[m] . . . *Al. A.* Confitemini domino filius israhel qu[i di]cit//

          Letania Maior ad S. Laurentium (25 April), with a prayer for St.
          Valentine. The upper margin has been torn away with the loss of the first
          ten lines of the column.

f. 3vb   [*Oratio ad crucem.* Deus qui culpas nostras . . .] //consolatione gaudere.
          Per. *A.* Parce domine parce . . . *Oratio ad +.* Parce domine quaesumus
          parce populo . . . *A.* Iniquitates nostrę [domine] multiplicate . . . *A.* Ex-
          clamemus omnes ad dominum . . . *A.* [Redime] domine de interitu . . . *A.*
          Exaudi nos domine . . . *Or. in atrio.* Adesto domine supplicationibus nos-
          tris . . . intercedente//

          Letania Maior. The upper margin has been torn away with the loss of the
          first nine lines of the column.

f. 4ra   *Post com.* [Quaesumus domine sal]utarib[us repleti . . . adiuue]mur. Per.

          Apostles Philip and James (1 May). The upper margin has been torn away
          with the loss of the first two lines of the column.

f. 4ra   *Mensis maii die iii inventio sanctae + et n[atale] sanctorum alexandri. eventii
          et theodoli* (corr. ex *theodori*) *atque iuuenalis.* Nos autem gloriari . . . *Ps.*
          Deus misereatur nobis [*supra:* nostri] et bene. *Or.* Deus qui in preclara
          salutifere crucis . . . Praesta quaesumus omnipotens deus. ut qui sanc-
          torum tuorum alexandri euentii [et] theodoli. atque beati iuuenalis . . . *Ad
          galathas.* Fratres. Confido de uobis in domino . . . autem conturbat//

          Sts. Alexander, Eventius, Theodolus, and Juvenal (3 May) and the Inven-
          tion of the Cross (3 May). The lesson is from Galatians 5.10.

f. 4rb   [prae]//dico quid adhuc . . . ego mundo. All. V. Dominus [re]gnauit de-
          corem . . . [beginning of rubric faded] *evg require a*[. . .] *in mense sept. in
          sancta cruce. Off.* Deus enim firmauit . . . [*Sec.*] S//[acrificium]

          Sts. Alexander, Eventius, Theodolus, and Juvenal (3 May) and the Inven-
          tion of the Cross (3 May). The lesson is from Galatians 5.11–12 and 6.12–
          14. The upper and lower margins have been torn away with the loss of the
          first three lines and the last five lines of text.

f. 4va   [*Sec.* Super has] //quaesumus hostias domine benedictio copiosa ... *Co.*
          [Spiritu]s ubi uult spirat et uocem ... *Post co.* Repleti alimonia cælesti
          ... [*Post co.*] Refecti participatione ... effectum. Per.

          Sts. Alexander, Eventius, Theodolus, and Juvenal (3 May) and the Inven-
          tion of the Cross (3 May). The upper margin has been torn away with the
          loss of the first two lines of text.

f. 4va   *Dominica ii. post octauam paschę.* Iubilate deo omnis terra ... *Ps.* Dicite
          deo. *Or.* Deus qui errantes ut in uiam ... iustitiæ//

          Second Sunday after the Octave of Easter. The lower margin has been
          torn away with the loss of the last five lines of text.

f. 4vb   [*L.* Obsecro uos ...] //et peregrin[os abstinere uos] a carnalibus ... Non
          tantum bonis//

          Second Sunday after the Octave of Easter. The lesson is from 1 Peter
          2.11–19. The upper margin has been torn away with the loss of the first
          two lines of text.

Parchment (stained and damaged). 4 folios (fols. 1 and 2 and fols. 3 and 4 form two
bifolia). Fol. 1 measures 248 x 55 mm; fol. 2, 360 x 247 mm; fol. 3, 301 x 249 mm;
fol. 4, 340 x 266 mm (written space 278 x 165 mm). 2 columns. 31 lines. Dry-point
ruling. Double vertical bounding lines with an extra vertical bounding line between
the two columns. Pricking in outer margin.
    Written in Caroline minuscule by two scribes, one on fols. 1–2 and the other on
fols. 3–4. There are two 7-line initials on fol. 2, set apart from the text; they are in
red outline with a center shaft filled with red and are decorated with foliate
ornamentation. 1- and 2-line prayer initials alternate red and brown and are written
on the inner vertical bounding line; the red initials are sometimes filled with yellow.
1-line chant initials are in brown rustic capitals, occasionally highlighted with red.
1-line initials within lessons are in brown rustic capitals with round *D.* Rubrics are
written in red rustic capitals mixed with minuscules and round *E.* Punctuation
consists of the punctus and punctus interrogativus (and a diacritical mark appears
over the interrogative word in a question, in the Beneventan fashion). Accents in
the same ink as the text.
    There are 2- to 10-line initials on fols. 3–4; several are in brown outline colored
with red and yellow, and others are in red outline colored with yellow or green. The
first letter after the initials is in brown rustic capitals with round *E.* 1-line chant
initials are in brown rustic capitals with round *E,* some filled with yellow, and are
set apart from the text when they occur at the beginning of a line. Rubrics are

written in red rustic capitals with round *E* and are marked with a horizontal yellow line. Punctuation consists of the punctus.

The bifolium 1/2 was used as a wrapper for a volume measuring at least 305 x 210 mm. The inscription "Vol. 10 / III.2.A / 3.III.2" is written on fol. 2r. A sixteenth-century hand has written inscriptions between the columns on fol. 2r. The bifolium 3/4 formed a portion of a wrapper of a volume measuring ca. 415 x 285 mm.

Zinniker 128–1 and 128–2.

MS 482.20   S. Germany or N. Italy, s. X/XI
Bible, Mark, or Lectionary or Missal   Pl. 83

The speakers in the text are noted by letters above the first word of quoted text: "T" for Jesus, "C" for the narrator, and "I" for other speakers. These letters indicate the different ways to read the words of the speakers in the passage during Holy Week, in this case, Feria III. According to Notker Balbulus, "T" indicates that Jesus's words are to be said slowly (*trahere* or *tenere*); "C" indicates that the narrator's words are to be said quickly (*celeriter*); and "I" indicates that the other speakers' words should be read with a lowering of pitch (*inferius*). See Karl Young, "Observations on the Origin of the Mediaeval Passion-Play," *Publications of the Modern Language Association* 25 (1910): 309–54.

f. 1r   //[singillati]m; Numquid ego . . . in diem illum cum illud bibam//

          Mark 14.19–29. The upper margin has been trimmed with the loss of approximately four lines of text.

f. 1v   //negabo; (C) Similiter autem et omnes . . . Et reuersus denuo//

          Mark 14.31–40. The upper margin has been trimmed with the loss of approximately four lines of text.

f. 2r   //filius hominis . . . apud uos in tem//[plo]

          Mark 14.41–49. The upper and outer margins have been trimmed with the loss of approximately four lines of text.

f. 2v   //rel[. . .] Et cogitanes [*sic*; *for* conuenientes] om[nes] . . . dicens [. . .]//

Mark 14.53–60. The upper and outer margins have been trimmed with the loss of approximately four lines of text.

Parchment (fols. 1r and 2v are worn from use in a binding). 2 folios (bifolium). Fol. 1 measures 219 x 188 mm; fol. 2 measures 218 x 98 mm (written space originally ca. 215 x 150 mm). 1 column. 16 of ca. 20 lines remaining; an extra line has been written in the lower margin of fol. 1r. Dry-point ruling.

Written in Caroline minuscule. 1-line initials are in brown rustic capitals and are not set apart from the text. Punctuation consists of the punctus and punctus versus.

The fragment was used as a pastedown in the binding of a volume measuring ca. 282 x 200 mm.

Zinniker 133–2.

MS 482.21

transferred to Beinecke MS 481.25, fols. 7, 9, 10, and 12

MS 482.22

transferred to Beinecke MS 481.39, fols. 1 and 2

MS 482.23

transferred to Beinecke MS 481.45, fols. 2 and 3

MS 482.24A

transferred to Beinecke MS 481.46, fol. 1

MS 482.24B

transferred to Beinecke MS 481.26, fol. 1

MS 482.25
Psalter (Gallican)

Southern Germany or Austria, s. XII[1]
Pl. 84

f. 1   //meo uirtutem. Auertisti faciem tuam a me ... et anni mei in gemi//
         [tibus]

         Psalms 29.8–30.11.

f. 2   //psalterio decem ... domine super nos; quemadmo//[dum]

         Psalm 32.2–22.

Parchment. 2 folios (bifolium). 198 x 140 mm (written space 165 x 110 mm). 1
column. 18 lines. Dry-point ruling on the hair side. Double vertical bounding lines.
    Written in late Caroline minuscule. One 3-line initial at the beginning of Psalm
30, set apart from the text between vertical bounding lines, in silver highlighted
with blue and green. Initials at the beginning of verses are in red square capitals,
with occasional use of enlarged minuscule n and uncial A and round D and E,
which in places has oxidized into a silver color; they are set apart from the text
between double bounding lines when they occur at the beginning of a line. Psalm
30 begins with a full line of brown rustic capitals. Punctuation consists of the punctus, punctus elevatus, and one punctus flexus, but the punctus elevatus and punctus flexus may be later alterations of original punctus. Later gothic hands have
made corrections and liturgical additions in the margin of fol. 1r.
    The fragment was used as a pastedown in the binding of a volume measuring ca.
283 x 198 mm.
    Zinniker 134.

MS 482.26
Antiphonary

Southern Germany, s. XII
Pl. 84

f. 1r   [A. Te qui in spiritu ...] //purificas humana contagia ... A. Baptista
         contremuit et ... A. Capud draconis saluator ... A. Magnum mysterium
         declaratur ... In evang. A. Precursor iohannes exultat ... In ii v. A. Ante
         luciferum genitus. R. In columbe specie. In evang. A. Christo datus est
         ... ei in ęternum.

         Epiphany, from lauds to second vespers. A slightly later hand has added
         additional chants for second vespers in the upper margin of the leaf.

f. 1r   *Dominica i post Theophaniam.* A. Fili quid fecisti ... A. Puer iesus profi-
          ciebat ... et homines alleluia.

          First Sunday after Epiphany.

f. 1r   *Dominica ii.* A. Nuptię facte sunt ... A. Quid mihi et tibi ... A. Deficiente
          uino iussit ... conuersę sunt. alleluia.

          Second Sunday after Epiphany.

f. 1r   *Dominica iii.* A. Cum autem descendisset ... A. Domine si tu uis ... A.
          Domine puer meus ... A. Domine non sum ... A. Tantum domine dic
          ... A. Multi ueniunt ab oriente ... in regno cęlorum. alleluia.

          Third Sunday after Epiphany. There are no neumes for "Domine puer
          meus ... "

f. 1r–v   *Dominica iiii.* A. Ascendente iesu in nauiculam ... A. Domine salua nos
          ... A. Surgens iesus imperauit ... mirati sunt uniuersis.

          Fourth Sunday after Epiphany.

f. 1v–2   *Dominica. Respons. de spalmis* [sic]. R. Domine ne in ira ... V. Timor et
          tremor ... R. Deus qui sedes ... V. Tibi enim derelictus ... R. Exurge
          domine deus meus ... V. Tibi enim. R. A dextris est mihi ... V. Conserua
          me domine ... R. Notas mihi fecisti ... V. Conserua me domine. R.
          Custodi nos domine ... V. Mirifica misericordias tuas ... R. Diligam te
          domine ... V. Laudans inuocabo dominum ... R. Domini est terra ... V.
          Ipse super maria ... R. Ad te domine leuaui ... V. Neque irrideant me
          ... R. Audiam domine uocem ... V. Domine dilexi decorem ... R. Afflicti
          pro peccatis ... V. Domine deus israhel ... R. Peccata mea domine ... V.
          Quoniam iniquitatem meam ... R. Adiutor meus esto ... V. Neque des-
          picias me ... R. Domine puer meus ... V. Domine non sum ... *Feria. ii.*
          R. Quam magna multitudo ... V. Perfecisti eis qui ... R. Benedicam
          domino in omni ... V. In domino laudabitur ... R. Delectare in domino
          ... V. Spera in domino ... R. Auribus percipe domine ... V. Dixi custo-
          diam uias ... R. Statuit dominus supra ... V. Expectans expectaui do-
          minum ... R. Ego dixi domine ... V. Domine ne in ira ... R. Sedes tua
          deus ... V. Dilexisti iusticiam et ... *Feria. iii.* R. Abscondi tamquam au-
          rum ... V. Quoniam iniquitatem ... R. Paratum cor meum ... V. Exurge
          gloria mea ... R. Adiutor meus tibi ... V. Eripe me de inimicis ... *Feria.
          iiii.* R. Exaudi deus deprecationem ... V. Dum anxiaretur cor ... R. Deus

in te . . . *V.* Esto mihi domine . . . *R.* Repleatur os meum . . . *V.* Gaudebunt
labia mea . . . *R.* Gaudebunt labia mea . . . *V.* Sed et lingua . . . *Feria v. R.*
Cogitaui dies antiquos . . . *V.* Illuxerunt coruscationes tuę . . . *R.* Domine
deus propitius . . . *V.* Adiuua nos deus . . . *R.* Deuastauit uineam me//[am]

Psalm responsories for use between Epiphany and Septuagesima (Sunday
through Feria V).

Parchment. 2 folios. 294 x 200 mm (written space 247 x 160 mm). 2 columns. Fol.
1 has 29 lines, and fol. 2 has 30 lines. Dry-point ruling. Double vertical and single
horizontal bounding lines. Three vertical lines in intercolumn.

Written in Caroline minuscule. 1-line initials at the beginning of responses are
in square capitals, with occasional use of round D, in thick brown ink dotted or
filled with orange; they are not set apart from the text. 1-line initials at the beginning of antiphons and verses are brown rustic capitals highlighted with orange.
Rubrics are written in orange rustic capitals and are set apart from the text when
they occur at the beginning of a line. Punctuation consists of the punctus. Interlinear neumes for chants with full text are in the St. Gall style.

Zinniker 8, 88.

MS 482.27   Germany, s. XII/XIII
Capitula (Breviary?)   Pl. 85

f. 1r   [multi]//tudo et mente confusa est . . . loquentes. *Aliud.* Parthi et medi
          . . . mesopotamiam. iudeam.//

          Capitula for sext of Pentecost, including Acts 2.6 and 2.9.

f. 1v   //in nobis. quo[niam] de spiritu sancto dedit nobis. *Aliud.* Caritas dei dif-
          fusa est . . . nobis.

          Capitula for an unidentified office, including 1 John 4.13 and Romans 5.5.

f. 1v   *Feria iiᵃ. Cap.* Aperiens petrus os suum dixit;//

          Capitulum for an unidentified Feria II, from Acts 10.34.

f. 2   //tenebrę nunc autem lux . . . ambulate.

          Capitulum for an unidentified Feria III, from Ephesians 5.8.

f. 2   *Feria 4ta*. Stabiles estote et inmobiles ... in domino.

Capitulum for an unidentified Feria IV, from 1 Corinthians 15.58.

f. 2   *Feria quinta*. Sobrii estote et uigilate ... fortes in fide.

Capitulum for an unidentified Feria V, from 1 Peter 5.8.

f. 2   *Feria vi^{ta}*. Nos qui diei sumus ... galeam salutis quod est uinculum pacis.

Capitulum for an unidentified Feria VI, from 1 Thessalonians 5.8.

f. 2   *Sabbato*. Exhibete uos deo ... iusticie deo. *Aliud*. Omnes uos filii ... tenebrarum.

Capitula for an unidentified Saturday, from Romans 6.13 and 1 Thessalonians 5.5.

f. 2   *In priuatis diebus ad i^{a} ca*. Domine miserere nostri ... tribulationis. *Aliud ad primam*. Omnes enim quicumque ... in christo iesu domino nostro. *Ad terciam.//*

Capitula from Isaiah 33.2 and Romans 10.13.

Parchment. 2 folios. Fol. 1 measures 90 x 147 mm; fol. 2 measures 277 x 204 mm (written space 200 x 135 mm). 1 column. 13 lines; fol. 1 preserves only 5 lines. Ruled in lead. Single vertical bounding lines.

Written in late Caroline minuscule bordering on early gothic. 1- and 2-line initials at the beginning of lessons are in red, and the 1-line initials are set apart from the text when they occur at the beginning of a line. Rubrics are written in red minuscule. The rubrics on fol. 2r are in a fifteenth-century hand. The name "petrus" on fol. 1v is written in brown rustic capitals. Punctuation consists of the punctus and punctus elevatus. Accents are in the same ink as the text.

The fragments were used as the wrapper (fol. 2) and a pastedown (fol. 1) in the binding of a volume measuring ca. 147 x 90 mm. On the upper margin of fol. 2r, a fifteenth-century gothic cursive hand has written a Bible passage, "bene]dictus deus et pater domini nostri iesu christi qui benedixit nos in [omni benedictione spirit]uali in celestibus in christo," (Galatians 1:3=Ephesians 1:3). A modern hand has written the number "50" in pencil in the lower right corner of fol. 2v and "51" in the lower left corner of fol. 1v.

Zinniker 114–1 and 114–2.

MS 482.28   Southern Germany, s. XI/XII
Antiphonary   Pl. 85

f. 1r   [A. Domus] //mea domus orationis est . . . docens in templo.

Feria III of the first week of Quadragesima. The outer margin has been
trimmed with loss of text.

f. 1r   *Feria i*[*iii.*] A. Generatio hęc praua . . . *i.* A. Sicut fuit ionas . . . *iii.* A. Cum
[immun]dus spiritus . . . *vi.* A. Dixit quidam ad iesum . . . *viiii.* A. Per arma
iusti[cie]. *In ev.* A. Si quis fecerit uoluntatem . . . et mater est.

Feria IV of the first week of Quadragesima. The outer margin has been
trimmed with loss of text.

f. 1r   *Feria quinta.* A. Si manseritis in sermone . . . A. Si ueritatem dico . . . dei
audit.

Feria V of the first week of Quadragesima. The outer margin has been
trimmed with loss of text.

f. 1r–v *Feria vi.* A. Angelus domini de[scende]bat . . . *i.* A. Dom[ine] non habeo
. . . *iii.* A. Qui me sanum . . . *Ad vesp. In e.* A. Vade ia[m et noli] peccare
. . . contingat.

Feria VI of the first week of Quadragesima. The outer margin has been
trimmed with loss of text.

f. 1v   *Sabbato.* [A. As]sumpsit iesus discipulos . . . *i.* A. Domine bonum est . . .
[*iii.*] A. Faciamus hic tria . . . *vi.* A. Descendentibus illis de monte . . . *viiii.*
A. Visionem quam uidistis . . . *vesp.* A. Nemini [dixe]ritis uisionem . . . a
mortuis resurgat.

Saturday of the first week of Quadragesima. The outer margin has been
trimmed with loss of text.

f. 1v   [Dom]inica ii. Ad vesperam. R. Dum exiret iacob. *ymnus.* [*u*]*ersus ut supra.*
In evang. A. Nemini dixeritis. *Invitat.* [Quoniam d]eus magnus dominus
. . . *Ps.* Venite. *ymnus et uersus ut supra.* [R. T]olle arma tua . . . V. Cum-
que uenatu aliquid . . . [R. E]cce odor filii . . . sicut harenam maris//

Second Sunday of Quadragesima. The outer margin has been trimmed
with loss of text.

Parchment. 1 folio (a portion of the conjugate leaf is preserved with some text). 235 x 137 mm (written space 197 x ca. 125 mm); conjugate leaf measures 235 x 27 mm. 1 column. 19 lines. Dry-point ruling. Double vertical and horizontal bounding lines.

Written in Caroline minuscule. On fol. 1v, there are portions of a 3-line square capital "T" in orange, not set apart from the text. Initials of the antiphons beginning feriae IV and VI are 1-line rustic capitals in orange. Initials of responses and of the antiphon beginning feria V are thick brown uncials filled with red. Other 1-line initials are brown rustic capitals highlighted with red. Rubrics are written in orange rustic capitals. Liturgical directions are written in brown minuscule highlighted with red. The first line of the first response of the second Sunday of Quadragesima is written in brown rustic capitals highlighted with red. Punctuation consists of the punctus. Interlinear neumes for chants with full text are in the St. Gall style.

The fragment was once used as a pastedown in the binding of a volume measuring ca. 235 x 165 mm.

Zinniker 140–1.

MS 482.29

transferred to Beinecke MS 481.51, fol. 16

MS 482.30

transferred to Beinecke MS 481.49, fol. 2

MS 482.31   Melk, Austria, s. XII[1]
Antiphonary   Pl. 86

f. 1r   //*In natale sancti pantaleonis mart*[*yris.*] Adest beati pantaleonis . . . *Invitat.*
            Christum regem uenite . . . A. Pantaleon senatoris eustorgii . . . Ps. Beatus
            uir. A. Hunc magister eius eufrosinus . . . A. Presbiter nomine ermolaus
            . . . v. Gloria et honore. [R.] Senator quidam nomine eustorgius . . . V.
            Hunc tradidit eufrosino . . . R. Erat quidam presbiter . . . V. Intellexit presbiter in puero . . . R. Pantaleon sicut arbor . . . V. Sic enim erat plenus . . .
            A. Dedit illi dominus . . . A. Intellexit clamorem . . . A. Per pantaleonem
            necdum . . . est nomen tuum. R. U//

St. Pantaleon (27 July), from first vespers to the first nocturn of matins. The lower portion of the leaf has been trimmed with loss of text.

f. 1v //R. Sanctus pantaleon de foueto ... V. Sanctis qui a miximiano [sic] ... R. Beatus pantaleon tetigit ... V. Qui sanas egrotos ... R. Mox ut cecus ... V. Quod cum pantaleon ... In mat. l. Senator quidam nomine eustorgius ... A. Acceptumque discipulum pantaleonem ... A. Fuit itaque quidam presbiter ... A. Et respiciens beatus pantaleon ... A. Gratias tibi ago domine ... In evangelio. A. Apparitores osculantes manus ... A. Beatus pantaleon tenuit ... in domum suam gaudens//

St. Pantaleon, from the third nocturn of matins to lauds. The lower portion of the leaf has been trimmed with loss of text.

Parchment. 1 folio. 130 x 214 mm (original written space uncertain; width of written space: 190 mm). 1 column. 16 lines remaining of an uncertain original. Drypoint ruling. Double vertical and single horizontal bounding lines.

   Written in late Caroline minuscule. 2-line initials at the beginning of the office, of the responsorial liturgy, and of lauds are in red square capitals and are not set apart from the text. 1-line initials at the beginning of responses are in thick black square capitals highlighted with red. Other 1-line initials are in brown rustic capitals highlighted with red. Rubrics are written in red in a mixture of rustic capital and minuscule forms. Punctuation consists of the punctus. Interlinear neumes in the St. Gall style are on the recto and only occasionally on the verso. Some of the neumes on the recto may be later additions.

   According to Alois Haidinger there are fragments from the same antiphonary in the library of Melk.

   The fragment was used as a flyleaf in the binding of a volume measuring ca. 214 x 115 mm.

   Zinniker 43–2.

MS 482.32   Germany, s. XII
Antiphonary   Pl. 86

f. 1r //sixtus decio respondit miser ... A. Responderunt felicissimus et agapitus ... A. Cumque sanctus sixtus felicissimus atque agapitus ... comminuta est.

Sts. Sixtus, Felicissimus, and Agapitus (6 August), second vespers. The upper right corner of the recto has been torn with loss of text.

f. 1r–v *De sancto laurencio.* A. Leuita laurencius bonum opus ... [Ps.] Laudate
... *v.* Gloria et honore. A. Confitebor tibi domine ... *vitor.* Venite adoremus regem ... [Ps.] Venite. A. Quo progrederis sine filio ... *v.* Beatus
laurencius dixit. A. Noli me derelinquere ... *v.* Quid in me ... Ps. Quare
fremuerunt. A. Non ego te ... *v.* Beatus laurencius dixit. Ps. Cum
inuocarem. *v.* Gloria et honore. [R.] Levita laurencius bonum opus ... V.
Dispersit dedit pauperibus ... R. Puer meus noli timere ... V. Liberabo te
de manu ... [R. Str]inxerunt corporis membra ... V. Carnifices uero
urgentes ... A. Beatus laurencius orabat ... *v.* Quia acusatus non negaui
... [Ps.] Verba mea. A. Dixit romanus ad beatum ... *v.* Aferens autem urceum ... [Ps.] Domine dominus. A. Beatus laurencius dixit ... *v.* Quia
ipse dominus nouit ... Ps. In domino confido. [*v.*] Posuisti. [R.] Noli me
derelinquere ... V. Nos quasi senes ... R. Beatus laurencius dixit ... V.
Quoniam ad te orabo ... R. Beatus uir laurencius ... V. Qui potuit transgredi ... A. Strinxerunt cor//[poris]

St. Laurence (10 August), from first vespers to the third nocturn of matins. The upper left corner of the verso has been trimmed with loss of text.

f. 2 //[Ps.] Laudate dominum. A. Ornatam in monilibus ... [Ps.] Lauda anima
mea. A. Is[ta est] speciosa ... [Ps.] Laudate dominum. A. Tota pulchra es
... [Ps.] Lauda hierusalem. R. Felix ualde. [V.] Ora. A. Virgo prudentis-
sima quo ... [Ps.] Magna. [A. I]bo michi ad montem ... *vitatorium.* In
onore beatissime marie ... [Ps.] Venite. A. Exaltata es sancta dei genitrix
... Ps. Domine deus. A. Paradisi porte per te ... Ps. Celi enarrant. [A.]
Sicut mirra electa ... [Ps.] Domini est terra. [*v.*] Specie tua. R. Vidi speciosam sicut ... V. Que est ista que ascendit ... R. Sicut cedrus exaltata
... [V.] Et sicut cinamomum ... R. Que est [ista que] processit ... V. Et
sicut dies ... A. Specie tua et ... [Ps.] Eructauit cor. A. Adiuuabit eam
deus ... [Ps.] Deus noster. A. Sicut letancium omnium ... R. Beatam me
dicent omnes ... [V.] Et misericordia eius ... R. Ornatam in monilibus
... V. Astitit regina a dextris ... R. Ista est speciosa ... [V.] Specie tua et
... A. Dignare me laudare ... [Ps.] Dominus regnabit. A. Gaude maria
uirgo ... [Ps.] Cantate domino. A. Post partum uirgo ... [Ps.] Cantate ii.
[A.] Adiuuabit eam//

Assumption of the Virgin (15 August), from first vespers to the third nocturn of matins. The upper corner of the inner margin has been trimmed
with loss of text.

Parchment (stained and damaged). 2 folios. Fol. 1 measures 205 x 144 mm (with
strip of conjoint leaf measuring 205 x 10 mm); fol. 2 measures 208 x 138 mm

(written space 183 x 110 mm). 1 column. 25 lines. Dry-point ruling. Single vertical and double horizontal bounding lines.

Written in late Caroline minuscule. 2-line initials at the beginning of responsorial liturgy are in red square capitals and are written on the vertical bounding line. 1-line initials are in brown rustic capitals, with uncial forms of M and round forms of E and sometimes D, and are not set apart from the text. Rubrics are written in red minuscule and are set apart from the text when they occur at the beginning of a line. Punctuation consists of the punctus and the punctus elevatus (rare). Interlinear neumes in the St. Gall style.

Both fragments were used as pastedowns in the binding of a volume measuring ca. 208 x 140 mm; they both preserve a pair of rust stains from the binding clasps, near the edge of the leaf in fol. 1 and in the middle of fol. 2.

Fol. 1 was formerly Zinniker 142; fol. 2 was formerly Beinecke MS 482.33, Zinniker 38.

MS 482.33

transferred to Beinecke MS 482.32, fol. 2

MS 482.34

transferred to Beinecke MS 481.52, fols. 3, 4, 5, 7, and 11

MS 482.35

transferred to Beinecke MS 481.54, fol. 2

MS 482.36   Germany, s. XII
Bible, Genesis   Pl. 87

f. 1r   [haedo]//s optimos; ut faciam ex eis ẹscas . . . et pergens affer [qu]e dixi. Abiit et//

Genesis 27.9–14. All margins have been trimmed with loss of text.

f. 1v   //osculum fili mi. Accessit et osculatus . . . et qui benedixerit tibi bened//
           [ictionibus]

           Genesis 27.25–29. All margins have been trimmed with loss of text.

Parchment. 1 folio. 86 x 115 mm (written space originally ca. 274 x 165 mm). 1
column. 8 lines remaining of an original ca. 28. Dry-point ruling.
       Written in late Caroline minuscule. 1-line initials are written in brown rustic
capitals. Punctuation consists of the punctus, some of which a later hand has altered to punctus elevati.
       The fragment was once sewn into the spine of a binding.
       Zinniker 108.

MS 482.37   Germany, s. XII
Bible, Leviticus   Pl. 87

f. 1ra   [q]//ui sanctifico uos . . . sex diebus facietis opus.//

           Leviticus 22.32–23.3. Only the bottom five lines of the leaf remain.

f. 1rb   //pro peccato. duosque agnos anniculos hostias pacificorum . . . Legitimum
           sempiternum erit in cunctis//

           Leviticus 23.19–21. Only the bottom six lines of the leaf remain.

f. 1va   //mensis septimi. quando . . . et ramos ligni den//[sarum]

           Leviticus 23.39–40. Only the bottom six lines of the leaf remain.

f. 1vb   [male]//dixerit deo suo portabit . . . nomen domini [morte m]oria//[tur]

           Leviticus 24.15–16. Only the bottom five lines of the leaf remain.

Parchment. 1 folio. 110 x 295 mm (written space originally ca. 375 x 230 mm). 2
columns. 5–6 lines remaining of original ca. 45. Dry-point ruling. Double vertical
bounding lines surround both columns.
       Written in late Caroline minuscule. Punctuation consists of the punctus and
punctus elevatus. Accents are in the same ink as the text. Chap. 23 begins with the
number "lxxvi" in red.
       The fragment was used in the binding of a volume measuring ca. 265 mm in

height. A modern hand has written "T41" in pencil in the lower left corner of the recto.

Zinniker 65–2.

MS 482.38   Germany, s. XII
Lectionary   Pl. 88

f. 1rb   [spo]//lia eius. Noluit autem asahel omittere . . . noluit declinare. Tu.

              2 Kings 2.21–23; lesson for Feria III of an unidentified feast. The inner
              and lower margins have been trimmed with the loss of the inner column
              and bottom line of text.

f. 1rb–va   *Feria iiii.* Percussit ergo abner asahel . . . in sepulchro patris sui in
              bethleem. Tu.

              2 Kings 2.23–31; lesson for Feria IV of an unidentified feast. The inner
              and lower margins have been trimmed with the loss of the inner column
              and bottom line of text.

f. 1va   *Feria v.* Facta est ergo longa concertatio inter domum . . . ad te uniuersum
              israhel.

              2 Kings 3.1–12; lesson for Feria V of an unidentified feast.

f. 1va   *Feria vi.* Sermonem quoque intulit abner . . . quęrebatis dauid. ut re//
              [gnaret]

              2 Kings 3.17; lesson for Feria VI of an unidentified feast. The inner and
              lower margins have been trimmed with the loss of the inner column and
              bottom line of text.

Parchment (stained and creased). 1 folio. 340 x 157 mm (written space originally
ca. 322 x 230 mm). 1 (outer) of 2 columns remaining. 39 lines remaining of an
original ca. 40 lines. Dry-point ruling; double vertical bounding lines. Prickings in
outer margin.

Written in late Caroline minuscule. 2- and 3-line initials at the beginning of
lessons are written in red uncials and are set apart from the text between the
double bounding lines. 1-line initials are written in brown rustic capitals and are set
apart from the text between the double bounding lines when they occur at the

beginning of a line. Rubrics are written in red rustic capitals. Punctuation consists of the punctus, punctus elevatus, and punctus interrogativus.

The fragment was used in the binding of a volume measuring ca. 291 mm in height. There is an undeciphered inscription on the recto in a fifteenth-century cursive gothic hand.

Zinniker 135.

MS 482.39
Bible, Minor Prophets

Germany, s. XIII
Pl. 88

f. 1ra   //ipse uocabit nomen meum. et ego exaudiam ... exibunt aque uiue de ie//[rusalem]

Zacharias 13.9–14.8. The upper margin has been trimmed with loss of text.

f. 1rb   //gentium. aurum et argentum ... domini exercituum in die illa. *Explicit Zacharias propheta; Incipit prologus in malachyam prophetam;*//

Zacharias 14.14–21. The upper margin has been trimmed with loss of text.

f. 1va   //est dominus usque in eternum ... est nomen meum in gentibus dicit dominus//

Malachi 1.4–11. The upper margin has been trimmed with loss of text.

f. 1vb   [ster]//cus sollempnitatum uestrarum ... Disperdat dominus uirum qui fe//[cerit]

Malachi 2.3–12. The upper margin has been trimmed with loss of text.

Parchment (rubbed and stained). 1 folio. 175 x 257 mm (written space originally ca. 305 x 193 mm). 2 columns. 22 of ca. 40 lines remaining. Ruled in ink. Double vertical bounding lines.

Written in gothic script (littera textualis). 2-line round E of Zach. 14.1 in red, written on the vertical bounding line. The chapter also begins with the number "XIIII" in alternating blue and red. 1-line initials are in brown highlighted with red. Rubrics are written in red in a slightly larger and more formal littera textualis. Punctuation consists of the punctus, punctus elevatus, punctus versus, and punctus interrogativus, many of which are added, altered, or highlighted in red. Accents have been added in red ink. The rubricator has also made a number of corrections to the text, as has another contemporary hand in brown ink.

The fragment was once used as the wrapper for a volume measuring ca. 155 x 100 mm.

Zinniker 116.

MS 482.40   Southern Germany, s. XII[1]
Noted Breviary   Pl. 89

f. 1r   [et ad]//iecit dominus loqui . . . terrę tuę o emmanuel. R. Sicut mater con-
          solatur . . . V. Dabo in syon . . . *vel* V. Deus a libano. [L.] Congregamini
          populi et uincemini . . . et in petram scanda//[li]

          Second Sunday of Advent, second nocturn of matins. The lessons are
          from Isaiah 8.5–8 and 8.9–14.

f. 1v   [R. Hierusalem] //plantabis uineam in montibus . . . V. Deus a libano ue-
          niet . . . [v] Gloria patri. quia de medio. *Ad cantica.* A. Dicite pusillaminis
          [*sic for* pusillanimis] confortamini . . . *Cantica.* Ecce dominus in fortitudine
          ueniet. v. Ex syon species. *Secundum lucam.* In illo tempore. Dixit dominus
          iesus discipulis suis. Erunt signa in sole et luna . . . *Omelia b. gregorii.* Do-
          minus ac redemptor noster paratos nos inuenire desiderans . . . prae con-
          fusione sonitus//

          Second Sunday of Advent, second nocturn of matins, with lesson from
          Gregory, *Homiliae xl in evangelia*, Homily I.1 (on Luke 21.25–32; PL
          76.1077–78); R. Étaix, ed., CCSL 141 (1999), 5–6.

f. 2r–v   [mo]//uebitur. sed et cum clamauerint ad eum . . . Non posuisti hęc super
          cor tuum neque recordata es nouissimi tui. *In euang.* A. De cęlo ueniet
          . . . A. Ecce rex ueniet . . . captiuitatis nostrę.

          Feria II of the second week of Advent, matins and second vespers. The
          lesson is from Isaiah 46.7–47.7.

f. 2v   *Feria tercia.* Audi me israhel et iacob quem ego uoco . . . et non fuisset
          attritum nomen eius a facie mea.//

          Feria III of the second week of Advent, matins. The lesson is from Isaiah
          48.12–19.

Parchment. 2 folios. 191 x 155 mm (written space originally ca. 196 x 110 mm). 1 column. 20 of an original ca. 23 lines remaining. Dry-point ruling. Double vertical bounding lines.

Written in two sizes of late Caroline minuscule, with a smaller script for the chants and a larger one for the lessons. 1- and 2-line initials at the beginning of lessons are in red square capitals, with round *E*, and are set apart from the text between double bounding lines when they occur at the beginning of a line. 1-line initials are in brown rustic capitals and are not set apart from the text. Rubrics are written in red rustic capitals with uncial A. Punctuation consists of the punctus. Accents have been added by a later hand. Interlinear neumes in the St. Gall style. On fol. 2r, the tonary letters "yh" are in the inner margin next to the *in evangelio* antiphon, and "o" is next to the following antiphon.

The fragments were used as the pastedown (fol. 2) and flyleaf (fol. 1) in the binding of a volume measuring ca. 192 x 139 mm. A modern hand has written the number "91" in the lower right margin of fol. 2v.

Zinniker 7 and 6.

MS 482.41   Southern Germany, s. XII
Noted Breviary   Pl. 89

f. 1   [V. Ora pro] //populo interueni pro clero . . . R. Beata es uirgo . . . V. Aue
          maria. *In iii.* N. A. Gaude maria uirgo . . . *Ps.* Cantate .i. A. Dignare me
          laudare . . . *Ps.* Dominus regnabit. A. Post partum uirgo. *Ps.* Cantate .ii.
          Lectio sancti evangelii secundum lucam. In illo tempore. Intrauit iesus in
          quoddam castellum . . . in domum suam. *Omelia lectionis eiusdem.* Lec [*sic;*
          for Hec] lectio fratres karissimi pulcherrima racione dilectionem dei et
          proximi . . . maria. R. Ornatam in monilibus . . . V. Astitit regina a dextris
          . . . [L.] Que etiam sedens [*word erased*] secus pedes domini . . . miserere
          nobis. R. Beatam me dicent omnes . . . V. Et misericordia eius . . . [L.] Ac-
          tiua enim uita est panem esurienti tribuere . . . anhelet. R. Felix namque
          es . . . V. Ora pro populo . . . *In matutine laudibus.* A. Assumpta est maria
          . . . A. Maria uirgo assumpta est . . . A. In odorem ungentorum [*sic*] . . . A.
          Benedicta filia tu . . . A. Pulchra es et decora . . . *Capit.* Transite ad me
          omnes . . . *Aliud.* Spiritus meus super mel dulcis . . . *Aliud.* Dilectus meus
          loquitur . . . propera amica mea columba//

          Assumption of Mary (15 August), from the second nocturn of matins to
          lauds. The lessons for the third nocturn are from Paul the Deacon's Hom-
          iliary, Homily II.70, an adaptation of Bede's *Expositio in Lucam*, III.10 (on
          Luke 10.38); see Grégoire, 465–66.

Parchment. 1 folio. 205 x 165 mm (written space 165 x 120 mm). 1 column. 28 lines. Dry-point ruling on the hair side. Double vertical bounding lines. Prickings are preserved in the outer, upper, and lower margins.

Written in two sizes of Caroline minuscule, with a smaller script for the chants and a larger one for the lessons. 2- and 3-line initials at the beginning of lessons are in red square capitals and are set apart from the text between double vertical bounding lines. 1-line initials at the beginning of chants are in brown rustic capitals, with uncial M, dotted or highlighted with red, and are set apart from the text when they occur at the beginning of a line. Rubrics are written in red rustic capitals except for the homily rubric which is partially in minuscule. Punctuation consists of the punctus. Interlinear neumes in the St. Gall style. The name "maria" has been supplied twice on the recto by a later hand.

The fragment was used in the binding of Lambach, Stiftsbibliothek, Ccl 282 (the shelfmark "282" is written in ink in the lower margin of the verso; the number "282P" is written in a modern hand in pencil in the lower margin of the verso).

A modern hand has written the number "140" in pencil in the lower right corner of the recto.

Zinniker 17.

Bibliography:
Babcock, *Reconstructing a Medieval Library*, 108 and fig. 30.

MS 482.42

transferred to Beinecke MS 481.66, fols. 1 and 4

MS 482.43

transferred to Beinecke MS 481.78, fol. 2

MS 482.44
Ps-Isidore, *Decretales* (excerpts)

Western Germany, s.XII[1]
Pl. 90

The fragment contains an unidentified collection of excerpts from the *Decretals* (on collections of excerpts from the *Decretals*, see H. Fuhrmann, *Einfluß und Verbreitung der pseudoisidorianischen Fälschungen*, 3 vols., MGH Schriften 24 [Stuttgart,

1972], 2:411–15). It is not listed in Schafer Williams, *Codices Pseudo-Isidoriani: A Paleographico-Historical Study*, Monumenta Iuris Canonici, Series C: Subsidia 3 (New York, 1971).

f. 1r   //aut contubernia aut stupra . . . non dubitate.

         Evaristus, Letter 1; P. Hinschius, ed., *Decretales Ps.-Isidorianae* (Leipzig, 1863), 88.

f. 1r   *Item.* Preterita mala et illicita . . . corripiantur.

         Evaristus, Letter 1; Hinschius, 88.

f. 1r   *Idem episcopis egypti in ea epistola unum nos fratres.* Sicut non debet . . . causa coniungat.

         Evaristus, Letter 2; Hinschius, 90.

f. 1r–v   *Item.* Sicut uxori non licet . . . innupta maneat.

         Evaristus, Letter 2; Hinschius, 90.

f. 1v   *Item.* Si adulterata fuerit . . . innupta permaneat.

         Evaristus, Letter 2; Hinschius, 90.

f. 1v   *Item.* Audiuimus quosdam infamatos . . . honoribus arce//[ri]

         Evaristus, Letter 2; Hinschius, 91.

f. 2r   //rationabiliter discernatur.

         Zephirinus, Letter 1; Hinschius, 132.

f. 2r   *Item.* De occultis alieni cordis . . . quemquam dampnare.

         Zephirinus, Letter 1; Hinschius, 132.

f. 2r   *Episcopis egypti in epistola. Tantam a domino.* Non bonum est detrahentibus . . . excutere palum.

         Zephirinus, Letter 2; Hinschius, 134.

f. 2r   *Item.* Ve ue illis qui detrahunt . . . ministerium agunt.

          Zephirinus, Letter 2; Hinschius, 134.

f. 2r   *Calistus papa. benedicto episcopo in epistola. Fraternitatis amore.* Nullus doc-
          tor per scripta . . . accusatori respondeat.

          Calixtus, Letter 1; Hinschius, 136.

f. 2r–v   *Episcopis galliȩ in epistola. Plurimorum relatu.* Excommunicatos a sacerdo-
          tibus . . . excommunicationi subiacebit.

          Calixtus, Letter 2; Hinschius, 138.

f. 2v   *Item.* Quo alterius terminos . . . uires ullas habebit.

          Calixtus, Letter 2; Hinschius, 138–39.

f. 2v   *Item.* Si quis metropolitanus . . . aliquid agere tempta//[uerit]

          Calixtus, Letter 2; Hinschius, 139.

Parchment. 2 folios (bifolium). 146 x 107 mm (written space 110 x 75 mm). 1 column. 16 lines. Dry-point ruling on the hair side. Double vertical and single horizontal bounding lines. Prickings in outer, upper, and lower margins.
     Written in Caroline minuscule. 1-line initials are in red square capitals, with
round *E* and enlarged minuscule *n*, and are set apart from the text between double
bounding lines; one initial between double bounding lines is in brown. Rubrics are
written in red minuscule. Punctuation consists of the punctus and punctus elevatus.
     The bifolium was formerly used as the wrapper of a volume measuring ca. 123 x
75 mm. On the spine is written "Casus Conscientiae Ad(am) Burghaber. s.j." Numerous editions of this work from 1654–1773 are cited in Augustin de Backer, *Bibliothèque des écrivains de la Compagnie de Jésus — Bibliographie*, vol. 2, ed. Carlos
Sommervogel (Brussels, 1890, rpt. Louvain, 1960), 387, chap. 11.
     A modern hand has written the number "49" in pencil in the outer margin of
fol. 2v.
     Zinniker 14.

Bibliography:
Babcock, *Reconstructing a Medieval Library*, 32, note 34.

MS 482.45
Lectionary for the Mass

Italy, s. XII[2]
Pl. 90

f. 1ra   //quem u[elle]t uocari ... qui audierant in corde suo//

Luke 1.62–66 (John the Baptist, 24 June). The upper margin has been trimmed with loss of text.

f. 1rb   //uisitauit et fecit ... plebi suæ.

Luke 1.68 (John the Baptist). The upper margin has been trimmed with loss of text.

f. 1rb   *In natale sanctorum iohannis et pauli. sequentia sancti lucae.* In illo tempore. Dixit iesus discipulis suis. Attendite a fermento ... locuti estis in cu// [biculis]

Luke 12.1–3 (Sts. John and Paul, 26 June).

f. 1va   [osten]//dam autem uobis quem timeatis ... multis passeribus pluris e//[stis]

Luke 12.5–7 (Sts. John and Paul). The upper margin has been trimmed with loss of text.

f. 1vb   *Sequentia sancti iohannis.* In illo tempore. Dixit iesus symoni petro. Symon iohannis diligis me ... Symon iohannis amas me?//

John 21.15–17 (Vigil of Sts. Peter and Paul, 28 June).

Parchment (recto badly faded from use in a binding). 1 folio. 255 x 218 mm (written space originally ca. 220 x 155 mm). 2 columns. 16 lines remaining of an original ca. 21. Dry-point ruling. Prickings in the outer margin.

Written in a protogothic minuscule. 3-line initials "I" at the beginning of lessons are in red and are set apart from the text. Other 1-line initials are in brown uncials and are not set apart from the text. Rubrics are written in red minuscule with some capital forms (*H* and *Q*). Punctuation consists of the punctus and punctus interrogativus.

The fragment was used as a wrapper for a volume measuring ca. 160 x 110 mm. On the spine is written "Jo. de Turrecremata in Psalm" with the shelfmark "229" and in another hand the date "1524". Juan de Torquemada's (1388–1468) *Expositio in Psalterium* was printed in Venice in 1524 by Stefano da Sabbio.

Zinniker 133–1.

MS 482.46   Southern Germany or Austria, s. XI^{ex}
Gradual   Pl. 91

f. 1r   //Uocem iocunditatis annunciate ... *Ps.* Iubilate deo omnis ... Alleluia.
          [*v.*] Surrexit dominus uere ... *Of.* Benedicite gentes alleluia. *Co.* Cantate
          domino ... [*faded:* alleluia].

          Fifth Sunday after Easter. Fol. 1r is mostly illegible.

f. 1r   *In natale sancti ambrosii episcopi.* ... Protexisti. *Per to*[*tum.*] Alleluia. Inueni
          dauid.

          St. Ambrose (4 April). Fol. 1r is mostly illegible.

f. 1r–v   *Sanctorum Tiburcii et Valeriani martirum.* S[ancti tui domine] ... *Ps.*
          [Exaltabo.] Alleluia. G[audete iusti] ... *Of.* [Confitebuntur celi] mirabilia
          tua domine ... *V.* Misericordias tuas domine ... *V.* Quoniam quis in nu-
          bibus ... *Co.* Gaudete iusti in domino ... alleluia.

          Sts. Tiburtius and Valerian (14 April).

f. 1v   *De sancto leone.* Sacerdotes dei. *Gr.* Iurauit dominus. *Tr.* Beatus uir. *Of.*
          Veritas mea. *Co.* Fidelis seruus. *Si post paschalem ebdomadam.* Protexisti.
          Per totum. Alleluia. Iurauit *alterum de Pascha.*

          St. Leo (? IX, Pope, 19 April).

f. 1v   *Natalis georgii martyris.* Protexisti me deus ... *Ps.* Exaudi deus orationem
          meam cum deprecor//

          St. George (23 April).

f. 2r   [Sancti spiritus] //domine corda nostra mundet ... *Of.* Intonuit de cęlo.
          Co. Spiritus sanctus docebit ... dixero uobis alleluia alleluia.

          Feria II after Pentecost. The outer margin of fol. 2 has been trimmed with
          loss of text. Fol. 2r is mostly illegible.

f. 2r   [*Feria iii*] A[ccipite iocunditatem glorie] ... *Ps.* Attendite popul[us] ...
          Alleluia. P[...]. *Of.* P[ortas celi]. *Co.* Spiritus qui a patre ... alleluia.

          Feria III after Pentecost. The outer margin of fol. 2 has been trimmed with
          loss of text.

f. 2r–v   *Feria quarta. Ad [priorem missam] festive agitur.* Spiritus domini. *Per to-*
[*tum.*] Alleluia. Emittes spiritum. Alleluia. Veni sanctę spiritus. *Ad pub-*
licam m[*issam.*] Deus dum egredieris . . . *Ps.* Exurgat [deus et di]ssipentur
. . . Alleluia. Emittes spiritum. Alleluia. Sancti spiritus. [*Of.* . . .] spiritum.
Co. Pacem meam do uobis . . . alleluia.

Feria IV after Pentecost. The outer margin of fol. 2 has been trimmed
with loss of text.

f. 2v   *Feria quinta.* [Spiritus] domini. *Per totum.* Alleluia. Emittes spiritum. Alleluia. Spiritus domini repleuit . . . uocis.

Feria V after Pentecost. The outer margin of fol. 2 has been trimmed with
loss of text.

f. 2v–3r *Feria sexta.* [Spiritus] domini. *Per totum.* Alleluia. Emittes spiritum. Alleluia. Veni sancte spiritus. [*Int.*] Repleatur os meum . . . *Ps.* In te domine
speraui . . . Alleluia. Paraclytus. *Of.* Lauda anima. *Co.* Spiritus ubi uult
. . . alleluia.

Feria VI after Pentecost. The outer margin of fol. 2 has been trimmed
with loss of text.

f. 3r   *Sabbato. Ad priorem missam que festive agitur.* Spiritus domini. *Per totum.*
Alleluia. Emittes spiritum. Alleluia. Sancti spiritus. *Ad publicam missam.*
Caritas dei diffusa est . . . *Ps.* Domine deus salutis . . . Alleluia. Emittes spiritum. Alleluia. Spiritus domini. Alleluia. Paraclytus. Alleluia. Veni sancte
spiritus. Alleluia. Benedictus es dominus deus patrum. *Tr.* Laudate dominum. *Of.* Emittes spiritum. *Co.* Non uos relinquam . . . alleluia.

Saturday after Pentecost.

f. 3v   *Sanctorum Petri et Marcellini.* C[lama]uerunt iusti. *Gr.* Clama[uerunt] iusti
et . . . *V.* Iuxta est . . . Alleluia. Mirabilis deus. *Of.* Letamini. *Co.* Iustorum
anime.

Sts. Peter, Marcellinus, and Erasmus (2 June). Fol. 3v is mostly illegible.

f. 3v   *Bonifatii et socii eius.* Multe tribulationes. *Gr.* Exultabunt sancti. Alleluia.
Iudicant sancti. *Of.* Gloriabuntur. *Co.* Anima nostra.

St. Boniface (5 June).

f. 3v   *Sanctorum primi et feliciani.* Sapientiam sanctorum narrant . . . *Ps.* Exultate
iusti in domino . . . *Gr.* Iustorum anime in manu . . . *V.* Visi sunt oculis in-
sipientium//

Sts. Primus and Felician (9 June).

Parchment (badly damaged from mildew and from use in a binding). 3 folios (fols.
2 and 3 are a bifolium). 238 x 180 mm (written space 188 x 125 mm). 1 column. 16
lines. Dry-point ruling. Double vertical bounding lines.

Written in Caroline minuscule. The 3- and 4-line initials at the beginning of
Masses are in two styles: several initials are composed of hollow intertwining vines
in red outline on a blue and green background; other initials are plain red square
capitals. 1-line initials are in thick brown square capitals. 1-line initials of Psalm
incipits are in brown rustic capitals. Rubrics are written in red rustic capitals; liturgical directions are in brown rustic capitals, as are the first few words of each
Mass. Punctuation consists of the punctus. Interlinear neumes are in the St. Gall
style. Liturgical notes have been written in the margin of fol. 3v in a fifteenth-century cursive gothic hand.

Fol. 1 was used as a flyleaf for a volume measuring 238 x 167 mm. The bifolium
was used as a pastedown in the binding of a volume measuring ca. 300 x 215 mm.
Both fragments preserve a set of five rust stains in an X-pattern.

Zinniker 117.

MS 482.47   Southern Germany or Austria, s. XII^{med}
Gradual   Pl. 91

f. 1r   //Respice domine in testamentum . . . *Ps.* Ut quid deus repulisti . . . *Gr.*
Respice domine. Alleluia. Uenite exultemus domino . . . Preoccupemus
faciem eius . . . *Of.* In te speraui. *Co.* Panem de celo . . . suauitatis.

Thirteenth Sunday after Pentecost.

f. 1r–v *Dominica xiiii.* Protector noster aspice deus . . . *Ps.* Quam dilecta taber-
nacula . . . *Gr.* Bonum est confidere. Alleluia. Quoniam deus magnus . . .
[*Of.*] Inmittit angelus. *Co.* Panem quem ego.

Fourteenth Sunday after Pentecost.

f. 1v   *Dominica xv.* Inclina domine aurem tuam . . . *Ps.* Letifica animam serui tui

... *Gr.* Bonum est confiteri. Alleluia.//

Fifteenth Sunday after Pentecost.

Parchment. 1 folio. 249 x 157 mm (written space 183 x 120 mm). 1 column. 15 lines. Dry-point ruling (very faint). Double vertical bounding lines. Prickings in lower margin.

Written in late Caroline minuscule. 2- and 3-line Mass initials are in red square capitals and are written on the vertical bounding lines. 1-line initial "A" of Alleluias is in red and is not set apart from the text. Other 1-line initials are in brown square capitals, not set apart from the text. Rubrics are written in red rustic capitals. The first line of each Mass is written in brown rustic capitals. Punctuation consists of the punctus. Interlinear neumes in the St. Gall style. A later hand has added reference numbers in Roman numerals over the abbreviated chants.

Zinniker 31.

MS 482.48   Southern Germany or Austria, s. XIII[1]
Gradual   Pl. 92

f. 1r–v   [allel]//uia. A. Cum iocunditate exibitis ... A. De hierusalem exeunt ...
           A. Ego sum deus ... A. Populus syon conuertimini ... [A.] Exclamemus
           omnes ad dominum ... [A] Parce domine parce ... [A.] Iniquitates
           nostre domine ... [A.] Oremus dilectissimi nobis ... alleluia.

           Letania maior.

f. 1v   *Incipiunt officia pro defunctis.* Requiem eternam dona eis domine ... *Ps.* Te
           decet ymnus deus ... *Gr.* Requiem eternam dona eis domine ... *V.* In
           memoria eterna ... *Tr.* De profundis clamaui ... *V.* Fiant aures tue ... *V.*
           Si iniquitates obseruaberis ... *Off.* Domine iesu christe ... omnium fide-
           lium defunctorum//

           Mass for the Dead.

f. 2   //patris amen. *Laus angelica.* Kyrie leyson. Christe leyson. Kyrie leyson.
           Kyrie. leyson ymac. *Laus angelica.* Gloria in excelsis deo. Kyrie leyson ...
           Ter. *Laus.* Gloria in excelsis deo ... *Laus angelica.* Kyrie leyson ... *Laus
           angelorum.* Gloria in excelsis deo ... Kyrie leyson. Christe leyson. Kyrie
           leyson. *Laus angelica.* Gloria in excelsis deo ... in gloria dei patris amen.//

           Holy Saturday.

Parchment. 2 folios (bifolium; a portion of a folio number "[. . .]viii" is preserved in the upper left corner of fol. 2v). 223 x 181 mm (written space 189 x 120 mm). 1 column. 24 lines. Dry-point ruling. Double vertical bounding lines. Prickings in the outer margins.

Written in late Caroline minuscule. 2-line initials are in red and green and are written on the inner vertical bounding line. 1-line initials of Kyries and of antiphons on fol. 1 are in red and are not set apart from the text when they occur at the beginning of a line. 1-line initials of hymn verses and of chants on fol. 1v are in brown rustic capitals, highlighted with red, and are set apart from the text when they occur at the beginning of a line. Rubrics are written in red rustic capitals. The words "Kyrie" and "Gloria" usually have a rustic capital "R". Punctuation consists of the punctus. Hyphenation is in the same ink as the text. Interlinear neumes are in the St. Gall style.

The bifolium was used as a wrapper for a volume measuring ca. 195 x 150 mm. Zinniker 29.

MS 482.49

transferred to Beinecke MS 481.48, fols. 4, 5, 7, and 8

MS 482.50

transferred to Beinecke MS 481.35, fol. 2

MS 482.51   Southern Germany or Austria, s. XII
Gregory the Great, *Moralia in Iob*   Pl. 92

f. 1   //aliud quam facies uidetur . . . audentium difficultate praepediri. maledicit dicens.//

Gregory the Great, *Moralia in Iob*, IV. pref. 22–112; M. Adriaen, ed., CCSL 143 (1979), 158–61.

Parchment (recto stained and worn from use in a binding). 1 folio. 305 x 212 mm (written space 235 x 145 mm). 1 column. 33 lines. Dry-point ruling. Double vertical and horizontal bounding lines. Prickings in outer, upper, and lower margins.

Written in late Caroline minuscule. 1-line initials are in brown rustic capitals filled or dotted with red; the lower loop of the letter "g" is usually dotted with red. Punctuation consists of the punctus, punctus elevatus, and punctus interrogativus.

The fragment was used as a wrapper for a thick volume measuring ca. 175 x 95 mm. The name "Laymann" and the letter "C" are written on the spine.

Zinniker 127.

MS 482.52   Germany, s. XII^{med}
Alan of Farfa, Homiliary   Pl. 93

f. 1ra   [Inc: Sacramentum dilectissimi salutis nostrae quam pretio sanguinis sui uniuersitatis conditor aestimauit . . . neces]//se est ut in agro illius cor[dis in quo] huius mali planta con[ualuit] . . . et gloria in//

Alan of Farfa, Homily II.20 (Ascension) = Leo Magnus, *Tractatus septem et nonaginta*, Tractatus 74.124–31; A. Chavasse, ed., CCSL 138A (1973), 461. See Grégoire, 170. The upper and right halves of the column have been trimmed with loss of text.

f. 1rb   [Inc: Glorificatio domini nostri iesu christi resurgendo et ascendendo completa est . . .] //Habemus ergo deum . . . [au]deret. quando quidem//

Alan of Farfa, Homily II.21 (Ascension) = Augustine, Sermon 263; PL 38.1209. See Grégoire, 170. The upper and left halves of the column have been trimmed with loss of text.

f. 1va   //uicit leonem. qui . . . [acce]pit. Gaudebat//

Homily II.21; PL 38.1210. The upper and right halves of the column have been trimmed with loss of text.

f. 1vb   [asce]//ndit in celum . . . celum nisi qui//

Homily II.21; PL 38.1210. The upper and left halves of the column have been trimmed with loss of text.

Parchment. 1 folio (cut into two fragments with top half and the portion between the two columns missing). Fol. 1a measures 182 x 85 mm with a strip from the conjoint leaf measuring 182 x 25 mm; fol. 1b measures 185 x 108 mm (written space originally ca. 265 x 235 mm). 2 columns. 15 lines remaining of an original ca. 29 lines. Ruling not visible. Pricking in the outer margin.

Written in late Caroline minuscule. 1-line initials are in brown rustic capitals. Punctuation consists of the punctus, punctus elevatus, and punctus interrogativus. Hyphenation and accents have been added by a later hand.

The fragments were used as wrappers for a volume measuring ca. 155 x 90 mm. The middle portion which formed the spine of the volume has been worn away.

Zinniker 65.

MS 482.53   Southern Germany or Austria, s. XII/XIII
Homiliary   Pl. 93

Although these three homilies are found in Paul the Deacon's homiliary, they occur here in a different order.

f. 1r   [Inc: Redemptoris nostri praecursor quo tempore praedicationis uerbum acceperit . . .] //cur ea[nd]em uim a diebus iohannis baptiste . . . misericordie pignus tenemus? Prestan[t]e domi[no] nostro iesu christo; qui cum patr[e] et spiritu s[ancto uiu]it et regnat in saecula saeculorum. Amen.

          Gregory the Great, *Homiliae xl in evangelia*, Homily I.20.14–15, on Luke 3.1–11 (Saturday after the Third Sunday of Advent); PL 76.1168–70; R. Étaix, ed., CCSL 141 (1999), 168–69 = Paul the Deacon's Homiliary, Homily I.13; see Grégoire, 432. The outer margin has been torn with loss of text. The lower margin has been trimmed with the loss of one line of text.

f. 1r–v   *Dominica iiii^a [secun]dum iohannem*. In [illo tempore]; Miserunt iudei ab iherosolimis . . . quia non sum ego christus et rel. *Omelia Beati Gregorii de eadem lectione*. Ex huius nobis lectionis uerbis fratres karissimi iohannis h[umilitas] commendatur . . . Qui inter hec mysterium//

          Gregory the Great, *Homiliae xl in evangelia*, Homily I.7.1–3, on John 1.19–28 (Fourth Sunday of Advent); PL 76.1099–101 = Paul the Deacon's Homiliary, Homily I.8; see Grégoire, 431. The outer margin has been torn with loss of text. The lower margin has been trimmed with the loss of one line of text.

f. 2   [Inc: Cum esset desponsata mater eius maria ioseph. quae fuit necessitas ut desponsata esset maria ioseph . . .] //et iusto; qui pene licentia maritali . . . ex illius condempnatione//

          Pseudo-Origen, Homily I, on Matthew 1.18–25 (Christmas Eve, 24

December); E. Benz and E. Klostermann, *Origenes Werke* (Leipzig, 1941), 12:241.3–244.15 = Paul the Deacon's Homiliary, Homily I.15; see Grégoire, 432–33. The outer corners of the leaf have been trimmed with loss of text. The lower margin has been trimmed with the loss of one line of text.

Parchment. 2 folios (bifolium). 277 x 215 mm (written space originally ca. 274 x 180 mm). 2 columns. 36 lines remaining of an original 37 lines. Dry-point ruling. Single vertical bounding lines. Prickings in inner margin.

Written in early gothic script (littera textualis). 3-line initial *I* and 2-line round *E* are in red and are written on the vertical bounding line. Rubrics are written in red in the same script as the text. The first letter ("M") of the Bible lesson on fol. 1r is in red. Punctuation consists of the punctus, punctus elevatus, and punctus interrogativus. Hyphenation is in the same ink as the text.

The bifolium was used as the wrapper of a volume measuring ca. 200 x 160 mm. The title "Theologia moralis" is written on the spine.

Zinniker 121.

MS 482.54   Southern Germany, s. XII^{med}
Honorius of Autun, *Imago Mundi*   Pl. 94

f. 1   //quod solus luceat ceteris stellis obscuratis ... usque ad firmamentum celestis//

Honorius of Autun, *Imago Mundi*, I.72–80; PL 172.139–40 = Book 1, chs. 77–85, ed. Valerie Flint, *Archives d'Histoire Doctrinale et Littéraire du Moyen Age*, vol. 49 (1982), 7–153, here pp. 77–9. The text scribe has also written two interlinear glosses on fol. 1r. A different but contemporary hand has added chapter headings in the margins.

Parchment. 1 folio. 203 x 154 mm (written space 166 x 95 mm). 1 column. 26 lines. Dry-point ruling. Double vertical and horizontal bounding lines. Pricking in outer margin.

Written in late Caroline minuscule. 1-line initials are in brown rustic capitals, with enlarged minuscule *m*, *n*, and *h*, and are set apart from the text between the vertical bounding lines when they occur at the beginning of a line; the initials that begin new chapters are dotted with orange. Punctuation consists of the punctus. Hyphenation is in the same ink as the text. The marginal chapter headings are written by a contemporary hand in brown minuscule and are encircled in orange, with an orange line connecting each circle. The same orange is used to adorn the chapter initials and to mark roman numerals in the text.

The fragment was used as the wrapper for a volume measuring ca. 136 x 75 mm.

Some of the books in the Lambach library were bound in this method (cf. Beinecke 481.93), suggesting the possibility that this leaf also comes from Lambach (see Babcock, *Reconstructing a Medieval Library*, 28–32). The hand of the marginal chapter headings is similar to that of other Lambach scribes. The Lambach library catalogue in Cml XIX lists several works by Honorius but not the *Imago mundi* (see Holter [1956], 273, and *MBKÖ*, 5:57).

Zinniker 55.

Bibliography:
Babcock, *Reconstructing a Medieval Library*, 102 and fig. 16.

MS 482.55   Southern Italy, s. XIII[in]
Lectionary or Missal   Pl. 94

f. 1ra   [I]//nduet pro torace iustitiam . . . equitatem. [I]bunt directi promissionis; et ad certum locum deducet illos dominus deus noster.

          Wisdom 5.19–20; 5.22. The inner margin has been trimmed with loss of text.

f. 1ra   *L. libri sap.* Reddet deus mercedem laborum . . . [tr]anstulit illos mare//

          Wisdom 10.17–18. The inner and lower margins have been trimmed with loss of text.

f. 1rb   //sunt repromissiones. Obturauerunt ora leonum . . . Alii uero ludibria et uerbera experti. in//[super]

          Hebrews 11.33–36. The lower margin has been trimmed with loss of text.

f. 1va   //*L. libri sap.* Expectatio iustorum lettitia [*sic*]. spes autem impiorum peribit . . . peruersa; Simplicitas iustorum diriget eos et sup//[plantatio]

          Proverbs 10.28–32; 11.3. The lower margin has been trimmed with loss of text.

1vb   //*Lectio libri apocalipsis beati Iohannis apostoli.* In diebus illis. Responde[ns] unus de senioribus dix[it] mihi . . . die ac nocte in templo e//[ius]

          Apocalypse 7.13–15. The lower and inner margins have been trimmed with loss of text.

Parchment. 1 folio. 157 x 211 mm (original dimensions uncertain; width of written space 160 mm). 2 columns. 14 lines remaining (original number uncertain). Drypoint ruling on the hair side. Double vertical and horizontal bounding lines.

Written in Beneventan script. 3- and 4-line initials are written on the inner vertical bounding line. One of them is a plain red square capital "I"; the others are brown square capitals filled with red foliate ornamentation. 1-line initials are brown, highlighted with red, and are set apart from the text when they occur at the beginning of a line. The rubrics are written in red minuscule. Punctuation consists of the punctus, punctus elevatus, and punctus versus.

According to Virginia Brown (letter of 22 March 1999), the text of this leaf contains the alternate readings for "Natale plurimorum martyrum," as the same readings are found for this feast in other Beneventan missals (e.g., Vat. lat. 6082, Montecassino 127, and Ottob. lat. 576), where they appear in roughly the same order, the exception being that Heb. 11.33–36 is placed after Apoc. 7.13–15 in the three parallels cited. The date recorded above (sec. XIII^{in}) was suggested by Prof. Brown.

The fragment was used as a wrapper for a volume measuring ca. 157 x 102 mm. The number "64" is written on the spine and the same hand has written "vol. 1 / III.6.E / 18" on the front cover of the volume. On the back cover other hands have written "Il nome" and "Il Biracc . . ." in ink. A modern hand has written the number "40" in pencil.

It is possible that this leaf is the one listed by E. A. Lowe, "A New List of Beneventan Manuscripts," in *Collectanea Vaticana in honorem Anselmi M. Card. Albareda*, Studi e Testi 220 (Vatican City, 1962), 224: "Hüsler Collection: Lectionarium. «saec. XI». One folio. (Bischoff)." The Hüsler leaf is reported as untraced by Virginia Brown, "A Second New List of Beneventan Manuscripts (1)," *Medieval Studies* 40 (1978): 239–89, here 283. Around 1955 Bischoff visited Hüsler in Lucerne, and on that occasion saw the leaf that is now MS 482.3 (see description above) as well as other items in Hüsler's possession. It may have been on that same visit that he saw the Beneventan lectionary leaf he reported to Lowe. It appears that Lowe did not see the fragment, but only had the report of it from Bischoff (which may account for the discrepancy in dating). Since the Reverend Zinniker (the original compiler of the collection of fragments now comprising MS 481 and MS 482) lived, like Hüsler, in Lucerne, and clearly acquired at least one other fragment from him, MS 482.3, it is not impossible that other fragments in Zinniker's collection also came from Hüsler, and that MS 482.55 is the missing Hüsler Beneventan fragment.

Zinniker 109.

Bibliography:
    Brown, V., "A Second New List of Beneventan Manuscripts (2)," *Medieval Studies* 50 (1988): 584–625, here 609.

Shailor, B., "Another Fragment of Beneventan Script," *Manuscripta* 25 (1981): 49–50.

MS 482.56

transferred to Beinecke MS 481.92, fols. 4 and 5

MS 482.57   Italy, s. XIII[in]
Medical Recipes   Pl. 95

The recipes are mostly gynecological, including several for tumors and swelling of the vulva, one of which the author says he has used on his sister Arsinoe. The text ends in the middle of fol. 2r; the originally blank portions of fol. 2r and 2v have been inscribed by other hands.

f. 1r   Largely illegible, but seems to be recipes similar to those on fol. 1v.

f. 1v   //storacis scrupulos .vi. opii. scrupulos .i. et semis . . . da maxima primo scrupulus .i. media scrupulus semis. Ad re//

          Medical recipes for tumors or swelling of the vulva.

f. 2r   //impone. ¶Ad duritiam uberum et inflacionem et ulcera . . . cum aqua laua. Expl.

          Medical recipes for hardness of the breasts, ulcers, and cancers, increasing milk, so a girl will not grow breasts nor a boy testicles, and so that the hands and neck will be white.

f. 2r   ¶Si uis scire utrum aliquis sit leprosus nec non . . . ¶Si uis facere mulierem . . . uel accetum potauerit.

          Medical recipes for ailments such as leprosy and hydropsy.

f. 2v   Largely undecipherable. Added in a different hand in the lower margin of fol. 2v, written upside down, there is a portion of a poem in a thirteenth- or fourteenth-century hand on the sounds made by various animals: "Ast pardus fellit pullat vultur leo ruit / Ast onager mugilat bos mugit. . . ."

Many of the pairings of animal and verb are similar to those in the poem "Iam vernali tempore . . ." (*Carmina Burana* 132; see Wilhelm Meyer, et al., *Carmina Burana*, vol. 1.2: *Die Liebeslieder*, 2nd ed. [Heidelberg, 1971], 220–21). On other poems of this type, see Wilhelm Wackernagel, *Voces variae animantium*, 2nd ed. (Basel, 1869).

Parchment. 2 folios (bifolium). 152 x 109 mm (written space 119 x 78 mm). 1 column. 30 lines. Ruling in lead. Pricking in outer margin.

Written in early gothic script (littera textualis). The added entries on fol. 2r are written in a French or Italian cursive hand, s. XIV^2. The upper portion of fol. 2v is written in littera textualis currens, s. XIII; the verses on animals are in a littera textualis, s. XIII/XIV. Punctuation consists of the punctus and punctus elevatus. Hyphenation is in the same ink as the text.

The bifolium was used as a pastedown in a binding measuring ca. 212 x 145 mm and bears the number "301" (fol. 2r).

Zinniker 35.

MS 482.58   Germany, s. XII
Noted Missal   Pl. 95

f. 1r–v   //*viii k. feb. Conuersio sancti pauli. preiecti martyr.* Scio cui credidi . . . [*Or.*] Deus qui uniuersum mundum beati pauli apostoli tui . . . *Al.* Martyris tui praeiecti nos quaesumus domine interuentio gloriosa commendet . . . *Lectio actuum apostolorum.* In diebus illis. Saulus adhuc spirans minarum et cedis in discipulos domini . . . quoniam hic est christus. *Gr.* Qui operatus est petro . . . V. Gracia dei in me . . . *Secundum matheum.* In illo tempore. Dixit symon petrus ad iesum. Ecce nos relinquimus omnia . . . possidebit. *Secreta.* Apostoli tui pauli precibus . . . *Secr.* Suscipe domine propicius orationem nostram . . . *Co.* Amen dico uobis . . . [*Ad compl.*] Sanctificati domine salutari mysterio . . . *Ad compl.* Votiua domine pro beati martyris tui praeiecti passione . . . praesidium. Per.

Conversion of St. Paul (25 January) and St. Praejectus (25 January). The lessons are from Acts 9.1–22 and Matthew 19.27–29.

f. 1v   *Oct. agnetis virginis. V.* Vultum tuum deprecabuntur . . . *Ps.* Eructauit cor meum. *Or.* Deus qui nos annua beatę agnete . . . *Of.* Diffusa est gracia . . . *Secreta.* Super has quaesumus domine hostias benedictio . . . *Co.* Simile est regnum . . . una preciosa//

Octave of St. Agnes (28 January).

f. 2r   [*L. Uenit iesus in partes* ...] //autem quem me esse dicitis? Respondens symon petrus ... et in cęlis. *Secr.* Ecclesię tuę quaesumus domine preces ... *Ad co.* Lętificet nos domine munus acceptum ... largitatem. Per.

             Chair of St. Peter (22 February). The lessons are from Matthew 16.15–19. Incipits for the Offertory and the Communio have been entered in the margin but have been mostly trimmed away.

f. 2r–v   *vi k mar. mathię apostoli.* Deus qui beatum mathiam apostolorum tuorum collegio ... *L. actuum apostolorum.* In diebus illis; Exsurgens petrus in medio fratrum dixit ... undecim apostolis. *Secundum lucam.* In illo. Designauit dominus. et alios septuaginta duos ... mercede sua. *Secr.* Deus qui proditoris apostatę ruinam ... *Ad co.* Praesta quaesumus omnipotens deus; ut per hęc sancta ... et pacem. Per.

             St. Matthias (24 February). The lessons are from Acts 1.15–26 and Luke 10.1–7. The incipits for the antiphon and the rubric *per to*[*tum*] have been entered in the margin but have been mostly trimmed away.

f. 2v   *Non. mar. Perpetuę et felicitatis.* Da nobis domine deus noster sanctorum martyrum palmas ... *Secreta.* Intende domine munera quaesumus altaribus tuis ... *Ad compl.* Praesta nobis domine quaesumus intercedentibus sanctis tuis ... capiamus. Per.

             Sts. Perpetua and Felicity (7 March).

f. 2v   *iiii id. mar. gregorii papae. A.* Sacerdotes dei benedicite ... *Ps.* Benedicite omnia opera domini. *Or.* Deus qui animę famuli tui gregorii ... *Tr.* Beatus uir qui ... *V.* Potens in terra ... *V.* Gloria et diuitiae ... *Secreta.* Annue nobis domine ut intercessione beati gregorii ... [*Co.*] Fidelis seruus et prudens ... *Ad co.* Deus qui beatum gregorium pontificem ... exempla. Per.

             St. Gregory (12 March).

f. 2v   *xiii. k. aprilis. Guthberti episcopi.* Omnipotens sempiterne deus qui in meritis sancti tui guthberti ... *Secr.* Hęc tibi domine quaesumus beati guthberti ... *Ad compl.* Deus qui nos sanctorum tuorum temporali facis ... sorte salutis. in qua illi//

             St. Cuthbert (20 March).

Parchment. 2 folios (bifolium). 255 x 168 mm (written space 217 x 125 mm). 1

column. 37 lines. Dry-point ruling (very faint). Double vertical bounding lines.

Written in two sizes of late Caroline script, with a larger script for the lessons and prayers and a smaller script for the chants. 1- and 2-line initials are in red square capitals, with round D, and are set apart from the text when they occur at the beginning of a line. Other 1-line initials are in brown rustic capitals. Rubrics are written in red minuscule, with occasional rustic capital and uncial forms. Punctuation consists of the punctus and punctus elevatus. Hyphenation and accents are in the same ink as the text. Interlinear neumes are in the St. Gall style.

The bifolium was used as a wrapper of a volume measuring ca. 323 x 120 mm and has the inscription "Mein Ungect(?) Register Anno 1569".

Zinniker 124.

MS 482.59   Southern Germany or Austria, s. XIII
Sacramentary   Pl. 96

f. 1r   [Pater noster qui es in caelis . . .] //et in terra. Panem nostrum cotid[ia]-
        num da nobis . . . Libera nos quesumus [domine a]b omnibus malis . . . Per
        [*added later*: eundem] dominum nostrum iesum christum . . . qui tecum
        uiuit et regnat . . . [P]er omnia saecula saeculorum. Amen. Pax domini sit
        semper uobiscum. Et cum spiritu tuo.

        Canon of the Mass. The upper margin has been trimmed with loss of text.

f. 1r–v   *In uigilia natiuitatis domini missa.* Deus qui nos redemptionis nostre annua
          expectacione letificas praesta . . . *Secr.* Da nobis quaesumus omnipotens
          deus . . . *Compl.* Da nobis quaesu[mus] domine. unigeniti filii tui . . . po-
          tamur. Qui tecum.

          Christmas Eve (24 December).

f. 1v   *In gallican[tu]* Deus qui hanc sacratissimam noctem ueri luminis . . . *Secr.*
         Accepta tibi sit domine quaesumus hodierne festiuitatis oblatio . . . *Pre-
         fatio.* UD eterne deus. Quia per incarnati uerbi mysterium noua mentis
         . . . *Infra actionem.* Communicantes et noctem sacratissimam celebrantes
         qua beate marie//

         Christmas (25 December).

Parchment. 1 folio. 215 x 154 mm (written space originally ca. 207 x 134 mm). 1 column. 19 lines remaining of an original 20 lines. Ruled in ink. Double vertical bounding lines.

Written in early gothic script (littera textualis). 6-line Romanesque initial *D* in brown, not set apart from the text, with intertwining brown vines ending in leaves. The letter and vines are decorated with bands, filled with circles, one of which has a 5-pointed asterisk in the center compartment. 2-line initials are in red square capitals. 1-line initials, written on the inner vertical bounding line when they occur at the beginning of a line, are in red square capitals. Rubrics are written in red in the same script as the text. The first line of the mass for Christmas Eve is written in red capitals. The name "maria" on fol. 1r is written with an uncial M and a rustic capital *R*. Punctuation consists of the punctus and punctus elevatus. Hyphenation is in the same ink as the text.

A modern hand has written the number "95" in pencil in the lower right corner of the verso.

Zinniker 63.

MS 482.60   Southern Germany, s. XII
Missal   Pl. 96

f. 1   [dili]//gamus inuicem; deus in nobis manet et caritas eius in nobis perfecta est . . . ut qui diligit deum. diligat et fratrem suum. R. Ego dixi domine . . . V. Beatus qui intellegit . . . Alleluia *v*. Verba mea auribus . . . *Lucam*. In illo tempore. Dixit iesus discipulis suis. Homo quidam erat diues et induebatur purpura et bisso . . . Fili recordare quoniam recepisti dona in uita tua; et lazarus//

Sunday after Holy Trinity. The lessons are from 1 John 4.12–21 and Luke 16.19–25.

Parchment. 1 folio. 221 x 155 mm (written space 162 x 112 mm). 1 column. 21 lines. Dry-point ruling.

Written in two sizes of late Caroline minuscule, with a smaller script for the chants and a larger one for the lessons. 3-line initial "I" at the beginning of the lesson is in red, set apart from the text. 1-line chant initials are in red uncials and are not set apart from the text. 1-line initials within the lessons are in brown rustic capitals highlighted with red and are not set apart from the text. Rubrics are written in red minuscule. Punctuation consists of the punctus and punctus elevatus.

The fragment was used as the wrapper for a volume measuring ca. 150 x 87 mm. On the spine is written "Genera . Declinationes . Praeterita duplice".

A modern hand has written "x42" in pencil in the lower margin of the recto.

Zinniker 100–1.

MS 482.61

transferred to Beinecke MS 481.40, fol. 1

MS 482.62

transferred to Beinecke MS 481.44, fol. 1

MS 482.63   Germany, s. XII^{in}
Commentary on Priscian's *Institutiones Grammaticae*   Pl. 97

f. 1   //ratione sed hac potius necessitate factum esse quia sine nomine et uerbo
           illa orationem non perficiunt ... sed etiam per se posita obtinent locum
           nominum pronomina. ideo etiam constructionem eorum nominum sibi
           defendit ut sicut nomina intransitiue//

           Unidentified commentary on Priscian, *Institutiones grammaticae*, XVIII.1–
           32; Keil, 2:210.1–222.26. The bottom margin is trimmed with the loss of
           a few lines of text.

f. 2r   //sint eedem uoces preteriti perfecti et futuri ... Inueniuntur tamen. .i.
           licet donatus uoluerit hanc conuenientiam esse inter optatiuum et sub-
           iuntiuum. tamen cum indicatiuo qui et uoce et significatione magis est
           remotus ab eo habet subiunctiuus hanc conuenientiam quod alter ex illis
           ponitur pro altero.

           Commentary on unidentified grammatical text.

f. 2r   De ortographia. Quia tempora et tenorem nec spiritum quae insepara-
           biliter ipsam sillabam comitantur. non cognosco. multo minus signifi-
           cationem cognosco ... Quia he sole. quasi perfectio orationis ex nomine
           et uerbo et ceteris constantis partibus soli nomini et uerbo innititur.

           Commentary on Priscian, *Institutiones grammaticae*, II.14–15; Keil,
           2:53.18–54.6.

f. 2r   Augustinus diffinit sensus est passio corporis per se ipse ipsam latens
           animam. Itaque ipsa uis anime. usque ad ultimam lineam ipsarum aurium

porrigitur . . . Cum antedico. tango. innuo alicuius corporis occursum pati. Cum uero tangor uim ipsam animę meę. accedere et occurrere corpori alicui et sic diligenter attendens in ceteris uerbis ad sensum pertinentibus inuenies significationes ipsis uocibus contrarias.

Commentary on Priscian, VIII.7; Keil, 2:373.

f. 2r–v   Deriuatorum nominum .viiii. sunt species. hę patronomicum. possessiuum. comparatiuum. superlatiuum. diminutiuum. denominatiuum. verbale. participiale. adverbiale. Patronimicum est quod a propriis tantummodo deriuatur patrum nominibus . . . Nunc dicit. In latinis autem dictionibus non solum his supra dictis utimur scilicet possessiuis. sed etiam quibusdam propriis latinorum. scilicet quae a latinis dictionibus informantur. Ut sunt ea. quę desinunt in .rius. uel//

Commentary on Priscian, II.32–49; Keil, 2:62.15–75.2.

Parchment. 2 folios (bifolium). 223 x 161 mm (original dimensions and written space uncertain; width of written space: 140 mm). 1 column. 60 lines remaining of an uncertain original. Dry-point ruling on the hair side. Single vertical bounding lines. Prickings in outer margin.

Written in Caroline minuscule in a minute, highly abbreviated scholastic hand. 1-line initials are in brown and are set apart when they are at the beginning of the line. The lemmata are set apart from the preceding commentary by paragraph marks in brown. Punctuation consists of the punctus.

The fragment was used as a flyleaf in the binding of a volume measuring ca. 294 x 210 mm. A modern hand has written the number "39" in pencil in the outer margin of fol. 2v. Another hand has written in pencil "70" in the lower left corner of fol. 1r and "71" in the lower left corner of fol. 2r.

Zinniker 28.

MS 482.64   Germany, s. XIII[1]
Canticles (from a Psalter)   Pl. 97

f. 1r–v   //sanctitate; terribilis atque laudabilis . . . in medio eius.

Exodus 15.11–19.

f. 1v   //Ca. Domine audiui; auditionem tuam et timui . . . ante pedes eius stetit et mensus//

Habakkuk 3.2–6.

Parchment. 1 folio. 179 x 121 mm (written space 135 x 85 mm). 1 column. 22 lines. Dry-point ruling. Double vertical and horizontal bounding lines. Prickings in outer margin.

Written in late Caroline minuscule. 3-line initial "D" ("Domine") is in red with blue flourishes and is not set apart from the text. 1-line initials are in red square capitals, with round E, and are not set apart from the text. Rubrics are written in red rustic capitals. Punctuation consists of the punctus and punctus versus. Hyphenation is in the same ink as the text.

This fragment was used as the binding of a book measuring ca. 102 x 63 mm with the title "Summa etc" written on the spine.

Zinniker 110–1

MS 482.65
Psalter (Gallican)

f. 1r   //Diligi[t misericordiam . . . terra.] Verbo [domini . . . eius] om[nis . . . eo-
         rum.] Cong[regans . . . ponens] in t[hesauris abyssos.] Time[at dominum
         . . . inhabit]ant//[es]

Psalm 32.5–8. Almost the entire leaf has been trimmed, with the loss of all but a few letters.

f. 1v   [adiut]//or [et protector . . . no]mi[ne . . . quemadmo]dum//

Psalm 32.20–22. The letter -d from the rubric of Psalm 33 ([*Psalmus Da-vi*]d) is also preserved. Almost the entire leaf has been trimmed, with the loss of all but a few letters.

f. 2r   [expul]//si sunt nec potuerunt stare . . . pasceris in diuitiis eius//

Psalms 35.13–36.3. The upper and lower portions of the leaf have been trimmed with loss of text.

f. 2v   [inten]//derunt arcum suum . . . super diuitias peccatorum multas//

Psalm 36.14–16. The upper and lower portions of the leaf have been trimmed with loss of text.

Parchment. 2 folios (1 bifolium; with two leaves of text missing between them). Fol. 1 measures 66 x 43 mm; fol. 2 measures 65 x 202 mm (written space originally ca.

205 x 145 mm). 1 column. 7 lines remaining of an original ca. 25 lines. Dry-point ruling. Double vertical bounding lines.

Written in late Caroline minuscule. The Psalms are written according to verse lines. 3-line initial "N" ("Noli") at the beginning of Psalm 36 is a square capital in orange and is not set apart from the text. 1-line initials at the beginning of verses are in orange and are set apart from the text between double bounding lines. Rubrics are written in orange rustic capitals. The first line of Psalm 36 is written in brown capitals with uncial and rustic capital forms. Punctuation consists of the punctus and punctus elevatus. A contemporary hand has written ". . . viam" with neumes in the margin of fol. 2r.

The fragment was used in the binding of a volume measuring at least 245 mm in height. A modern hand has written the number "26" in pencil in the gutter between fols. 1v and 2r.

Zinniker 79–2.

MS 482.66   Southern Germany, s. XII²
Psalter (Gallican)   Pl. 98

f. 1   //Dominus illuminatio mea . . . Adiutor meus esto ne derelinquas//

Psalm 26.1–9.

Parchment. 1 folio. 190 x 132 mm (written space 128 x 80 mm). 1 column. 19 lines. Dry-point ruling. Double vertical bounding lines.

Written in late Caroline minuscule. The Psalm is written according to verse lines. 8-line initial "D" ("Dominus") is in red outline and is filled with intertwining vines in red outline. The spaces between the vines are filled with blue and green wash. The style is reminiscent of Regensburg decoration. The letters of the first two words of the Psalm are written on four lines to the right of the initial in 1-line square capitals that alternate between red and blue highlighted with red. The first line of text beneath the initial is written in brown rustic capitals with occasional use of round E. 1-line initials at the beginning of verses are written in red square capitals and are set apart from the text between vertical bounding lines. Punctuation consists of the punctus. Hyphenation is in the same ink as the text. Line fillers and line dividers are in red.

Zinniker 61.

MS 482.67   Germany, s. XII
Psalter (Gallican)   Pl. 99

f. 1   //causam meam de gente non sancta . . . qui oderunt nos diripiebant//

            Psalms 42.1–43.11.

f. 2   //Et secundum multitudinem . . . super altare tuum uitulos.//

            Psalm 50.3–21. A later hand has added "Gloria patri . . ." at the end of
            Psalm 50.

f. 3   //es susceptor meus . . . dedisti hereditatem timentibus nomen//

            Psalms 58.17–60.6. A fifteenth-century gothic hand has made a correc-
            tion to the text and traced over the last two words on fol. 3v. The margins
            of the leaf have been trimmed with loss of text in the outer margin.

Parchment. 3 folios (fols. 1 and 2 form a bifolium, probably the outer of a quire of
8; there are ca. 6 leaves missing between fols. 2 and 3). Fol. 1 measures 173 x 121
mm; fol. 2, 174 x 98 mm; fol. 3, 174 x 81 mm (written space 132 x 80 mm). 1 column. 19 lines. Dry-point ruling. Double vertical bounding lines.
    Written in late Caroline minuscule. 3-line initials at the beginning of Psalms,
one a round D and the other a square capital D, are in red, which in places has
oxidized to a silver color; the initials are written on the inner vertical bounding
line. 1-line initials at the beginning of verses are in red square capitals, with round
forms of D and E, which in places has oxidized to a silver color; they are set apart
from the text between the vertical bounding lines when they occur at the beginning
of a line. Rubrics are written in red rustic capitals. The first line of each Psalm is
written in brown rustic capitals. Punctuation consists of the punctus.
    The fragments were used in a binding. The bifolium, measuring 218 x 174 mm,
was probably used as a flyleaf.
    A modern hand has written the number "4" in the upper right corner of fol. 1r
and the number "16" in the upper left corner of fol. 3r.
    Zinniker 138–1 and 138–2.

MS 482.68

transferred to Beinecke MS 481.88, fols. 2 and 3

MS 482.69

transferred to Beinecke MS 481.91, fol. 1

MS 482.70	Southern Germany or Austria, s. XII
Sacramentary	Pl. 99

f. 1r   [*Secr.*] //Munera tuẹ misericors deus maiestati . . . Ad [*co.*] Diuina libantes mysteria quaesumus domine ut eorum . . . gaudemus presentia. Per.

Mass for a saint whose relics are held in the church. The upper and outer margins have been trimmed with loss of text.

f. 1r   A[*lia.*] Propitiare quaesumus domine nobis famulis tuis . . . *Secr.* Suscipiat clementia tua quaesumus . . . [*Ad co.*] Diuina domine libantes mysteria quaesumus domine que . . . donis reficia[mur. Per.]

Mass for a saint whose relics are held in the church. The outer margin has been trimmed with loss of text.

f. 1r   Omnipotens sempiterne deus qui me peccatorem . . . *S*[*ecr.*] Deus qui nos pastores in populo uocari uoluisti . . . [*Ad co.*] Sumentes domine deus salu-tis nostrẹ sacramenta . . . proficiat salutem. [Per.]

Mass for a priest. The outer margin has been trimmed with loss of text.

f. 1r–v   Omnipotens mitissime deus respice propitius preces nostras . . . *S*[*ecr.* Has tibi domine deus offerimus oblationes . . .] sancti spiritus inluminare dig-neris. Per. *Ad compl.* [Per hoc quaesumus] domine sacrificium quod . . . temptationibus. Per.

Mass requesting the grace of the Holy Spirit. The outer margin has been trimmed with loss of text. The upper margin has also been trimmed with the loss of two lines of text.

f. 1v   *Pro temptatione carnis.* [Ur]e igne sancti spiritus quaesumus domine renes nostros . . . *Sec.* Disrumpe domine uincula [pecc]atorum nostrorum . . . *Ad co.* [Domine a]diutor et protector noster refloreat caro nostra . . . com-prehendat. Per.

Mass on the temptation of the flesh. The outer margin has been trimmed with loss of text.

f. 1v   *Pro congregatione.* [O]mnipotens semper deus qui facis mirabilia magna . . . *Sec.* Hostias domine famulorum tuorum placatus . . . *Ad co.* Quos celesti recreas [mun]ere perpetuo . . . redemptione concede. Per.

Mass for the congregation. The outer margin has been trimmed with loss of text.

f. 1v   *Pro episcopo nostro.* [Deu]s omnium fidelium pastor et rector famulum tuum episcopum nostrum . . . *Sec.* Oblatis quaesumus domine placare muneribus et famulum tuum . . . protectione guberna. Per.//

Mass for the bishop. The outer margin has been trimmed with loss of text.

f. 2r   [Praetende domine fidelibus tuis . . .] //auxilii ut et te toto corde perquirant . . . *Secr.* Propitiare domine supplicationibus nostris et has oblationes quas tibi pro incolomitate . . . *Ad co.* Da famulis tuis quaesumus domine omnibus episcopis. presbyteris. diaconibus . . . euellantur. Per.

Mass for the living. The upper margin has been trimmed with the loss of two lines of text.

f. 2r–v   *Alia.* Omnipotens sempiterne deus per quem salus mundi . . . *Secr.* Hostias domine quas tibi pro salute nostra et pace . . . *Al.* Omnipotens sempiterne deus qui uiuorum dominaris simul et mortuorum . . . *Secr.* Deus cui soli cognitus est numerus electorum . . . *Ad co.* Purificent nos quaesumus omnipotens et misericors deus . . . omnium peccatorum. Per.

Mass for the living and the dead. The upper margin has been trimmed with the loss of two lines of text.

f. 2v   *Alia.* Sanctorum tuorum intercessionibus quaesumus domine et nos protege . . . orthodoxorum quorum commemorationem agimus. et quorum corpo//[ra]

Mass for the living and the dead.

Parchment. 2 folios (bifolium). Fol. 1 measures 214 x 123 mm; fol. 2 measures 214 x 176 mm (written space originally ca. 195 x 125 mm). 24 of an original 26 lines remaining. Dry-point ruling on flesh side. Double vertical bounding lines. Pricking in outer margin.

Written in late Caroline minuscule. 2-line initials at the beginning of each Mass are in red square capitals and are written on the vertical bounding lines. 1-line initials are in red square capitals and are set apart from the text between double bounding lines when they occur at the beginning of a line. Rubrics are written in red rustic capitals. Punctuation consists of the punctus.

The bifolium was used as a flyleaf in the binding of a volume measuring ca. 302 x 210 mm. On fol. 2v there is an inscription in a fifteenth-century hand.

Zinniker 99.

MS 482.71

transferred to Beinecke MS 481.109, fols. 3 and 4

MS 482.72   Germany, s. XII/XIII
Missal   Pl. 100

f. 1ra   *Secreta.* Hostias tibi domine pro sanctorum tuorum ... *Post co.* Sumpti
         sacramenti quaesumus domine ... derelinquat. et in//

         Common of Saints. The upper portion of the leaf has been trimmed with
         loss of text.

f. 1rb   [Fratres. Omnis namque pontifex...] //pro homini[bus] ... et populo; ita
         et//[iam]

         Lesson from Hebrews 5.1–3. The upper portion and the inner margin of
         the leaf have been trimmed with loss of text.

f. 1va   //ferimus suppli[cationibus] ... *Post co.* [...]one sollempni[...] confessoris
         [...]amenti et cor//

         Unidentified secreta and postcommunio (Common of a Confessor?). The
         upper portion and the inner margin of the leaf have been trimmed with
         loss of text.

f. 1vb   //adiuuemur meritis. cuius castitatis ... *vel.* Qui gloriatur *ut supra.* Domine
         deus meus exaltasti. *Require lucie virginis. Graduale ut supra. ewangelium.*
         Simile est regnum celorum thesauro. *Require lucie virginis.* [*Off.*]

Offerentur. *Secreta*. Hostias domine quas tibi offerimus . . . intercedente//

Common of Virgins. The lesson incipits are from Sirach 51.13, 2 Corinthians 10.17, and Matthew 13.44. The upper portion of the leaf has been trimmed with loss of text.

Parchment. 1 folio. 113 x 155 mm (original dimensions and written space uncertain; width of one column: 85 mm). 2 columns (only a portion with a small amount of text of the second column is preserved). 7 lines remaining (original number uncertain). Ruled in lead. Single vertical bounding lines.

Written in late Caroline minuscule. Three lines of a large initial F (?) that is half green and half red are preserved on fol. 1r. 1-line initials at the beginning of prayers are in red square capitals, with round D, and are written on the vertical bounding line. Smaller 1-line initials are in brown rustic capitals highlighted with red. Rubrics are written in a mixture of red capitals and minuscule forms. Liturgical directions are written in brown minuscule, with some rustic capital forms, and are dotted with red. Punctuation consists of the punctus and punctus elevatus. Hyphenation is in the same ink as the text.

The fragment was formerly used as a pastedown in the binding of a volume measuring ca. 155 x 101 mm. A modern hand has written the number "43" in pencil in the lower left corner of fol. 1r.

Zinniker 100–2.

MS 482.73

transferred to Beinecke MS 481.108, fols. 1, 4, 5, and 8

MS 482.74   Germany, s. XII²
Homiliary (of Paul the Deacon?)   Pl. 100

These fragments may represent a manuscript of Paul the Deacon's Homiliary, since all three homilies are found there; however, since no two homilies appear together on a single leaf, it cannot be verified that they occur in the same order as in Paul the Deacon's Homiliary. We have foliated the leaves as though they were from a copy of Paul's Homiliary.

f. 1r   [Inc: Iohannes baptista et praecursor domini saluatoris quem . . .] //diligentius intuendum est. quia . . . redeuntis crebra luce re//[ficiantur]

Bede, Homily I.15.134–45; D. Hurst, ed. CCSL 122 (1955), 109 (Feria IV after Epiphany) = Paul the Deacon, Homily I.49. See Grégoire, 439.

f. 1v   [ope]//ratur unus atque idem spiritus . . . paulo post; quia apud uos//

Bede, Homily I.15.162–72; Hurst, 109–10.

f. 2r   [Inc: Docente in monte domino discipuli uenerunt ad eum . . . ad]//orans dominum dicat ad eum . . . sperasti; mundus effectus es.//

Origen, Homily 2 (on Matt. 8.1–13); E. Benz and E. Klostermann, *Origenes Werke* (Leipzig, 1941), 12:249.1–8; PL 95.1191 (Third Sunday after Epiphany) = Paul the Deacon, Homily I.61. See Grégoire, 441.

f. 2v   //eum centurio. rogans eum et dicens . . . aiebat michi seruus est; et ego crea//[toris]

Origen, Homily 2; Benz and Klostermann, 251.3–9; PL 95.1192.

f. 3r   [Inc: Cum in toto mundo uirgineus flos . . .] //est quod anulo fidei agnes se asserit . . . per litteras traduntur exempla; ut//

Pseudo-Ambrose, Sermon 48; PL 17.701 (St Agnes, 21 January) = Paul the Deacon, Homily I.62. See Grégoire, 441.

f. 3v   [diabo]//lum superatum quotiens contra uirginem . . . dominum meritis virginis tenebatur et exi//[bat]

Pseudo-Ambrose, Sermon 48; PL 17.703–4.

Parchment. 3 folios. Fol. 1 measures 150 x 135 mm; fol. 2, 117 x 155 mm; fol. 3, 179 x 164 mm (written space originally ca. 355 x 235 mm; width of written space of 1 column: 110 mm). 1 column remaining of an original 2. Fol. 1 preserves 16 lines, fol. 2 preserves 12 lines, and fol. 3 preserves 19 lines of an original ca. 38. Ruled in lead (very faint). Single vertical bounding lines. Prickings in the outer margin.

Written in late Caroline minuscule. 1-line initials are written in brown rustic capitals and are not set apart from the text. Punctuation consists of the punctus, punctus elevatus, and punctus interrogativus. Hyphenation is in the same ink as the text.

The fragments were used to reinforce the spine of a binding.

Zinniker 108.

MS 482.75
Decretales

Germany, s. XII
Pl. 101

f. 1r   //facere quicquam nisi quod uiderit patrem facientem.

End of an unidentified text, quoting John 5.19.

f. 1r   *Non in calice aut uinum solum aut aqua sola offeratur.* Alexander successor euaristi dixit. Non debet enim ut a patribus accepimus . . . infirmitas humanę naturę. Nichilominus statuimus et iudicamus. nulli sacerdotum esse licitum una die uni altari plus quam tres missas superponere . . . Bonifacius uero archiepiscopus et martyr semel tam//

The first portion of the text (to "infirmitas humanę naturę") is from the Synod of Tribur (895), chap. 19: J. F. Schannat and J. Hartzheim, ed., *Concilia Germaniae* (Cologne, 1760, rpt. 1970), 2:397. In the margin next to the rubric the text hand has written "Ex concilio triburiensi" in black ink. This is followed with no break by a passage that is not found in the Synod of Tribur but is similar to PL 114.943. The other side of the leaf has been completely erased, and the lower and outer margins have been trimmed with loss of text.

Parchment. 1 folio. 195 x 136 mm (original dimensions and written space uncertain; width of written space: 80 mm). 1 column (of original 2). 24 lines remaining (of an uncertain original). Ruled in lead. Double vertical and single horizontal bounding lines; extra vertical bounding line in margin.

Written in late Caroline minuscule. 2-line capital "A" ("Alexander") is a red square capital set apart from the text between the double vertical bounding lines. 1-line initials are in brown capitals, with enlarged minuscule *n*, and are not set apart from the text. The rubric is written in red minuscule. Punctuation consists of the punctus.

The fragment was used as a pastedown in the binding of a volume measuring ca. 195 x 125 mm. A modern hand has written bibliographical information concerning the Synod of Tribur (mistakenly ascribing it to the year 859) in pencil in the outer margin. Another hand has written the number "94" in pencil in the lower margin of the fragment.

Zinniker 83.

MS 482.76   Germany, s. XII
Vergil, *Aeneid*   Pl. 101

The fragment includes the Pseudo-Ovidian prologue to Book 3, of which it omits
line 10. The text of the prologue agrees with that in Wolfenbüttel, Herzog-August-
Bibliothek, Gudianus lat. 70 (Lyon, s. IX).

f. 1r   //Puluere per pedes traiectus lora tumentes . . . Incidit aut rapidus// [mon-
            tano flumine torrens]

            Vergil, *Aeneid*, 2.273–305; *P. Vergili Maronis opera*, ed. R. A. B. Mynors,
            OCT (Oxford, 1969), 135–36. The lower margin has been trimmed with
            the loss of the last line of text and a portion of the next to last line.

f. 1v   //Praecipitesque trahit siluas. stupet inscius alto . . . [Addunt se socios
            ripeus et] maximis armis//

            Aeneid, 2.307–39; Mynors, 136–37. The lower margin has been trimmed
            with the loss of the last line of text and a portion of the next to last line.

f. 2r   //Tunc sic affa[ri] et curas. his demere dicis . . . C[essi et sublato montis
            genitore petiui]//

            Aeneid, 2.775–804; Mynors, 151. The upper margin has been trimmed
            with loss of three lines of text. Almost all the text has been erased from
            when the leaf was used in a binding.

f. 2v   //Regis ad hospitium . . . poliphemo urguente recepit.//

            Pseudo-Ovidian Prologue III.4–9; A. Reise, ed., *Anthologia Latina* (Leipzig,
            1869), 1:3. The upper margin has been trimmed with loss of three lines of
            text.

f. 2v   //Postquam res asię priamique euerte[re gentem] . . . Conatus ra[mis] te-
            gerem. ut frondentibus ar[a]s//

            Aeneid, 3.1–25; Mynors, 153.

Parchment. 2 folios. Fol. 1 measures 170 x 99 mm; fol. 2 measures 170 x 76 mm
(written space originally ca. 172 x 62 mm). 1 column. Fol. 1 preserves 33 lines, and
fol. 2 preserves 31 lines of an original 34. Lead ruling. Double vertical bounding
lines. Prickings in outer margin.

Written in late Caroline minuscule. A portion of the initial "P" ("Postquam") of Book 3 is preserved, written in red and partially set apart from the text. 1-line initials at the beginning of verses are in brown in a mixture of rustic capital and uncial forms and are set apart from the text between the vertical bounding lines. Punctuation consists of the punctus.

A leaf from the same manuscript was sold to a private collector by Maggs Bros. Ltd., in 1982 (see Maggs Bros., *Many Kinds of Learning* [Sale Catalogue 1025, March 1982], lot 167, pl. 2). This leaf preserves Book 1.513–43 and 547–76, and was earlier sold by E. von Scherling (Leiden): *Rotulus*, 4 (Winter 1937): 23, item 1878.

Folio 2 of the Beinecke fragments was used as the spine in the binding of a book measuring ca. 146 x 83 mm. Folio 1 and the Maggs leaf formed the wrappers for the front and back covers of this volume.

Bibliography:
Babcock, *Reconstructing a Medieval Library*, 32, note 34.

MS 482.77   Lambach, Austria, s. XII^{ex}
Rufinus of Aquileia, *Historia monachorum*   Pl. 102

The text of this leaf varies from the standard text of the *Historia monachorum* by omitting chapters 29.5.1–32.1. Other copies of the text that show the same omission are Vienna, Österreichische Nationalbibliothek, s.n. 3610, fols. 66–112, a manuscript of the twelfth century (formerly Lambach, Stiftsbibliothek, Cml CXIII), and Brussels, Bibliothèque Royale, MS 8216–18, a ninth-century manuscript from St. Florian (see E. Schulz-Flügel, ed., *Tyrannius Rufinus Historia monachorum sive De vita sanctorum patrum* [Berlin, 1990], 124–25).

f. 1r   //imaginibus ludentes. requirit ab eis si in oratione uel edificandi cogitationes habuerint ... accedentium ad altare uel indignitates uel merita praelaterent.

Rufinus, *Historia Monachorum*, chap. 29.4.11–16 (St. Macarius); Schulz-Flügel, 373–74; PL 21.459–60.

f. 1r–v   *Incipit de s. Piamone*. Uidimus et alium quendam presbyterum ammirabilem nomine piamonem. ... ut solito sanior redderetur.

Historia Monachorum, chap. 32.2–8 (St. Piamon [Poemen]); Schulz-Flügel, 383–84; PL 21.459–60.

f. 1v   *Incipit de sancto Iohanne.* Erat in ipsis locis et uir sanctus ac totius gratiẹ
         dono repletus iohannes nomine ... ut quacumque mesticia. quocumque
         tedio ob//[pressa]

         Historia Monachorum, chap. 33.1 (St. John); Schulz-Flügel, 384; PL
         21.459–60.

Parchment (stained and with several large holes resulting from imperfection in the
parchment). 1 folio. 215 x 160 mm (written space 193 x 130 mm). 1 column. 25
lines. Ruled in lead. Single vertical bounding lines.

Written in late Caroline minuscule. 1-line initials at the beginning of chapters
are in red uncials and are not set apart from the text. Other 1-line initials are in
brown, once filled with red, and are a mixture of uncial, rustic capital, and enlarged
minuscule forms; they are set apart from the text when they occur at the beginning
of a line. Rubrics are written in red rustic capitals, with uncial M and enlarged
minuscule or round E. A line divider is in brown filled with red. Punctuation consists of the punctus. Hyphenation is in the same ink as the text.

Other leaves of the same manuscript are preserved as flyleaves in Lambach,
Stiftsbibliothek, Cml XLIV, Cml XLV, and Cml IL. The manuscript may have been
one of the "Duo volumina in vitas patrum" listed in the Lambach library catalogue
in Cml XIX (see Holter [1956], 274, and MBKÖ, 5:57). This fragment was used in
the binding of a volume measuring ca. 215 x 142 mm, perhaps Lambach Ccl 284.
On the recto in the lower margin there is a faint pencil notation "284" that is similar to other pencil notations of Lambach shelf numbers on other Beinecke leaves,
and the measurement of the leaf is consistent with the measurements of other
Lambach manuscripts that are similar in size to Lambach Ccl 284 (Ccl 283 measures 220 x 145; see its description in Holter [1959], 262).

A modern hand has written the number "50" in pencil in the lower right corner
of the verso.

Zinniker 90.

Bibliography:
Babcock, *Reconstructing a Medieval Library,* 102 and fig. 28

MS 482.78   Italy, s. XIII[1]
Verba Seniorum (Vitae Patrum)   Pl. 102

The *Verba Seniorum* comprises chapters 5–7 of the *Vitae Patrum,* a collection of
Saint's Lives gathered together by H. Rosweyde in 1615 (reprinted by Migne, PL
73–74). The *Verba Seniorum* circulated separately in the Middle Ages, often under

the name *Vitae Patrum*, *Vitas Patrum* or *Adhortationes Sanctorum Patrum*. See C. M. Batlle, *Die 'Adhortationes Sanctorum Patrum' ('Verba Seniorum') im lateinischen Mittelalter* (Münster, 1971).

f. 1   [ue]//ra que audisti. Et ille dixit ei. Etiam pater uerum est . . . Exiens ergo frater. dixit illi; quia//

Vitae Patrum, 5.10.37–39; PL 73.919–20.

Parchment. 1 folio. 315 x 230 mm (written space 223 x 165 mm). 2 columns. 29 lines. Dry-point ruling. Single vertical bounding lines.

Written in a rounded early gothic script (littera textualis). 2- and 3-line initials are in red with red and blue penwork and are written on the vertical bounding line. 1-line initials are in brown uncials, with enlarged minuscule n, and are not set apart from the text. Punctuation consists of the punctus, punctus elevatus, and colon. Accents and hyphenation are in the same ink as the text.

The fragment was used as the wrapper of a copy of the *Liber de divitiis* ascribed to Pope Sixtus III, measuring ca. 175 x 123 mm. The title "de Divitiis S.Sisti" is written on the spine with the shelf mark "O 25."

Zinniker 64.

MS 482.78A   Southern Germany or Austria, s. XIII/XIV
Antiphonary   Pl. 103

f. 1   [R. Bonum certamen certaui . . . coro]//na iusticie. V. Scio cui credidi . . . R. In omnem. *In iu° n°* A. Saulus qui et paulus . . . V. Ostendens quia hic . . . Ps. Exaudi deus deprecationem. A. Ne magnitudo reuelationum . . . V. Nam uirtus in infirmitate . . . Ps. Exaudi deus orationem. A. Reposita est michi . . . V. Cooperante gratia spiritus . . . Ps. Te decet. A. Exaltabuntur. Ps. Confitebimur. A. Lux orta. Ps. Dominus regnauit exultet. A. Custodiebant. Ps. Dominus regnauit irascantur. *v.* Constitues eos. R. Reposita est michi . . . V. Scio cui . . . R. Audistis enim conuersationem . . . V. Habundantius enim emulator . . . R. Cum autem placuit . . . V. Continuo non acquieui . . . R. Constitues eos. *Ad cant.* Ter virgis cesus . . . V. Nocte ac die . . . R. Saulus autem magis . . . V. Fuit autem cum discipulis . . . R. Gracia dei sum . . . sed gratia eius//

St. Paul (30 June), from the first to the third nocturn of matins.

Parchment. 1 folio. 266 x 194 mm (written space 231 x 155 mm). 1 column. 18 lines. Ruled in lead. Single vertical and horizontal bounding lines.

Written in gothic script (littera textualis). Initials of antiphons and responses are 1-line red capitals and are not set apart from the text. 1-line initials for verses and Psalm incipits are in brown highlighted with red and are not set apart from the text. Rubrics are written in red in the same script as the text. Punctuation consists of the punctus. Hyphenation is in the same ink as the text. Interlinear neumes are in the St. Gall style, somewhat surprising in a manuscript of this date. Differentiae in roman numerals with neumes in the St. Gall style are in the outer margins for antiphons with full text.

A modern hand has written in black ink the letter "S" in the upper left corner, "B" in the upper right corner, and "H.2 27." in the upper center margin of the recto.

Zinniker 54–1.

MS 482.79   S. France or N. Italy, s. XIV
Commentary on Ps.-Gilbert of Poitiers, *Lib. VI principiorum*   Pl. 103

f. 1   //eadem enim forma communicat et non communicat in eodem esse natura cum subiecto ... quia immutare est materiam agere praeterea dicit boethius quid ille qui destruit nihil aliud facit//

Unidentified commentary on Pseudo-Gilbert of Poitiers, *Liber sex principiorum*, I.11–II.21 (information on the text was supplied by Professor Timothy Noone of Catholic University); L. Minio-Paluello, ed., *Aristoteles Latinus*, 1.7 (Bruges–Paris, 1966), 37–39.

Parchment. 1 folio. 287 x 195 mm (written space 250 x 165 mm). 2 columns. 65 lines. Ruled in lead. Single vertical and double horizontal bounding lines. Prickings in outer margin.

Written in a small gothic script with frequent abbreviations (scriptura notularis). Spaces are left for two 2-line initials, not set apart from the text, but they have not been added. 1-line initials are in brown capitals and are not set apart from the text. Quotations from the text are underlined in brown. Paragraph marks are in brown and are set apart from the text when they occur at the beginning of a line. Punctuation consists of the punctus. Hyphenation is in the same ink as the text.

A modern hand has written the number "88" in pencil in the lower right corner of the recto.

Zinniker 87.

MS 482.80

transferred to Beinecke MS 481.111, fol. 2

MS 482.81   Germany, s. XIII
Bible, Leviticus   Pl. 104

f. 1ra   //tam indigena quam colonus . . . quia non fuit libera//

            Leviticus 18.26–19.20. The upper margin has been trimmed with loss of
            text.

f. 1rb   [exprobre]//tis ei sed sit inter uos . . . cum muliere in fluxu menstruo et
            releua//[uerit]

            Leviticus 19.33–20.18. The upper and outer margins have been trimmed
            with loss of text.

f.1va   //morte moriantur [lapidibus ob]ru[ent] . . . quae ipsi offerunt//

            Leviticus 20.27–22.3. The upper and outer margins have been trimmed
            with loss of text.

f. 1vb   //absque liberis [reuersa fuerit ad] domum patris sui . . . mense primo
            quartadecima//

            Leviticus 22.13–23.5. The upper margin has been trimmed with loss of
            text.

f. 2ra   //[quo] obtulistis manipulos primitiarum . . . uniuscuiusque diei exceptis
            sabbatis//

            Leviticus 23.15–38. The upper margin has been trimmed with loss of text.

f. 2rb   //uespere usque in mane coram [domino] . . . Quae sponte gignit//

            Leviticus 24.3–25.5. The upper and outer margins have been trimmed
            with loss of text.

f. 2va   //ueris tanto minoris empcio . . . sed quasi mercennarius//

Leviticus 25.16–40. The upper and outer margins have been trimmed with loss of text.

f. 2vb   //usque ad iubeleum secundum hos reddet ... incassum labor uester non profe//[ret]

Leviticus 25.51–26.20. The upper margin has been trimmed with loss of text.

Parchment (fols. 1v and 2r are stained and obscured by pieces of wood and leather from use in a binding). 2 folios. 205 x 142 mm (written space originally ca. 235 x 150 mm). 2 columns. 36 lines remaining of an original ca. 54 lines. Ruled in lead. Single vertical bounding lines.

Written in gothic script (littera textualis). Spaces are left within the text for 1-line initials but they have not been added. Other 1-line initials are in brown and are not set apart from the text. Punctuation consists of the punctus and is extremely rare. Hyphenation is in the same ink as the text.

A modern hand has written the number "3373" in pencil in the upper right corner of fol. 2v. Another modern hand has written the number "261" in green crayon in the lower margin of fol. 1r.

Both fragments were used as pastedowns in the binding of a volume measuring ca. 205 x 142 mm.

Zinniker 107–1 and 107–2.

MS 482.82   Germany, s. XIV
Bible, Kings and Wisdom   Pl. 104

f. 1   [sa]//muel ad ysai. Numquid iam completi sunt filii ... Quod cum audisset eliab//

1 Kings 16.11–17.28.

f. 2   //eius scrutator est uerus ... Dabitur enim illi fi//[dei]

Wisdom 1.6–3.14.

Parchment. 2 folios (bifolium). 213 x 150 mm (written space 152 x 110 mm). 2 columns. 33 lines. Ruled in ink. Single vertical and double horizontal bounding lines. Prickings in outer margins.

Written in gothic script (littera textualis). 1-line initials of each verse are in brown highlighted with red and are not set apart from the text. Punctuation consists of the punctus and punctus elevatus.

A modern hand has written the number "12" in the upper left corner of fol. 2v.

The bifolium was used as a pastedown in the binding of a volume measuring ca. 300 x 200 mm.

Zinniker 130.

MS 482.83 Northern France (?), s. XIII[1]
Gospel Harmony, Matthew and Luke (with commentary) Pl. 105

The text from the New Testament is written in sections in short lines (40 mm width) surrounded above, below, and on the right with an unidentified commentary. In the bottom margin on both sides, another scribe has added two columns of 13 lines of another unidentified commentary.

f. 1r //[u]obis r[eg]num dei et dabitur genti . . . sicut prophetam eum habebant.

Matthew 21.43–46.

f. 1r Mt. *lec.* Et respondens iesus iterum . . . nuptias filio suo. *Luc.* Et uocauit plures. Et hora cene misit seruos . . . et nolebant uenire. *Luc.* Et ceperunt simul omnes excusare.

Matthew 22.1–2; Luke 14.16–17 and Matthew 22.3; Luke 14.18.

f. 1r–v Primus dixit villam . . . nunciauit haec domino suo.

Luke 14.18–21.

f. 1v Iterum mis[it alios seruos] dicens . . . et contumelia affectos occiderunt.

Matthew 22.4–6.

f. 1v Rex autem cum audisset . . . fuerunt digni. Ite ergo//

Matthew 22.7–9.

Parchment (badly stained, especially the verso which is almost illegible). 1 folio. 320 x 225 mm (written space 231 x 157 mm). 2 columns. 26 lines of biblical text and 52 lines of commentary. Dry-point ruling.

Written in early gothic script (littera textualis). Each section from the Bible begins with a 2-line initial in red that is set apart from the text. The corresponding sections of the commentary begin with a 1-line red initial that is not set apart from the text. Other 1-line initials in both the text and the commentary are in black and are not set apart from the text. Rubrics are written in red in the same script as the text. The lemmata in the commentary are underlined with red. Canon table numbers are written in black in the margins and are surrounded by red boxes. Punctuation consists of the punctus. Hyphenation is in the same ink as the text.

Zinniker 136–1.

MS 482.84   Northern France (?), s. XIII
Bible, Commentary on Wisdom   Pl. 105

f. 1   //Sicut patuit quando istam scientiam eis quos repleuit dedit . . . dicit
          dominus (dominus *expunx. man. alt.*) sapiens quia mors nec est nec a
          condi//

Unidentified commentary on Wisdom 1.8–13.

Parchment. 1 folio. 297 x 197 mm (written space 206 x 144 mm); strip of conjoint folio (without any text) measures 270 x 20 mm. 2 columns. 61 lines. Ruled in lead. Single vertical bounding lines. Prickings in upper and lower margins.

Written in a small gothic script with frequent abbreviations (littera textualis currens), below the top line. 1-line initials are in black and are not set apart from the text. Punctuation consists of the punctus. Quotations from Wisdom are underlined in black.

This fragment was used as a wallet binding for a codex measuring 180 x 120 x 15 mm. The number "146" is written on the spine of the volume, possibly referring to Lambach Cml CXLVI. The modern location of Cml CXLVI is unknown, and its measurements are uncertain; however, since the Lambach library was organized by size, Cml CXLVI should measure ca. 180 x 120–140 mm, a range consistent with the size of the book covered by this fragment.

Zinniker 112.

Bibliography:
Babcock, *Reconstructing a Medieval Library,* 114 and fig. 63.

MS 482.85

transferred to Beinecke MS 481.100, fol. 2

MS 482.86   Germany, s. XIII
Breviary   Pl. 106

f. 1r   //tu[i a]tque pontificis meritis et intercessione letificas ... *Oro.* Da quae-
         sumus omnipotens deus ut qui beati N. martyris tui atque pontificis sol-
         lempnia ... *Or.* Preces populi tui quaesumus domine clementer exaudi
         ... *Or.* Deus qui nos annua beati N. martyris ... uirtutem quoque pas-
         sionis imitemur. Per.

         Common of a Martyr Bishop.

f. 1r   *Item de martyribus. lectio prima.* Psalmus qui cantatur domino uidetur sanc-
         tis martyribus conuenire ... pertinere intelligamus. Qui seminant//

         Common of Martyrs. The lesson is from Augustine, Sermon 31 (PL
         38.192). The lower half of the leaf has been trimmed with loss of text.

f. 1v   //pertineant. Nulli enim tantum inpenderunt ... Perit manus ubi non perit
         pilus? Perit ca//[put]

         Common of Martyrs; the lesson from Augustine, Sermon 31 continues
         (PL 38.193). The lower half of the leaf has been trimmed with loss of text.

f. 2r   //tribulationibus fuerunt. Nam ut eorum lacrimas christus consolaretur
         ... quando faciebat quod non faceret//

         Common of Martyrs; the lesson from Augustine, Sermon 31 continues
         (PL 38.193–94) . The lower half of the leaf has been trimmed with loss of
         text.

f. 2v   [exsul]//tantis sunt non plorantis ... et uenit leticia sine fine mansura. tu.
         autem. *Secundum lucam.* In illo tempore. Descendens iesus de monte stetit
         in loco campestri ... *Omelia uenerabilis bede presbyteri.* Et ipse eleuatis ocu-
         lis in discipulos dicebat ... etsi generaliter//

         Common of Martyrs. The lesson from Augustine, Sermon 31 ends (PL

38.194). The reading is from Luke 6.17–18. The lesson for the third nocturn is from Bede, Homily III.69 (on Luke 6.20, PL 94.448 = *In Lucae
euangelium expositio* II.6, D. Hurst, ed., CCSL 120 [1960], 137). The lower
half of the leaf has been trimmed with loss of text.

Parchment (stained and covered with remnants of paper from use in a binding). 2
folios. Fol. 1 measures 185 x 280 mm; fol. 2 measures 187 x 272 mm (written space
originally ca. 293 x 190 mm). 1 column. 14 lines remaining of an original ca. 27
lines. Ruled in ink. Single vertical and double horizontal bounding lines.

Written in gothic script (littera textualis). 2- and 3-line initials at the beginning
of lessons are in red uncials; only the initial "I" ("In illo tempore") is set apart from
the text. The initials for the prayers are in red and are 3-line initials when they
occur at the beginning of a line and 1-line initials when they occur within a line. 1-
line initials within lessons are in black and are not set apart from the text. Rubrics
are written in red in the same script as the text. Punctuation consists of the punctus, punctus elevatus, and punctus interrogativus. Hyphenation is in the same ink
as the text.

Fol. 1 was used as a pastedown and fol. 2 as a flyleaf in the binding of a volume
measuring ca. 280 x 187 mm. The inscription "Spizzenbuch" is written in red in the
upper margin of fol. 1r. The number "1809" is written next to it in blue ink.

Zinniker 102–1 and 102–2.

MS 482.87   Germany, s. XIV[1]
Breviary   Pl. 106

f. 1r   [R. Ecce iam uenit plenitudo tem]//poris in quo misit deus filium . . . V.
         Propter [nimiam caritatem] suam qua dilexit . . . *Lec. v^a*. Consurge con-
         surge induere fortitudinem . . . R. Uirgo israhel reuerter[e] ad ciuitates
         . . . V. In caritate perpetua . . . *Lectio v*//[*i^a*]

         Fourth Sunday of Advent, second nocturn of matins. The upper margin
         has been trimmed with the loss of one line of text.

f. 1v   //et uenient in syon laudantes . . . consolabor uos. R. Iuraui dicit dominus
         . . . V. Iuxta est salus . . . Gloria. *Quando uigilia natalis domini in hac . . . Se-
         cundum iohannem*. In illo tempore. Miserunt iudei ab ierosolimis sacer-
         dotes et leuitas . . . [L.] Ex huius nobis lectionis uerbis fratres karissimi io-
         hannis humilitas commendatur . . . elegit solide subsistere in se ne//

         Fourth Sunday of Advent, from the second to the third nocturn of matins.

The lessons for the second nocturn are from Isaiah 51.11–12. The lessons for the third nocturn are from Gregory the Great, *Homiliae xl in Evangelia*, I.7 (on John 1.19; PL 76.1099; R. Étaix, ed., CCSL 141 [1999], 46) = Paul the Deacon's Homiliary, Homily I.8 (see Grégoire, 431). The upper margin has been trimmed with the loss of one line of text.

Parchment. 1 folio. 138 x 100 mm (written space originally ca. 118 x 78 mm). 1 column. 18 lines remaining of an original 19 lines. Ruled in ink. Single vertical bounding lines; double horizontal bounding lines.

Written in gothic script (littera textualis). The initials of the lessons are slightly enlarged and are set apart from the text; they alternate blue with red penwork or red with blue penwork. Initials at the beginning of verses are highlighted with red. Rubrics are written in red in the same script as the text; liturgical directions are written in black and are underlined in red. Punctuation consists of the punctus. Hyphenation is in the same ink as the text.

The fragment was used as a pastedown in the binding of a volume measuring ca. 138 x 100 mm.

Zinniker 44–3.

MS 482.87A

transferred to Beinecke MS 481.97, fols. 2 and 3

MS 482.88   Germany, s. XIII^{ex}
Calendar and Computus   Pl. 107

Perhaps made for a Cistercian monastery, given that the feasts of *Roberti abb.* (29 April) and of *Petri ep. et conf.* (8 May) have twelve lessons. On 19 April the calendar notes the death of "Regis Richardi feria iii^a post octavam pasce."

f. 1   //aprilis habet dies xxx^a . . . xi d *ii kl* petronille virginis.//

            Calendar for April and May.

f. 2   //A natale domini usque xl . . . dies bisextus.//

            Computus tables for determining the dates of Septuagesima, Quadragesima, Easter, Rogation, and Pentecost.

Parchment. 2 folios (bifolium). 156 x 100 mm (written space 130 x 90 mm). 5 columns. 35–38 lines. The calendar is ruled in lead. Computus tables are ruled vertically with red ink.

Written in gothic script (littera textualis). On fol. 1 columns 3 and 4 are written in red, as is the slightly enlarged "A" indicating a Sunday on every seventh line in column 2. The enlarged abbreviations for the words "kalendae", "nonae", and "idus" are also red. The script in the columns of the computus tables alternates black and red. Punctuation consists of the punctus.

The bifolium was used as a wrapper for a volume measuring ca. 125 x 80 mm. There are a number of pen trial in later hands, one of which reads "Ich."

Zinniker 139–1.

MS 482.89

transferred to Beinecke MS 481.98, fol. 1

MS 482.90

transferred to Beinecke MS 481.99, fols. 1, 4, 5, and 6

MS 482.91   Germany, s. XIII^{ex}
Humbert of Romans, *Liber Constitutionum Sororum O. P.*   Pl. 107

The consuetudines for Dominican nuns were issued at the Valenciennes Chapter of 1259; see E. Brett, *Humbert of Romans: His Life and Views of Thirteenth-Century Society* (Toronto, 1984), 74–79. The text here is divided into lessons.

f. 1r   [Inc: Quoniam ex precepto regule] //iubentur sorores habere cor unum et animam unam in domino . . . *lectio*. Ad hec tamen in conuentu suo . . . *lectio*. Declaramus autem quod constitutiones . . . nisi propter preceptum uel contemptum.

          Humbert of Romans, *Liber constitutionum sororum ordinis Praedicatorum*, preface; ed. in *Analecta sacri ordinis fratrum Praedicatorum* 3 (1897): 337–48, here 338. The upper margin has been trimmed with the loss of the first two lines of text.

f. 1r–v   De officio ecclesie capitulum .i. . . . De concessione domorum. *xxi*.

Liber constitutionum sororum, capitula; ed. 338–39. The upper margin has
been trimmed with the loss of the first two lines of text.

f. 1v   [*lecti*]*o. De officio ecclesie.* Audito primo signo surgant sorores . . . *lectio.*
Tempore quo bis reficiuntur sorores . . . usque ad signum. similiter et
post//

Liber constitutionum sororum, chap. 1; ed. 339.

f. 2   //alii deputatas quamuis non animo retinendi sine licentia acceperit . . .
minores uidebitur iustum esse. *De grauiori culpa. xx.* Grauior culpa est .si
qua per contumaciam uel manifestam rebellionem . . . *lectio.* Pro huiusmodi culpis que rea fuerit . . . *lectio.* Talis quam diu erit in hac penitentia
. . . *lectio.* Eodem modo penitere debet . . . *lectio.* Si que tamen non mali-
tiose . . . eius uicario significetur. *lectio. De grauissima culpa. xxi.* Grauissima
culpa est. incorrigibilitas illius que nec culpas timet . . . pro culpis uero
minoribus istis. poterit interdum//

Liber constitutionum sororum, chaps. 19–21; ed. 344–45.

Parchment. 2 folios. Fol. 1 measures 214 x 158 mm; fol. 2 measures 211 x 162 mm
(written space 182 x 126 mm). 2 columns. The number of lines varies from 26 to
29 lines, with an original 31 lines in some columns on fol. 1. The leaves are ruled
vertically in lead, but there is no horizontal ruling.

Written in gothic script (littera textualis). 3-line initials at the beginning of
chapters are in red with red ornamentation and are not set apart from the text. 1-
line initials in the capitula list are in red and are not set apart from the text. Other
1-line initials are in black highlighted with red and are not set apart from the text.
Rubrics are written in red in the same script as the text. Paragraph marks in red are
occasionally used in the margins to mark the beginning of a new lesson. Punctuation consists of the punctus and punctus elevatus.

A modern hand has written the number "39" in the lower margin of the verso.
Zinniker 106–1 and 106–2.

MS 482.92   Italy, s. XIII[med]
Lectionary   Pl. 108

f. 1r   //Et hic mensis est sextus illi que uocatur sterilis . . . Fiat michi; secundum
uerbum tuum.

Luke 1.36–38 (Feria V of the third week of Advent).

f. 1r   *Feria vi. Sequentia sancti euangelii; secundum lucam.* In illo tempore. Exurgens maria; abiit in montana cum festinatione ... Et exultauit spiritus
meus in deo salutari meo.

Luke 1.39–47 (Feria VI of the third week of Advent).

f. 1r–v   *Sabbato in xii. lectione. Sequentia sancti euangelii; secundum lucam.* Anno
quintodecimo imperii tyberii cesaris ... Et uidebit omnis caro; salutare
dei.

Luke 3.1–6 (Saturday of the third week of Advent).

f. 1v   *Dominica iiii. de aduentu domini. Sequentia sancti euangelii; secundum iohannem.* In illo tempore. Miserunt iudei ab hierosolimis sacerdotes et leuitas
... Hec in bethania facta sunt trans iordanem; ubi erat iohannes bap-
tizans.//

John 1.19–28 (Fourth Sunday of Advent).

Parchment. 1 folio. 303 x 240 mm (written space 257 x 155 mm). 1 column. 23
lines, though on the verso three lines have been added to the bottom. Ruled in
lead. Single vertical bounding lines. Prickings in upper and lower margins.

Written in gothic script (littera textualis), above the top line. One 4-line and
two 3-line initials are in red, decorated with blue penwork, and are set apart from
the text. 1-line initials at the beginning of verses are in brown uncials highlighted
with red and are not set apart from the text. Rubrics are written in red in the same
script as the text, with capital Q. Punctuation consists of the punctus, punctus
elevatus, and punctus interrogativus. Hyphenation and accents are in the same ink
as the text. There are three signs that occur over syllables of words, one similar to
a backwards "3", one similar to a squarish, backwards "C," and the third a virgule;
perhaps these are pitch or accent marks or some other type of aid for reading aloud.

The fragment was used as a flyleaf in the binding of a volume measuring ca. 303
x 218 mm.

Zinniker 1.

MS 482.93

transferred to Beinecke MS 481.102, fol. 2

MS 482.94

Gregory IX, *Decretales*

Italy, s. XIII²
Pl. 108

f. 1   [dignita]//tibus spolietis. Innoce[n]cius iii in concilio generali Quia nonnulli propter inopiam . . . ut passo iniuriam et ecclesie satisfieri//

Gregory IX, *Decretales*, 5.5.4–5.6.14; E. Friedberg, ed., *Corpus iuris canonici*, 2: *Collectiones decretalium* (Leipzig, 1922), 770–75.

Parchment (the parchment is stained from leather from its use in a binding). 1
folio. 282 x 222 mm (written space 225 x 130 mm). 2 columns. 50 lines. Ruled in
lead. Single vertical bounding lines.

Written in gothic script (littera textualis). There are guide letters for initials at
the beginning of each capitulum, but the initials have not been added; no spaces
have been left for them, so they would have been set apart from the text. 1-line initials are in red and are not set apart from the text. The heading of titulus VI is
written in red. Punctuation consists of the punctus. Paragraph marks are in red ink,
brackets in brown. Corrections have been added by several contemporary hands.
Running title on recto "V9" (i.e., "*Quintus*").

The fragment was used as a flyleaf in the binding of a volume measuring ca. 282
x 214 mm from the Abbey of Sts. Peter and Paul in Melk. The verso bears the inscription "Catalogo Monasterii Mellicensis hunc librum inscripsi".

Zinniker 93.

MS 482.95

Augustine, Sermon 69

Germany, s. XIII
Pl. 109

f. 1ra   [Inc: Unde hic labor. Audiuimus in euangelio dominum exhilaratum
spiritu dixisse deo patri . . . uiden]//tis. ut illum deum uidere concupis-
camus de quo dicit scriptura . . . [E]t difficile est quidem ut eum//

Augustine, Sermon 69 (on Matthew 11.28–29); PL 38.441. The lower
margin has been trimmed with loss of text.

f. 1rb   [insipi]//entes estis in populo. et stulti aliquando sapite? . . . Non ergo ubi
hoc promittas; uelis nolis ui//[det]

Sermon 69; PL 38.441. The lower margin has been trimmed with loss of
text.

f. 1va   //ab oculis dei? Si non uis recedere ab eis . . . ibi est qui dixit; celum et//

Sermon 69; PL 38.442. The lower margin has been trimmed with loss of text.

f. 1vb   //sciebat. Unde me nosti? Ait ei dominus. Cum esses . . . in carne peccati. nascimur qua[m]//

Sermon 69; PL 38.442. The lower margin has been trimmed with loss of text.

Parchment. 1 folio. 198 x 258 mm (written space originally ca. 290 x 190 mm). 2 columns. 17 lines remaining of an original ca. 34 lines. Ruled in ink. There is double horizontal ruling for each line.

Written in early gothic script (littera textualis), below the top line. 1-line initials are in brown highlighted with red and are not set apart from the text. Punctuation consists of the punctus, punctus elevatus, and punctus interrogativus. Hyphenation is in the same ink as the text.

The fragment was used as a wrapper for a volume measuring ca. 167 x 110 mm. There is an eighteenth- or nineteenth-century inscription (visible under ultra-violet light) in the upper right corner of the recto that has been offset from the volume in the binding of which the fragment was used.

Zinniker 82.

MS 482.96   Senigallia, Italy, after December 1237
Copy of a Judicial Decision   Pl. 109

Jacobus was bishop of Senigallia from 1232 to 1270 (see C. Eubel, *Hierarchia Catholica Medii Aevi* [Regensburg, 1913], 1:446). Sinibaldus was cardinal priest of St. Laurentius in Lucina from 1227 to 1243 (see Eubel, 6–7 and 43).

f. 1r   In dei nomine amen. Ego Jacobus senegal. episcopus a domino senibaldo cardinali . . . a consilio generali ciuitatis seneg.// [*last line of document stained*]

Authenticated notarial copy of a decision of Bishop Jacobus of Senigallia, extracted from the protocols in the hand of the notary Benven[uto], by the notary Iohannes filius condam Iuliani, delegate of the rector of the Marca d'Ancona, Cardinal Sinibaldo, concerning a case between the monasteries of S. *Iohannes peneclaria* and S. *Iacobus in burgo*, both in

Ancona. The verso contains the date and a brief description of the contents.

Parchment. 1 folio. 615 x 246 mm (written space 560 x 235 mm). 70 lines. 1 column.

Written in notarial script by the notary Johannes, son of Julianus. The document begins with a flourished initial "I". 1-line initials are in brown. The notary's sign is in the center of the lower margin. Punctuation consists of the punctus and punctus elevatus. Hyphenation is in the same ink as the text.

Zinniker 16.

MS 482.97   Italy, s. XIV
Johannes de Deo, *Liber Poenitentiarius*   Pl. 110

See A. D. Sousa Costa, "Animadversiones criticae in vitam et opera canonistae Ioannis de Deo," *Antonianum* 33 (1958): 76–124, here 104–8; idem, *Doutrina penitencial do canonista João de Deus* (Braga, 1956), which has a list of known manuscripts (11–14; MS 482.97 is not cited); and idem, *Um mestre português em Bolonha no século XIII* (Braga, 1957). An updated list of manuscripts is in M. Bloomfield et al., *Incipits of Latin Works on the Virtues and Vices, 1100–1500 A.D.* (Cambridge, Mass., 1979), 34–35, no. 0238 (MS 482.97 is not cited).

f. 1r   //Quintum uitium est quod p[rae]lati inuident subditis et subditi praelato
          ... sumant sed leprosis et//

          Johannes de Deo, *Liber Poenitentiarius*, chaps. 20–24; excerpts from these chapters are printed in PL 99.1107–8. The verso, which contains the end of chap. 24 and chaps. 25–28, is almost completely illegible from the fragment's use in a binding. The lower margin has been trimmed with the loss of one line of text.

Parchment (verso badly stained from use in a binding). 1 folio. 282 x 198 mm (written space originally ca. 265 x 152 mm). 2 columns. 67 of 68 lines remaining. Lead ruling. Single vertical bounding lines, with an extra vertical bounding line between the two columns.

Written in a rounded gothic script (littera textualis). There are spaces with guide letters for 2-line initials, not set apart from the text, but they have not been added. Rubrics are written in red in the same script as the text. Guides for the rubricator are in the margins in light brown ink. Punctuation consists of the punctus. A late sixteenth- or early seventeenth-century German hand has added marginalia to the recto.

Zinniker 47.

MS 482.98   Italy, s. XIII^ex
Justinian, *Digesta,* with glossa ordinaria of Accursius   Pl. 110

f. 1   [prae]//stat que tamen [*sic*] corpore implenda sunt . . . circa munera quoque municipalia subeunda idem. honor senec//[tuti]

Justinian, *Digesta,* 50.5.2–50.6.6; T. Mommsen and P. Krueger, edd., *Corpus iuris civilis* (Berlin, 1928), 1.900–1. The outer margin has been trimmed with loss of a portion of the commentary.

Parchment (the verso is damaged from use in a binding). 1 folio. 277 x 222 mm (written space of main text 212 x 115 mm). 2 columns of text surrounded by 2 columns of commentary. 47 lines (main text). Lead ruling. Single vertical bounding lines.

Text of the *Digest* in a rounded gothic script (littera textualis), that of the commentary in a smaller hand (notularis), perhaps later. Initials of the names of authorities alternate 1- and 2-line red and blue capitals, set apart from the text. The first word of each section begins with a 1-line capital alternating red and blue, not set apart from the text. Guide letters for both initials are written in light brown ink. Punctuation consists of the punctus. The number "X.I.I" is written in black ink in the upper right corner of the recto.

Zinniker 47–1.

MS 482.99   Italy, s. XIII
Justinian, *Digesta,* with glossa ordinaria of Accursius   Pl. 111

f. 1va   //in ueram quantitatem fideiussor teneatur . . . P[aulus. l.] Quotiens uictore cau//[tum]

Justinian, *Digesta,* 2.8.2–2.8.6; T. Mommsen and P. Krueger, ed., *Corpus iuris civilis* (Berlin, 1928), 1.50. The lower margin has been trimmed with the loss of approximately five lines of text. The recto is mostly illegible but includes text from *Digesta* 2.7.4 to the rubric of 2.8 in the first column and 2.8.1–2.8.2 in the second column.

f. 1vb   //et diuus pius et etiam pomponius ... Qui mulierem adhibet ad satis-
dandum non uidetur//

Justinian, *Digesta*, 2.8.7–2.8.8; Mommsen and Krueger, 1.50–51. The lower margin has been trimmed with the loss of approximately five lines of
text.

Parchment (the recto is badly stained and rubbed from use in a binding). 1 folio.
184 x 232 (width of written space 115 mm). 2 columns of text surrounded by two
columns of commentary. 30 lines remaining of an original ca. 35 lines. Lead ruling.
Single vertical bounding lines.
    Written in a rounded gothic script (littera textualis). Later marginal and inter-
linear notes. Initials of the names of authorities are 2- and 3-line blue capitals with
red penwork and are set apart from the text. The initials of the first word of each
section are 1-line red capitals and are not set apart from the text. 1-line initials
within the text are in black and are not set apart from the text. Rubrics are written
in red in the same script as the text. Paragraph marks are either red, blue, or black
and are set apart from the text when they occur at the beginning of a line. Punctuation consists of the punctus. Hyphenation is in the same ink as the text.
    The fragment was used as part of a wrapper for a volume measuring ca. 200 x
150 mm.
    Zinniker 50–1.

MS 482.100   Germany, s. XIII/XIV
Prayers (in Latin and Middle High German)   Pl. 111

f. 1r   //Ad manus. Salue salue iesu bone. fatigatus in agone ... Ecce me tibi
prae//[sento]

Rhythmica oratio; PL 184.1321, col. 1. The lower margin has been trimmed
with the loss of the bottom two lines of text.

f. 1v   //qui praesto as amantibus ... crucis torrida. Salue latus//

Rhythmica oratio; PL 184.1321, cols. 1–2. The lower margin has been
trimmed with the loss of the bottom two lines of text.

f. 2   //[*faded*: scatet fons cruoris qui corda lauat] sordida ... ut te nobis im-
partires ut//

Rhythmica oratio; PL 184.1321, col. 2–1322.

f. 3–4r   //herre. daz du got unsere herre bist ... Und glouben von der kraft des
           vaters enphahe vermugentheit aller dinge da ich muge sprechen. *Omnia*
           possum in eo qui me confortat. Ach herre nu minne in mir. bekenne in mir
           ... me belibet. Ein ents[. . .]ken p//

           Unidentified prayers in Middle High German. The lower margin of fol. 4
           has been trimmed with the loss of the bottom two lines of text.

f. 4v   //[. . .]senden. ein leben [. . .] lebenden ... ieze gedenkest. [. . .]den du[. .]
           meiner vergessen//

           Unidentified prayers in Middle High German. The verso is badly stained
           and is illegible in many places. The lower margin has been trimmed with
           the loss of the bottom two lines of text.

Parchment (badly stained and rubbed from use in a binding). 4 folios (fols. 1 and 4
and fols. 2 and 3 form bifolia). Fols. 1 and 4 measure 105 x 100 mm; fol. 2 measures
142 x 100 mm; fol. 3 measures 143 x 102 mm (written space 96 x 60 mm). 1 column. 19 lines, with 17 lines remaining on fols. 1 and 4. Ruling in lead. Single vertical bounding lines.
    Written in gothic script (littera textualis). 1-line initials are in black capitals
highlighted with red and are not set apart from the text. Sections within the *Rhyth-*
mica oratio are marked by paragraph marks in red. Rubrics in the prayers are written
in black minuscule and underlined in red. Punctuation consists of the punctus. Hyphenation is in the same ink as the text.
    The bifolia were glued together and formed the wrapper for one board in the
binding of a volume measuring ca. 195 x 150 mm.
    Zinniker 44–1 and 44–2.

MS 482.101   Italy (Bologna ?), s. XIV[1]
Justinian, *Digesta*, with glossa ordinaria of Accursius   Pl. 112

f. 1   //filio qui apud hostes est ... permitti posteriore capite non permit//[tit]

           Justinian, *Digesta*, 28.2.29. T. Mommsen and P. Krueger, ed., *Corpus iuris*
           civilis (Berlin, 1928), 1.414.

Parchment. 1 folio. 319 x 216 mm (written space 285 x 183 mm). 1 column surrounded on all four sides by the commentary. 40 lines of text and 79 lines of commentary. Ruled in lead.

Written in two sizes of gothic script (littera textualis), with a larger script for the text and a smaller script for the commentary (notularis), possibly by a different hand. Later marginal and interlinear notes in a cursive hand. 1-line initials are enlarged minuscule forms, preceded by a paragraph mark in blue. Running chapter number "II" in the upper center of both sides is red and blue. Punctuation consists of the punctus and is very rare.

The fragment was used as a binding and bears the inscription "Ammts Winsen an der Lühe / Haubt Inventarium / Von Ostern Anno 1667 bis Ostern 1668". Winsen is located approximately 15 miles southeast of Hamburg, on the southern bank of the Luhe. Hartmut Hoffmann (letter of 12 October 1997) suggests the possibility that the fragment derives from the archive of the Duke of Braunschweig-Lüneburg, to whom the Amt Winsen belonged.

Zinniker 137.

MS 482.102   Germany, s. XIII[1]
Sacramentary   Pl. 112

f. 1r   //[*faded:* . . .] ac sociorum eorundem precibus consequamur. Per.

        Mass for an unidentified saint and companions.

f. 1r   *Emmerami episcopi.* Deus qui non (*sic*) annua beati emmerammi martyris tui . . . [*Sec.*] Donis celestibus da quesumus domine libera nos . . . *Compl.* Repleti alimonia quesumus domine intercedente beato emmerammo . . . mereamur. Per dominum nostrum iesum christum filium.

        St. Emmeram (22 September).

f. 1r–v   *Cosme et damiani.* Magnificet te domine sanctorum tuorum cosme et damiani beata sollempnitas . . . *Sec.* In tuorum domine preciosa morte iustorum . . . [*Compl.*] Sit nobis domine sacramenti tui perceptio . . . [ex]-ploramus. Per dominum nostrum.

        Sts. Cosmas and Damian (27 September). The outer corners of the leaf have been trimmed with loss of text.

f. 1v   *Michahelis archangeli.* Deus qui miro ordine angelorum misteria hominumque dispensas . . . [M]unus populi tui domine quesumus dignanter assume . . . [B]eati archangeli tui michahelis intercessione suffulti . . . et mente. Per dominum nostrum iesum christum.

Archangel Michael (29 September). The outer corners of the leaf have
been trimmed with loss of text.

f. 1v   *Ieronimi episcopi*. Deus qui beatum ieronimum confessorem sacerdotemque
           . . . *Sec*. Supplicationis nostre hostias domine deus omnipotens . . . dig-
           neris. Per dominum nostrum ihesum christum.//

           St. Jerome (30 September).

f. 2r   [Concede quaesumus omnipotens deus ut sicut apostolorum tuorum . . .
           pro]//merenda maiestatem tuam . . . *Sec*. Muneribus nostris apostolorum
           symonis et iude festa . . . *Compl*. Sumpto domine sacramento suppliciter
           . . . eternam. Per dominum nostrum.

           Vigil of Sts. Simon and Jude (27 October).

f. 2r   *In die sancto*. Deus qui nos per beatos apostolos tuos . . . *Sec*. Gloriam do-
           mine sanctorum apostolorum perpetuam . . . *Compl*. Perceptis domine
           sacramentis suppliciter rogamus . . . medelam. Per dominum.

           Sts. Simon and Jude (28 October).

f. 2r–v   *Vigilia omnium sanctorum*. Domine deus noster multiplica super nos . . .
           Sec. Altare tuum domine deus . . . sollempnia praeuenimus. Per dominum
           nostrum.

           Vigil of All Saints (31 October).

f. 2v   *In die sancto*. Omnipotens sempiterne deus qui nos om[nium sanc]torum
           merita . . . *Sec*. Munera tibi domine nostre deuocionis offerimus . . . *Compl*.
           Adesto nobis domine martirum deprecatione . . . suffragari. Per dominum
           nostrum.

           All Saints (1 November).

f. 2v   *Cesarii martyris*. Deus qui nos beati martyris tui cesarii . . . *Sec*. Hostias tibi
           domine beati cesarii . . . [*Compl*.] Huius nos domine perceptio sacramenti
           mundet//

           St. Caesarius (1 November).

Parchment (badly stained and damaged from use in a binding). 2 folios (bifolium).

225 x 210 mm (written space 190 x 140 mm). 1 column. 21 lines. Ruled in ink. Single vertical bounding lines.

Written in early gothic script (littera textualis), below the top line. 2-line initials at the beginning of each Mass and 1-line initials for other prayers are in red and are written on the vertical bounding line. Rubrics are written in red in the same script as the text, with occasional use of uncial or rustic capital forms. Punctuation consists of the punctus. Hyphenation is in the same ink as the text.

The fragment was used as the wrapper for a copy of Abraham Gorlaeus's *Dactyliotheca* that measured ca. 190 x 145 mm. The partially damaged inscription "Gorlæi Dactyliotheca" is written on the spine.

Zinniker 98.

MS 482.103   Germany, s. XIV[1]
Sermons   Pl. 113

f. 1r   [Inc: Acquisierat sibi fratres genus humanum astutia diabolicae fraudis
           . . .]//super eum spiritus sanctus. hoc enim ostensum est in tempore aaron
           in figura. Dominus enim praecepit moysi de singulis tribubus auferri . . .
           Suscipiamus regem hodie uenientem praeparemus habitacula pastorum
           contra imperatorem talem qui dignetur nos recipere in celeste ierusalem
           qui uiuit etc.

           Hildebert of Le Mans, *Sermones de tempore*, Sermon 11 (On Tit. 3.5;
           Christmas; 25 December); PL 171.392–94. The lower margin has been
           trimmed with the loss of two lines of text.

f. 1r–v   [U]alde honorandus est beatus iohannes qui supra pectus domini in cena
           [*deleted*: domini] recubuit. beatus iohannes cuius festa hodie celebramus
           magnam gratiam inuenit apud deum . . . suscitando mortuos. sanando in-
           firmos. illuminando cecos. et alia signa faciendo.

           Unidentified sermon on John the Evangelist (27 December). The lower
           margin has been trimmed with the loss of two lines of text.

f. 1v   [P]ostquam consummati sunt dies octo ut circumcideretur puer uocatum
           est nomen eius iohannes. In hac die octaua de nativitate christi celebra-
           mus . . . cum confessione et non sequitur sed orat cum//

           Unidentified sermon on the Circumcision (1 January). The lower margin
           has been trimmed with the loss of two lines of text.

Parchment. 1 folio. 195 x 175 mm (written space originally ca. 187 x 150 mm). 2 columns. 31 lines remaining of an original 33. Ruled in ink. Single vertical bounding lines.

Written in an informal gothic script (approaching a littera textualis currens). Spaces have been left at the beginning of the homilies for 2-line initials, not set apart from the text, but they have not been added. 1-line initials are in brown and are not set apart from the text. Punctuation consists of the punctus. A contemporary hand has made some corrections to the text in a darker ink.

The fragment was used as a pastedown in the binding of a volume measuring at least 175 x 195 mm. A modern hand has written the number "9" in pencil in the upper left corner of the recto.

Zinniker 112.

MS 482.104   Trent, Italy, 3 August 1233
Judicial Decision   Pl. 113

Aldricus, who is named in line 7, was bishop of Trent from 1232 to 1247; see C. Eubel, *Hierarchia Catholica Medii Aevi* (Regensburg, 1913), 1:497.

f. 1   Anno domini millesimo ducentesimo trigesimo tercio. Indicione sexta. die mercurii. tercio intrante augusto. tridente. in palatio episcopatus, in presencia domini iacobi. Zordani causidicorum … Ego rolandinus qui zacaranus vocor notarius domini regis otonis interfui et rogatus scripsi.

Notarial redaction of a judgment emanating from the podestà of Trento, Riprandus Otonis Rici, by order of Bishop Aldricus of Trento concerning a controversy between Maius filius quondam Romedii and Niger filius Gonterii over easement to the stable of Maius (which Niger has obstructed with a hedge). On the verso the word "nichil" and the year "1233" are written in contemporary hands.

Parchment. 1 folio. 340 x 142 mm (written space 322 x 135 mm). 1 column. 37 lines. No visible ruling.

Written in notarial script by Rolandinus. At the opening of the document there is a design in brown ink resembling a chalice. A cross stands above the entire document. The initial "E" of the notary's signature is a 2-line square-shaped capital in black ink, decorated with dots and not set apart from the text (his *signum tabellionis*). Punctuation consists of the punctus and, at the end of the document, the punctus versus.

Zinniker 57.

MS 482.105
Duties of the Cellarer of the Church of St. Victor, Xanten

Germany, s. XIII
Pl. 114

f. 1r   //pasche usque ad festum barbare. dandus est caseus. excepta uigilia omnium sanctorum . . . Item notandum quod cum quondam essent .v. termi-
ni ad soluendum dictos denarios pro ut//

Duties of the Cellarer of the Church of St. Victor in Xanten; C. Wilkes,
*Quellen zur Rechts- und Wirtschaftsgeschichte des Archidiakonats und Stifts
Xanten*, Veröffentlichungen des Vereins zur Erhaltung des Xantener
Domes E. V. 3 (Bonn, 1937), 71–72. The upper margin has been trimmed
with the loss of one line of text.

Parchment. 1 folio. 324 x 250 mm (written space originally ca. 283 x 185 mm). 1
column. 21 lines remaining of an original 22 lines. Ruled in lead. Single vertical
bounding lines.

Written in early gothic script (littera textualis). 1-line initials are in black,
highlighted with red, and are not set apart from the text. Rubrics are written in red
in the same script as the text in the margins. Punctuation consists of the punctus,
some of which are in red.

The leaf was used as a pastedown in the binding of a volume measuring ca. 324
x 225 mm.

Zinniker 119.

MS 482.106
Antiphonary (in Latin and German)

Germany, s. XIV/XV
Pl. 114

f. 1   [R. Quomodo fiet istud . . . spi]//ritus sanctus superueniet . . . [V.] Ideoque
quod nascetur . . . Gloria patri et . . . *In mat. laud.* An. Quando uenit ergo
. . . An. Uerbum supernum a patre . . . An. Beatus auctor seculi . . . An.
Clausa parentis uiscera . . . An. Domus pudici pectoris . . . *Ad bn.* A. Hec
est dies . . . femina intulit//

Annunciation (25 March), from the third nocturn of matins to lauds,

f. 2r   [R. Induta est caro . . .] //mea. V. Dies mei sicut . . . R. Memento mei
domine quia . . . V. De profundis clamaui . . . uocem meam.

Responsories from the book of Job and Psalms. This text has been added
by a fifteenth-century hand.

f. 2v   Du min junger wilt du wissen wie lang zwischend wienacht und vasnacht
          ... So ist die lange grosse zile nebent zu unt der roten zal die guldin zal.

          Computistical table for calculating the time between Christmas and
          Shrove Tuesday, with explicatory note in German.

Parchment. 2 folios (bifolium; paginated 23–24 and 27–28 in purple in a modern
hand). 315 x 230 mm (written space 240 x 165 mm). 1 column. 11 lines. Ruled in
ink. Single vertical bounding lines.
     Written by three scribes in gothic script (littera textualis); one scribe copied fol.
1, another copied fol. 2r, and a third copied fol. 2v. 2-line initials at the beginning
of the antiphons on fol. 1 are in red; the guide letters for these initials are still visible in light brown ink, and some have been ornamented, including one with a
crude figure of a person. 2-line initials at the beginning of verses on fol. 1 are in
black with black penwork and highlighted with red; one is decorated with the figure
of an animal with a human head. 1-line initials on fol. 1 are in black filled with red.
1- and 2-line initials on fol. 2 are in brown with some brown ornamentation. Fol. 2v
begins with a very crude 2-line round D in red. The rubrics on fol. 1 are written in
red in the same script as the text; rubrics have not been added to fol. 2r, but there
are guide letters in light brown ink. Hyphenation is in the same ink as the text.
Musical notation is in black and on fol. 1 is on a 4-line staff in black; on fol. 2r it is
on a 5-line staff in black. Punctuation consists of the punctus. The lines in the
table on fol. 2v are in black, except for the outer boundaries and the roman numerals which run down the left column, which are in red. The quire signature "xx
sexternus" is written in brown ink in the center of the lower margin of fol. 1r.
     Zinniker 27.

MS 482.107   Southern Germany, s. XIV/XV
Antiphonary   Pl. 115

f. 1r   [A.]//Cosmas et damianus anthimius ... coronati sunt.

          Sts. Cosmas and Damian (27 September), second vespers.

f. 1r–v   *In festo sancti michahelis archangeli* A. Omnes fideles christi ... A. Angelus
          archangelus michahel ... A. Data est potestas ... micha//[helo]

          Archangel Michael (29 September), first vespers.

f. 1v   [ar]//changele dei michahel ... A. Uiuit michael archangelus ... R. Te
          sanctum dominum ... V. Cherubin quoque et seraphi//[m]

Archangel Michael, first nocturn of matins.

f. 2r   //runt decorari martirio. A. Eligunt terris sygone . . . *in eu.* A. In hoc ergo
          loco . . . *In ii. v.* A. Adest namque beati dyonisii . . . triumphans agon//[em]

          St. Dionysius (9 October), from lauds to second vespers.

f. 2v   //de manu domini. A. Et facta est comes . . . gloria tibi domine.

          St. Dionysius, second vespers.

f. 2v   *De s. gallo.* Uenerabilis gallus diaconum . . . habitationibus oportunus//

          St. Gall (16 October), vespers.

Parchment. 2 folios (originally a bifolium). 354 x 300 mm (written space 344 x 205
mm). 1 column. 8 lines remaining of an original 9 lines. Ruled in ink.
    Written in gothic script (littera textualis formata). The offices of Archangel
Michael and of St. Gall begin with 2-line initials in red and blue, not set apart from
the text. The inside of the letters is decorated with an animal on a red and green
ground surrounded by red and blue penwork and white dots; the outside of the
letters is surrounded by red and blue penwork. 2-line initials of antiphons and responses alternate red and blue; the 2-line initial of the verse is in brown highlighted
with red. The left margins of both versos are decorated with red and blue designs,
which are topped by an animal head in red on fol. 1v. Musical notation is in black
on a 5-line staff in black. Punctuation consists of the punctus.
    The bifolium was used as wrapper for a volume measuring ca. 300 x 200 mm
that contained a copy of Eusebius, *Opera Omnia* ("Eusebii opera omnia" is written
on the spine).
    Zinniker 76 and 45.

MS 482.108   Switzerland(?), s. XIII
Lessons for the Mass (from a Lectionary or Missal)   Pl. 115

f. 1ra   //est preceptum. *Sanctorum Basilidis* [?] *naboris et nazarii martyrum* [?].
          Attendite a fermento. *Sancti anthonii confessoris euangelium.* Uos estis sal.
          Sanctorum marci et marcellini martyrum euangelium. Cum audieritis.

          Incipits of lessons for Sts. Basilides, Nabor, and Nazarius (12 June), for St.

Anthony (13 June), and for Sts. Mark and Marcellian (18 June). The upper margin has been trimmed with loss of text.

f. 1ra   *Sanctorum geruasii et protasii martyrum secundum marcum.* In illo tempore. Cum egrederetur iesus de templo . . . Non relinquetur.//

               Sts. Gervase and Protase (24 June); the lesson is from Mark 13.1–3.

f. 1rb   //uidete ne quis uos seducat. Multi enim uenient . . . et in omnes gentes primum oportet praedicari//

               Sts. Gervase and Protase, lesson continued (from Mark 13.7–10). The upper margin has been trimmed with loss of text.

f. 1va   //et eritis odio omnibus . . . in finem hic salvus erit.

               Sts. Gervase and Protase, lesson continued (from Mark 13.13). The upper margin has been trimmed with loss of text.

f. 1va   *In vigilia sancti iohannis baptiste inicium sancti euangelii secundum lucam.* Fuit in diebus herodis regis iudee sacerdos quidam nomine zacharias . . . Factum est autem//

               Vigil of St. John the Baptist (23 June); the lesson is from Luke 1.5–8.

f. 1vb   //turbatus est uidens . . . ut conuertat corda//

               Vigil of St. John the Baptist, lesson continued (from Luke 1.12–17)

f. 2ra   [ue]//nerunt circumcidere puerum; et uocabant eum . . . et super omnia montana iudee. diuul//[gabantur]

               St. John the Baptist (24 June); the lesson is from Luke 1.58–65.

f. 2rb   Attendite a fermento. *In vigilia apostolorum petri et pauli secundum Iohannem.* In illo tempore. Dixit symoni petro iesus. Symon iohannis diligis me plus hiis? . . . et dicit ei. Domine tu//

               Vigil of Sts. Peter and Paul (28 June), lesson from John 21.15–17.

f. 2va   [Cathe]//dra sancti petri. *In commemoratione sancti pauli euangelium sicut supra in conuersione eiusdem. In octaua sancti iohannis euangelium sicut in die.*

Per octavam apostolorum euangelium. Hoc est preceptum. *In octaua aposto-lorum. secundum matheum.* In illo tempore. Iussit iesus discipulis suis as-cendere in nauiculam ... iactabatur fluctibus. Erat enim contrarius//

Octave of the Apostles; the lesson is from Matthew 14.22–24.

f. 2vb   //tu es iube me uenire ad te super aquas ... Vere. filius dei es.//

Octave of the Apostles, continued; the lesson is from Matthew 14.28–33.

f. 2vb   *Placiti et Sigisbert.* Descendens iesus de monte. *Procopii.* Nemo [*illegible*]. *Udalrici episcopi.* Sicut lumbi. *Diuisio apostolorum.* Conuocatis iesus xi [*sic*] apostolis. [*illegible*].

Lessons for the feasts of Sts. Placid and Sigisbert (July 11); Procopius (July 8 or 9); Ulric (July 4); and Dispersion of the Apostles (July 15) added in the lower margin in a late fifteenth-century hand. The commemoration of Placid and Sigisbert, the founders of the abbey of Dissentis in the diocese of Chur, suggests a Swiss provenance.

Parchment. 2 folios (bifolium). 190 x 206 mm (written space originally ca. 208 x 152 mm). 2 columns. 16 lines remaining of an original ca. 25 lines. Ruled in ink. Single vertical bounding lines.

Written in gothic script (littera textualis). The words "In illo tempore" begin with a 7- to 8-line initial "I" in blue with red penwork, set apart from the text. The initials of the lessons are 1-line red or blue initials decorated with blue or red pen-work. 1-line initials within lessons are in black highlighted with red. Rubrics are written in red in the same script as the text. Punctuation consists of the punctus and punctus elevatus. Hyphenation and accents are in the same ink as the text. There are symbols similar to neumes above some of the text, perhaps aids for reading aloud.

The fragment was used as a wrap-around binding for a book belonging to one "Iohannes Ienatschius notarius," whose name is written on fol. 2v. Fifteenth- and sixteenth-century hands have added various marginalia.

Zinniker 51.

MS 482.109   Germany, s. XIV
Ludolphus de Luco, *Flores Grammaticae*   Pl. 116

The *Flores grammaticae* consists of around 1020 hexameters. It was written by

Ludolphus de Luco of Hildesheim (see line 933, "Hildeshemiensis uel teutuni-
cusque ludolphus") between 1280 and 1306 (see *Verfasserlexikon*, 5: cols. 965–67).

f. 1   //Dic homo uel capra sic pone uocancia uerba . . . Ad synodum quartus is
            quintus dicimus ue secundus

            Flores grammaticae, vv. 869–904 (numbering from the edition of J. Amer-
            bach?, Basel, ca. 1489–94). The upper and outer margins have been
            trimmed with the loss of portions of the commentary.

f. 2   //Inquisitiuus eciam sextum bene ponis . . . Signare locum uersus debet tibi
            quorsum//

            Ludolphus de Luco of Hildesheim, *Flores grammaticae*, vv. 905–40.

Parchment. 2 folios (bifolium; the inner bifolium of a quire). Fol. 1 measures 234
x 130 mm; fol. 2 measures 234 x 168 mm (written space 161 x 65 mm). 1 column.
18 lines for the main text. Ruled in ink. Single vertical and double horizontal
bounding lines.
    Main text written in gothic script (littera textualis). The commentary is added
in a contemporary or slightly later hand in littera cursiva currens, both marginally
and interlinearly. 1-line initials of each verse are in brown, filled with red, and are
written with the text inside the single bounding line. There are frequent paragraph
marks in red preceding the initials outside of the bounding line. Punctuation consists of the punctus. The commentary also has paragraph marks in red. We are
grateful to Ursula Bauermeister of the Bibliothèque Nationale in Paris for information and for a microfilm of the BN copy of the Amerbach edition of Ludolphus
(= BNCI L 259).
    The bifolium was used as a flyleaf in the binding of a volume measuring ca. 299
x 210 mm.
    Zinniker 53.

MS 482.110   Germany, s. XIV
Missal   Pl. 116

f. 1r   //atio sancta misterii. et pariter nobis expiationem tribuat et munimen.
            Per.

            Feria III after the twelfth Sunday after Pentecost.

f. 1r   *Feria iiii^a. Ad corinthios.* Fratres. Non praedicamus nos metipsos. sed domi-
          num nostrum iesum christum. Nos autem seruos uestros . . . *Secundum* M.
          [. . .] secuti sunt eum duo ceci . . . infirmitatem.

          Feria IV after the twelfth Sunday after Pentecost. The lessons are from 2
          Corinthians 4.5–10 and Matthew 9.27–35.

f. 1r–v   *Feria vi^a. Ad corinthi.* Fratres. Fugite ab ydolorum cultura . . . *Secundum* M.
          [. . .] iesus exprobrare ciuitatibus in quibus facte sunt . . . quam tibi.

          Feria VI after the twelfth Sunday after Pentecost. The lessons are from 1
          Corinthians 10.14–17 and Matthew 11.20–24.

f. 1v   *Dominica xiii^a. Oratio.* Omnipotens sempiterne deus da nobis fidei spei et
          caritatis augmentum . . . *Ad galathas.* Fratres. Abrahe dicte sunt promis-
          siones et semini eius . . . *Secundum lucam.* In illo tempore dixit iesus dis-
          cipulis suis. Beati oculi qui uident que uos uidetis . . . Quis horum trium
          uidetur//

          Thirteenth Sunday after Pentecost. The lessons are from Galatians 3.16–
          22 and Luke 10.23–36.

Parchment (the fragment has been torn into two pieces). 1 folio (foliated "CIX" on
the recto). The upper portion measures 180 x 280 mm, and the lower portion
measures 187 x 280 mm (original measurements are ca. 367 x 280 mm with a written space of 273 x 182 mm). 2 columns. 14 (upper) and 15 (lower) of 29 lines.
Only faint traces of ruling, perhaps in ink. Single vertical bounding lines. The horizontal text rulings continue into the upper margin for the foliation.
    Written in gothic script (littera textualis). 3-line initials at the beginning of
lessons alternate blue with red flourishes or red with no flourishes and are written
on the vertical bounding line. 1-line initials at the beginning of verses are black,
highlighted with red dots. Punctuation consists of the punctus and punctus interrogativus. Hyphenation is in the same ink as the text. Folio number "CIX" in top
center of recto alternates blue and red.
    These fragments were used as the binding of a volume measuring ca. 173 x 105
mm.
    Zinniker 101-1 and 101-2.

MS 482.111   Italy, s. XIV
Missal   Pl. 117

f. 1r–v   [*Lectio ad hebreos*. Fratres Christus assistens pontifex . . .] //huius crea-
           tionis. Neque per sanguinem . . . *Gr*. Eripe me de inimicis meis . . . *V*. Lib-
           erator meus domine . . . *Tr*. Sepe expugnauerunt me . . . *V*. Dicat nunc
           israhel . . . *V*. Et enim non potuerunt ... *V*. Supra dorsum me . . . *Secundum
           iohannem*. In illo tempore. Dicebat iesus turbis iudeorum. et principibus
           sacerdotum . . . *Off*. Confitebor tibi domine . . . *Sec. or*. Hec munera quae-
           sumus domine et uincula nostre prauitatis . . . *Co*. Hoc corpus quod . . .
           Post co. Adesto nobis domine deus noster . . . praesidiis. Per.

           Palm Sunday. The lessons are from Hebrews 9.11–15 and John 8.46–59.

f. 1v   *Feria ii. Introitus*. Miserere mei domine . . . *Ps*. Conculcauerunt me inimici
           . . . *Or*. Sanctifica quaesumus domine nostra ieiunia . . . *Lec. ione prophete*.
           In diebus illis factum [est *add. man. alt*.] uerbum dei ad ionam prophetam
           secundo dicens. Surge . . . Et cepit ionas introire in ciuitatem itinere//

           Feria II after Palm Sunday. The lesson is from Jonas 3.1–4.

Parchment. 1 folio. 285 x 230 mm (written space 255 x 160 mm). 2 columns. 29
lines on the recto; 32 lines on the verso. Ruled in ink. Single vertical bounding
lines.
     Written in two sizes of a rounded gothic script (littera textualis), a larger script
for the lessons and prayers and a smaller script for the chants. 2-line initials of
prayers and lessons alternate red and blue and are set apart from the text. 1-line
initials within lessons, of chants, and the first letters following a 2-line initial are
brown and yellow. Rubrics are written in red in a cursive script. Punctuation consists of the punctus. A contemporary hand has made corrections in black ink.
     This fragment was used as a flyleaf in the binding of a volume measuring ca. 285
x 183 mm.
     Zinniker 144.

MS 482.112   Germany, s. XIV
Missal   Pl. 117

f. 1ra   //Dominus uobiscum. Oremus. *Oratio*. Deus qui tribus pueris mitigasti
           flammas ignium . . . *Ad Thesalonicenses*. Fratres. Rogamus uos. corripite
           inquietos . . . Hec est enim uoluntas dei in christo iesu; in omnibus uobis.//

Saturday after the First Sunday of Quadragesima. The lesson is from 1 Thessalonians 5.14–18. The lower margin has been trimmed with loss of text.

f. 1rb   //nix. Et ecce apparuit illis moyses et helyas ... neminem uiderunt nisi solum iesum.//

Saturday after the First Sunday of Quadragesima. The lesson is from Matthew 17.2–8. The lower margin has been trimmed with loss of text.

f. 1va   //*Dominica ii*ᵃ. *Oratio*. Deus qui conspicis omni nos uirtute ... *Ad Thessalonicenses*. Fratres. Rogamus uos et obsecramus in domino iesu; ut quemadmodum accepistis a nobis ... suum uas possidere in sanctificati//[one]

Second Sunday of Quadragesima. The lesson is from 1 Thessalonians 4.1–4. The lower margin has been trimmed with loss of text.

f. 1vb   //fili dauid; filia mea male a demonio uexatur ... magna est fides tua; fiat ti//[bi]

Second Sunday of Quadragesima. The lesson is from Matthew 15.22–28. The lower margin has been trimmed with loss of text.

Parchment. 1 folio (foliated "XXXI" in red in the upper center of the recto). 185 x 293 mm (width of written space 178 mm). 2 columns. 17 lines remaining. Ruled in ink. Single vertical and triple horizontal bounding lines.

Written in gothic script (littera textualis formata). 2- and 3-line initials at the beginning of lessons and prayers alternate blue decorated with red penwork and red with no flourishes (the blue is faded); they are written on the vertical bounding line. 1-line initials beginning the second word of the lessons alternate red and blue and are not set apart from the text. Other 1-line initials are brown highlighted with red strokes and dots. Rubrics are written in red in the same script as the text. Punctuation consists of the punctus and punctus elevatus. Hyphenation added by a later hand.

The fragment was used as a wrapper for a volume measuring 150 x 95 mm. The number "i 83" is written on the spine.

Zinniker 73.

MS 482.113
On Virtues and Vices

Germany, s. XIV¹ (lower text: s. X/XI)
Pl. 118

The text on the virtues and the vices has been written as a palimpsest over an earlier text. The lower text, scraped away but faintly visible in some areas, is illegible.

f. 1r   //origo luxurie mater nausie. Ebrietas aufert memoriam dissipat sensum confundit intellectum. [C]oncitat libidinem inuoluit linguam corrumpit sanguinem uitam diminuit . . . Torpor est ex languentis animi pigricia remissa in ocio tocius corporis habitudo.//

Unidentified text on drunkenness and other vices.

f. 1v   //roris liuore ore et amaritudinis imperio quassate mentis contricio luctus est . . . Indignacio est ex turbida quaedam//

Unidentified text on various vices.

f. 2r   //cia est uirtus quae carnales declinans se in diuinos colligens amplexus uirginitas est porte genialis . . . ut obliuiscaris bonum tuum o domine si ego admisi//

Unidentified text on various virtues.

f. 2v   //suplicio quorum mens in hac uita numquam uoluit carere peccato . . . illi qui fecit me et te me//

Unidentified text on various virtues.

Parchment. 2 folios (bifolium). 112 x 103 mm (width of written space 75 mm). 1 column. 21 lines remaining. Ruled in ink. Single vertical and horizontal bounding lines. Prickings in outer margin; prickings in lower margin remain from the earlier text. The lower text was apparently written in one column with a written space measuring at least 195 x 90 mm and with at least 28 lines.

The upper text is written in gothic script (littera textualis currens). 1-line initials are in brown and are not set apart from the text. There is space for a 2-line initial on fol. 1r, but it has not been added. Punctuation consists of the punctus. Authorities for specific passages in the upper text are written in the outer margins (for example, "au" or "aug" for Augustine, "Bo" for Boethius). The lower text is written in Caroline minuscule.

The fragment was used as a pastedown in the binding of a volume measuring ca. 206 x 112 mm.

Zinniker 107–3.

MS 482.114
Heinrich Seuse, *Buchlein der Ewigen Weisheit*
(in Middle High German)

SW Germany or N. Switzerland, s. XIV^{med}
Pl. 118

This manuscript was probably written during or shortly after the lifetime of the author (1295–1366), and is among the earliest known copies of the *Buchlein*. The dialect of this fragment is a combination of Swabian and Alemannic, indicating an origin in the transitional zone between the two dialects, in Southwestern Germany or Northern Switzerland. Because it is written in this combination dialect, the text has many variants from the standard Middle High German text.

ff. 1–2 //und vallent . . . in der suezzen//

    Heinrich Seuse, *Buchlein der Ewigen Weisheit*, chaps. 6–7; K. Bihlmeyer, ed., *Heinrich Seuse: Deutsche Schriften* (Stuttgart, 1907), 220.19–224.15.

ff. 3–4 //selbes ein . . . und siech es//

    Buchlein der Ewigen Weisheit, chaps. 7–9; Bihlmeyer, 228.14–232.2.

Parchment. 4 folios (fols. 1 and 4 and fols. 2 and 3 form bifolia). Fol. 1 measures 171 x 121 mm; fol. 2 measures 134 x 125 mm; fol. 3, 134 x 75 mm; fol. 4, 172 x 76 mm (written space 132 x 95 mm). 1 column. 36 lines. Ruled in ink. Pricking in outer margin.

Written in gothic script (littera textualis). 3-line initials at the beginning of chapters are in red and are not set apart from the text. 1-line initials are in black, highlighted with red, and are not set apart from the text. Rubrics are written in red in the same script as the text. Punctuation consists of the punctus and virgule.

Contemporary (or slightly later) page numbers in Roman numerals in the upper margins of fols. 1r, 2r, and 4r identify them as pp. 14, 16, and 20 of the manuscript. The folio number on fol. 3r (originally p. 18) has been cut away. This numbering is consistent with the length of the work. The *Buchlein* would have filled around 60 folios.

These fragments were used as the binding of a volume measuring ca. 160 x 100 mm.

Zinniker 105.

Bibliography:
Enders, M., *Das mystische Wissen bei Heinrich Seuse* (Paderborn, 1993), 246–316.

MS 482.115   Germany, s. XV
Rituale   Pl. 119

f. 1   //*Corpus et sanguis domini nostri dicendo.* Corpus et sanguis domini nostri
           iesu christi prosit anime tue ... *Sequitur oratio.* Propitietur dominus cunc-
           tis iniquitatibus tuis. Amen. Et sanet omnes langores [*sic*] tuos Amen.
           ... *Quando quis uoluerit inungi oleo sancto dicat septem psalmos penitenciales
           et letaniam et post dicit. Oratio* Omnipotens sempiterne deus qui dixisti per
           beatum apostolum tuum iacobum infirmatur quis in uobis ... [*text illegible*]
           ungatur inter scapulas dicendo. In nomine patris. et filii et spiritus sancti
           ... ut per hanc [text illegible]//

           Order of visiting the sick. The prayer "Omnipotens sempiterne ..." is
           nearly identical to the prayer found in *Das Rheinauer Rituale* (*Zürich Rh
           114, Anfang 12.Jh.*), ed. Gebhard Hürlimann, Spicilegium Friburgense 5
           (Freiburg, Schweiz, 1959), 147.

Parchment. 1 folio. 216 x 163 mm (written space 140 x 130 mm). 1 column. 14
lines. Ruled in ink. Prickings in outer margin.
    Written in gothic script (littera textualis). 2-line initials in red are surrounded
by and filled with brown circles and flourishes. 1-line initials are in brown. Rubrics
are written in red in the same script as the text. Punctuation consists of the punctus. Hyphenation is in the same ink as the text.
    The fragment was used as the binding of a volume measuring ca. 122 x 75 mm.
Zinniker 129–1.

MS 482.116   Germany, s. XV²
Antiphonary   Pl. 119

f. 1   //*Commune de sanctis et primo de apostolis ad ves. super psalmos an.* Estote
           fortes in bello ... R. Fuerunt sine querela ante dominum ... V. Tradide-
           runt corpora sua ... *Aliud Rm.* Uos estis sal terre ... V. Videant opera ves-
           tra bona//

           Common of Apostles, first vespers.

Parchment. 1 folio. 346 x 238 mm (written space 268 x 186 mm). 1 column. 8
lines. Ruled in red ink. Double vertical bounding lines.
    Written in a rounded gothic script (littera textualis formata). The 4-line initial
at the beginning of the office is blue and red with blue and red flourishes. 2-line

initials at the beginning of responses alternate blue and red; 2-line initials at the beginning of verses are brown with brown and yellow flourishes. 1-line initials within verses are in brown and are highlighted with red. Rubrics are written in red in the same script as the text. Punctuation consists of the punctus. Hyphenation is in the same ink as the text. Musical notation is on a four-line staff.

The leaf was used as the wrapper for the binding of a volume measuring ca. 191 x 145 mm.

Zinniker 143.

MS 482.117   Germany, s. XV
Bible, Matthew   Pl. 120

ff. 1–2   //[*portion of first line illegible*: omne peccatum et] blasphemia remittetur
            hominibus . . . ex omni genere piscium congreganti//

            Matthew 12.31–13.47. The outer margin of fol. 2 has been trimmed with
            loss of text.

Parchment. 2 folios (bifolium). Fol. 1 measures 161 x 121 mm; fol. 2 measures 161 x 86 mm (written space 115 x 71 mm). 1 column. 32 lines. Ruled in ink. Single vertical bounding line. Additional ruling in upper margin for running titles. Prickings in outer margin.

Written in a minute gothic script (littera cursiva libraria). 1-line initials at the beginning of verses are in black, filled with red. Running titles ("Matheus") are written in red in the center of the upper margin. Punctuation consists of the virgule in red. Hyphenation is in the same ink as the text. Paragraph marks are in red.

The fragment was used as a flyleaf in the binding of a volume measuring 207 x 146 mm. A fifteenth- or sixteenth-century hand has written three proverbs in a cursive gothic script in the gutter between the two folios, "Doctrine pater usus est doctrina . . .", "Pluribus intentus minor est ad singula . . .", and "Deficit ambobus qui uult . . ." (given fully in Walther, *Sprichwörter*, nos. 6201, 21629, and 5306 resp.), and "Segnius inritant a(?) . . ." (unidentified).

Zinniker 109.

MS 482.118   Germany, s. XV
Breviary   Pl. 120

f. 1   //hominibus supersticiosam sectam . . . [R.] Dum deambularet dominus. *ut*

supra. [L.] Andreas respondit. Ego su[m] qui praedico uerbum ... R. Uenite post m[e] ... V. D[um] deambularet dominus ... [L.] Proconsul
dixit. Ista supersticio ... R. Mox ut [uo]cem domini ... V. [Ad] unius iussionis ... [L.] Proconsul iussit eum ... R. Homo dei ducebatur//

St. Andrew (30 November), matins. The lessons are from an unidentified
Passio S. Andreae. The outer margin has been trimmed with loss of text.

f. 2v   //[*recto illegible:*]suetum et pium. A. *Ad primam et ad terciam de primo
          nocturno. Ad vi.* A. Mox ut uocem domini ... *Ad ix.* A. Domine iesu
          christe magister ... *In secunda uespera mat. laud. ew. an.* Cum uenisset be-
          atus andreas ... suscipias me discipulum//

St. Andrew, lauds through second vespers. The recto is illegible.

Parchment (fols. 1v and 2r are badly stained from use in a binding). 2 folios (bifolium; at least one bifolium is missing between fols. 1 and 2). 149 x 111 mm (written
space 107 x 85 mm). 1 column. 17 lines. Ruled in lead. Double vertical bounding
lines.

Written in a hybrid gothic script (littera textualis with frequent but not consistent use of cursive forms of *d*, *b*, *l*, and *t*; *s* and *f* do not descend below the base
line). 1-line initials at the beginning of lessons are in red and are written on the
inner vertical bounding line when they occur at the beginning of a line. Other 1-
line initials are in brown highlighted with red. Rubrics are written in red in the
same script as the text; liturgical directions are written in brown and are underlined
in red. Punctuation consists of the punctus and virgule.

The fragment was used as the wrapper of a volume measuring ca. 123 x 75 mm.
Zinniker 139–2.

MS 482.119

transferred to Beinecke MS 481.136, fol. 2

MS 482.120   Italy, s. XV[2]
Cicero, *Orationes Philippicae*   Pl. 121

f. 1v   //nec ueientum rex eos quos modo nominaui quam ser. sulpicium occidit
          antonius ... neque eius sentenciæ periculum uitaturum. cuius ipse//

Cicero, *In M. Antonium oratio Philippica* IX, 7–9; ed. P. Fedeli (Leipzig, 1982), pp. 119.20–120.12.

f. 2r [mor]//talium turpissimus esset antonius? . . . cui testis est per literas brutus eum princi//[pem]

Cicero, *In M. Antonium oratio Philippica* X, 22–24; Fedeli, 130.13–131.7.

Parchment. 2 folios (bifolium; the fragment has been cut in half horizontally but with no text missing; one side of the bifolium, comprising fols. 1r and 2v, is entirely erased). 207 x 145 mm (written space 171 x 113 mm). 1 column. 26 lines. No visible ruling.

Written in a round humanistic bookhand. 1-line initials are in brown square capitals and are not set apart from the text. Punctuation consists of the punctus, punctus elevatus, and punctus interrogativus. Hyphenation is in the same ink as the text.

Zinniker 56.

MS 482.121 Germany, s. XV²
Missal Pl. 121

f. 1ra //saluatore nostro deo; qui omnes homines uult saluos fieri . . . in fide et ueritate. In christo iesu domino nostro. *Eum.* Respondens iesus dixit. Confiteor tibi domine.

Feria V after the Fifth Sunday after Pentecost. The lessons are from 1 Timothy 2.3–7 and Matthew 11.25.

f. 1ra *Feria vi^a. Lectio e beati iacobi apostoli.* Karissimi. Quod proderit si fidem quis dicat . . . autem eis quae necessa//[ria]

Feria VI after the Fifth Sunday of Pentecost. The lesson is from James 2.14–16.

f. 1rb [*Or.* Deus uirtutum cuius . . .] //augmentum. et ut quae bona sunt nutrias ac pietatis studio que sunt nutrita custodias. Per. *Ad romanos.* Fratres. Quicumque baptisati sumus in christo iesu . . . christus resurgens a mortuis; iam//

Sixth Sunday after Pentecost. The lesson is from Romans 6.3–9.

f. 1va   //[*first line illegible*] habundauerit iustitia [uestra] plusquam scribarum ...
          Offr. Perfice [gressus meos] ... uerba mea mirifica//

          Sixth Sunday after Pentecost. The lesson is from Matthew 5.20–24.

f. 1vb   //*Feria iiii ad hebreos.* Fratres. Habemus gratiam per quam seruiamus ...
          Mementote praepositorum//

          Feria IV after the Sixth Sunday after Pentecost. The lesson is from He-
          brews 12.28–13.7.

Parchment. 1 folio (foliated "CXXVII"). 198 x 273 mm (written space originally ca.
320 x 187 mm). 2 columns. 22 lines remaining of an original ca. 42. Ruled in ink.
Single vertical bounding lines.
    Written in gothic script (littera textualis formata). 2-line initials are in red and
are not set apart from the text. 1-line initials are in brown highlighted with red.
Rubrics are written in red in the same script as the text. The foliation is written in
red in the upper center of the recto. Punctuation consists of the punctus and punctus elevatus. Hyphenation is in the same ink as the text.
    The fragment was used as the binding of a volume measuring ca. 145 x 88 mm.
Zinniker 50–2.

MS 482.122   Germany, s. XV
Lessons for the Mass (from a Lectionary or Missal)   Pl. 122

f. 1r   //Et consurgent filii ... hic saluus erit.

          Matthew 10.21–22.

f. 1r   *Secundum lucam.* In illo tempore. Descendens iesus de monte ... est in
          celo//

          Luke 6.17–23.

f. 1r–v   *Secundum lucam.* In illo tempore. Dixit iesus discipulis suis Attendite a
          fermento ... coram angelis dei.

          Luke 12.1–8.

f. 1v   *Secundum lucam.* In illo tempore. Dixit iesus turbis iudeorum et prin-
         cipibus sacerdotum . . . dei dixit Mittam//

         Luke 11.47–49.

Parchment. 1 folio. 381 x 263 mm (written space 259 x 182 mm). 2 columns. 24
lines. Ruled in ink. Single vertical bounding lines.
    Written in gothic script (littera textualis formata). 1- and 3-line initials at the
beginning of lessons are in red. Initials at the beginning of verses are in brown
highlighted with red. Rubrics are written in red in the same script as the text. Punctuation consists of the punctus. Hyphenation is in the same ink as the text. Foliation from the fifteenth century is in upper margin of the recto: "CLXXI".
    The fragment was used as the binding of a volume measuring ca. 210 x 150 mm.
Zinniker 48.

MS 482.123   France, s. XV²
Book of Hours   Pl. 122

f. 1r   //contra hostes tuos. Domine exaudi orationem meam. Oremus. *Oratio.*
         Protege domine famulos tuos . . . *An.* Sancti dei. *v.* Letamini. Oremus.
         Oratio. Tribue quesumus domine omnes sanctos tuos . . . deo gracias//

         Hours of the Virgin, end of Terce. The right margin next to the text has
         a decorative gold border with flowers in green and blue and a butterfly in
         blue, grey, and black. Two 2-line initials are in gold; one is on a blue
         ground filled with salmon, and the other is on a salmon ground filled with
         blue.

f. 1v   Full-page miniature of mediocre quality depicting the Adoration of the
         Magi, for the beginning of Sext. The border in the left and lower margins
         is gold and is decorated with vines, grey leaves, flowers in red and light
         blue, and grotesques. The miniature has been damaged by rubbing and
         water.

f. 2r   Full-page miniature of low quality depicting the Office of the Dead. A
         body lies on its shroud in the center of the scene. At the top of the mini-
         ature, Christ sits enthroned, surrounded by angels (all only faintly visible,
         drawn in brown on a gold background). Immediately below, on a back-
         ground of blue sky, the Archangel Michael and a demon fight over the
         soul of the deceased, which floats between them. Below the body, demons

torment souls in Hell. The border in the left and lower margins are decorated with flowers, leaves, an owl, and a hedgehog on a gold ground.

f. 2v   //missionem cunctorum tribue peccatorum ... Amen. Requiescant in
         pace. Amen.

         Office of the Dead. The border in the right margin has flowers on a gold
         ground.

f. 3   //dominice. Ut digni efficiamur ... *Oratio.* Deus qui ecclesiam tuam beati
         domini [*sic* for dominici] confessoris tui ... *De beato francisco confessore.*
         O Sancte francisce sydues aureum ... V. Ora pro nobis beate francisce
         ... *Oratio.* Deus qui ecclesiam tuam beati francisci ... gaudere. Per
         christum.

         Suffrages. Suffrage for St. Dominic and St. Francis. The border in the
         right margin of the recto and the left margin of the verso is decorated with
         leaves and flowers on a gold ground. The suffrage for St. Francis begins
         with a 4-line initial in gold on a blue ground filled with salmon. The ora-
         tions begin with a 2-line initial in gold on a salmon ground filled with
         blue.

Parchment. 3 folios. 124 x 89 mm (written space 68 x 45 mm). 1 column. 16 lines.
Ruled in red ink. Single vertical and horizontal bounding lines.
    Written in a hybrid gothic script mixing elements of littera bastarda and littera
cursiva formata. See above for descriptions of decoration. Rubrics are written in red
in the same script as the text. Punctuation consists of the punctus. Hyphenation is
in the same ink as the text.
    Zinniker 74–1, 74–2, and 23–2.

MS 482.124   Germany, s. XV
Book of Hours   Pl. 123

f. 1   //O beate paule apostole doctor gencium deprecare pro me ... *Ant.*
         Gloriosi principes terre quomodo in vita sua dilexerunt se ... *v.* In omnem
         terram ... Et in fines orbis terre uerba eorum.//

         Suffrage for St. Paul.

Parchment. 1 folio. 118 x 83 mm (written space 83 x 50 mm). 1 column. 15 lines.
Ruled in ink. Single vertical and double horizontal bounding lines.

Written in gothic script (littera textualis). Historiated 7-line initial "O" on the recto, not set apart from the text, is in blue with white highlights, filled by a depiction of the apostle Paul standing on a green field with a gold ground. Paul holds a sword in his right hand and a book in his left. The details of the face are suggested by simple black lines, and red dots adorn the cheeks and mouth. The folds of Paul's red robe are modeled with fine shading, and his gown is intricately embroidered in gold and green. The initial is contained within a square frame, with opposite corners outlined green with yellow highlights, filled with red, or dull yellow with brown highlights, filled with red. The 2-line initial at the beginning of the antiphon is in red, surrounded by brown penwork, and is not set apart from the text. 1-line initials are in black and are not set apart from the text. Rubrics are written in red in the same script as the text. Punctuation consists of the punctus. Hyphenation is in the same ink as the text.

Zinniker 23–1.

MS 482.125   Germany, s. XV
Hymnal   Pl. 123

f. 1r   //scandere mente ... semper in euum. Amen.

             End of unidentified hymn.

f. 1r   *ympnus.* Ihesu nostra redempcio amor ... credimus. Gloria tibi domine qui as(cendisti).

             Anon., s. VII/VIII (Ascension); AH 51.85; Schaller-Könsgen 7657.

f. 1r   *De sancto spiritu.* Ueni creator spiritus ... omni tempore. Amen.

             Anon. s. IX/X, perhaps Rabanus Maurus (Pentecost); AH 50.144; Schaller-Könsgen 17048.

f. 1r   *Ad noctur. ympnus.* Iam christus astra ... Deo patri sit gloria eiusque soli fi(lio).

             Anon., s. IV/V (Pentecost); AH 51.92; Schaller-Könsgen 7471.

f. 1r–v   *Ad laudes ympnus.* Beata nobis gaudia ... salutos recreet. Amen.

             Anon., s. X (Pentecost); AH 51.91; Schaller-Könsgen 1617.

f. 1v   *De corpore christi.* Sacris sollempniis iuncta . . . inhabitas. Amen.

          Thomas Aquinas (Corpus Christi); AH 50.387.

f. 1v   Pange lingua gloriosi corporis . . . Tantum ergo//

          Thomas Aquinas (Corpus Christi); AH 50.386.

Parchment. 1 folio. 323 x 245 mm (written space 230 x 161 mm). 2 columns. 31 lines. The horizontal text lines were ruled with lead, and the margins were ruled in ink. Single vertical and horizontal bounding lines.

     Written in a formal gothic script (littera textualis formata). 2- to 12-line initials at the beginning of hymns are in red; only those that begin with the letter "I" are set apart from the text. 1-line initials at the beginning of verses are in red and are not set apart from the text. Rubrics are written in red in the same script as the text. Punctuation consists of the punctus.

     The fragment was used as part of a wrapper for a volume measuring ca. 228 x 177 mm.

     Zinniker 136–2.

MS 482.126   Germany, s. XV
Initial   Pl. 124

f. 1r   Historiated initial "R" (for the introit "Resurrexi et adhuc . . ." of Easter); the initial is blue with white highlights on a gold ground contained within a square green border. The inside of the letter depicts Christ rising from a coffin surrounded by three sleeping guards; two women kneel behind the sepulchre. Christ holds a staff with a red banner in his left hand. In the background there are hills, trees, and a castle. The remainder of the leaf has been cut away.

f. 1v   [Vidi aquam egredientem]//de templo a late[re dextro, alleluia: et omnes ad] quos peruenit a[qua ista salui facti sun]t et dicent alle//[luia]

          Chant for the sprinkling of water in Paschaltide. The remainder of the leaf has been cut away.

Parchment. 1 folio. (partial: fragment is the size of the initial). 81 x 70 mm (original dimensions and written space uncertain). 1 column. 3 lines remaining of an uncertain original number. Ruled in lead.

Written in gothic script (littera textualis). For decoration of the initial, see above.
Musical notation in black on a 4-line staff of lead, yellow, lead, and red lines.
Zinniker 78.

MS 482.127   Italy, s. XV
Initial   Pl. 125

f. 1r   Large, illuminated initial "D" or "O" in blue, pink, green, and red on a
          gold ground, with elongated marginal flourishes ending in gold balls out-
          lined and decorated with black. The remainder of the leaf has been cut
          away.

f. 1v   [do]//mine//

          Unidentified chant. The remainder of the leaf has been cut away.

Parchment. 1 folio. 242 x 152 mm (original dimensions and written space uncertain). 1 column. 1 line remaining of an uncertain original number. Ruled in lead.
     Written in gothic script (littera textualis formata). For decoration, see above.
Musical notation in black on a 4-line staff in red. There is no punctuation.
     Zinniker 62.

MS 482.128   Low Countries or W. Germany (?), s. XV
Antiphonary   Pl. 126

f. 1r   //tabantur flentes dom[. . .] Uobis//

          Unidentified chants. Almost the entire leaf surrounding the initial "U"
          has been trimmed with loss of text.

f. 1v   [V. Lustris sex qui . . .] //in cruce leuatur immolan[dus . . . A.] O mors ero
          [. . .] inferne. P. Miserere. euoue. A. [Plangent eum quasi unigenitum]
          quia innocens dominus occisus est//

          Holy Saturday, lauds. The upper, lower, and inner margins have been
          trimmed with loss of text.

Parchment. 1 folio. 121 x 147 mm (original dimensions and written space uncertain). 1 column. 4 lines remaining of an uncertain original number. Ruled in ink.

Written in gothic script (littera textualis formata). The 4-line initial "U" is in blue and red. Some of the sketched flourishes outside of the letter have been traced in red and filled with green, others merely filled with green, and some only traced with red. Inside the letter a floral pattern has been sketched and partially completed; the spaces have been filled with green, but only part of the sketch has been traced with red. The 2-line initial "O" is red with sketched flourishes only partially completed and filled with green. Rubrics are written in red in the same script as the text. Quadrata notation is in black on a 4-line staff in red. Punctuation consists of the punctus.

Zinniker 51–1.

MS 482.129   Germany, s. XIV
Missal   Pl. 126

f. 1r–v   [All. ...] //as nostras omnibus horis ... V. [...]a. Item. Dispo[sui tes]ta-
          mentum electis meis ... V. [...]a. Item. Iste est [...]te deum ... V. [...
          Item]. Inueni dauid seruum meum ... V. [...] Item al. Amauit eum do-
          minus ... V. [...] Item. Iste sanctus digne ... V. [...] Item. Iustum [...]
          dominus ... V. [...] Item. N. dilectus ... V. Iustus germinabit ... V. [...]
          It. Beatus uir qui auffert ... V. [...] Item. Gaudete [iusti in] domino ...
          Seqn. [A]d laudes saluatoris ... Seqn. Psallens deo. Seq. Uictime. Tr. Be-
          atus uir qui timet ... V. Potens in terra erit ... V. Gloria et diuitie ... Tr.
          Desiderium anime eius tribuisti ... V. Quoniam praeuenisti eum ... V.
          Posuisti super caput ... Offt. Inueni dauid seruum meum ... Offt. Ueritas
          mea et misericordia mea ... Off. Desiderium anime eius tribuisti ... Off.
          Gloria et honore coronasti ... Offert. Confitebuntur celi mirabilia ... Co.
          Beatus seruus quem cum uenerit ... Co. Posuisti in capite eius ... Com-
          mo. Domine quinque talenta ... Communio. Fidelis seruus ... Co. Semel
          iuraui in sancto meo ... C[o.] Magna est gloria eius ... decorem impon[es
          super eum domine.]

          Common of Confessors. The inner margin has been trimmed with loss of
          text.

f. 1v   Oro. Omnipotens sempiterne deus qui es sanctorum ... Secre. Praesta
          quaesumus omnipotens deus. ut nostre humilita[tis obla]tio ... [Secr.]
          Sancti N. confessoris tui atque pontificis annua ... L. l. Sap.//

          Common of a Confessor Bishop. The inner margin has been trimmed with
          loss of text.

Parchment (recto stained and verso covered with glue from use in a binding). 1 folio (foliated "cclxxxxiii" in the center of the upper margin of the verso). 405 x 248 mm (written space originally ca. 281 x ca. 190 mm). 2 columns. 28 lines. Ruled in ink. Single vertical and double horizontal bounding lines.

Written in two sizes of gothic script (littera textualis), with a larger script for the prayers and a smaller script for the chants. 1- and 2-line initials alternate red and blue and are not set apart from the text except for the initial "I" and the shafts of initials "P". Rubrics are written in red in the same script as the text. The running headlines "[c]on" / "fessoribus" on the recto and "Com" / "mu[ne]" on the verso are written in red in the upper margins above the two columns. The foliation on the verso is written in red roman numerals in the center of the upper margin. Punctuation consists of the punctus and punctus elevatus. Hyphenation is in the same ink as the text.

The fragment was used as the wrapper of a volume measuring ca. 203 x 145 mm. The inscription on the spine reads "Au[.]altys Caus[.] / No 3."

Zinniker 126.

MS 482.130   Austria, s. XV²
Missal   Pl. 127

f. 1r   //[. . . proderi]t homini si lucretur mundum totum et detrimentum faciet
         . . . cum angelis sanctis. *Off.* Posuisti domine. *Secre.* Oblatis quaesumus
         domine placare muneribus et intercedente beato crisogono . . . *Com.*
         Magna est. *Complen.* Tui domine percepcione sacramenti . . . insidiis. Per.

         St. Chrysogonus (24 November). The lesson is from Mark 8.36–38.

f. 1r   *Katherine uirginis.* Gaudeamus. *Oratio.* Deus qui dedisti legem moysi . . .
         Epistola. Confitebor tibi domine. *Gr.* Audi filia. Alleluia. *V.* [. . .] *Sequen-*
         tia. Sanctissime uirginis uotiua festa recolamus . . . *Eu.* Simile est reg[num]
         celorum thesauro. *Off.* Filie regum. *Secre.* Munera domine sacrificii
         praesentis . . . *Co.* Simile est. *Complen.* Sumptis domin[e] salutis eterne
         . . . expellat. Per.

         St. Catharine of Alexandria (25 November). The lessons are from Sirach
         51.1 and Matthew 13.44.

f. 1r–v *Uirgilii episcopi.* Statuit ei dominus. *Or[atio. Da]* quaesumus omnipotens
         deus [. . .] uirgilii confessoris . . . *Epistola.* Dedit dominus confessionem.

Gr. Ecce sacerdos. Alleluia. V. Iurauit dominus. *Sequentia.* Rex regum.
Ewangelium. Homo quidam nobilis. *Off.* Ueritas mea. *Secre.* Beati confessoris tui atque pontificis uirgilii quaesumus domine ueneranda sollem-
nitas ... *Co.* Beatus seruus. *Complen.* Beati uirgilii confessoris tui atque
pontificis domine praesentibus ... capiamus. Per dominum.

St. Virgil, Bishop of Salzburg (27 November); the lessons are from Sirach
47.9 and Luke 19.12.

f. 1v   *Incipit commune sanctorum primo in uigilia unius apostoli officium.* Ego autem
sicut oliua fructificaui ... *Ps.* Quid [gloriaris in malitia ...] *Oratio.* Concede nobis omnipotens deus uenturam ... *Lectio libri sapientie.* Beatus uir
qui inuentus est ... omnis ecclesia. *Lectio libri sapientie.* Benedictio domini
super caput ... sanctum fecit illum. et ele//[git]

Common of an Apostle. The lessons are from Sirach 31.8–11 and 44.25–
45.4.

f. 2r–v [*Secundum iohannem.* ... Hoc est preceptum meum ...] //uos ut eatis et
fructum afferatis ... det uobis. *Secundum iohannem.* In illo tempore. Dixit
iesus discipulis suis. Hec mando uobis ut diligatis inuicem ... me gratis.
Secundum marcum. In illo tempore. Dixit iesus discipulis suis. Facilius est
camelum per foramen acus transire ... uitam eterna[m.] *Secundum lucam.*
In illo tempore. Designauit dominus et alios septuagin[ta] duos discipulos
... mercede sua. *Off.* Constitues eos principes ... *Off.* In omnem terram
... *Off.* Michi autem nimis ... *Secre.* Sacrandum tibi domine munus ...
Co. Amen dico uobis quod ... *Co.* Uos qui [se]cuti estis ... *Complen.*
Beati apostoli tui ... letantes. Per.

Common of an Apostle. The lessons are from John 15.16; John 15.17–25;
Mark 10.25–30; and Luke 10.1–7. The outer margin has been trimmed
with a slight loss of text.

f. 2v   [I]n *die plurimorum apostolorum. Oratio.* Deus qui nos per beatos apostolos
... *Secre.* Gloriam domine sanctorum apostolorum ... *Complen.* Perceptis
domine sacramentis suppliciter ... ad medelam. Per.

Common of Apostles.

f. 2v   *De pluribus martyribus officium.* Intret in conspectu ... *Ps.* Deus uenerunt
gentes ... *Introitus.* Salus autem iustorum ... *Ps.* Noli emulari in ...
Introitus. Sapientiam sanctorum narrant ... *Ps.* Exaltate iusti in ...

[*Introitus.*] Clamauerunt iusti et dominus exau//[diuit]

Common of Martyrs.

Parchment. 2 folios. Fol. 1 measures 345 x 238 mm; fol. 2 measures 349 x 230 mm (written space 269 x 197 mm). 2 columns. 32 lines. Ruled in ink. Single vertical bounding lines.

Written in a formal gothic script (littera textualis formata). There is a 7-line initial "E" on fol. 1v in pink with red and white highlights, on a gold ground, most of which has flaked away revealing an orange base; the initial is filled with a green latticework and is framed by a two-tone blue square. Green and blue vines with pink flowers extend from the initial into the lower margin (the left margin has been trimmed away), and the forks in the vines were once filled with gold wedges, although now only the orange base remains, with brown strokes radiating outwards. Other 1- to 4-line initials are in red and are not set apart from the text. 1-line initials within lessons and of some of the chants are in brown, stroked with red, and are not set apart from the text. Rubrics are written in red in the same script as the text. Punctuation consists of the punctus. Hyphenation is in the same ink as the text.

The leaves were once used as wrappers for the binding of a volume measuring ca. 317 x 200 mm.

Fol. 1 was formerly Zinniker 131; fol. 2 was Beinecke MS 482.134, Zinniker 104.

MS 482.131   Germany, s. XV^2
Missal   Pl. 127

f. 1ra   [s]//ic et sic locu[ta est puella de] terra Israhel … Venit [ergo naama]n cum equis//

Feria II of the third week of Quadragesima. The lesson is from 2 Kings 5.4–9. The bottom margin has been trimmed with the loss of approximately eight lines. The inner margin has been trimmed with loss of text.

f. 1rb   //manu sua locum lepre et curaret me … in uniuersa terra. nisi tamen dominus deus israhel. Gr. Deus uitam meam annunciaui … V. Miserere michi domine … homo tota die bellans//

Feria II of the third week of Quadragesima. The lesson is from 2 Kings 5.11–15. The bottom margin has been trimmed with the loss of approximately eight lines.

f. 1va   [L. In illo tempore. Dixerunt pharisei ad iesum. Quanta audiuimus facta
          in capharnaum . . .] //in israhel. quando clausum est celum . . . medium
          illorum ibat. *Offr.* Exaudi deus orationem . . . *Secr.* Munus quod tibi do-
          mine . . . *Co.* Quis tabit [*sic for* dabit] ex syon salutare israel . . . *Compl.*//

          Feria II of the third week of Quadragesima. The lesson is from Luke 4.23–
          30. The bottom margin has been trimmed with the loss of approximately
          eight lines.

f. 1vb   [*Int.* Ego clamaui quoniam . . .] //tuam et exaudi . . . [*Ps.*] Exaudi domine
          [iusticiam] . . . [*Or.*] Exaudi [nos omnipotens et] misericors . . . [*L.*] In
          diebus [illis. Mulier] quedam clam[abat ad helise]um . . . ostium cum
          i//[ntrinsecus]

          Feria III of the third week of Quadragesima. The lesson is from 4 Kings
          4.1–7. The bottom margin has been trimmed with the loss of approxi-
          mately eight lines. The inner margin has been trimmed with loss of text.

Parchment (the recto is stained and the verso is covered in glue from use in a
binding). 1 folio (foliated "xliiii"). 241 x 211 mm (written space originally ca. 265
x 200 mm). 2 columns. 28 lines remaining of an original ca. 36. Ruled in ink. Single
vertical bounding lines.
    Written in two sizes of gothic script (littera textualis formata), with a larger
script for the lessons and prayers and a smaller script for the chants. The 2-line
initial beginning the Mass of Feria III is a blue uncial and is not set apart from the
text. The 8-line initial "I" beginning the lesson is red and is set apart from the text.
1-line initials are uncials in red or black highlighted with red and not set apart from
the text. Rubrics are written in red in the same script as the text. Punctuation
consists of the punctus. Hyphenation is in the same ink as the text. The foliation
is written in red roman numerals in the center of the upper margin of the recto.
    The fragment was used as the wrapper of a volume measuring ca. 160 x 93 mm.
Zinniker 120.

MS 482.132   Austria, s. XV
Index from a Missal   Pl. 128

The Sanctorale includes the feast day (27 March) and translation (24 September)
of St. Rupert, patron saint of Salzburg.

f. 1   *Dominica .i. in aduentu do.* Dominica secunda . . . *Pro defunctis totaliter.*//

Index of the temporale, sanctorale, and Common of saints. The fragment has been cut in half with the loss of approximately two lines of text in the middle.

Parchment (the verso is badly damaged from use in a binding). 1 folio (cut in half). The upper portion of the folio measures 130 x 230 mm; the lower portion measures 137 x 230 mm (written space originally ca. 215 x 157 mm). 2 columns. The upper portion preserves 16 lines, and the lower portion preserves 10 lines of an original ca. 28 (column b of the verso has an extra line at the bottom). Ruled in ink. Single vertical bounding lines.

Written in gothic script (littera textualis formata) in red and black ink. The 1-line initials at the beginning of each line are in red or in black highlighted with red. The feasts of Advent, the canon and prefaces of the Mass, the first Sunday after Easter, the beginning of the sanctorale, and all the items of the Commons are written in red. Other important feasts days such as Christmas, Epiphany, Easter, and Pentecost begin with a paragraph mark in red. Punctuation consists of the punctus.

The fragments were used as binding covers for a volume measuring ca. 228 x 138 mm. An inscription on the recto reads "Mon. Typ. 4° 1486 / N.8 / Hain 2205. Proctor 4602.", referring to a copy of Avicenna's *Canon* (Venice: Petrus Maufer et Socii, 1486) = GKW 3120. In the same place there is also a 17th-century inscription that reads "Wilhelm Barthun" and one from the sixteenth century that is undeciphered.

Zinniker 49–1 and 49–2.

MS 482.133   Germany, s. XV^2
Missal   Pl. 128

f. 1r   //[b]inos ante faciem suam in omnem [ci]uitatem ... appropinquauit in uos regnum dei. *Secundum lucam xii.* I[n] illo tempore. Facta est contencio inter discipulos ... super thronos duodecim iudicantes duodecim tribus israhel.

Common of Apostles. The lessons are from Luke 10.1–9 and Luke 22.24–30.

f. 1r–v   *Commune de pluribus martyribus.* Clamauerunt iusti et dominus ... *Ps.* Benedicam dominum ... *Gr.* Gloriosus deus in sanctis suis ... *V.* Dextera tua domine ... Alleluia. *V.* Letamini in domino ... *Sequencia.* Agone triumphali militum regis ... *Offr.* Letamini in domino ... *Co.* Ego uos elegi ... *De pluribus martyribus oro.* Deus qui nos concedis ... *Scr.* Munera tibi domine nostre deuocionis ... *Comp.* Praesta nobis quaesumus domine

intercedentibus sanctis . . . *Alia oro.* Da quaesumus omnipotens deus ut
qui beatorum martyrum tuorum N. . . . *Scr.* Hostias tibi domine beatorum
martyrum tuorum N. . . . *Comp.* Quaesumus omnipotens deus ut qui ce-
lestia alimenta . . . *lectio libri sapientie iii.* Iustorum anime in manu dei . . .
regnabit dominus illorum in perpetuum. *lectio libri sapientie ecc. ii.* Metuentes deum sustinete misericordiam . . . pius et misericors [. . .] *hebreos.*
Fratres. Rememoramini pristinos dies . . . [*rest of lesson too stained to read*]//

Common of Martyrs. The lessons are from Wisdom 3.1–8, Sirach 2.7–13,
and Hebrews 10.32–38. The sequence is by Notker Balbulus (von den
Steinen, 82; Schaller-Könsgen 499).

f. 2r   //[*first few words illegible*] *Secundum lucam vi.* I[n illo] tempore. Descendens iesus de monte in loco campestri . . . merces uestra multa est in
caelo. *Secundum lucam x.* I[n] illo tempore. Dixit iesus discipulis suis. Attendite a fermento pharyseorum . . . confitebitur in illo coram angelis dei.
S. lucam xxi. In illo tempore. Dixit iesus discipulis suis. Cum audieritis
proelia et sediciones . . . de capite uestro non peribit.

Common of Martyrs. The lessons are from Luke 6.17–23, Luke 12.1–8,
and Luke 21.9–18.

f. 2r–v *In comm. unius martyris. Int.* Iustus ut palma florebit . . . *Ps.* [*too stained to
read*: Bonum est(?)] . . . *Gr.* Posuisti domine super caput . . . *V.* Desiderium anime eius tribuisti . . . Alleluia. *V.* Posuisti domine super caput
. . . *Sequentia.* Hic sanctus cuius hodie celebrantur sollemnia . . . *Offr.*
Gloria et honore coronasti . . . *Co.* Qui uult uenire . . . et sequatur me.

Common of a Martyr.

f. 2v   *In comm. unius martyris non pontificis oro.* Praesta quaesumus omnipotens
deus. ut qui beati N. martyris . . . *Secreta.* Oblatis quaesumus domine placare muneribus et intercedente beato N. . . . *Compl.* Sit nobis domine
reperacio . . . *Alia oratio.* Adesto domine supplicacionibus nostris . . . *Scr.*
Muneribus nostris quaesumus domine precibusque susceptis . . . *Comp.*
Sumpsimus domine sancti martyris tui N. . . . consequantur. Per.

Common of a Martyr not a Bishop.

f. 2v   *In comm. unius martyris et pontificis or.* Deus qui nos beati N. martyris tui
. . . *Scr.* Munera tibi domine dicata sanctifica . . . *Comp.* Hec nos communio domine purget a crimine et intercedente . . . *Alia oro.* Praesta

quaesumus omnipotens deus ut qui beati N. martyris tui atque pontificis
... *Scr.* Hec hostia quaesumus domine emundet nostra delicta ... *Comp.*
Refecti participatione muneris sacri quaesumus domine ... *Ad corinthios*
[*sic*]. Nemo militans deo. implicat se negociis secularibus ... dominus in
omnibus intellectum. *Ad corinthios ii.*//

Common of a Martyr Bishop. The lesson is from 2 Timothy 2.4–7.

Parchment (badly damaged and stained from use in a binding). 2 folios (originally
a bifolium; foliated "clxxxi" and "clxxxiiii"). 380 x 277 mm (written space 283 x
195 mm). 2 columns. 37 lines. Ruled in lead. Single vertical bounding lines.

Written in two sizes of gothic script (littera textualis), with a larger script for the
lessons and prayers and a smaller script for the chants. 6- to 7-line initials "I" at the
beginning of lessons are in red and are set apart from the text. Other 1-, 2-, and 3-
line initials are in red and are not set apart from the text. 1-line initials within
lessons are in black highlighted with red. Rubrics are written in red in the same
script as the text. Punctuation consists of the punctus. Hyphenation is in the same
ink as the text.

When they formed a bifolium, the fragments were used as the binding of a volume measuring ca. 305 x 200 mm. On fol. 1r and on fol. 2v there are mirror images
of an unidentified printed text that offset onto the parchment while the leaves were
serving as binding material.

Zinniker 70, 71.

MS 482.134

transferred to Beinecke MS 482.130, fol. 2

MS 482.135   Southern Germany or Austria, s. XIV
Missal   Pl. 129

f. 1r   [*Secr.* Omnipotens sempiterne deus qui curam de omnibus ...] //quam
           offerimus uisitacionem specialem ... [*Co.*] Beata uiscera. [*Post co.*] Omni-
           potens sempiterne deus qui commemorationem ... per eundem.

           Visitation of Mary (2 July).

f. 1r–v   [*Int.* P]rotexisti me deus a conuentu malignancium ... [*Ps.*] Exaudi deus

orationem meam ... Gloria patri. Protexisti. [*Or.* D]eus qui nos beati.
[*Lec.* B]eatus uir qui inuentus est sine macula ... omnis ecclesia sanctorum. [A]lleluia. [*Gr.*] Iustus ut palma florebit ... [*Lec.* I]n illo [tem-
pore.] dixit iesus discipulis suis. Si quis uult post me uenire ... donec
uideant regnum dei. [*Off.*] Confitebuntur celi mirabilia ... [*Co.*] Letabitur
iustus in domino ... alleluia. alleluia.

Mass for an unidentified martyr. The lessons are from Sirach 31.8–11 and
Matthew 16.24–28.

f. 1v   [*Or.* D]eus qui sanctam nobis huius diei solempnitatem pro commemo-
racione beati martyris tui panthaleonis ... [*Secr.* P]resencia munera quaesumus domine serena ... ut sancti spiritus per//

St. Pantaleon (27 July).

f. 2r   [*Lec.* Sciens iesus quod iam omnia ... al]//terius qui crucifixus est ...
uerum est testimonium eius. [*Off.* I]nsurrexerunt in me ... [*Secr.* D]omi-
ne iesu christe fili dei uiui qui pro redempcione mundi crucis lignum ...
[*Co.* F]oderunt manus meas et pedes ... [*Post co.* D]omine ihesu christe
fili dei u[i]ui qui pro redempcione mundi crucis patibulum ... gaudiaque
eterna introire mereamur. Qui//

Mass on the five wounds of Christ. The lesson is from John 19.32–35.

f. 2v   *Ad* [. . .] *missa de passione domini. hec indulgencie a sanctis patribus uiris apostolicis confirmate sunt. Quicumque christianus missam de quinque vulneribus
christi semel per tempus uite sue cum contritione cordis ligni* [?] *legi* [?] *audierit
numquam anima eius portas mortis introibit. Item a quolibet domino spiritu
sancto petro in d*[?] *fuerunt et erunt in XL dies indulgentiarum opt*[?] *Inno-
centius quartus confirmauit.* [*Or.* O]mnipotens sempiterne deus miserere
famulo tuo ... [*Secr.* P]roficiat quaesumus domine hec oblatio ... [*Post
co.* S]umentes domine perpetua sacramenta salutis ... protegas. Per.

Mass for the living. The rubric is faded.

f. 2v   [*Or.* O]mnipotens sempiterne deus respice propicius ad preces nostras
... temptacione cogitacio//

Votive Mass in time of temptation.

Parchment (fols. 1r and 2v are damaged from use in a binding; pieces of paper and wood are still attached to them). 2 folios. Fol. 1 measures 310 x 208 mm; fol. 2 measures 310 x 188 mm (written space 217 x 160 mm). 2 columns. 20 lines. Ruled in ink. Single vertical and double horizontal bounding lines.

Written in two sizes of gothic script (littera textualis formata) with a larger script for the lessons and prayers and a smaller script for the chants. There are spaces for initials and rubrics, but none have been added except for the lengthy rubric on fol. 2v. 1-line capitals within lessons are black, not set apart from the text, and adorned with black penwork. Punctuation is very rare and consists of the punctus. Hyphenation is in the same ink as the text. Accents were added by a later hand.

Zinniker 115.

MS 482.136   Germany, s. XIV/XV
Missal   Pl. 129

f. 1 //dabit illi; Aut si petierit ouum numquid porriget illi scorpionem . . . petentibus se. *Off.* Confitebor domino nimis in ore . . . *Secr.* Hec munera quaesumus domine; et uincula nostre . . . *Com.* Petite et accipietis . . . [*Post co.*] Uota nostra quaesumus domine pio fauore . . . crescamus. Per.

Great Litany. The lesson is from Luke 11.11–13.

f. 1r–v *Anne matris marie.* Gaudeamus. *lxxii. Or.* Deus qui beate Anne tantam gratiam donare . . . *Lectio libri sapientie.* Mulierem fortem quis inueniet . . . et beatissimam praedicauerunt. uir eius//

St. Anne (26 July). The lesson is from Proverbs 31.10–28.

Parchment (stained). 1 folio (foliated "xxxiiii"). 237 x 199 mm (written space 185 x 126 mm). 1 column. 25 lines. Ruled in ink. Single vertical bounding lines.

Written in two sizes of gothic script (littera textualis formata), with a smaller script for the chants and a larger one for the prayers and lessons. 2-line initials at the beginning of Masses and lessons and 1-line initials at the beginning of chants and prayers alternate red and blue uncials and are not set apart from the text. 1-line initials within the lessons are in brown highlighted with red. The rubrics are written in red in the same script as the text. The folio number is written in red roman numerals in the center of the upper margin of the recto. Punctuation consists of the punctus, punctus elevatus, and punctus interrogativus. Hyphenation is in the same ink as the text.

The fragment was used as part of the wrapper for the binding of a volume measuring ca. 191 x 150 mm.

Zinniker 132.

MS 482.137 (printed)   Bamberg, Germany, 1490
Missale Bambergense (Johann Sensenschmidt)   Pl. 130

From the dimensions of the typeface and the width of the columns, this fragment
of a missal printed on parchment appears to have come from the Missale Bam-
bergense (Bamberg: Johann Sensenschmidt, 1490), Hain *11302.

f. 1ra   //secundum multitudinem misericordie. V. Magnus dominus et laudabilis
          ... in monte sancto eius. *Oratio.* Deus in quo uiuimus ... *Lectio Jeremie
          prophete. xiiii..* In diebus illis://

          Mass for rain.

f. 1rb   [num]//quid sunt in sculptilibus gencium qui pluant ... fecisti omnia hec:
          domine deus noster. *Grad.* Oculi omnium in te sperant ... V. Aperis tu
          manum tuam ... Alleluia. V. Confitemini domino quoniam bonus.
          quoniam//

          Mass for rain. The lesson is from Jeremiah 14.22.

f. 1va   //turbe: ut discumberent super ... quatuor milia hominum.//

          Mass for rain. The lesson is from Matthew 15.35–38.

f. 1vb   [*Post co.* Da nobis quaesumus domine pluuiam ...] //per hec sancta que
          sunt ... celestibus dignanter infunde. Per dominum.

          Mass for rain.

f. 1vb   *Pro serenitate. Introitus.* Misereris omnium domine ... *Ps.* Miserere mei
          deus ... confidit anima mea.//

          Mass for fair weather.

Parchment (stained). 1 folio. 164 x 230 (written space originally ca. 294 x 187
mm). 2 columns. 12 lines remaining of an original 30 lines.
    Printed in two sizes of gothic typeface: 196, and 156 leaded to 196 (see
Catalogue of Books Printed in the XVth Century; these are Proctor types 10 and 11).
The larger type is for the lessons and prayers and the smaller type is for the chants.
2-line initials at the beginning of Masses, prayers, and lessons and 1-line initials at
the beginning of chants are in red, not set apart from the text, and are adorned
with balls. 1-line initials of verses and within lessons are in black and are not set

apart from the text. Rubrics are printed in red in the same script as the text. Punctuation consists of the punctus, the colon, and the punctus interrogativus. Hyphenation is in the same ink as the text.

The fragment was used as the wrapper of a volume measuring ca. 126 x 80 mm and bears the inscription "Iacobeo Nusbaumer [. . .] 1652".

Zinniker 129–2.

Bibliography:

Catalogue of Books Printed in the XVth Century Now in the British Museum (London, 1963), 1:175.

Proctor, R., An Index to the Early Printed Books in the British Museum: From the Invention of Printing to the Year 1500 (London, 1960), 71, no. 788.

MS 482.138   France, s. XV
Legal Document   Pl. 130

f. 1r   Guillielmi besseti praesentibus anthonio oyselli et stephan[*margin trimmed*]metum bosonacti alias naclart de tanemo habitato . . . petri arnati sue uxoris cum suis pareriis p//

A notarial deed, concerning a land transaction involving the family Cassard. A marginal note indicates that the notary is Petrus Omandus. The outer and lower margins have been trimmed with loss of text. The verso is blank.

Parchment. 1 folio. 213 x 168 mm (original dimensions and written space uncertain). 1 column. 39 lines of an uncertain original number. Ruled in ink. Double vertical bounding lines.

Written in gothic cursive script. 1-line initials are written in brown and are not set apart from the text. Punctuation consists of the punctus.

The fragment was used as the wrapper in the binding of a volume measuring ca. 140 x 80 mm.

Zinniker 70.

MS 482.139   Rovereto, Italy, 22 January 1505
Legal Document   Pl.131

f. 1r   In christi nomine amen. anno a natiuitate eiusdem millesimo quingentesimo quinto; indictione octaua, die mercurii uigesimo secundo mensis ianuarii, Roueredi uallis . . . rogatus scribere publice scripsi.

A document related to Rovereto (?), diocese of Trent, transferring the debts that are owed to Nicolaus de Francinis, with names and debts listed. Docket on verso.

Parchment. 1 folio (scroll). 640 x 235 mm (written space 597 x 217 mm). 1 column. 95 lines. Ruled in lead.

Written in Humanistic notarial script. The document begins with a 7-line initial "I" in brown which is not set apart from the text. 1-line initials within the text are in brown and are not set apart from the text. Punctuation consists of the punctus, the comma, and the punctus versus. Hyphenation is in the same ink as the text.

In the upper left corner of the verso the number "58" has been written and crossed out in red (cf. MSS 482.141 and 482.142).

Zinniker 19.

MS 482.140   Germany, s. XIV[1]
Sequentiary   Pl. 131

f. 1r–v   [Inc: Natus ante saecula . . .] //luminis uetustas mundi depulerit genitus tenebras . . . Ut ipsos diuinitatis tue participes deus facere digneris unice dei.

Notker Balbulus (Christmas, 25 December); AH 53.15; von den Steinen, 12; Schaller-Könsgen 10034.

f. 1v   *De sancto stephano sequencia.* Hanc concordi famulatu colamus . . . O stephane signifer regis summi//

Notker Balbulus (St. Stephen, 26 December); AH 53.215; von den Steinen, 14; Schaller-Könsgen 6070.

f. 2r–v   [Inc: Congaudent angelorum chori gloriosae uirgini . . . concin]//unt prophetarum chorus iubi[lat] . . . esse digneris per euum.//

Notker Balbulus (Assumption of Mary, 15 August); AH 53.104; von den Steinen, 66; Schaller-Könsgen 2596.

f. 2v   //Interni festi gaudia nostr[a] . . . cernens in gloria.//

Adam of St. Victor (St. Augustine, 28 August); AH 55.74; RH 9054; Walther 9494.

Parchment (fol. 1 is stained on the verso and has a large hole from use in a binding). 2 folios. Fol. 1 measures 315 x 207 mm; fol. 2 measures 250 x 127 mm (written space 212 x 148 mm). 1 column. 8 lines. Ruled in ink. Single vertical bounding line.

Written in gothic script (littera textualis formata). 2-line initials at the beginning of sequences are in red, decorated with blue penwork, and are written on the vertical bounding line. 1-line initials at the beginning of verses alternate red and blue. Rubrics are written in red in the same script as the text. Punctuation consists of the punctus. Hyphenation is in the same ink as the text. Musical notation in black on a four-line staff in red.

Fol. 1 was used as the wrapper of a volume measuring at least 187 x 163 mm. Fol. 2 was used as part of a wrapper for a volume measuring ca. 205 in height.

Zinniker 123–1, 123–2.

MS 482.141
Legal Document

Diocese of Trent, Italy, 5 August 1488
Pl. 132

f. 1r   In christi nomine amen. anno domini millesimo quatuorgentesimo octuagesimo octauo indictione sexta die martis quinto mensis augusti super campo plebis blezi tridentis diocesis . . . rogatus a partibus scribere ea publice scripsi et me subscripsi.

Settlement of a land dispute. The notary is named Luterius. Docket on verso.

Parchment (the first five lines of the document are badly stained). 1 folio (scroll). 394 x 243 mm (written space 274 x 212 mm). 1 column. 47 lines. Ruled in lead.

Written in Italian notarial script. The document begins with a 6-line initial "I" in brown, not set apart from the text. 1-line initials are written in brown and are not set apart from the text. Punctuation consists of the punctus and the colon. Hyphenation is in the same ink as the text.

In the upper left corner of the verso the number "80" has been written and crossed out in red (cf. MSS 482.139 and 482.142).

Zinniker 41.

MS 482.142
Legal Document

Trent, Italy, 25 November 1514
Pl. 132

f. 1r   In christi nomine amen anno natiuitatis eiusdem millesimo quingentesimo
quartodecimo indictione secundi die sabbati vigesimoquinto mensis no-
uembris tridenti in orto monasterii ecclesie sancti marci ciuitatis tridenti
existente ex opposito stube ipsius monasterii, praesentibus petrobono filio
magistri leonis ... Ego simon filius q. egregii uiri d. girardi mirare(?) ...
scripsi et me subscripsi.

Contract for sale of property by Bernardino a Buscho to the monastery of
St. Mark in Trent. The notary is Simon, son of Girardus Mirara(?). Docket on verso.

Parchment. 1 folio (scroll). 616 x 277 mm (written space 535 x 235 mm). 1 column. 69 lines. Dry-point ruling.
    Written in Italian notarial minuscule. The document begins with a 7-line initial
"I" in brown, not set apart from the text. 1-line initials within the text are in brown
and are not set apart from the text. Punctuation consists of the colon. Hyphenation
is in the same ink as the text.
    In the upper left corner of the verso there are traces of red ink, suggesting that
there was once a number here similar to those on MSS 482.139 and 482.141.
    Zinniker 92.

MS 482.143
Legal Document (in German)

Tyrol, s. XV^{ex}
Pl. 133

f. 1r   //Ich Nicklas und ich hanns des benennten Nicklasen eenickle Bekennen
offenlich an dem brieue als pawleirt de[... hof] am graben ze dietenhaim
für uns unser erben und nachkomen von wegen der zwaÿung des uëldes
am Reise[...] das in den benennten hoff am graben gehört daran am äche
aker gelegen ist die der kirchen ze brawnnegk ... den obgenennten für-
namen und weisen Jörigen pürrenpeken das er als ain ambman unser
gnädigen heërschaft sein insigel an den br[ieue] gehengt hat im und sein
erben anschaden des sind gezeugen die erberen.

A contract concerning land near Bruneck.

f. 1r   Retulit mihi quidam frater ordinis minorum nomine paulus de conuentu
montis syon in iherusalem, quia anno 1481 tanta tempestas fulgorum ...
ad nihilum redactum sit/

A description in Latin of the damage to Mohammed's tomb in Mecca by a storm in 1481. This text is written perpendicular to the document and was added when the fragment was being used as a flyleaf.

f. 1v   Dye hernach vi puncta und articula hat der erczpischof von kolen gefrag unsern gnädigisten herren Maximilianum den romischen kunig in seiner kronung ze ache anno domini 1486, quinta die. aprilis Wiltu den häligen gelauben . . . und der meinen am pesten finden mag, dem allerhäligisten vater dem Römischen//

An account of the coronation of Emperor Maximilian I at Aachen in 1486, written in a southern German dialect. The text is excerpted from the account printed in *Dessen Krönung* ([Augsburg:] Anton Sorg, after 4 April 1486), a iv verso–a v verso (Goff M-390). The text is continued on the back pastedown in the binding of Beinecke Library, Zi +4486, copy 2, in which this fragment was once a flyleaf. See also A. Huyskens, "Die Krönung König Maximilians I. in Aachen 1486 nach einem noch unbekannten Frühdruck," *Zeitschrift des Aachener Geschichtsvereins* 64/65 (1951/2): 72–99.

Parchment. 1 folio. 177 x 286 mm (original dimensions and written space uncertain). 16 lines (original document). No visible ruling.

Written in a cursive gothic script (littera cursiva) in a hand similar to that of the scribe who wrote the document in MS 482.144. The first word of the document ("Ich") is enlarged, with the initial "I" trailing down the margin of the entire text. There is no punctuation. The Latin text is written in a gothic bastarda script with punctus and virgule used as punctuation.

The fragment was used as a flyleaf in the back cover of Beinecke Library, Zi +4486, copy 2 (compilation of HC *6924, Hain 3567=GKW 4818, and Hain 11759). The flyleaf was removed from the binding before 1946, when the incunable was acquired by Yale. This book was once in the possession of the Poor Clares at Brixen; an inscription on the recto of the fragment reads "Iste liber est sororum ordinis s. clare in runkada prope brixinam."

Zinniker 58.

MS 482.144   Enneberg, Tyrol, s. XV[ex]
Legal Document (in German)   Pl. 133

f. 1r   Ich Nicklas Mesnër an der pharr inn Ennebergs Ich Nicklas Ich Hainreich

seine prüder Ich caspar Riedlär ich dorothea sein eeleich wirttin für uns
und mit vollen gewalt anstat unsers swager ... petter von Rost aus en-
nebergß das e[r sein] Insigel an den brieff gehenngt hat im und sein erben
an allen schaden des sind gezeugen die erbern[en.]

A document concerning tenure of land.

f. 1r   Anno domini a natiuitate christi 1486; Feria quinta post dominicam
          inuocauit quae fuit 16 February electus est Illustrissimus princeps Maxi-
          milianus Archidux austrie et burgundie etc. in Regem Romanorum Franc-
          furt per omnes electores sacri impery concorditer ... corona ferrea a
          Nurenberga ad hoc allata actus dominica misericordia domini quae fuit 9
          aprilis anni supradicti.

          Account of the election of Maximilian, Archduke of Austria and Duke of
          Burgundy, as Emperor of the Holy Roman Empire in 1486 (his coronation
          is described in the related fragment, MS 482.143). This text was written
          perpendicular to the legal document when the fragment was being used as
          a flyleaf.

f. 1v   Nota quod dubitatum est aliquando utrum quando papa mandat de aliquo
          nouiter canonizato festum celebrari ... Nota quod prelati dicuntur mem-
          bra ecclesie ... Nota quod pallium arciepiscopale ... Ego episcopus.

          A brief description of how one is to celebrate the feast of a newly canon-
          ized saint, and a brief metaphorical discussion of the Church hierarchy as
          a body with Rome as its head.

Parchment. 1 folio (partial). 286 x 205 mm (original dimensions uncertain). 1 column. 30 lines (original document). Dry-point ruling.
     Written in a cursive gothic script (littera cursiva), similar to that of the scribe
who wrote the document in MS 482.143. The document begins with a flourished
initial. There is no punctuation.
     The fragment was used as the front flyleaf in the binding of Beinecke Library, Zi
+4486, copy 2 (compilation of HC *6924, Hain 3567=GKW 4818, and Hain
11759). It was taken out of the volume before 1946, when the book was acquired
by Yale. The book formerly belonged to the Poor Clares at Brixen; an inscription on
the verso, which was used as the recto when the fragment was a flyleaf, reads "Iste
liber est sororum ordinis sancte clare in brixinam." To this a later hand has added
"H. 46." A fifteenth-century note reads "Anno a natiuitate domini 1460 a magistro
heinrico carthusiensi edita siue compilata est Cronica quam fasciculum temporum
appelauit." The *Fasciculus Temporum* is contained in Beinecke Library, Zi +4486,

copy 2, the contents of which are noted in partially erased twentieth-century pencil notations on the verso.

Zinniker 2.

MS 483.1   Spain, s. XV/XVI
Noted Missal   Pl. 134

f. 1   [Credo in unum deum . . . ado]//ratur et conglorificatur . . . Et uitam uen-
          turi seculi. Amen. *In festis prime secunde tertie et quarte dignitatis prephatio.*
          Per omnia secula seculorum. Amen . . . ut admitti iubeas deprecamur
          supplici//

          Ordo missae.

Parchment. 1 folio. 411 x 292 mm (written space 301 x 209 mm). 2 columns. 24 lines, or 8 lines with musical notation. Ruled in ink and lead.

Written in a formal gothic script (littera textualis formata) without feet on the minims. One 9-line initial "P" ("Per") on fol. 1r, not set apart from the text, in varying shades of blue with foliate decoration in white filigree. In the loop of the letter a peacock in blue and grey with green and gold feathers stands underneath a red rose. The letter is on a gold geometric ground bordered in green and decorated with green and red flowers. The text on the recto is bordered on all four sides and in the center margin with a gold band filled with blue diamonds alternating with circles filled with flowers. The remainder of the border is filled with flowers or red penwork designs. In the center of the border in the lower margin there is a green and red wreath filled with blue in which there was once the figure of a statue, now erased; surrounding the wreath are two diamonds containing quails. 1- and 3-line initials are in black and are not set apart from the text. Rubrics are written in red in the same script as the text. Musical notation is in black on 4-line staves in red. Punctuation consists of the punctus. Hyphenation is in the same ink as the text.

Gift of Henrietta C. Bartlett in 1954. According to De Ricci, the leaf was given to Bartlett by Beverly Chew, who gave another leaf from the same manuscript to Mrs. W. Lanman Bull of New York (see De Ricci, 2:1668).

Bibliography:
De Ricci, 1:173, no. 1.

MS 483.2
Book of Hours (in Latin with rubrics partially in French)

France, s. XV
Pl. 135

f. 1r   //omnium fidelium mentes dirige in uiam salutis eterne. Per.

            Unidentified office.

f. 1r   *De saint laurens* A. Laurentius ingressus est martir . . . *v.* Dispersit dedit
            pauperibus. R. Iusticia eius manet . . . *Oratio.* Da nobis quaesumus om-
            nipotens deus uiciorum nostrorum flammas . . . superare. Per.

            St. Laurence (10 August).

f. 1r–v   *De s. nicolas* A. Amicus dei nicholaus pontificali . . . *v.* Ora pro nobis beate
            nicholae. R. Ut digni efficiamur . . . *Oratio.* Deus qui beatum nicholaum
            pontificem tuum . . . liberemur. Per.

            St. Nicholas (6 November).

f. 1v   *De saincte* [sic] *katherine* Ant. Virgo sancta katherina . . . *v.* Diffusa est
            gratia . . . R. Propterea benedicit te . . . *Oratio.*//

            St. Catharine of Alexandria (25 November).

Parchment. 1 folio. 165 x 122 mm (written space 95 x 60 mm). 1 column. 15 lines.
Ruled in red ink for both text and marginal decorations. Single vertical and horizontal bounding lines.

   Written in two sizes of gothic script (littera textualis formata). 2-line initials in
gold, not set apart from the text, on a blue ground decorated with white filigree.
The initials are filled with red and decorated with white filigree. 1-line initials are
black highlighted with yellow. Rubrics are written in red in the same script as the
text. Punctuation consists of the punctus. Hyphenation is in the same ink as the
text. The outer margin is modestly decorated with vine tendrils in black with green
and gold leaves and blue, red, and pink flowers and berries.

   Gift of Henrietta C. Bartlett in 1954.

Bibliography:
   De Ricci, 1:173, no. 2.

MS 483.3
Book of Hours

France, s. XV
Pl. 135

f. 1r   //*De sancto nicholao ant.* Beatus nicholaus adhuc puerulus ... *v.* Ora pro
         nobis beate nicholae ... *Oracio.* Deus qui beatum nicholaum ... libe-
         remur. Per christum dominum nostrum. amen.

St. Nicholas (6 November). The bottom two lines are blank.

f. 1v   *De sancta katherina. ant.* Ave gemma claritatis ... *v.* Specie tua et ...
         [*Oracio*] Deus qui dedisti legem ... et precibus ad montem qui//

St. Catharine of Alexandria (25 November).

Parchment. 1 folio. 185 x 138 mm (written space 108 x 74 mm). 18 lines. Ruled in
red ink for text and for marginal decorations.

Written in gothic script (littera textualis). Two miniatures of mediocre quality,
one for each saint. The miniature of St. Nicholas shows him in bishop's clothing,
holding a staff and a book, and standing next to a tub with two children in it. St.
Catharine is depicted as crowned, holding a book and a sword; on the floor behind
her is the wheel upon which she was tortured. The floor in each miniature is
checkered with yellow and light orange, and the wall is dark red with gold flowers
on the bottom and blue-grey on the top. The antiphons and orations begin with a
2-line initial in gold on an alternating ground of blue with white filigree or red with
white filigree. Initials on blue grounds are filled with red, and initials on red
grounds are filled with blue. 1-line initials are black and are highlighted with
yellow. Punctuation consists of the punctus. Hyphenation is in the same ink as the
text. Rubrics are written in red minuscule. The upper, lower, and outer borders are
decorated with blue and gold vines, red vines with blue and red or gold and blue
berries, and yellow vines with green and purple thistles. A thin black vine stem
with gold flowers is in the inner margin on the recto only. The border in the outer
margin is of a higher quality than that of the upper and lower margins, which
appear to be later additions.

Gift of Henrietta C. Bartlett in 1954.

Bibliography:
    De Ricci, 1:173, no. 3.

MS 483.4   Northern France or Low Countries, s. XV
Book of Hours (Litanies)   Pl. 136

f. 1   //Sancte gereon cum sociis tuis or. . . . Sancte ambrosi or.//

Litany, includes the following saints: Gereon and companions, Cosmas, Damian, Fabian, Sebastian, Gervase, Protase, Crispin, Crispinian, Chrysogonus, Leodegarus, Lambert, Christopher, Thomas, Demetrius, Blaise, Livinus, Firminus, Silvester, Gregory, Leo, Hilary, Martin, Nicholas, Augustine, and Ambrose.

Parchment. 1 folio. 130 x 93 mm (written space 88 x 63 mm). 1 column. 14 lines. Ruled in red ink. Single vertical and horizontal bounding lines.

Written in gothic script (littera fere bastarda). Each line begins with a 1-line initial "S" in gold on alternating grounds of red and blue. The names of the saints are written on the same line as "Or[a pro nobis]" but are separated from it by line fillers of alternating bands of red and blue decorated with gold penwork. There is no punctuation.

Gift of Henrietta C. Bartlett in 1954.

Bibliography:
De Ricci, 1:173, no. 4.

MS 483.5   Low Countries, s. XV^2
Gradual (in Latin with rubrics partially in Dutch)   Pl. 136

f. 1r   //*In uigilia sancti andree apostoli.* Comt die uig[ilie] Andriese up den sondach so salmen dit naeruolg[. . .] in der octauen metten. Alleluia. Dilexit andream. A. Dominus secus ma[re gali]lee . . . *Ps.* Celi en//[arrant]

Vigil of St. Andrew (29 November). The outer and lower margins have been trimmed with loss of text.

f. 1v   //*V.* [Dilexit] andream dominus in . . . *Offertorium.* Michi autem nimis. *Communio.* [Uenite] post me faciam . . . at illi continuo relictis reti//[bus]

St. Andrew (30 November). The outer and lower margins have been trimmed with loss of text.

Parchment. 1 folio (foliated "CX" on the recto). 183 x 158 mm (the original written space is uncertain). 1 column. 6 lines remaining. Ruled in ink.

Written in gothic script (littera textualis formata). 4-line historiated initial "D" ("Dominus") in blue on a dark red ground bordered with gold. The initial, of workshop quality and badly rubbed and damaged by water, shows Christ standing on the shore with Andrew and Peter in a boat. The 2-line initial at the beginning of the Psalm is in black highlighted with yellow. 1-line initials and the first letter after the historiated initial are in black capitals highlighted with red. The extant margins on the recto are decorated with blue and gold vines from which come pink, green, and gold flowers. Rubrics are written in red in a less formal script than the text. Punctuation consists of the punctus. Words and syllables are separated by horizontal strokes in red. The foliation is written in red in the center of the upper margin of the recto.

Gift of Henrietta C. Bartlett in 1954. According to De Ricci, Bartlett obtained this fragment from Maggs.

Bibliography:
De Ricci, 1:173, no. 5.

MS 483.6–7   Italy, s. XIV/XV
Initial

De Ricci records two manuscript numbers for this fragment; however, it contains only one initial.

Initial "N", measuring 62 x 67 mm, in light pink decorated with white foliate patterns around the outer edge of the letter and white dots around the inner edge; the ends of the letter terminate in green and yellow. The letter is on a gold geometric ground that is outlined in black and filled with green, pink, and red leaves attached to a blue vine and with balls that are half white and half blue or green.

A portion of musical notation in black ink on a red staff is preserved on the other side of the folio.

Parchment. 1 fragment. 68 x 80 mm. Ruled in ink.
Gift of Henrietta C. Bartlett in 1954.

Bibliography:
De Ricci, 1:173, nos. 6–7.

MS 483.8–9   England, s. XIII
Initials (from a Psalter)

These initials are from the same manuscript as MSS 483.11–14 (see description below).

> Two 2-line initials "L" (measuring 35 x 30 mm) and "H" (measuring 35 x 27 mm) in blue decorated with foliate ornamentation outlined in brown and colored with green. The initials are for the beginning of psalm verses.

Parchment. 2 fragments. (For further description of the manuscript from which these initials come, see below under MSS 483.11–14.)

One letter "o" is preserved, following the "H", written in gothic script in black ink.

Gift of Henrietta C. Bartlett in 1954.

Bibliography:
De Ricci, 1:173, nos. 8–9.

MS 483.10   France (?), s. XV
Initials

> A series of initials from a manuscript of moderate quality attached by a gold border, beginning with a 5-line initial "D" underneath which is a 2-line initial "U," 1-line initials "Q," "Q," "H," "Q," and "G," and a 2-line initial "U." The initial "D" is in dark red decorated with white penwork and on a gold ground; it is filled with blue and white vines in an s-shape that is attached to red flowers decorated with white penwork. The 2-line initials are in gold; the first is on a blue ground decorated with white penwork and is filled with red decorated with blue penwork, and the second is on a red ground decorated with blue penwork and is filled with blue decorated with white penwork. The 1-line initials alternate between blue surrounded and filled with red penwork and gold surrounded and filled with blue penwork. The letters are attached by a vertical strip of gold and blue with both ends terminating in blue and red vines with blue, red, and gold flowers.
>
> A portion of an unidentified text is preserved on the other side of the fragment.

Parchment. 1 fragment. 160 x 42 mm (height of written space originally ca. 110 mm). Originally ca. 21–22 lines. Ruled in ink.

Written in gothic script (littera textualis).
Gift of Henrietta C. Bartlett in 1954.

Bibliography:
De Ricci, 1:173, no. 10.

MS 483.11–14 England, s. XIII
Initials (from a Psalter)

Judging from the initials partially preserved on the backs of these fragments, they come from the same manuscript as the initials in MSS 483.8–9.

483.11r //curam tuam [et ipse te enut]riet; non da[bit in aeternum] fluctu-
atio//[nem]

Psalm 54.23.

483.11v //M//[iserere]

Psalm 56.2.

483.12r //E//[xaudi]

Psalm 16.1.

483.12v //ut non [moveantur u]estigia [mea ego cl]amaui//

Psalm 16.5–6.

483.13r [mag]//nus super omnem [subiecit po]pulos nobis; [et gentes sub] pedibus
nostris//

Psalm 46.3–4.

483.13v //M//[agnus]

Psalm 47.2.

483.14r //E//[xaltabo]

Psalm 29.2.

483.14v [r]//efugii ut [saluum me] facias. [Quoniam fortitu]do mea et//

    Psalm 30.3–4.

Parchment. 4 fragments. Each initial measures ca. 44 x 45 mm (width of written space of one column of text originally ca. 95 mm). 2 columns. Ruled in lead.

    Written in gothic script (littera textualis). Four 3-line initials from the beginning of Psalms. The first two initials are blue uncials on a square pink ground bordered in green. The second two are pink uncials on a square blue ground bordered in green; the "M" on MS 483.13 has a ground containing a diaper pattern with gold dots at the interstices and red crosses in the spaces. All four initials are filled with gold in which there are pink, green, or blue vines with white, yellow, or pink flowers. The initials on MS 483.11r ("I" from a verse in Psalm 55) and MS 483.12v ("P" of Psalm 16.11) are 2-line capitals in red decorated with foliate ornamentation outlined in brown and colored with green; they are set apart from the text. These initials are very similar in design, decoration, and size to the initials in MSS 483.8–9. Punctuation includes the punctus and punctus elevatus. Hyphenation is in the same ink as the text.

    Gift of Henrietta C. Bartlett in 1954.

Bibliography:
    De Ricci, 1:173, nos. 11, 12, 13, and 14.

MS 483.15
Missal, use of Sarum

England, s. XV
Pl. 137

The format, script, and especially the initials of this fragment are similar to those of the Sacramentary in MS 483.16, suggesting that they are originally from companion volumes.

f. 1ra   [L. Nolo fieri uos . . . conscient]//iam. Si [quis autem dixeri]t hoc immo-la[ticium] . . . omnia in gloriam [dei facite. *Se*]*cundum matheum*. [Di]xit iesus turbis iude[orum homo qu]idam habuit duos fi[lios] . . . Ille autem//

    Feria IV after the Twenty-fourth Sunday after Trinity. See J. Wickham Legg, *The Sarum Missal* (Oxford, 1916), 195–96. The lessons are from 1 Corinthians 10.27–31 and Matthew 21.28–29. The upper and inner margins have been trimmed with loss of text.

f. 1rb   //Quis ex duobus fecit uoluntatem patris? . . . Qui habet aures audiendi; audiat.

Feria IV after the Twenty-fourth Sunday after Trinity. The lesson is from Matthew 21.31. The upper margin has been trimmed with loss of text.

f. 1rb   *Dominica xxv*. Officium*. Dicit dominus. *Oratio*. Excita quaesumus domine tuorum fidelium uoluntates . . . *Lectio Ieremie prophete*.//

Twenty-fifth Sunday after Trinity (Sunday before Advent).

f. 1va   //In diebus illis saluabitur iuda et israhel habitabit . . . *Gr*. Liberasti nos. Alleluia. V. Timebunt gentes nomen tuum . . . V. In exitu israhel . . . V. Confitebor tibi domine//

Twenty-fifth Sunday after Trinity (Sunday before Advent). The lesson is from Jeremiah 23.6–8. The upper margin has been trimmed with loss of text.

f. 1vb   [*Secr.*] //Sacrifi[cium tibi domine] celebran[dum] . . . [*Post co.*] Anime nostre quaesumus omnipotens deus . . . [lumi]naria fulgeam[us. Per. *Cum prolixum fuerit infra i*[*nceptionem*] *historie*. Deus omnium. *et* [*aduentum domini. officium.*] Dicit dominus. *Per iii. d*[*ominicas cantetur*] *ut supra notatum est. Cum* [*uero breue fuerit*] *semper proxima dominica ante* [*aduentum quando de dominica agitur*] *cantetur*. Dicit dominus. [*cum oratione. Ex*]cita quaesumus. *Epistola*. E//[cce]

Twenty-fifth Sunday after Trinity (Sunday before Advent). The upper and inner margins have been trimmed with loss of text.

Parchment. 1 folio. 220 x 161 mm (written space ca. 218 x 150 mm). 2 columns. 19 lines remaining of an original ca. 24 lines. Ruled in lead.

Written in gothic script (littera textualis). There are three 2-line initials in blue with red penwork trailing up and down the entire margin of the column; the initials are not set apart from the text. 1-line initials are in brown and are not set apart from the text. Rubrics are written in red in the same script as the text. Punctuation consists of the punctus and punctus elevatus. Hyphenation is in the same ink as the text.

A strip of paper is attached with binding string to the outer margin of the verso on which there is an inscription in a sixteenth-century hand that reads "Anno domini 1562. et Anno iiii^{to}. domine Elizabethe etc." On the recto there is an inscription in a sixteenth-century hand that reads "A valuacion and [. . .]cion of the revenues of Foxyde[. . .] anno 4to Eliz." A modern hand has written "Fr[ance]. 1450–1500" in the lower margin of the verso.

Gift of Henrietta C. Bartlett in 1954.

Bibliography:
    De Ricci, 1:174, no. 15.

MS 483.16   England, s. XV
Sacramentary   Pl. 137

The format, script, and especially the initials of this fragment are similar to those of
the Missal in MS 483.15, suggesting that they are originally from companion
volumes.

f. 1ra   //omnibus sanctis tuis . . . *Post co.* Sumpsimus domine beate marie semper
           uirginis . . . consecramur per eundem.//

           Prayers for an unidentified Mass. The lower margin has been trimmed
           with loss of text.

f. 1rb   //oblata sanctifica; et propicius esto omnibus inuocantibus . . . *Post co.*
           Purificent nos semper et muniant [*corr. from:* muneant] tua sacramenta
           . . . secundum carnem//

           Prayers for an unidentified Mass. The lower margin has been trimmed
           with loss of text.

f. 1va   //sanctis percimus ueraciter porcionem. Qui tecum. *Secr.* Clemenciam
           tuam domine suppliciter exoramus . . . *Post co.*//

           Prayers for an unidentified Mass. The lower margin has been trimmed
           with loss of text.

f. 1vb   [domi]//ne deus qui uiuorum dominaris . . . pietatis tue clemencia qui//

           Prayers for an unidentified Mass. The lower margin has been trimmed
           with loss of text.

Parchment. 1 folio. 141 x 206 mm (width of written space ca. 150 mm). 2 columns.
13 lines remaining. Ruled in ink. Single vertical or horizontal bounding lines.
    Written in gothic script (littera textualis). 2- and 3-line initials alternate red
with blue penwork and blue with red penwork, and are not set apart from the text.
Rubrics are written in red minuscule. Punctuation consists of the punctus and
punctus elevatus.

The fragment was used as a flyleaf in the binding of a volume measuring ca. 206 x 141 mm, from which there are remnants of sewing string. There is an inscription in the outer margin of the verso in a sixteenth-century English hand which reads "A Kallender of Evidence of Lands in Essex and Suffolk." This inscription is in a hand that is similar to the inscription on MS 483.17. A modern hand has written "Fr[ance]. 1450–1500" in pencil in the upper right corner of the recto.

Gift of Henrietta C. Bartlett in 1954, who acquired it from E. H. Dring in June 1923.

Bibliography:
De Ricci, 1:174, no. 16.

MS 483.17 England, s. XV
Noted Breviary, use of Sarum Pl. 138

f. 1ra   [A. Quomodo stet istud angele ... conci]//piendo non pertuli ... *Ps.* Magnificat. *uel A. O. Or. dominicalis.*

Feria IV of the third week of Advent, second vespers. The upper margin has been trimmed with loss of text.

f. 1ra   *Feria vᵃ inuit.* Regem uenturum. *Ps.* Uenite. *ymnus.* Uerbum supernum pro[diens]. *An de nocturno illius ferie versus lectiones et responsae per ordinem dicuntur. In laudibus.* A. De syon ueniet ... *Ps.* Miserere. A. Conuertere domine aliquantulum ... *Ps.* Domine//

Feria V of the third week of Advent, matins and lauds.

f. 1rb   [R. Praecursor pro nobis ... aeter]//num et in seculum seculi. [V.] Ipse est rex iusticie ... R. Modo ueniet dominator ... V. Orietur in diebus ... R. Vi//[debunt gentes iustum]

Feria VI of the third week of Advent, matins. The upper margin has been trimmed with loss of text.

f. 1va   [A.] //Ego autem ad dominum ... *Ps.* Laudate. *Ca.* Ecce dies ad ... *ymnus.* Uox clara *versiculus.* Uox clamantis. *Antiph.* Ex quo facta est ... *Ps.* Benedictus. *Or.* Excita quaesumus domine potenciam tuam ... *Hec oratio dicitur ad has matutinas tantum ad alias vero horas dicitur oratio dominicalis. Ad uesperas A. O. Ps. Magnus. Or. dominicalis post uesperas huius ferie non potest incipi.* O sapientia.

Feria VI of the third week of Advent, from lauds to second vespers. The upper margin has been trimmed with loss of text.

f. 1va   *Sabbato. Inuitat.* Prope est. Ps. Uenite. *ymnus.//*

Saturday of the third week of Advent, matins.

f.1vb   [*v.* Super quem] //continebunt reges os suum ... *v.* Gloria patri et filio ... *versiculus.* Emitte agnum domine. *In laud. Ant.* Ueniet dominus in potestate ... Ps. Miserere. A. Intuemini quantus sit ... ad saluandos po//[pulos]

Saturday of the third week of Advent, from matins to lauds. The upper margin has been trimmed with loss of text.

Parchment. 1 folio. 222 x 331 mm (width of written space 291 mm). 2 columns. 19 lines of text (or 7 lines of text with musical notation) remaining. Ruled in ink. Single vertical and double horizontal bounding lines.

Written in gothic script (littera textualis). 2-line initials are in blue with red penwork or in black with black penwork and are not set apart from the text. 1-line initials are in black, not set apart from the text. Rubrics are written in red minuscule. Punctuation consists of the punctus. Hyphenation is in the same ink as the text. Musical notation is in black on 4-line staves in red.

In the sixteenth century the leaf was used in a binding of a book with the title "The revenues of lands in Essex and Suffolk Late B[?]." This inscription is similar to a contemporary one on MS 483.16. There are several other notes in sixteenth-century English hands, including a quotation from book I of St. Ambrose's *De virginitate* (PL 16.273): "Ambro: libro quarto de virginibus Nos nova omnia que Christus non docuit iure dampnamus quia fidelibus via Christus est. Si igitur Christus non docuit quod docemus, etiam id detestabile iudicamus." A modern hand has written "England, 1450" in pencil in the lower right corner of the verso.

Gift of Henrietta C. Bartlett in 1954.

Bibliography:
De Ricci, 1:174, no. 17.

MS 483.18   Italy, s. XV
Antiphonary   Pl. 138

This leaf is from the same manuscript as MS 483.19.

f. 1   //Et omnes. seuouae. Alleluia. seoae. *Feria vᵃ*. Memento domine dauid
            ... sanctificatio mea. Et omnis mans//[uetudinis]

            Feria V throughout the year, second vespers.

Parchment (torn at the bottom and patched with modern parchment and paper).
1 folio. 352 x 268 mm (written space 275 x 192 mm). 2 columns. 20 lines. Ruled in
lead. Single vertical bounding lines.

    Written in a formal, rounded Italian gothic script (littera textualis formata). The
6-line initial "M" ("Memento") at the beginning of the Psalm is in gold, on a square
ground of blue decorated with white filigree; the initial is not set apart from the
text. The inside of the initial contains a miniature of good quality, though now
damaged by water, depicting David kneeling against a mauve background and
looking up to the hand of God. 1-line initials at the beginning of Psalm verses and
antiphons alternate in red and blue uncials and are set apart from the text. Other
1-line initials and the first letter after the 6-line initial are in black highlighted with
red and are not set apart from the text. Rubrics are written in red capitals in the
margin. Punctuation consists of the punctus and punctus elevatus. Musical notation is in black on 4-line staves in red.

    Modern hands have written "18/- 50" in the lower left, "6" in the lower right,
and "101" in the upper left corner of the recto.

    Gift of Henrietta C. Bartlett in 1954.

Bibliography:
De Ricci, 1:174, no. 18.

MS 483.19   Italy, s. XV
Antiphonary   Pl. 139

This leaf is from the same manuscript as MS 483.18.

f. 1   //ymnus. Aurora iam spargit polum terris ... *v*. Repleti sumus mane ... *R*.
            Et exultauimus. *Ad v*. Illuminare domine hiis ... *P*. Benedictus. Dixit
            dominus. seoe. Alleluia. seuouae. Dixit dominus domino meo ... Tecum
            principium in//

            Saturday throughout the year, lauds and second vespers.

Parchment. 1 folio. 362 x 268 mm (written space 276 x 193 mm). 2 columns. 20
lines. Ruled in lead. Single vertical bounding lines.

Written in a formal, rounded Italian gothic script (littera textualis formata). The 7-line initial "D" ("Dixit") at the beginning of the Psalm is in light tan and gold on a square ground in blue with white filigree; the initial is not set apart from the text. The inside of the initial contains a miniature that is badly rubbed, depicting Christ holding a book on a mauve ground. The first line of the Psalm is written in 1-line white capitals on a rectangular red ground. The first letter of the next line is a 1-line black capital highlighted with red. Guide letters for the artist are in the margin in red. 1-line initials are black capitals highlighted with red and are not set apart from the text. Punctuation consists of the punctus and punctus elevatus. Hyphenation is in the same ink as the text. Musical notation is in black on 4-line staves in red.

Modern hands have written the number "78" in the upper left corner of the recto, "10/6" and "[?]00" in the lower left corner of the verso, and "13" in the lower right corner of the verso.

Gift of Henrietta C. Bartlett in 1954.

Bibliography:
De Ricci, 1:174, no. 19.

MS 483.20   Italy, s. XIV
Dynus de Mugello, *Super Infortiato et Digesto Novo*   Pl. 139

The first part of the text of this fragment follows fairly closely the printed text of the commentary by Dynus de Mugello (d. 1298), a teacher of law at Bologna, although in many minor instances it agrees more closely with the quotations attributed to Dynus by Albericus de Rosate (d. 1360) in his commentary. The extensive commentary on *Si is qui ducenta* (*Digest* 34.5.13), which takes up half of column 2 on the recto and all of the verso, is not found in the printed edition of Dynus, but it does appear in the edition of Albericus's commentary, where it is attributed to Dynus.

f. 1r   //uel ante moram uel uerius dic quod ibi nihil erat faciendum per lega-
         tarium . . . praeterea non fuit legata species eius generis du(bii). *De rebus
         dubiis.* In .l. fundum seianum in glossa alternatiue ibi ponitur condici-
         onaliter . . . dicas quod ibi fuit copulatiua hic disiunctiua.

         Dynus de Mugello, *Super infortiato et digesto nouo* (Lyon, Jacob Myt, 1513;
         rpt. Bologna, Forni Editore [Opera iuridica rariora, 17], 1971), fols. [l$_8$] ver-
         so–m[$_1$] verso. The commentary is on Justinian, *Digesta*, 34.4.3–5.12; ed. T.
         Mommsen and P. Krueger, *Corpus iuris civilis* (Berlin, 1928), 1:531–35.

f. 1r–v   Si is qui ducenta. §utrum pro euidencia dicendorum primo notandum est
           ... et scilicet de condi. insci. vel si heredi. plures. respondeo ue//[rum]

           Dynus de Mugello in Albericus de Rosate, *Commentarii in secundam in-
           fortiati partem* (Venice, 1586; rpt. Bologna, Forni Editore [Opera iuridica
           rariora, 24], 1978), fols. 105v–6r. The commentary is on Justinian, *Di-
           gesta*, 34.5.13; Mommsen and Krueger, 1:535.

Parchment. 1 folio. 400 x 262 mm (written space 305 x 189 mm). 2 columns.
81–84 lines. Ruling (lead?) not visible.

Written in a cramped and inelegant gothic script (scriptura notularis). Two 2-
line initials alternating red and blue, decorated with red penwork and not set apart
from the text. Rubrics are written in red gothic cursive. The lemmata are marked
with alternating red and blue paragraph marks, and some of them are underlined in
brown. Another hand has added a running series of letters from "i" to "z" and then
"a" to "l" in the margin next to each lemma. Punctuation consists of the punctus.
Hyphenation is in the same ink as the text.

The fragment was folded in half and used as the wrapper of a volume measuring
ca. 263 x 200 mm. There are several sixteenth-century inscriptions on the recto,
including "Westhall, supervisio manorii(?)," which may refer to Westhall in Suffolk, England, and seems to be the title for the volume bound by the fragment. The
names "Robert," "Thomas," and "Alsoppe" also appear on the recto. On the verso
a sixteenth-century hand has written abstracts of accounts.

Gift of Henrietta C. Bartlett in 1954.

Bibliography:
De Ricci, 1:174, no. 20.

MS 483.21   France or Low Countries, s. XV
Book of Hours (Office of the Dead)   Pl. 140

f. 1   [Magnificat anima mea . . .] //exultauit spiritus meus . . . semini eius in se-
            cula. A. Absolue domine animas . . . *Inuitatorium.* Regem cui omnia uiuunt
            . . . *Ps.* Uenite exulte. A. Dirige domine deus. *psalmus.* Uerba mea auribus
            percipe . . . Quoniam ad te orabo domine ma//[ne]

            Office of the Dead, from vespers (the Canticle of the Virgin: Luke 1.47–
            55) to the first nocturn of matins (Psalm 5.1–4).

Parchment. 1 folio. 169 x 125 mm (written space 86 x 59 mm). 1 column. 14 lines.
Ruled in ink. Single vertical and horizontal bounding lines.

Written in two sizes of gothic script (littera textualis formata), with a larger script for the canticle and Psalm and a smaller script for the chants. The 2-line initial at the beginning of the Psalm and the 1-line initials at the beginning of the Psalm verses are in gold on a ground that alternates between red with blue penwork and blue with white penwork. The interior of the letters on the red ground are filled with blue with white penwork, and the interiors of those on blue grounds are filled with red with blue penwork. 1-line initials at the beginning of chants are in brown. Rubrics are written in red in the same script as the text. Punctuation is rare and consists of the punctus. Hyphenation is in the same ink as the text.

Gift of Henrietta C. Bartlett in 1954. The fragment is not listed in De Ricci (1:173–74).

MS 484.1   France or Italy, s. XII^{in}
Commentaries on the Psalms   Pl. 140

The fragment preserves Arnobius the Younger's commentaries on Psalms 58–61 and 64–65 and Jerome's commentary on Psalm 66. K.-D. Daur and G. Morin record this mixture of commentaries in four other manuscripts: Venice, Biblioteca Marciana, 45 (I, xciv) and Florence, Bibliotheca Laurentiana, Plut. XVIII.xx, both dated by Daur and Morin to the eleventh or twelfth century, and Vatican City, Bibliotheca Vaticana, Ottobon. lat. 478 and Vat. lat. 317, both dated by Daur and Morin to the sixteenth century (see Daur, CCSL 25 [1990], xx–xxii and Morin, *Études, Textes, Découvertes*, Anecdota Maredsolana 2.1 [Maredsous, 1913], 257–63). Two contemporary corrections in the Beinecke fragment are also found in the Florence manuscript, with which the Beinecke fragment shares several other readings.

f. 1   [Inc: Quando domus corporis tui a principe huius mundi ...] //mei
          confido. Exultans mane ... De quorum nos consiliis et uiolentiis. liberat
          dominus iesus christus; qui regnat cum patre et spiritu sancto; per omnia
          saecula saeculorum. Amen.

          Arnobius, *Commentarii in Psalmos*, 58.38–50; K.-D. Daur, ed., CCSL 25
          (1990), 83–84. CPL 242.

f. 1r–1v Prostratis hostibus uictoriam nos docuit domino reputare ... quia tu ad
          nichilum rediges omnes tribulantes nos; qui regnas in saecula saeculorum.
          Amen.

          Arnobius, *Commentarii in Psalmos*, 59; Daur, 84–85.

f. 1v   Ecclesiam supra petræ soliditatem fundatam. Et turrem fortitudinis factam
             . . . redde uota tua de die in diem domino iesu christo; qui regnat cum pa-
             tre et spiritu sancto in saecula saeculorum. Amen.

             Arnobius, *Commentarii in Psalmos*, 60; Daur, 85–86.

f. 1v   In omnibus psalmis mysticus exuberat sensus . . . irruitis in homines. et
             sicut paries//

             Arnobius, *Commentarii in Psalmos*, 61.1–9; Daur, 86.

f. 2r   [Inc: In Hebraeo non habet nec Hieremiam nec Aggaeum . . . epu]//lan-
             tur. ita ut etiam fines deserti pinguescant . . . clamabunt arietes et oues si-
             mul. ymnum dicentes christo filio dei; qui regnat cum patre et spiritu
             sancto. in unitate deitatis; et in trinitate unitatis. in saecula saeculorum.
             Amen.

             Arnobius, *Commentarii in Psalmos*, 64.40–end; Daur, 91.

f. 2r–2v   Iudeorum terra sola iubilat deo . . . Benedico te. qui non amouisti precem
             meam. nec misericordiam tuam a me; qui regnas cum patre et spiritu
             sancto. per omnia saecula saeculorum. Amen.

             Arnobius, *Commentarii in Psalmos*, 65; Daur, 91–93.

f. 2v   Deus misereatur nobis et benedicat nos . . . uiam tuam et scientiam tuam.
             nosse non possumus.//

             Jerome, *Tractatus in Psalmos*, 66.1–27; G. Morin, ed., CCSL 78 (1958),
             34–35.

Parchment. 2 folios (bifolium; probably one bifolium missing between fols. 1 and 2).
299 x 209 mm (written space 264 x 159 mm). 2 columns. 31 lines. Ruled in dry-
point on the flesh side before folding. Double horizontal and outer vertical bounding lines; single inner vertical bounding lines. Prickings in upper and lower margins.
      Written in Caroline minuscule. 2- and 3-line initials at the beginning of each
commentary are in red uncials and are not set apart from the text; they are frequently decorated with balls or cross-hatching. 1-line initials are in brown uncials
with occasional use of rustic capital forms such as H and D and of enlarged
minuscule n. The first several words of each commentary are written in brown
rustic capitals. Punctuation consists of the punctus, punctus elevatus, and punctus
versus. Hyphenation is in the same ink as the text. Accents were added by a later

hand. Quotations are marked by double wavy lines in the left margin opposite each line containing a quotation. A contemporary hand has made corrections in a lighter ink on both folios. On fol. 2r there are marginalia in a fifteenth-century hand.

Modern hands have written "83" and "Saec. [*erased*]. Francia (Corbie?)" in pencil on the recto. Gift of Edmund T. Silk; purchased from Kraus in 1948.

Bibliography:
Kraus, H. P., *List no. 109* (New York, [1947]), no. 23.

MS 484.2   Southern Germany(?), s. IX$^{2/4}$
South German Homiliary   Pl. 141

f. 1r   [Inc: Gaudeamus . . .] //Quas itaque laudes debita pietati dei . . . commen-
          dare dignatur in cẹlis. Quod ipse præstare dignetur dominus omnipotens
          qui uiuit et regnat per omnia saecula saeculorum. amen.

          Homily II.27 (On the Nativity of Mary, 8 September); see G. Folliet,
          "Deux nouveaux témoins du sermonnaire carolingien récemment recon-
          stitué," *Revue des Études Augustiniennes* 23 (1977): 155–98, here 194.

f. 1v   Temporibus ualeriani et galliani principum cyprianus episcopus erat
          cartagine . . . Postquam eius sententiam. multitudo fratrum//

          Homily II.28 (On the Passion of St. Cyprian, 14 September); see Folliet,
          194.

Parchment. 1 folio. 214 x 154 mm (written space 200 x 120 mm). 1 column. 23 lines remaining of an original 25 lines. Dry-point ruling. Double vertical bounding lines.

Written in Caroline minuscule, which Bischoff (on the basis of his inspection of other leaves of the same manuscript) dated to the second quarter of the ninth century. Holter (1957), 441, no. 9, reports that Bischoff attributed the manuscript to Italy. Bischoff later expressed reservations about this attribution: "Die Schrift . . wirkt fremdartig; dass sie italienisch sein muss, wage ich nicht mehr zu behaupten," *Schreibschulen*, 2:42–43.

The homily on fol. 1v begins with a 3-line initial "T" outlined in orange and filled and surrounded with brown; it is set apart from the text. 1-line initials are in orange uncials and are set apart from the text between the double vertical bounding lines. Punctuation consists of the punctus and punctus versus.

Other leaves from this manuscript are preserved as Beinecke MS 482.4 (1 leaf), Lambach, Stiftsbibliothek, Fragment 8/1-8 (14 leaves), and in the bindings of Vienna, Österreichische Nationalbibliothek, s.n. 3620 (1 leaf and binding strips; formerly Lambach Ccl 436), s.n. 3622 (binding strips), and in the binding of a manuscript illustrated in Holter (1957), pl. 185, and given the shelfmark Ccl 480 (according to Holter [1989], cat. no. IX.02, this manuscript is now Kremsmünster CC 417). See Holter (1989), 210–11, cat. nos. IX.01–02 and Bischoff, *Schreib-schulen*, 2:42–43, where MS 484.2 is misidentified as "MS 3."

A modern hand has written the number "35" in pencil on the verso. In the upper left corner of the recto the number "2" is written in red. Gift of Thomas E. Marston; purchased from Kraus in 1948. The leaf was earlier in the possession of E. von Scherling (Leiden); cf. idem, *Rotulus*, 4 (winter 1937): 21, item 1873.

Bibliography:
Babcock, *Reconstructing a Medieval Library*, 92 and fig. 48.
Kraus, H.P., *List no. 109* (New York, [1947]), no. 10.

MS 484.3   Northern Italy, s. IX$^{1/3}$
Pseudo-Augustine, Sermons (Alan of Farfa, Homiliary?)   Pl. 141

Both of these sermons are found in Alan of Farfa's Homiliary and in the same order as they are found here; however, since they are both Pseudo-Augustinian sermons and because of the early date of the fragment, it is not certain that they are truly from Alan's Homiliary and not from some other collection of sermons.

f. 1r   [Inc: Piscatoris et persecutoris sacratissimum diem ...] //ligno suspen-
         ditur. Paulus pro christo gladio trucid[at]ur ... si uolumus caulas intrare
         pastoris.

         Ps-Augustine, Sermon 205 (Sts. Peter and Paul, 29 June); PL 39.2126–27
         = Alan of Farfa, Homily II.47. See Grégoire, 175.

f. 1r–v *In natale apostolorum quorum supra.*
         Filioli mei audite nos et liberate uos ... Paulus submisus//

         Ps-Augustine, Sermon 204; PL 39.2124 (Sts. Peter and Paul) = Alan of
         Farfa, Homily II.48. See Grégoire, 175. A later hand has added "sermo
         sancti augustini" in brown ink to the rubric.

Parchment. 1 folio. 288 x 204 mm (written space 267 x 190 mm). 2 columns. 31 lines. Dry-point ruling on the hair side. Double vertical bounding lines.

Written in Caroline minuscule, which Bischoff has dated to the first third of the ninth century (letter of 5 October 1985). The homily begins with a 7-line decorated initial "F" outlined in brown and filled with orange, dark orange, ochre, and olive green; it is set apart from the text. 1-line initials are in brown uncials and are set apart from the text between double vertical bounding lines. The rubric is written in red uncials which in places has oxidized to a silver color. The first line of the sermon is written in brown uncials. Punctuation consists of the punctus and punctus versus. A leaf has been drawn in red in the space between the columns on the verso.

A modern hand has written the number "5" in pencil on the verso. In the upper margin of the recto a modern hand has written "Verona, saec. IX, Augustinus Sermones" in pencil. Gift of the Yale University Library Associates; purchased from Kraus in 1948.

Bibliography:
Kraus, H. P., *List no. 109* (New York, [1947]), no. 16.

MS 484.4   Italy, s. X/XI
Ars Laureshamensis, *Expositio in Donatum maiorem*   Pl. 142

This fragment preserves a portion of an anonymous commentary on Donatus's *Ars maior*, edited by B. Löfstedt as the *Ars Laureshamensis* (CCCM 40A [Turnhout, 1978]; MS 484.4 not cited). Löfstedt attributes the commentary to a tenth-century Irishman (cf. L. Holtz, "Sur trois commentaires irlandais de l'*Art Majeur* de Donat au IXe siècle," *Revue d'Histoire des Textes* 2 [1972]: 45-72). The portion preserved here, on how to distinguish between nouns and participles and on the comparison of adjectives, is on part II of Donatus's grammar ("De octo partibus orationis") and is preserved in two other manuscripts: Vatican City, Bibliotheca Vaticana, Palatinus lat. 1754 (Lorsch, s. X) and Munich, Bayerische Staatsbibliothek, Clm 14488 (Northern Italy, s. X/XI).

f. 1   [Inc: Notandum est quia in capite uniuscuiusque libri ... ge]//nerale est
            quod in diuersas species ... extrinsecus forte uenient//[ium]

            Ars Laureshamensis, *Expositio in Donatum maiorem*; B. Löfstedt, ed.,
            CCCM 40A (1978), 22.4-25.98. The inner margin of the leaf has been
            trimmed with the loss of a few letters.

Parchment. 1 folio (later foliation "61" in upper right corner of recto). 284 x 210 mm (written space 263 x 148 mm). 1 column. 31 lines. Dry-point ruling on the hair side. Double vertical bounding lines; horizontal text-rulings extend through the prickings in outer margin.

Written in Caroline minuscule. 1-line initials are brown rustic capitals, with occasional use of enlarged minuscule *h* and *e*, and are not set apart from the text. Punctuation consists of the punctus and punctus interrogativus. Double quotation marks are within the text.

A fifteenth-century inscription in Italian is written on fol. 1v: "Celi mei li quali hanno hauto paura de la nebia non sonno andati a la vingna." A modern hand has written the number "77" in pencil on the recto. Gift of the Yale University Library Associates; purchased from Kraus in 1948.

Bibliography:
Kraus, H. P., *List no. 109* (New York, [1947]), no. 22.

MS 484.5   N. France or Germany, s.XII^2
Boethius, *De syllogismo categorico, De differentiis topicis*   Pl. 142

f. 1r   [Inc: Multa Graeci ueteres posteris in consultissimis reliquere tractatibus
           ... contra]//ria patiuntur. Hec de categoricorum sillogismorum categoricis
           ... per tractata sunt.

           Boethius, *De syllogismo categorico*, Book I; PL 64.810.

f. 1r–v   Superioris igitur series uoluminis quod ad categoricorum sillogismorum
           propositiones attinebat ... quia uidetur uniuersalis conuersa affirmatio//

           De syllogismo categorico, Book II; PL 64.809–12.

f. 2r–v   //Quartus modus tertiẹ figure ... in rebus mendaciumque meditabitur.
           Explicit liber boetii de cathegoricis silogismis.

           De syllogismo categorico, Book II; PL 64.827–32.

f. 2v   Si quis operis titulum diligens æxaminator inspiciat cum de topicis dif-
           ferentiis conscribamus ... locorum qui eisdem facul//[tatibus]

           Boethius, *De differentiis topicis*, Book IV; PL 64.1205.

Parchment. 2 folios (bifolium; probably the outer bifolium of a quire, with six folios missing between fols. 1 and 2). 225 x 160 mm (written space 189 x 110 mm). 1

column. 37 lines. Ruled in lead. Single vertical bounding lines. Prickings in upper margin.

Written in a highly abbreviated, late Caroline script. 2- and 3-line initials at the beginning of each section are red and are written on the vertical bounding line. 1-line initials are brown rustic capitals, with uncial M and enlarged minuscule *e*. The explicit is written in brown rustic capitals, with some use of uncial and minuscule forms. There are nine diagrams, one outlined in red. Punctuation consists of the punctus.

The fragment was used as a pastedown in the binding of a volume measuring ca. 304 x 206 mm. Three rust holes remain in the corners. A modern hand has written the number "98" in pencil on the recto. Gift of Clarence W. Mendell; purchased from Kraus in 1948.

Bibliography:
Kraus, H. P., *List no. 109* (New York, [1947]), no. 62.

MS 484.6   Italy, s. XI^in
Sacramentary   Pl. 143

f. 1r   //cede [rest of first line illegible].

             Unidentified prayer.

f. 1r   Omnium apostolorum intercessionibus ... Satiasti domine tuis donis ac datis reple nos ... patre et spiritu sancto.

             Prayers for before and after meals.

f. 1r   *Benedictio uuae siue fauae.* Benedic domine hos fructos nouos ... *Benedictio ad omnia quę uolueris.* Benedic domine creaturam istam ut ... percipiat. Per.

             Benedictions.

ff. 1r–2   Omnipotens sempiterne deus a cuius facie caeli distillant ... *Item alia pro paruulo energumino.* Domine sanctę pater omnipotens sempiterne deus uirtutem ... *Alia oratio super inerguminum baptizato.* Deus angelorum. deus archangelorum. deus prophetarum ... *Alia.* Deus conditor et defensor generis humani ... uirtutem diaboli fallacesque//

Prayers for the exorcism of people possessed by devils (including candidates for baptism).

Parchment (fols. 1r and 2v are badly stained from the fragment's use in a binding). 2 folios (bifolium). 272 x 175 mm (written space 200 x 115 mm). 1 column. 21 lines. Dry-point ruling on the hair side. Double vertical and single horizontal bounding lines. Prickings in upper and lower margins.

Written in Caroline minuscule. 2-line initials are red rustic capitals with a single round *D* and are set apart from the text between double bounding lines. 1-line initials are brown uncials and are set apart from the text between the double bounding lines when they occur at the beginning of a line. The rubrics are written in red rustic capitals. Punctuation consists of the punctus and punctus versus. Accents in the same ink as the text.

The bifolium was used as the wrapper for a volume measuring ca. 221 x 150 mm. There are several Latin notes on the fragment in sixteenth-century Italian hands. Modern hands have written "33" and "Saec. X^2. Italia settentrionale" in pencil on fol. 1v. Gift of Thomas E. Marston; purchased from Kraus in 1948.

Bibliography:

Kraus, H. P., *List no. 109* (New York, [1947]), no. 15.

Lutz, Cora E. "A Bifolium from the *Sacramentarium Gregorianum*," in eadem, *Essays on Manuscripts and Rare Books* (New Haven, 1975), 28–38 (with plates of each page).

MS 484.7   Italy, s. XIV/XV
Quintus Curtius Rufus, *Historiae Alexandri Magni*   Pl. 143

f. 1   //quicquid mortalitas cupiebat impleret ... esse uel subdere//

Quintus Curtius Rufus, *Historiae Alexandri Magni*, chaps. 10.5–6; ed. E. Hedicke (Leipzig, 1912), 374.7–377.13. The top line of text is illegible.

f. 2   [potu]//isset dum a pluribus ... copiisque praeesset que//

Chaps. 10.9–10; Hedicke, 384.6–387.12. The top line of text is illegible.

Parchment (stained, creased, and with numerous holes). 2 folios (bifolium; probably one bifolium missing between fols. 1 and 2). 307 x 211 mm (written space 195 x 105 mm). 1 column. 33 lines. Dry-point or lead ruling on the hair side. Single horizontal and vertical bounding lines. Prickings in upper, lower, and outer margins.

Written in a rounded gothic bookhand (gothico-humanistica). 1-line initials are brown capitals and are not set apart from the text. There are brief notes on the text written in the margins in a cursive humanistic script of the fifteenth century. Punctuation consists of the punctus. Running headlines ("L[iber]" / "X") in red and blue appear in the center of the upper margin.

The bifolium was used as the wrapper for a volume measuring ca. 214 x 155 mm. The inscription "Pratica di M. Guglielmo Pagnini" appears on the back of the cover (bottom of fol. 2r); the number "6" is written on the spine, which is mostly destroyed, along with remnants of other numbers ("23" and "17"). There are several illegible inscriptions on the front cover. The number "I.1947" is written in a modern hand on the inner flap. Miscellaneous names, accounts, and pen-trials are written on the outer covers and the inside flaps, of which the following are legible: "Jo. Bastiano Franch," "Antonio," "Di Giovanni," "Antonio Franch," "Ambrogio Franch di (?)villa [?]," and "Havendomi mostrato in gran tempo," the last with a drawing of a face.

Modern hands have written in pencil the number "54" at the top of fol. 1r, "Lombardy, saec. XV" at the bottom of fol. 1v, and the number "6013" in pencil in the lower outer margin of fol. 2r. Gift of the Yale University Library Associates; purchased from Kraus in 1948.

Bibliography:
Kraus, H. P., *List no. 109* (New York, [1947]), no. 104.

MS 484.8   France or Italy, s. XII[1]
Bible, Luke   Pl. 144

f. 1   //adprehendit omnes et magnificabant deum . . . ab omni iudea et hierusalem. Et maritima//

          Luke 5.26–6.17.

f. 2   //et unum helie nesciens quid diceret . . . Rogate ergo dominum//

          Luke 9.33–10.2.

Parchment. 2 folios (bifolium; probably the outer of a quire, with six folios missing between fols. 1 and 2). 284 x 212 mm (written space 190 x 110 mm). 1 column. 30 lines. Dry-point ruling on the hair side. Double vertical and triple horizontal bounding lines. Additional single vertical ruling in inner and outer margins to accommodate canon table numbers. Prickings in upper, lower, and outer margins.

Written in Caroline minuscule. 1- and 2-line initials alternate in red and green uncials and are set apart from the text between double vertical bounding lines. 1-line initials are brown uncials and are not set apart from the text. The running title "Secundum" / "Lucam" is written in brown rustic capitals in the upper margin. Punctuation consists of the punctus, punctus elevatus, punctus versus, and punctus interrogativus. Hyphenation is in the same ink as the text. Canon table numbers are written in the left margins in red roman numerals.

The bifolium was used as the wrapper for a volume measuring ca. 245 x 185 mm. An inscription in ink in the lower margin of fol. 2v reads "1689 Montdol(?)." Modern hands have written in pencil the number "100" in the upper left corner of fol. 1r and "9/47 10/2" in the upper margin of fol. 2v. Gift of the Yale University Library Associates; purchased from Kraus in 1948.

Bibliography:
Kraus, H. P., *List no. 109* (New York, [1947]), no. 50.

MS 484.9   France, s. XII[1]
Gregory the Great, *Homiliae xl in evangelia*   Pl. 144

ff. 1–2r   [Inc: Sancti euangelii, fratres karissimi, breuis est lectio recitata . . . fu]//
            isset orbata. Numquam ego . . . carnalia desideria in mente trucidamus.

            Gregory the Great, *Homiliae xl in evangelia*, Homily I.3.3–end (on Matt.
            12.46–50); PL 76.1087–89; R. Étaix, ed., CCSL 141 (1999), 22–25. The
            first two lines of the leaf are illegible.

ff. 2r–4v   *Lectio sancti euangelii secundum matheum.*
            In illo tempore. Misit iesus duodecim discipulos suos . . . in die iudicii
            quam illi ciuitati.
            Homelia leccionis eiusdem habita ad populum in baselica [sic] *sancti stephani.*
            Cum constet omnibus fratres karissimi. quia redemptor noster in mundum
            pro redemptione gentium uenit . . . ei bonis actibus cum festinatione pre-
            paremur.

            Homily I.4 (on Matt. 10.5–15); PL 76.1089–92; Étaix, 26–32.

ff. 4v–6v   In illo tempore. Ambulans iesus iuxta mare galilee . . . relictis retibus et
            patre secuti sunt eum.
            [A]udistis fratres karissimi. quia ad unius iussionis uocem. petrus et an-
            dreas relictis retibus. secuti sunt redemptorem . . . quandoque ad propria
            contempnenda perducatur.

Homily I.5 (on Matt. 4.18–22); PL 76.1092–95; Étaix, 33–37.

ff. 6v–8v   In illo tempore. Cum audisset iohannes in uinculis opera christi . . . qui
non fuerit scandalizatus in me.
[Q]uerendum nobis est fratres karissimi. iohannes propheta et plusquam
propheta qui uenientem ad baptisma dominum ostendit . . . denuntiat.
cum uerba sanctẹ//

Homily I.6.1–6.6 (on Matt. 11.2–6); PL 76.1095–98; Étaix, 38–43.

Parchment. 8 folios (4 bifolia). 266 x 192 mm (written space 200 x 125 mm). 1 column. 25 lines. Dry-point ruling on the hair side before folding. Double vertical and
single horizontal bounding lines. Prickings in upper, lower, and outer margins.
  Written in late Caroline minuscule. At the beginning of Homily 4 (fol. 2r) there
is a 3-line initial "C" sketched, but not completed, in brown ink with foliate decoration, not set apart from the text; it may be a later addition. 1-line initials are
brown uncials and are set apart from the text between double bounding lines when
they occur at the beginning of the line. The rubrics for Homily 4 and its lesson are
written in red minuscule mixed with uncial forms, with red line-filler. A contemporary hand has supplied omitted text on fol. 2v. There are no initials or rubrics for
the other homilies, but a later hand has added a 3-line initial "I" in brown to the
beginning of each lesson. Punctuation consists of the punctus, punctus elevatus,
and punctus interrogativus. Hyphenation is in the same ink as the text. Accents
were added by a later hand. On fol. 2v there are three interlinear Latin glosses in
a fifteenth-century hand. Other fifteenth-century hands have added marginal notations and figures of heads on fols. 7v–8r.
  A modern hand has written the number "94" in pencil on fol. 1r. Gift of the
Yale University Classical Club; purchased from Kraus in 1948.

Bibliography:
Kraus, H. P., List no. 109 (New York, [1947]), no. 33.

MS 484.10   Italy, s. XI/XII
Passio S. Felicitatis (from a Passionary?)   Pl. 145

f. 1r   [Inc: Temporibus Antonini imperatoris . . .] //misera si tibi . . . impietas
est. et//

Passio S. Felicitatis (10 July); Acta Sanctorum, Iul. 3:12; BHL 2853. Only
the upper portion of the inner column remains.

f. 1v   //Nos si transitorium ... et in sempi//[ternum]

> *Passio S. Felicitatis*; *Acta Sanctorum, Iul.* 3:12–13. Only the upper portion
> of the inner column remains.

Parchment. 1 folio. 188 x 130 mm (width of written space of one column 80 mm;
original written space ca. 350 x 175 mm). 1 of 2 columns remaining. 18 of ca. 36
lines remaining. Dry-point ruling on the hair side. Double vertical and horizontal
bounding lines.

Written in an inelegant Caroline minuscule. 1-line initials are brown rustic
capitals and are not set apart from the text. Punctuation consists of the punctus,
punctus elevatus, and the punctus versus.

Modern hands have written "74," "Saec. XI" and "Saec. XII" in pencil on the
recto. Gift of the Yale University Library Associates; purchased from Kraus in
1948.

Bibliography:
Kraus, H. P., *List no. 109* (New York, [1947]), no. 36.

MS 484.11   Italy, s. XII[1]
Gregory the Great, *Homiliae xl in evangelia*   Pl. 145

f. 1ra   [Inc: Lectio sancti evangelii quae modo in auribus vestris lecta est ...]
            //Nam piscatorem petrum ... corruptionem carnis excesserat//

> Gregory the Great, *Homiliae xl in evangelia*, Homily II.24.1–2; PL 76.1184–
> 85; R. Étaix, ed., CCSL 141 (1999), 197–98. The upper and lower mar-
> gins have been trimmed with loss of text.

f. 1rb   //resurgeret. mitti quidem rete ad piscandum iubet ... In ista uero pis-
            catione et multi pisces//

> Homily II.24.3; PL 76.1185; Étaix, 198. The upper and lower margins
> have been trimmed with loss of text.

f. 1va   //additur et quanti scilicet et centum quinquaginta tribus ... per trigonum
            decem et septem et ueniunt quin//[quaginta]

> Homily II.24.4; PL 76.1186; Étaix, 199–200. The upper and lower margins
> have been trimmed with loss of text.

f. 1vb   //haec uero et haesterna sancti euangelii lectio ... Qui enim assari ut
          pisc//[is]

          Homily II.24.5; PL 76.1186–87; Étaix, 201. The upper and lower margins
          have been trimmed with loss of text.

Parchment. 1 folio. 200 x 298 mm (written space originally ca. 392 x 238 mm). 2
columns. 25 lines remaining of an original ca. 50 lines. Dry-point ruling on hair
side. Double vertical bounding lines.
    Written in late Caroline minuscule. 1-line initials are brown uncials, with
occasional use of enlarged minuscule n, and are set apart from the text between
double bounding lines when they occur at the beginning of a line. Punctuation
consists of the punctus, punctus elevatus, and punctus interrogativus. Hyphenation
is in the same ink as the text.
    A modern hand has written "97" in pencil on the verso. Gift of the Yale Uni-
versity Library Associates; purchased from Kraus in 1948.

Bibliography:
    Kraus, H. P., *List no. 109* (New York, [1947]), no. 48.

MS 484.12   Italy, s. XI/XII
Homilies (Haimo of Halberstadt?)   Pl. 146

f. 1r–v   //tantum locuntur. et filio aliquando patris et filii et spiritus sancti pariter
          mentionem faciunt ... Et quem antea hominem credebant. hoc signum
          uidentes deum uerum hominem essę crediderunt iesum christum domi-
          num nostrum.

          Homily on John 2.1–11 (here 2.6–11) for the Second Sunday after Epi-
          phany. This homily is similar to Homily 18 attributed to Haimo of Hal-
          berstadt in PL 118.135–37 (Inc: Miracula domini et saluatoris nostri
          quandocunque leguntur ...) but is much expanded. The lower margin has
          been trimmed with the loss of the bottom line of text.

f. 1v   *Dominica III lectio sancti evangelii secundum mattheum.*
          In illo; Cum descendisset iesus de monte. secute sunt eum turbe multe et
          reliqua.
          Superior textus ęuangelii. narrat quod dominus in montem sedens. octo
          beatitudines discipulos docuit ... Post incarnationem uero secute sunt
          eum turbe multę ex omnibus nationibus//

Homily on Matthew 8.1 for the Third Sunday after Epiphany. This homily is similar to Homily 19 attributed to Haimo of Halberstadt in PL 118.137. The lower margin has been trimmed with the loss of the bottom line of text.

f. 2   [p]//salmista. Accedite ad eum inluminamini; Et facies uestre non confundentur . . . Sic iusti in hoc saeculo inter populum habitantes//

Homily on Matthew 8.23–26 for the Fourth Sunday after Epiphany. This homily is similar to Homily 20 attributed to Haimo of Halberstadt in PL 118.151–54 (Inc: In huius lectionis serie utriusque suae naturae ueritatem . . .). The lower margin has been trimmed with the loss of the bottom line of text.

Parchment. 2 folios. 292 x 208 mm (written space originally ca. 297 x 198 mm). 2 columns. 39 of 40 lines remaining. Dry-point ruling on the hair side. Double vertical bounding lines.

Written in Caroline minuscule. On fol. 1v there is a very fine 3/4-page decorated initial "I" in red and yellow on a purple, blue, and orange ground, with vine-stem decoration lightly washed with yellow. The design of the initial is very similar to that in F. Avril and Y. Zaluska, *Manuscrits enluminés d'origine italienne*, 1: VIe–XIIe *siècles* (Paris, 1980), pl. XXVII, no. 71 (from a central Italian manuscript of s. XII^1). 1-line initials are either in red rustic capitals or brown rustic capitals highlighted with red; they are not set apart from the text. Rubrics are written in a mixture of red minuscule and rustic capitals. Punctuation consists of the punctus and punctus elevatus. Double quotation marks are within the text. Accents are in the same ink as the text.

A modern hand has written the number "92" in pencil on fols. 1v and 2r. Gift of the Yale University Library Associates; purchased from Kraus in 1948.

Bibliography:
Kraus, H. P., *List no. 109* (New York, [1947]), no. 12.

MS 484.13   France or Italy, s. XI^{in}
Noted Breviary   Pl. 146

f. 1r   //qui ueniunt ad nos in uestimentis ouium . . . de illo diuina procurante prouidentia.

Excerpts from Augustine, *De sermone domini in monte*, II.78.1784–79.1829; A. Mutzenbecher, ed., CCSL 35 (1967), 176–78.

f. 1v   In illo tempore. Dixit iesus discipulis suis. Adtendite a falsis prophetis . . . regnum cælorum. *In eug. A.* Attendite a falsis prophetis . . . A. Non omnis qui dicit michi domine . . .

The lesson is from Matthew 7.15–21, and the antiphons seem to be for the seventh Sunday after Pentecost.

f. 1v   *In sancti apolenaris leccio.* Deus cuius prouidentia in sui. Nemo militans deo implicat se negotiis . . . legittime certauerit. R. Pulchra facie. *hym.* Festa sacrata praesulis . . . Inter eadem famina perrexit ad emiliam//

Undetermined office for St. Apollinaris (23 July). The lesson is from 2 Timothy 2.4–5. The hymn is printed in AH 14.98 (Schaller-Könsgen 5078).

Parchment. 1 folio. 348 x 238 mm (written space 258 x 157 mm). 1 column. 28 lines. Dry-point ruling on the hair side. Double vertical and single horizontal bounding lines. Prickings in upper margin.

Written in two sizes of Caroline minuscule, with a larger script for the lessons and hymn and a smaller script for the antiphons and responses. On fol. 1v there are decorated initials "I" (7-line) and "F" (8-line), outlined in orange and colored with green and yellow, set apart from the text. 1- and 2-line initials are orange uncials and are set apart from the text. Other 1-line initials are brown rustic capitals, highlighted with orange, and are set apart from the text when they occur at the beginning of a line. 1-line initials within the hymn are a mixture of orange uncials and rustic capitals and are set apart from the text when they occur at the beginning of a line. Rubrics are written in orange minuscule. Interlinear neumes in the St. Gall style. Punctuation consists of the punctus, punctus elevatus, and punctus interrogativus. Accents and diacritical marks over double *i* by later hands.

The folio was folded in half and used as the first two flyleaves in a volume measuring ca. 239 x 173 mm. The contents of the volume are described in the inner margin of the recto in a sixteenth-century cursive hand as "Magister Iohannes de Sancto Amando summa super regnum [*sic, for* regimen] acutorum morborum," referring to the commentary by John of St. Amand (died before 1312) on Hippoccrates' *De regimine morborum acutorum* (see L. Thorndike and P. Kibre, *A Catalogue of Incipits of Mediaeval Scientific Writings in Latin*, 2nd ed. [Cambridge, Mass., 1963], 1623; P. Kibre, *Hippocrates Latinus* [New York, 1985], 23; and L. Thorndike, *A History of Magic and Experimental Science*, 8 vols. [New York, 1929–58], 2:510–13).

Modern hands have written the number "12" and "Saec. XI in. Francia" in pencil on the recto. Gift of the Yale University Library Associates; purchased from Kraus in 1948.

Bibliography:
Kraus, H. P., *List no. 109* (New York, [1947]), no. 29.

MS 484.14   Italy, s. XI/XII
Remigius of Auxerre, *Homiliae* (*Expositio super Mattheum*)   Pl. 147

No edition of these homilies has been printed. They are described by J. Villar, "L'*Expositio Remigii super Mattheum* en el cod. 548 de la Biblioteca de Catalunya," *Estudis Universitaris Catalans* 22 (1936): 263–81, who provides a list of incipits, and Barré, *Homéliaires*, 125–30, who provides a list of manuscripts in which they occur, most of which were produced in Italy in the eleventh and twelfth centuries. See also Stegmüller 7227.

f. 1r–v   [Inc: In hoc loco sancti euangelistae uaria narrauerunt . . .] //palma martyrii coronati sunt . . . Videntes quippe secuti sunt. quia bonum quod intellexerunt operari studuerunt.

Remigius, Homily on Matthew 20.29–34 (here 20.31–34); Villar, 279, no. 72; Barré, *Homéliaires*, no. r76, see p. 275. The lower margin has been trimmed with the loss of the bottom line of text.

f. 1v   *Dominica de adventu domini. CI.*
Et cum adpropinquasset hierosolimam uenit bethfage. et cetera.
Narrat sanctus euangelista superius dominum egressum a galilea . . . hye-rusalem interpretatur uisio paci//[s]

Remigius, Homily on Matthew 21.1–9 (here 21.1); Villar, 279, no. 73; Barré, *Homéliaires*, no. r77, see p. 258. The lower margin has been trimmed with the loss of the bottom line of text.

Parchment. 1 folio. 333 x 230 mm (written space ca. 325 x 210 mm). 2 columns. 39 of 40 lines remaining. Dry-point ruling on the hair side. Double vertical and triple horizontal bounding lines.

Written in late Caroline minuscule. 2-line initial "E" ("Et") is a red uncial highlighted with yellow and written on the inner vertical bounding line. 1-line initials are a mixture of brown uncials, rustic capitals, and enlarged minuscule forms, usually filled with yellow; they are frequently set apart from the text between the double bounding lines when they occur at the beginning of a line. The rubric is written in red minuscule. Punctuation consists of the punctus, punctus elevatus, and punctus interrogativus, some of the last altered from punctus by a corrector.

Hyphenation is in the same ink as the text.

Modern hands have written the number "19" and "Saec. XI ineunte" in pencil on the verso and "Saec. XII¹" on the recto. Gift of the Yale University Library Associates; purchased from Kraus in 1948.

Bibliography:

Kraus, H. P., List no. 109 (New York, [1947]), no. 61.

MS 484.15   Southern Italy, s. X/XI
Passionary (*Passio S. Cassiani*)   Pl. 14

The two lives of St. Cassian in this fragment are also found together in Rome, Bibliotheca Casanatensis, 1408, nos. 40–1, a manuscript copied in Beneventan script in Benevento in the twelfth century (see A. Poncelet, *Catalogus codicum hagiographicorum latinorum bibliothecarum Romanarum praeter quam Vaticanae* [Brussels, 1909], 258–59).

f. 1r   [Inc: Sylla forum statuit Cornelius . . .] //re uulnerem stillant . . . domum reuertor cassianum predico.

          St. Cassian (13 August); Prudentius, *Peristephanon*, Book IX.58–106; BHL 1625. The upper margin has been trimmed with the loss of the first line of text.

f. 1r–v   Hinc d[octus prudentius dum taliter] gesta . . . nunc scinditur nunc//

          Passio S. Cassiani; BHL 1626b. The upper margin has been trimmed with the loss of the first line of text.

Parchment. 1 folio. 413 x 308 mm (written space originally ca. 385 x 245 mm). 2 columns. 35 of 36 lines remaining.

Written in Beneventan script. The Prudentius life is written in poetic stanzas. Six-line decorated initial is outlined in brown, not set apart from the text. 1-line initials are brown uncials; in the Prudentius text, they are set apart from the text, but in the prose life they are set apart only when they occur at the beginning of a line. Punctuation consists of the punctus, punctus elevatus, and punctus versus.

According to V. Brown, another leaf from this manuscript is preserved in Sweet Briar (Virginia) College Library, MS 2 (letter of 17 October 1994). The Sweet Briar leaf contains Pseudo-Ildefonsus, Homily 7 (PL 96.269; Inc: [Celebritas hodierni diei nos admonet . . .ma]//ria mulier esse non potuit . . . amen.) and Pseudo-

Augustine, Homily 194 (PL 39.2104–6; Inc: Adest nobis diem dilectissimi optatus dies . . . fingunt sabelli peperit paruulum//). These two texts are in Alan of Farfa's Homiliary (Homilies II.64–65) for the feast of the Assumption of the Virgin Mary (15 August). They occur with the prose *Passio S. Cassiani* in Rimini, Biblioteca Gambalunghiana, 4.A.I.i, a manuscript written in Italian Caroline script of the end of the eleventh or beginning of the twelfth century (see A. Gattucci, "Codici agio-grafici riminesi: Il Passionario della Biblioteca Gambalunghiana," *Studi Medievali* 10 [1969]: 269–331 and BHL 5355cb and 5355cc). According to De Ricci, the Sweet Briar leaf was obtained in 1931 from Rappoport in Rome (see De Ricci, 2:1855, no. 2; see also Faye and Bond, 525).

The Beinecke fragment was used as the wrapper of a volume measuring ca. 308 x 207 mm. There are various pen trials, including two in Greek, both of which read πρόσταγμα ἔθετο, a quotation from Psalm 148.6.

Modern hands have written in pencil "Sec. XI 1ª metà probabilmente Monte Casino" on the recto and the number "24" on the verso. Gift of the Yale University Library Associates; purchased from Kraus in 1948. The leaf was earlier sold by E. von Scherling (Leiden), cf. *Rotulus* 1.4 (December 1931): 75, item 1269.

Bibliography:

Kraus, H. P., *List no. 109* (New York, [1947]), no. 24.

Lohrmann, D., "Zwei Passionare des 12. Jahrhunderts aus der Kapitelbibliothek von Benevent," *Quellen und Forschungen aus italienischen Archiven und Bibliotheken* 46 (1966): 455–75.

Lowe, E. A., *The Beneventan Script: A History of South Italian Minuscule*, 2nd ed. by Virginia Brown, 2 vols. (Rome, 1980), 2:107.

MS 484.16   Italy, s. XII^{in}
Paul the Deacon, Homiliary   Pl. 148

f. 1r   [Inc: Heri celebrauimus temporalem sempiterni . . . mi]//serante saluetur. Nam et sancta scriptura dicit . . . Adiuti(??) gratia christi domini salu-atoris.//

          Paul the Deacon, Homily I.27 (St. Stephen Protomartyr, 26 December) = Fulgentius, Sermon 3; PL 65.731–2; J. Fraipont, ed., CCSL 91A (1968), 905–9. See Grégoire, 435.

f. 1r–v   *Item in natale eiusdem beati martiris stephani. omelia sancti maximi episcopi.* Lectio actuum apostolorum que nobis hodie lecta est . . . praesumimus accedere ad altare. Non timentes//

Paul the Deacon, Homily I.28 (St. Stephen Protomartyr) = Caesarius, *Sermo* 219; G. Morin, ed., CCSL 104 (1953), 867–69. See Grégoire, 435.

Parchment. 1 folio. 493 x 340 mm (written space 358 x 229 mm). 2 columns. 45 lines. Dry-point ruling on the hair side. Single vertical bounding lines; single upper and triple lower horizontal bounding lines. Prickings in upper, lower, and outer margins.

Written in Caroline minuscule. 7-line initial "L" is in red, the horizontal stroke decorated with two round balls; the initial is set apart from the text. 1-line initials are brown uncials and are not set apart from the text. The rubrics are written in red in the same script as the text, but in a larger module. Punctuation consists of the punctus.

The fragment was used as a wrapper to keep notarial documents. It bears the dates "1529 usque 1534" and a column listing the years 1524 through 1534. Other inscriptions read "Secundum prothocollum" and "Ser Vincentius Striuinat[. . .]."

Modern hands have written "39" and "Saec. XII ineunte" in pencil on the recto. Gift of the Yale University Library Associates; purchased from Kraus in 1948.

Bibliography:
Kraus, H. P., *List no. 109* (New York, [1947]), no. 35.

MS 484.17   Italy, s. XII^med
Paul the Deacon, Homiliary   Pl. 148

f. 1r   [Inc: Quod resurrectionem dominicam discipuli tarde crediderunt . . .] //intentionem mentis in uera lucę soliditate. Ecce ad cęlum . . . Non autem deserit desiderium nostrum ipse qui dedit, iesus christus dominus noster. qui uiuit et regnat cum patre in unitate spiritus sancti deus. per omnia saecula saeculorum amen.

Paul the Deacon, Homily II.28 (Ascension) = Gregory the Great, *Homiliae xl in evangelia*, Homily 29; PL 76.1219; R. Étaix, ed., CCSL 141 (1999), 254. See Grégoire, 458.

f. 1r–v   *Dominica post ascensionem domini. Lectio sancti evangelii secundum iohannem* In illo tempore. Dixit iesus discipulis suis. Cum autem uenerit paraclitus . . . a patre spiritum ueritatis. et reliqua.
Omelia uenerabilis bede presbiteri de eadem lectione
Ex multis sancti euangelii locis inuenimus quia discipuli ante aduentum sancti spiritus . . . illis hoc peccatum. Arbitra//[ntur]

Paul the Deacon, Homily II.29 (First Sunday after the Ascension) = Bede, Homily II.16; D. Hurst, ed., CCSL 122 (1955), 290–93. See Grégoire, 458.

Parchment. 1 folio. 503 x 386 mm (written space 435 x 242 mm). 2 columns. 48 lines. Dry-point ruling on hair side. Single vertical and double horizontal bounding lines; text-rulings extend into the inner margin. Prickings in outer and lower margins.

Written in late Caroline minuscule. On fol. 1r there is a fine 7-line decorated initial "E" in yellow filled with red geometric penwork on a ground of blue, green, and dark red, with four vine stems originating from the lower bar of the "E" (cf. K. Berg, *Studies in Tuscan Twelfth-Century Illumination* [Oslo, 1968], pls. 123–24 for initials of roughly similar design and pl. 135 for the general arrangement of the vine stem); it is not set apart from the text. A guide letter appears in the margin opposite the decorated initial. 1-line initials are black uncials and are not set apart from the text. The first line of the sermon is written in 2-line black uncials; the second line and the words "In illo tempore" are written in 1-line black uncials. The rubrics are written in red uncials. Punctuation consists of the punctus. Hyphenation and accents were added by a later hand.

The fragment was folded in half and used as a flyleaf (upper portion) and pastedown (lower portion) in a volume measuring ca. 386 x 253 mm. Scraps from a late twelfth- or early thirteenth-century manuscript that were also used in the binding are preserved glued onto this fragment. A modern hand has written the number "27" in pencil on fol. 1r. Gift of the Yale University Library Associates; purchased from Kraus in 1948.

Bibliography:
Kraus, H. P., *List no. 109* (New York, [1947]), no. 54.

MS 484.18   France or Switzerland, s. XII^2
Bible, Genesis   Pl. 149

f. 1   [Inc: Frater ambrosius tua mihi munuscula perferens . . . in]//terrogauit sacerdotes legem . . . Responditque. Quomodo possum.//

          Jerome, *Epistula ad Paulinum*; I. Hilberg, ed., CSEL 54 (1910), 447.17– 451.10; see Stegmüller 284.

f. 2r   //et interfecto aman qui interpretatur iniquitas . . . semper cogitat esse moriturum. Explicit epistola.

Epistula ad Paulinum; Hilberg, 461.12–465.9.

f. 2r–v   *Incipit prefacio sancti Ieronimi presbyteri in libro Genesis*
          Desiderii mei desideratas accepi . . . eos transferre sermonem. Explicit
          prefatio.

          Jerome, *Praefatio in Pentateuchum*; Stegmüller 285.

f. 2v   *Incipiunt Capitula*
          .i. De lucis exordio . . . et de morte ioseph. Expliciunt capitula.

          Capitula.

f. 2v   In principio creauit deus . . . lucem quod esset//

          Genesis 1.1–4.

Parchment. 2 folios (1 bifolium; probably one bifolium missing between fols. 1 and
2). 422 x 340 mm (written space 320 x 222 mm). 2 columns. Fol. 1 has 33 lines;
fol. 2 has 65 lines. Dry-point ruling. Double outer and single inner vertical bounding lines; additional ruling between columns. Single horizontal bounding lines.
Prickings in all margins.

     Written in two sizes of gothic bookhand (littera textualis). The preface on fol.
2r begins with a 10-line decorated initial "D" in red interlace on a green geometric
ground with a blue ground for the central portion of the vine stem. The text of
Genesis begins with a half-page decorated initial "I" in the same style. 1-line initials
in the prefatory materials are occasionally red and set apart from the text or are
black and set apart when they occur at the beginning of a line. The first letter of
each chapter heading is a red round "D" and is set apart from the text with roman
numerals in red. The first three lines of biblical text alternate between red capitals
filled with green and decorated with blue penwork and blue capitals decorated with
red penwork; there is also one green capital decorated with red penwork. Rubrics
are written in red in the same script as the text. Line fillers are in red. Punctuation
consists of the punctus, punctus elevatus, and punctus interrogativus. Hyphenation
is in the same ink as the text. Accents were added by a later hand. A fourteenth-
century cursive hand has written "lectio prima" next to the beginning of Genesis 1.1.

     The fragment was used as the outside wrapper for the binding of a volume
measuring ca. 350 x 240 mm. Traces of an inscription on the spine read "Sup[. . .]."
Modern hands have written "25" and "Saec. XII Germania meridiana [?] Suizzera"
in pencil on fol. 2r. Gift of the Yale University Library Associates; purchased from
Kraus in 1948.

Bibliography:
Kraus, H. P., *List no. 109* (New York, [1947]), no. 59.

MS 484.19   Italy, s. XII[1]
Bible, Sirach   Pl. 149

The text includes the headings for chapters LXXXII through LXXXVII, which correspond to *forma a* of *Series* A of the capitula (see *Biblia sacra iuxta latinam vulgatam versionem*, ed. H. Quentin et al., vol. 12: *Sapientia–Sirach* [Rome, 1964]). The variant reading "benefacit" in the heading for Chapter LXXXII is also found in Vatican, Bibliotheca Apostolica, Vat. Lat. 10511 (Italy, c. 1100).

f. 1   //ualidum. qua[m] census immensus . . . in omnia opera altissimi. Duo duo.//

Sirach 30.15–33.15.

Parchment. 1 folio. 424 x 317 mm (written space 390 x 245 mm). 2 columns. 46 of 47 lines remaining. Dry-point ruling on the hair side. Single vertical and horizontal bounding lines. Prickings in outer margin.

Written in a late Caroline minuscule. 3- to 7-line initials are red uncials and are set apart from the text. 1-line initials are black uncials and are set apart from the text when they occur at the beginning of a line. Chapter headings are written in red minuscule in a larger module. Punctuation consists of the punctus, punctus elevatus, punctus versus, and punctus interrogativus. Hyphenation was added by a later hand.

Modern hands have written "10" and "Saec. XII. Scriptura carolina. Italia" in pencil on fol. 1r. Gift of the Yale University Library Associates; purchased from Kraus in 1948.

Bibliography:
Kraus, H. P., *List no. 109* (New York, [1947]), no. 55.

MS 485.1   Italy, s. XVI; XIX/XX
Gradual   Pl. 150

f. 1   [*Off.* Aue maria . . .]//Uentris tui. Alleluia. [*Co.*] Ecce virgo concipiet . . . emanuel. Al//[leluia]

Fourth Sunday of Advent. The other side of the leaf cannot be read since it is pasted onto a board.

Parchment. 1 folio. 500 x 358 mm (written space 400 x 260 mm). 1 column. 5 lines. Ruled in lead.

Written in a formal gothic bookhand (littera textualis formata), with musical notation in black on a four-line staff in red. The parchment and writing appear to be from the sixteenth century, but the decoration was added in modern times. There is a 2-line initial "U" ("Uentris") in blue, green, and purple on a gold ground and containing the figure of an angel striking a tambourine. Foliage decorations in the same colors as the initial extend from the initial into the left margin; similar decorations are in the lower margin. 1-line initial "E" ("Ecce") is a red capital. Punctuation consists of the punctus.

The fragment is pasted down onto stiff cardboard measuring ca. 471 x 402 mm. Gift of E. P. Adair, 1960.

MS 485.2   Northern Italy, s. XV
Breviary   Pl. 150

f. 1   [A. Conuersus est furor tunc] //et consolatus es me. An. Laudate dominum de celis. Ps. Ipsum. Ca. Nox praecessit dies autem ... ambulemus. *hymnus.* Splendor paterne glorie. de luce lucem proferens ... Letus dies hic// [*catchword*: transeat]

Feria II throughout the year, lauds. The capitulum is from Romans 13.12–13. On the hymn see Schaller-Könsgen 15627.

Parchment. 1 folio. 565 x 377 mm (written space 405 x 265 mm). 1 column. 14 lines. Ruled in ink.

Written in a formal gothic bookhand (littera textualis formata). The 2-line initial "S" ("Splendor") at the beginning of the hymn is in olive-green, green, and red with white filigree and is filled with purple, blue, and red foliage decorated with white filigree. The initial is on a gold ground outlined in black and is surrounded by green, blue, and orange foliage that extends into the margin with gold balls. 1-line initials alternate blue and red. The first letter after the 2-line initial and after the 1-line initial "N" ("Nox") are 1-line black capitals filled with yellow. Rubrics are written in red in the same script as the text and are occasionally highlighted with yellow. Punctuation consists of the punctus, punctus elevatus, and punctus flexus. Hyphenation is in the same ink as the text. The catchword is in the center of the lower margin.

Gift of James T. Babb, 1957.

MS 485.3
Antiphonary

Spain, s. XVI
Pl. 150

f. 1   [A. Non diebus neque . . .] //colloquiis diuinis et oratione . . . Ca. Magnificat Seculorum. In i°. noct. Ana. Cecilia virgo almachium . . . Ps. Domine deo Seculorum. [A.] Expansis manibus orabat . . . Ps. Celi enarrant.//

St. Cecilia (22 November), matins.

Parchment. 1 folio (the folio number "[.]05" was added by a later hand in the upper right margin of the recto). 788 x 560 mm (written space 600 x 373 mm). 1 column. 6 lines. Vertical ruling in dry-point and horizontal ruling in lead. Prickings in upper, outer, and lower margins.

Written in a formal gothic bookhand (littera textualis formata), with musical notation in black on a five-line staff in red. On the recto there is a 2-line initial "C" ("Cecilia") in red and blue on a rectangular ground of red and blue penwork, not set apart from the text. The 2-line initial "E" ("Expansis") on the verso and the 1-line initials are black and are not set apart from the text. Rubrics are written in red in the same script as the text, but in a smaller module. Punctuation consists of the punctus. Hyphenation is in the same ink as the text.

Gift of Victor O. Freeburg, 1953.

MS 485.4
Gradual (or Missal)

Spain or Italy, s. XV
Pl. 150

f. 1   [Co.] //Signa eos qui . . . Co. Dico autem uobis amicis . . . persequuntur. In natale unius martiris officium.//

Common of Martyrs and rubric for the Common of a Martyr.

Parchment. 1 folio. 711 x 500 mm (written space 600 x 390 mm). 1 column. 5 lines. Ruled in lead.

Written in a formal gothic bookhand (littera textualis formata) with musical notation in brown on 4-line staves in red. 1-line initials alternate red with brown penwork and blue with red penwork. The 1-line initial at the beginning of the rubric is a blue capital with red penwork, and the rubric is written in red in a smaller version of the text script. Words and syllables are divided by red horizontal strokes. Punctuation consists of the punctus. The musical notation for "Dico autem uobis . . ." has been entirely changed by a later hand, which also rewrote several letters of the text.

The number "147" is written in ink in the outer margin of the recto, along with two other numbers that have been crossed out.

Gift of Dr. Morton J. Loeb, 1956. According to Dr. Loeb, the leaf is from a sixteenth-century Spanish manuscript "originally used by the Choristers of the Cathedral of Jaen in Southern Spain."

MS 485.5   Spain, s. XVI or later
Antiphonary   Pl. 150

f. 1   [*hymnus*. Summe deus clementie ... rum]//pimus, ditemur omnes affati, donis ... Pręsta pater piissime ... *Ana.* Quia mirabilia. *Tempore pasch. Ana.* Alleluia. *Ps.* Cantate domino canticum nouum: quia mirabilia ... Psallite domino in citha//[ra]

Saturday throughout the year, matins.

Parchment. 1 folio (foliated "48"). 635 x 425 mm (written space 477 x 297 mm). 1 column. 14 lines. The boundary lines were first ruled in lead and then rewritten with double lines in red ink; the minim lines are ruled in lead, and the rulings separating each text line are in red ink.

Written in a formal gothic bookhand (littera textualis formata). On the recto there is a 4-line initial "C" ("Cantate"), not set apart from the text, in red and blue on a ground outlined in purple and decorated with purple foliage on red crosshatching. 1-line initials at the beginning of the hymn and the psalm are red and are not set apart from the text. Other 1-line initials are black and are not set apart from the text. Rubrics are written in red in the same script as the text. Running titles ("Ad Matutinum" and "Sabbato") are written in red in the center of the upper margin; the folio number "48" is also written in red in the upper center of the recto. Punctuation consists of the punctus and the comma. Hyphenation is in the same ink as the text.

On the recto there are two unidentified numbers: "715" in pencil in the upper left corner and "175 Pt" in ink in the lower margin.

Gift of Dr. Morton J. Loeb, 1956.

MS 485.6   Italy, s. XIV
Gradual   Pl. 150

f. 1r   [*Off.* Deus] //deus meus ad te ... *Co.* Ego sum pastor bonus ... alleluya.

Second Sunday after Easter.

f. 1v   *Dominica iii̅ᵃ post pascha. Introitus.* Iubilate deo omnis terra ... *Ps.* Dicite
         deo quam terribilia ... in multi//[tudine]

Third Sunday after Easter.

Parchment. 1 folio (foliated "224"). 510 x 382 mm (written space 370 x 255 mm).
1 column. 6 lines. Ruled in ink with double vertical bounding lines.
    Written in gothic script (littera textualis). One 4-line initial "I" ("Iubilate"), the
body of which is divided into three columns of blue, blue-grey, and light brown,
each column decorated with a different pattern of white filigree. The crossbars of
the letter are orange, decorated with white filigree and tipped with green; the bottom crossbar extends down the left margin where it ends in blue-grey, green, and
orange. 1-line initials and the letters of "Iubilate" following the initial alternate red
with blue penwork and blue with red penwork. The first letter of the rubric is a blue
uncial with red penwork, and the rest of the rubric is written in red. Punctuation
consists of the punctus. Musical notation is in black on 4-line staves in red. The
folio number "224" is written in the upper right corner of the recto in ink by a later
hand.
    The notation "LB. 57443" is written in pencil in the upper left corner of the
recto.
    Gift of Dr. Morton J. Loeb, 1956.

Indices

*Numbers in the index entries refer to the manuscript
number rather than to the page number.*

Index I

Manuscripts by Places and Periods

Index II
Dated Manuscripts

Index III
General Index

Index IV
Illuminators and Scribes

Index V
Provenance

Index VI
Other Manuscripts Cited

Index VII

A: *Incipits of Non-Liturgical Texts*

Ecclesiam supra petræ soliditatem fundatam. Et turrem fortitudinis factam, 484.1

Egreditur de hiericho turbis eductis, 481.12

Epiphaniam id est apparitionem domini saluatoris, 481.8

Epistola domini nostri iesu christi descendens de cęlo super altari sancti petri, 481.94

Erat in ipsis locis et uir sanctus ac totius gratię dono repletus iohannes nomine, 482.77

Et cum adpropinquasset hierosolimam uenit bethfage, 484.14

Ex huius nobis lectionis uerbis frs kmi iohannis humilitas commendatur, 482.53

Ex multis sancti euangelii locis inuenimus quia discipuli ante aduentum sancti spiritus, 484.17

Excommunicatos a sacerdotibus, 482.44

Fateor sanctitate uestrae timueram ne frigus, 481.34

Filioli mei audite nos et liberate uos, 484.3

Frater ambrosius tua mihi munuscula perferens, 484.18

Fur di valluntsuch — scribe an ain zedel, 481.77

Gaudeamus, 484.2

Glorificatio domini nostri iesu christi resurgendo et ascendendo completa est, 482.52

Grauior culpa est .si qua per contumariam uel manifestam rebellionem, 482.91

Grauissima culpa est. incorrigibilitas illius que nec culpas timet, 482.91

Gregorius episcopus seruus seruorum dei de ipsis habendo fiduciam, 481.103

Gregorius hac urbe romana patre giordano, 481.15

Guillielmi besseti praesentibus anthonio oyselli et, 482.138

Heri celebrauimus temporalem sempiterni, 484.16

Hinc doctus prudentius dum taliter gesta, 484.15

Hortatur uos fratres sacra scriptura ad medi-

camenta animę uestrę per confessionem, 481.78

Ich Nicklas Mesnër an der pharr inn Ennebergs 482.144

Ich Nicklas und ich hanns des benennten Nicklasen eenickle, 482.143

Illuminatio domini nostri iesu christi saluatoris de celo facta est, 481.42, 481.43

In christi nomine amen anno domini, 482.141

In christi nomine amen anno a natiuitate, 482.139

In christi nomine amen anno natiuitatis, 482.42

In dei nomine amen. Ego Jacobus senegal. episcopus a domino senibaldo cardinale, 482.96

In Hebraeo non habet, 484.1

In hoc loco sancti euangelistae uaria narrauerunt, 484.14

In huius lectionis serie utriusque suae naturae ueritatem, 484.12

In insula quae nautae, 481.16

In omnibus psalmis mysticis exuberat sensus, 484.1

In quatuor euangelii uel potius quatuor libris, 481.10

Iohannes baptista et praecursor domini, 481.38; 482.74

Iudeorum terra sola iubilat deo, 484.1

Lautante [?] Reo et contumace existente, 481.79

Lectio actuum apostolorum que nobis hodie lecta est, 484.16

Lectio sancti evangelii quae modo in auribus vestris lecta est, 484.11

Lecturus hęc quę de trinitate disserimus. prius oportet, 481.20

Malum punicum, 481.96

Miracula domini et saluatoris nostri quandocunque leguntur, 484.12

Miserunt iudei ab iherosolimis, 482.53

Misit iesus duodecim discipulos suos, 484.9

Multa Graeci ueteres, 484.5

Multis ergo modis dilectissimi fratres dominus noster, 482.4

Index VII

B. Incipits of Liturgical Texts

The entries follow the orthography of the manuscripts, as reported in the description of each manuscript above. This means that there are sometimes multiple entries for the same incipit, listed under the different spellings. In using this index, the reader should be careful to consider all possible spellings for a word.

A dextris est mihi, 482.26
A solis ortu, 481.51 *ter*; 481.52
A solis ortus cardine, 481.119
A summo celo, 481.102
A summo cęlo, 481.24
Ab eis enim sanctorum martyrorum, 481.25
Ab inicio et ante secula creata sum, 481.135
Ab insurgentibus in me, 481.51
Ab occultis meis, 481.51
Ab oriente uenerunt, 481.52, 481.67
Abrahe dicte sunt, 482.110
Abscondi tamquam aurum, 482.26
Absolue domine animas, 483.21
Absolue quaesumus domine nostrorum uincula, 481.91, 481.108
Absterge deus, 481.49
Absterget deus omnem lacrimam, 481.25 *bis*, 481.95, 481.114
Accepta sit tibi domine sacrate, 481.109
Accepta tibi sit domine nostrae deuotionis, 481.92
Accepta tibi sit domine quaesumus, 481.109 *bis*, 482.59
Acceptabis sacrificium iusticie, 481.48
Acceptumque discipulum pantaleonem, 482.31
Accipe quaesumus domine munera, 481.109
Accipiens, 481.52
Accipiens symeon, 481.25, 481.52
Accipiens symeon puerum, 481.25, 481.52
Accipite iocunditatem glorie, 482.46
Actiones nostras quaesumus domine et aspirando, 481.91

Actiua enim uita, 482.41
Ad annuntiandum mane, 481.48 *bis*
Ad dominum cum tribularer, 481.31, 481.48, 481.51
Ad dominum uigiles, 481.51
Ad hanc uocem, 481.25
Ad hęc beata agnes, 481.25
Ad hoc tantum, 481.25 *quinquiens*
Ad laudes saluatoris, 482.129
Ad nutum domini, 481.51
Ad omnia quae mittam, 481.97
Ad te domine, 481.31 *bis*
Ad te domine clamabo, 481.51, 481.52, 481.129
Ad te domine leuaui, 481.18, 481.48 *quinquiens*, 482.26
Ad te leuaui, 481.48 *bis*, 481.51
Ad te nos domine clamantes, 481.92
Ad unius iussionis, 481.51, 482.118
Adducentes autem puerum, 481.25
Adducentur in leticia, 481.133
Adducentur regi uirgines, 481.133 *bis*
Adest beati pantaleonis, 482.31
Adest namque, 481.51
Adest namque beati Dyonisii, 482.107
Adesto deus unus, 482.14
Adesto domine supplicacionibus, 482.133
Adesto domine supplicationibus, 481.24, 481.120, 481.138, 482.19
Adesto nobis domine deus, 482.111
Adesto nobis domine martirum deprecatione, 482.102
Adesto quaesumus domine supplicacio-

Conserua me domine, 481.51, 482.26 *bis*
Conserva populum tuum deus, 481.92
Consolamini consolamini popule, 481.64
Consolemur nos ergo inuicem, 481.26
Constantes estote uidebitis, 481.51, 481.52
Constitues eos, 481.25, 481.51 *ter*, 482.78A
    bis, 482.130
Constitutus a deo, 481.52
Consurge consurge induere, 481.64, 482.87
Continet in gremio, 481.25, 481.52 *bis*
Continuo non acquieui, 482.78A
Contumelias, 481.41
Conuersus est furor, 485.2
Conuersus ezechiel ad, 481.51
Conuerte nos deus salutaris noster, 481.91
Conuertere domine, 481.25, 481.31 *bis*,
    481.51, 481.129, 483.17
Conuocatis iesus xi apostolis, 482.108
Converte nos deus salutaris noster, 481.108
Cooperante gratia spiritus, 482.78A
Corde et animo, 481.51 *ter*
Corona aurea, 481.136
Corpora sanctorum in pace, 481.95
Corpus et sanguis domini, 482.115
Cosmas et damianus anthimius, 482.107
Cottidie apud, 481.41
Crastina die delebitur, 481.52
Credidi, 481.25 *ter*, 481.51, 481.95, 482.14
Credimus sanctam trinitatem, 482.14
Credo in unum deum, 483.1
Crescit ut in nobis, 481.66
Crucem sanctam subiit, 481.51 *ter*
Crucifixus resurrexit, 481.51 *bis*
Crucifixus surrexit a mortuis, 481.51
Crucis, 481.52
Crux benedicta nitet, 481.25, 481.51
Crux est murus obsessorum, 481.115
Cuius prostibulum, 481.23, 481.66
Cuius pulchritudinem sol, 481.25 *bis*,
    481.49 *bis*, 481.52
Cuius pulcritudinem sol, 481.52
Cum ab scolis reuertitur, 481.25
Cum ad horam, 481.25
Cum appollo esset Corinthi, 481.134
Cum artifices de paruitate, 481.25
Cum audieritis, 482.108, 482.133
Cum autem complacui, 481.49
Cum autem descendisset, 481.18 *bis*, 482.26

Cum autem placuit, 482.78A
Cum autem uenerit, 481.51
Cum campidonam sanctus uenisset, 481.23
Cum diuersis signis et miraculis diuinitatis,
    481.25
Cum dominus ad, 481.51
Cum egrederetur iesus, 482.108
Cum enim eundem, 481.25
Cum ergo natus esset iesus, 481.25
Cum esset iesus annorum duodecim, 481.67
Cum factus esset, 481.52
Cum factus esset iesus annorum duodecim
    481.25, 482.19
Cum immundus spiritus, 482.28
Cum inuocarem, 481.23, 481.25 *quater*,
    481.48, 481.49, 481.51, 481.52,
    481.114, 482.32
Cum invocarem, 481.64
Cum iocunditate exibitis, 482.48
Cum iocunditate natiuitatem, 481.51 *bis*
Cum praeclara sanctissimi uiri columbani
    qui et columba, 481.25
Cum primates militarium gentium, 481.97
Cum proficiscendi tempus, 481.25
Cum psalmis deo, 481.23, 481.66
Cum scirem ego, 481.66
Cum sub diocletiano tiranno, 481.23,
    481.66
Cum transacto infantię, 481.23
Cum turba plurima, 481.19, 481.132
Cum turbe irruerent, 481.121
Cum uenerit filius, 481.51
Cum uenisset beatus andreas, 482.118
Cum uenisset paulus romam, 481.97
Cum uero peruenisset, 481.51
Cum uideris nudum, 481.25
Cum uidisset beatus, 481.51
Cumque abisset ruben, 481.51
Cumque bone indolis uir, 481.25 *bis*
Cumque carnifices ducerent, 481.51
Cumque complesset apostolus, 481.25
Cumque intuerentur in celum, 481.48
Cumque obduxero nubibus, 481.51
Cumque sanctus sixtus, 482.32
Cumque uenatu aliquid, 481.51, 482.28
Cumque uidissent ioseph, 481.51
Cunctis diebus uitae, 481.51
Cura ergo ut inchoauimus, 481.25

Metuentes deum sustinete misericordiam, 482.133
Michi autem nimis, 482.130, 483.5
Minor sum cunctis, 481.25
Mirabantur autem de eo, 481.25
Mirabile misterium de, 481.18
Mirabilia testimonia, 481.51
Mirabilis, 481.25, 481.49
Mirabilis deus, 481.37, 481.48, 481.95, 482.46
Mirabilius namque est cælum, 481.26
Mirifica misericordias tuas, 482.26
Miserere, 481.51 *bis*, 481.52, 482.128, 483.17 *bis*
Miserere mei, 481.19, 481.51
Miserere mei deus, 481.48 *bis*, 481.51, 482.137
Miserere mei deus miserere, 481.51 *bis*
Miserere mei deus qui, 481.51
Miserere mei domine, 482.111
Miserere mei fili, 481.51
Miserere mei secundum eloquium, 481.48
Miserere michi domine, 482.131
Miserere quaesumus domine famulis, 481.138
Misereris omnium domine, 481.48, 482.137
Misericordia domini, 481.25, 481.48
Misericordia tua subsequatur, 481.18
Misericordias, 481.18
Misericordias domini in eternum, 481.101
Misericordias tuas domine, 482.46
Misericors et miserator domine, 481.92
Miserunt iudei ab ierosolimis, 482.87, 482.92
Misit de celo, 481.48
Misit deus manum, 481.97
Misit dominus angelum, 481.66
Misit dominus uerbum, 482.19
Missus est gabriel, 481.25 *bis*, 481.51 *bis*, 481.52 *ter*, 481.68
Missus sum, 481.25
Missus sum ad oues, 481.25
Modicum et non, 481.48, 481.51
Modo ueniet dominator, 481.51, 483.17
Mortem enim, 481.52
Mox ut cecus, 482.31
Mox ut uocem, 481.51, 482.118 *bis*
Moyses et Aaron, 481.51

Mulier cum parit, 481.51
Mulier quedam clamabat, 482.131
Mulierem fortem quis, 481.37, 482.136
Multe tribulationes, 482.46
Multi enim sunt, 481.19, 481.26
Multi ueniunt ab oriente, 482.26
Multiplica quaesumus domine per haec diuina mysteria, 481.92
Multitudo languentium, 481.25, 481.101
Multotiens enim desiderabat, 481.25
Mundi cordis amatorem, 481.23, 481.66
Mundus autem gaudebit, 481.97
Munera domine oblata sanctifica, 481.91, 481.108
Munera domine sacrificii praesentis, 482.130
Munera domine tibi dicata, 481.92
Munera nostra domine aput clementiam, 481.109
Munera nostra domine sacrificii praesentis que tibi offerimus, 481.31
Munera nostra quaesumus domine natiuitatis, 481.109
Munera plebis tuae quaesumus domine, 481.92
Munera quaesumus domine oblata sanctifica, 481.134
Munera tibi domine dicata sanctifica, 482.133
Munera tibi domine nostre deuocionis, 482.102, 482.133
Munera tua nos deus a delectationibus, 481.92
Munera tuę misericors deus, 482.70
Muneribus nostris apostolorum, 482.102
Muneribus nostris quaesumus domine, 481.92 *bis*, 481.108, 482.133
Munus populi tui domine, 482.102
Munus quod tibi domine, 482.131
Mysteria nos domine sancta purificent, 481.92
Mysteria nos tua domine, 481.121
N. dilectus, 482.129
Nam cum sanctę mulieris, 481.24
Nam et ego, 481.51
Nam ipsius ad uocem, 481.23
Nam uirtus in infirmitate, 482.78A
Nascetur nobis paruulus, 481.25, 481.51

Plates

Plates

PLATE 1

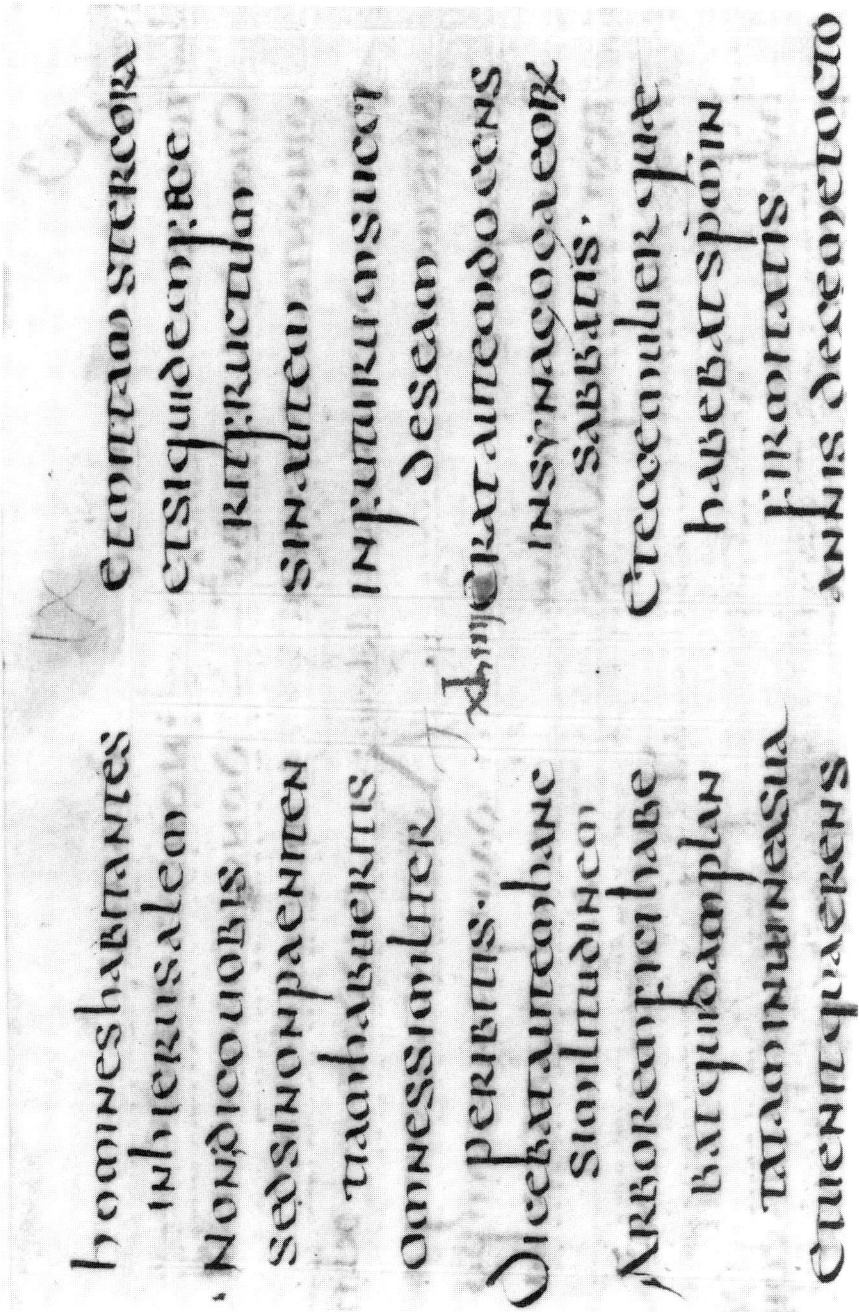

HOMINESHABITANTES
INHIERUSALEM
NONDICOUOBIS
SEDSINONPAENITEN
TIAMHABUERITIS
OMNESSIMILITER
PERIBITIS DICEBATAUTEMHANC
SIMILITUDINEM
ARBOREAPICIHABE
BATQUIDAMPLAN
TATAMINUINEASUA
ETUENITQUAERENS

ETOITAO STERCORA
ETSIQUIDEOMFECE
RITFRUCTUM
SINAUTEM
INFUTURUMSUCCI
DESEAM ERATAUTEADOCENS
INSYNAGOGAEORK
SABBATIS
ETECCEMULIERQUAE
HABEBATSPMIN
FIRMITATIS
ANNISDECEOETOCTO

MS 481.1, f. 1v, Italy, s. VIIᵉˣ

PLATE 2

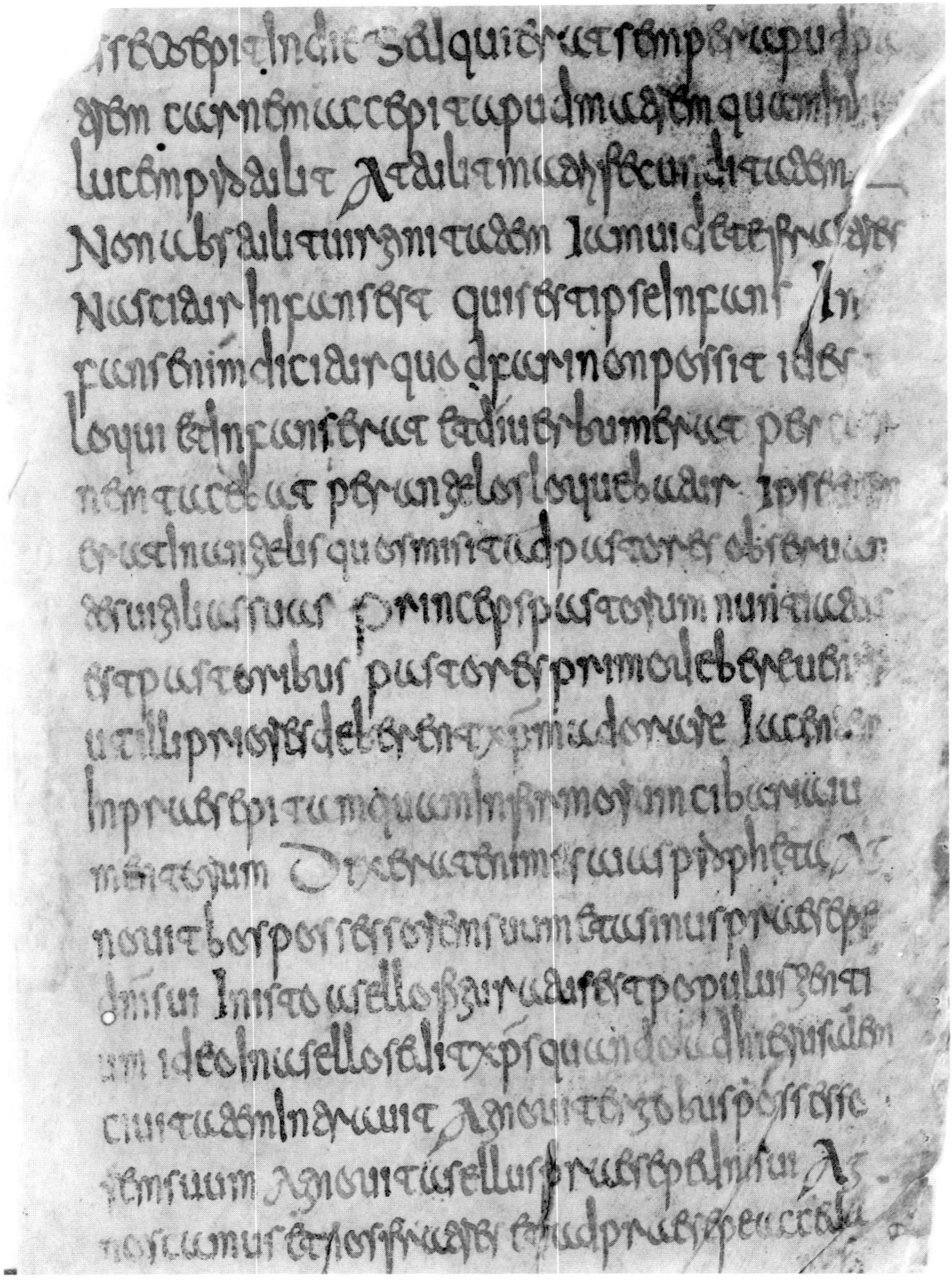

...recepit Indie scd̄ qui erat tempus et apud dm̄
erem carnem accepit apud dm̄ autem quantum
lucem prestabit. A talia mea secundum dm̄
Non umbra... tunc in tenebris lumen de tenebris
Nascitur infans est qui erat ipse infans. Infans enim dicitur quod loqui non possit. Ideo
loqui et infans erat et diu verbum erat per quod
non tacebat per angelos loquebatur. Ipse erat
erat in angelis qui... ad pastores observa...
...princeps pastorum nuntiatur
et pastoribus pastores primo leberent uehi
ut illi priores deberent xpm adorare lucem...
In praesepi tum quam infirmos in cibum...
ministerium. Dies erat enim... prophetia...
novit bos possessorem suum et asinus praesepe
dn̄i sui. In isto... populus...
um ideo in isto... xps quia dd̄... ad...
ciuitatem Ingrauit. Agnouit ergo bos possesse
... Agnouit uitellus praesepe dn̄i sui
noscamur et... et ad praesepe ...

PLATE 3

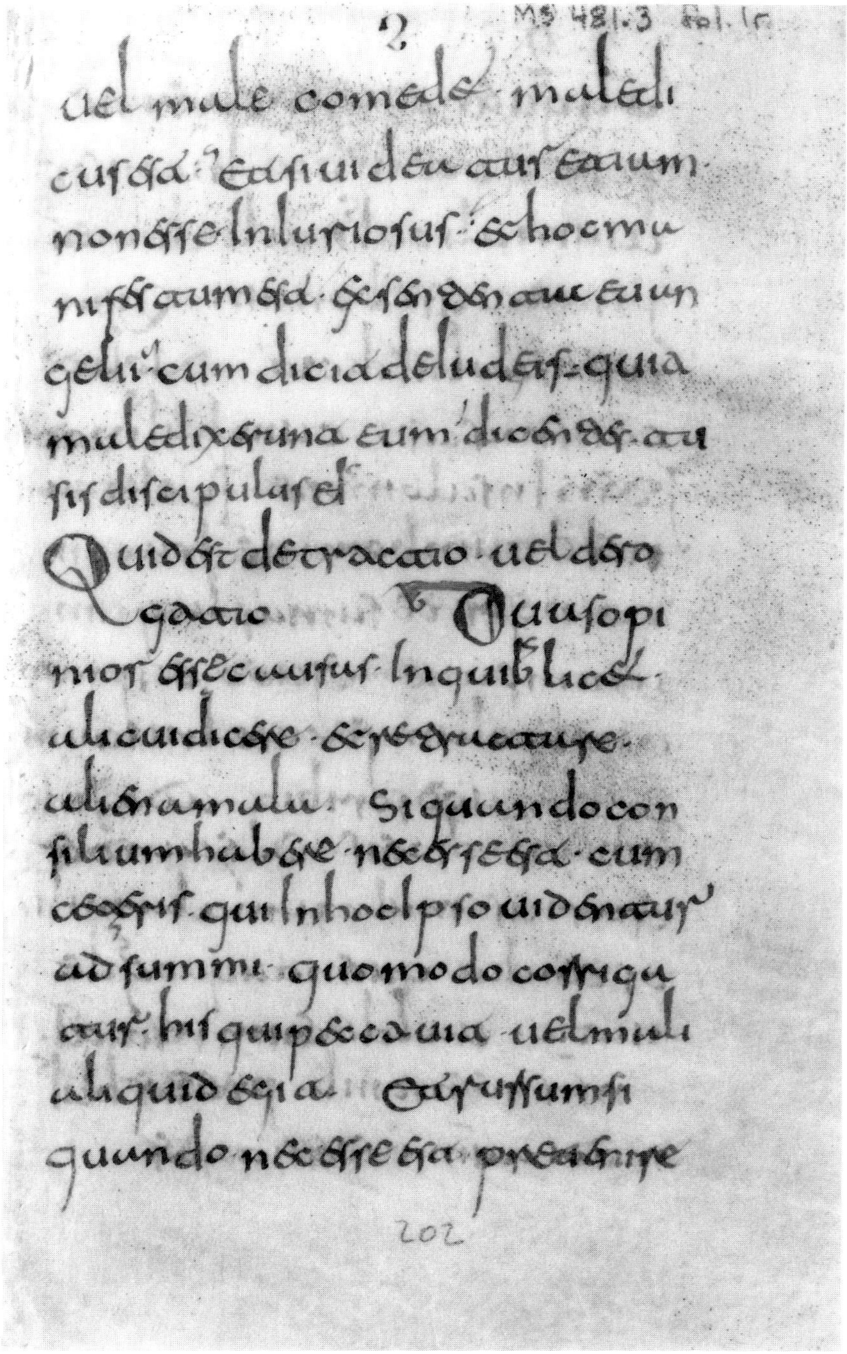

uel male comedo maledi

cussd̄ eas ui deū aut eaum

non esse Inluriosus et hoc mu

nis aum sed ꝗs̄ deū aut eaun

gelui cum dicia deludas quia

maledixerina eum dicsi deū au

sis discipulas et

Quid est detractio uel dero

gacio Quusopi

mor etetuusus Inquib lice

ulicui dicere et reguucaupe

ulidnamalui Siquando con

silium habere nec essa cum

cogris qui In hoc lpso uidniauy

adsummi quomodo corrigu

aur his quipseca uia uelmuli

aliquid egia exiussumsi

quando nec essa ea proauure

MS 481.3, f. 1r, Northeastern Spain, s. IX/X

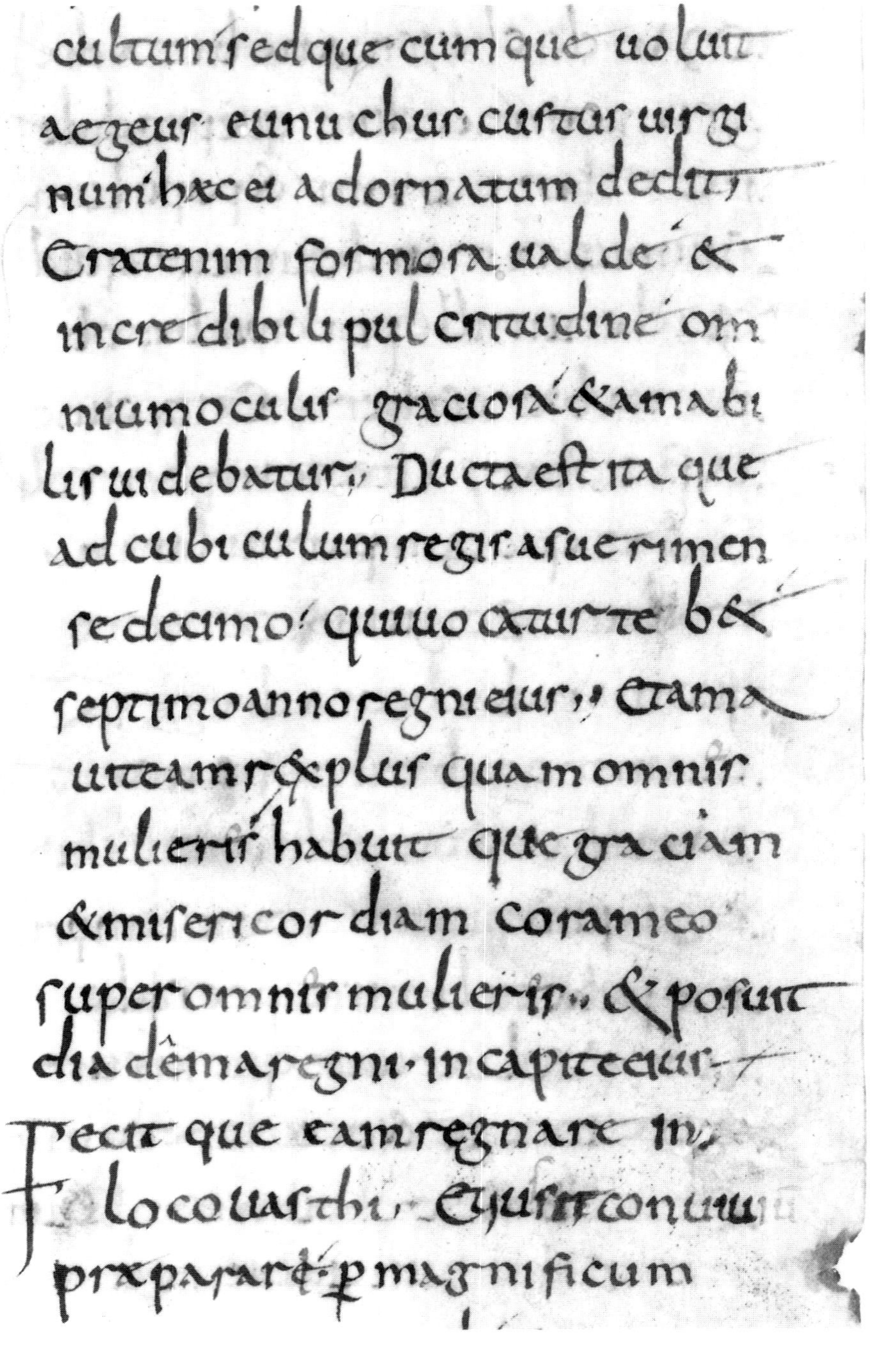

PLATE 4

cultum sed quecumque uoluit
acciperet eunuchus custos uirgi
num hec ei adornatum dedit.
Erat enim formosa ualde &
incredibili pulcritudine om
nium oculis graciosa & amabi
lis uidebatur. Ducta est itaque
ad cubiculum regis assueri men
se decimo quiuocatur tebeth
septimo anno regni eius. Et ama
uit eam rex plus quam omnis
mulieris habuit que graciam
& misericordiam coram eo
super omnis mulieris. & posuit
diadema regni in capite eius.
fecit que eam regnare in
loco uasthi. Eiusque conuiuium
preparari p magnificum

MS 481.4, f. 1r, Northeastern France (Rheims?), s. IX[in]

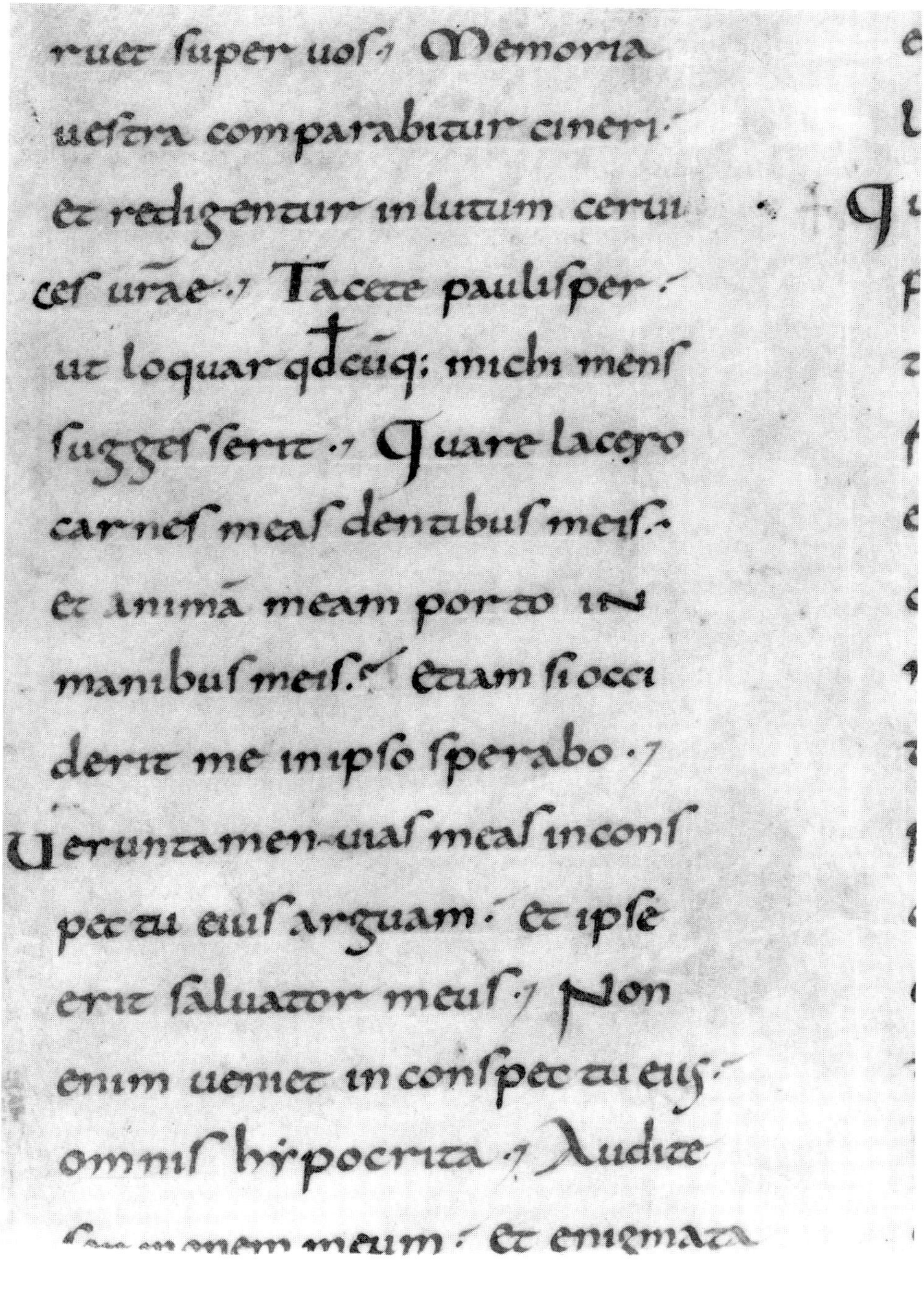

PLATE 5

ruet super uos; Memoria
uestra comparabitur cineri·
et redigentur in lutum ceruí
ces urae·; Tacete paulisper·
ut loquar qdcuq; michi mens
suggesserit·; Quare lacero
carnes meas dentibus meis·;
et animam meam porto in
manibus meis·; etiam si occi
derit me inipso sperabo·;
Ueruntamen uias meas inconsp
pectu eius arguam· et ipse
erit saluator meus·; Non
enim ueniet in conspectu eius·
omnis hypocrita·; Audite
sermonem meum· et enigmata

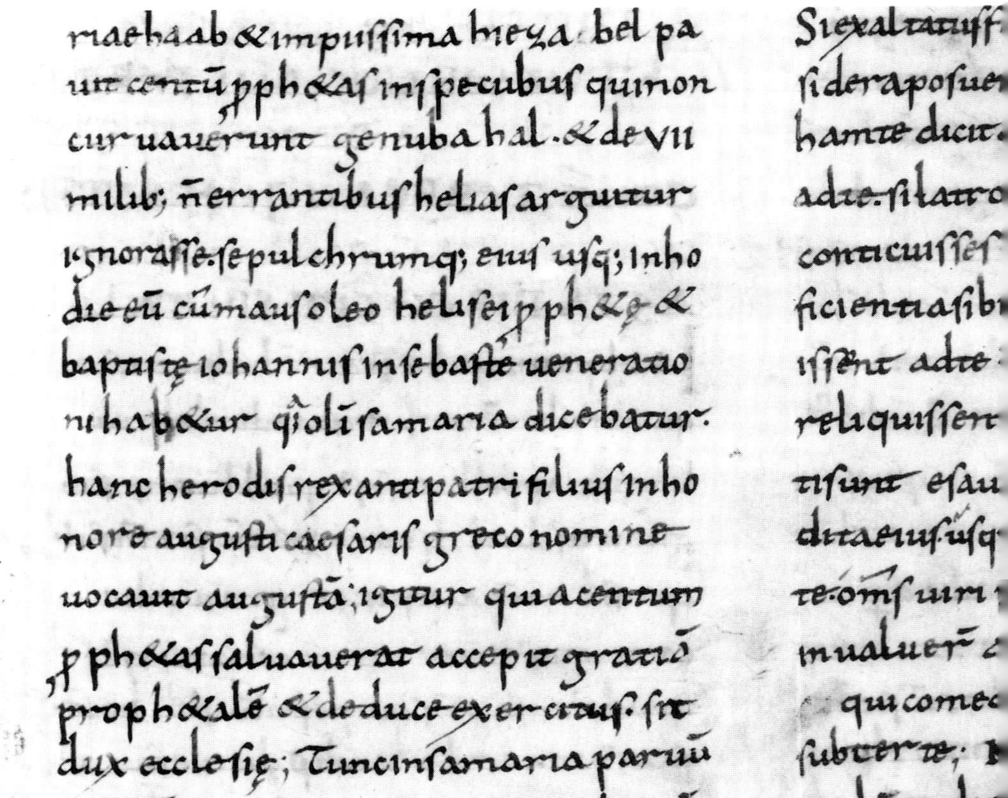

PLATE 6

riaebaab & impuissima ieza bel pa
uit centu pph & as in specubus quinon
curuauerunt genuba hal . & de vii
milib; n errantibus helias arguitur
ignorasse sepulchrumq; eius usq; inho
die eu cu mauso leo heliseip ph & &
baptiste iohannis in sebaste ueneracio
ni habetur qi oli samaria dicebatur.
hanc herodis rex antipatri filius inho
nore augusti caesaris greco nomine
uocauit augusta igitur qui acentum
p ph & as saluauerat accepit gratio
proph & ale & de duce exercituus: sit
dux ecclesie; Tunc insamaria paruu
gregem pauerat Nunc in toto orbe xpi
pascit ecclesias & sicut stephanus co
rona meruit passionis sic hic seruitu
te dicu paulo apostolo nomine gloriat
quia abdias seruus dm in nro sonat
eloquio INCIPIT ABDIAS PRO
PHETA

VISIO ABDIE; HAEC DICIT
DNI DS AD E DOM; AUDITU
AUDIUIMUS ...

Si exaltatus f
sidera posue
ham te dicit
adte. si latro
conticuisses
ficientia sibi
issent adte
reliquissen
tis unt esau
dita eius usq
te oms uiri
mualuer
qu comec
subter te,
qud n indie
sapientes d
de monte es
iu meridie
te esau; Pr
xppter inu
Opere & te c
indie cus a
ebant alien
in grediebā

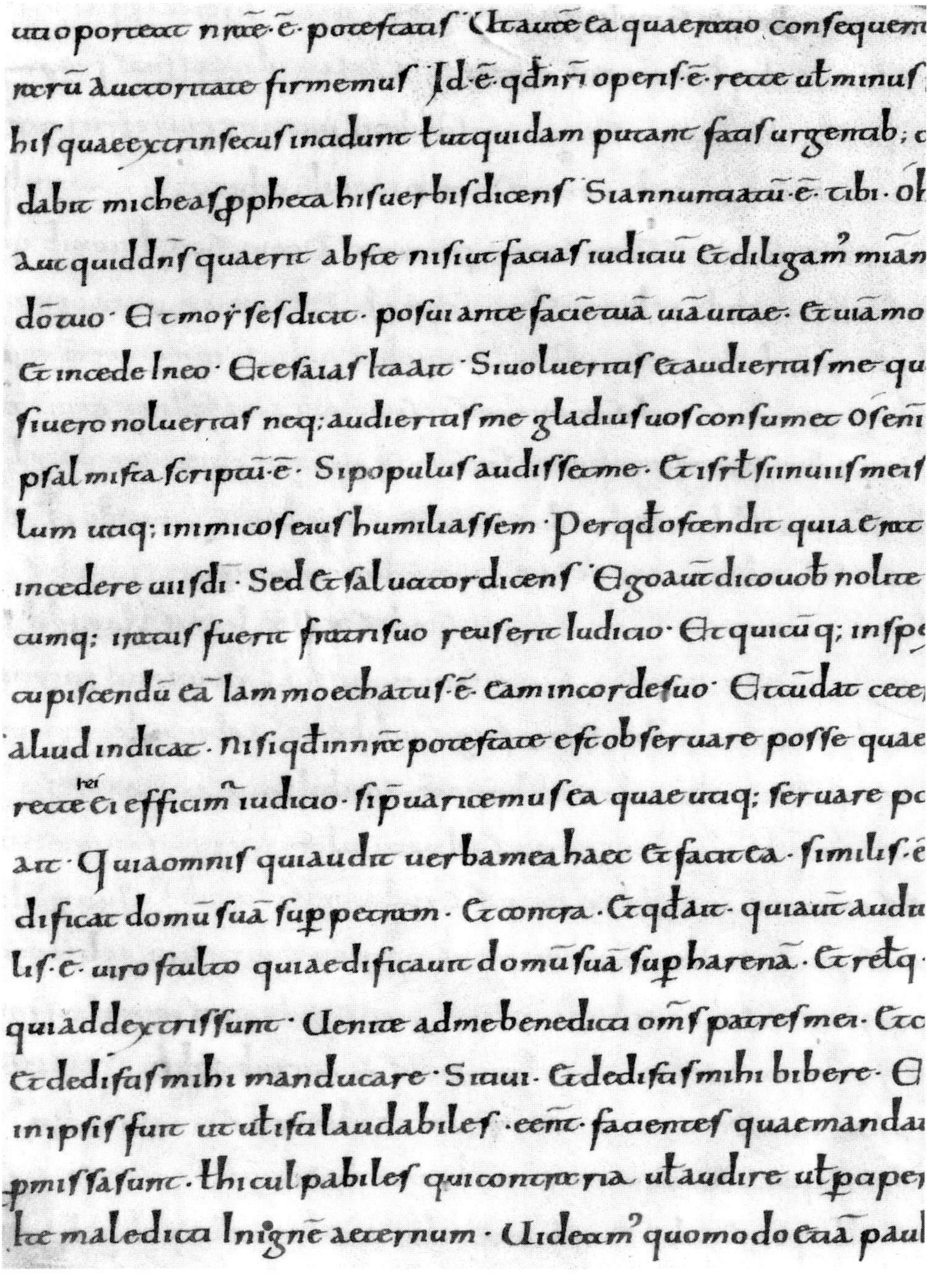

PLATE 7

...io oporteat n̄re e potestatis Ct autē ea quae ratio consequentī

rerū auctoritate firmemus Id ē qd n̄ri operis e recte ut minus

his quae extrinsecus inadunt tutquidam putant satas urgentab; c

dabit micheas ppheta his uerbis dicens Si annunciatū e tibi oh

Aut quid dn̄s quaerit abs te nisi ut facias iudiciū Et diligam miā

dō tuo Et tmo r ses dicit posui ante faciē tuā uiā uitae Et uiā mo

Et incede Ineo Et esaias teadit Si uolueritas Et audieritas me qu

si uero nolueritas neq; audieritas me gladius uos consumet O seī

psal mista scriptū e Si populus audisse me Et isrt si in uiis meis

lum utaq; inimicos eius humiliassem Per qd ostendit quia e rtc

incedere uiis di Sed Et sal uator dicens Ego autē dico uob nolite

cumq; iratus fuerit fratri suo reus erit iudicio Et quicū q; in sp

cupiscendū eā Iam moechatus e eam in corde suo Et tudat cete

aliud indicat nisi qd in n̄c potestate e observare posse quae

recte Et efficiā m iudicio si puaricemus ea quae utaq; seruare p

att Quia omnis qui audit uerba mea haec Et facit ea similis e

dificat domū suā suppetram Et contra Et qd ait quia aut audi

lis e uiro fatto quia edificauit domū suā sup harenā Et retq

quia ad dexteris sunt Uenite ad me benedicti oms patres mei Et c

Et dedi fas mihi manducare S tiui Et dedi fas mihi bibere El

in ipsis fuit ut utifa laudabiles ecnt facientes quae manda

pmissa sunt thi culpabiles qui contraria ut audire ut paper

te maledicta In igne aeternum Uideam quomodo etā paul

MS 481.7, f. 1v, Fulda, Germany, s. IX²/³

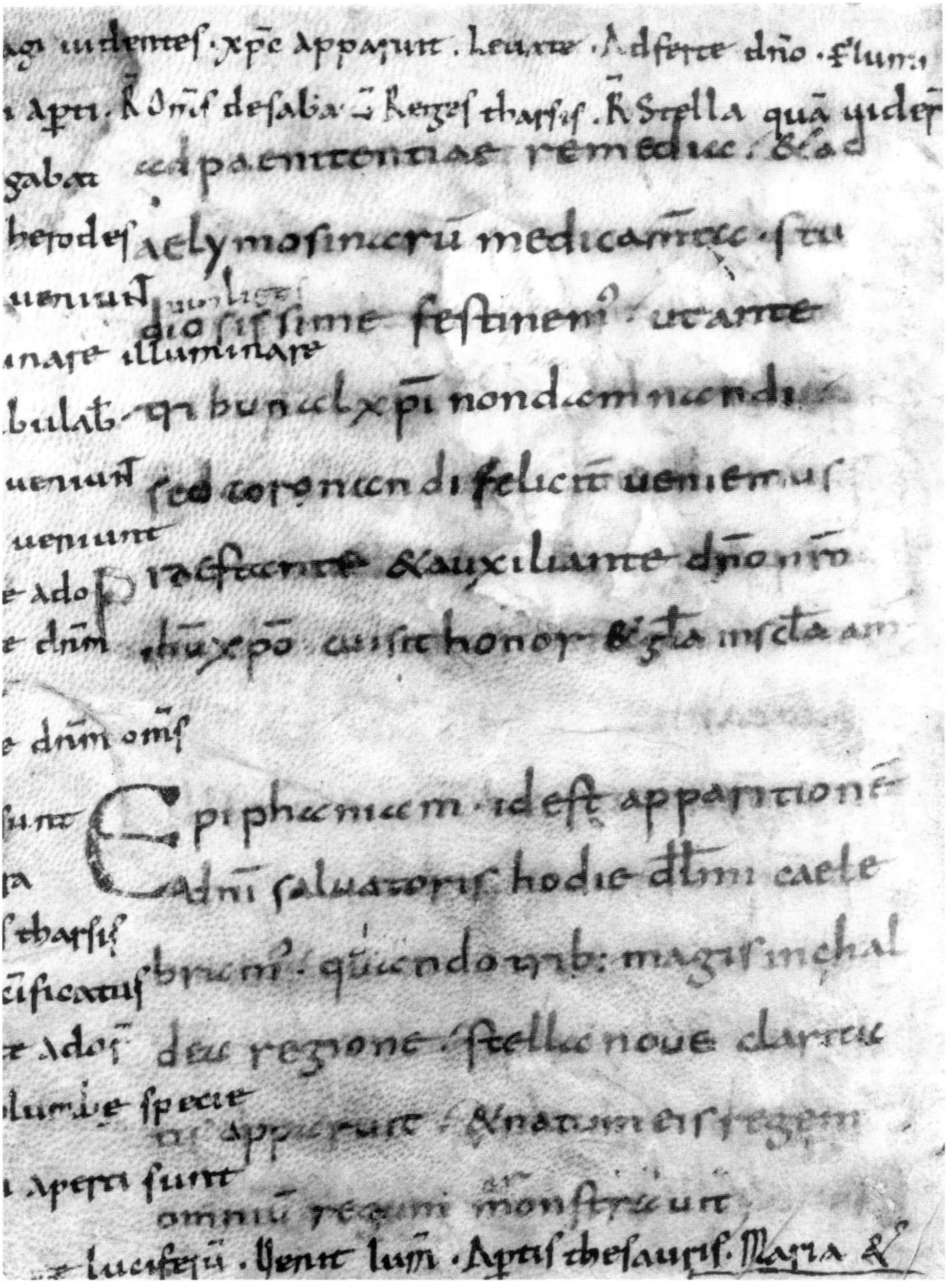

PLATE 8

MS 481.8, f. 1v, Southeastern Germany, s. IX$^{1/3}$

PLATE 9

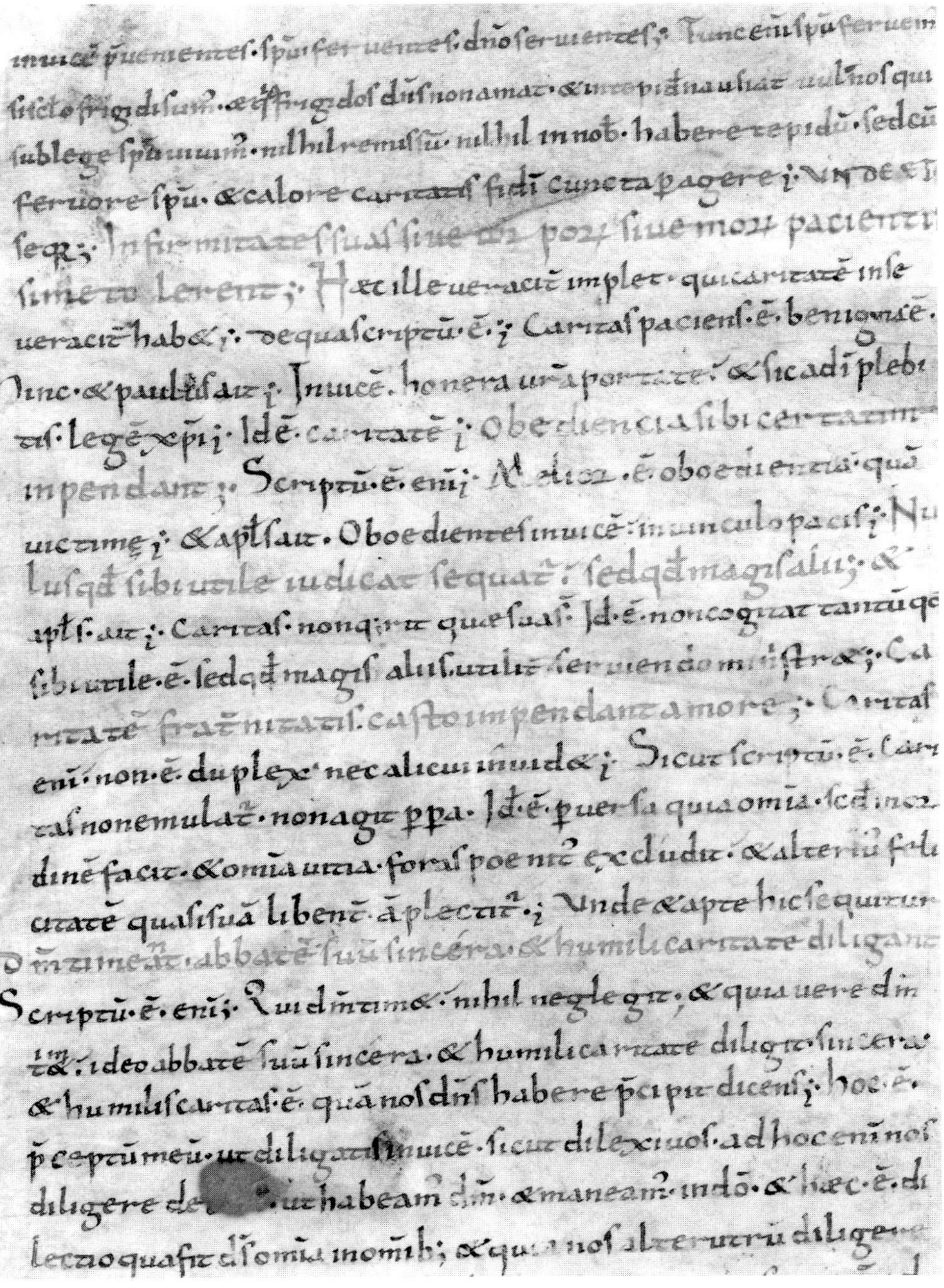

inuicē puenientes spu feruentes dño seruentes; Tunc ē spū seruen
siteo frigduam. & si frigidos dūs nonamat & nec pigna uult nec uult nos qui
sublege spū uiuam. nihil remissū. nihil in nob· habere tepidū· sed cū
feruore spū· & calore caritatis sidi cuncta pagere ; Vn dē s
seqr; In firmitates suas siue aī por siue mou pacientr
sine tedere lerent ; Hec ille ueracit implet· qui caritatē in se
ueracit habet ; de qua scriptū ē ; Caritas paciens ē· benigna ē·
Hinc· & paulus ait ; Inuicē honera uestra portate· & sic adi plebi
tis legē xpi; Idē caritate ; Obœdiencia sibi certatim
impendant ; Scriptū ē enī; Melior ē oboediencia quā
uictime ; & apts ait· Oboedientes inuicē in uinculo pacis; Nu
lus qd sibi utile iudicat sequat· sed qd magis aliu; &
apts ait ; Caritas non qrit que sua; Idē non cogitat tantū qe
sibi utile ē· sed qd magis aliis utile seruiendo ministre; Ca
ritatē fraternitatis casto impendant amore ; Caritas
enī non ē duplex nec alicui inuide ; Sicut scriptū ē· Cari
tas non emulat· non agit ppa· Idē puersa quia omia se inor
dine facat· & omia uetera foras poente excludit· & alter iū feli
citate qualis sua libent āplectat·; Vnde & apte hic sequitur
Dī timeat· abbatē suū sincera· & humili caritate diligant
Scriptū ē enī; Qui dī timet· nihil neglegit ; & quia uere dm̄
tit· ideo abbatē suū sincera· & humili caritate diligit sincera·
& humili caritatis ē quam nos dūs habere pcepit dicens; hoc ē·
pceptū meū· ut diligatis inuicē· sicut dilexi uos· ad hoc enī nos
diligere det· ut habeam dm̄· & maneam in dō· & hec ē di
lectio qua sit dī omia in omib; & quia nos alterutru diligere

MS 481.9, f. 1r, Southern France, s. IX^ex

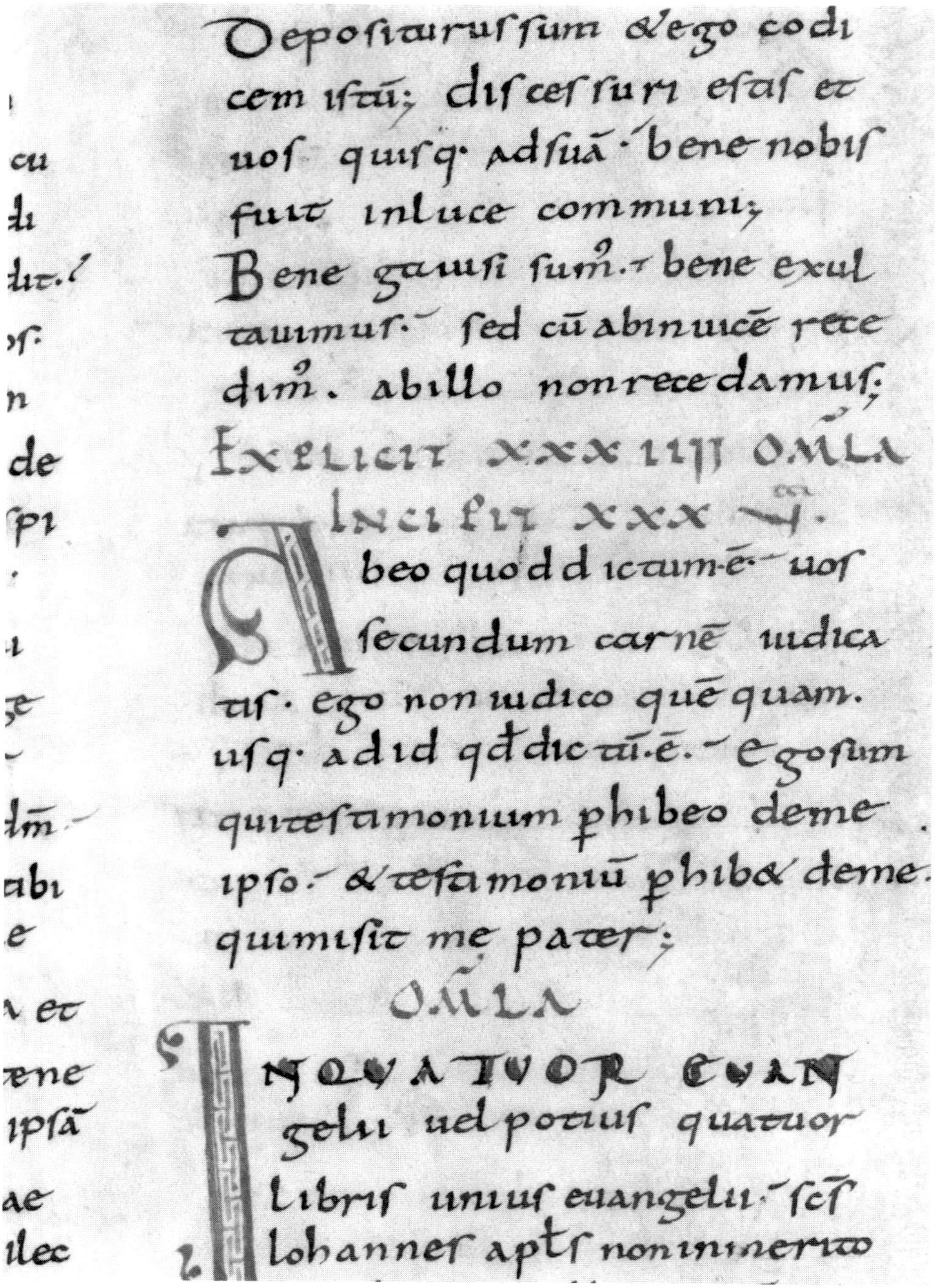

PLATE 10

Depositaturus sum & ego codi
cem istu; discessuri estis et
uos quisq; ad sua · bene nobis
fuit in luce communi;
Bene gauisi sum · & bene exul
tauimus · sed cu abinuice rece
dim . abillo non rece damus;
EXPLICIT XXX IIII OMLA
INCIPIT XXX V .
beo quod dictum e uos
secundum carne iudica
tis · ego non iudico que quam .
usq; ad id qd dictu e . ego sum
qui testimonium phibeo de me
ipso · & testimoniu phib& de me .
qui misit me pater;
OMLA
NOUATUOR EUAN
gelii uel potius quatuor
libris unius euangelii · sct
Iohannes apts non inmerito

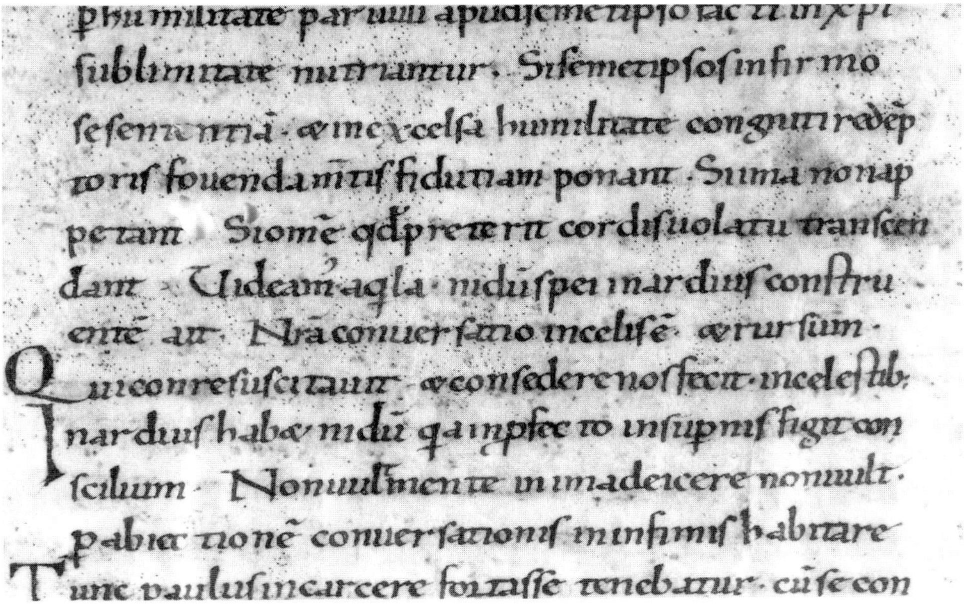

PLATE 11

p humilitate paruuli apud semetipso fac ti in xpi
sublimitate nutriantur. Si semetipsos infirmo
se sementia ce me excelsa humilitate congnit redep
toris fouenda mitis fiditiam ponant. Suma non ap
petant. Si ome q(ui)d p(ro)tte rit cordis suol atu transcen
dant. Uideam ag la nidus pei nardius constru
ente aut. N(ost)ra conuersatio incelis e ce rur sum.
Qui con resuscitauit ce consedere nos fecit in celestib;
In ardius habe nidu qa ipse to insup mis figit con
scilium. Nonuull mente in ima descere nonuult
p abitc tio ne conuersationis in infimis habitare
Tunc paulus in carcere fortasse tenebatur. cu se con

MS 481.11, f. 3r, Italy, s. XI[1]

ascha non sicut qui dam
estimant grecum nomen est
sed hebreum; Oportunissime
tamen occurrit in hoc nomine quedam
con gruentia utrariq(ue) linguarum
Qui eni(m) patitur pascha grece dicitur.
Ideo pascha passio putatae ut hoc no
men a passione sic appellatu(m) est. In sua

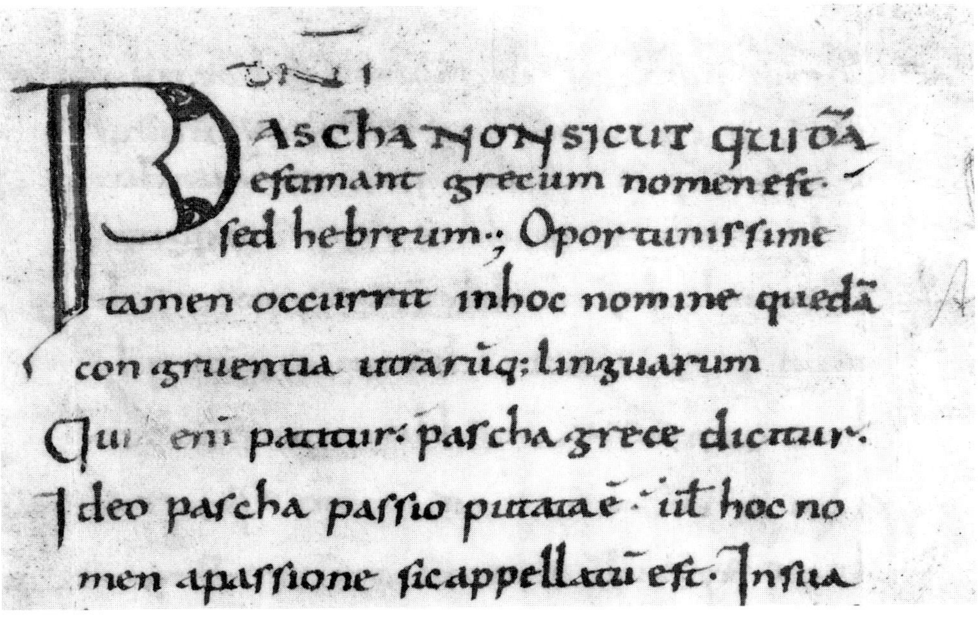

MS 481.12, f. 2r, Italy, s. X[1]

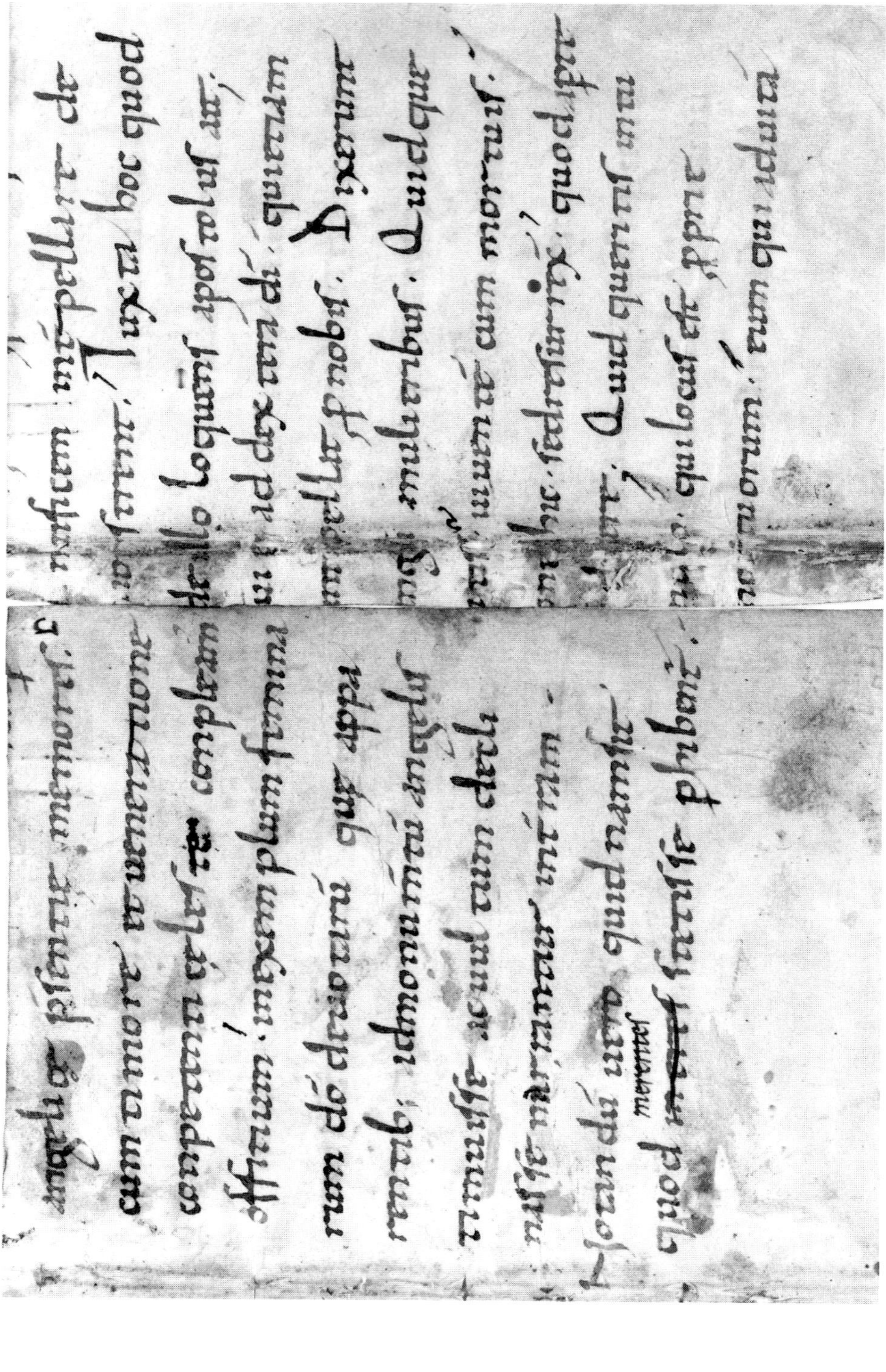

PLATE 12

MS 481.13, f. 1r,
Austria or Northern Italy, s. X²

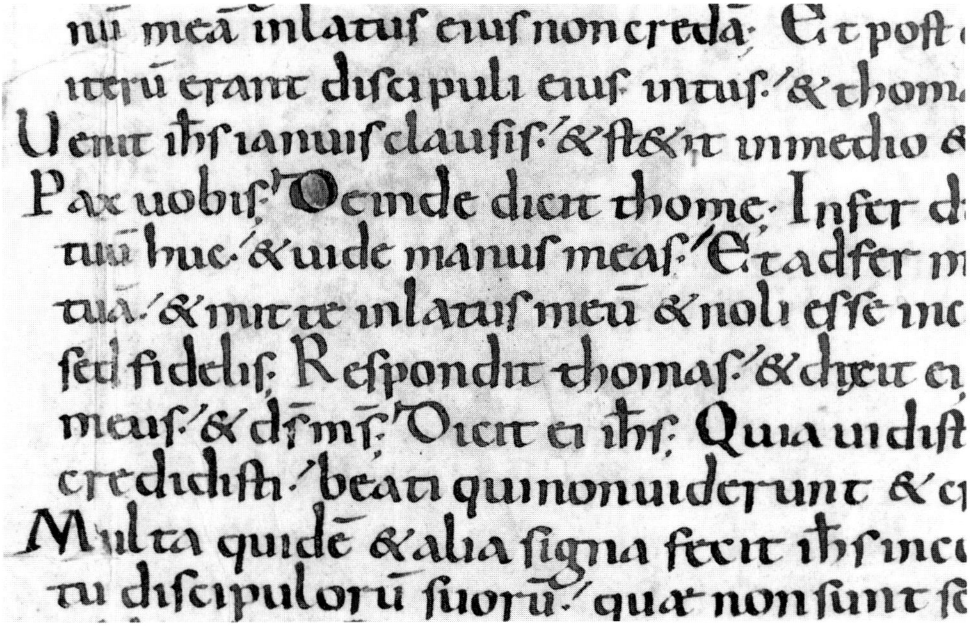

PLATE 13

nͥ mea inlatuſ eiuſ non credã. Et poſt
iterũ erant diſcipuli eiuſ intuſ. & thoma
Uenit ihſ ianuiſ clauſiſ. & ſt& in medio &
Pax uobiſ. Deinde dicit thome. Infer d
tuū huc. & uide manuſ meaſ. Et adfer m
tuã. & mitte in latuſ meū & noli eſſe inc
ſed fideliſ. Reſpondit thomaſ. & dixit ei
meuſ. & dſ mſ. Dicit ei ihſ. Quia uidiſt
credidiſti. beati qui non uiderunt & q
Multa quide & alia ſigna fecit ihſ in co
tu diſcipuloꝛū ſuoꝛū. quae non ſunt ſc

MS 481.14, f. 2r, Southern Germany, s. X[med]

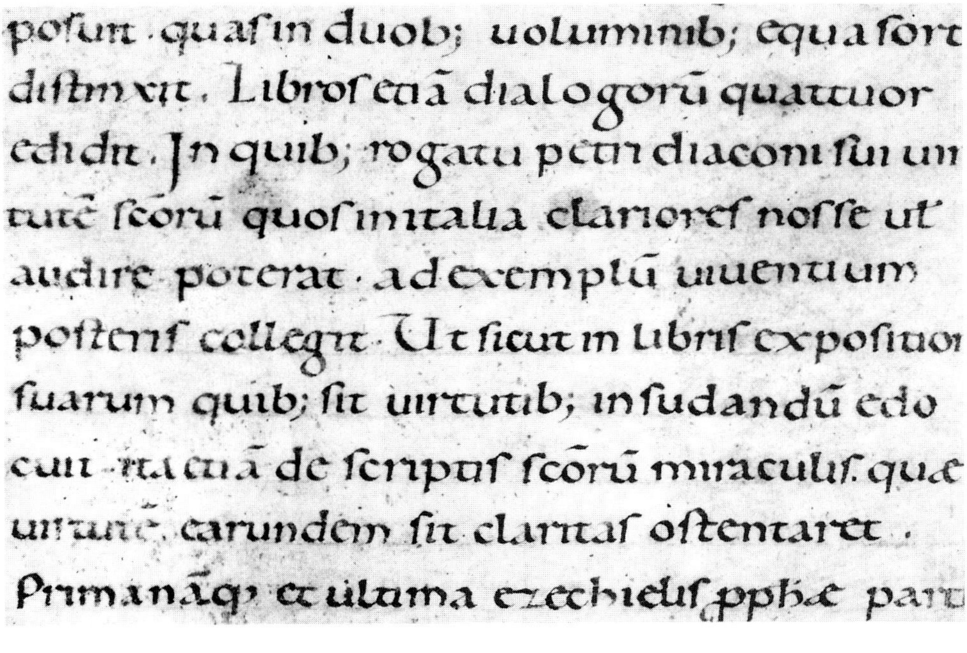

poſui. quaſ in duob; uoluminib; equa ſort
diſtinxit. Libroſ etiã dialogoꝛū quattuor
edidit. In quib; rogatu petri diaconi ſui uir
tute ſcoꝛū quoſ in italia clarioreſ noſſe ut'
audire poterat. ad exemplũ uiuentium
poſteriſ collegit. Ut ſicut in libriſ expoſitior
ſuarum quib; ſit uirtutib; in ſudandũ edo
cuit. ita etiã de ſcriptiſ ſcoꝛū miraculiſ. quae
uirtute. earundem ſit claritaſ oſtentaret.
Prima naꝗ; et ultima ezechieliſ ꝓꝑhe part

MS 481.15, f. 1v, Italy, s. XII[in]

PLATE 14

MS 481.16, f. 1v, Italy, s. XI^{4/4}

MS 481.17, f. 2v, Southern Germany, s. X¹

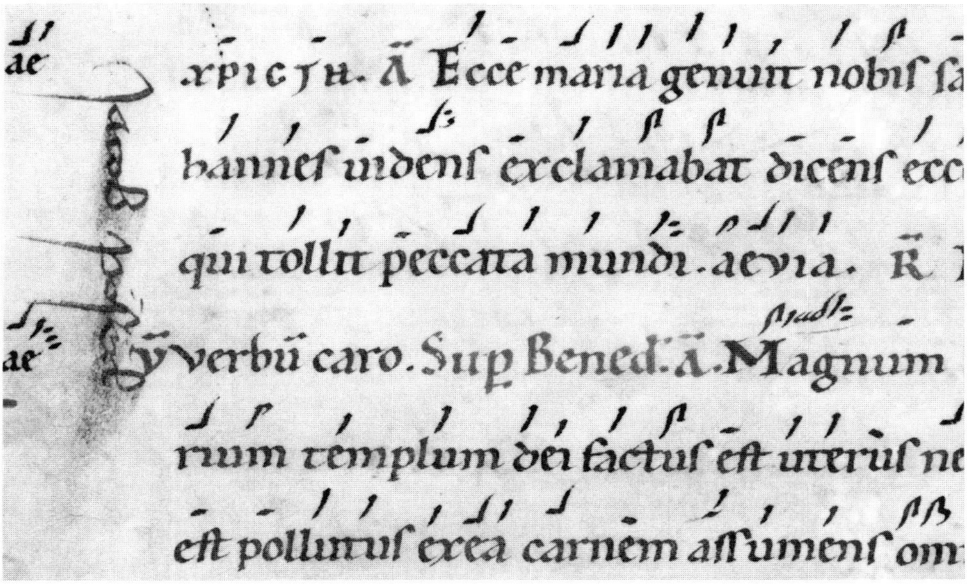

PLATE 15

MS 481.18, f. 1v, Austria (Lambach?), s. XII[med]

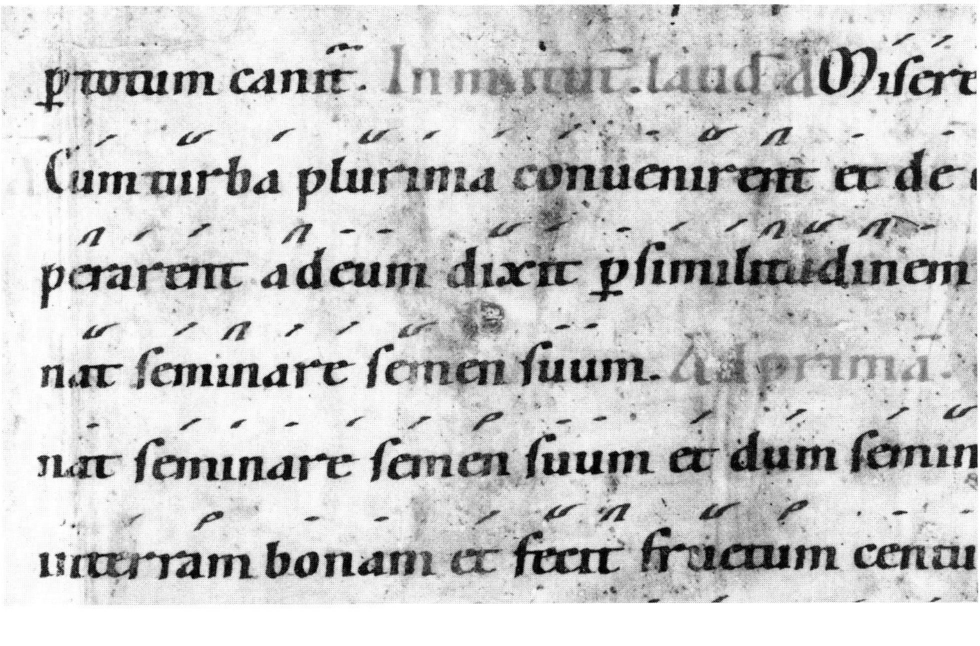

MS 481.19, f. 1r, Southern Germany or Austria, s. XII[1]

PLATE 16

MS 481.20, f. 1v, Southern Germany, s. X^2

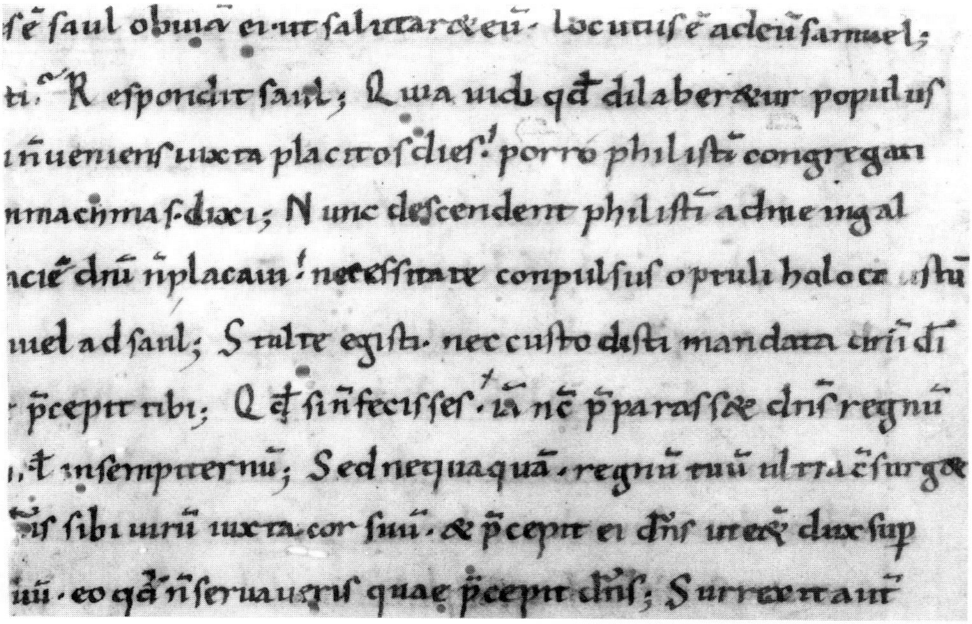

MS 481.21, f. 3v, Germany, s. X^{ex}

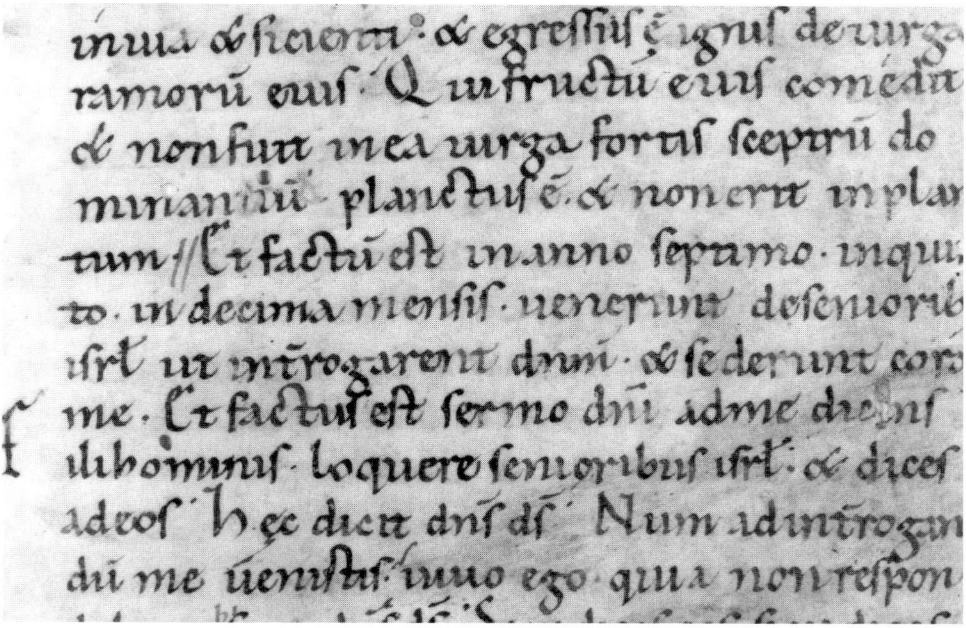

PLATE 17

inuia deficientiū: & egreſſuſ e ignuſ deuirga
ramorū euiſ · Quiſ fructū euiſ comedit
& nonfuit inea uirga fortiſ ſceptrū do
minantiū· planctuſ e & nonerit inplā
tum // Et factū eſt inanno ſeptimo · inquī
to · indecima menſiſ · uenerunt deſenioribꝰ
iſrł ut introgarent dnm · & federunt corā
me · Et factuſ eſt ſermo dni adme dicēſ
ilibominuſ· loquere ſenioribuſ iſrł · & diceſ
adeoſ · Hęc dicit dnſ dſ · Num adintrogā
dū me ueniſtiſ inuo ego · quia non reſpon

MS 481.22, f. 1r, Lothringia, s. XI^2

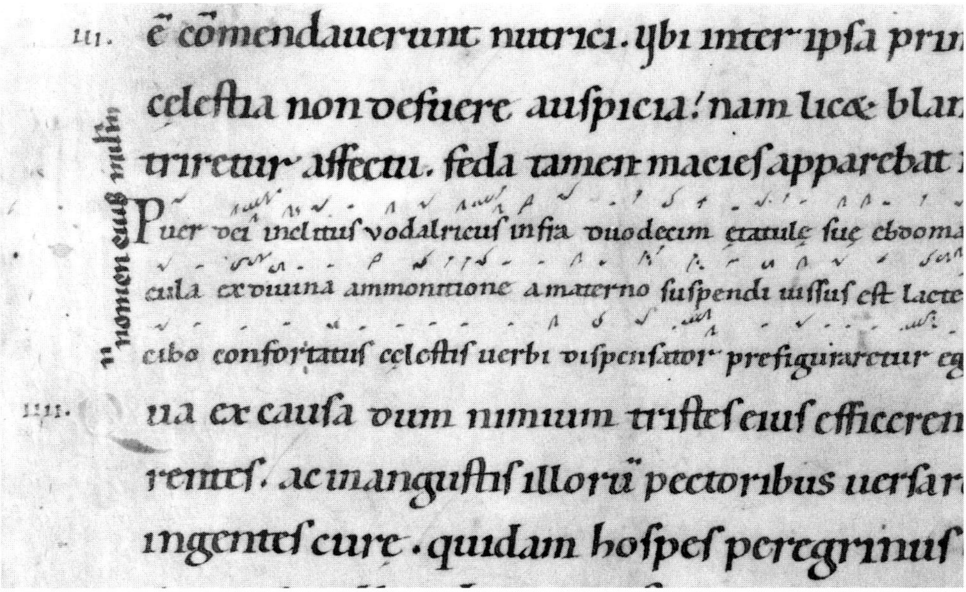

iii. ē comendauerunt nutrici. ybi inter ipſa pri
celeſtia non defuere auſpicia! nam licet blā
triretur affectu. feda tamen macieſapparebat
Puer dei mehtiuſ uodalricuſ infra duodecim etatule ſue eboma
cula exdiuina ammonitione amaterno fuſpendi iuſſuſ eſt lacte
cibo confortatuſ celeſtiſ uerbi diſpenſator prefiguraretur eg
iiii. ua excauſa dum nimium triſteſ eiuſ efficeren
remteſ. acinanguſtiſ illorū pectoribuſ uerſar
ingenteſ cure. quidam hoſpeſ peregrinuſ

MS 481.23, f. 2v, Southern Germany (Augsburg?), s. XI^{med}

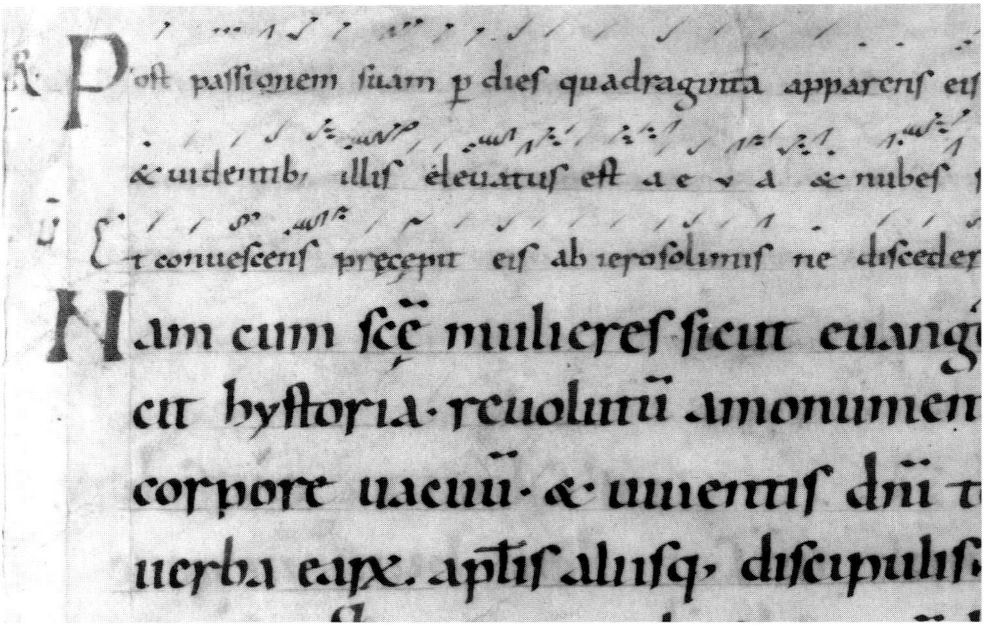

PLATE 18

Post passionem suam p dies quadraginta apparens ei...

& uidentib, illis eleuatus est a e v a & nubes...

Et conuescens precepit eis ab ierosolimis ne disceder...

Nam cum sce mulieres sicut euang...

eu hystoria · reuolutu amonumen...

corpore uacuu · & · uiuentis dni...

uerba eap. aptis aliisq, discipulis...

MS 481.24, f. 1v, Southern Germany, s. XI

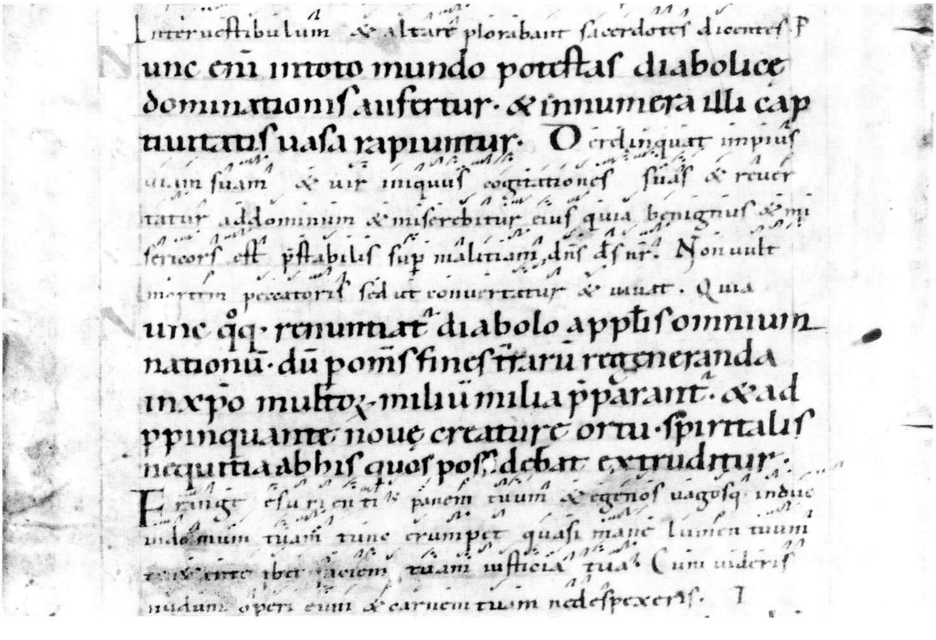

Inter uestibulum & altare plorabant sacerdotes dicentes P...
unc eni intoto mundo potestas diabolice
dominationis aufertur · & innumera illa cap
tiuitatis uasa rapiuntur. O relinquat impius
uiam suam & uir iniquus cogitationes suas & reuer
tatur addominum & miserebitur eius quia benignus & mi
sericors est pstabilis sup malitiam, dns dsnr. Non uult
mortem peccatoris sed ut conuertatur & uiuat. Quia
unc qq. renuntiat diabolo apptis omnium
nationu · du poms fines terrarum regeneranda
inxpo multox miliu milia pparaunt · & ad
ppinquante noue creature ortu spiritalis
nequitia abhis quos possidebat extruditur.
Frangit esurienti pane tuum & egenos uagosq induc
in domum tuam tunc erumpet quasi mane lumen tuum
... faciem tuam iusticia tual Cum uideris
nudum oper eum & carnem tuam ne despexeris. T

MS 481.25, f. 13v, Southern Germany, s. XI[2]

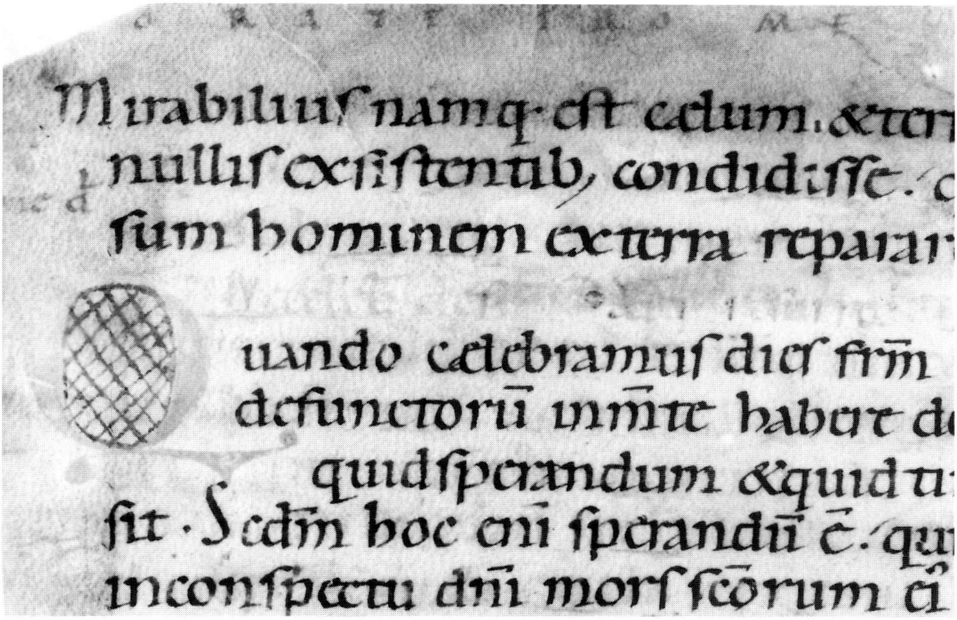

PLATE 19

Mirabiliuf namq̄ eſt cęlum . æter
nullif exſiſtentib, condidiſſe . c
ſum hominem ex terra repara

uando cęlebramuf dieſ frm
defunctoru inmte habet d
quidſpercandum &quid t
ſit . Secm hoc eni ſperandu e . qu
inconſpectu dni morf ſcorum e

MS 481.26, f. 1v, Southern Germany, s. XI/XII

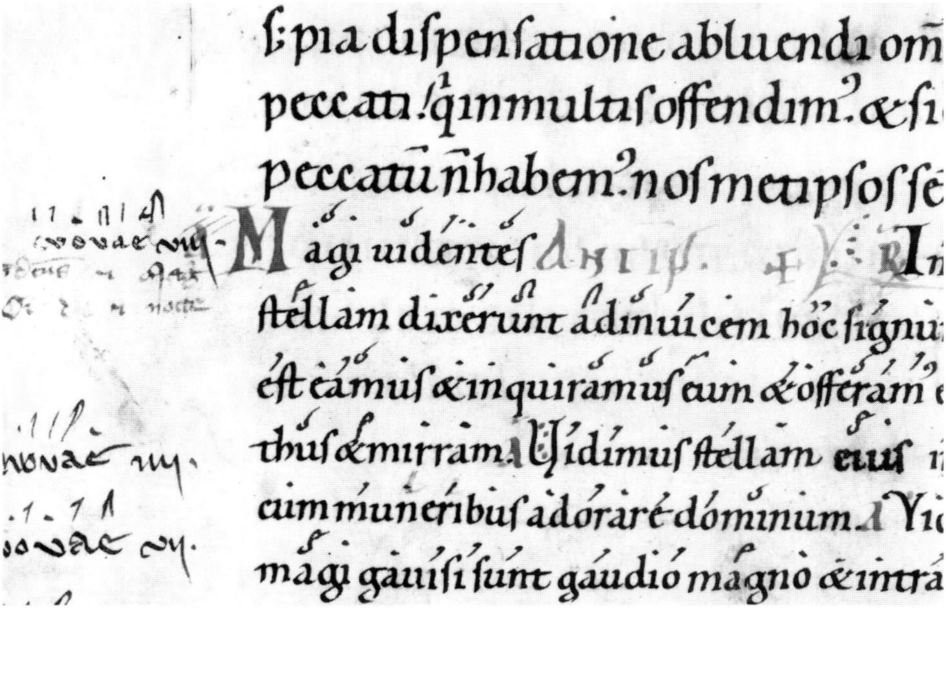

ſi pia diſpenſatione abluendi om
peccati ./q̄inmultifoffendim? æfi
peccatu n habem? nofmetipfoſſe
Magi uidenteſ
ſtellam dixerunt adinuicem hoc ſignu
eſt eamuſ & inquiramuſ eum & offeram
thuf & mirram . L̄ fidimuf ſtellam eiuſ i
cum muneribuſ adorare dominum . Vi
magi gauiſi ſunt gaudio magno & intra

MS 481.27, f. 1v, Southern Germany or Austria, s. XII

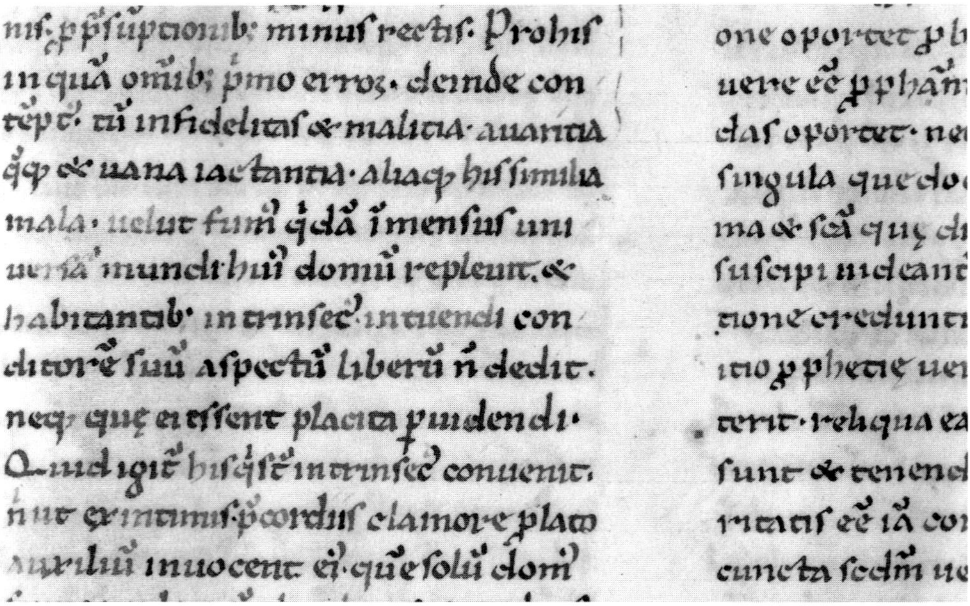

PLATE 20

nis ⁊ p psūptionib; minius rectis. Prohis
in quā omib; pmo erroz. deinde con
tēptc̄. tū infidelitas & malitia auaritia
qq ⁊ uana iactantia. aliaq hiis similia
mala. uelut fumi qdā imensus uni
uersa mundi huii domū repleunt. &
habitantib; intrinsec intuendi con
ditorē suū aspectū liberū n dedit.
neq; quę ei essent placita puidendi.
Quid igit hiisq̈ sc̄ intrinsec conuenit.
n ut ex intimis pcordiis clamore placo
auxiliū inuocent ei. quę solū domi

one oportet p h
uere cē p phām
das oportet. ne
singula que do
ma & scā quę d
suscipi indcanti
tione creduntu
itio p phetie uer
terit. reliqua ea
sunt & tenend
itatis ee iā con
cuncta sedm ue

MS 481.28, f. 2v, France (?), s. XII^{med}

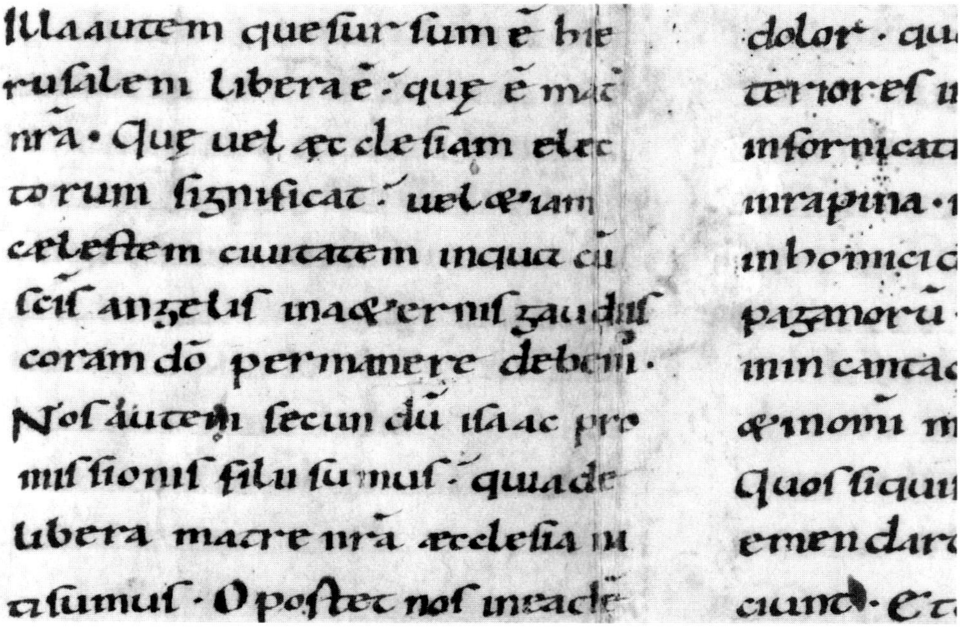

Illa autem que sursum ē hie
rusalem libera ē: quę ē mat
nra. Quę uel ęcclesiam elec
torum significat. uel ętiam
cęlestem ciuitatem inqua cū
scīs angelis inęternis gaudiis
coram dō permanere debem.
Nos autem secun dū isaac pro
missionis filii sumus. quia de
libera matre nra ęcclesia n
ascimus. O postea nos ineade

dolor. au
terrores u
infornicati
nrapina. i
in homicid
pzgmoru
min cantac
⁊ nomī m
Quos siqui
emendari
ciunt. Et

MS 481.29, f. 1v, France or Italy, s. X/XI

PLATE 21

pdu/at ad se; Et ascendit p gradus eius qz nobis pfiaentib; eo nob
pluis exaltat. quo altius z incomphensibilis esse cognoscitur; In uirtut
quippe nraru gradib; ipse ascendere dr qz tanto ipse sublimior nobi
dicitur quanto nr animu a rebus infimis separat; Seqr: Et men
lumen porte calamo uno latitudine. idest lum uniu calamo uno lati
dinem; Cur postqm dictu est lumen porte stati subiungitur
unu · nisi quia apte innuit quod adhuc inferius lumen aliud du
Porta aut a lumine surgit: ut porta sit. Sic porta dns · qs hu
te lum est. nisi illi antiq patres ex quoz pgenie dns incarnari

MS 481.30, f. 1v, Southern Germany, s. XII

co V ... tiamo festiutatis die dicebat iesus qui in
flumina deuentre eius fluent a que uiue Hoc au
de spiritu quem acceptari erant credentes in eu

Coll d sca kat
Deus qui moysi famulo tuo in monte syna legem de
in eodem loco p manus angelorum corpus bte
gmis z martyris tue mirabilit collocasti: tribue
meatis et pcibus ut ad montem uirtutum qui
pe ualeamus p eundem ... micra nra domine
tio que tibi offerimus in honore sce katerine ur
kant nobis quesumus eius pcibus uita ppetua et

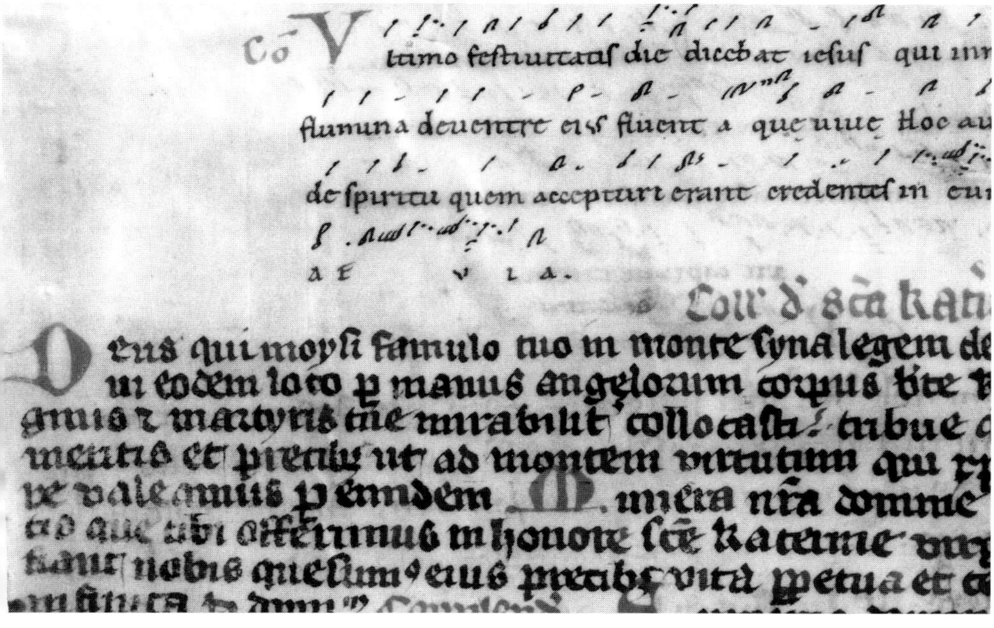

MS 481.31, f. 2v, Southern Germany, s. XII[1]

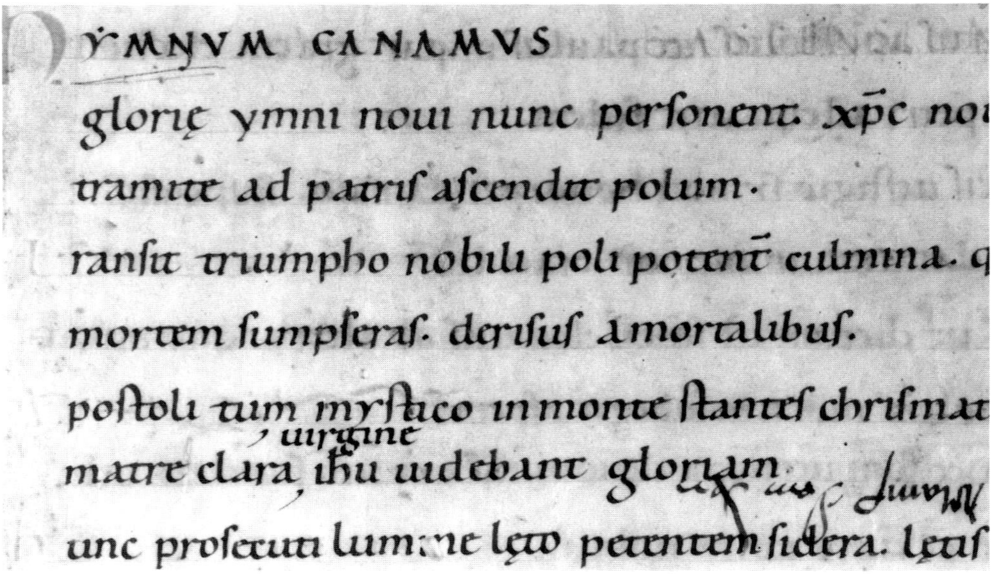

PLATE 24

YMNVM CANAMVS

gloriȩ ymni noui nunc personent xp̄c no
tramite ad patris ascendit polum.
ransit triumpho nobili poli potent̄ culmina. q
mortem sumpseras. derisus a mortalibus.
postoli tum mystico in monte stantes chrismat
                    uirgine
matre clara, ihu uidebant gloriam
unc prosecuti lumine lȩto petentem sidera. lȩtis

MS 481.36, f. 2r, Münster-Schwarzach or Lambach, s. XI^med

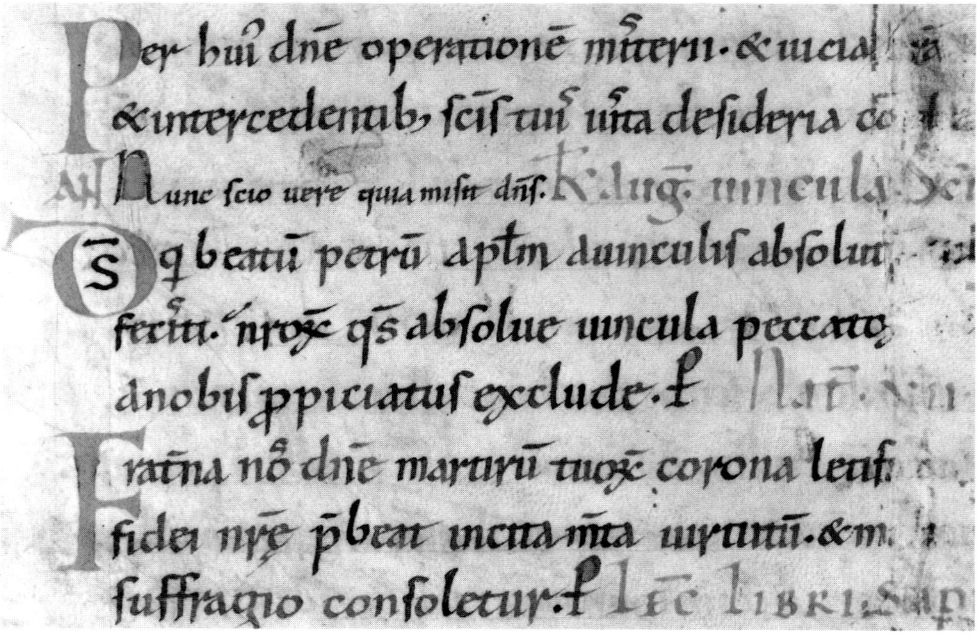

Per huii dn̄e operatione mitern. & uicia iā
& intercedentib; scīs tuī uīta desideria c̄o
une scio uere quia misit dn̄s. K. Iuḡ. uincula sc̄
q beatū petrū aptm dauinculis absolui rai
fecit. n̄roq̄ q̄s absolue uincula peccato
a nobis ppiciatus exclude. f
ratna non dn̄e martirū tuoq̄ corona lētis
fidei nre p̄beat incita mta uirtutū. & m.
suffragio consoletur. f lēc libri sap

MS 481.37, f. 1v, Germany, s. XI²

PLATE 21

pduat̄ ad se; Et ascendit p gradus eius qr nobis pficientib; eo nob
plius exaltat̄. quo altius ⁊ incōphensibilis esse cognoscitur; In uirtu
quippe n̄arū g̃dib; ipse ascendere dr̄ qr tanto ipse sublimior nob
dicitur: quanto nr̄ anim̄ a rebus infimis separat̄; Seqr̄ Et men
lumen portę calamo uno latitudinē. id est lm̄ uniꝰ calamo uno til
dinem; Cur postqm̄ dictū est lumen portę stat̄ subiungitur
unū· nisi quia apte innuit quod adhuc inferius lumen aliud du
Porta aut̄ a lumine surgit· ut porta sit· Siꝗ porta dn̄s· qs hi
te lm̄ est· nisi illi antiq patres ex quoꝗ ꝓgenie dn̄s incarnari

MS 481.30, f. 1v, Southern Germany, s. XII

Co̅ tǐmo festiuitatis die dicebat iesus qui in
flumina deuentre eius fluent a quę uiuę Hoc au
de spiritu quem accepturi erant credentes in eu

Coll̄ d̄ sc̄a kati

Deus qui moysi famulo tuo in monte syna legem de
in eodem loco p manus angelorum corpus bt̄e
ginis ⁊ martyris tue mirabilit̄ collocasti· tribue
mentis et precibus ut ad montem uirtutum qui p
pe valeamus p eundem Munera nr̄a domine
tio quę tibi offerimus in honore sc̄e katerine uꝛ
tiant nobis quesumꝰ eius precibus uita ꝑpetua et
in futura te domin̄ ꝛ Camplend

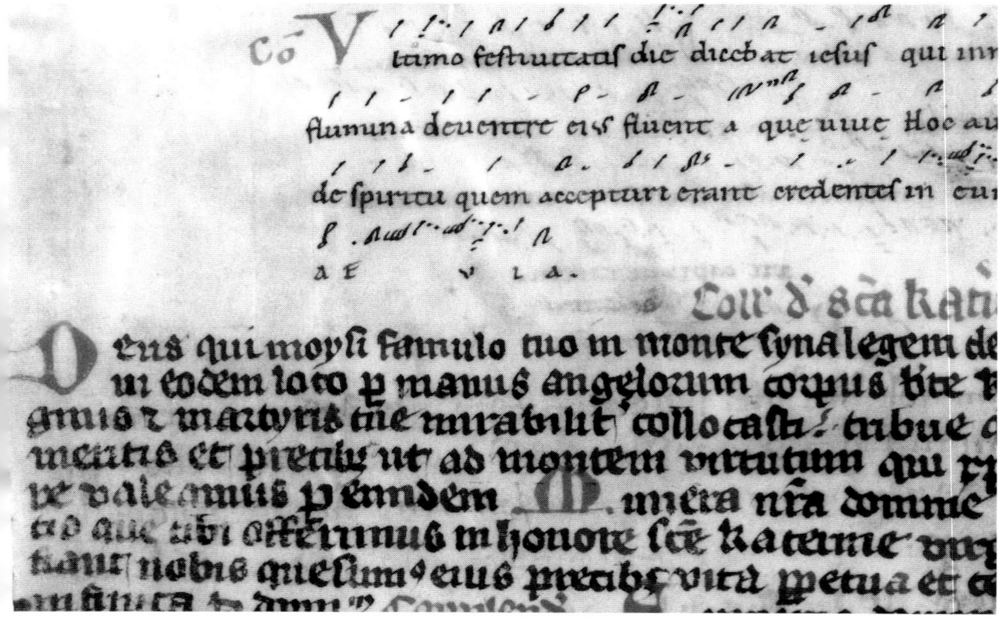

MS 481.31, f. 2v, Southern Germany, s. XII[1]

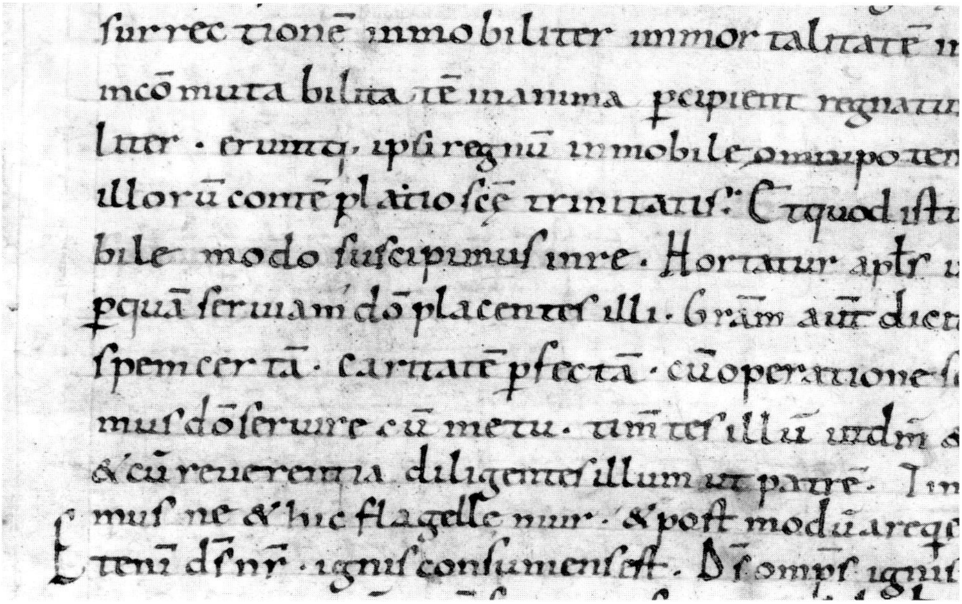

PLATE 22

MS 481.32, f. 1v, Italy, s. XI^2

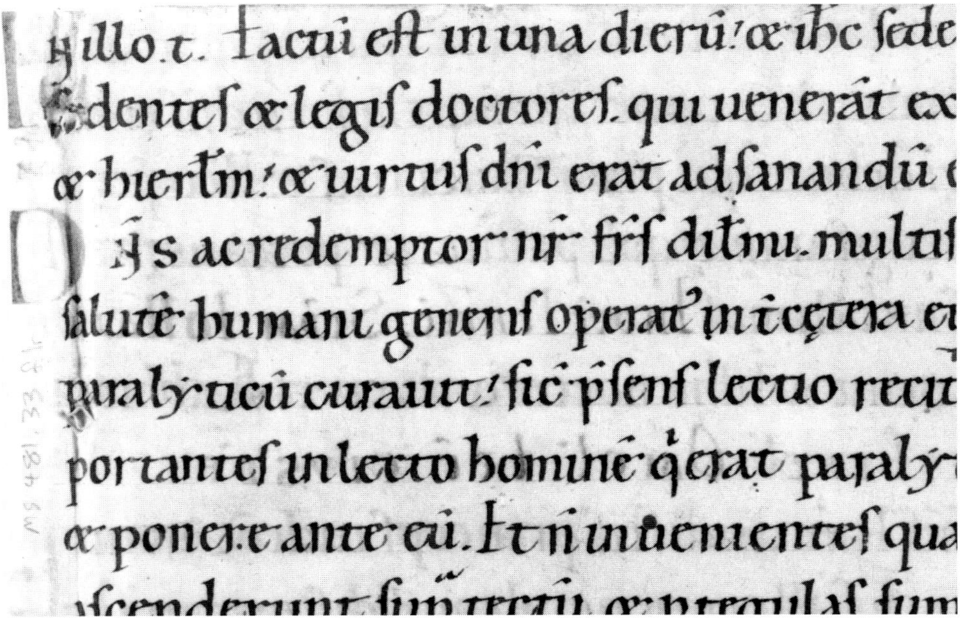

MS 481.33, f. 1r, Southern Germany or Austria, s. XII^{med}

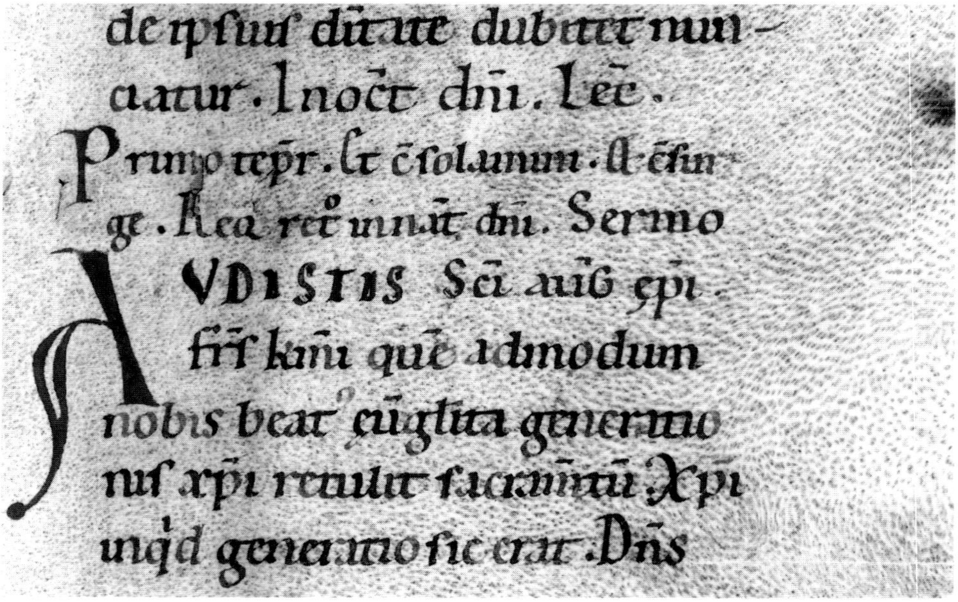

PLATE 23

de ipsius divitate dubitet nunciatur. In noct dni. Lec.
Primo tepr. & csolunum. A esin
ge. Aea reu innut dnu. Sermo
VDISTIS Sci auG epi.
frr knu que admodum
nobis beat euglita generatio
nis xpi retulit sacratu Xpi
unqd generatio sic erat. Dns

MS 481.34, f. 3r, Italy, s. XII[1]

Omelia Beati ambrosii epi Lec eiusde
ON D COMPNATUR
silentio incredulitas sacerdotis./ et fides ppharum
probatur oraculo. Clama in.
Et dix. Quid clamabo.
omns caro foenu. Unde iub
tis imperium. obtemparants
obsequium. sed abneganur affectum. obse
quentis oraculum. Credidit enim. quicquid
clamat exposcit. Et quia credidit ppham

MS 481.35, f. 1r, Italy, s. XII[in]

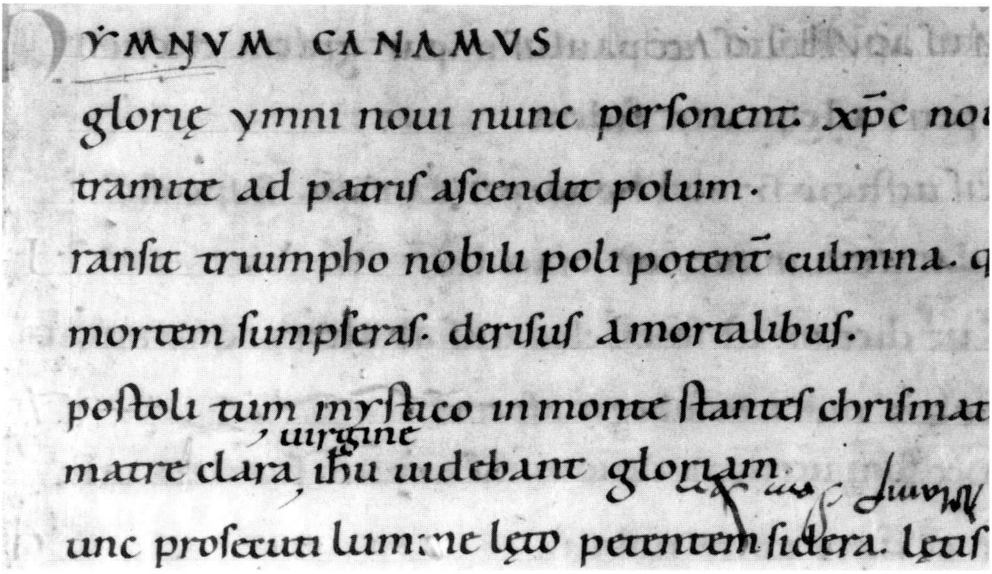

PLATE 24

YMNVM CANAMVS

glorię ymni noui nunc persononent. xpc no
tramite ad patris ascendit polum.
ransit triumpho nobili poli potent culmina. q
mortem sumpseras. derisus a mortalibus.
postoli tuim mystico in monte stantes chrismat
matre clara, ihu uidebant gloriam.
unc prosecuti lumine lęto petentem sidera. lętis

MS 481.36, f. 2r, Münster-Schwarzach or Lambach, s. XI[med]

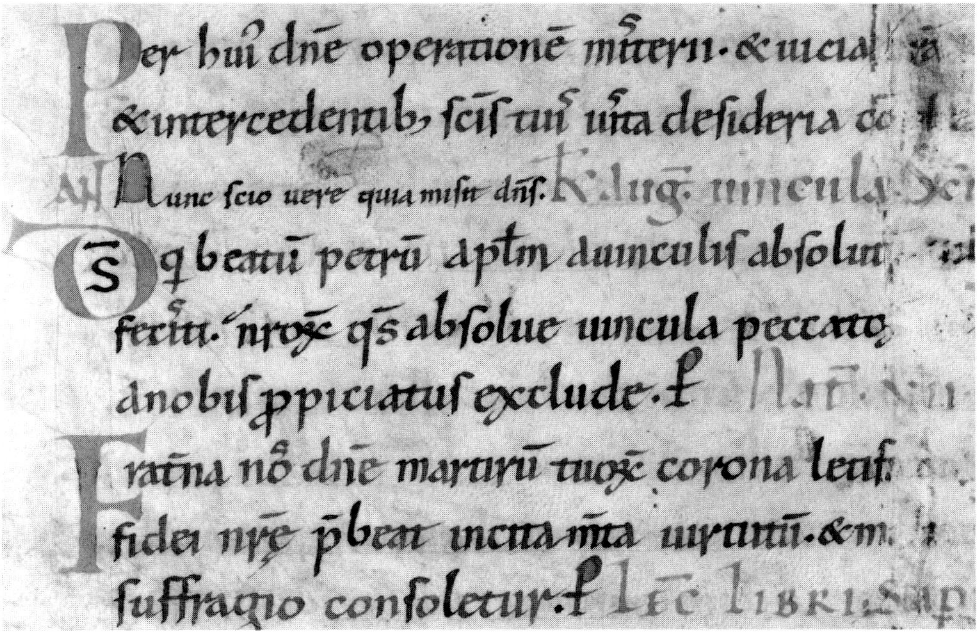

Per huī dne operatione mīteryi. & uicia
& intercedentib, scīs tuī uita desideria cō
une scio uere quia misit dūs.
q beatū petrū aptm uinculis absolui
fecit. nroę q̄s absolue uincula peccato,
a nobis ppiciatus exclude.
ratia nō dīe martyrū tuoę corona lętis
fidei nrę pbeat incitamta uirtutū. & m.
suffragio consoletur.

MS 481.37, f. 1v, Germany, s. XI[2]

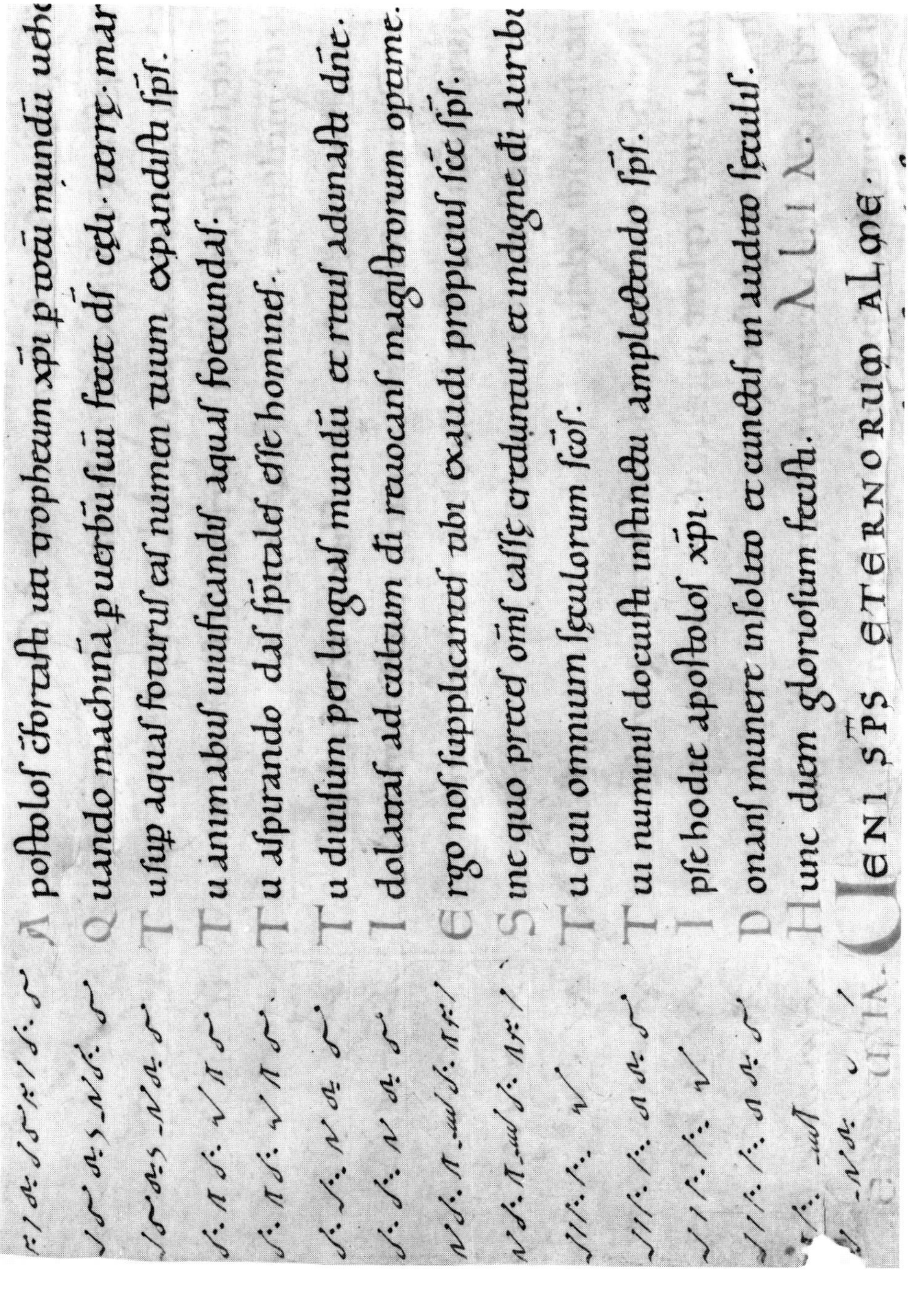

PLATE 26

Apoſtoloſ eforaſti uia tropheum xp̄i pꝛouā mundū uch...
Quando machinā pꝛuerbiſ fuū fecc d̄ſ ect̄a. uarꝏ. mar...
Tuſup aquaſ foaruſ eaſ numen tuum expandiſti ſp̄ſ.
Tu inimabuſ uuuficandſ aquaſ foecundaſ.
Tu aſpirando daſ ſp̄italeſ eſſe homineſ.
Tu diuiſūm per linguaſ mundū ex retuſ adunaſti d̄n̄e.
Idolatraſ ad cultum d̄i revocanſ magiſtrorum opame...
Ergo noſ ſupplicantſ tibi exuudi pꝛopicuſ ſc̄c̄ ſp̄ſ.
Sine quo preceſ om̄ſ caſſe creduntur ex indigne d̄i uurbe...
Tu qui omnium ſeculorum ſc̄oſ.
Tu numinſ docuiſti inſtinctu ampletendo ſp̄ſ.
Ipſe hodie apoſtoloſ xp̄i.
Donanſ munere inſolito ex cunctoſ in auditꝺ ſeculſſ.
Hunc diem glorioſum faciſ.

VENI SPS ETERNORUM ALME.

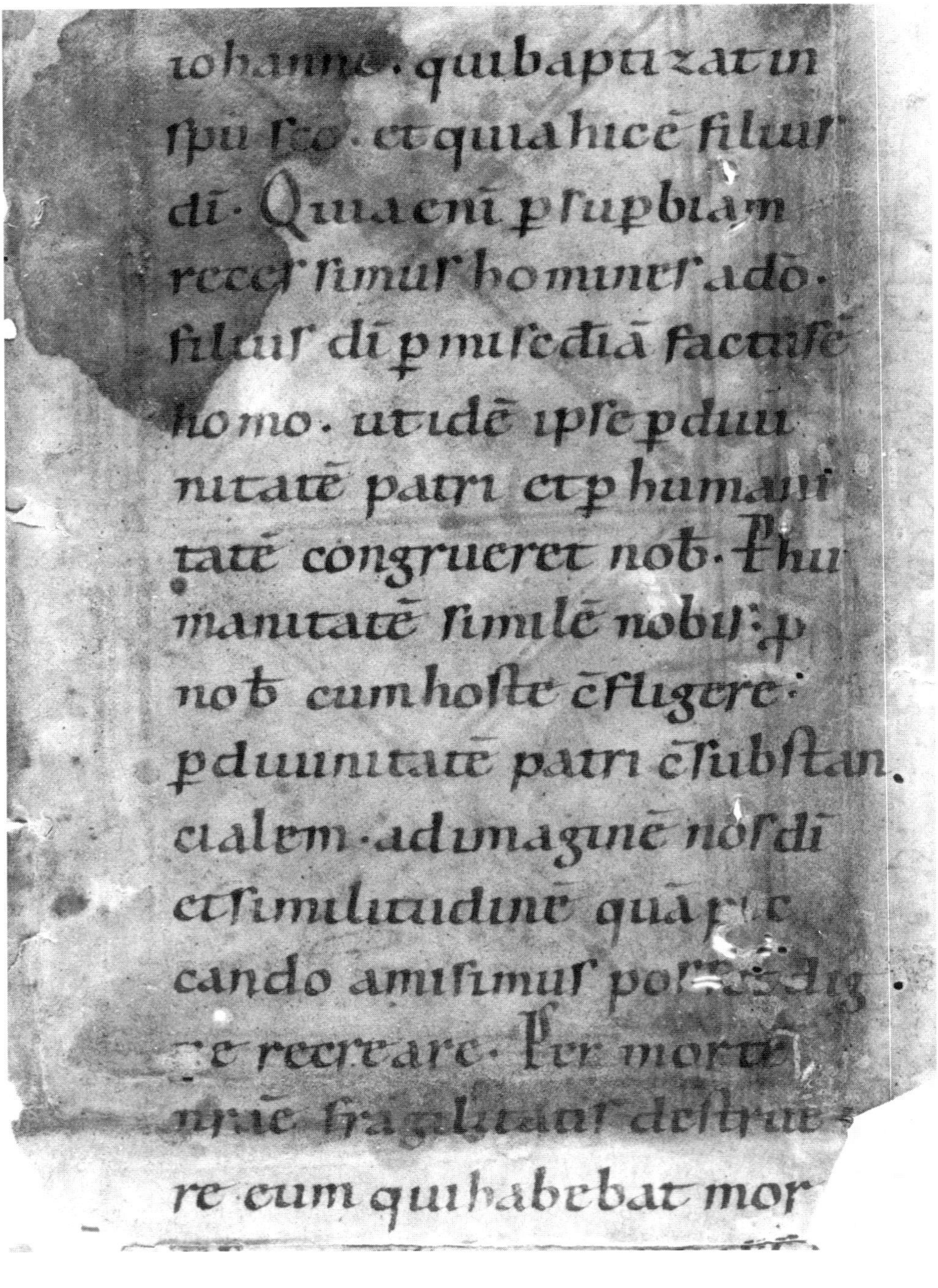

PLATE 25

iohanne · quibaptizat in
spu sco · et quia hic e filius
di · Quia enim p supbiam
recessimus homines a do ·
filius di p misedia factus e
homo · ut ide ipse p diuinitate patri et p humani-
tate congrueret nob · Thu-
manitate simile nobis: p
nob cum hoste efligere ·
p diuinitate patri e substan-
cialem · ad imagine nos di
et similitudine qua pec-
cando amisimus po...dis ·
...e recreare · Per mort...
...ie fragilitat destrue-
re eum qui habebat mor

MS 481.38, f. 1v, Germany, s. X/XI

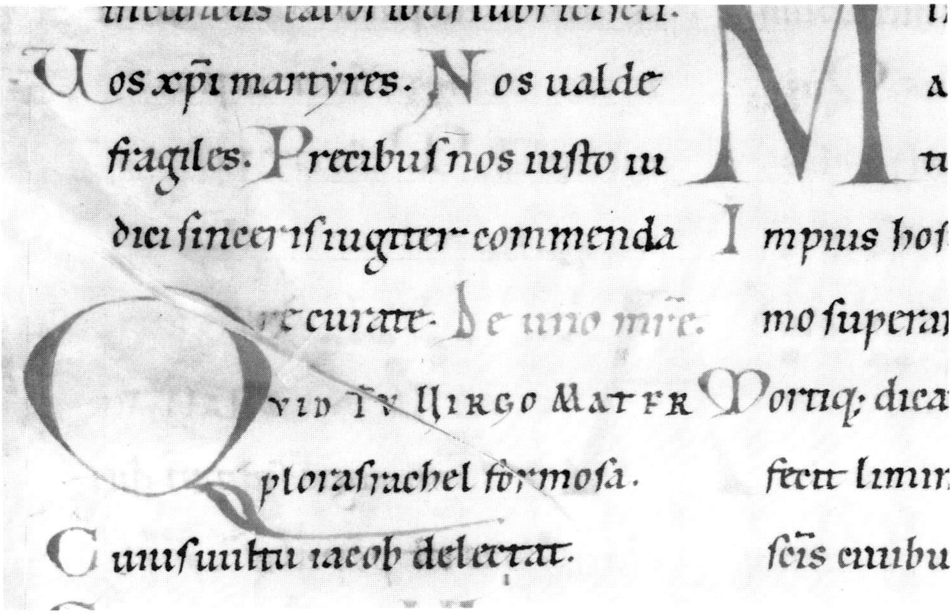

PLATE 27

MS 481.40, f. 1v, Kremsmünster, Austria, s. XII$^{3/4}$

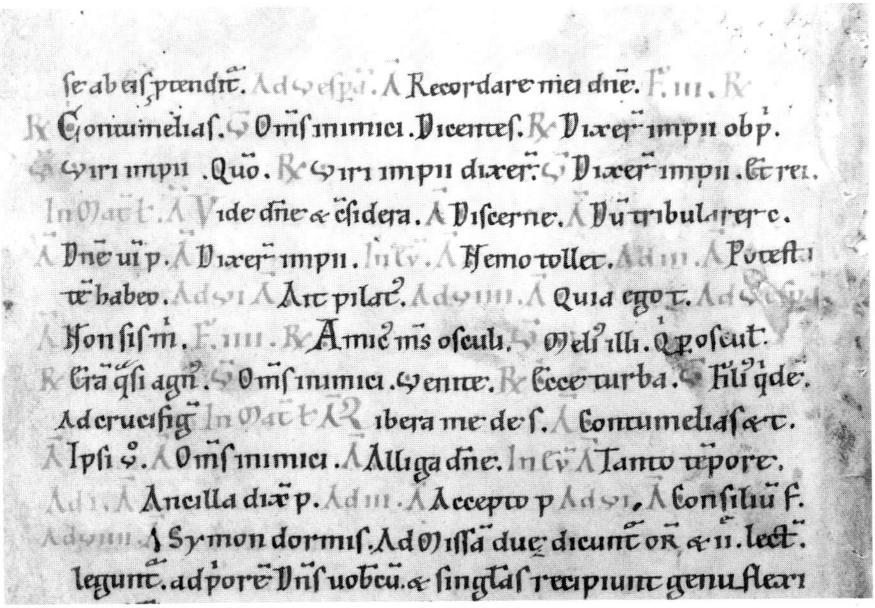

MS 481.41, f. 1v, Southern Germany, s. XII^{1}

PLATE 28

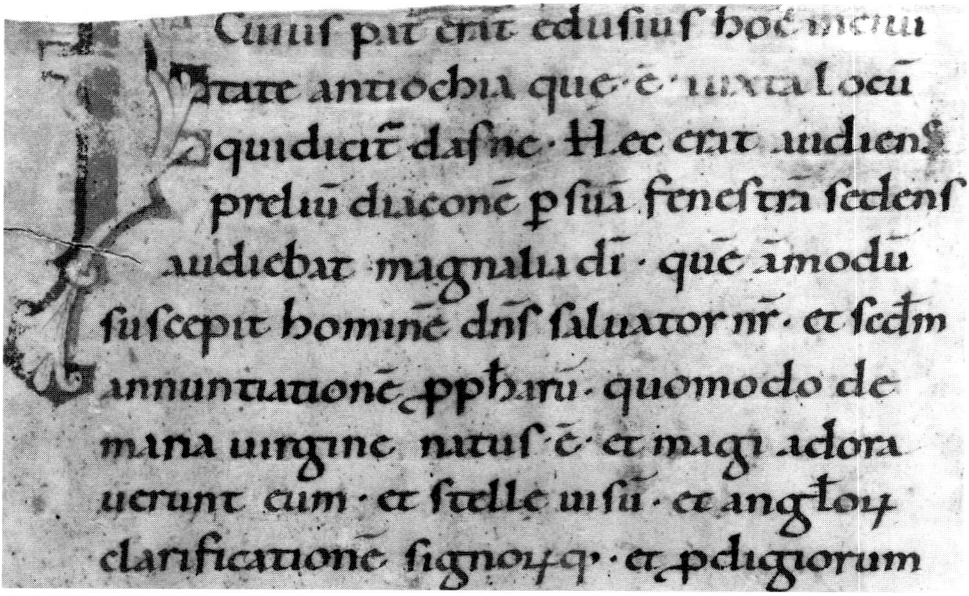

Cuiuf pat erit edufiuf hoc mear
itate antiochia que e iuxta locu
quidicat dafne · Hec erat audiens
preliu diacone p sua fenestra sedenf
audiebat magnalia di · que amodu
sufcepit homine dnf faluator nr · et fedm
annuntiatione ppharu · quomodo de
maria uirgine natuf e et magi adora
uerunt eum · et stelle uifu · et angtof
clarificatione signoyq · et pdigiorum

MS 481.42, f. 1r, Italy, s. XI^2

agnofcit · Df eni n manu factuf ha
bitat · nec in metallo · aut faxo cog
nofcit · hic q gentilif pptf cu pfecutio
ne xpiano intulerit · hac pena plec
tit · in cu facrilega fua mola iudican
di fct fluctib dermgatur · Paffio f
...cpi nr · et nifene uirg ·
LLVMINATIO dni nri ihu
xpi faluatorif de celo facta est

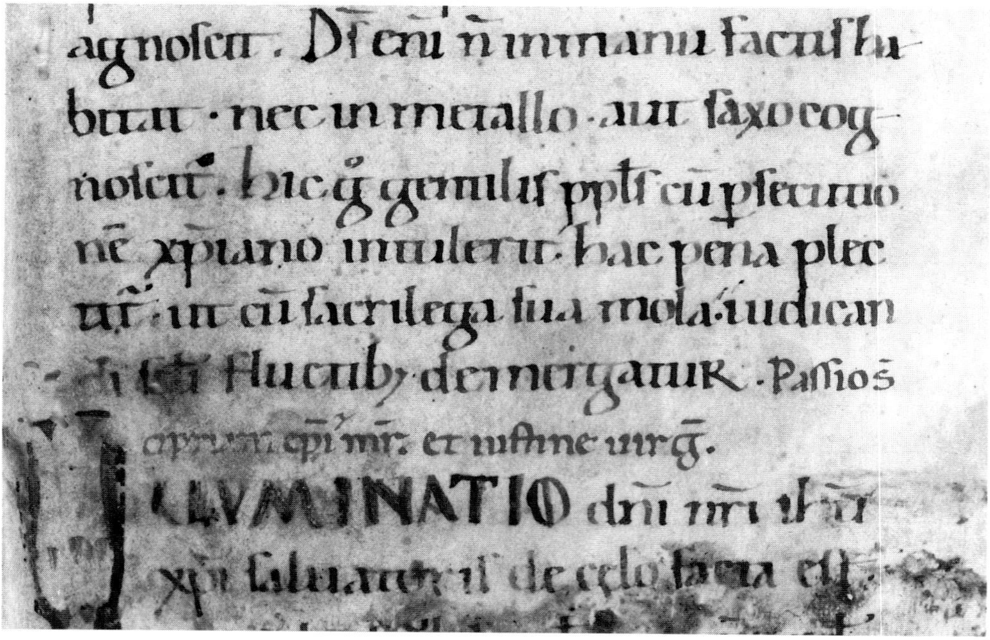

MS 481.43, f. 1r, Italy, s. XI^{ex}

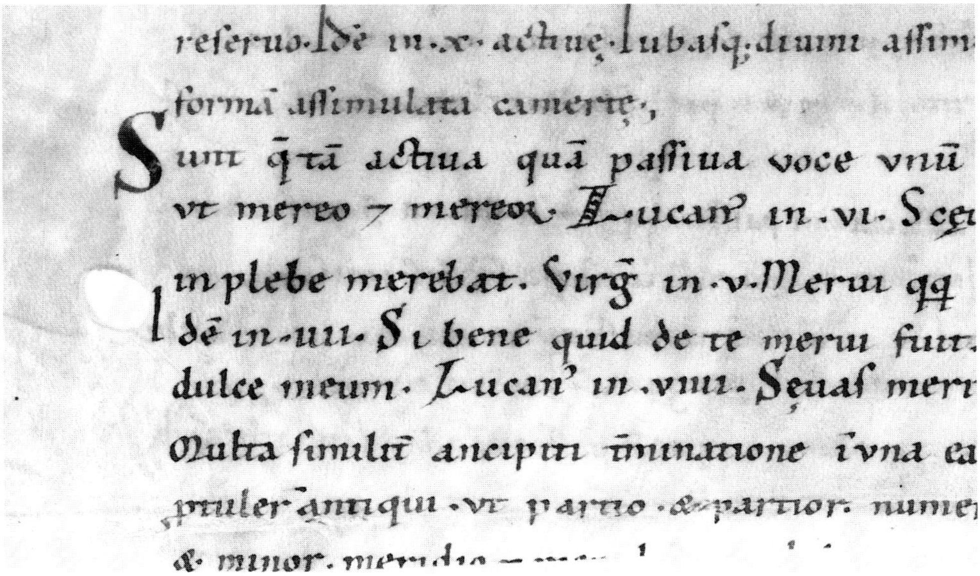

PLATE 29

MS 481.44, f. 2v, Western Germany, s. XI^2

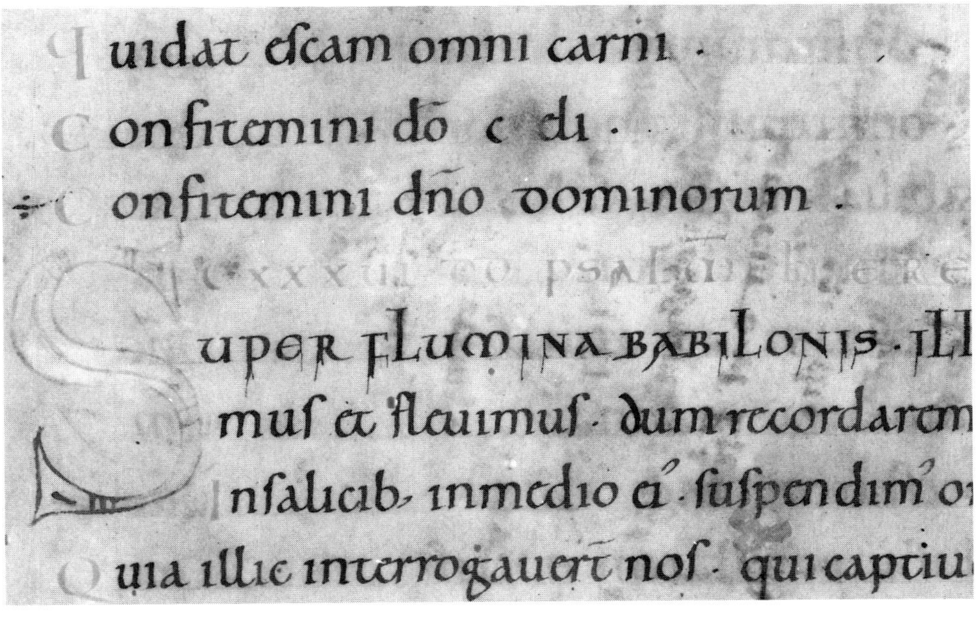

MS 481.45, f. 2v, Fulda, Germany, s. XI$^{2/3}$

PLATE 30

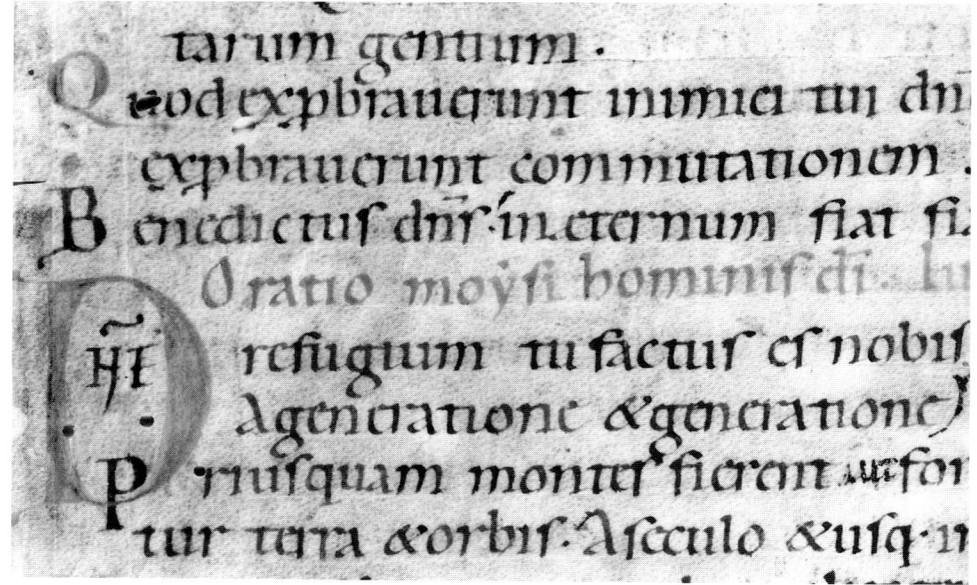

MS 481.46, f. 3r, Southern Germany, s. XI/XII

MS 481.47, f. 1r, Melk, Austria, s. XIII[1]

PLATE 31

MS 481.48, f. 1r, Lambach, Austria, s. XII^{ex}

PLATE 32

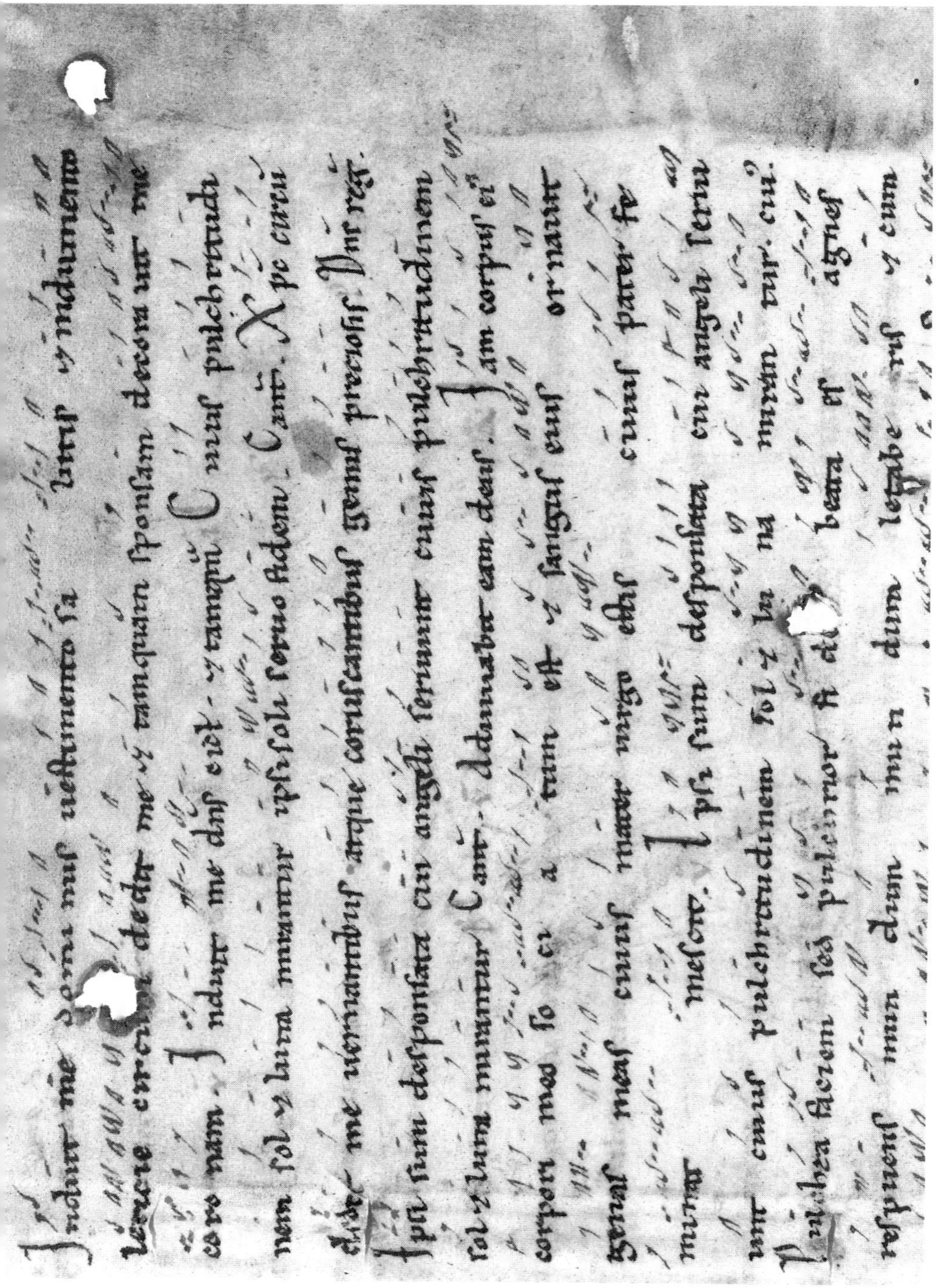

MS 481.49, f. 1r, Melk, Austria, s. XII

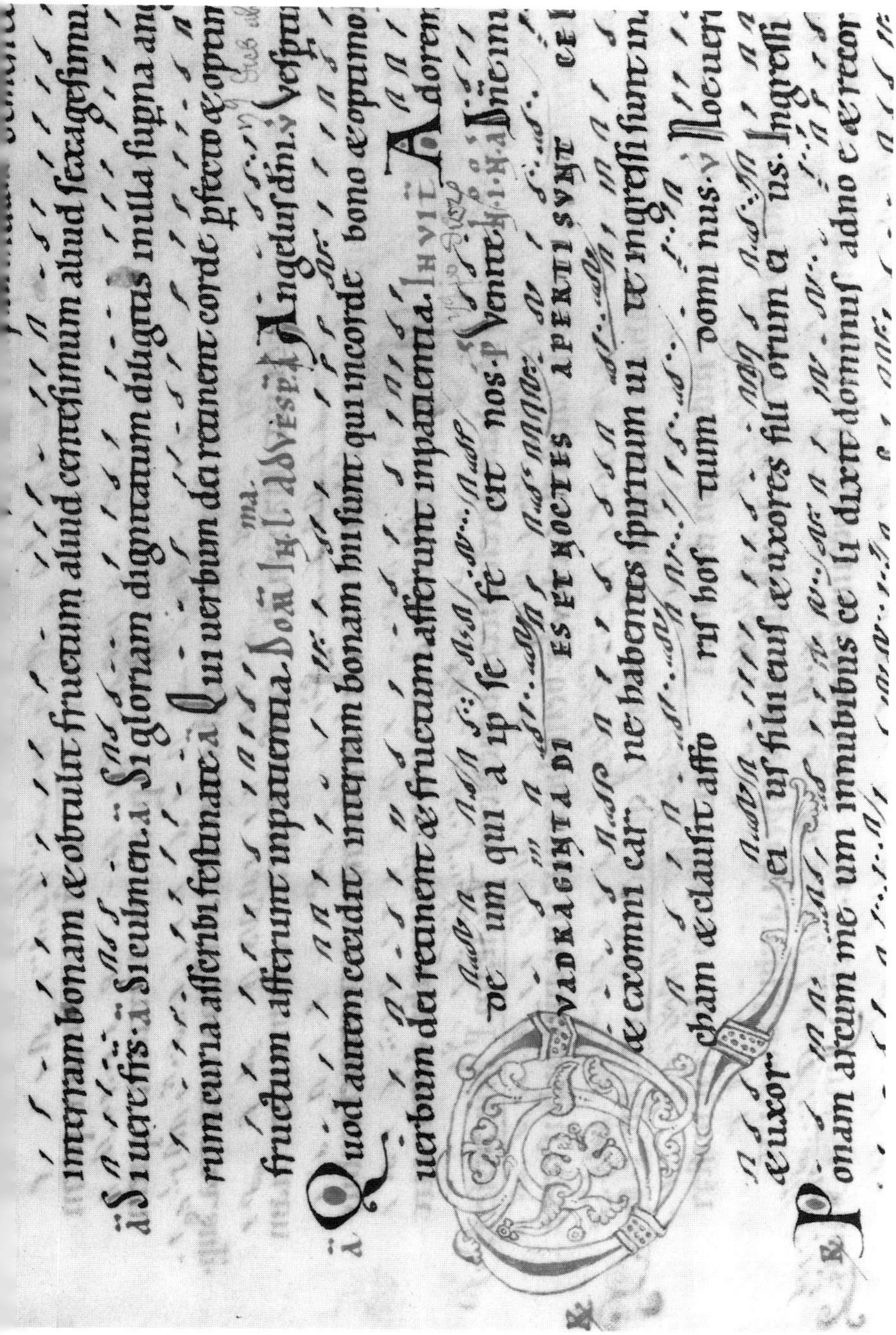

PLATE 33

...interiam bonam & obtulit fructum aliud centesimum aliud sexagesimum

...dñ In gressis ·a· Siculmen ·a· Si gloriam dignarum diligras in illa fugna ang...

rum curia asseribi festinanca ꝙ Qui uerbum dare tenent corde ꝓfecto & optim...

fructum afferunt in pacientia. Doñ In. ꟾ ꟾ ꟾ Ad uesp ·a· Angelus dñi uespra...

℟. Quod autem cecidit interam bonam hii sunt qui in corde bono & optimo

uerbum dare tenent & fructum afferunt in pacientia. In uit. A dorem...

Venite ꟾ ꟾ ꟾ ꟾ ꟾ Añ Diem...

VADRAGINTA DI ES ET NOCTES APERTI SVNT ce...

ꝯe um qui a ip se fe ... eat nos·P...

& excomunicar ne habentes spiritum ui & ingressi sunt in...

...cham & clausit asso ... rif hoc tum Domi nus ·v· Nocueri...

...cham ...

Euxor ea ur filii auf & uxores fili orum a us. Ingressi...

℟. Ponam arcum me um innubibus ce li dixit dominus adno e & recor...

MS 481.51, f. 8r, Lambach, Austria, s. XIIᵉˣ

PLATE 34

MS 481.52, f. 10v, Lambach, Austria, s. XII[2]

MS 481.53, f. 1v, Schaffhausen, Switzerland, ca. 1100

PLATE 35

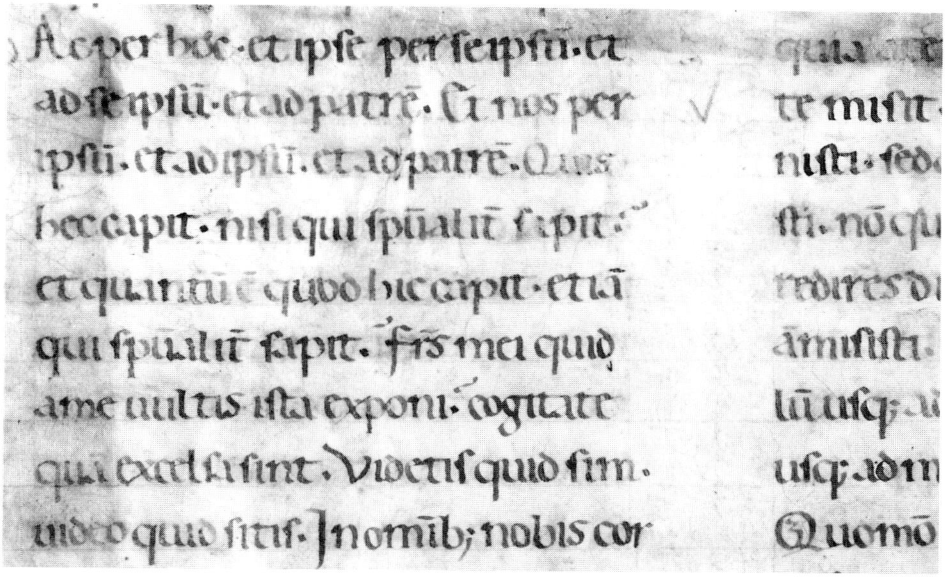

MS 481.54, f. 2v, Italy, s. XII[1]

MS 481.55, f. 2r, France, s. XIII[1]

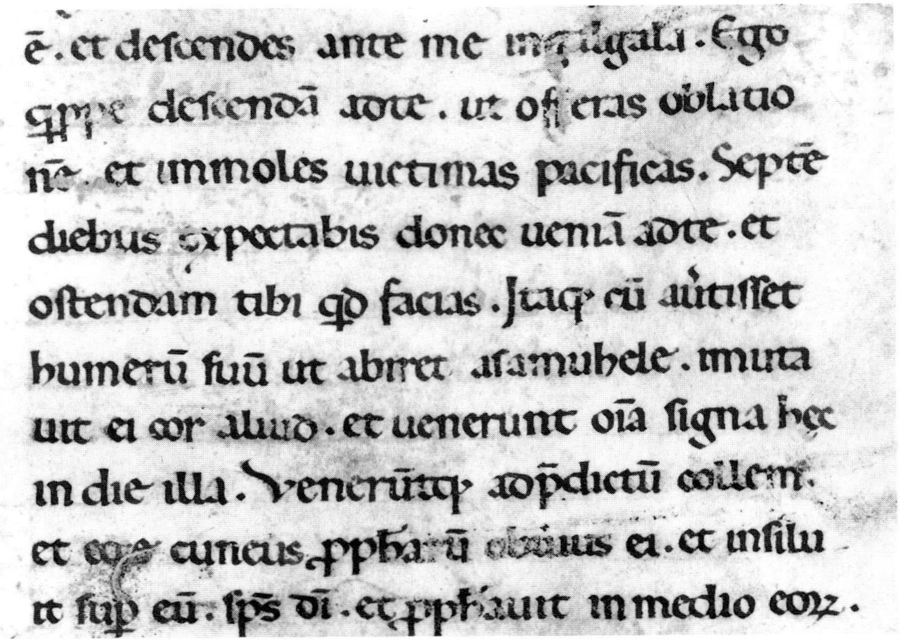

PLATE 36

ē. et descendes ante me in̄ ...dgala. Ego
q̄p̄e descendā ad te. ut offeras oblatio
ne. et immoles uictimas pacificas. Septē
diebus expectabis donec ueniā ad te. et
ostendam tibi qd facias. Itaq; cū aūtisset
humerū suū ut abiret asamuhele. muta
uit ei cor aliud. et uenerunt oīa signa hec
in die illa. Venerūtq; ad p̄dictū collem.
et eos cuneus ppharū obuius ei. et insilu
it sup eū. sps dī. et pphauit in medio eoz.

MS 481.56, f. 1r, Italy, s. XII[2]

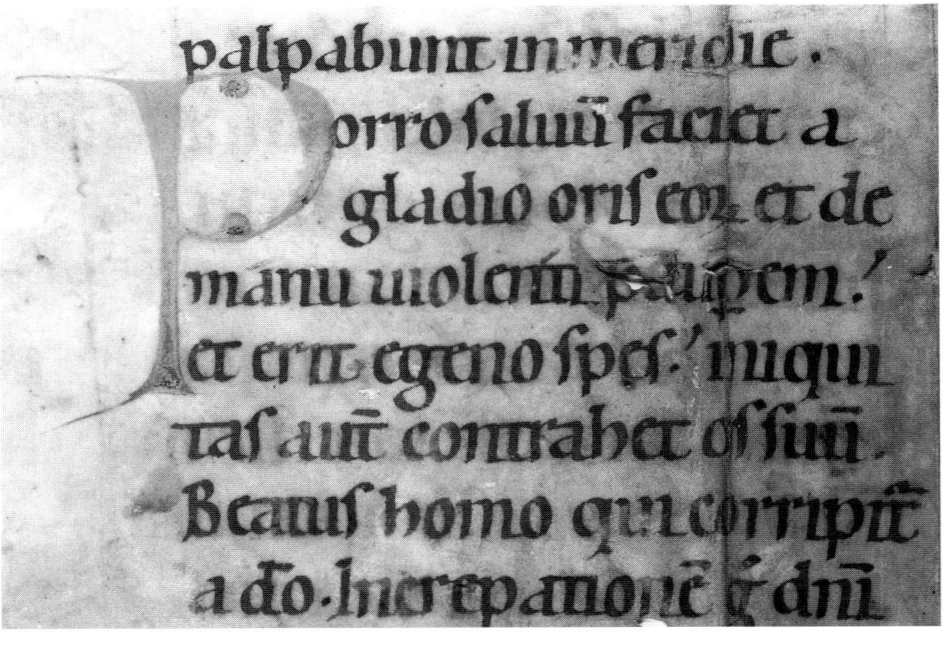

palpabunt in meridie.
Porro saluū faciet a
gladio oris eoz. et de
manu uiolenti p...pem!
et erit egeno spes! iniqui
tas aut contrahet os suū.
Beatus homo qui corripit
a do. Increpatione g dni

MS 481.57, f. 1v, Germany, s. XII

PLATE 37

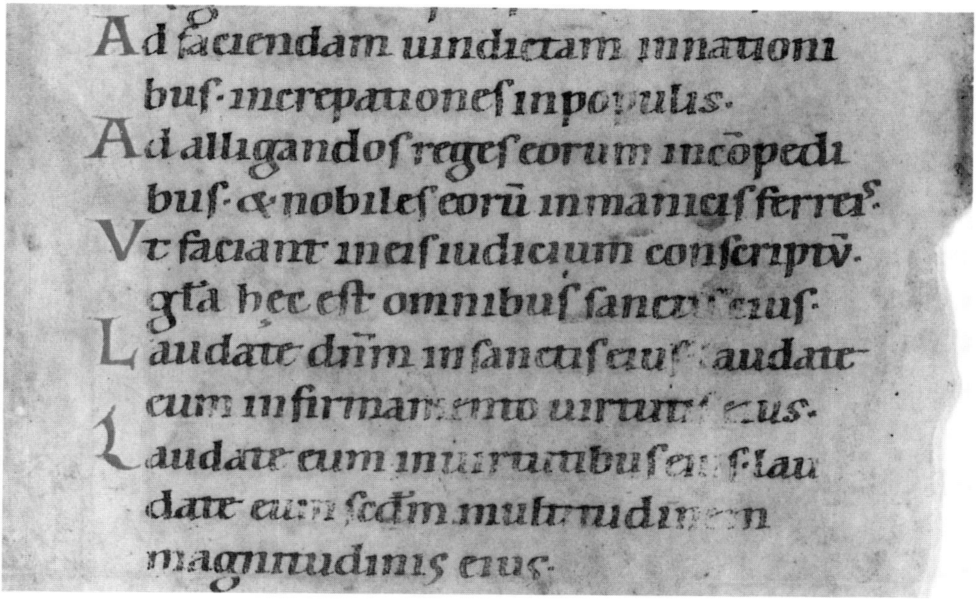

Ad faciendam uindictam innationi
bus· increpationes inpopulis·
Ad alligandos reges eorum incopedi
bus· & nobiles eorū inmanicis ferreis·
Vt faciant ineis iudicium conscriptū·
gła hec est omnibus sanctis eius·
Laudate dm̅m infanctis eius· audate
eum infirmamento uirtutis eius·
Laudate eum inuirtutibus eius· Lau
date eum sedm multitudinem
magnitudinis eius·

MS 481.58, f. 1v, Southern Germany or Austria, s. XII[1]

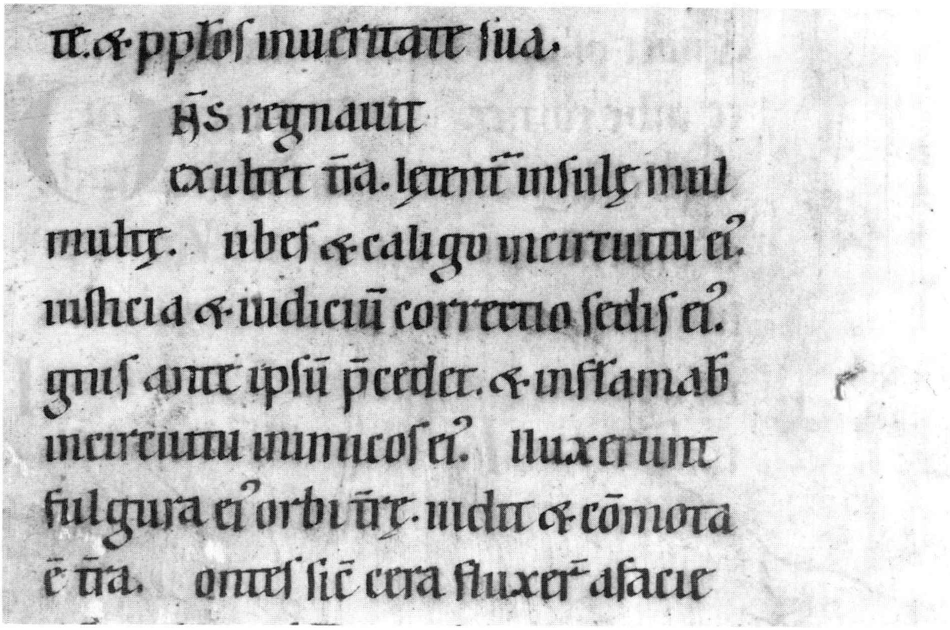

tc· & pplos inueritate sua·
H̄s regnauit
exultet tr̄a· letentur insule mul
multe· nubes & caligo incircuitu eī·
iusticia & iudiciū correctio sedis eī·
gnis ante ipsū p̄cedet· & inflamab
incircuitu inimicos eī· lluxerunt
fulgura ei? orbi tr̄e· uidit & comota
ē tr̄a· ontes sic cera fluxer̄ a facie

MS 481.59, f. 1r, Germany, s. XII[2]

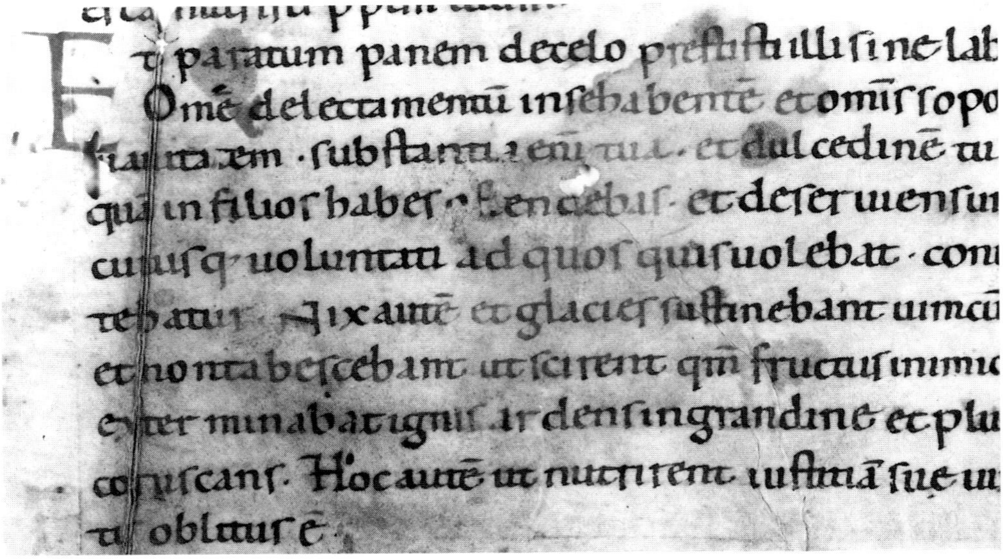

PLATE 38

...mu ppm...
t paratum panem decelo prestes illis sine lab
Ome delectamentu inse habente et omisso po
fta tarem · substantia enī tua · et dulcedine tu
qua in filios habes · Senaebus · et deseruiensu
cuiusq uoluntati ad quos quisuolebat · con
rebatur · Nix aute et glacies sustinebant uimcu
et honta bescebant ut scirent qm fructus inimic
exter minabatignis ardensingrandine et plu
coruscans · Hoc aute ut nutrirent iustitia sue u
t oblatus e ·

MS 481.60, f. 1r, Italy, s. XI[ex]

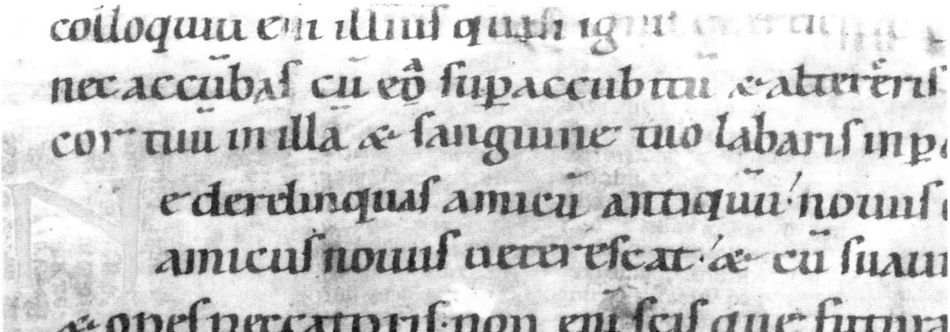

colloquiu ein illius qua ign...
nec accubas cu eo supaccubitu et atteret...
cor tuu in illa et sanguine tuo labaris inp...
e derelinquas amicu antiquu nouus...
amicus nouus ueterescat · ae cu suau...
et opes peccatoris non eni seis que futura
tibi iniuria iniustoru sciens qm usq ad
ge ab esto ab homine potestate habenti
timore moras et si accesseris ad illu no
auferat uita tua · Comunione mortis...

MS 481.61, f. 1r, Germany, s. XII[1]

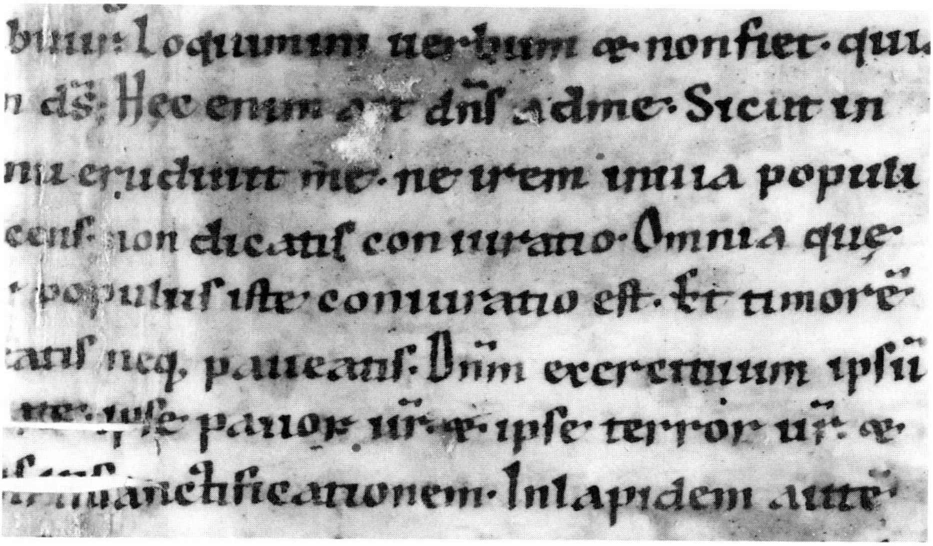

PLATE 39

MS 481.62, f. 1r, Southern Germany, s. XII

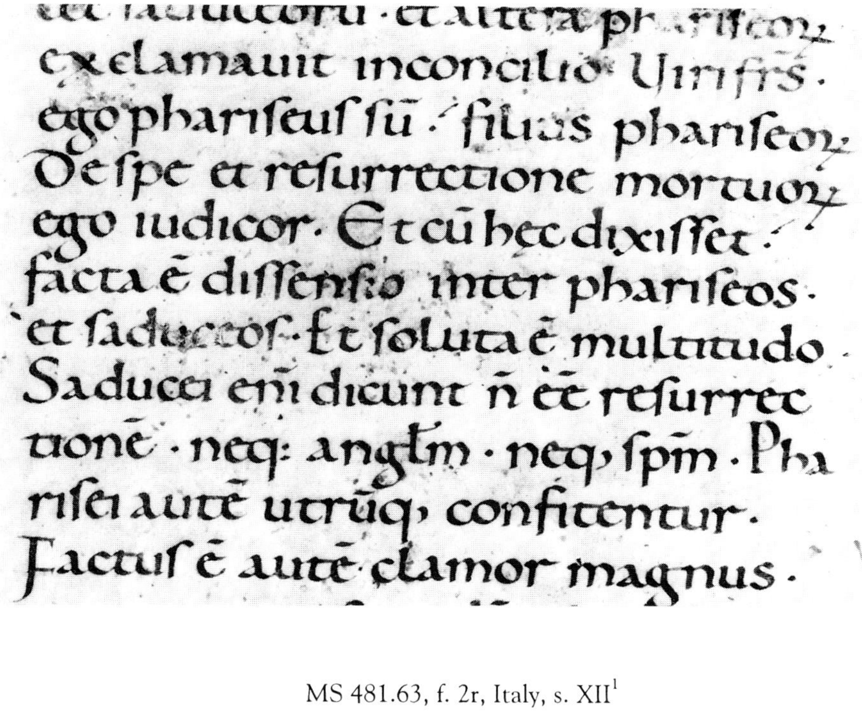

MS 481.63, f. 2r, Italy, s. XII[1]

PLATE 40

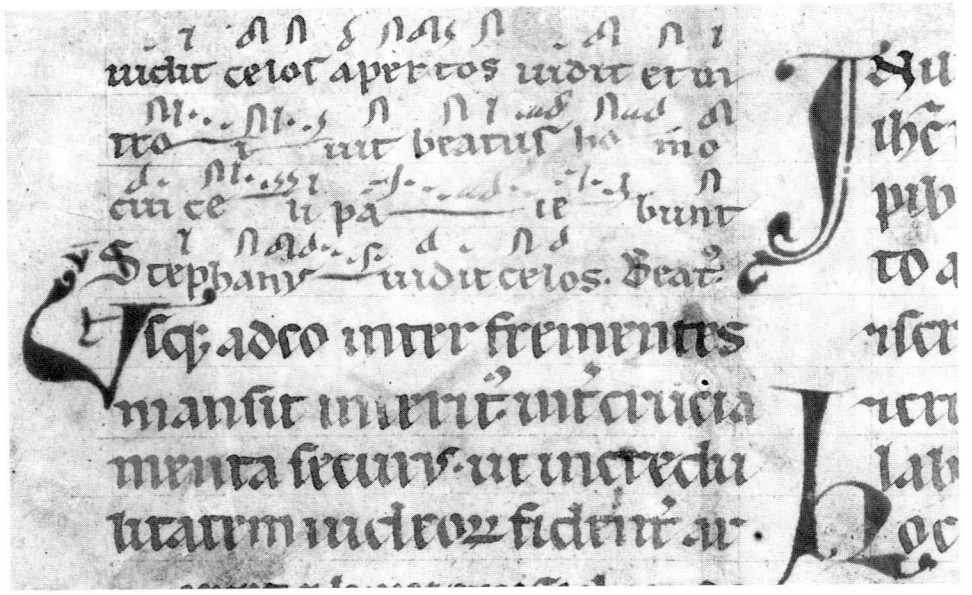

MS 481.64, f. 2v, Germany, s. XIII[1]

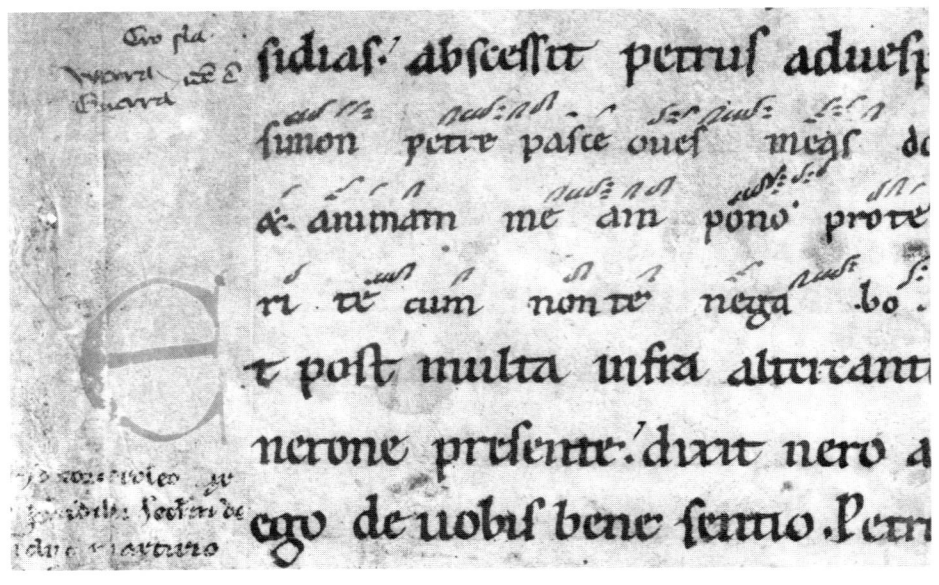

MS 481.65, f. 1v, Germany, s. XII[2]

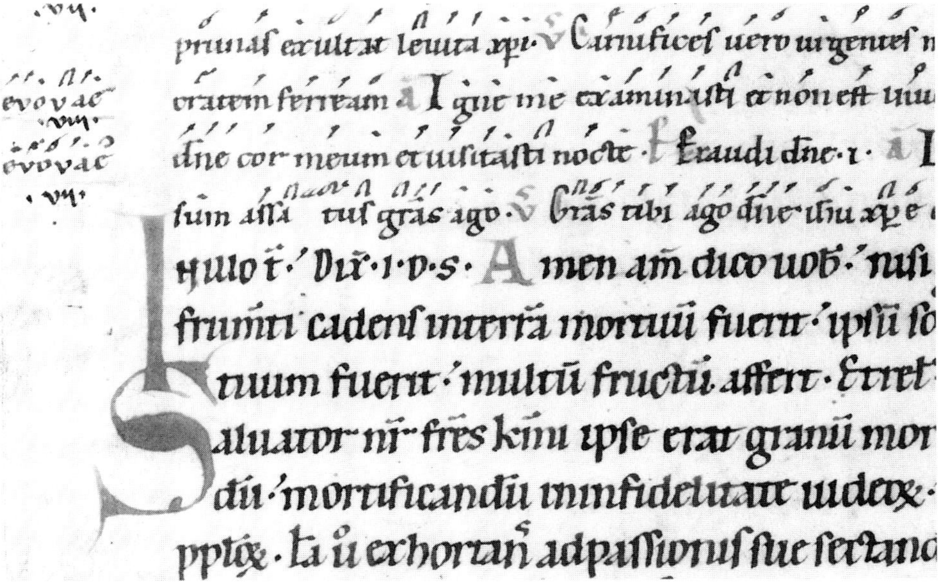

PLATE 41

prunus exultat leuita xpi · Carnifices uero urgentes n
cratem ferream · a I quic me exaîinasti cr non est iniu
dne cor meum et uisitasti nocte · t Exaudi dne · 1 · a I
sum asia tus gras ago · v Gras tibi ago dne iñu xpe ê
Hullo t̄ · Dir · 1 · v · s · A men am dico uob · nisi
frumti cadens interra mortuū fuerit · ipsū so
tuum fuerit · multū fructū affert · Et ret
aluator n̄r fr̄es k̄inu ipse erat granū mor
diu · mortificandū inīfidelitate uideox ·
pplox · ta u exhortan ad passionis sue sectand

MS 481.66, f. 3v, Lambach, Austria, s. XII[2]

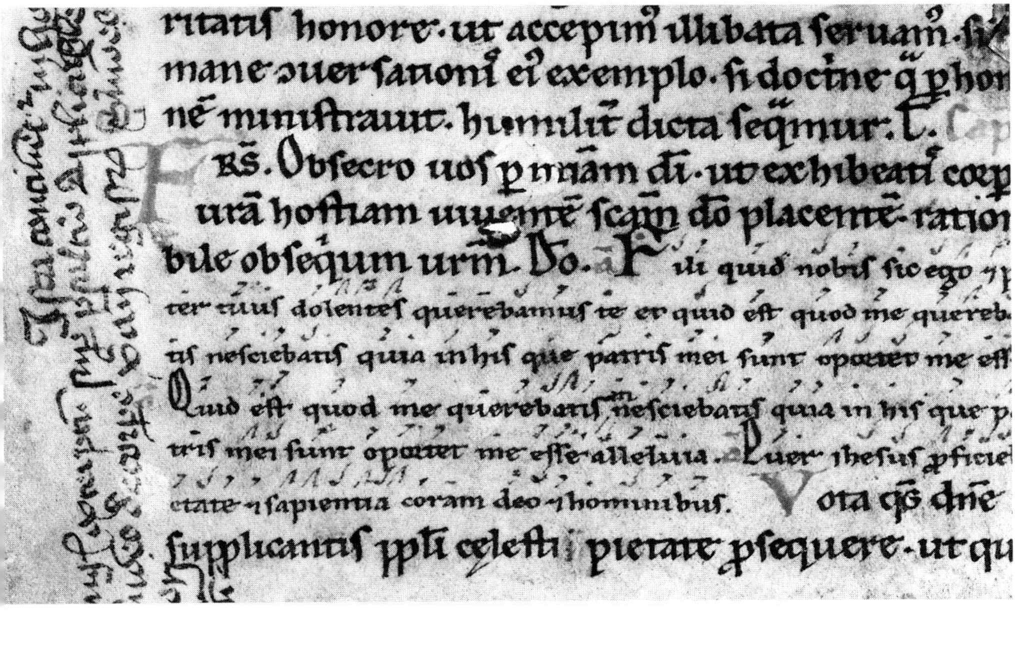

ritatis honore · ut accepim̄ illibata seruam̄ si
mane ouersationi ei exemplo · si doctrie q̄ phor
ne ministrauit · humilit̄ dicta seq̄mur · L ·
R̄S · Obsecro uos p m̄iam d̄i · ut exhibeati corp
urā hostiam uiuentē scām d̄o placentē ration
bile obseq̄um urm̄ · Do · F ui quid nobis sic ego
ter tuus dolentes querebamus te et quid est quod me quereb
us nesciebatis quia inhis que patris mei sunt oportet me es
Quid est quod me querebatis nesciebatis quia in his que p
tris mei sunt oportet me esse alleluia · Luer ihesus pficie
etate ī sapientia coram deo ī hominibus · Vota cp̄s d̄ne
supplicantis ipsi celesti pietate psequere · ut q

MS 481.67, f. 3v, Southern Germany or Austria, s. XII[2]

PLATE 42

ea hec est ut unu dm in trinitate. et trinitate in
unitate ueneremur. Neq; confundentes psonas.
neq; substantia separantes. Alia e eni psona patris.
alia filij. alia spc sci. Sed patris et filij et spc sci. una
est diuinitas. equalis gla. coeterna maiestas. Qualis
pater. talis filius talis spc scs. Increat pater. increat fili increat spc scs. Inmensus pat. inmensus filius. inmesus spc scs. Eternus pat. etn fili etn spc scs.
Et tam non tres eterni. sed unus eternus. Sicut n tres
increati. nec tres inmensi. sed un increat et un im-
mens. Similit omips pat. omips fili omips spc
scs Et tam non tres omipotentes. sed un omips.

MS 481.68, f. 2v, Germany, s. XII[2]

Inuenit eum in tra deserta in
loco horroris et uaste solitudi
nis. Circumduxit eum et
docuit. et custodiuit quasi pu
pillam oculi sui. Sic aqui
la puocans aduolandu pullo
suos. et subter eos uolitans. Ex
pandit alas suas et assupsit

M 105

132

MS 481.70, f. 1r, Germany, s. XIII[1]

PLATE 43

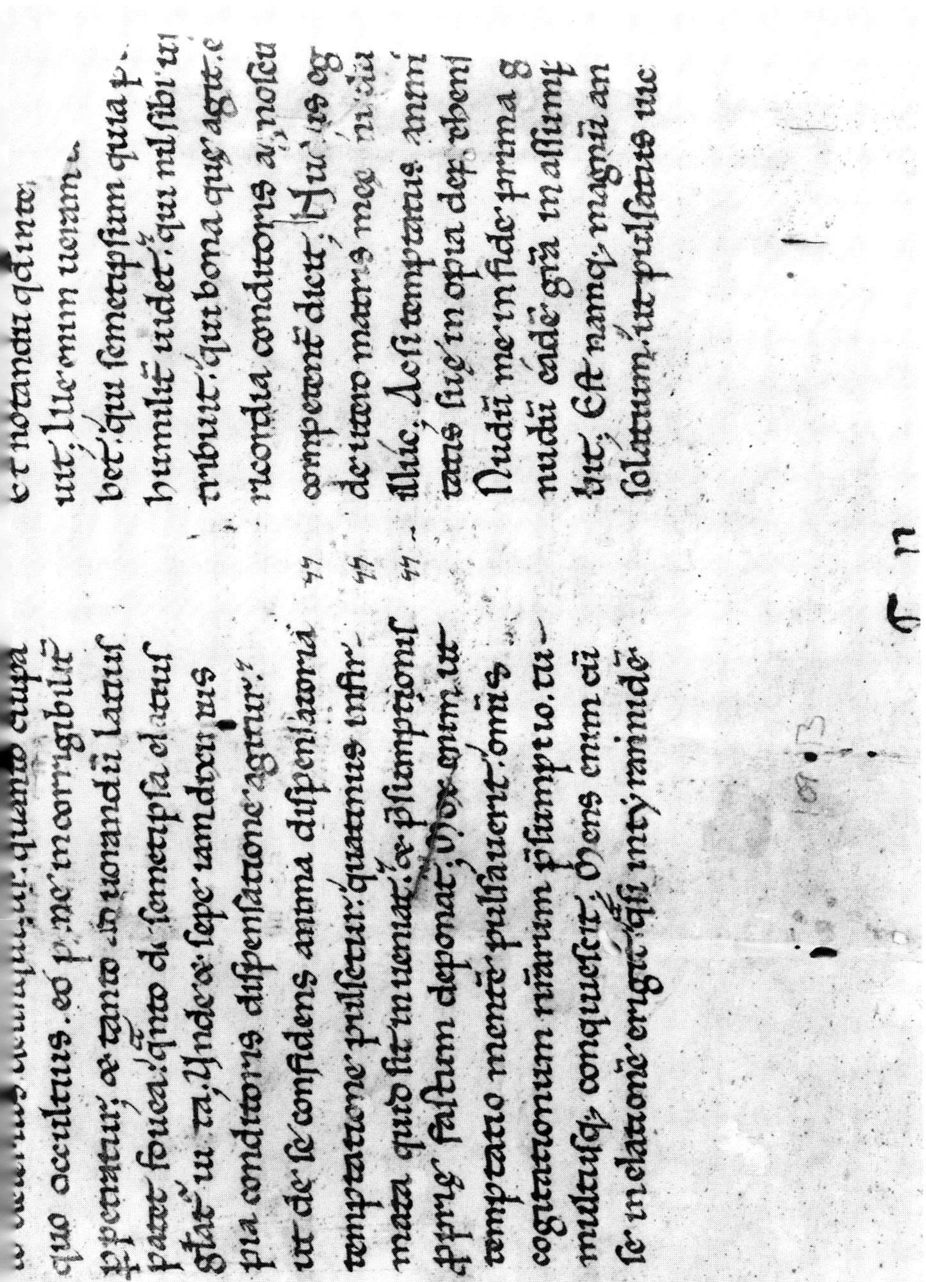

MS 481.71, f. 1v, France, s. XI/XII

PLATE 44

sub apostolicis & patriarcharum nominibus; arbitror dd eqna? & d eqnib; & n ipo
kalupsi iohannis apud nos scribit & multa diuinar scripturaru sacramota
restari; & necesse c ur tali scuris dic? & octo mha peruenit tcat cala
mox sub quo numero & in sedo. dc uicesimo psalmo l & n aturalis desecrip-
ta; grag; euange in describit; qub; ecca ide urbis saluatoris & struc .
ta est. Homon quog; ipsius cunaos; nequaquam crit ut pris-
hierosolima que interpretatur usio pacis; sed ad onansam.
quod in latmu sermonem uertitur domnus ibidem. qui
numquam precedat ab a. ut a priori populo ante discel
sit. tuterus ad discipulos. surgit abeamus hinc. & do
iudeos. relinquetur uobis domus uestra deserta. sed
eterna habeat possessionem. & sit c ipse possessio.
isdem discipulis repromittens: Ecce ego uobis
cum sum usq; ad consummationem seculi.

A ꞁ q c̄ c r̄ H . q . D

MS 481.72, f. 1v,
Southern Germany or Austria, s. XII[1]

PLATE 45

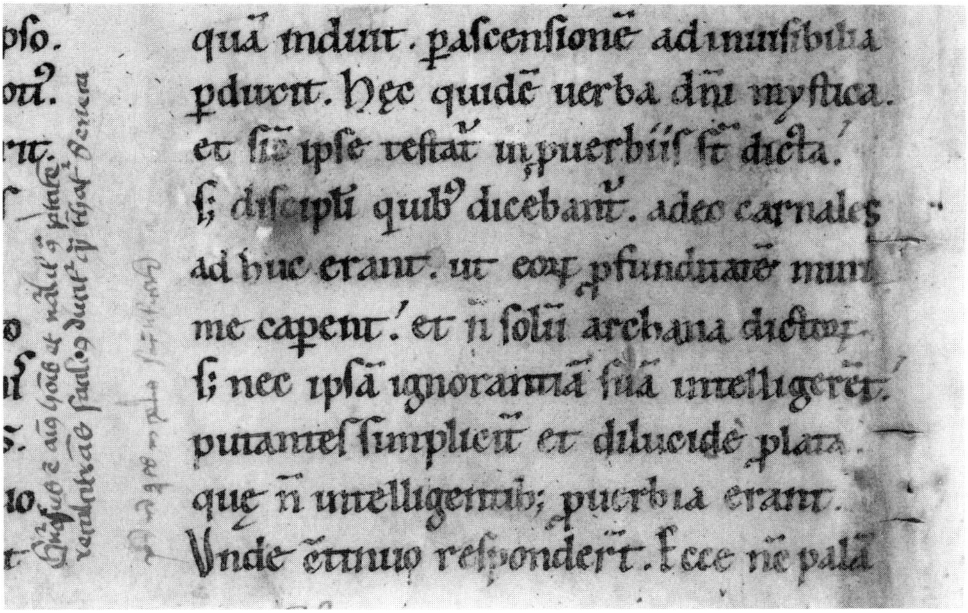

quā indunt . pascensionē ad inuisibilia
pduxit. Hęc quidē uerba dñi mystica.
et sīc ipse restat in puerbiis sr dicta.
s; discipli quib dicebant. adeo carnales
ad huc erant. ut eox pfunditatē mini
me capent. et n solū archana dictox;
s; nec ipsā ignorantiā suā intelligeret.
putantes simplicit et dilucide plata
que n intelligentib; puerbia erant.
Vnde etinuip respondert. Ecce nē pala

MS 481.73, f. 1v, Germany, s. XII

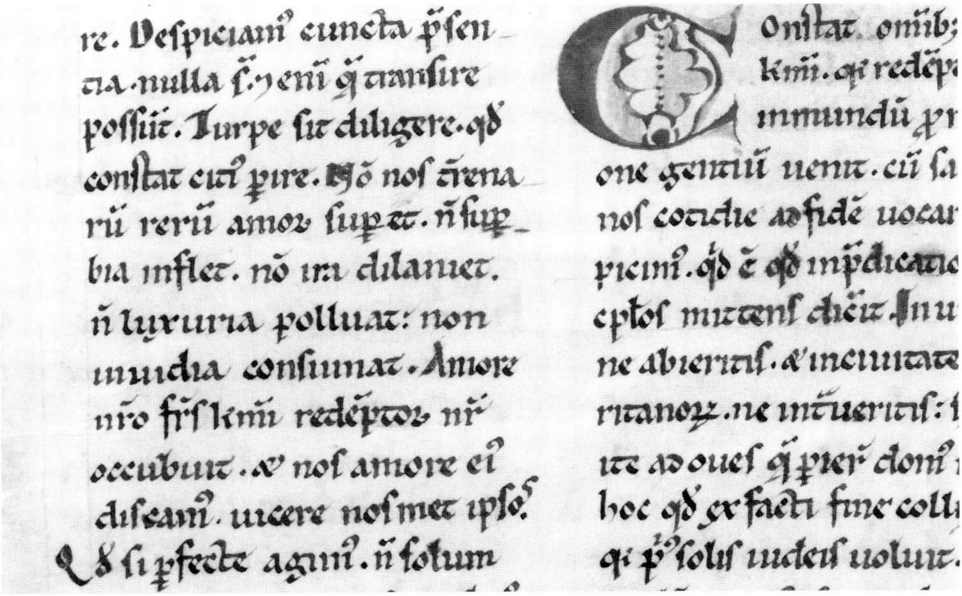

re. Despiciam cuncta psen
tia nulla s. y enī q transire
possiit. Turpe sit diligere qd
constat cu pire. Ideo nos terena
rū rerū amor supet. n sup
bia inflet. no ira dilaniet.
n luxuria polluat: non
inuidia consumat. Amore
nro srs kmi redeptox nr
occubuit. aut nos amore ei
discamī. uincere nosmet ipso?
Qs si pfecte agim. n solum

onstat omnib;
kmi. qt redep
immundū qr
one gentiū uenit. cū sa
nos cotidie aa fide uocar
picimi. qd e qd in pdicatie
eptos mittens dicit. In u
ne abieritis. a inciuitate
ritanox ne intueritis. I
ite ad oues q pter dom
hoc qd ex facti fine coll
qe p solis iudeis uoluit.

MS 481.74, f. 1r, Germany, s. XII/XIII

PLATE 46

iuiler · coluiuia toi poliu · ipciaiu iuuce of
bis terraru fine; De cortaneo oiariu;
are oiagnu est · qd ab occasu et oceano
fluit · et in meridie uergit · ft inde ad
septetrione tendit · et inde magnu appel
latur · qd cetera maria in coparatione eu minora
sunt · Istud e et meditraneu · qa p media terra
usq ad ortente pfundit · Europa et africa asia
q disterminans · Cui pme partis sinus · qui in
spanus pfundit · ybericus et balle ire appellat ·
De inde gallicus · qui narbonense p meia allu

MS 481.75, f. 1r, Germany, s. XII[2]

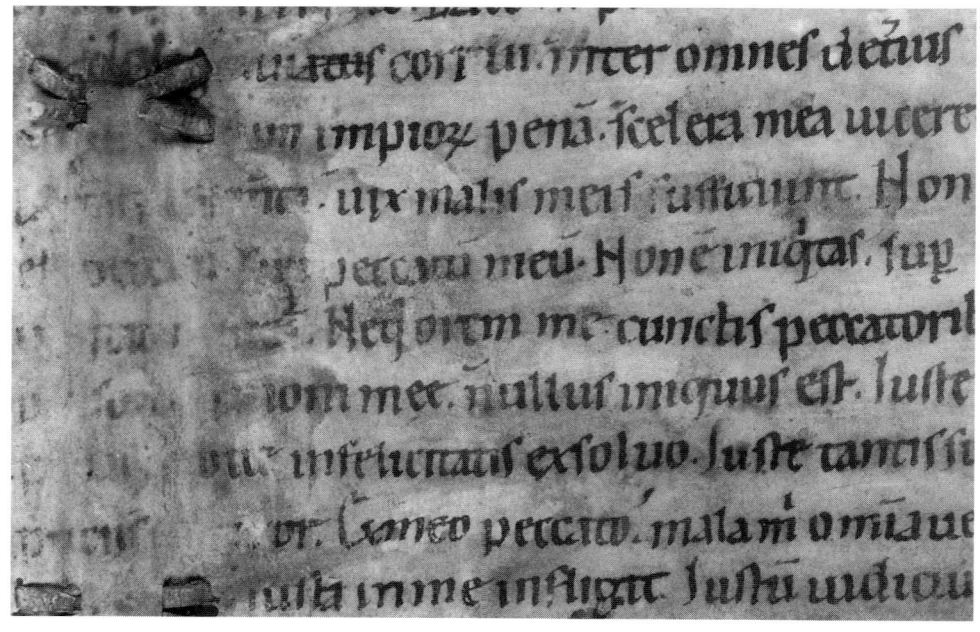

MS 481.76, f. 1r, Southern Germany, s. XII[2]

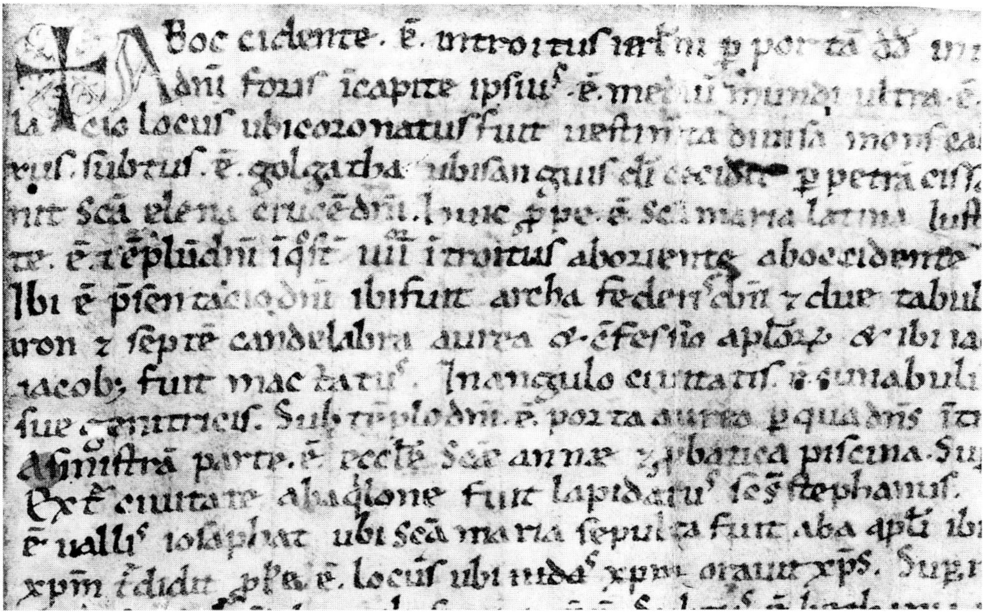

PLATE 47

MS 481.77, f. 1r, Italy, s. XII$^{1/4}$

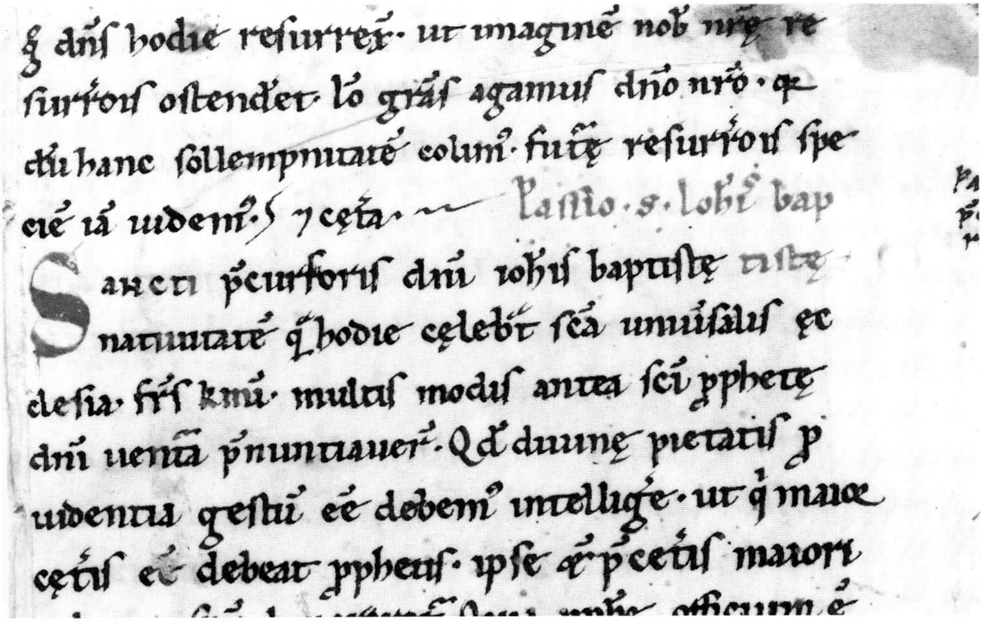

MS 481.78, f. 1r, Southern Germany or Austria, s. XII^{ex}

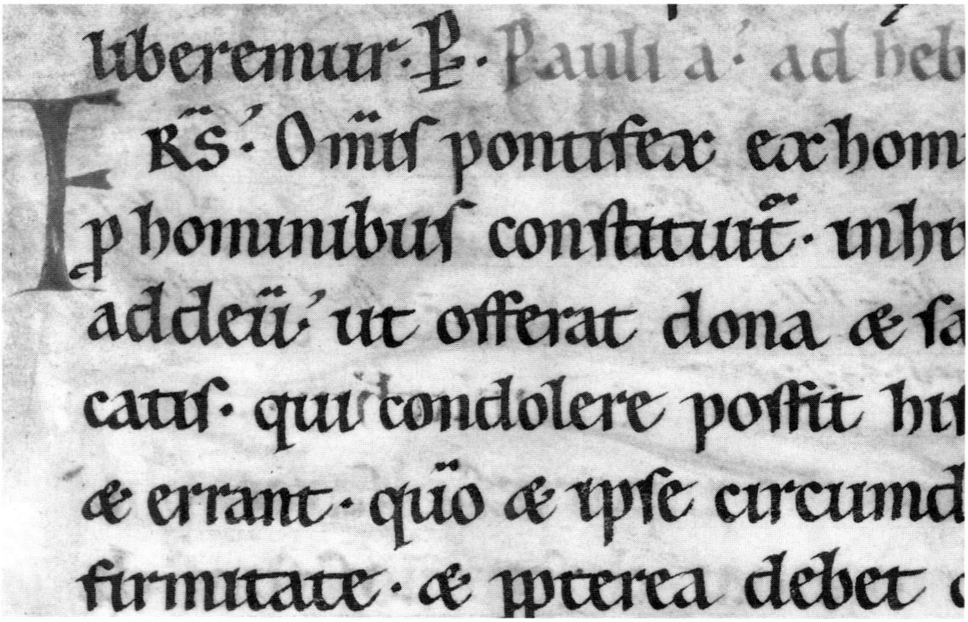

PLATE 48

liberemur · P · pauli a · ad heb

RS · Omnis pontifex ex hom

p hominibus constituit · inhi

ad deū · ut offerat dona & sa

catis · qui condolere possit hi

& errant · quō & ipse circumd

firmitate · & ipterea debet

MS 481.79, f. 2r, Germany, s. XII

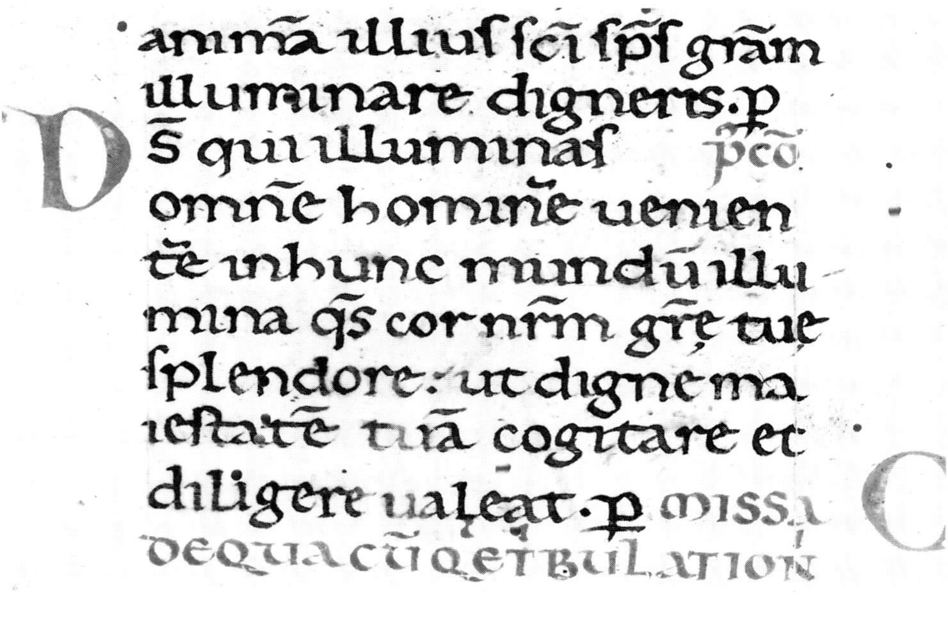

anima illius sci sps grām

illuminare digneris · p

s qui illuminas   pco

omnē hominē uenien

tē inhunc mundū illu

mina qs cor nrm gre tue

splendore · ut digne ma

iestate tuā cogitare et

diligere ualeat · p MISSA

DEQUACŪQ ET BULATION

MS 481.80, f. 1v, Italy, s. XII^med

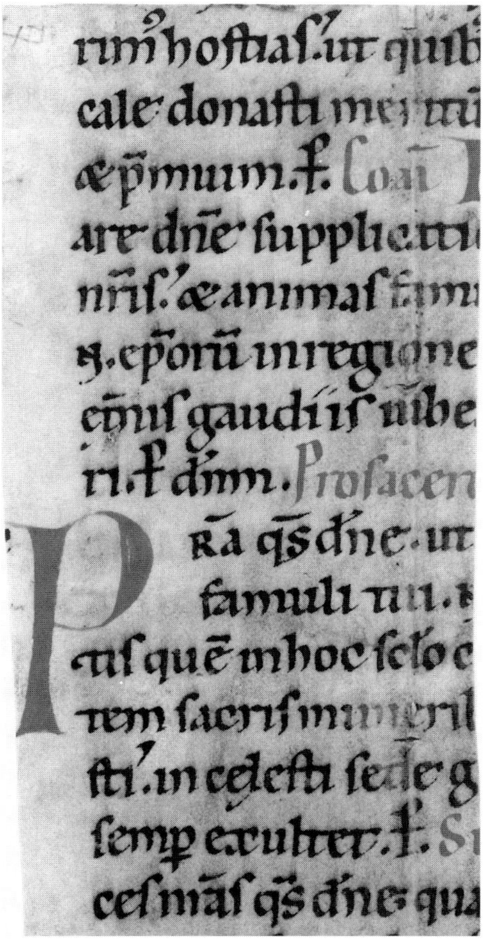

PLATE 49

rum hostias. ut quib̄
cale donasti me tru
æp̄muim.f. Coai
are dn̄e supplietti
nr̄is. ꝯ animas tam
ꝗ. epōrū in regione
cm̄is gaudiis nibe
ri.f dn̄m. Profacen
r̄a q̄s dn̄e. ut
famuli tui.
tus quē in hoc seło ꝯ
tem sacrisim̄inerib̄
sti. in celesti sede g
semp exultet. f. Si
ces mās q̄s dn̄e qua

MS 481.81, f. 1v, Southern Germany, s. XII[2]

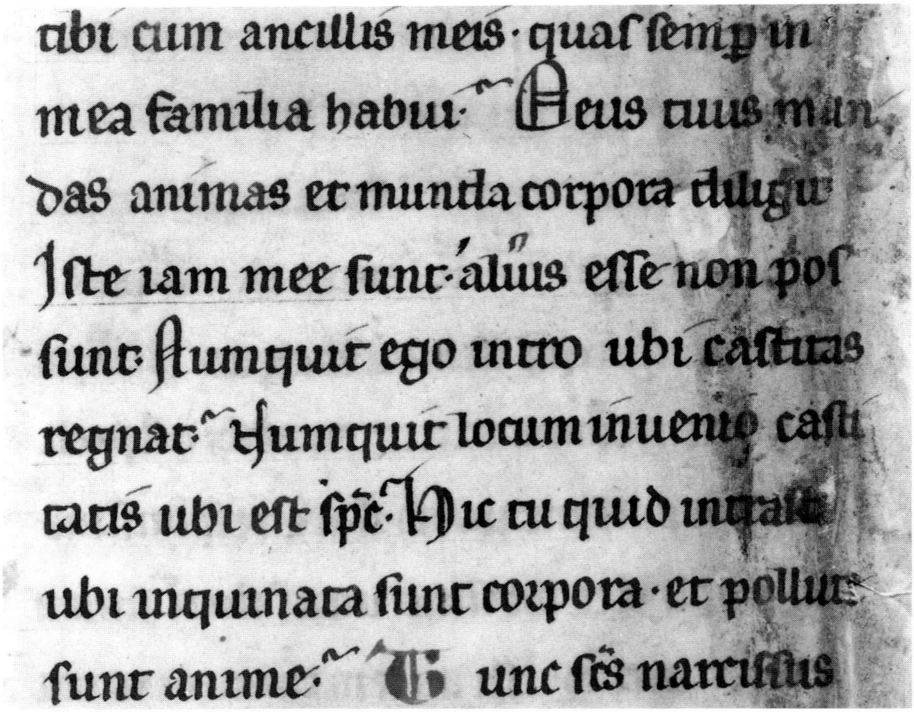

PLATE 49

tibi cum ancillis meis · quas semp in
mea familia habui· Deus tuus mun-
das animas et munda corpora diligit
Iste iam mee sunt· alius esse non possunt Nuumquit ego intro ubi castitas
regnat· Numquit locum invenio castitatis ubi est spc· Hic tu quid intras
ubi inquinata sunt corpora · et pollut-
sunt anime· Tunc scs narcissus

PLATE 50

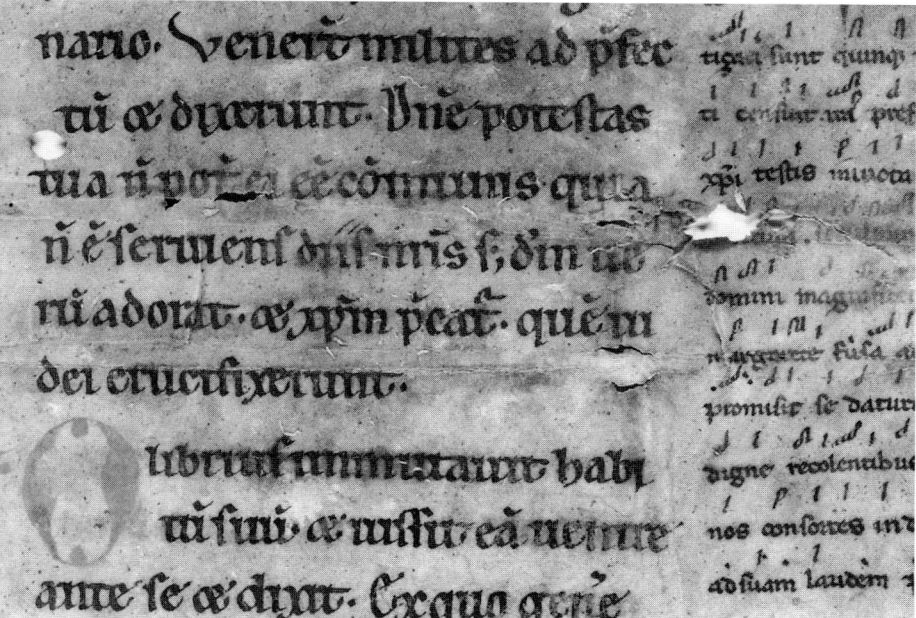

MS 481.83, f. 1r, Southern Germany, s. XII²

MS 481.84, f. 1r, Southern Germany, s. XII²

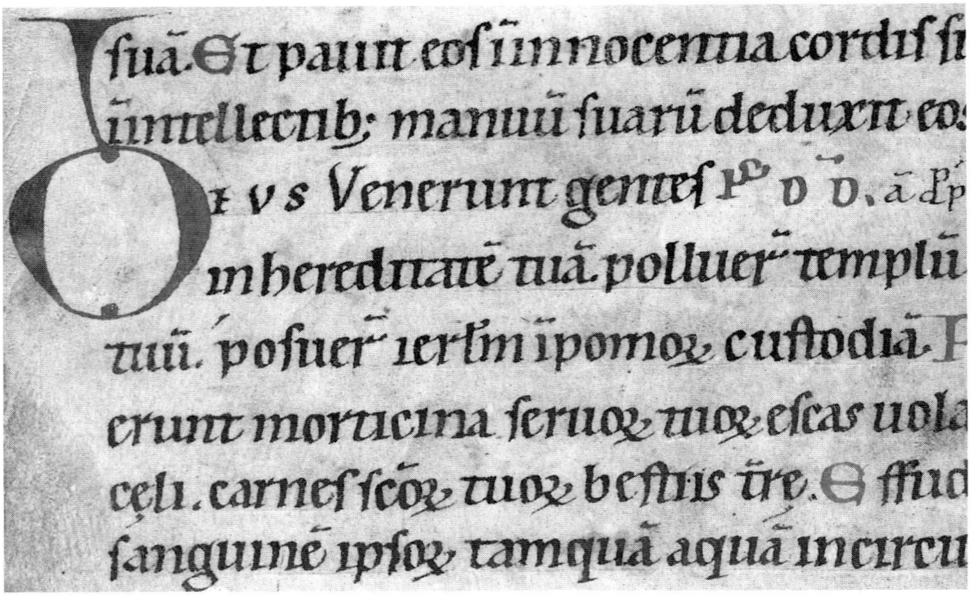

PLATE 51

suā. Et pauit eos ī innocentia cordis si
in intellectib; manuū suarū deduxit eos
t vs Venerunt gentes ḷo ḍ ̄ḍ. ā p̄p̄
in hereditatē tuā. polluerūt templū
tuū. posuerūt ierłm ipomoz custodiā
erunt morticina seruoz tuoz escas uola
celi. carnes scoz tuoz bestiis tre. Effud
sanguinē ipsoz tamquā aquā incircu

MS 481.85, f. 3r, Southern Germany or Austria, s. XII

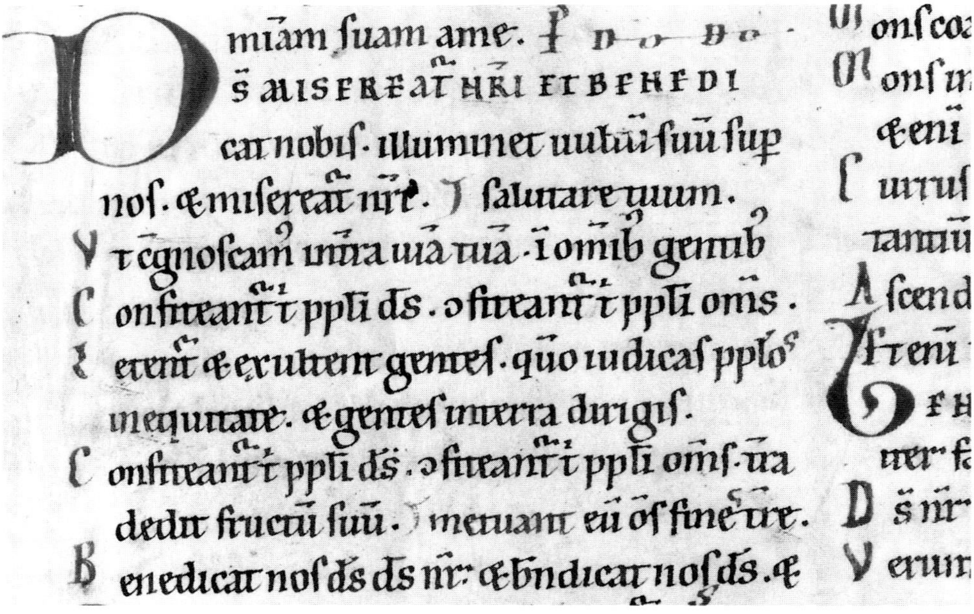

miam suam ame. ̄ ̄ onscoa
s misereat nri et benedi onsin
cat nobis. illuminet uultū suū sup æni
nos. & misereat nri. ̄ salutare tuum. untut
t cognoscam intra uia tua. i omib gentib tantū
onfiteant t ppli ds. ofiteant t ppli oms. Ascend
etent & exultent gentes. quo iudicas pplos treni
inequitate. & gentes interra dirigis. ̄ FH
onfiteant t ppli ds. ofiteant t ppli oms. tra uer f
dedit fructū suū. metuant eū oms fines tre. D s nr
enedicat nos ds ds nr; & bndicat nos ds. & erun

MS 481.86, f. 2r, Melk, Austria, s. XII/XIII

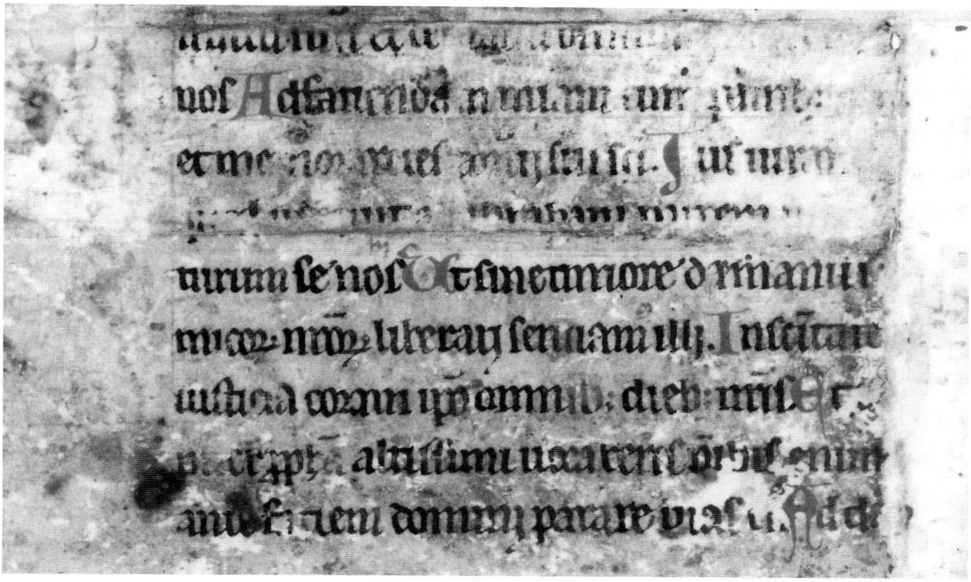

PLATE 52

MS 481.87, f. 1v, Germany, s. XIII[1]

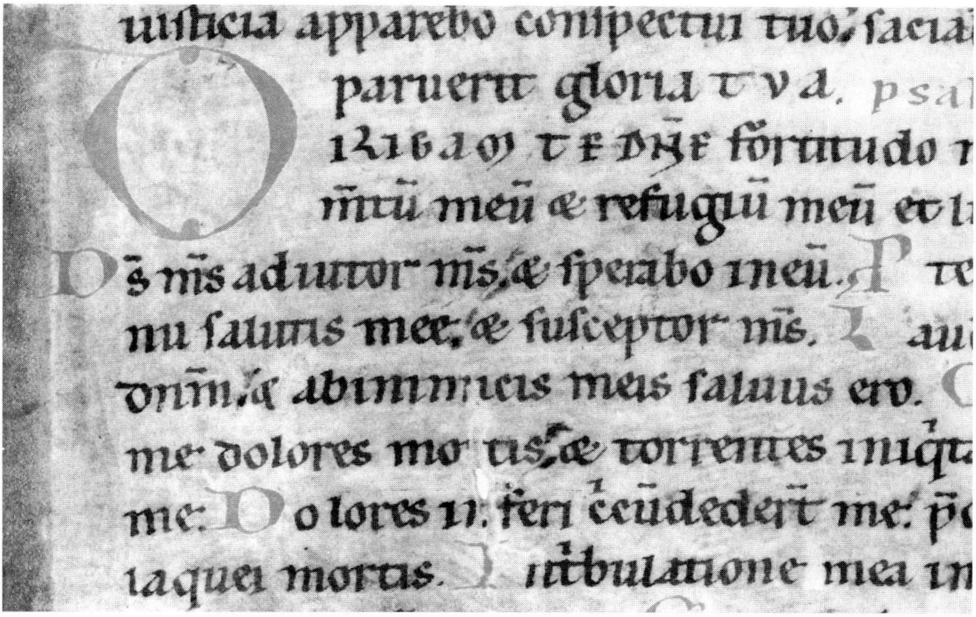

MS 481.88, f. 4r, Lambach, Austria, s. XII[ex]

PLATE 53

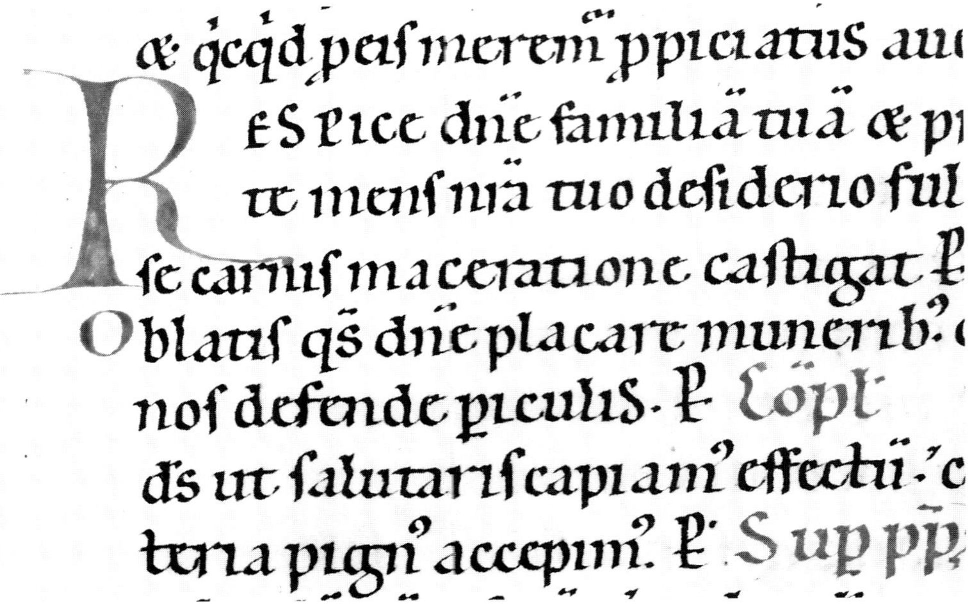

Ꝝ Ꝙ qᶜqd peⱦſ merem̄ ppiciatuſ au[

ES pice dn̄e familiā tuā œ p[

tᶜ menſ n̄ıā tuo deſideꝛio ful[

ſe carnıſ maceꝛatıone caſtıgat ꝑ[

Oblatıſ q̄ſ dn̄e placare munerıb' [

noſ defende pıculıſ . ꝑ Cōpl[

d̄ſ ut ſalutarıſ capıam̄ effectū · c[

teꝛıa pıgn̄ accepım̄ . ꝑ Supp p̄[

MS 481.91, f. 1v, Southern Germany or Austria, s. XII^2

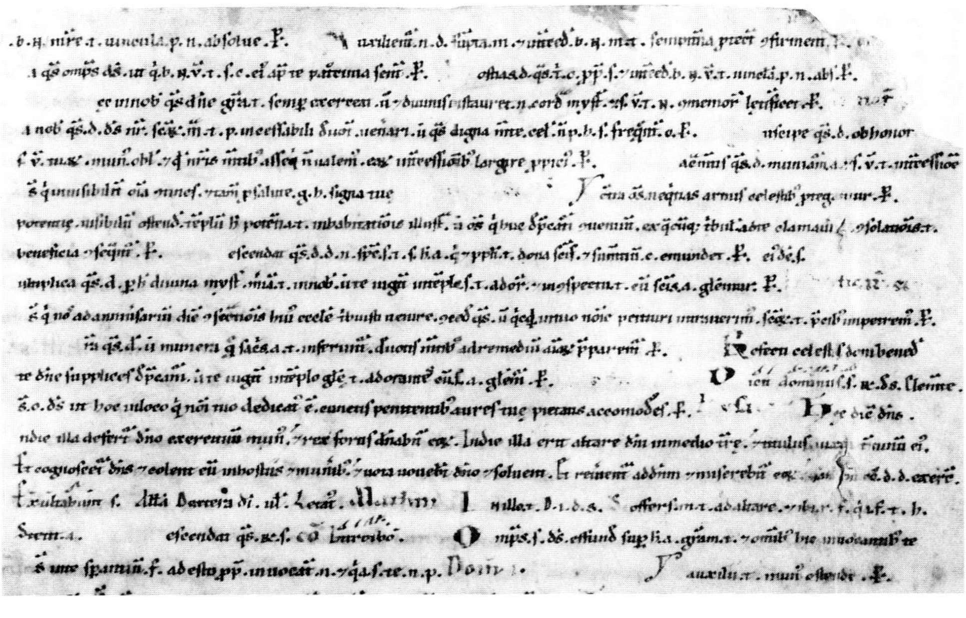

MS 481.92, f. 4v, Southern Germany or Austria, s. XII^{med}

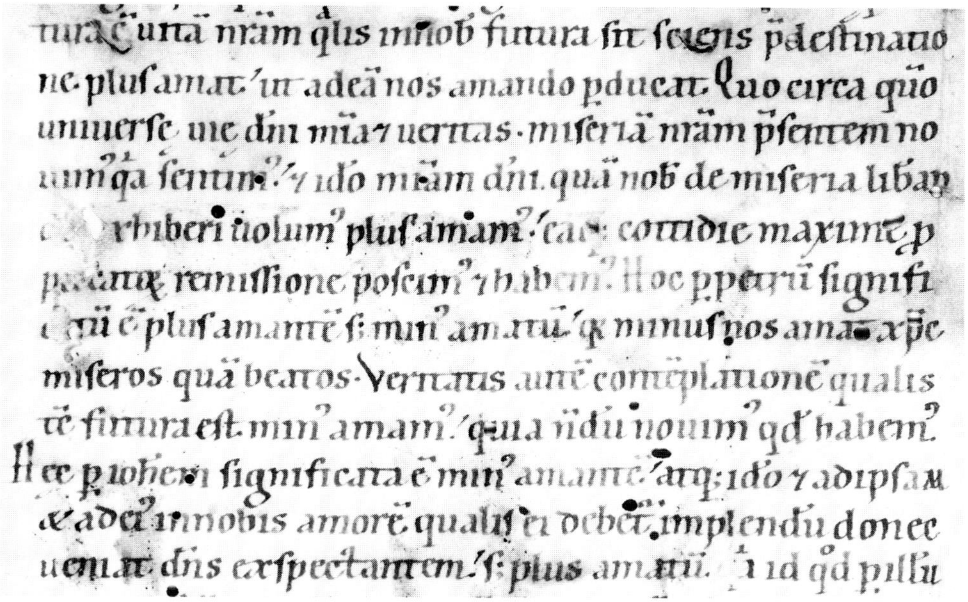

PLATE 54

turā c̄ urtā n̄rām q̄lis inn̄ob futura sit sciēis pdestinatio
ne·plus amat·ut adeā nos amando pducat. Quo circa quo
uniuerse·me dn̄i mīa ⁊ ueritas·miseriā n̄rām p̄sentem no
uin̄q̄a sentim̄·⁊ ideo mīam dn̄i·quā nob de miseria libar̄
c̄ ...nhiberi uolum̄ plus amiam̄·eac̄ cottidie maxime p
p....atuq̄ remissione poscim̄ ⁊ habem̄·Hoc p p̄tm̄ signifi
c̄ ...tn̄ c̄ plus amante si mn̄ amatū·q̄ minus nos ama x̄p̄e
miseros quā beatos·Veritatis aūt contēplatione qualis
tē futura est·mn̄ amam̄·quia n̄dū nouim̄ qd̄ habem̄·
Hec p uohem signiftcata c̄ mn̄ amante·atq̄ ideo ⁊ adipsam
ate adeā innobis amore qualis ea debet·implendū donec
ueniat dn̄s exspectantem·S̄ plus amatū·⁊ id qd̄ p̄sstu

MS 481.93, f. 1v, Lambach, Austria, s. XII^ex

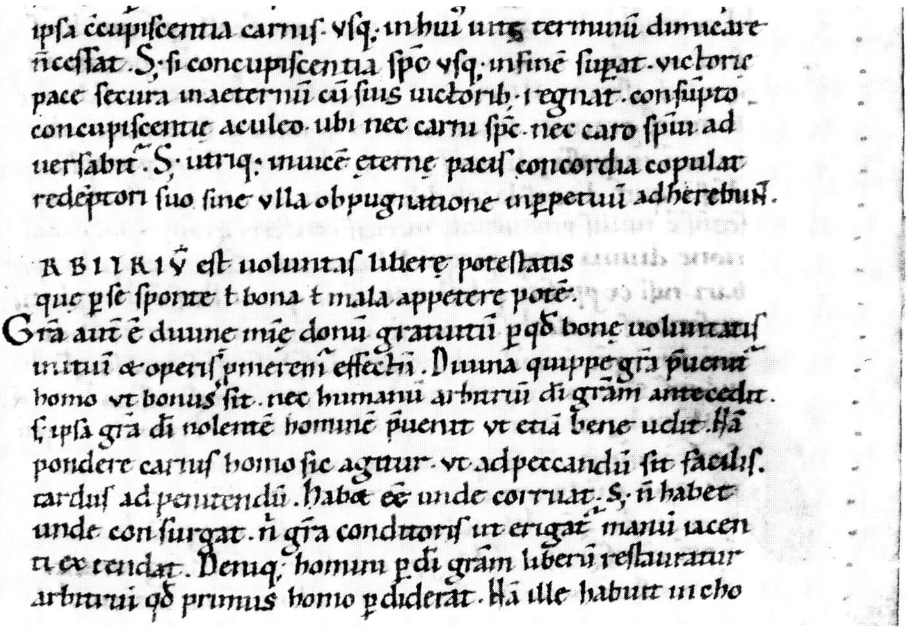

ipsa c̄cupiscentia carnis·vsq̄·in hui uitg terminū dimicare
ncessat·S̄ si concupiscentia sp̄o vsq̄·infine supat·victorie
pace secura inaeternū cū suis uictorib·⁊ regnat·consupto
concupiscentie aculeo·ubi nec carni sp̄e·nec caro sp̄u ad
uersabit·S̄·utriq̄·inuicē eterne pacis concordia copulat
redēptori suo sine ulla obpugnatione inppetuū adhērebuñ·

ARBITRIŪ est uoluntas libere potestatis
que p se sponte t bona t mala appetere pote·
Gr̄a aūt c̄ diuine mīe donū gratuitū pq̄d bone uoluntatis
initiū ⁊ operis p̄merentī effectu·Diuina quippe gr̄a p̄uenit
homo ut bonus sit·nec humanū arbitriū d̄i grām anteceda·
s̄ ipsā grā d̄i nolente homine p̄uenit ut etiā bene uelit·Iñ̄a
pondere carnis homo sic agitur·ut ad peccandū sit facilis·
tardus ad penitendū·habet ec̄ unde corruat·S̄·n̄ habet
unde consurgat·n̄ gr̄a conditoris ut erigat manū iacen
ti ex tendat·Deniq̄·homini p d̄i grām liberū restauratur
arbitriū qd̄ primus homo p̄diderat·Hā ille habuit in cho

MS 481.94, f. 1r, Germany, s. XII^in

PLATE 55

MS 481.95, f. 1v, Germany, s. XIII

MS 481.96, f. 2r, Germany, s. XIII

PLATE 56

MS 481.97, f. 1v, Germany, s. XIII

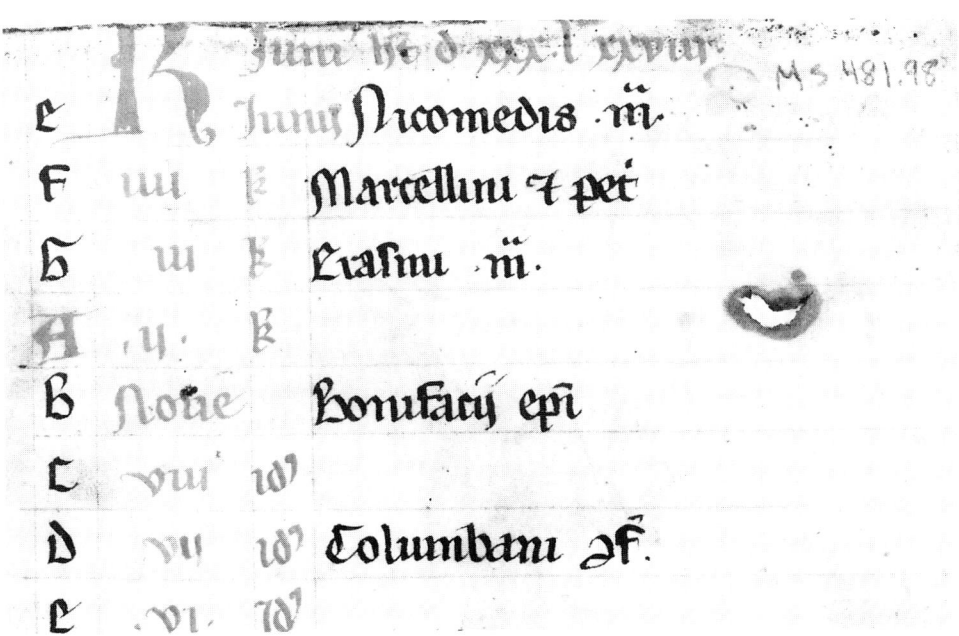

MS 481.98, f. 2r, Southern Germany, s. XIII[2]

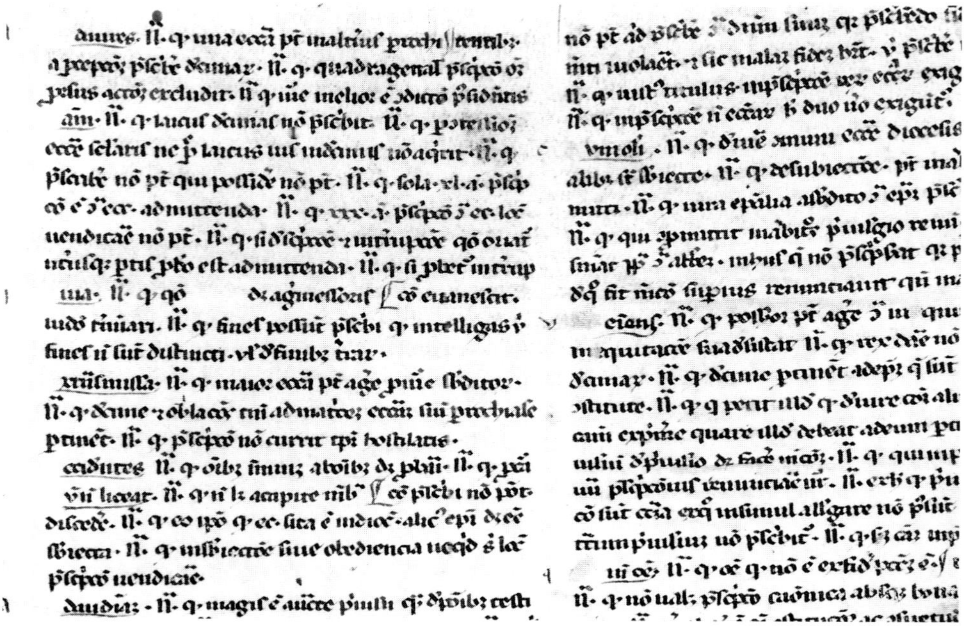

PLATE 57

MS 481.99, f. 6r, Italy, s. XIII[2]

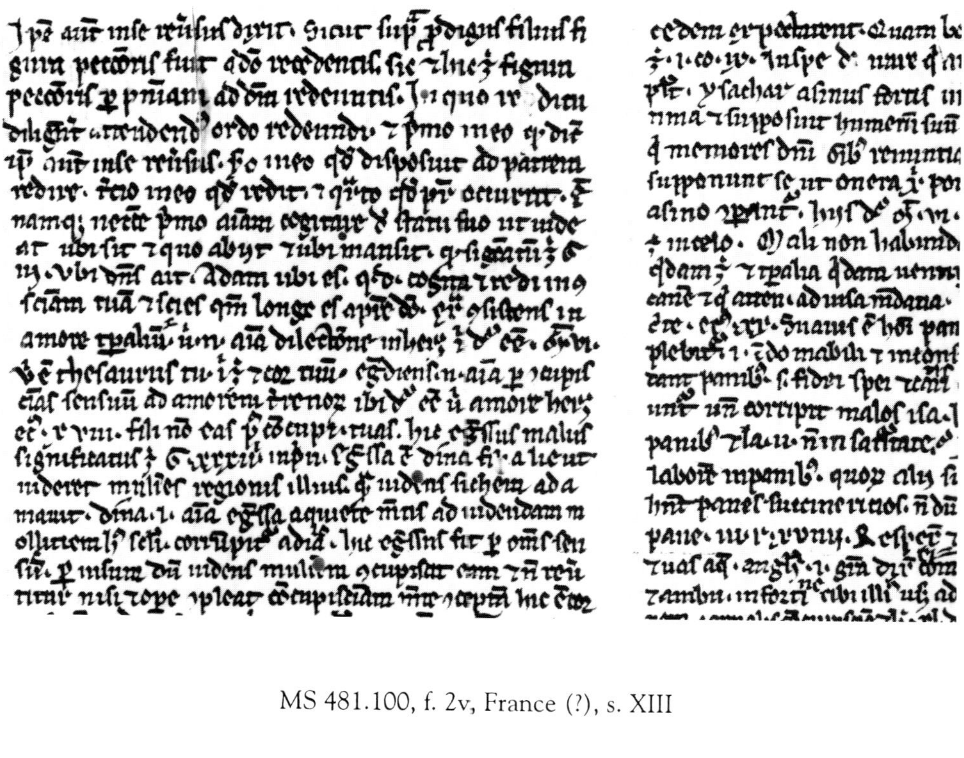

MS 481.100, f. 2v, France (?), s. XIII

PLATE 58

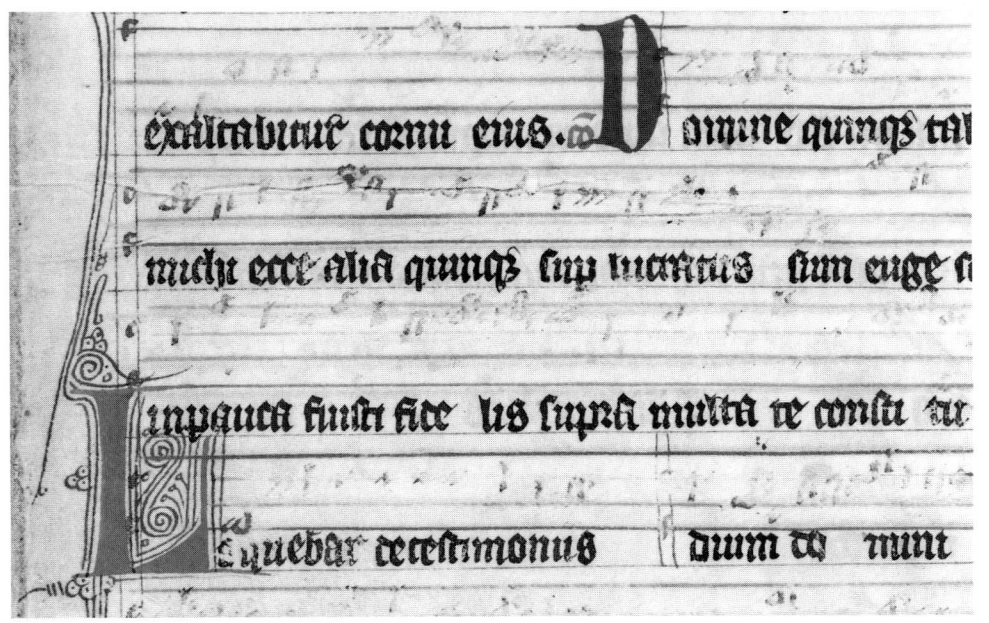

MS 481.101, f. 2r, Germany, s. XIII/XIV

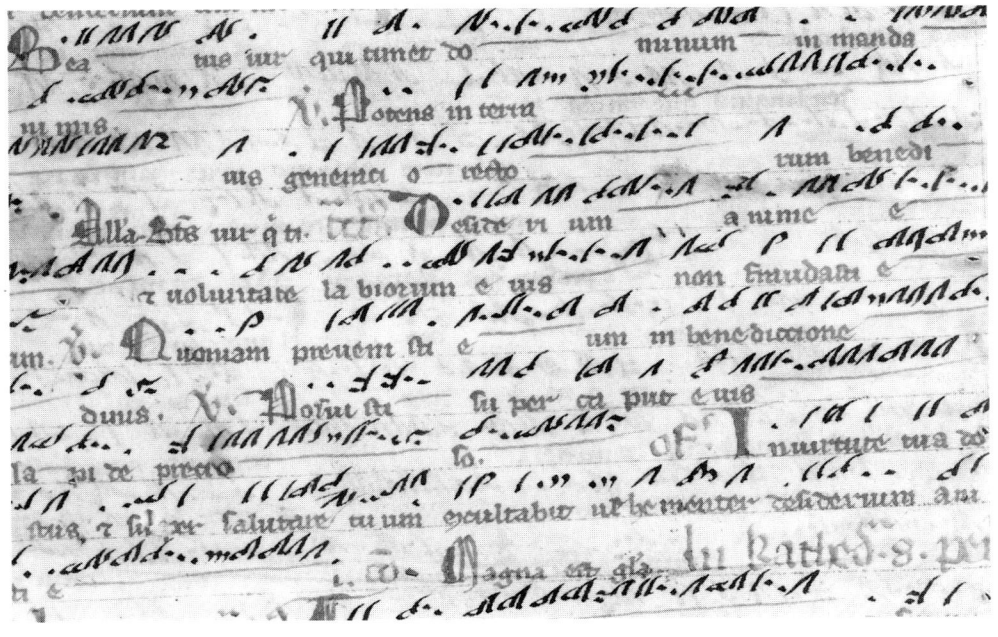

MS 481.102, f. 2r, Southern Germany or Austria, s. XIII^{ex}

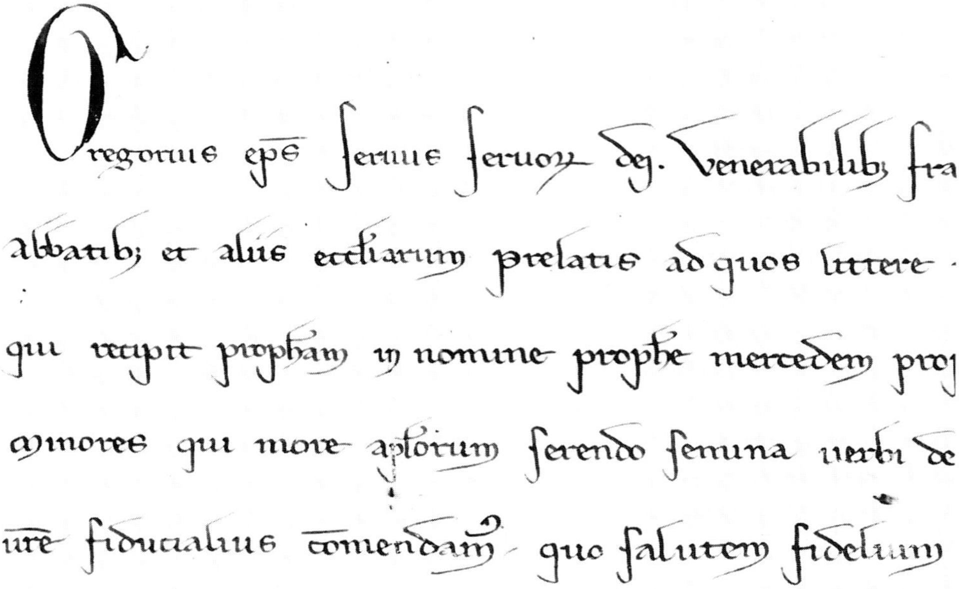

PLATE 59

Gregorius ep̄s seruus seruoꝝ dei. Venerabilibꜩ fra
albatibꜩ et aliis ecclarum prelatis ad quos littere ·
qui recipit prophaɱ in nomine prophe mercedem proj
aɱores qui more aⱊtorum serendo semina uerbi de
ūre fiduciahus comendaɱ· quo salutem fidelium

MS 481.103, f. 1r, Perugia, Italy, 14 July 1235

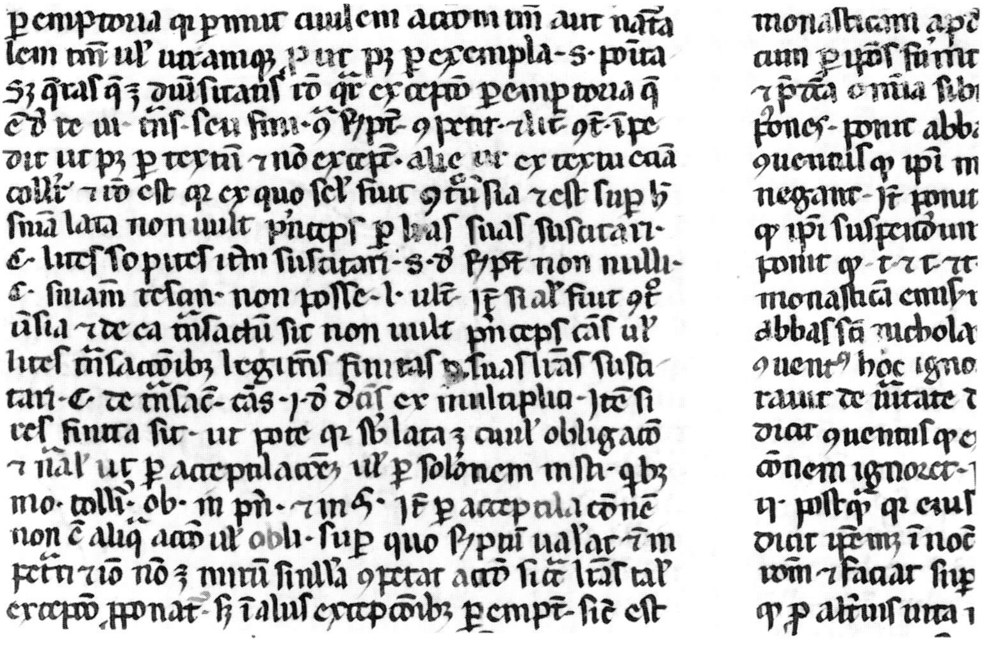

pemptoria q̄ pꝛimit auulem acaom tm̄ aut nāta
lem tm̄ ul' utramꝗꝫ p ut pꝫ pexempla· s· pꝺta
ꝫꝫ grās q̄ꝫ duisitans rō q̄r ex cꝺptō pempꝺruia q̄
ꝺd ꝺc ut tns̄· seu sim· ꝺ Ᵽꝓpt 9ꝺenr· ꝛlic gt· īpe
ꝺit ut pꝫ p ꝺexꝛni ꝛno ex cꝺptī· alie ur ex ꝺcꝛu caā
colli' ꝛ rō est qꝛ ex quo seꝯl' siut 9tū sia rest sup ꝝ
sua lata non uult pꝛincps p ꝝas suas susataꝛi
e· lites so pites idm susataꝛi· s· ꝺ Ᵽꝓpt non nulli
e· simam ꝺean· non posse· l· ult· if̄ sia siut gt
ūsia ꝛ ꝺe ca insactu sit non uult pꝛincps caꝯ ul'
lites insacpibꝫ legiꝺnis finitas ꝓ suas lias susa
taꝛi· e· ꝺc insac· cās· ꝓꝺ ꝺaꝯ ex inulaplia· ꝺe si
res sintra sit· ut pꝺꝛe qꝛ sb lata ꝫ cuul' obligacō
ꝛ ꝺal' ut p acꝛpulacꝛ ul' p solonem insi· qbꝫ
mo· tolli· ob· in pꝛi· ꝛ in ꝗ· if̄ p acꝛpula cōnē
non ē aliꝗ acō ul' obli· sup quo Ᵽꝓpt ualꝛac ꝛ in
fꝛen ꝛio nōꝫ niiru siulla ꝓꝺetar acō siꝛ liā tal
exꝺcꝺpō ꝑꝓnat· sꝫ talus exꝺcꝛpōibꝫ pempꝺ· sic est

monasticam apꝺ
cum p ꝝꝓs̄ siurnt
ꝛ ꝑꝺa ōnia sibi
fones· ꝑꝓnit abbꝛ
quentiis qꝺ ipi m
negant· sꝫ ꝑꝓnit
qꝛ ipi suspendun
ꝑꝓnit qꝛ ꝛꝛ ꝛꝛ
monastiꝛ cmisꝛ
abbas sā nicholꝛ
quent9 hoc igno
rauir ꝺc nūrare ꝛ
ꝺiar quentiis qꝛe
ōnem ignozcꝛ· ꝛ
iꝛ pȝstꝗ qꝛ cxul
ꝺiar ipꝺem ꝛ ī noc
rom ꝛ faciar sup
qꝫ p alrins urra ꝛ

MS 481.104, f. 1r, Italy, s. XIV

PLATE 60

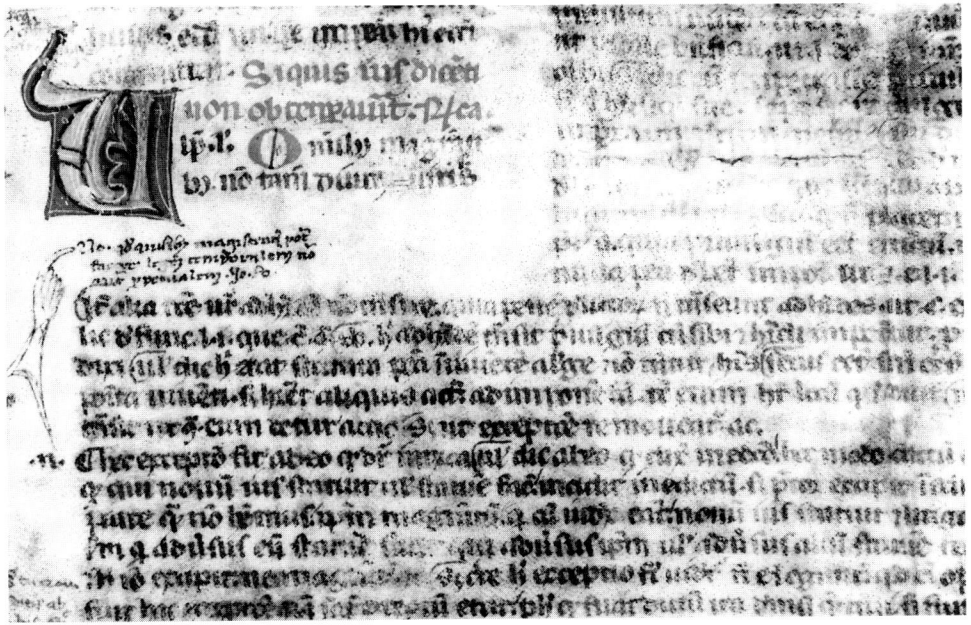

MS 481.105, f. 1r, Italy, s. XIV

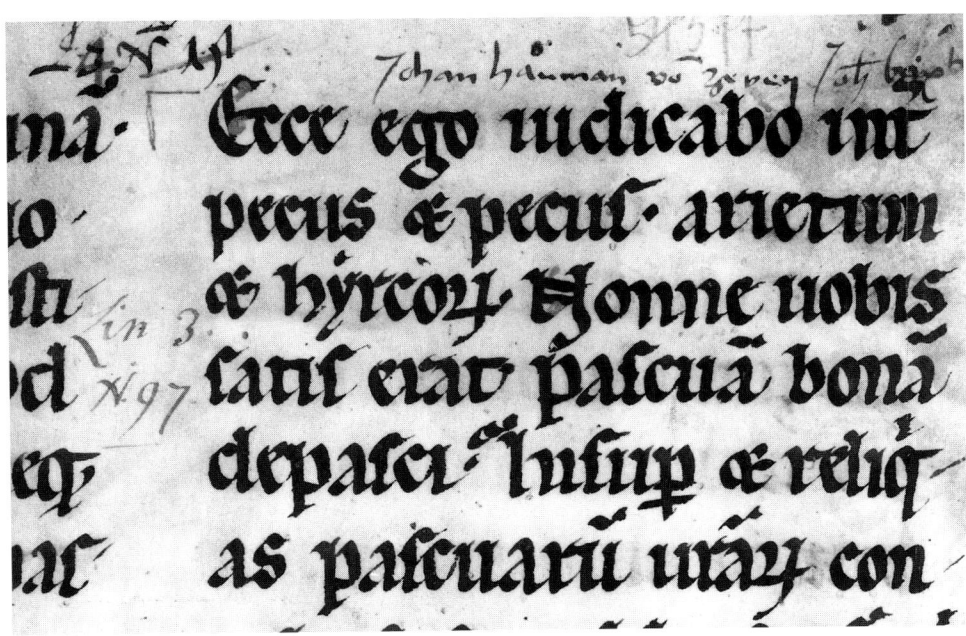

MS 481.106, f. 1v, Southern Germany, s. XIII

mee uenit.

rcumsperi & non erat auxiliator.

fuit qui adiuuaret.

t saluauit michi brachium meun

mea ipsa auxiliata est michi·

f nite & reuertaii ad dm̅m̅·q

& sanabit nos· pcuciet & cura

unficabit nos post duos dies

suscitabit nos· & uiuemus in co

MS 481.107, f. 1r, Germany, s. XIII

MS 481.108, fol. 8R

s̅ Rui ecclam tuam

annua quadragesimali obseruacioē

purificas· pta familie tuę? ut qd̅ are

obtinere nittitur·hoc bonus operibus prqua

tur .♣. acrificium quadra

gesimalis in ieu solempnit̅ immolamus te

due depcantes? ut cum epulas̅ restrictione

MS 481.108, f. 8r, Germany, s. XIII[1]

PLATE 62

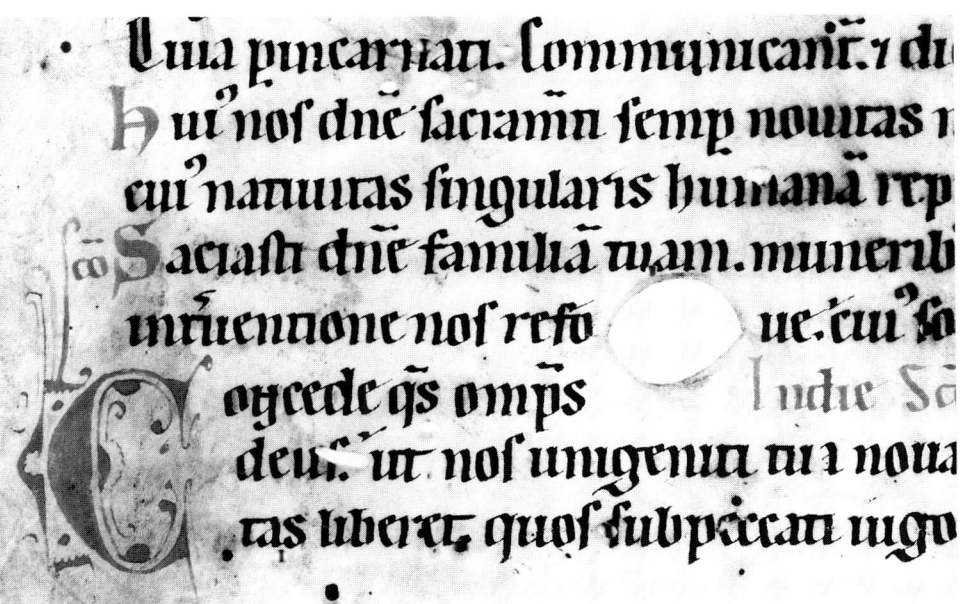

MS 481.109, f. 2v, Germany, s. XIII[1]

MS 481.110, f. 2r, France, s. XIII

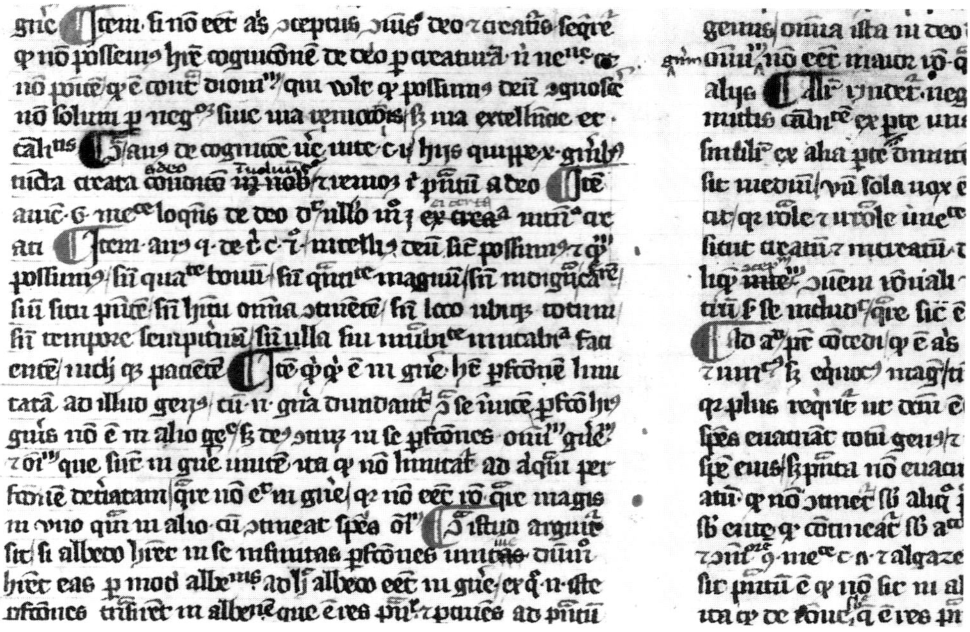

PLATE 63

MS 481.111, f. 2r, France, s. XIII^2

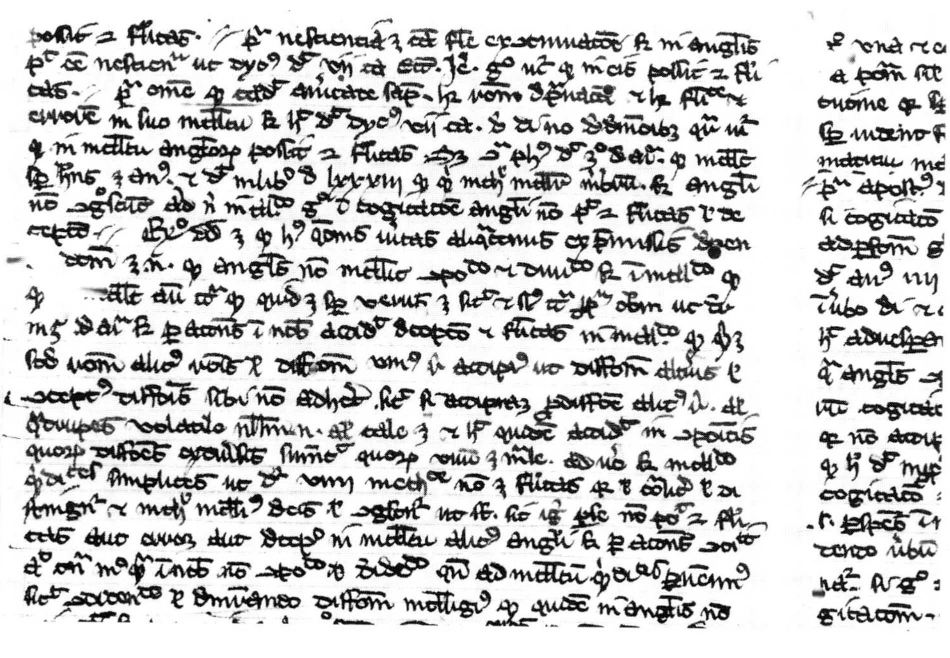

MS 481.112, f. 1v, Italy, s. XIII^{med}

PLATE 64

wol ein riter sin. von der tavelrunde. war ic[...]
ner stunde. der selben riter einen sach. da e[...]
hundert sper zebrach. vn zewelf frume rite[...]
vie. bêhher riter wrden nie. danne die selben
ter sint. biden citen was ich ein chint. do ich [...]
selben riter sach. wan div ritschaft geschach [...]
mines vater huse. von de chvnige artvse. [...]
er dar durch ritschaft. er het ellen vn chra[...]
hich der herre kawein. an sine schilte was[...]
guldin tavelrunde. geworht dah niemen ein[...]
des. em wassen de geliche. vinden also rich [...]
inne was gelovbet mith. von driden gemâlet
ein wiher hirh. vf eine berge guldin do se[...]
wassen daz was sin. der die riter alle vie [...]
tavel div dar vmbe gie. die neswrte de h[...]
man. als ich vernomen han. wan der m[...]
her arbeit. vn mit siner manheit. die s[...]
hat errungen. swem so was gelungen. de[...]
te die tavel rvnde. daz man da in chunde se[...]
hen vn wihen daz er zeder tavel rvnde s[...]
daz selbe wassen ich wol sach. do mir dâz [...]
leit geschach. in des riters schilte. den d[...]
bevilte. ern rite durch mich in den tot. ob[...]
den chlage des get mich not. wan er euch h[...]
te erloste. vns allen zetroste. ich het mi[...]
gar bewegen. nuwan durch den selben d[...]
ir werte benamen da tot gelegen.

PLATE 64

MS 481.114, f. 1r, Southern Germany or Austria, s. XIV[1]

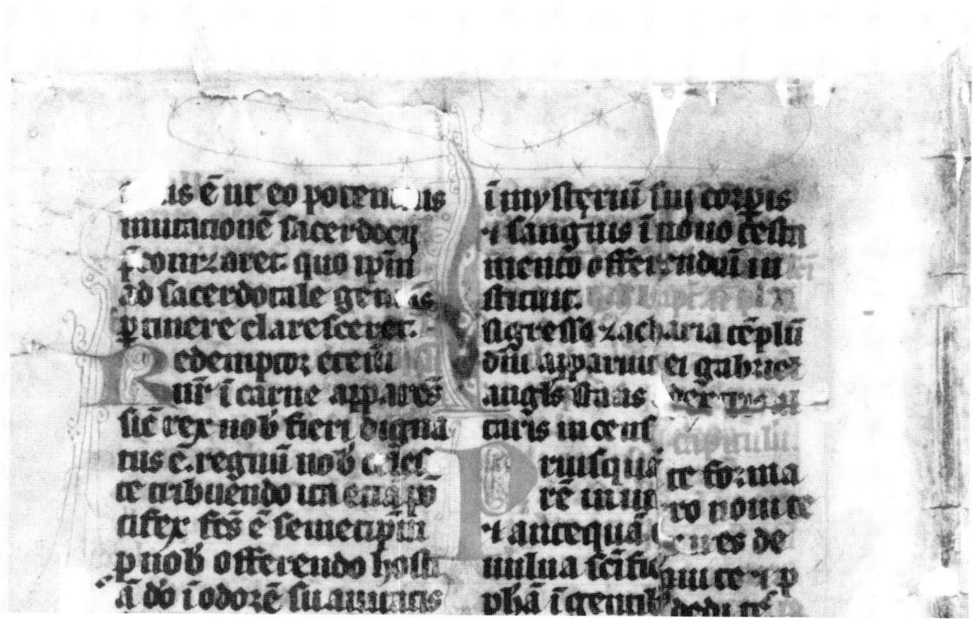

PLATE 65

MS 481.115, f. 2v, Germany, s. XIV[1]

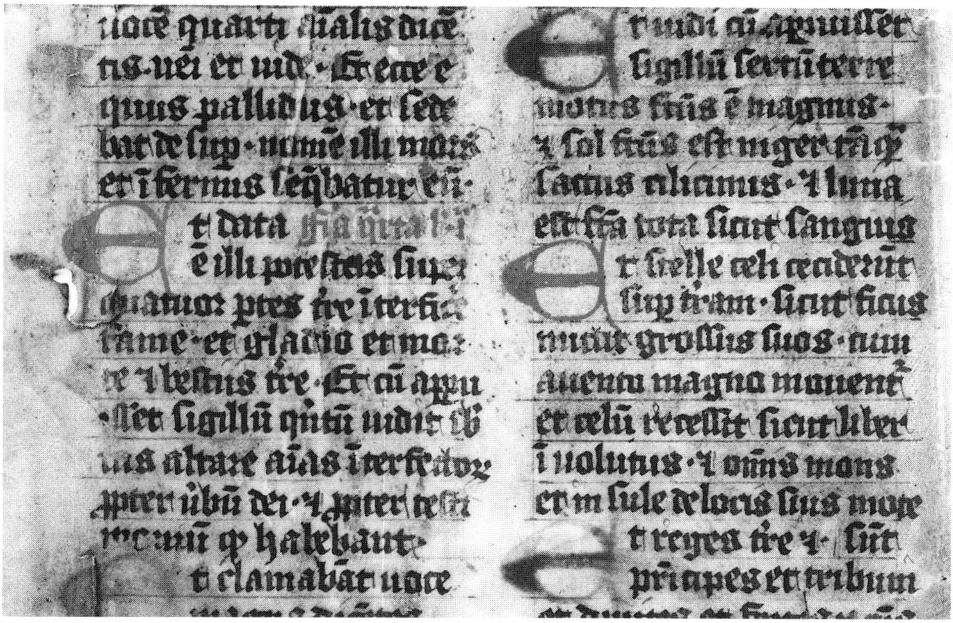

MS 481.116, f. 1r, Germany, s. XIV

PLATE 66

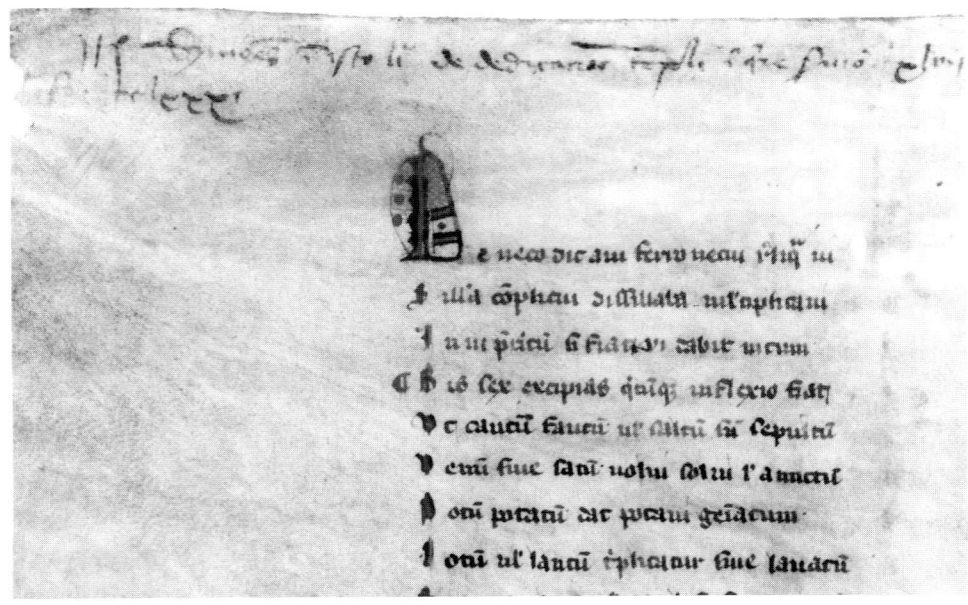

MS 481.117, f. 1v, France, s. XIV[1]

MS 481.118, f. 1v, Klosterneuburg, Austria, s. XV/XVI

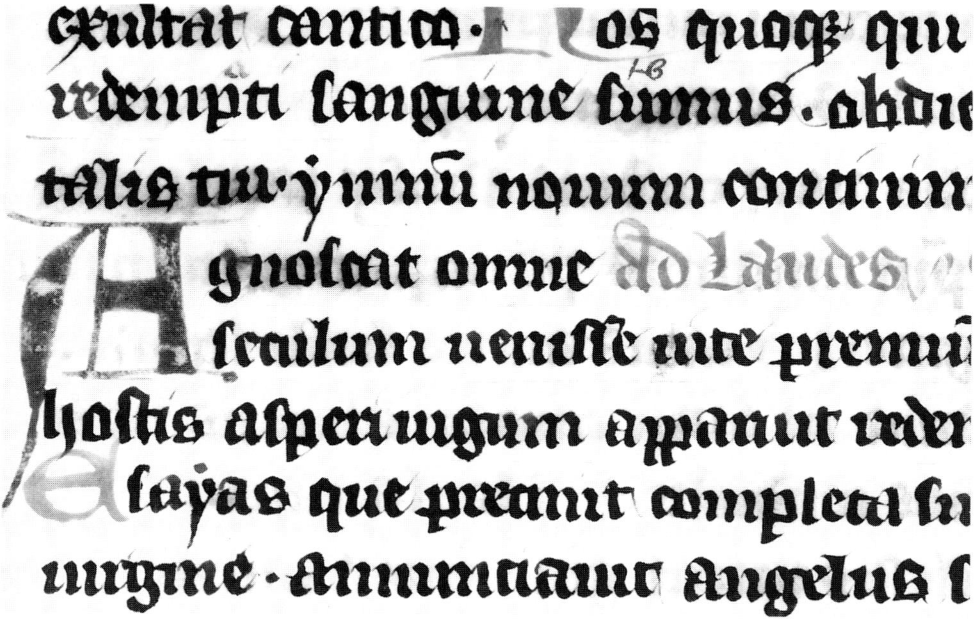

PLATE 67

exultat cantico · [L]os quoqȝ qui
redempti sanguine sumus · obdie
talis tui · ymnū nouum continiu
Agnoscat omne ad Laudes
seculum uenisse iure premui
hostis asperi iugum apparuit redet
sayas que premit completa su
uirgine · Annunciauit angelus [

MS 481.119, f. 1r, Germany, s. XIV

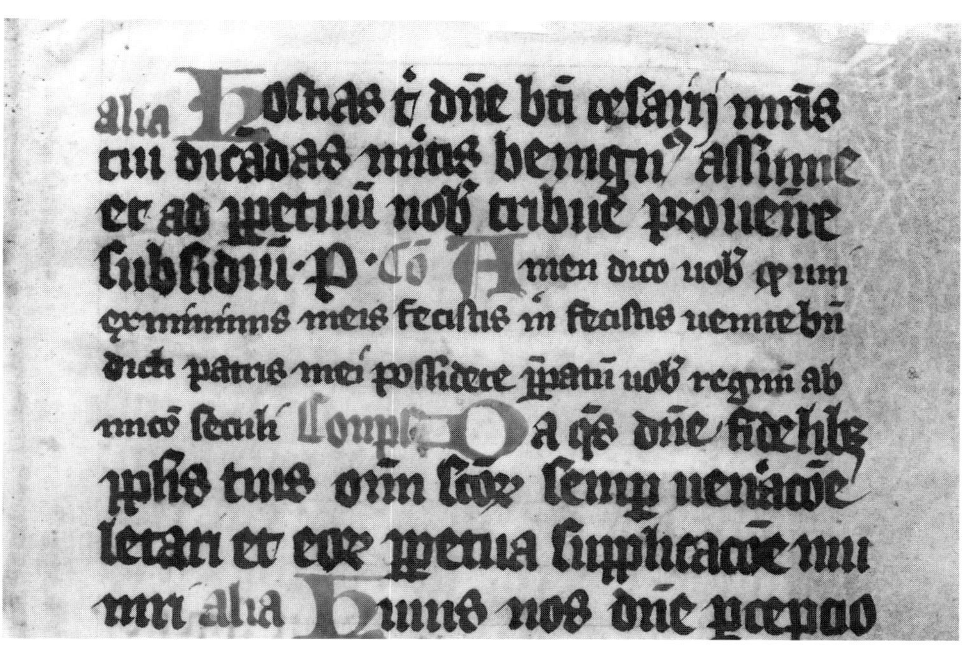

alia Hostias t̄ dn̄e bū cesarij mūs
tui dicadas mūas benign̄ assiqne
er ad p̄ctuū nob̄ tribue prouene
subsidiū · p · c̄o Amen dico uob̄ ꝗ un
examinimis meis feasti̅s in feastis uenite bn̄
dicti patris mei possidere ip̄atū uob̄ regnū ab
mco seculi Compl [O]a q̄s dn̄e fidelib̄
ip̄sis tuis omn̄ see̅ semp̄ uenia̅ce
letari er eoꝝ p̄etua su̅plicacōe mu
mm alia Huius nos dn̄e p̄epao

MS 481.120, f. 1r, Germany, s. XIV

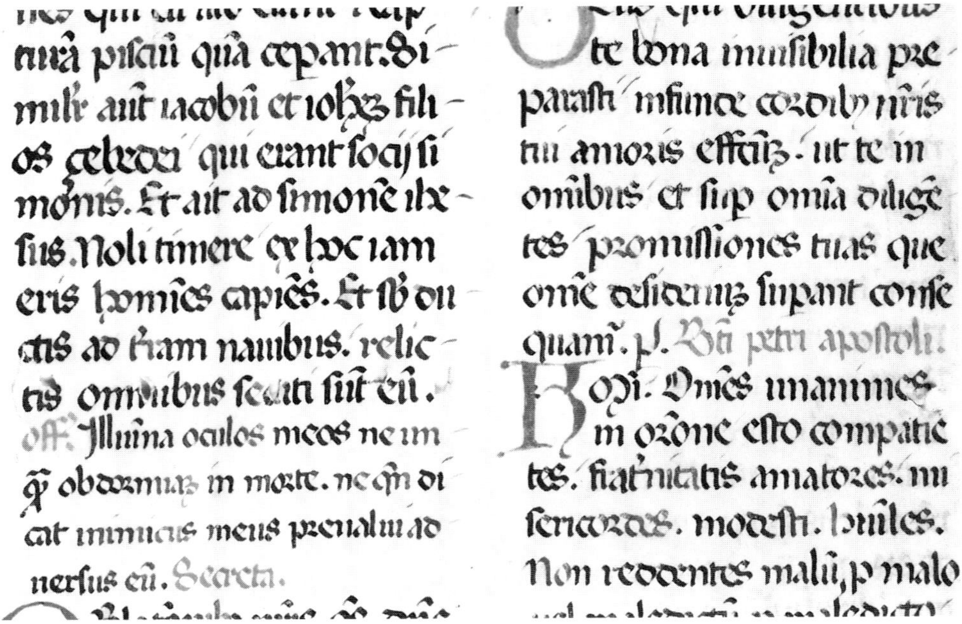

PLATE 68

MS 481.121, f. 1v, Italy, s. XIV

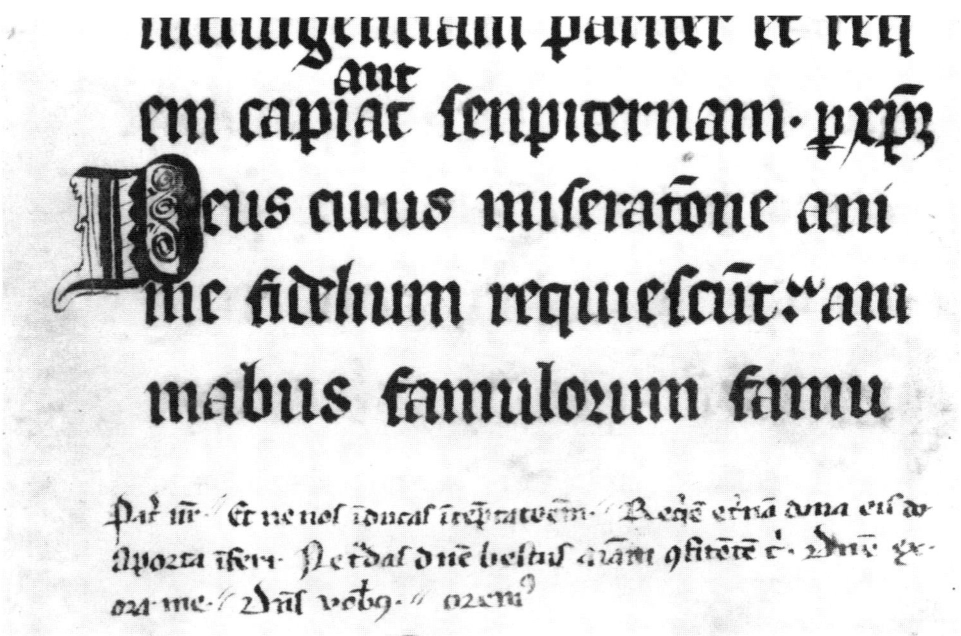

MS 481.122, f. 1v, Germany, s. XIV

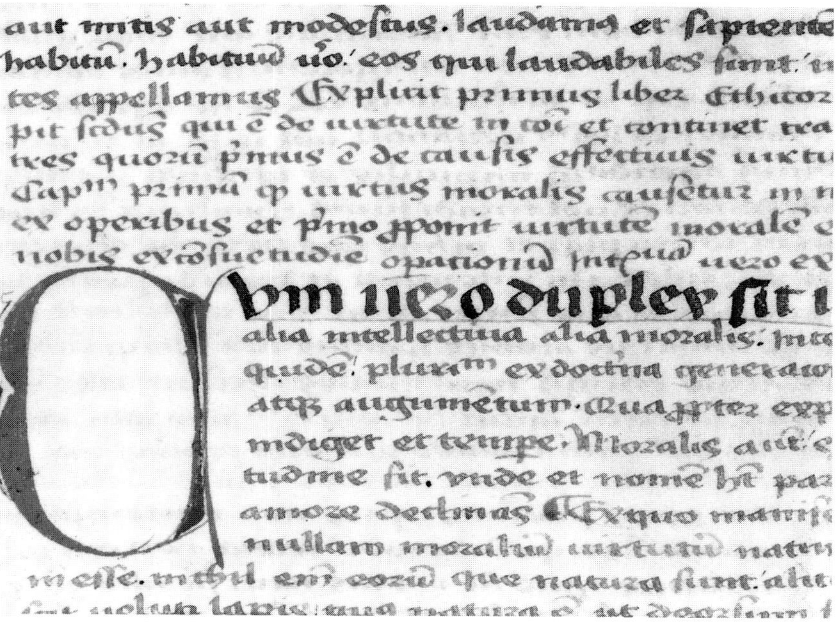

PLATE 69

MS 481.123, f. 1r, Spain, s. XV[1]

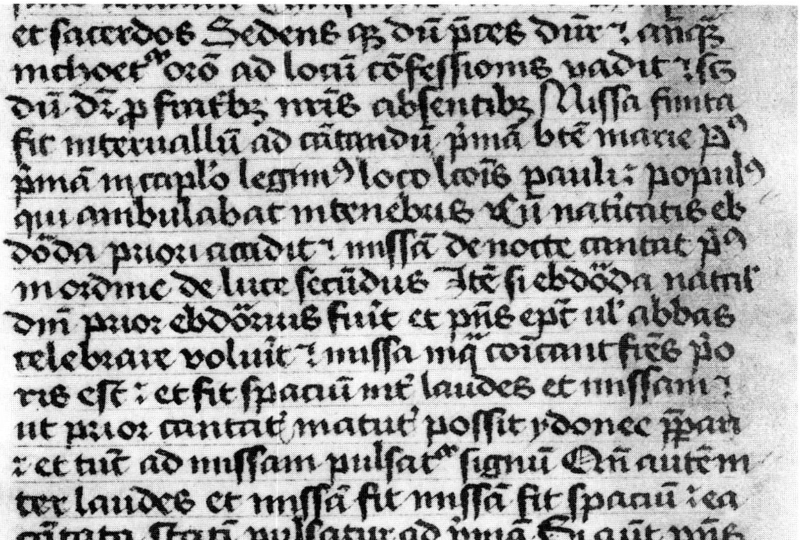

MS 481.124, f. 2r, Germany, s. XIV/XV

PLATE 70

MS 481.125, f. 1r, Germany, s. XV[1]

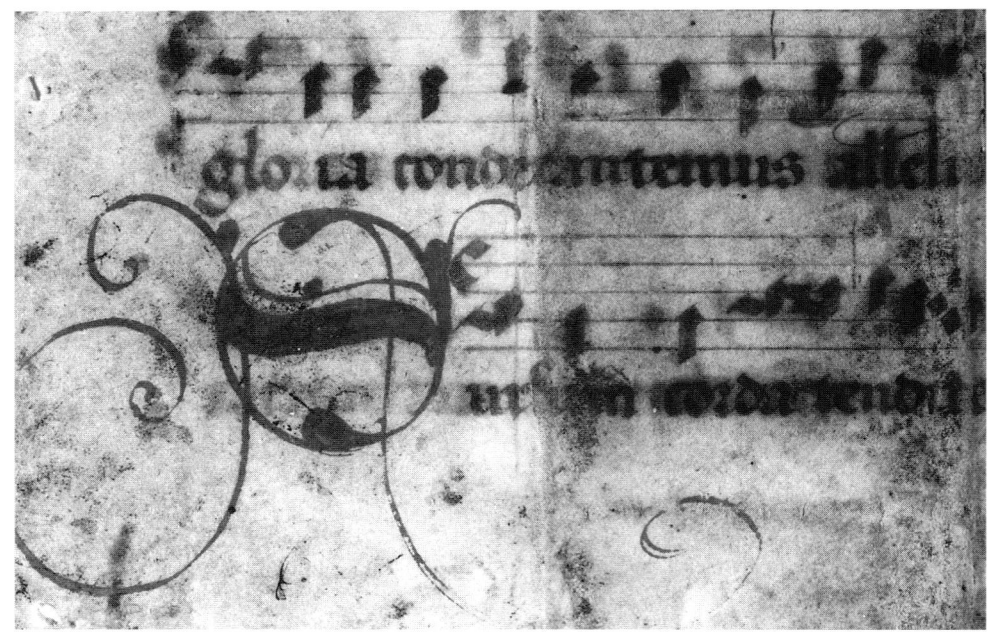

MS 481.126, f. 1r, Germany, s. XV[1]

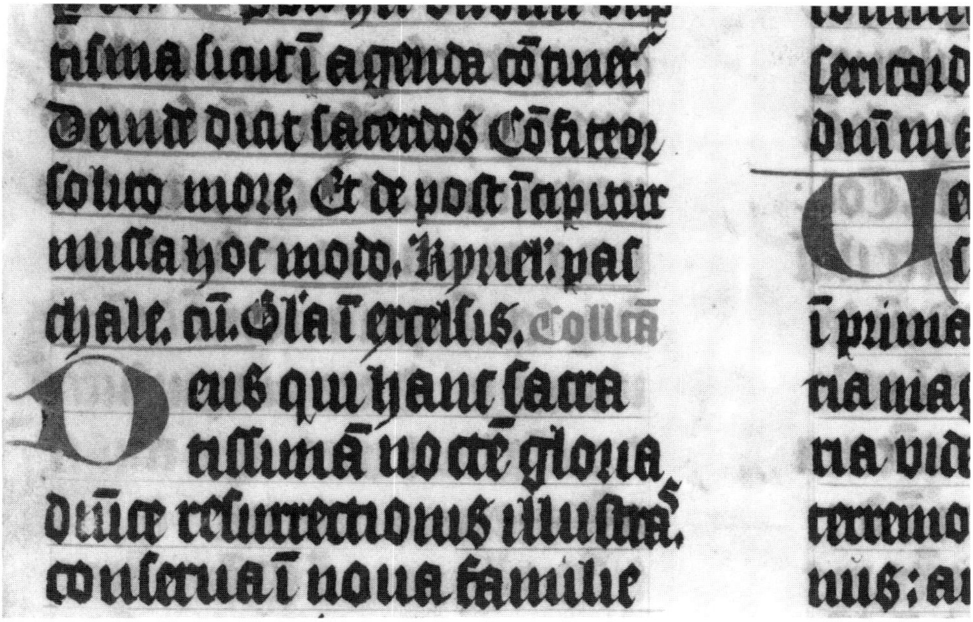

PLATE 71

MS 481.127, f. 1v, Southern Germany, s. XV

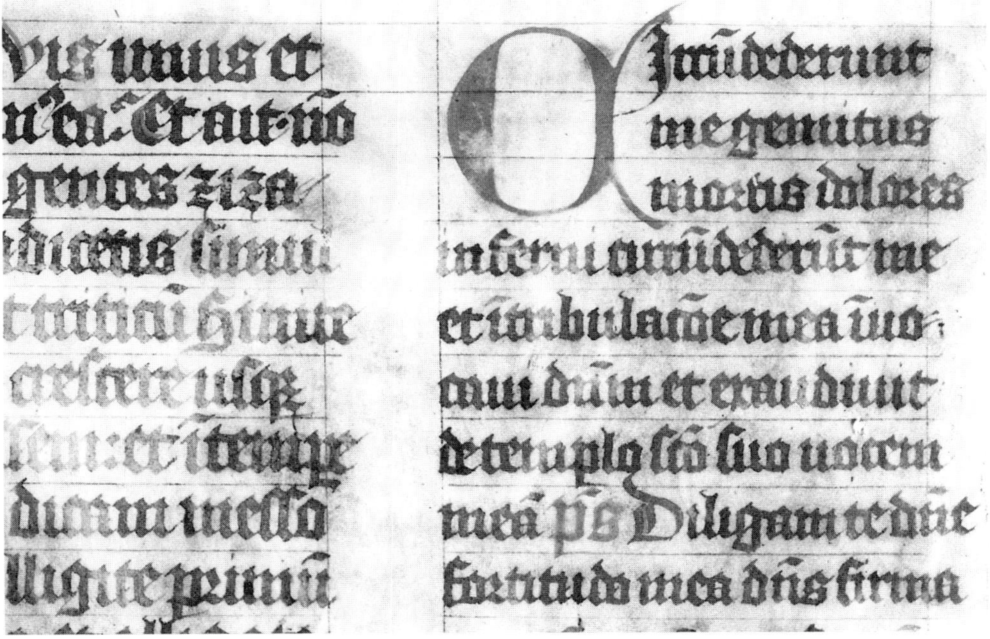

MS 481.128, f. 1v, Germany or Austria, s. XV[1]

PLATE 72

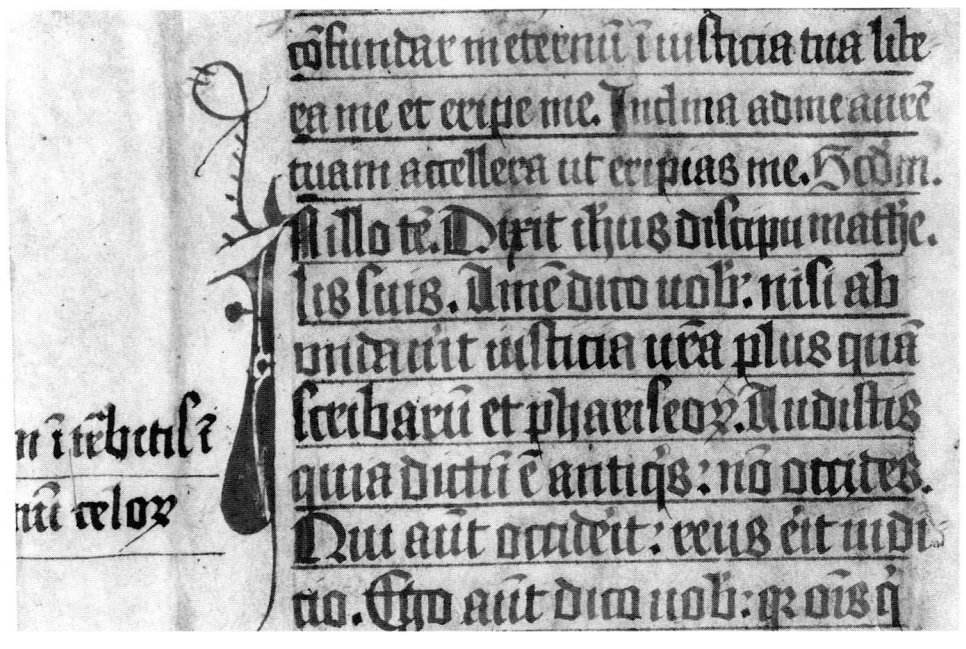

MS 481.129, f. 1v, Germany, s. XV

MS 481.130, f. 1r, Germany, s. XV[2]

PLATE 73

MS 481.131, f. 1v, Northern France (?), s. XVI[in]

MS 481.132, f. 1r, Germany, s. XV[2]

PLATE 74

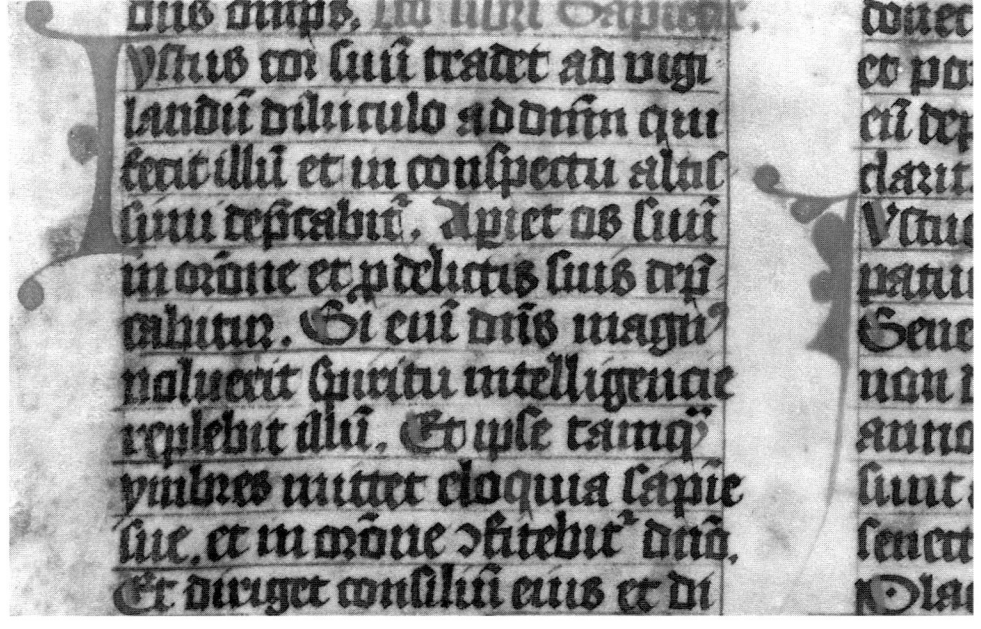

MS 481.133, f. 2v, Germany, s. XV

MS 481.134, f. 1r, Germany, s. XV[1]

PLATE 75

MS 481.135, f. 1r, England or France, s. XV

MS 481.136, f. 2r, Germany, s. XV

PLATE 76

MS 481.137, f. 1r, Germany, s. XV

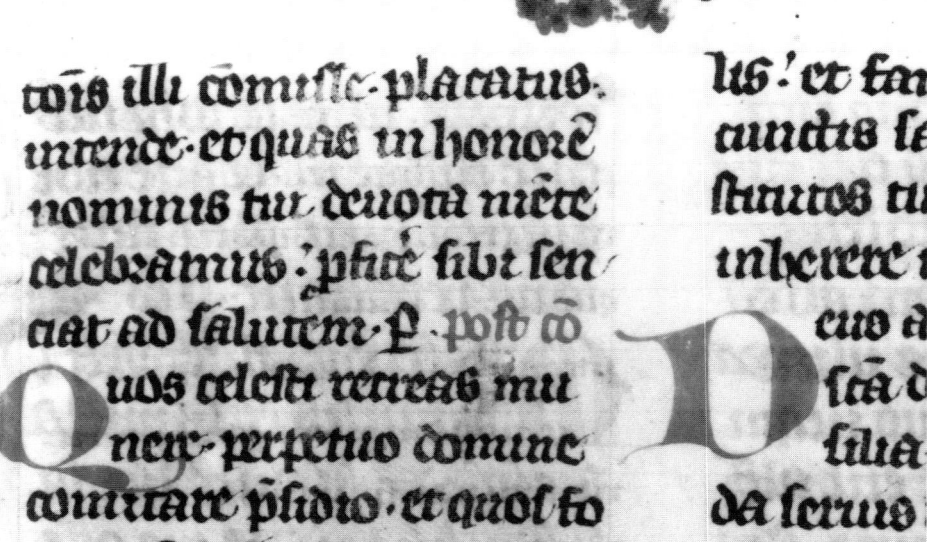

MS 481.138, f. 1r, Southern Germany, s. XV

PLATE 77

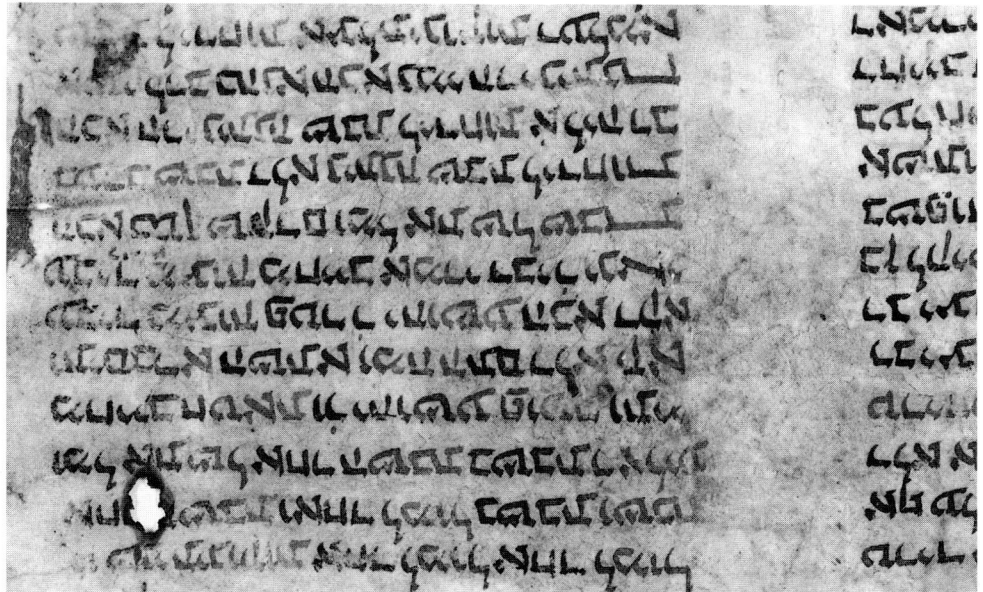

MS 481.143, f. 1v, Northern France or Germany, s. XIII

MS 481.144, f. 1r, Italy, s. XIII

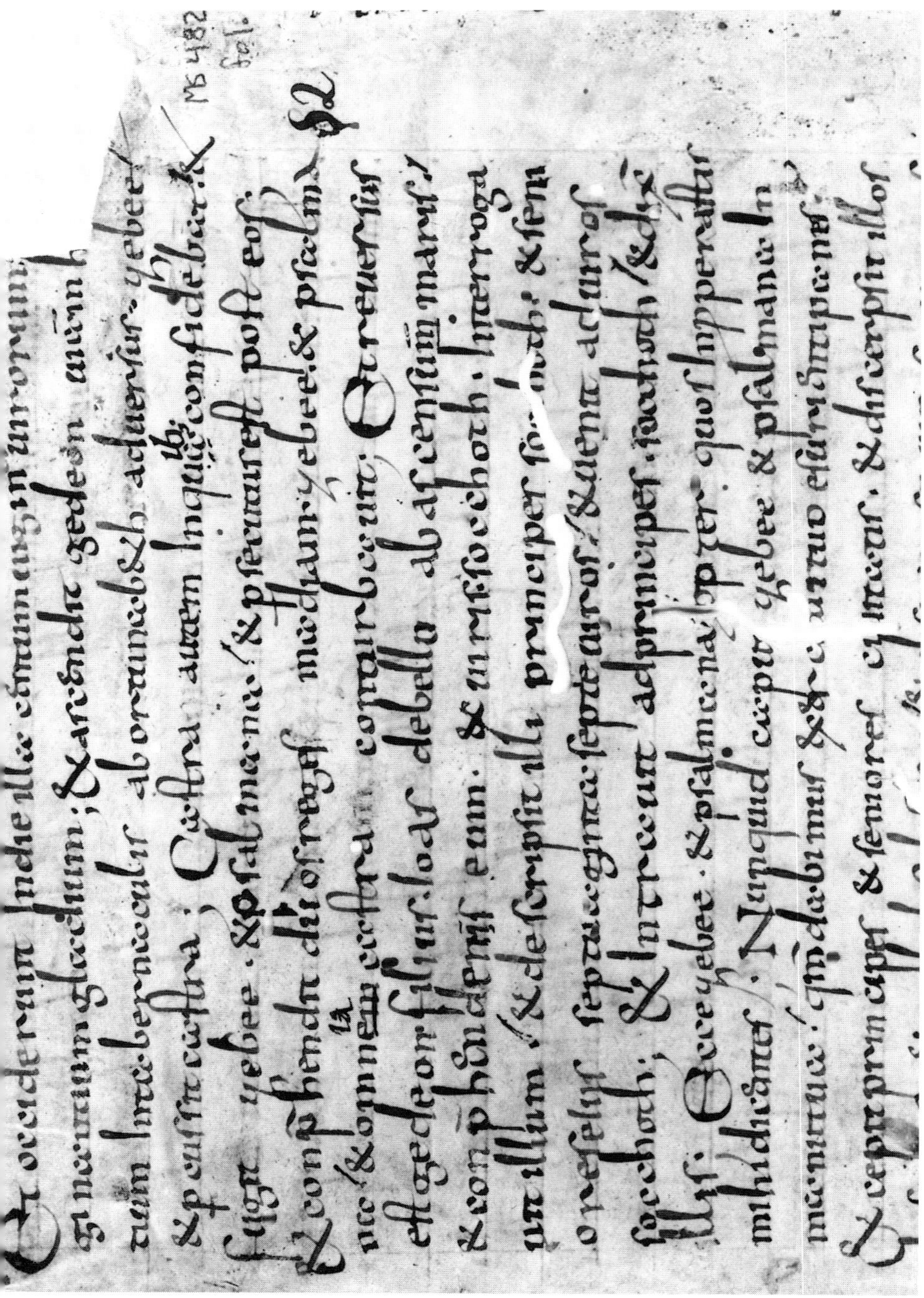

PLATE 78

MS 482.1, f. 1r,
Eastern France or Southwestern Germany, ca. 800

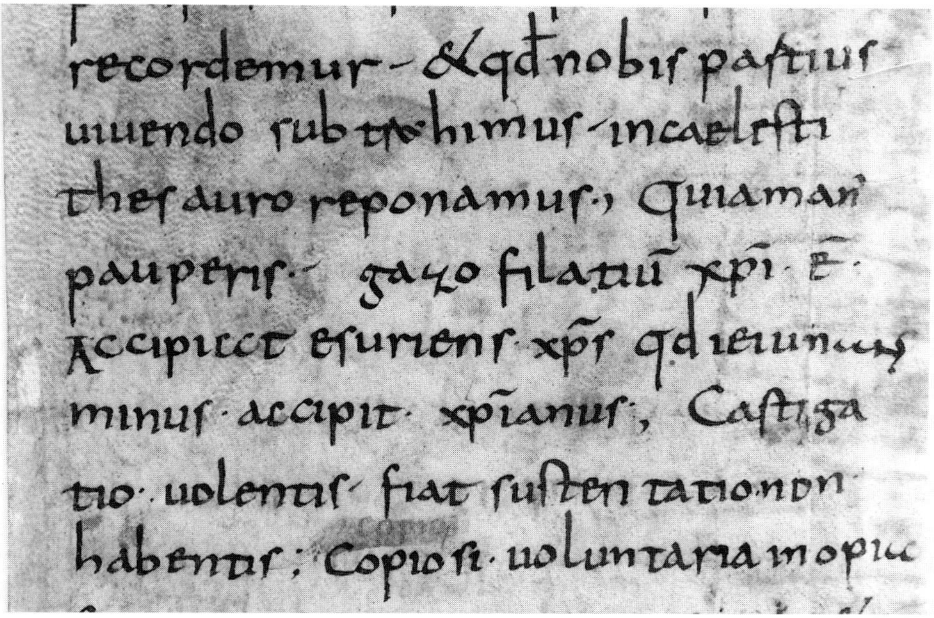

PLATE 79

MS 482.2, f. 1v, Southeastern Germany, s. IX$^{1/3}$

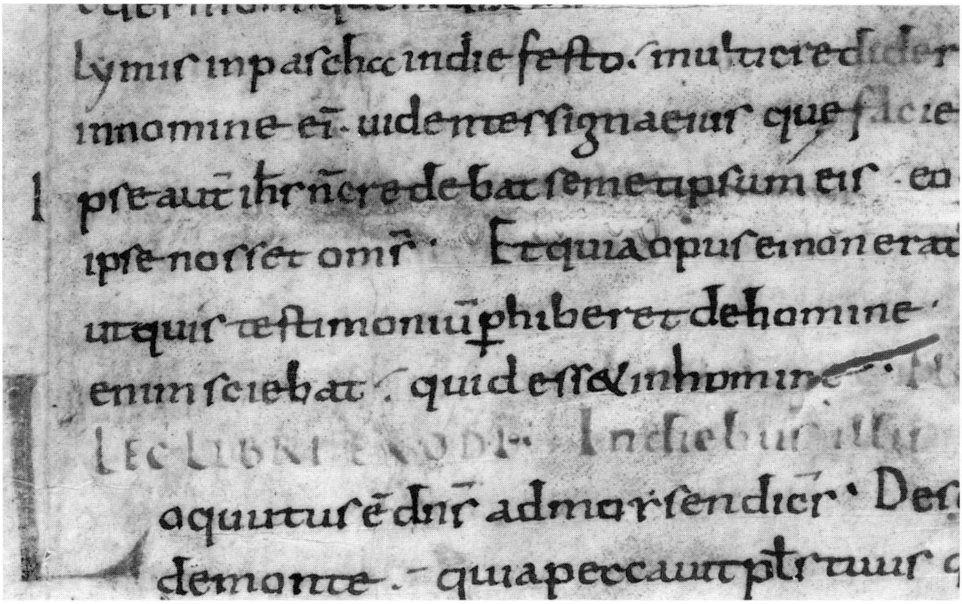

MS 482.3, f. 1r, Freising, Germany, s. IX$^{3/4}$

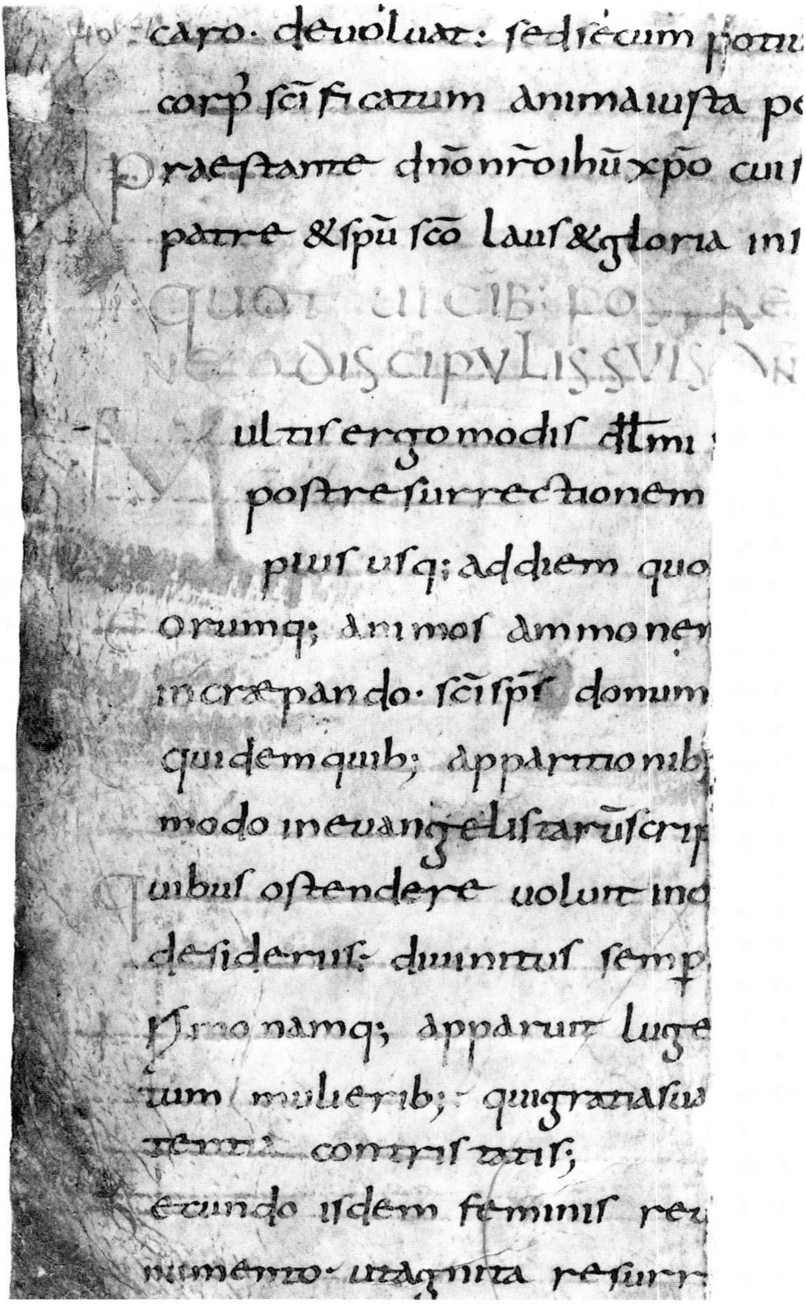

PLATE 80

caro devoluat· sed tecum potu
corp sci ficatum animal iusta p
praestante dno nro ihu xpo cui
patre & spu sco laus & gloria in

QUOT EII CIB POS AE
NE DISCIPVLIS SVIS IN

ultis ergo modis dtmi
post resurrectionem
plus usq; ad diem quo
orumq; animos ammone
increpando· sci spi donum
quidem quib; apparitionib;
modo in euangelistarum scrip
uibus ostendere uoluit ind
desideriis diuinitus semp
primo namq; apparuit luge
tum mulieribus· qui granasu
terrae contristatis;
ecundo isdem feminis re
numento· ut agnita resurr

MS 482.4, f. 1r, Southern Germany or Northern Italy, s. IX$^{2/4}$

PLATE 81

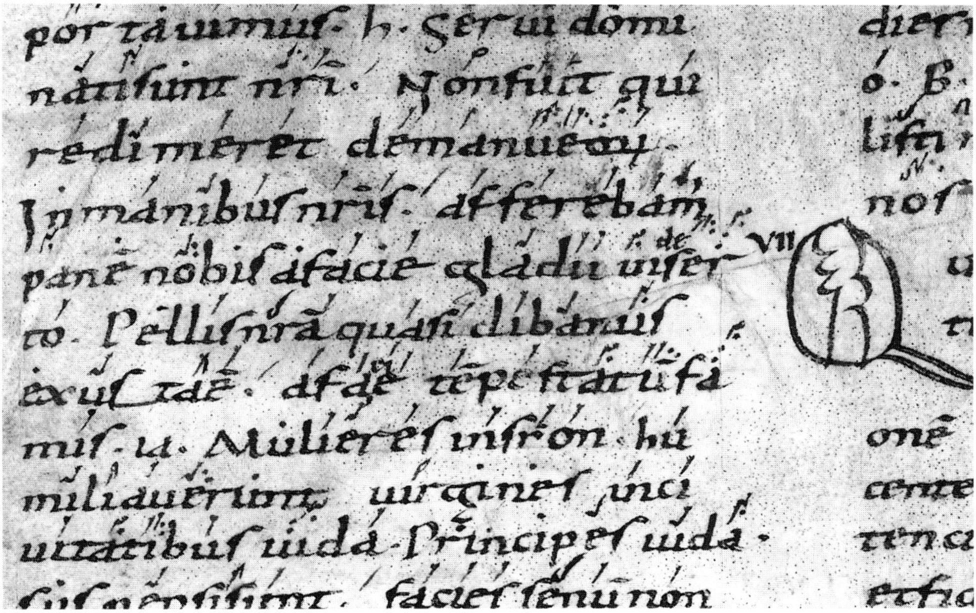

MS 482.8, f. 1v, Italy, s. X

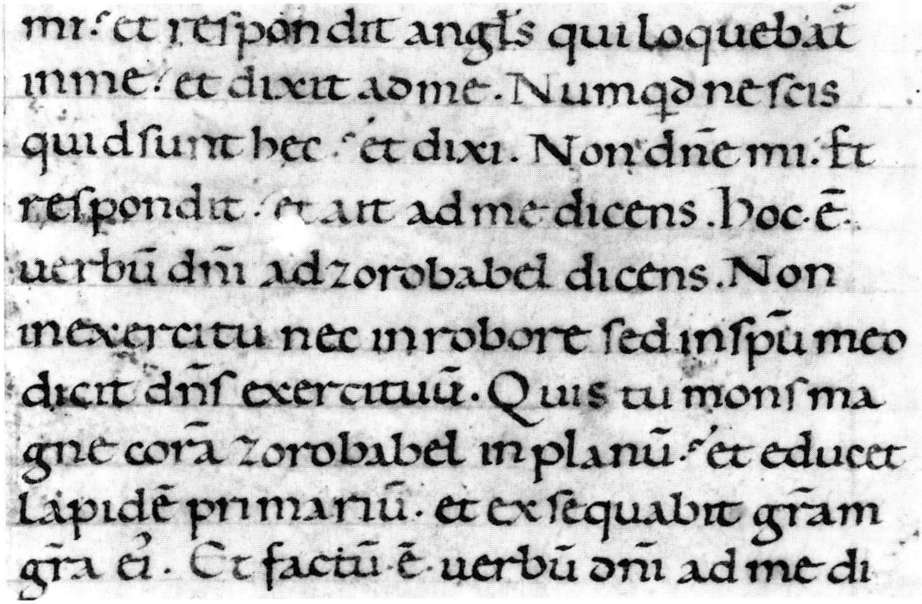

MS 482.12, f. 1r, Italy, s. XII[1]

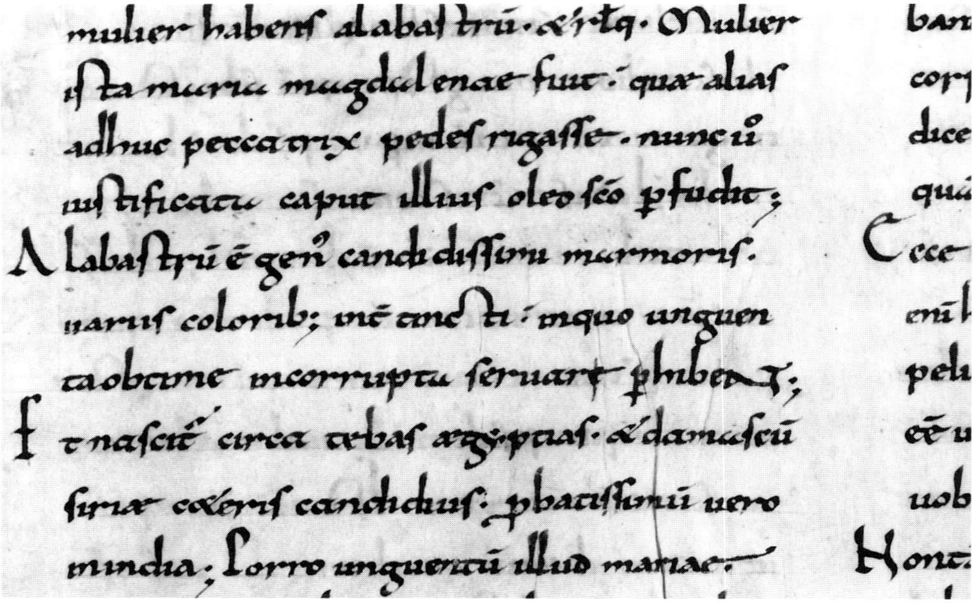

PLATE 82

mulier habens alabas tru . ... q̄ · Mulier   ban
ista maria magdalenae fuit: quae alias   cor
adhuc peccatrix pedes rigasse . nunc u̅   dice
iustificata caput illius oleo s̄c̄o p̄fudit;   qui
Alabastru̅ e̅ gen̅ candidissimi marmoris .   ece
uariis coloribus; unde & uti: inquo unguen   eni
ta obtime incorruptu seruare p̄hibe̅t;   peli
& nascet̅ circa tebas aegyptias . & damasceu̅   e̅ u
siriae exteris candidius: p̄batissimu̅ uero   uob
inindia; Porro unguentu̅ illud mariae: Hon

MS 482.13, f. 1r, France or Italy, s. X[1]

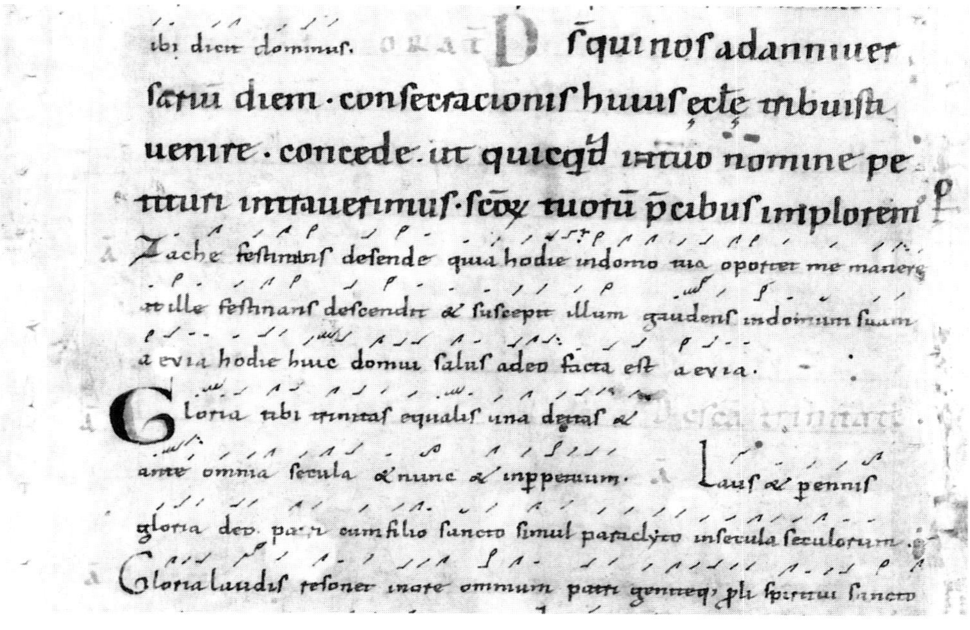

ibi dicit dominus.   ORAT   **D** s̄ qui nos ad anniuer
sariu̅ diem . consecracionis huius ecl̄e tribuisti
uenire . concede . ut quicq̄d in tuo nomine pe
tituri intrauerimus . sc̄o̅r̅ tuoru̅ p̄cibus imploremus
Zache festinans descende quia hodie indomo tua oportet me manere
& ille festinans descendit & suscepit illum gaudens indomum suu̅
alleluia hodie huic domui salus adeo facta est alleluia .
Gloria tibi trinitas equalis una deitas &
ante omnia secula &nunc & inperpetuum . Laus & perennis
gloria deo patri cumfilio sancto simul paraclyto insecula seculorum .
Gloria laudis resonet inore omnium patri genitoq; p̄li spiritui sancto

MS 482.14, f. 1r, Southern Germany, s. XI/XII

PLATE 83

Scō· scī evang̅ scdm ioh̄·
n̄ılı̄ : H✝aḇone sacrēıncha
na gal[...] vepaī maī ihu
ihı Voca[...] ē aū ihs. evoı
ıc palı eỏ adnupnaſ. f̄de
ficıente uıno. oıcıı maī ihu
ao eū. Vınū nonhabem.
ev dıcıı eı ihc. Quıd mıhı
ev tıbı ē mulıer· nondum

gla
fcıpulı
unıūfa repı
dıcıre·noı eı
narrabo uo
[e]cıı dn̄ſ aı
blata

MS 482.19, f. 2v, Italy, s. XI[2]

negabo; Sımılῑ aū eomſ dıcebaī
[i]oī ınpdưı· cuı nom̄ gethſemanı;
cıpulıſ ſuıſ; Sedete hıc· donec oπε; [l]
peī evıacobıī evıohannē ſecū· evcc̄
πe evecleſıe; ε̄ aıı ıllıſ; Tπıſῑıſ ē ı[a]
uſq; ad morπε; Suſῑınete hıc· ev[u]
ε̄ cū̄πoceſſſſ& paululū πcıdıı

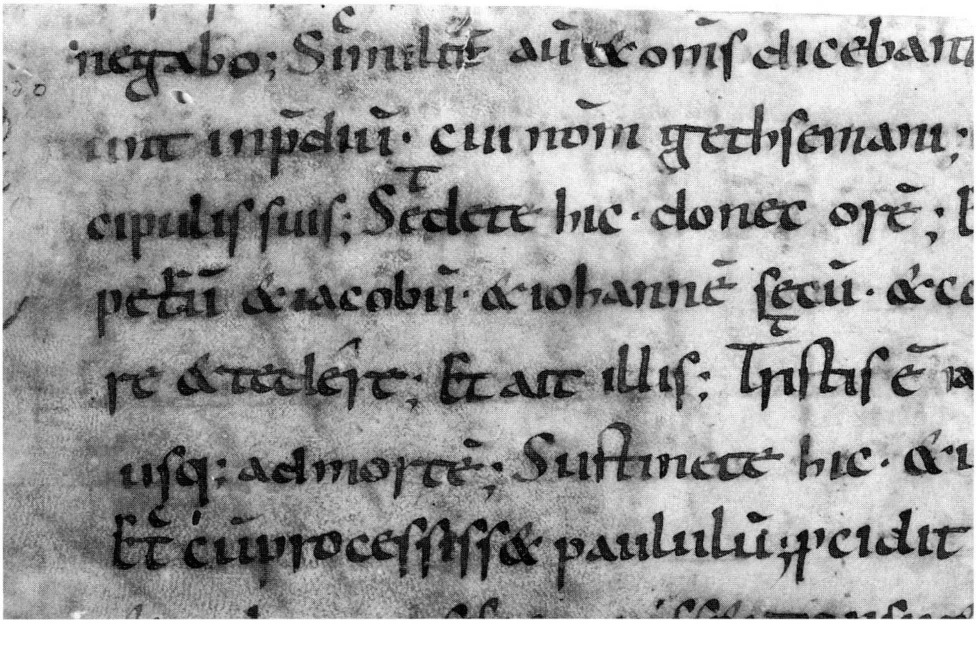

MS 482.20, f. 1v, Southern Germany or Northern Italy, s. X/XI

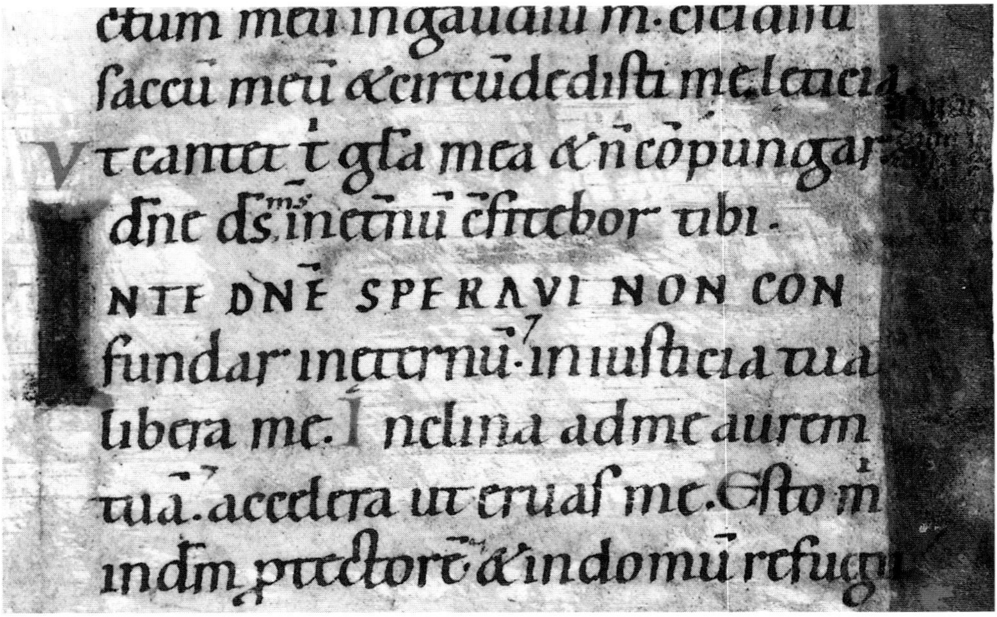

PLATE 84

MS 482.25, f. 1r, Southern Germany or Austria, s. XII[1]

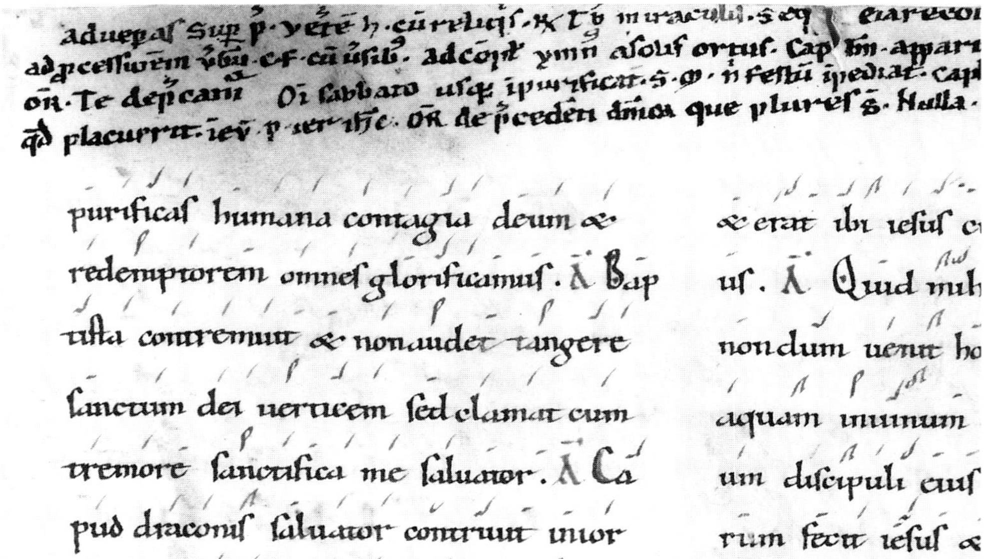

MS 482.26, f. 1r, Southern Germany, s. XII

PLATE 85

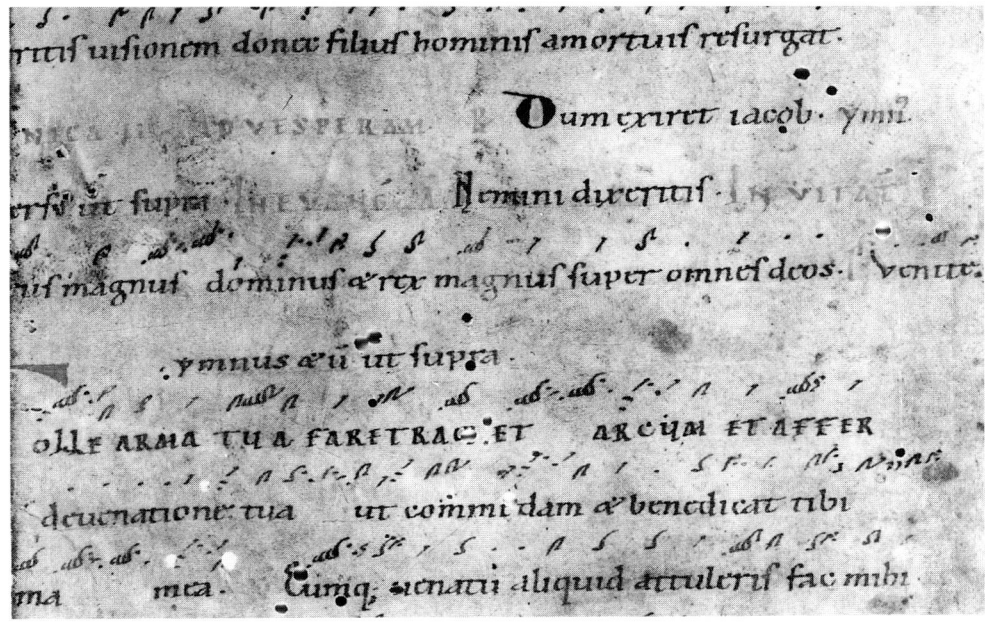

tenebre nimie aut lux in om(...)
filii lucis ambulate esf:. eta S (...)
les estote et in mobiles · habu(...)
tes in ope dm semp · scientes q(...)
labor ur non est in anis in d(...)

MS 482.27, f. 2r, Germany, s. XII/XIII

ritis uisionem donec filius hominis a mortuis resurgat.
...VESPERAM Dum exiret iacob · ymn̄
ersi ut supra Homini dixentis ·
is magnus dominus et rex magnus super omnes deos. Venite.
ymnus eū ut supra.
OLLE ARMA TUA FARETRAC · ET ARCUM ET AFFER
deuenatione tua ut commedam et benedicat tibi
ma mea. Cumq; uenati aliquid attuleris fac mihi

MS 482.28, f. 1v, Southern Germany, s. XI/XII

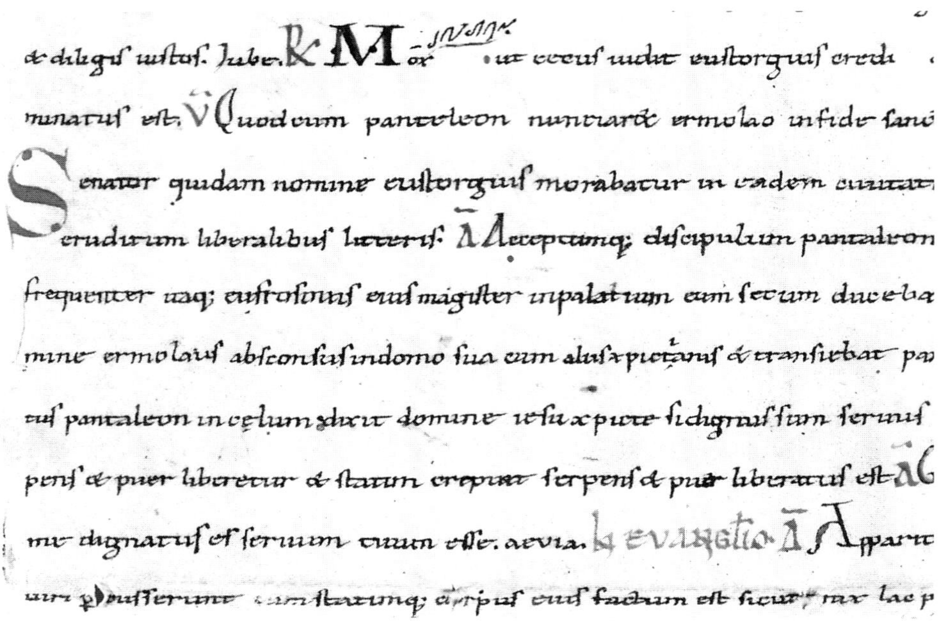

PLATE 86

MS 482.31, f. 1v, Melk, Austria, s. XII[1]

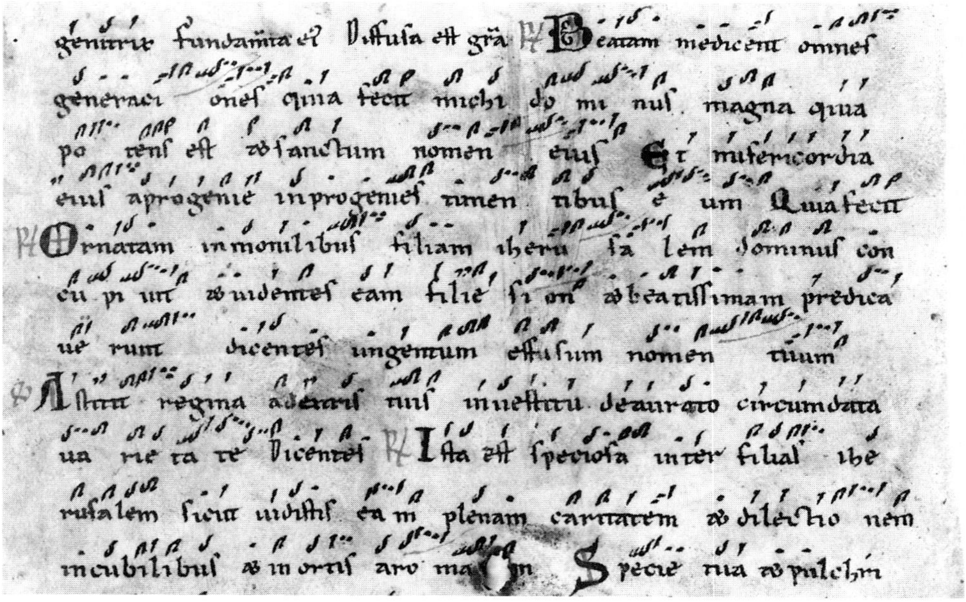

MS 482.32, f. 2v, Germany, s. XII

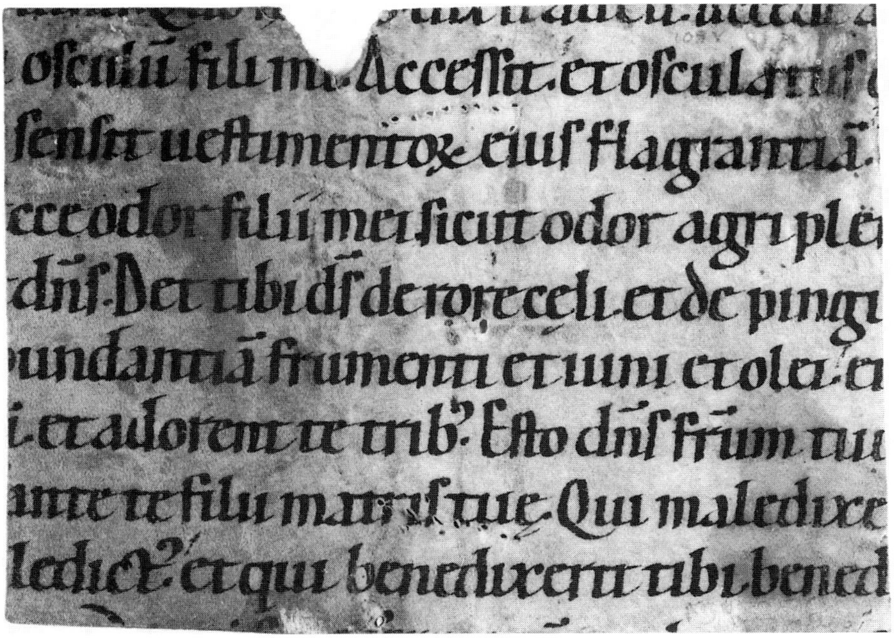

PLATE 87

osculū filiu mē Accessit. et osculatus
sensit uestimentog, eius flagrantiā
ecce odor filii mei sicut odor agri ple
dn̅s. Det tibi ds̅ de rore celi et de pingu
undantiā frumenti et uini et olei et
et adorent te trib. Esto dn̅s frm tu
ante te filii matris tue. Qui maledixe
ledic et qui benedixerit tibi bened

MS 482.36, f. 1v, Germany, s. XII

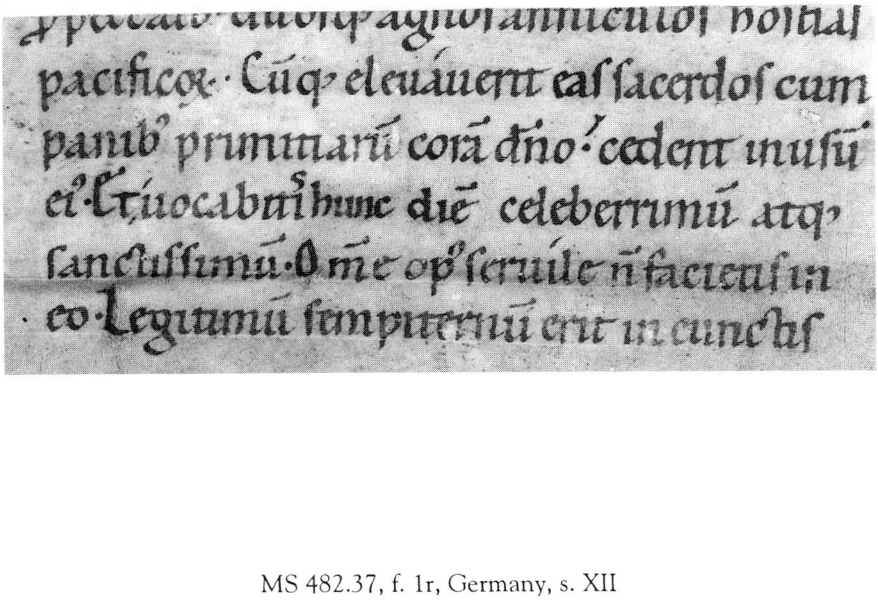

pecca duolq, agnos annuculos nostras
pacificos. Cūq, eleuauerit eas sacerdos cum
panib primitiaru̅ cora̅ dn̅o ‒ cedent in usū
ei. Et uocabitis hunc die̅ celeberrimū atq,
sanctissimū. O me op seruile n̅ facietis in
eo. Legitimu̅ sempiternū erit in cunctis

MS 482.37, f. 1r, Germany, s. XII

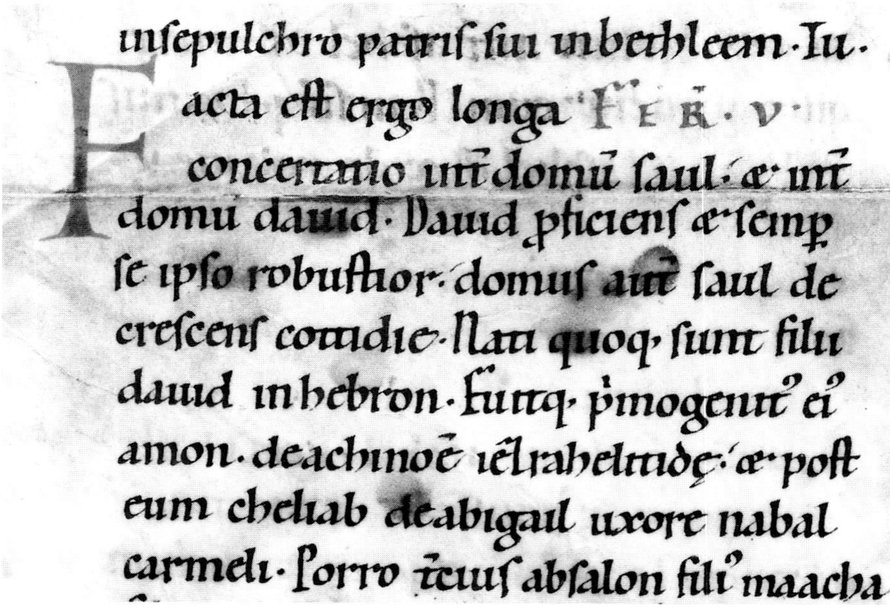

PLATE 88

in sepulchro patris sui in bethleem · Iu ·
facta est ergo longa FEB · v
concertatio inter domu saul · & inter
domu dauid · Dauid proficiens & sem̄p
se ipso robustior · domus aut saul de
crescens cottidie · Nati quoq; sunt filii
dauid in hebron · Fuitq; primogenit' ei'
amon · de achinoe iesraheltide; & post
eum cheliab de abigail uxore nabal
carmeli · Porro tercius absalon fili' maacha

MS 482.38, f. 1v, Germany, s. XII

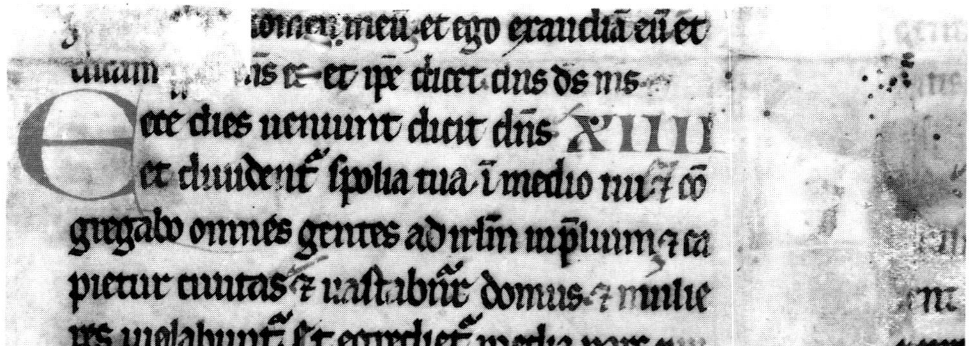

...omine meu · et ego exaudia eu et
dicam ... us es · et ipse dicet dns ds m's
Ecce dies ueniunt dicit dns XIII
et diuident spolia tua · in medio tui · & con
gregabo omnes gentes ad irlm in prelium · & ca
pietur ciuitas · & uastabunt domus · & mulie
res uiolabunt · Et egredietur media pars ciui
tatis in captiuitate; et reliquum ipli non aufer
ex urbe · Et egredietur dns et preliabit' contra gentes
illas · sic preliatus e in die certaminis · et stabi
pedes eius in die illa sup monte oliuarz; q est

MS 482.39, f. 1r, Germany, s. XIII

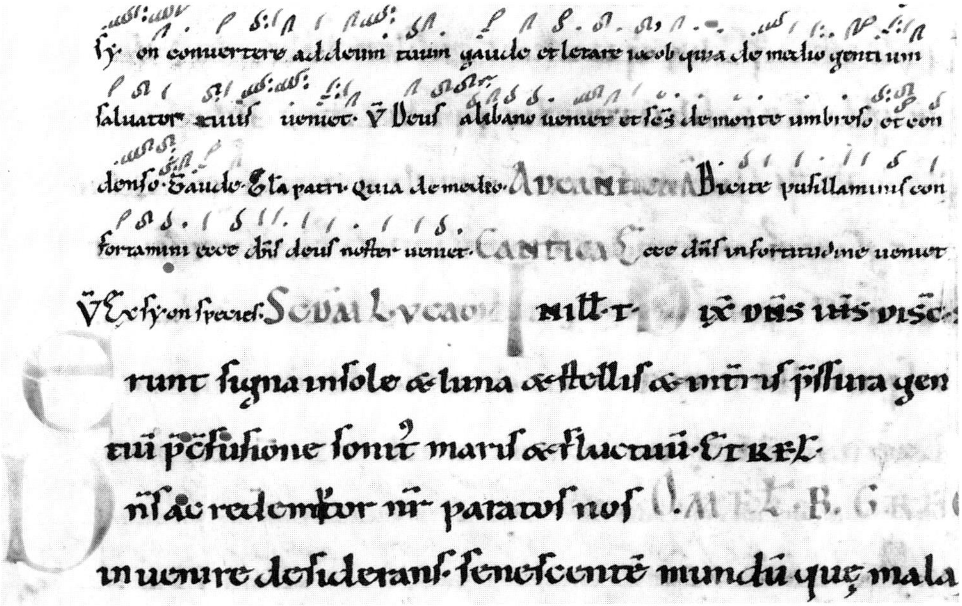

PLATE 89

MS 482.40, f. 1v, Southern Germany, s. XII[1]

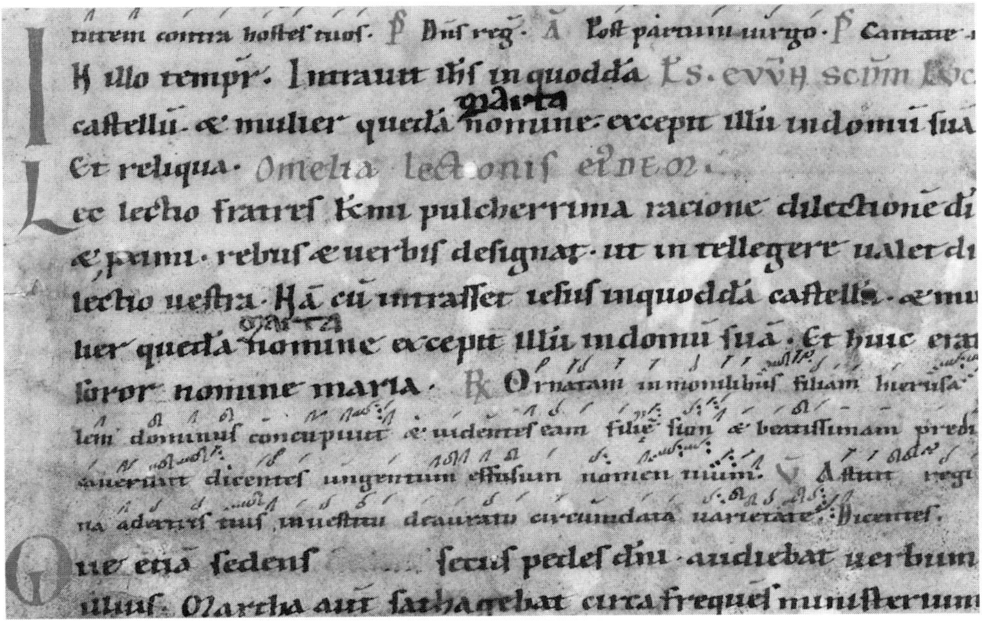

MS 482.41, f. 1r, Southern Germany, s. XII

PLATE 90

MS 482.44, f. 1r, Western Germany, s. XII[1]

MS 482.45, f. 1v, Italy, s. XII[2]

PLATE 91

MS 482.46, f. 1v, Southern Germany or Austria, s. XI^ex

MS 482.47, f. 1r, Southern Germany or Austria, s. XII^med

PLATE 92

MS 482.48, f. 2r, Southern Germany or Austria, s. XIII[1]

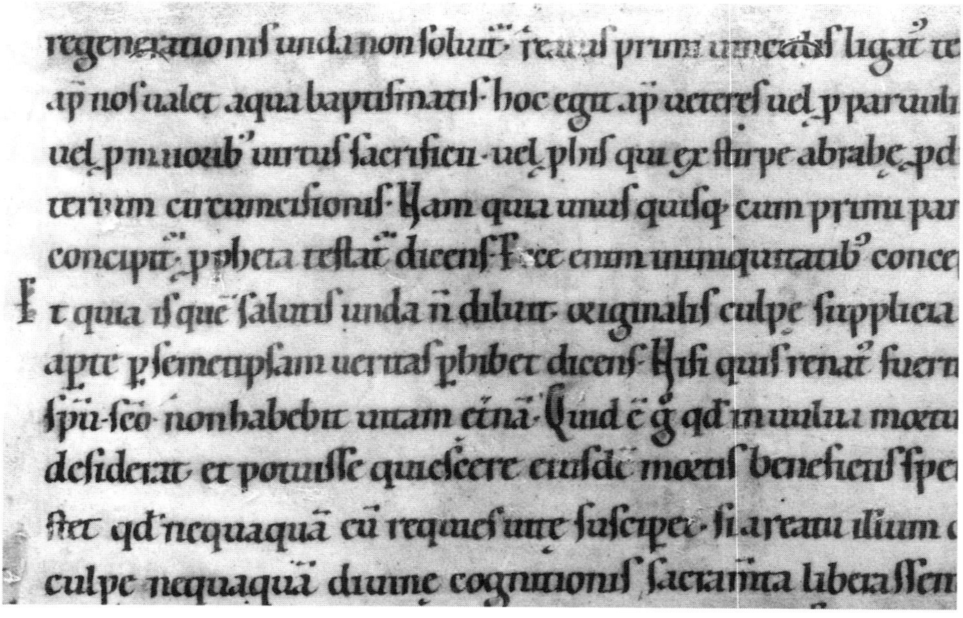

MS 482.51, f. 1v, Southern Germany or Austria, s. XII

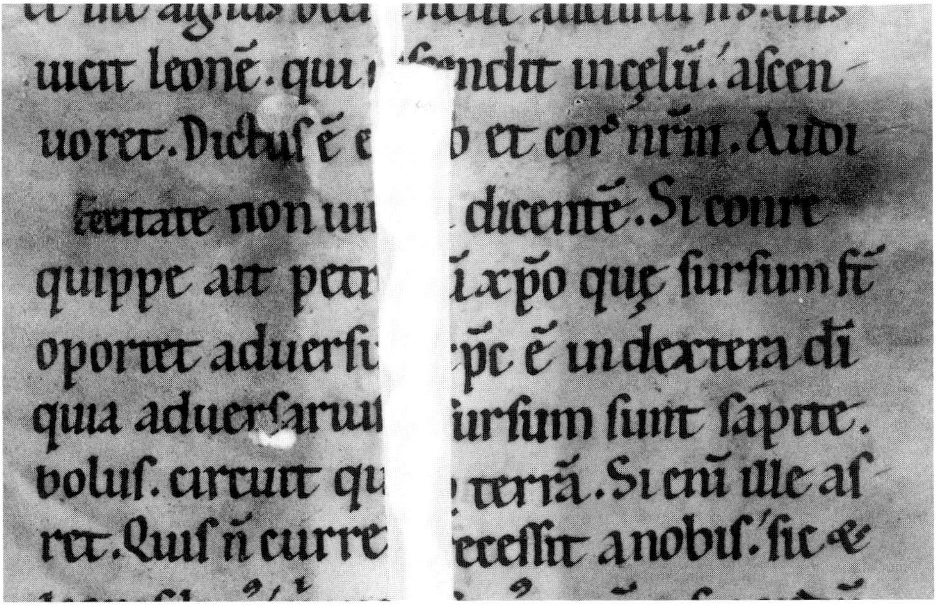

PLATE 93

MS 482.52, f. 1v, Germany, s. XII^{med}

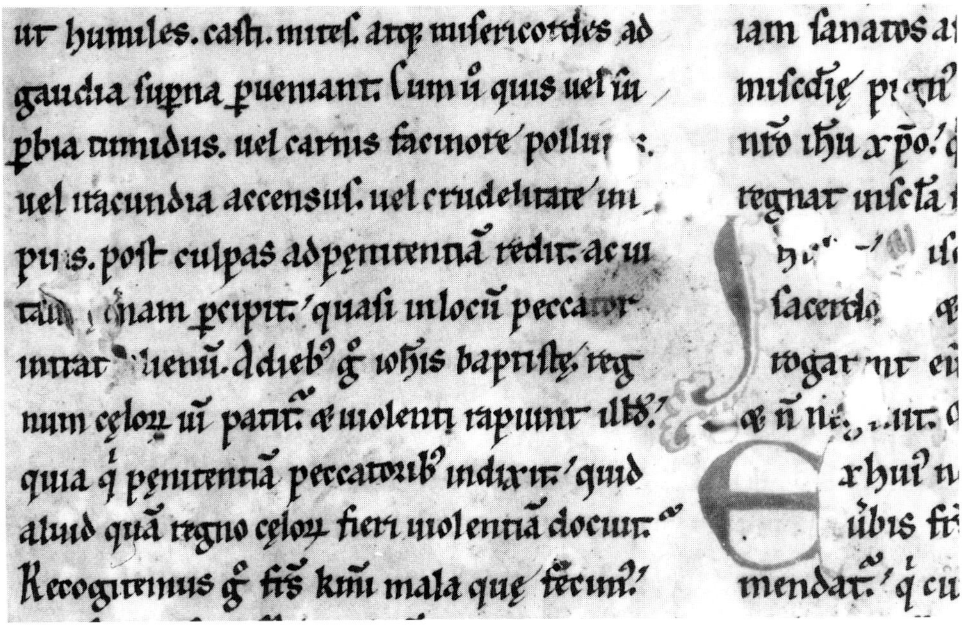

MS 482.53, f. 1r, Southern Germany or Austria, s. XII/XIII

PLATE 94

lonale parte ceti pagrans fac nobis longoi diei
ce estate · austrate u pcurrensi duert nobis bre
ues ce hieme · Sol iortu suo maculosus · ut subnu
be latens · pluuiale die psagit · Si palleat' te pes
tuosii · Si concauus uidet · ita ut medio fulgens ·
radiosad austru ce ad a quilone emittat · tem
pestate humida 7 uentuosa · Si pallidus' mui
gras nube soceidat aquilone uentu · Quintus
planeta e Marsce 7 pyrois globosus igne feru
dus · pcurrit signiferu ii annis · Sextus pla
neta e louis qui ce phenon rotundus te pat
Zodiacu pagans · xii annis · Septim' planeta e Sai nus dz 7 pheton · In cui ecortu p xxx ·

MS 482.54, f. 1r, Southern Germany, s. XII^med

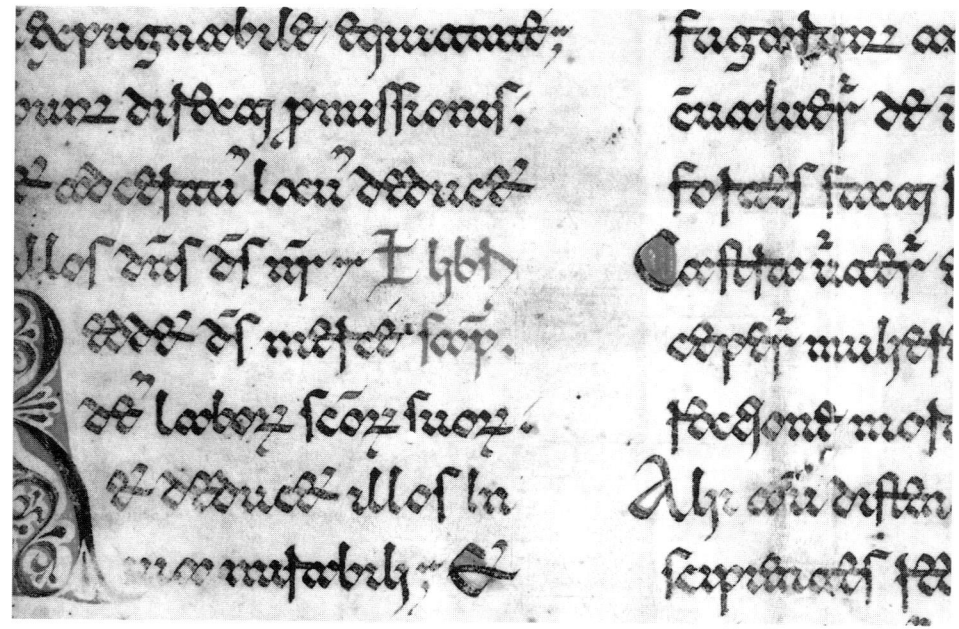

MS 482.55, f. 1r, Southern Italy, s. XIII^in

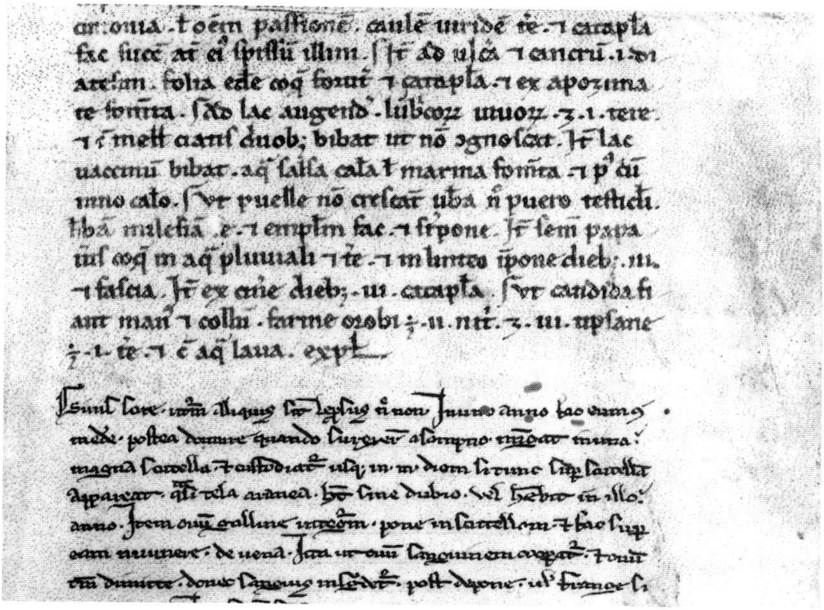

PLATE 95

MS 482.57, f. 2r, Italy, s. XIII[in]

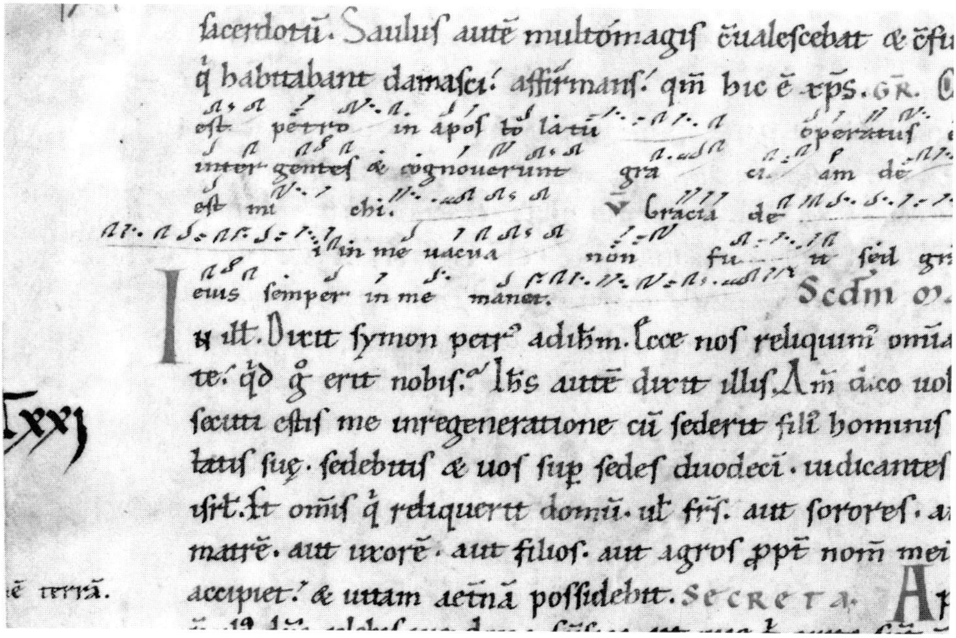

MS 482.58, f. 1v, Germany, s. XII

PLATE 96

eromia ícía ícíoz· meu· qr dui lit íemp nobiícu·

cu· í·

Redempriouií nře annua expecta

one íerificaí přa· ur unigenitu

ruum quem redemptoze íeu íuíe

muí· uentente quoqʒ iudice íecu

audeamuí· Dum nřm

a nobií qʒ ompt

MS 482.59, f. 1r, Southern Germany or Austria, s. XIII

íiç iíe Zʒ nos uon uuib3c mundo· Tum·

ň ett incaritate· í; pfecta caritaí foraf iuř

ar amořé· quō tumor penā babet· Q· au

rem timet· non é pfectuí incaritate· Hos

ʒ diligaun dm· quō ipíe ʒs pzī diíexit

nof· Sı qʒ dixerit quō diligo bm ʒ frařm íu

um odit· mendax é· Qui em ň diligit

frem íuū qué uidet· dm qué non uidet

quom poteit diligere· Cc hoc manda

tum habemus ab eo· ut qʒ diligit deū·

MS 482.60, f. 1r, Southern Germany, s. XII

PLATE 97

MS 482.63, f. 2r, Germany, s. XII^{in}

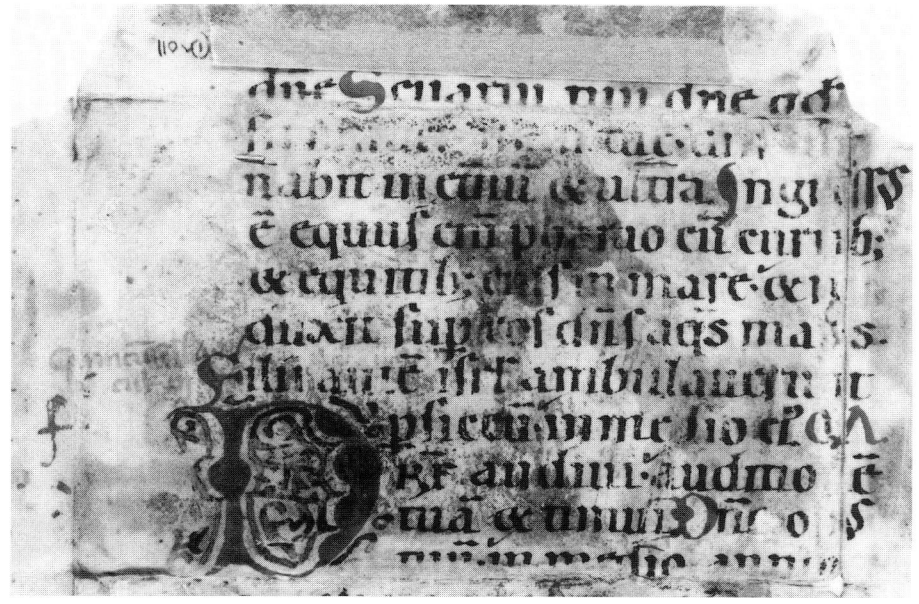

MS 482.64, f. 1v, Germany, s. XIII^{1}

PLATE 98

si sunt nec potuerunt stare ...
...o si eoy uerun inos alignant...
neq, helauerif facientes iniu...
...uo tamquam fenu uelocit...
& quemadmodu holera herbaru cu...
...era in dno & fac bonitate q in ha...
...pascens in diuiuis eius

MS 482.65, f. 2r, Southern Germany or Austria, s. XII[1]

OMI
NVS
ILLV
MINA

TIO MEA. ET SALVS MEA
quem timebo. S dabo.
D ns prector uite mee. aquo trepi
D um adpplant super me nocentes.
ut edant carnes meas.
...trbulant me inimici mei. iusi

MS 482.66, f. 1r, Southern Germany (Regensburg?), s. XII[2]

PLATE 99

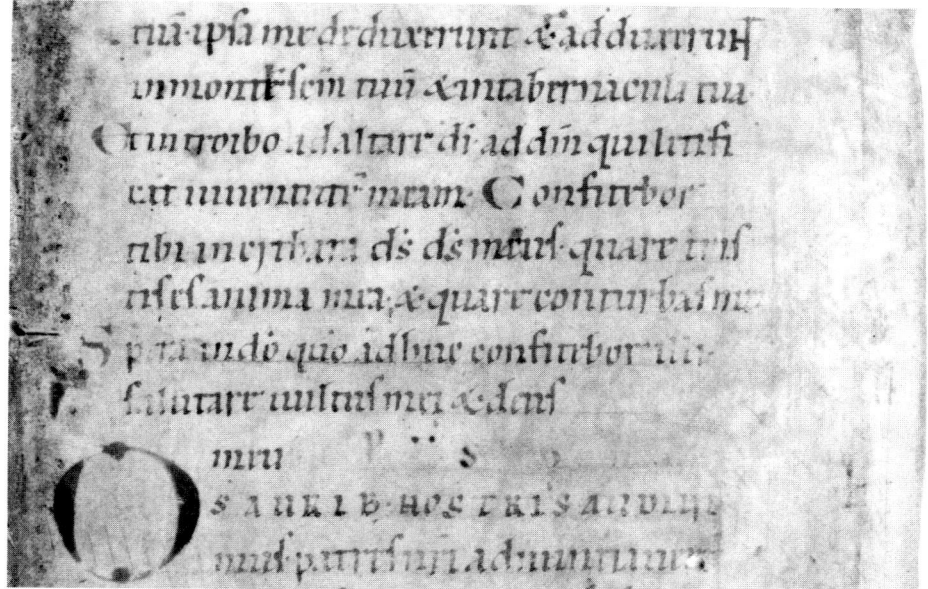

MS 482.67, f. 1r, Germany, s. XII

MS 482.70, f. 2v, Southern Germany or Austria, s. XII

PLATE 100

Hostias tibi dne p scoz s r. .
tuoz. y. comemoratione suppli
ces deferim. humilit depcantes.
ut et indulgentia nobis pariter
conferant et salutem. p. p o.
Sempti sacramti qs dne ppetua
nos tuicio no derelinquat. et in

pro num
sunt ad
crificia
possit h
qm et y
tate. et
et pplo

MS 482.72, f. 1r, Germany, s. XII/XIII

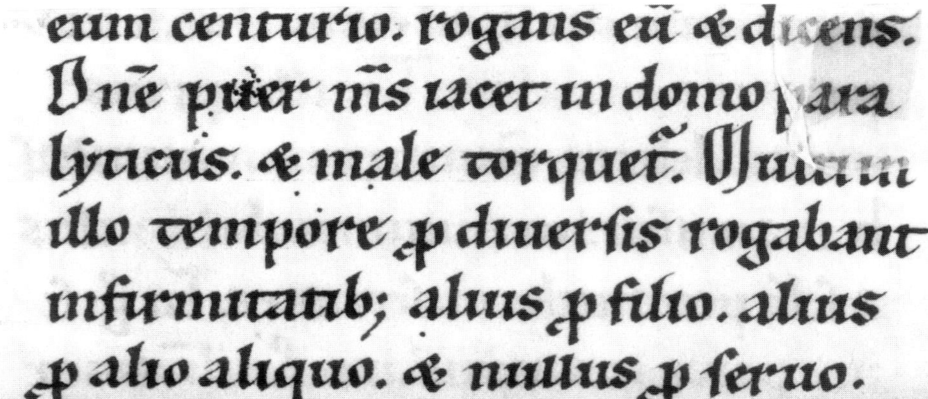

eum centurio. rogans eu & dicens.
Dne puer ms iacet in domo para
lyticus. & male torquet. Quia in
illo tempore p diuersis rogabant
infirmitatib; alius p filio. alius
p alio aliquo. & nullus p seruo.
nisi iste solus. & hoc ei adaugmen
tum beatitudinis ad coronam gte
erat. Quid enim cogitabat iste be
atus. quid estimabat iste in omni

MS 482.74, f. 2v, Germany, s. XII[2]

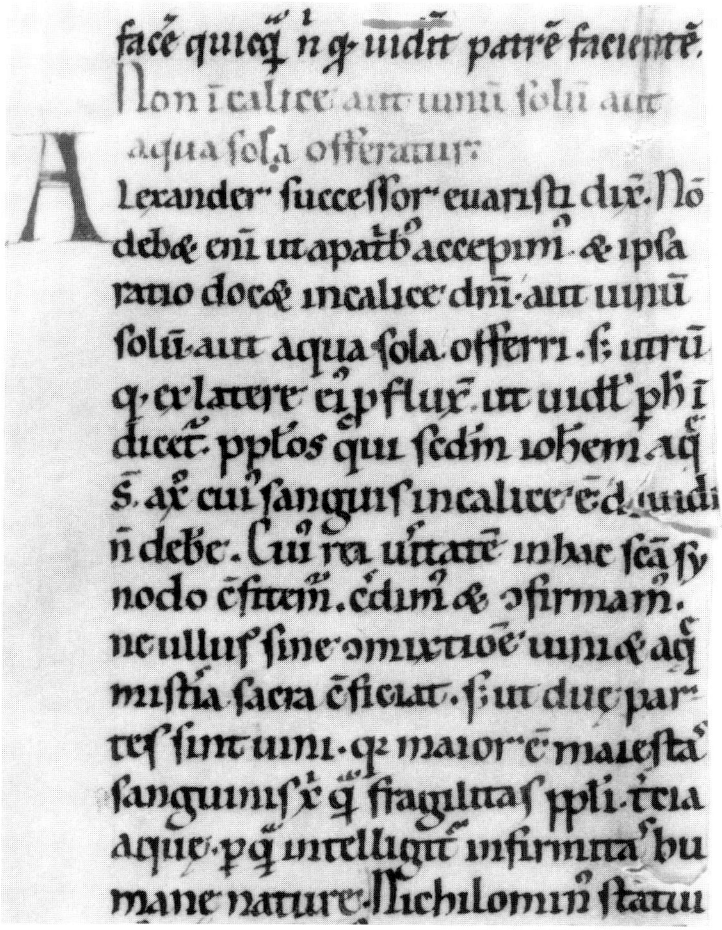

PLATE 101

facere quicq̃ n q̃ uidit patrẽ facientẽ.
Non ĩ calice aut uinũ solũ aut
aqua sola offeratur:
Alexander successor euaristi dix. Nõ
debet enĩ ut apatb̄ accepim̃. & ipsa
ratio docet incalice dn̄i. aut uinũ
solũ aut aqua sola. offerri. s̄: utrũ
q̃ ex latere ei̯ p̃flux. ut uidt̃ ph̄ ĩ
dicet. pp̃los qui sedm iohem aq̃
s̄. ax cui sanguis incalice ed uidi
n̄ debet. Cui ra uitatẽ inhac seã sy
nodo c̃sitem̃. edim̃ & c̃sirmam̃.
ne ullus sine c̃mixtioẽ uini & aq̃
mistia sacra c̃siciat. s̄ ut due partes sint uini. q̃ maiore e maiestã
sanguinis x̄ q̃ fragilitas p̃pli. tc̃ia
aquie. pq̃ intelligit infirmitas hu
mane nature. Nichilomĩ statui

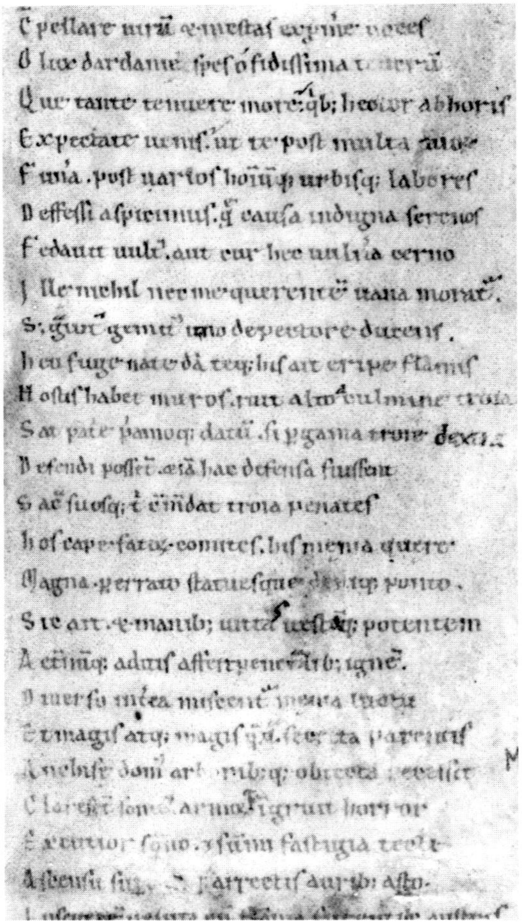

PLATE 101

C pellare uiru̅ e̅ me̅stas expme̅ uoces
O lux dardanie spes o fidissima te̅ ne̅ru̅
Q ue tante tenuere more̅ q̅b; hector abhoris
Expectate ue̅nis. ut te post multa tuo̅r
F unia . post uarios hoi̅u̅ q̅ urbisq; labores
D effessi aspicimus. q̅ causa indigna sereuos
F edauit uult̅. aut cur hec uulnia cerno
I lle mehil nec me querente̅ uana mora̅t̅.
S; grau̅ gemi̅t̅ imo depectore ducens .
h eu fuge nate dea teq; his ait eripe flamis
H ostis habet muros. ruit alto culmine trola
S at pate patriaq; datu̅ . si pgama troue dextra̅
D efendi posset. et̅a̅ hac defe̅sa fuisse̅t
S ac suosq; t̅ ci̅mdat troia penates
h os cape fatoy comites. his menia quere
M agna. peray statuesq̅ue desi̅y ponto .
S ic art. e manib; uitta uestaq; potentem
A et̅niq; adimis affert penetraib; igne̅.
D merso i̅n̅tea misce̅nt̅ mo̅ra tuoris
t̅ magis atq; magis qo̅ t̅cta parentis
A ne̅lu̅ie domi arboribusq; obtecta recessit
C lare̅tt̅ son̅. armoru̅̅̅ grui̅t horror
E xcutior so̅no. et su̅mi fastugia tecti
A scensu sup̅ . s; arrectis auryb; asto.
l nsu͠e̅ru̅ uelutu eu fla̅ma eu̅u̅u̅

PLATE 102

sacrificia offerret· tuditēāglīn di flamē iuxta a[l]
ariculaq; monachoꝝ accedentiū ad altare· ſcrībe
ba nomina ī libro q̄ tenebat ī manib; ſuis· q̄rundi ū
[ta] nī ſcrībentē· ſūq̄d ilaq̄ent obſeruans; ſenior q̄
q̄rū nī ſc[ri]ſſt; ſp̄ta q̄ſ cōpleta myſtia amiuq̄q; eoꝝ
uocans pſcrutat̄· q̄d eā ī occulto peccata ſuiſſ; adm[]
[E]t ī uenit ex cfeſſione eoꝝ unuq̄q; mortalis peccatiol[]
[T]ū ē hortat̄ ē eos agere peniteǹa ī ſeipſū cīe[]
ante dnīm pſternens dic· ac noctē ꝗ ipſe eoꝝ peccǎ[]
obnoxiꝰ flebat ſt tadiu pmanſit cū eas in luctu ꝟ[]

MS 482.77, f. 1v, Lambach, Austria, s. XII[ex]

[a]ut ad quendam ſolitari   ꝗ eum cum g[]
um· Erat enim ille habes   nex· et ſaluta[]
cum oīmibus caritatem· et   reſederunt· C[]
multi ueniebant ad eum·   peregrinus il[]
Nunciauit autem ei frīl[]   turis ſcīs· et
le· quēdam ꝺe abbate paſto   ſtibus· abbr[]
re· Qui audiens uirtutem   uertit faciem
anima eius· deſiderauit eū   ei dedit reſp[]
uidere· Cum aūt reuerſus   aūt ille quia
eet ille fr in egypto· poſt ali   tur cum eo·
[]   [] et dixit [i]

MS 482.78, f. 1v, Italy, s. XIII[1]

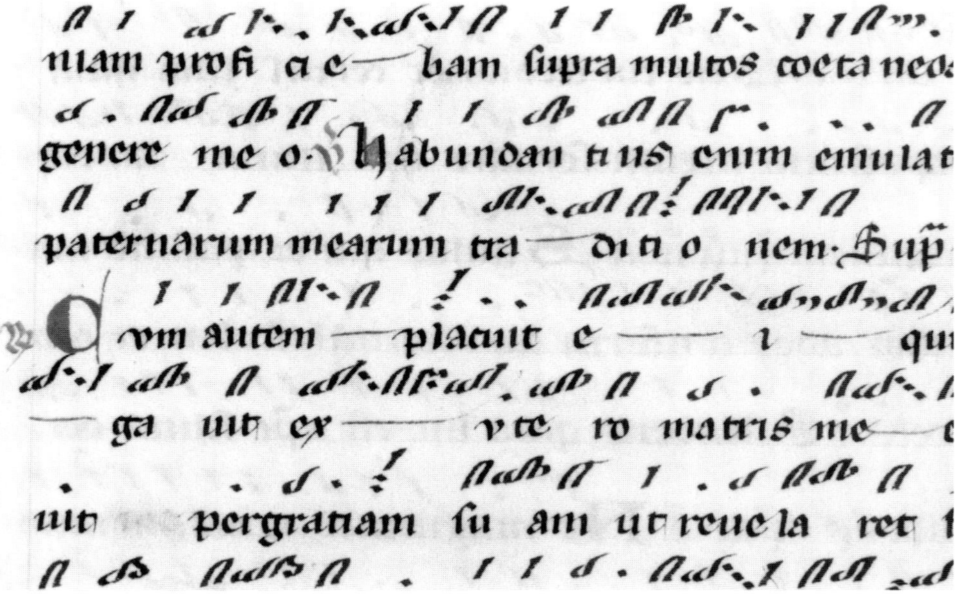

PLATE 103

niam pfofi a e — bam supra multos cocta nea

genere me o Habundan ti us enim emulat

paternarum mearum tra — di ti o nem. Sup

vm autem — placuit e — i qui

ga uit ex — v te to matris me

uit pergratiam su am ut reuela ret

MS 482.78A, f. 1v, Southern Germany or Austria, s. XIII/XIV

MS 482.79, f. 1r, Southern France or Northern Italy, s. XIV

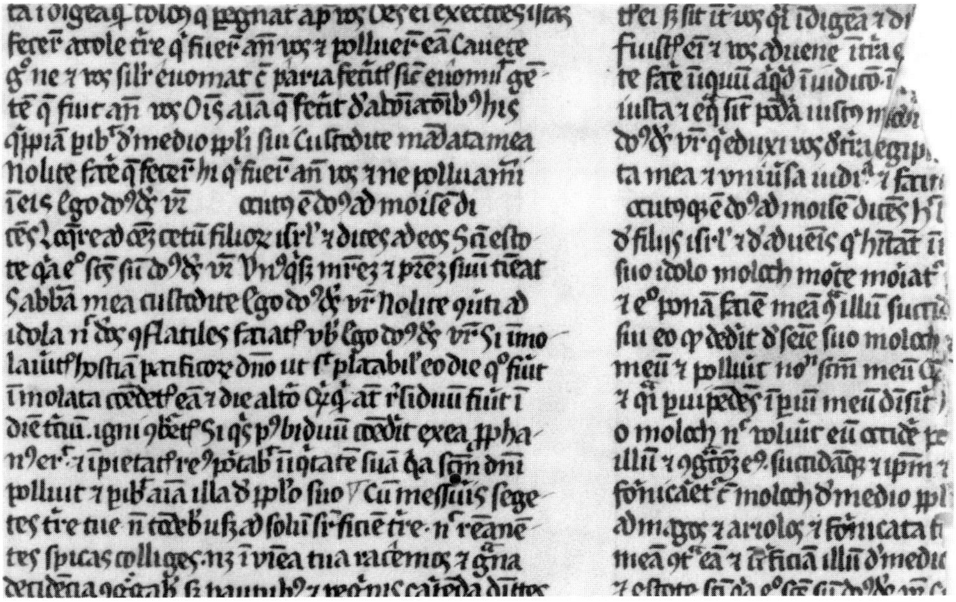

PLATE 104

MS 482.81, f. 1r, Germany, s. XIII

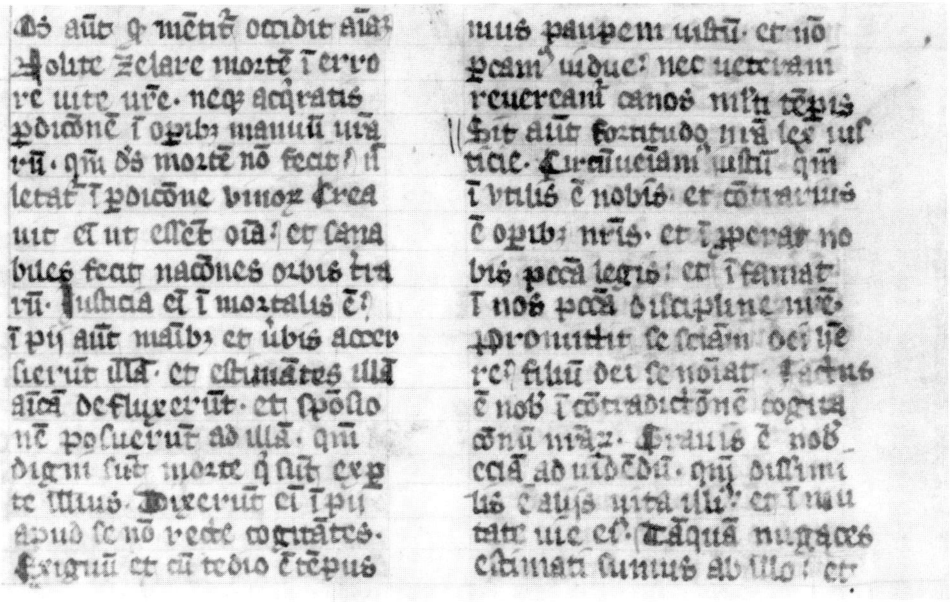

MS 482.82, f. 2r, Germany, s. XIV

PLATE 105

MS 482.83, f. 1r, Northern France (?), s. XIII[1]

MS 482.84, f. 1v, Northern France (?), s. XIII

PLATE 106

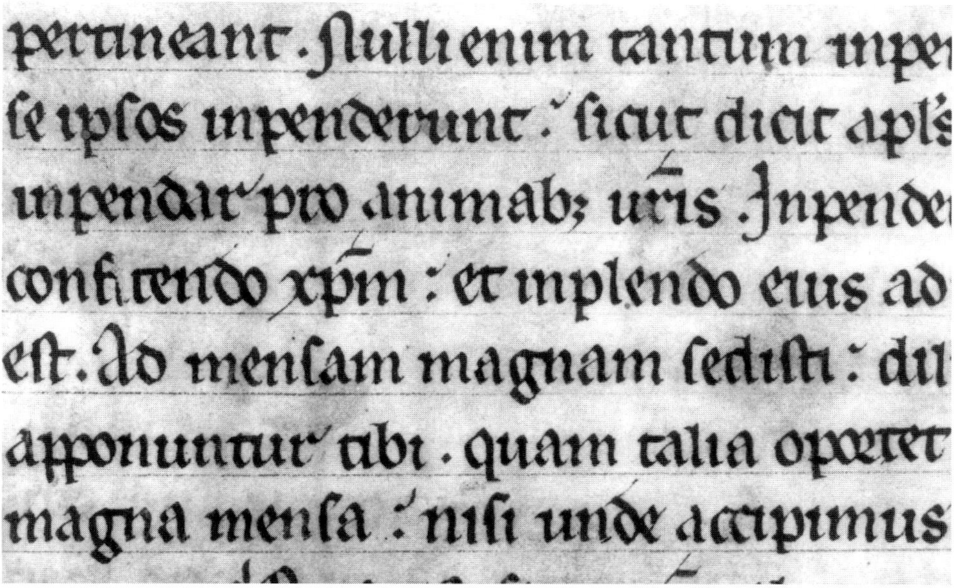

pertineant . Mulli enim tantum impe[r]
se ipsos inpenderunt : sicut dicit apl[s]
inpendar pro animab; u[est]ris . Inpende[re]
confitendo xpm : et implendo eius ad
est . Ad mensam magnam sedisti : dil[i]
apponuntur tibi . quam talia oportet
magna mensa : nisi unde accipimus

MS 482.86, f. 1v, Germany, s. XIII

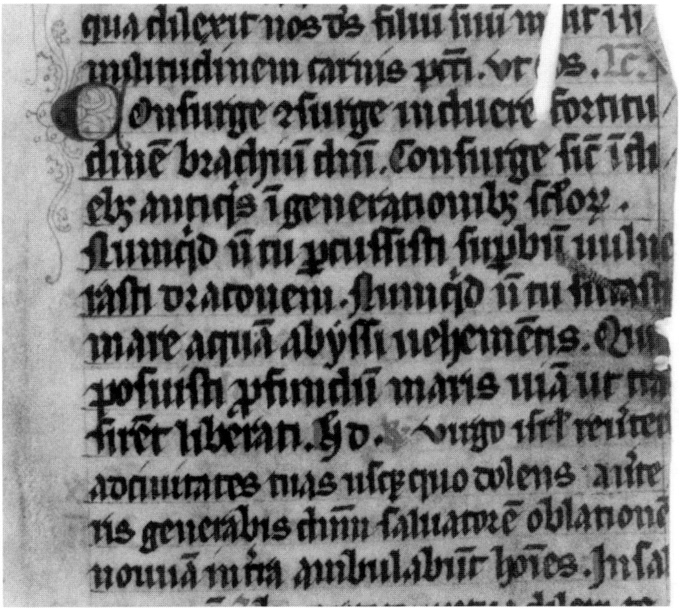

qua dilexit nos d[eu]s filiu[m] suu[m] in[?]
in[?]itudinem carnis p[ecca]ti . Vt [?]
onsurge [et] surge induere fortitu[dine]
dine brachiu[m] d[omi]ni . Confurge s[icu]t i[n]
els antiq[ui]s i[n] generationib; s[e]c[u]lo[rum] .
Numquid non tu percussisti s[u]p[er]bu[m] uuln[er]
asti draconem . Numquid non tu sic[c]asti
mare aqua[m] abyssi uehemens. Qu[i]
posuisti p[ro]fundu[m] maris uia[m] ut t[ra]n
siret liberati . H[oc] d[icit] . Virgo isr[ae]l reuerte[re]
ad ciuitates tuas usq[ue] quo deliciis . Quia [?]
nis generabis d[omi]n[u]m saluatore[m] oblatione[m]
nouua[m] in t[er]ra ambulabit ho[m]ines. In sal[ute]

MS 482.87, f. 1r, Germany, s. XIV[1]

PLATE 107

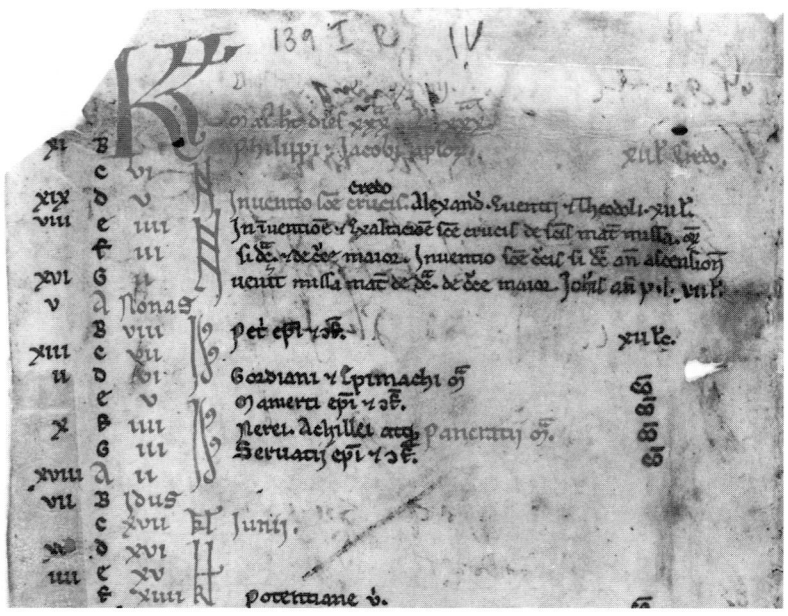

MS 482.88, f. 1v, Germany, s. XIII^ex

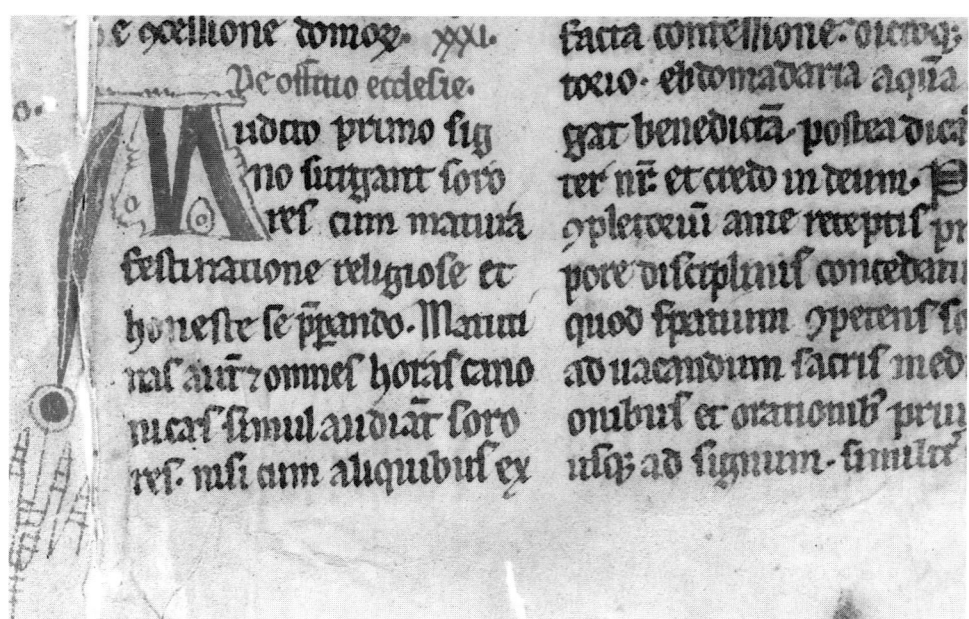

MS 482.91, f. 1v, Germany, s. XIII^ex

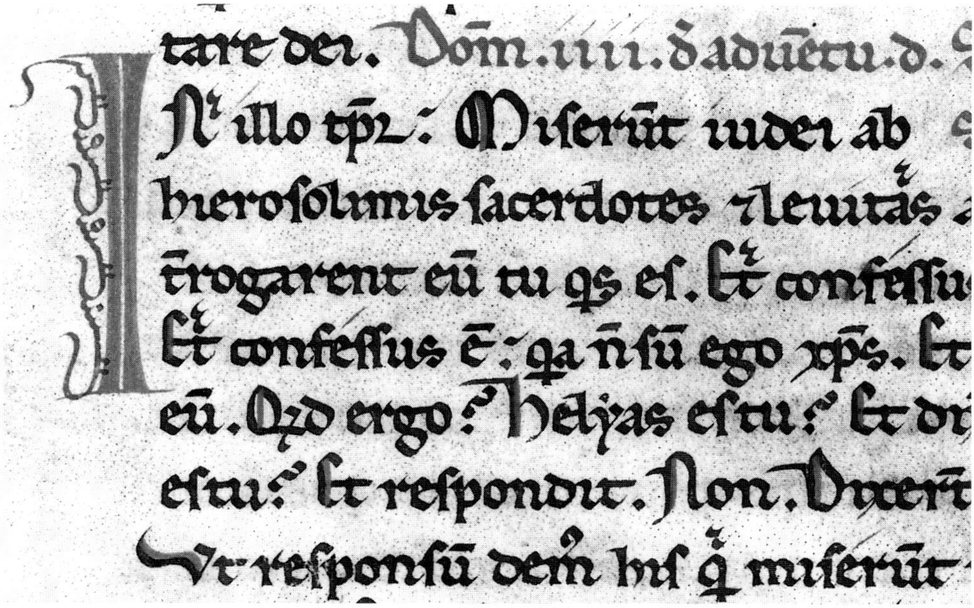

PLATE 108

MS 482.92, f. 1v, Italy, s. XIII[med]

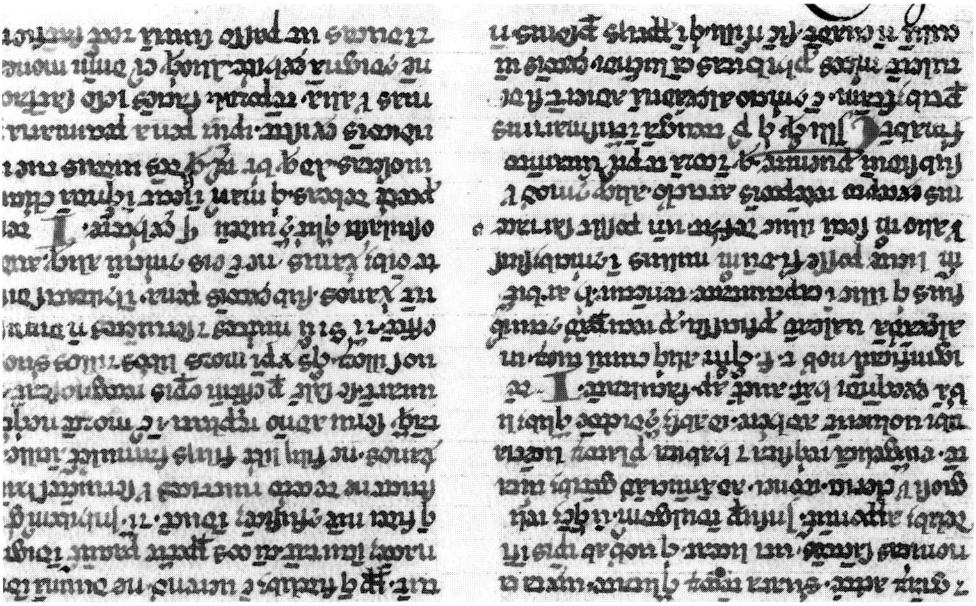

MS 482.94, f. 1v, Italy, s. XIII[2]

PLATE 109

aboculis dei. Si non uis
recedere abeis. multu la
boras. Audi dicente. ue
nite adme oms qui labo
rans. Non uis laborare
fugiendo. abillo fugis fu
gere non adillum. inueni
quo. et fuge. Si aut aptre
tea non potes abillo fuge

sciebat
ei dns
bore f
xpc in
uidebi
est eni
bore fi
hoc u
Recon

MS 482.95, f. 1v, Germany, s. XIII

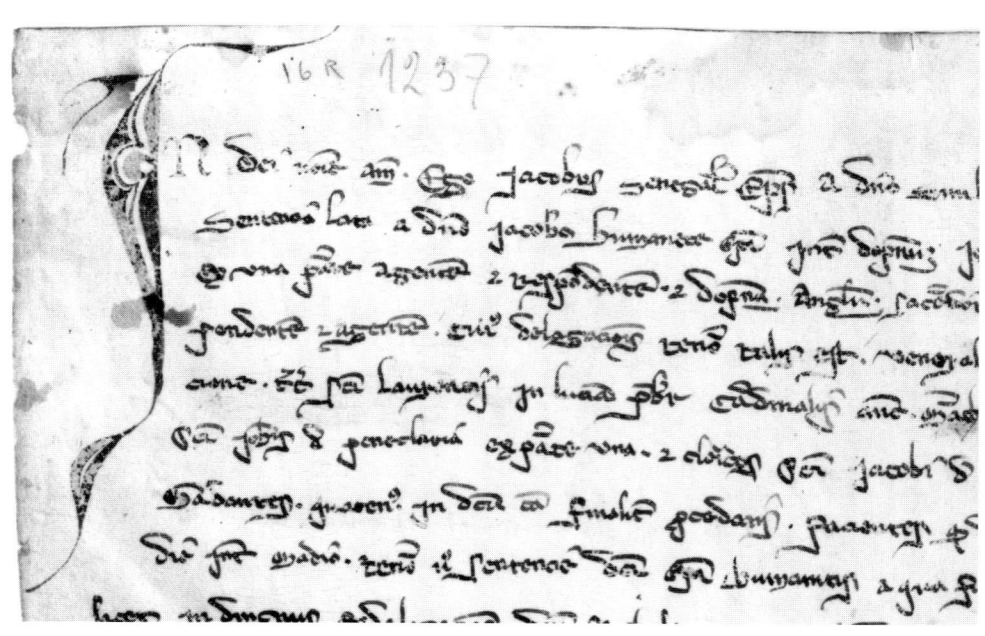

MS 482.96, f. 1r, Senigallia, Italy, after December 1237

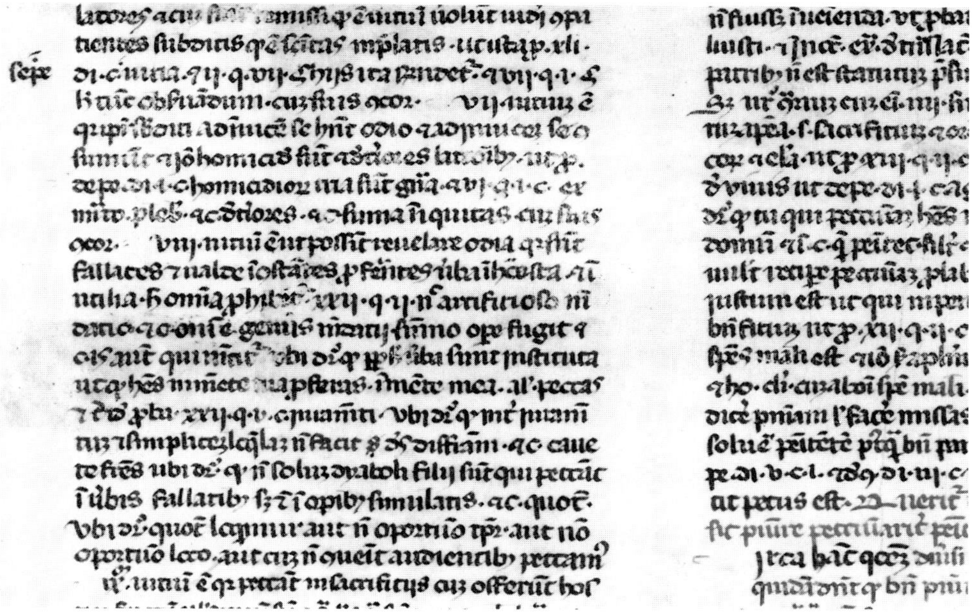

PLATE 110

MS 482.97, f. 1r, Italy, s. XIV

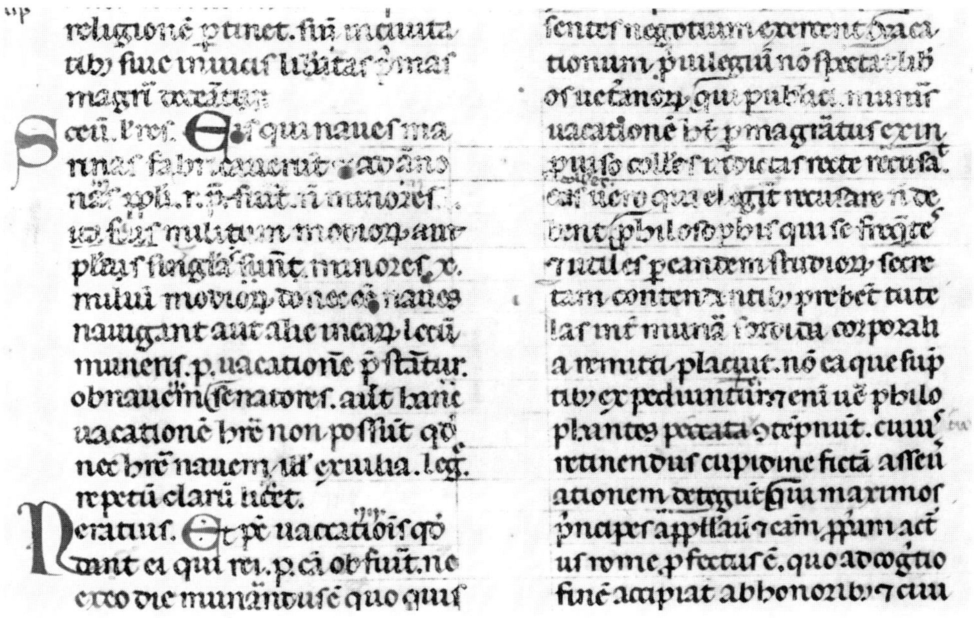

MS 482.98, f. 1r, Italy, s. XIII^ex

PLATE 111

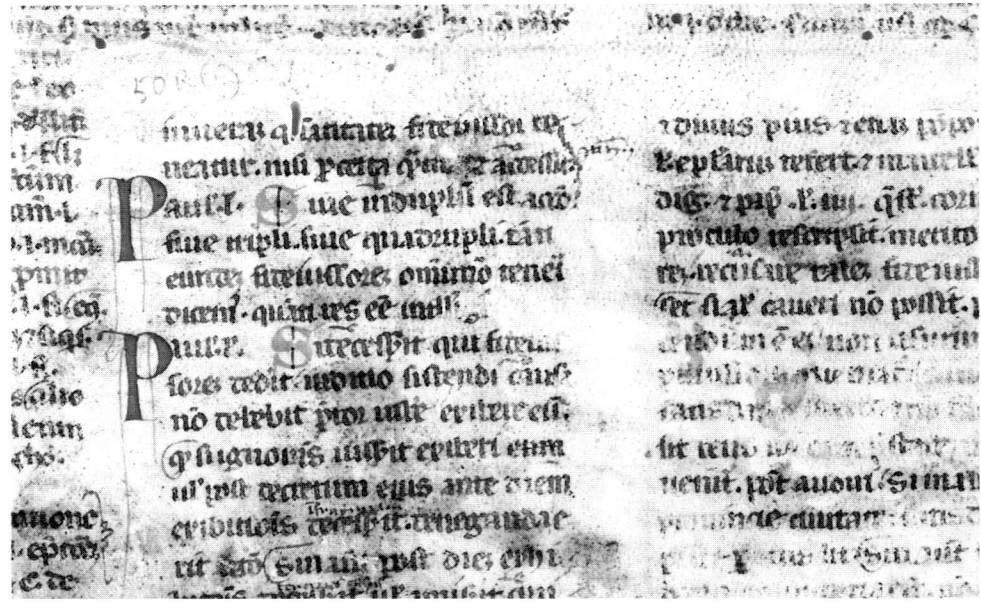

MS 482.99, f. 1v, Italy, s. XIII

MS 482.100, f. 4r, Germany, s. XIII/XIV

PLATE 112

MS 482.101, f. 1r, Italy (Bologna?), s. XIV[1]

MS 482.102, f. 2r, Germany, s. XIII[1]

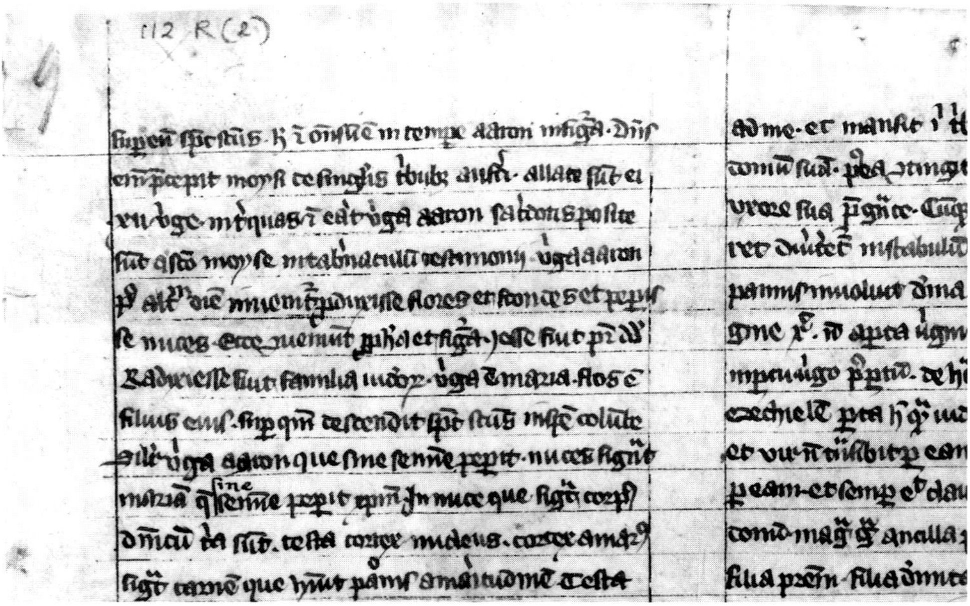

PLATE 113

MS 482.103, f. 1r, Germany, s. XIV[1]

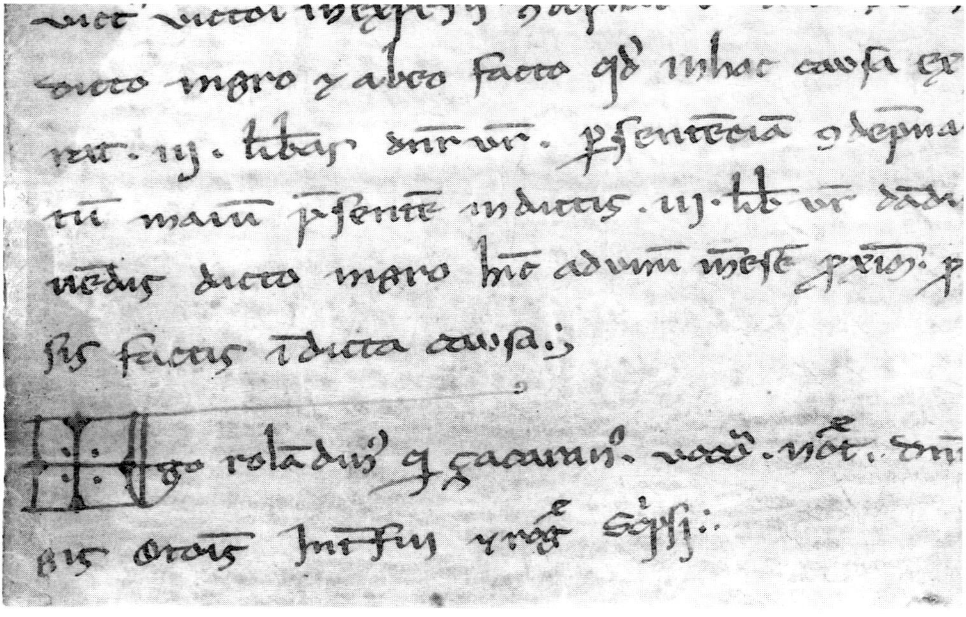

MS 482.104, f. 1r, Trent, Italy, 3 August 1233

PLATE 114

Scieñdum uero est quod . dn̄ . iam dicti qui
ad minus estimari detoto anno ad firmmam.
Suma redempcionis simplicis que debetur p
dictum est estimaz̃ ad minus ad . vj. fol̄ col̄ d
dari . i. mr̄ col̄ d prolardo . illis autē qui ñ
nibus i lardo vocaut anni debetur plena re

MS 482.105, f. 1v, Germany, s. XIII

MS 482.106, f. 1r, Germany, s. XIV/XV

PLATE 115

MS 482.107, f. 2v, Southern Germany, s. XIV/XV

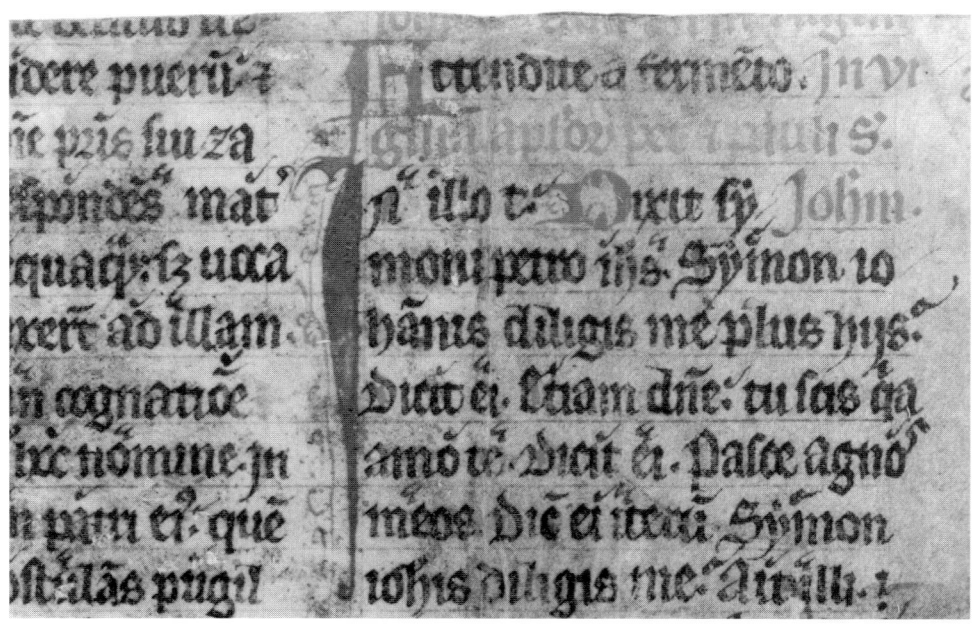

MS 482.108, f. 2r, Switzerland (?), s. XIII

PLATE 116

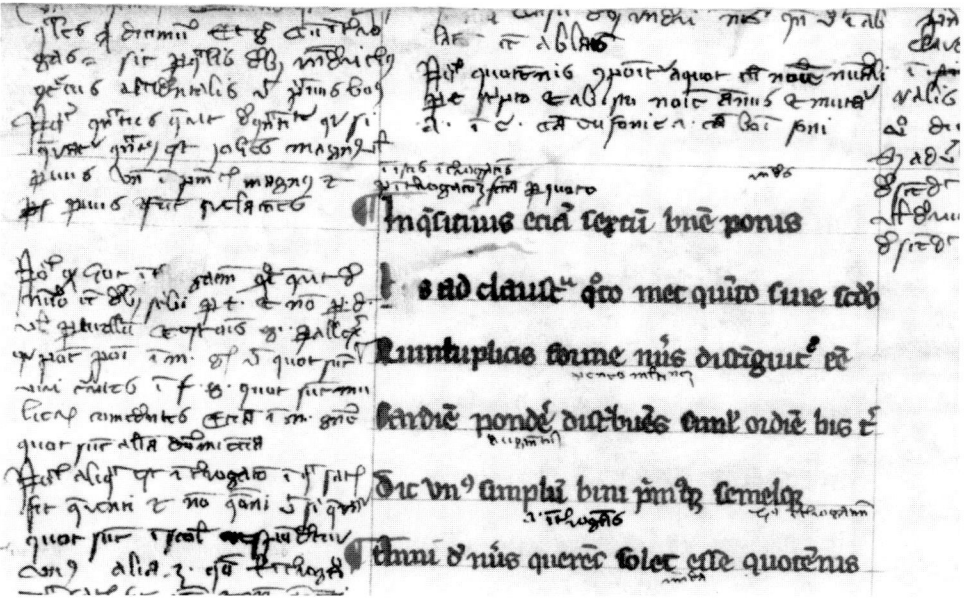

MS 482.109, f. 2r, Germany, s. XIV

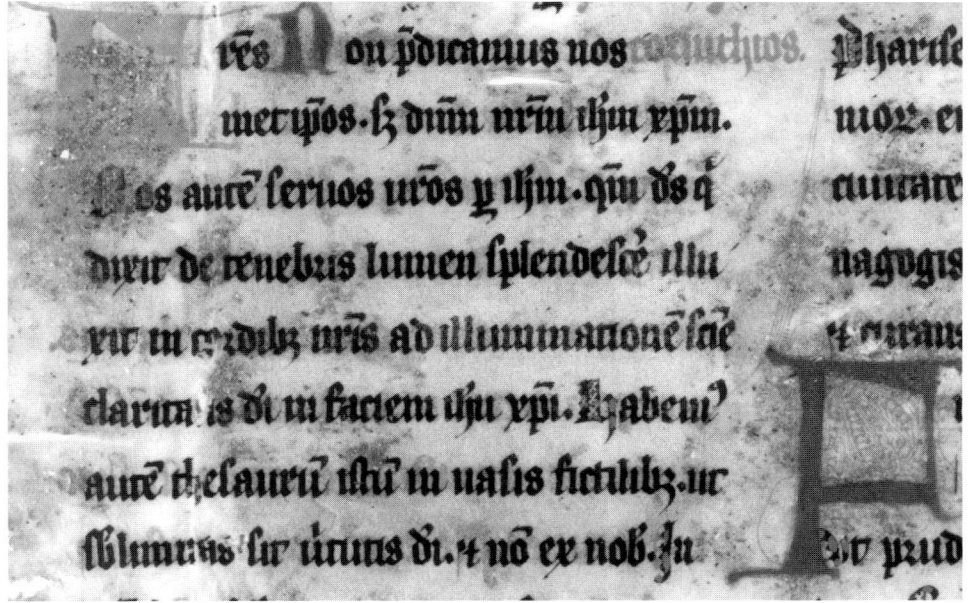

MS 482.110, f. 1r, Germany, s. XIV

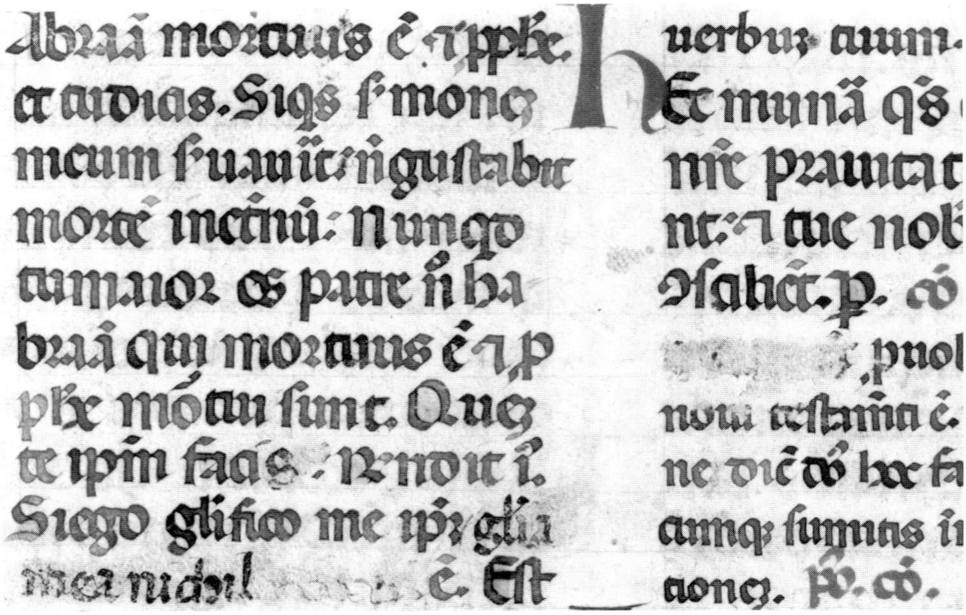

PLATE 117

MS 482.111, f. 1v, Italy, s. XIV

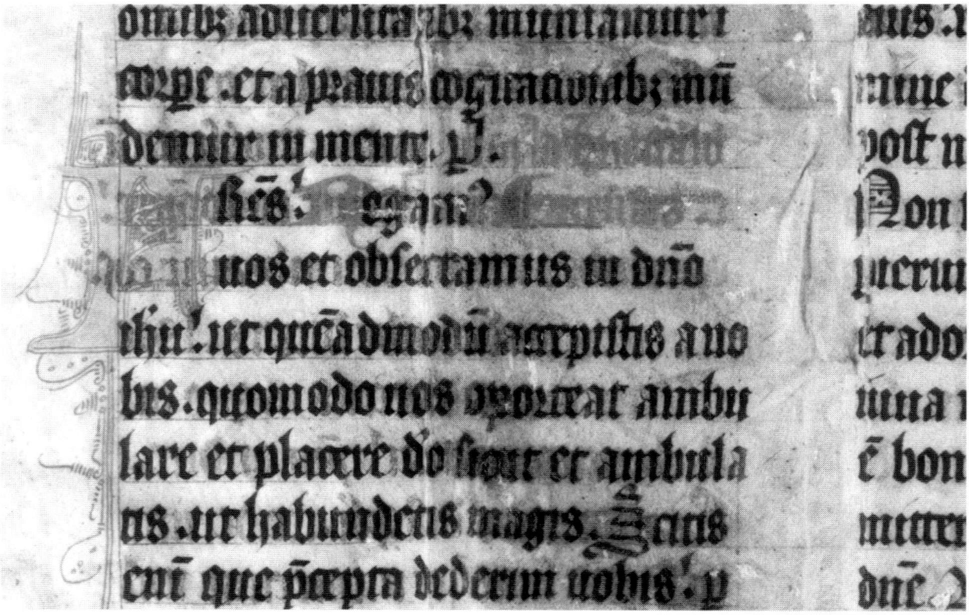

MS 482.112, f. 1v, Germany, s. XIV

PLATE 118

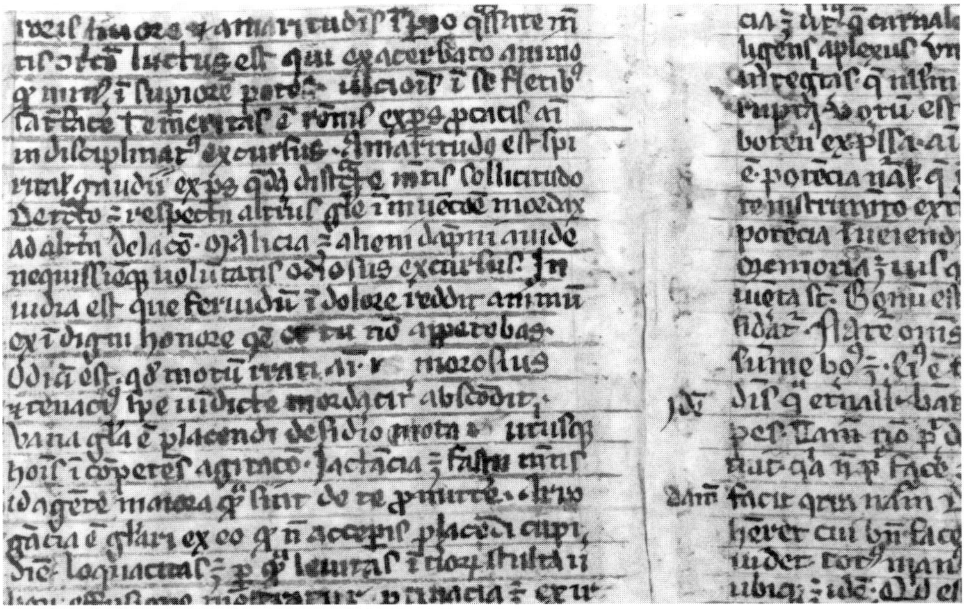

MS 482.113, f. 1v/2r, Germany, s. XIV[1]
(lower text: s. X/XI)

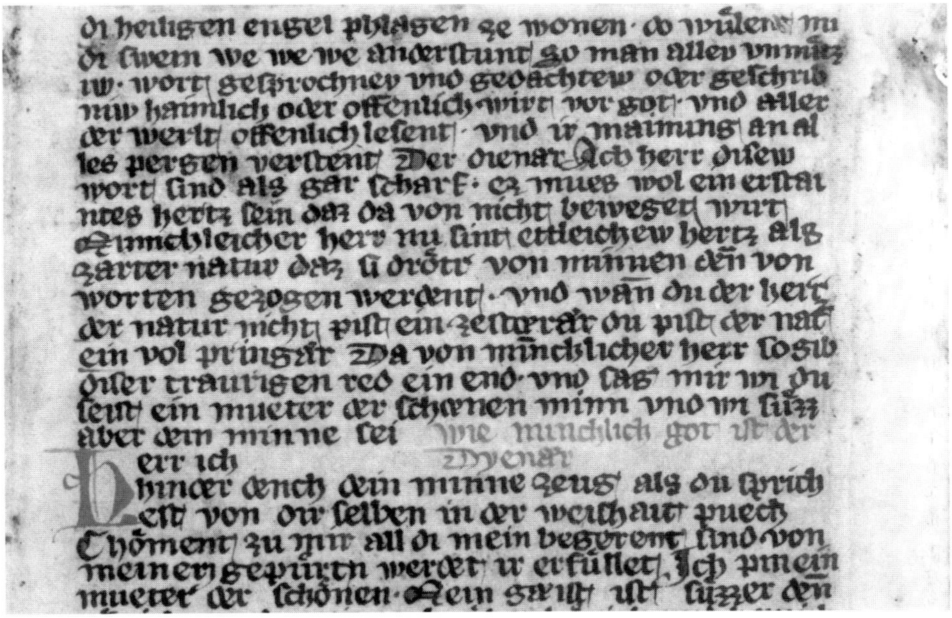

MS 482.114, f. 2r,
Southwestern Germany or Northern Switzerland, s. XIV[med]

PLATE 119

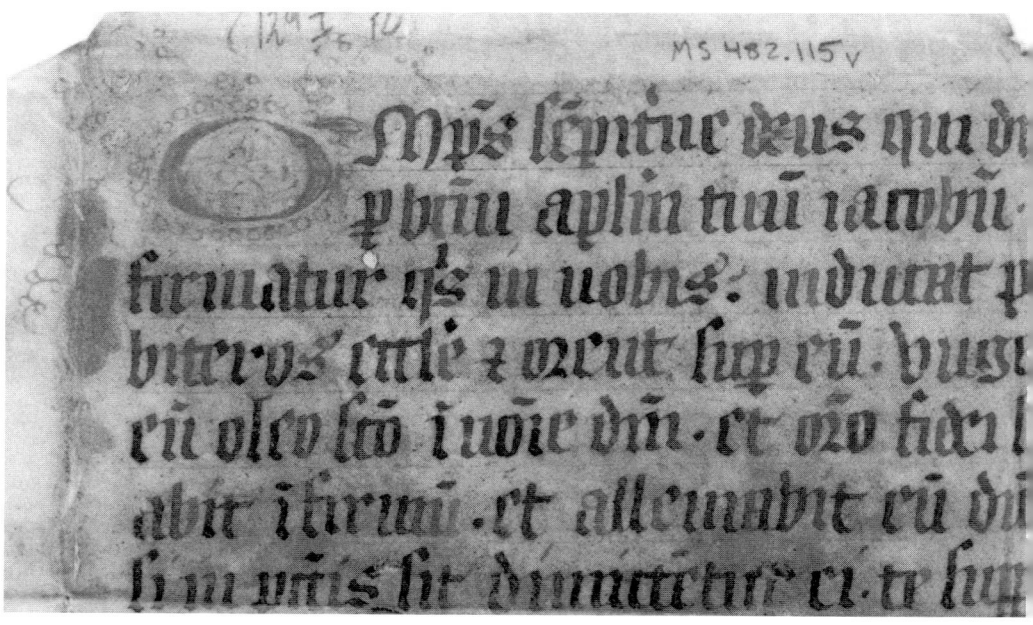

MS 482.115, f. 1v, Germany, s. XV

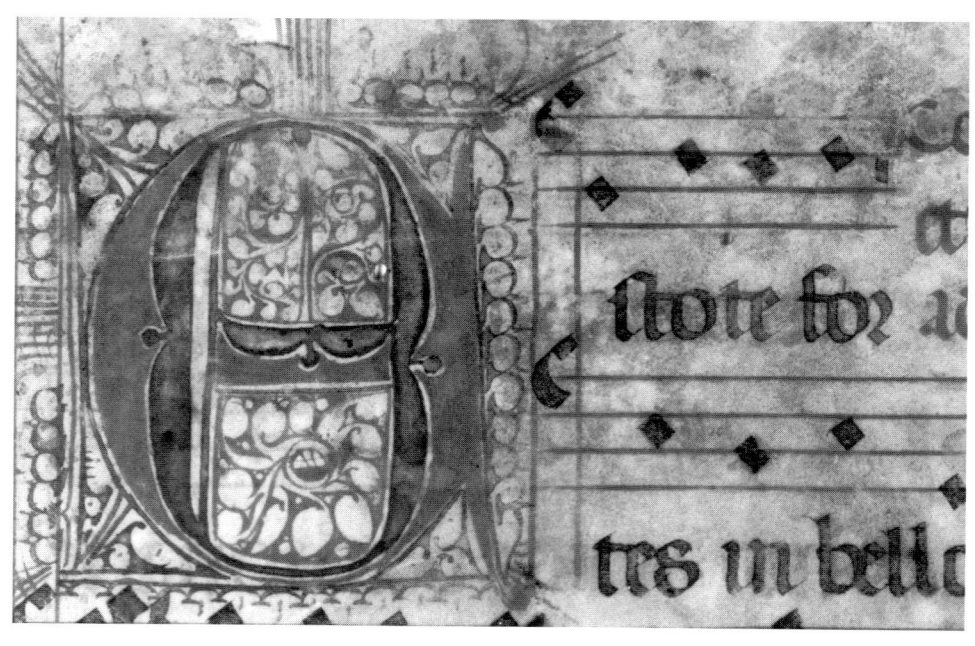

MS 482.116, f. 1r, Germany, s. XV[2]

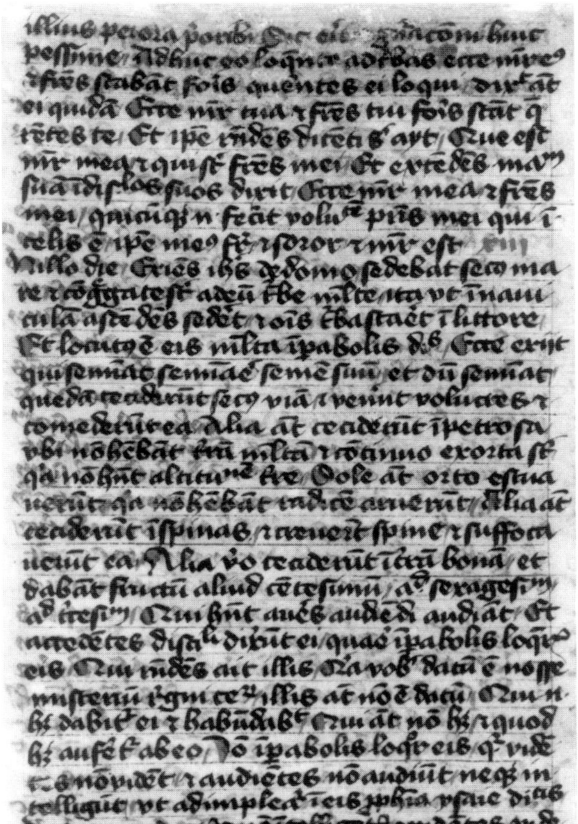

PLATE 120

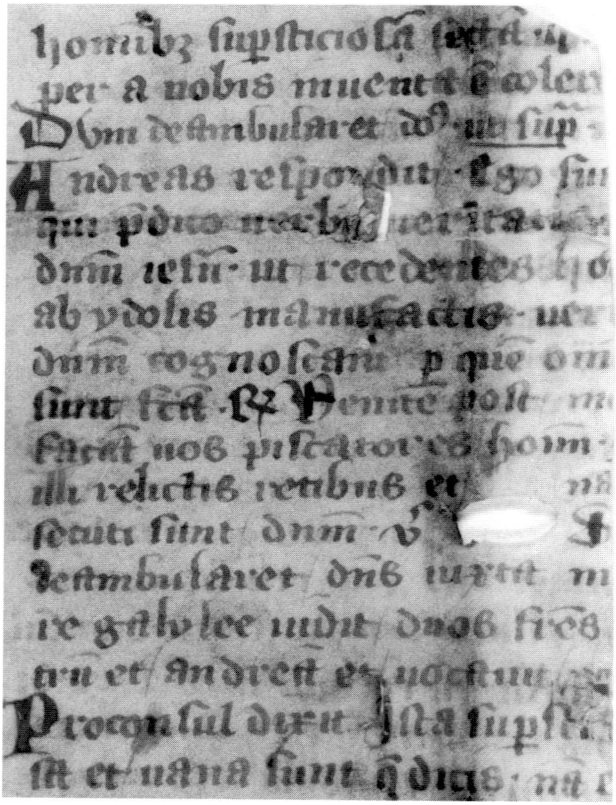

PLATE 120

homib3 supsticiosa sede
per a uobis mucnta colen
Dum deambularet do ur sup
Andreas respondit. Ego siu
qui pdico uerbis ueritas
dnm iesm ut recedentes ho
ab ydolis manufactis uer
dnm cognoscam p que om
sunt sca. R7 Venite post me
facit nos piscatores hoim
illi relictis reubus et na
secuti sunt dnm v S
deambularet dns iuxta m
re galvlee iudit dnos fres
tru et Andrea eu uocauit
Proconsul dixit Ista supst
sa et uana sunt q dicis, ut c

PLATE 121

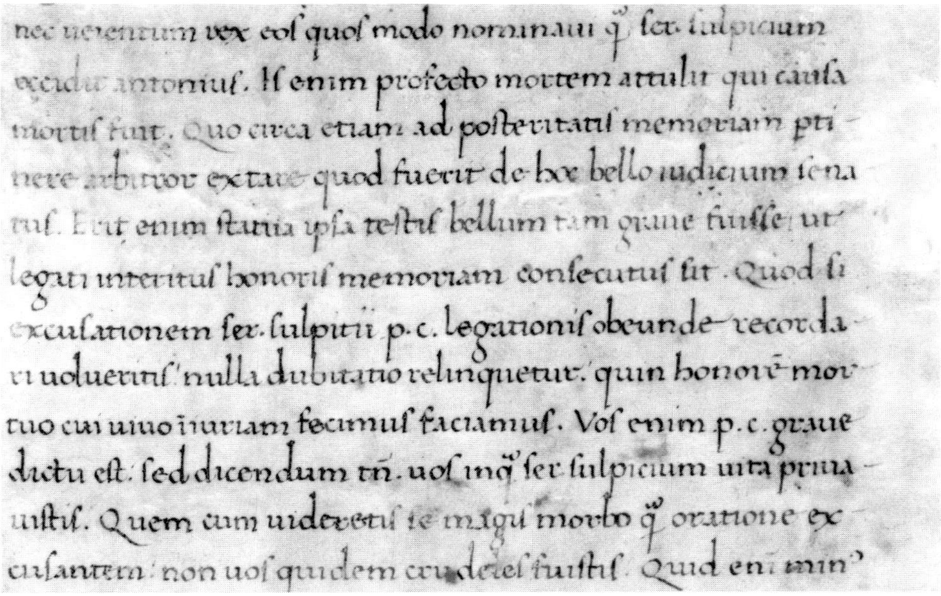

MS 482.120, f. 1v, Italy, s. XV^2

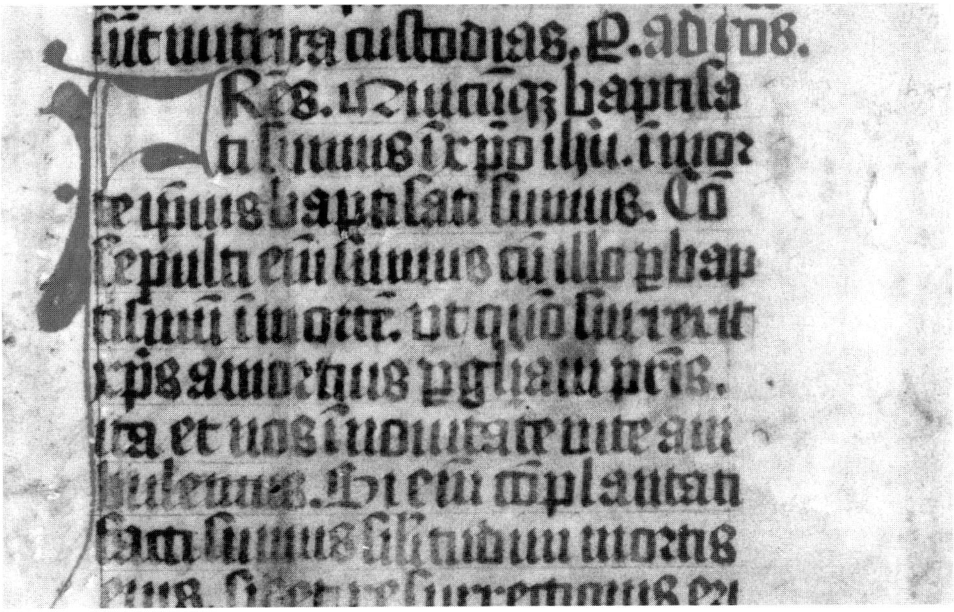

MS 482.121, f. 1r, Germany, s. XV^2

PLATE 122

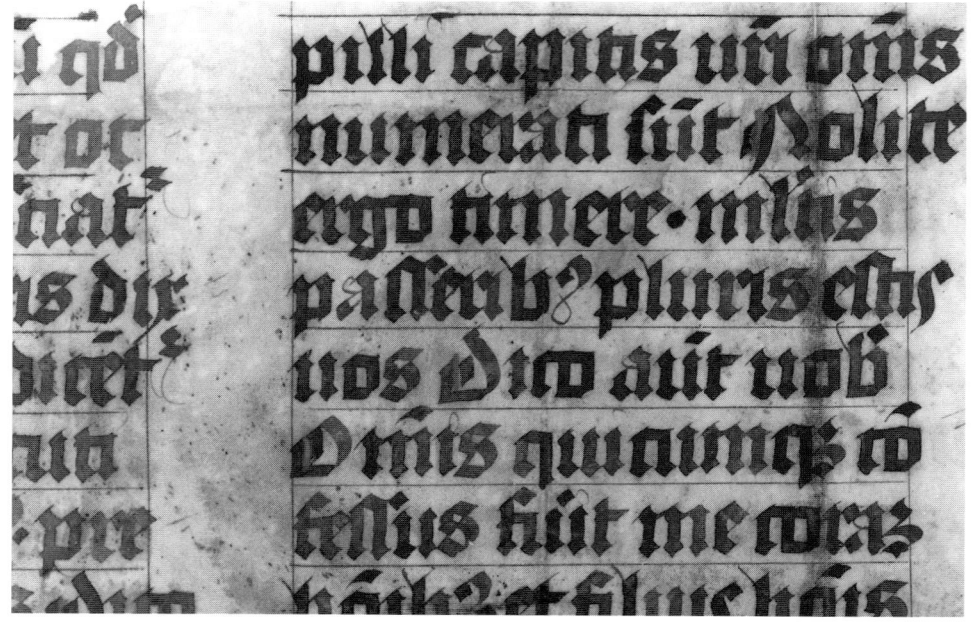

MS 482.122, f. 1v, Germany, s. XV

MS 482.123, f. 1r, France, s. XV[2]

PLATE 123

bře pau
le aplē
doctor
genūū
děpcaur
pro me
oīpcen
teui dm qui te de celo uocauit
r īfuam pstrauit de pseautore
feat uas electionis ut me p
ctauū ī malo eleuer ī bono et
ut ubox tuox erudinonibz e
doctos disci spuē fugitia huī
sēli gaudia ef ueuā lucem que
rps e ualeam apphende. A

MS 482.124, f. 1r, France, s. XV[2]

decz semp ui ewīn Ameq. ympuus
Uesū uza retempao amoz z deside
riuui deus creatoz dūr homo īfiue
tempoz pue te uoat demeuna
ot sezres uza ciuuua crudelem moz
tem pañes ut nos amozte solues
īfezu claustra peuetrans tuos
captuos redimens uictoz triūpho
uobili ad dextram pzis residēus
pa te cogat pietas ot mala

patemqz to
te p mo ū
ez te snamu
filiū te utr
tempoz A
Am kpt ac
uude ueuezat
datuzus spi
bat dies qi
ozbe uolut

MS 482.125, f. 1r, Germany, s. XV

PLATE 126

MS 482.128, f. 1r, Low Countries or Western Germany (?), s. XV

MS 482.129, f. 1v, Germany, s. XIV

PLATE 123

bīe pau
le aplē
doctor
genaū
deprcair
p̄ro me
oī p̄ oten
tein d̄m q̄u te de celo uocauit
ₑ fiīnam p̄ſtrauit de p̄ſeaitor e
ſeat uas electionis ut me p̄
ſtitaū ī malo elener ī bono et
ut ūłboꝛ tuoꝛ erudiaonibꝫ e
doctos diſcā ſpnē fuigūta hui'
ſāi gaudia er uerā lucein que
r p̄ s ē ualeam apꝓhendē. Ʒt

MS 482.124, f. 1r, France, s. XV[2]

----

dec̄ꝝ ſeiūp īn euiu Amey. ympuls   pacemꝗ̄ d̄

Ꝺeſu ūā reteinpao einoꝛ ꝫ deſide   te p̄ ino v

rium deus creatoꝛ b̄n̄ ḡouio īſīne   ez te ſn̄aūu

teinpoꝛ Ꝺ ue te uirt clemenaa   filūi te vtri

ꝟt feꝛres ūā eꝛuui̅ crudelein inoꝛ   teinpoꝛr Ꝏ

tein paries ut nos ainocte ſoluies   Ꝏin ꝑ̄pī̄ ac

Ꝺnfeꝛni clauſtra peiietraus tuos   unde ueuerat

captiuos reduineus uirtie triinpho   catuꝛzus ſpī

uobili ad deꝛtram p̄r̄is reſidēs   bat dies ꝗ

Ꝺp̄a te cogat pietas ꝟt mala   oꝛbe uoluti

MS 482.125, f. 1r, Germany, s. XV

PLATE 124

MS 482.126, f. 1r, Germany, s. XV

PLATE 125

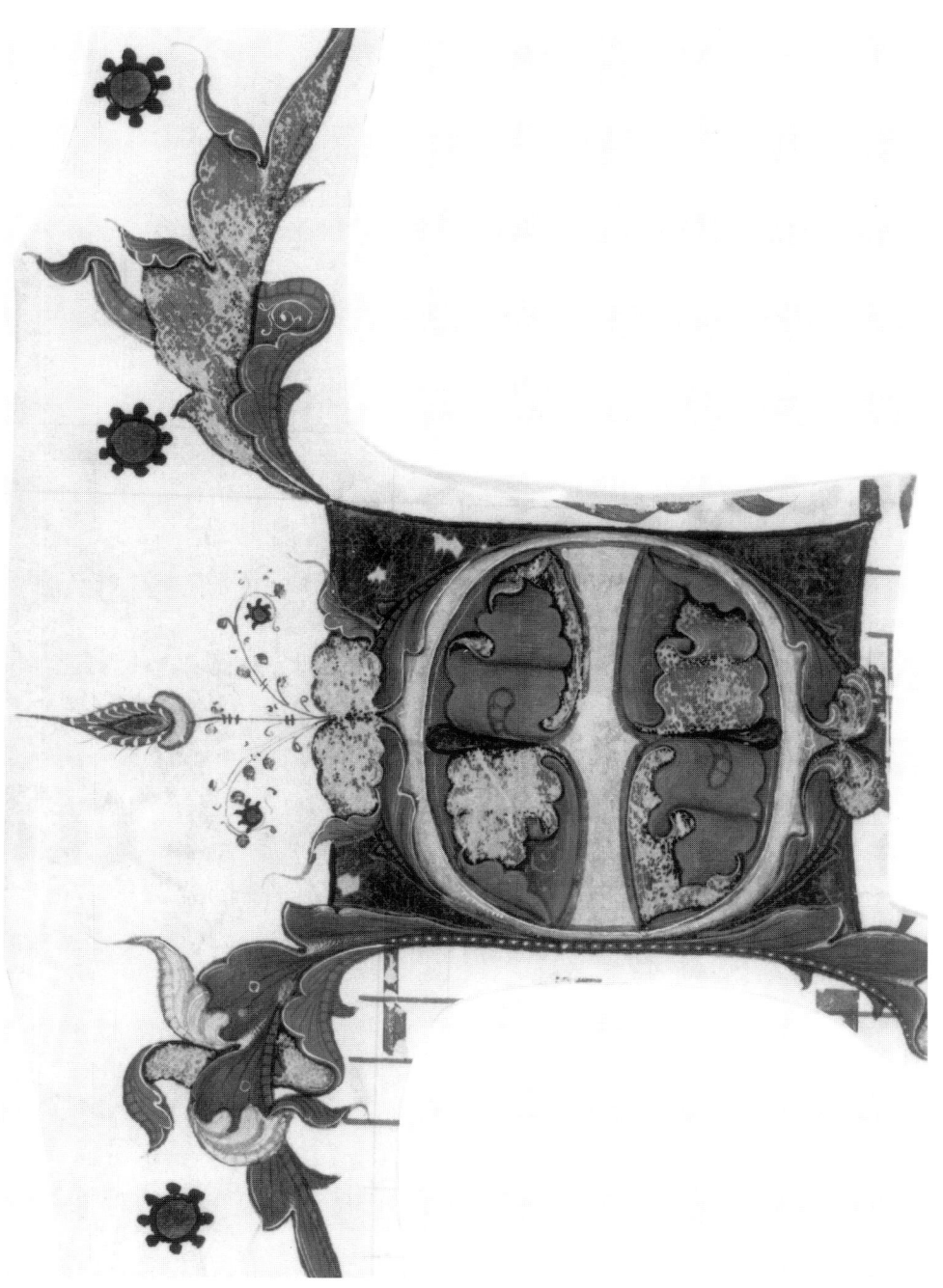

MS 482.127, f. 1r, Italy, s. XV

PLATE 126

MS 482.128, f. 1r, Low Countries or Western Germany (?), s. XV

MS 482.129, f. 1v, Germany, s. XIV

PLATE 127

MS 482.130, f. 1v, Austria, s. XV[2]

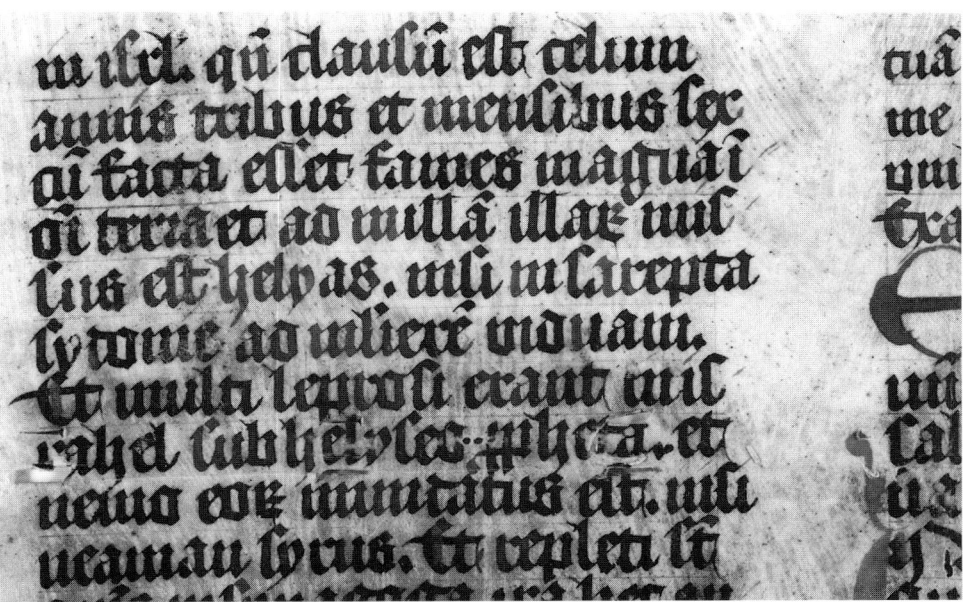

MS 482.131, f. 1v, Germany, s. XV[2]

PLATE 128

MS 482.132, f. 1r, Austria, s. XV

MS 482.133, f. 2v, Germany, s. XV[2]

PLATE 129

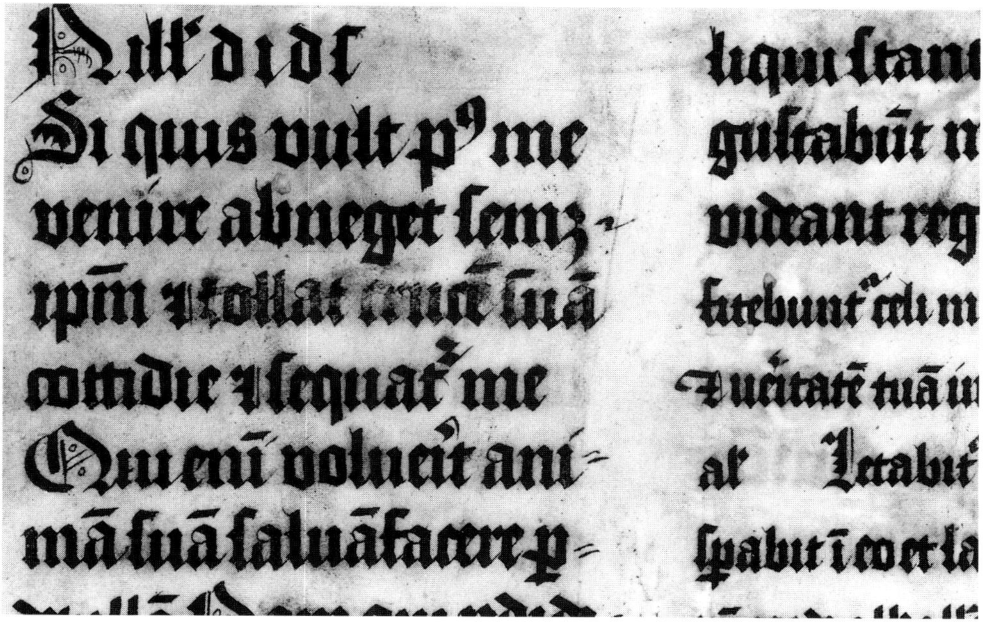

MS 482.135, f. 1v, Southern Germany or Austria, s. XIV

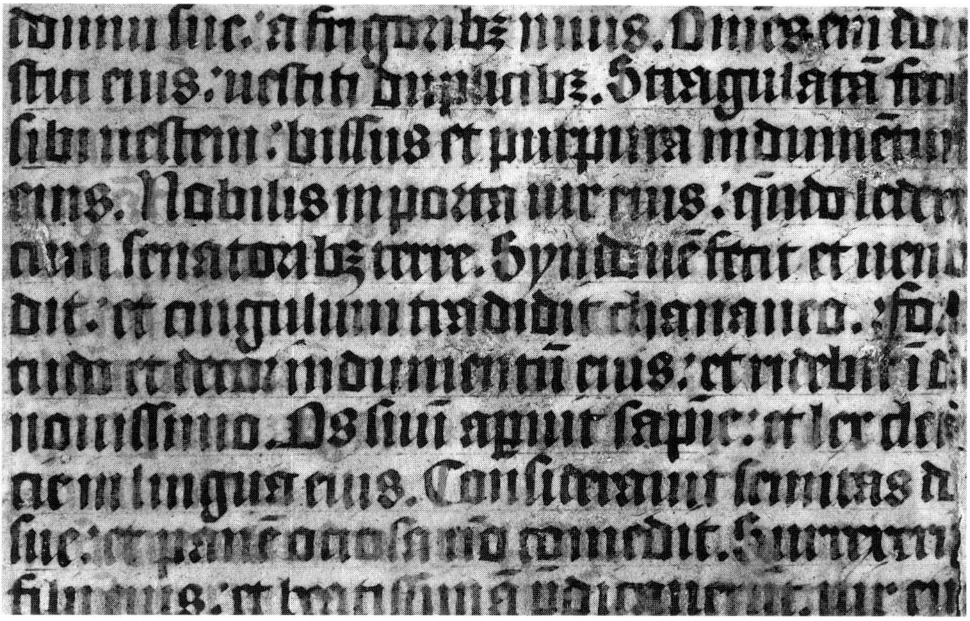

MS 482.136, f. 1v, Germany, s. XIV/XV

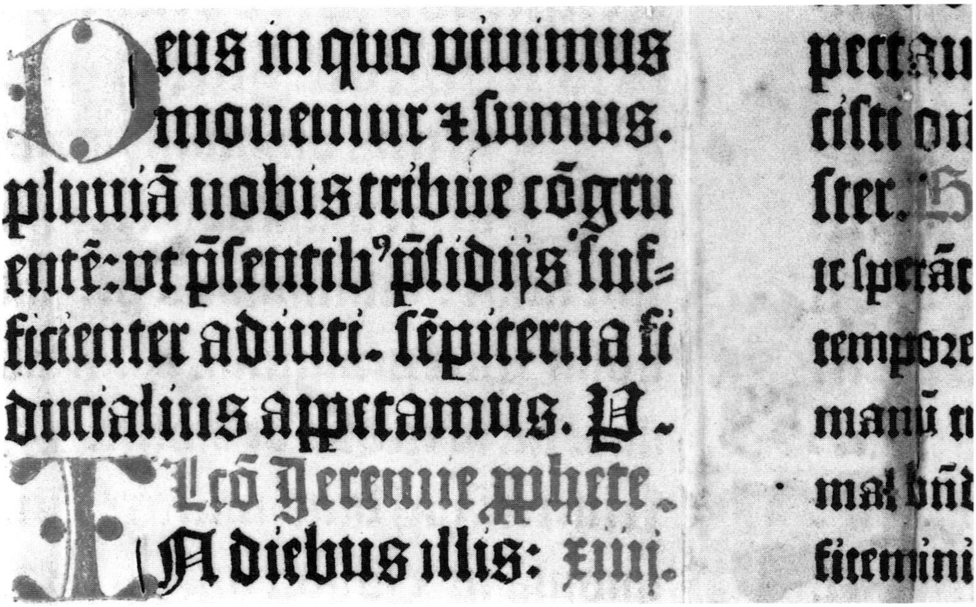

PLATE 130

MS 482.137, f. 1r, Bamberg, Germany, 1490

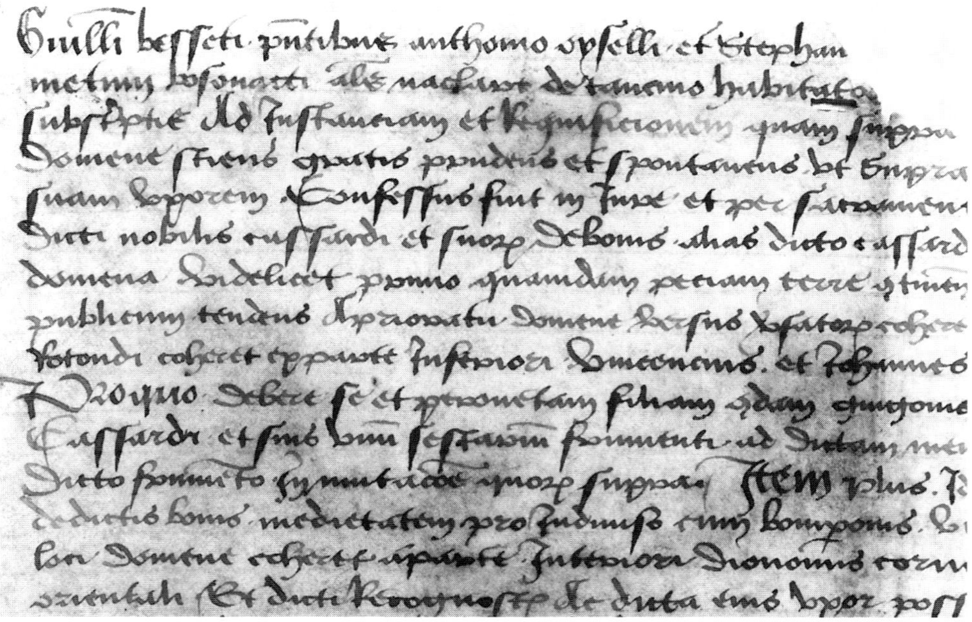

MS 482.138, f. 1r, France, s. XV

PLATE 131

MS 482.139, f. 1r, Rovereto, Italy, 1505

MS 482.140, f. 1r, Germany, s. XIV[1]

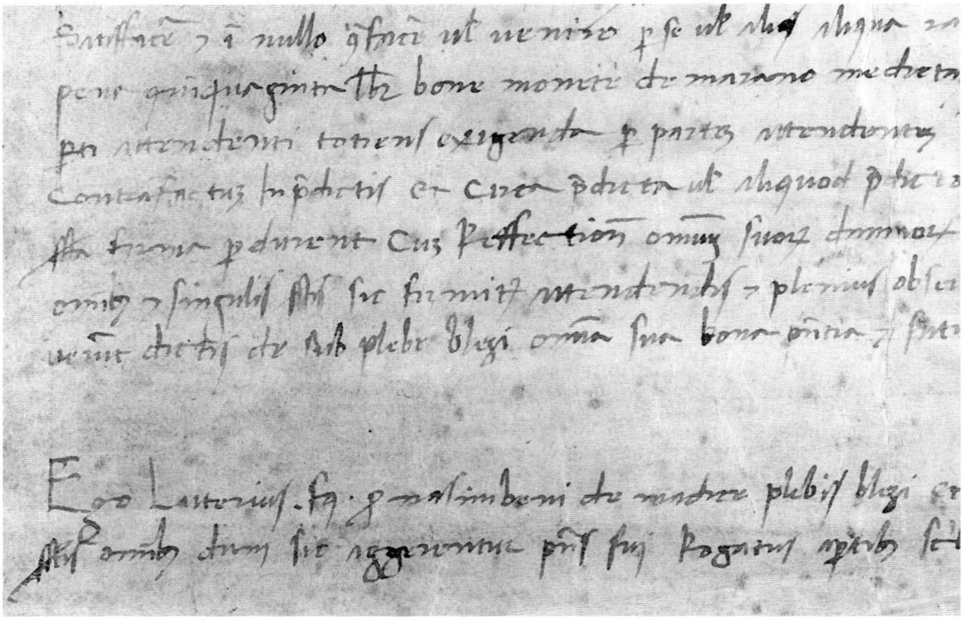

PLATE 132

MS 482.141, f. 1r, Diocese of Trent, Italy, 1488

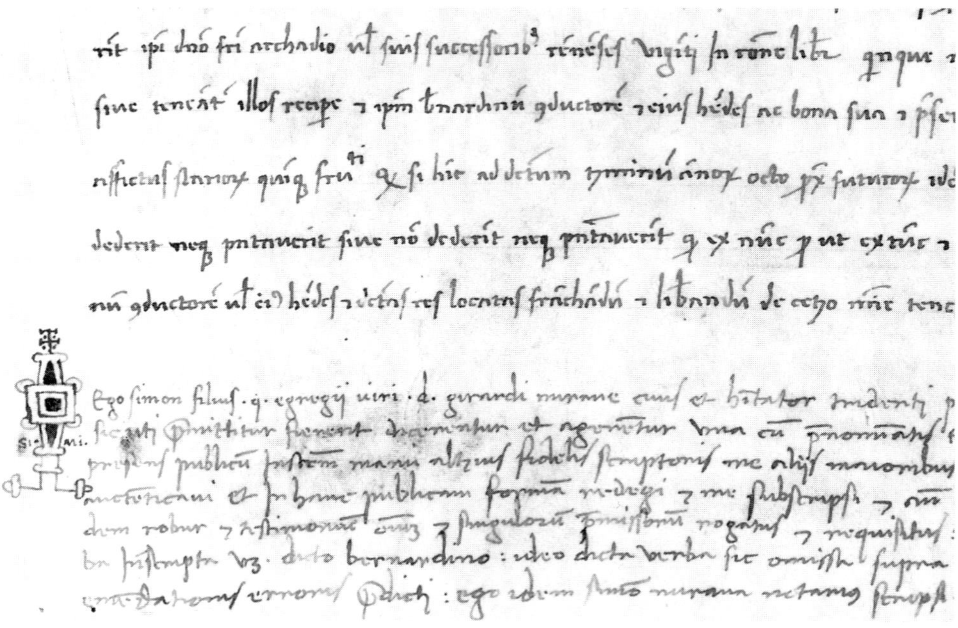

MS 482.142, f. 1r, Trent, Italy, 1514

PLATE 133

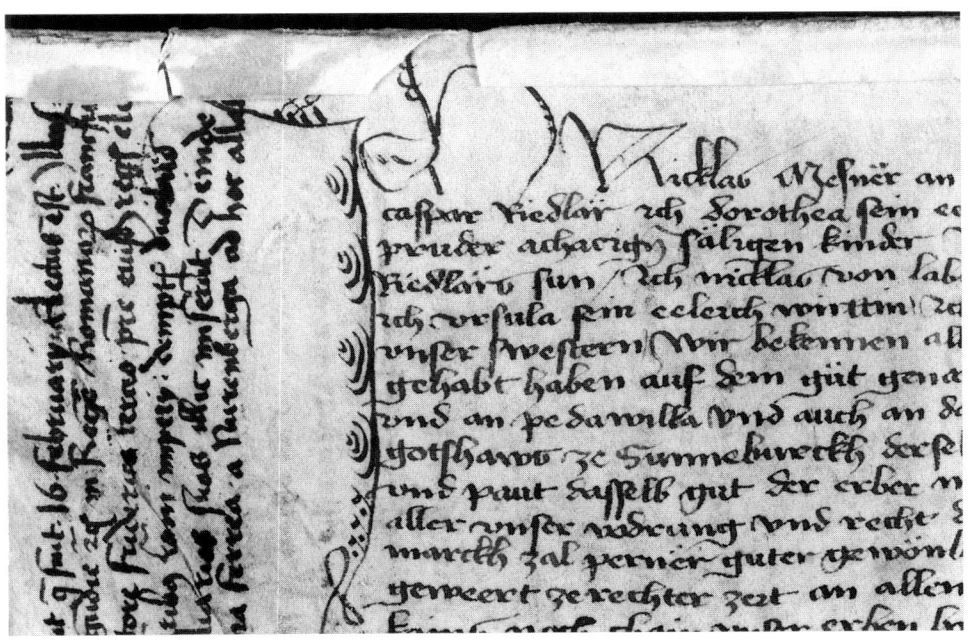

MS 482.143, f. 1v, Austria, s. XV^{ex}

MS 482.144, f. 1r, Tyrol, s. XV^{ex}

PLATE 134

MS 483.1, f. 1r, Spain, s. XV/XVI

PLATE 135

MS 483.2, f. 1r, France, s. XV

MS 483.3, f. 1r, France, s. XV

PLATE 136

MS 483.4, f. 1r, Northern France or Low Countries, s. XV

MS 483.5, f. 1r, Low Countries, s. XV[2]

PLATE 137

MS 483.15, f. 1v, England, s. XV

MS 483.16, f. 1r, England, s. XV

PLATE 138

MS 483.17, f. 1v, England, s. XV

MS 483.18, f. 1r, Italy, s. XV

PLATE 139

MS 483.19, f. 1v, Italy, s. XV

MS 483.20, f. 1r, Italy, s. XIV

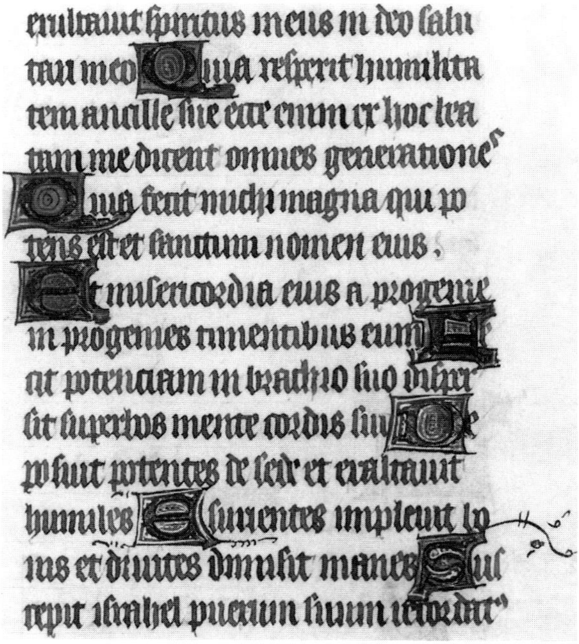

PLATE 140

exultauit spiritus meus in deo salu
tari meo Quia respexit humilita
tem ancille sue ecce enim ex hoc bea
tam me dicent omnes generationes
Quia fecit michi magna qui po
tens est et sanctum nomen eius ;
Et misericordia eius a progenie
in progenies timentibus eum
at potenciam in brachio suo disper
sit superbos mente cordis sui De
posuit potentes de sede et exaltauit
humiles Esurientes impleuit bo
nis et diuites dimisit manes Sus
cepit israhel puerum suum recordat'

MS 483.21, f. 1r, France or Low Countries, s. XV

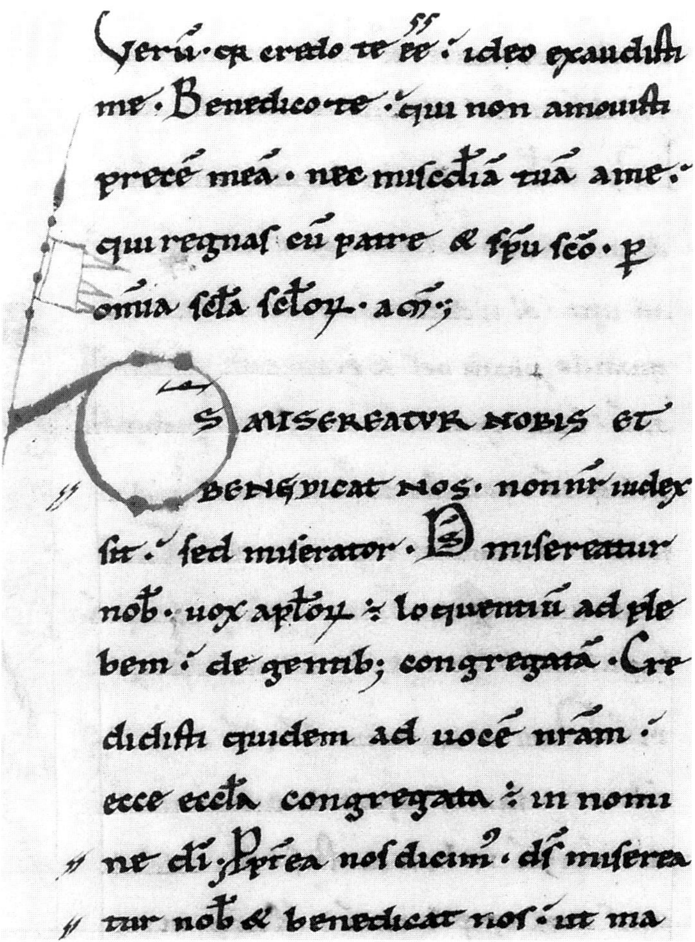

PLATE 140

Ueru̅ ex celo te te̅ : ideo exaudisti
me . Benedico te : qui non amouisti
prece̅ mea̅ . nec misedia̅ tua̅ a me :
qui regnas cu̅ patre & spu̅ sc̅o . p̅
om̅ia sec̅la sc̅lo̅y . am̅ ;

S ANISEREATVR NOBIS ET
  BENEDICAT NOS . non n̅r iudex
sit : sed miserator . D misereatur
nob . uox aptoy̅ ꝛ loquentiu̅ ad ple
bem : de gentib; congregata̅ . Cre
didisti quidem ad uoce̅ n̅ram :
ecce eccl̅a congregata ꝛ in nomi
ne d̅i ; p̅ ꝑea nos dicim̅ . d̅s miserea
tur nob & benedicat nos : ut ma

PLATE 141

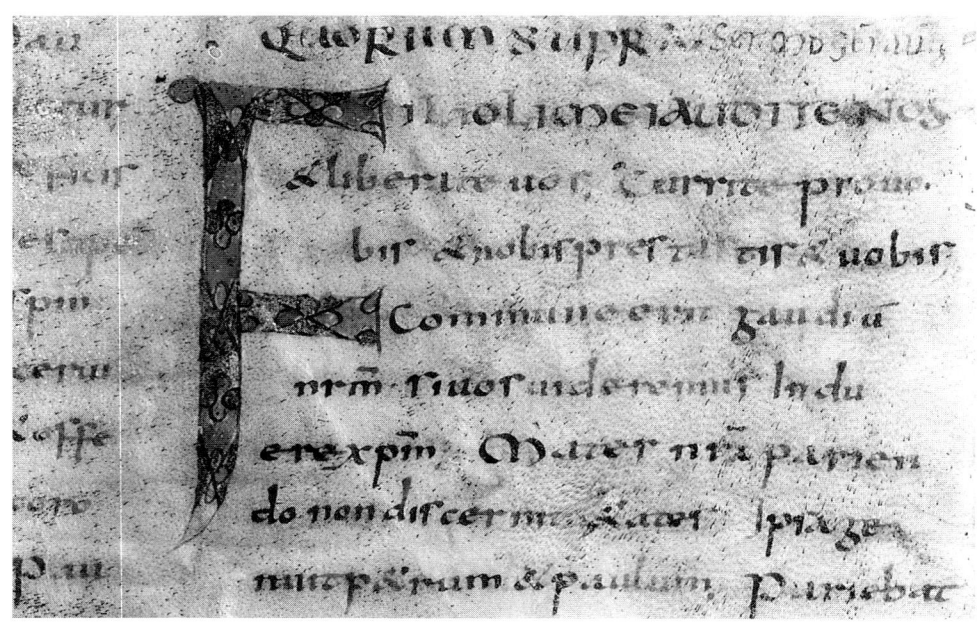

MS 484.2, f. 1v, Southern Germany (?), s. IX$^{2/4}$

MS 484.3, f. 1r, Northern Italy, s. IX$^{1/3}$

PLATE 142

nerale ē qđ in diuersas species potest diuidi· ut corp̄· animal· ꝶ

lia· ut lapis· homo· lignū Speciale ē quod a gn̄e diuiditur· ut l

gn̄u· ꝶ Alia facta de uerbo· ut doctor· lector· Verbale dr̄ nom̄

rbo nascitur· & in tor· sēp exit Fit autē ita Gerundi modi ultim

turi in tor· uestis· & facis nom̄· ut ē docendi· docendo· docendum

octū Tu· in tor· cuersa· fit doctor· Similiū legendi· legendo· leg

tui· Tu in tor· cuersa· fit lector ꝶ Alia participiis similia· ut de

is· potens· Participii simile nom̄ ē qđ sic sonat quasi participiū

iom ē· ut potens· Ecce hoc nomen quod ē potens· sic sonat quēa

participiū legens· Unde o dorest discerni· ex eo uidelicet quod

MS 484.4, f. 1r, Italy, s. X/XI

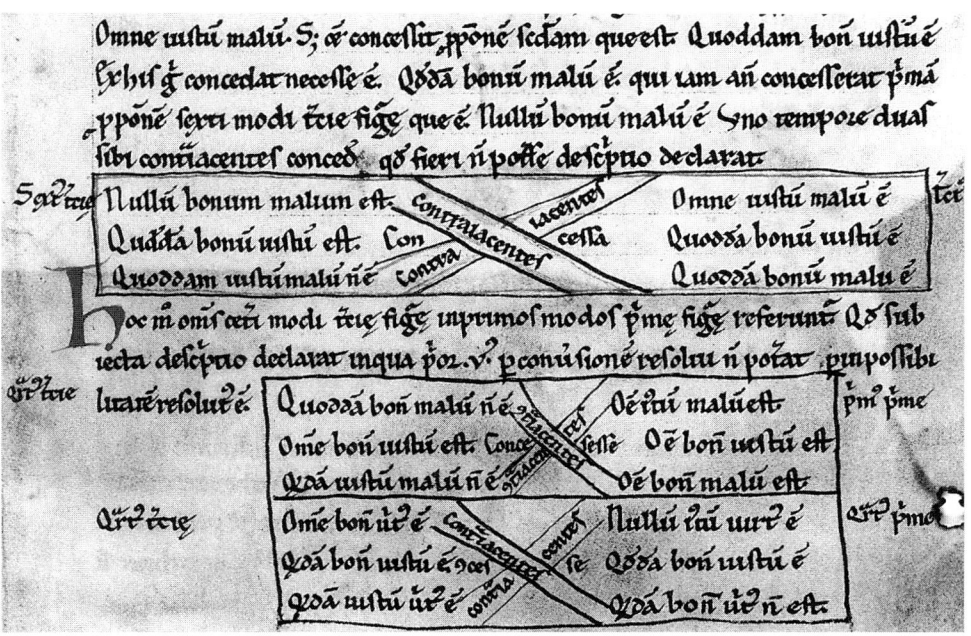

MS 484.5, f. 1r, Northern France or Germany, s. XII[2]

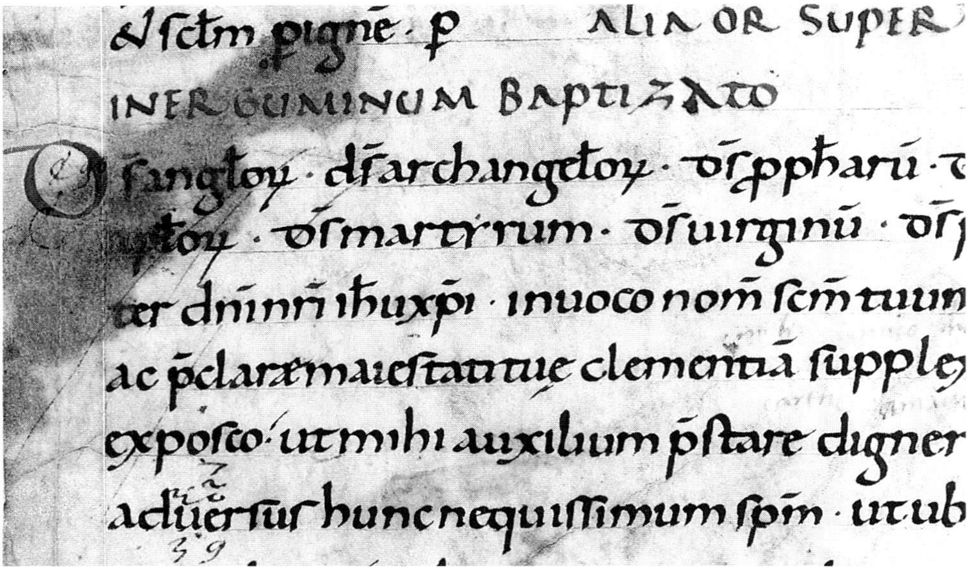

PLATE 143

el sctm pigne. p   ALIA OR SUPER
INERGUMINUM BAPTIZATO
O sanctoy. dsarchangeloy. dspphariu. t
toy. dsmartyrum. dsuirginu. ds
ter dninri ihuxpi. inuoco nom scm tuum
ac pclarcmaiestatit tue clemenriua supple
exposco. ut mihi auxilium pstare digner
adiuersus hunc nequissimum spm. utub

MS 484.6, f. 2r, Italy, s. XI^{in}

ala iina obequitait pcditibz cepit disdordie auctores quos
tueri tebebat Instictu poice ad supplicia exposces, minabat
q omnes turmas cu elephantis inductur se.stupebatimpuiso
malo pedites.ue plus in ipo meleagro erat aut consilij aut ai
turissimu cr pritibz uitebat erpectare poteius qua mouere
fortunaz Tum poica ut torpentes robnorios uidit tareen
tos. re qui meleagru eumpentu erconace que pma Hita
est poil morte alexandri secuti erat a cetis discbos elephatis
in cosp teu totius ceatus obicatiomes q beluaru pedibz obter
iti fiit nec philente philipp nec auctore. appbaturs id mo p
se iudicaturu qd ad plauset eueatus hoc bello re auitui macedo
nibz romen i pricipui fiut .. Meleager setro intellecta fran
te poice Tum quidem qripius corporis tuis no afferebat sag
nunc quietus steat. i mor dapnata sir salutis cu eius noie que

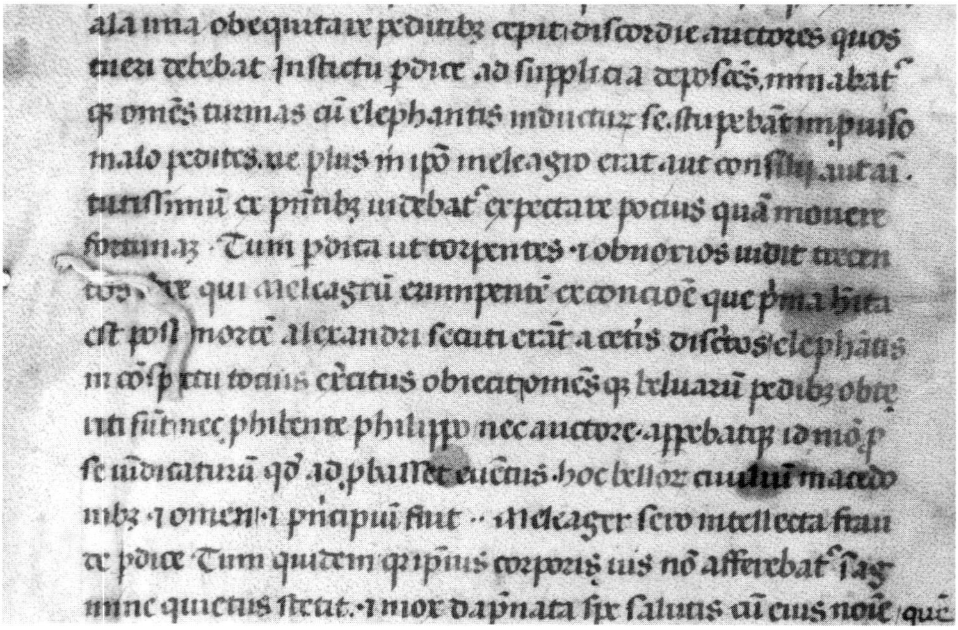

MS 484.7, f. 2v, Italy, s. XIV/XV

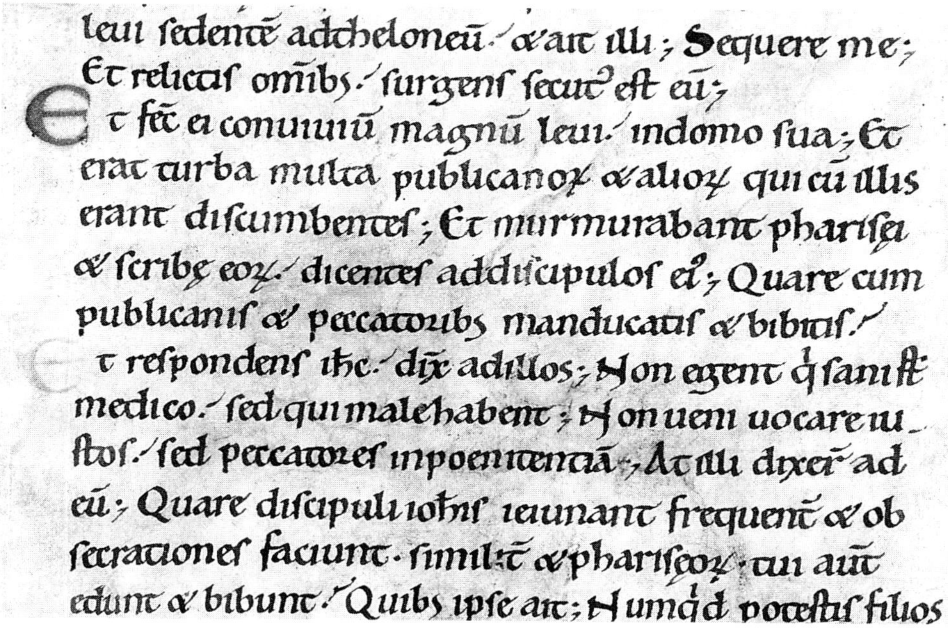

PLATE 144

leui sedente adcheloneū. & ait illi; Sequere me;
Et relictis omibs. surgens secut est eū;
t sec ei conuuiū magnū leui. indomo sua; Et
erat turba multa publicanox & alioy qui cū illis
erant discumbentes; Et murmurabant pharisei
& scribe eox. dicentes addiscipulos eī; Quare cum
publicanis & peccatoribs manducatis & bibitis;
t respondens ihc. dix adillos; Non egent q̇ sani st
medico. sed qui malehabent; Non ueni uocare iu_
stos. sed peccatores inpoenitentiā; At illi dixer ad
eū; Quare discipuli iohis ieiunant frequent & ob_
secrationes faciunt. similit & phariseox. tui aut
edunt & bibunt. Quibs ipse ait; Humqd potestis filios

MS 484.8, f. 1r, France or Italy, s. XII[1]

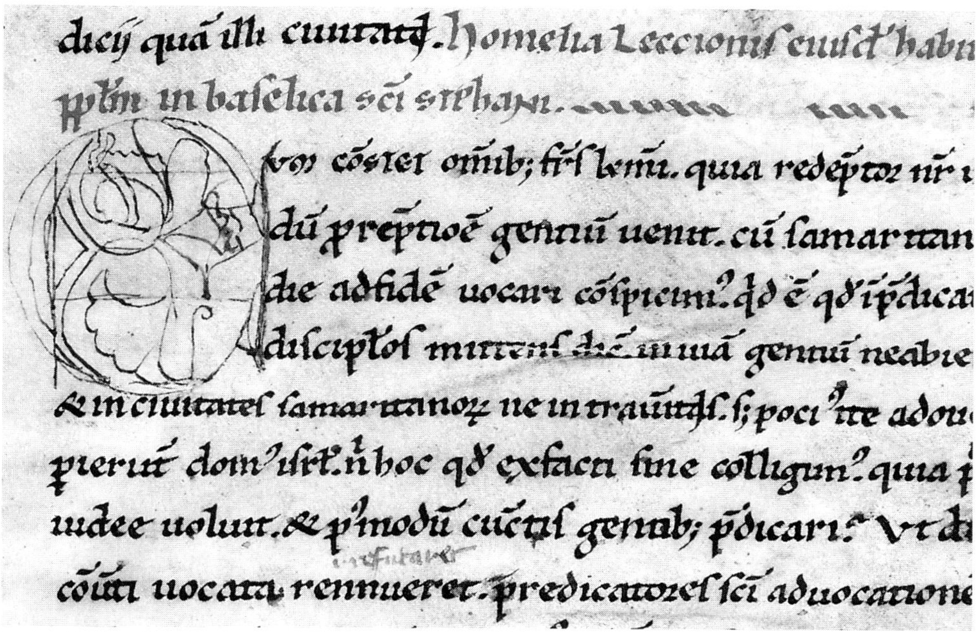

dieis quā illi ciuitati. Homelia Leccionis eiusd' habit
ipm in basilica sci stehani.
vos coster omib; frs leuiu. quia redemptor nr u
dū preptioe gentiū uenit. cū samaritan
die adfide uocari cospicim? qd e qd ipi dicat
disciplos mittens dic inuiā gentiū neabie
& in ciuitates samaritanox ne intrautis. s; poci ite adou
pierut dom' isrt. n hoc qd exfacti sine colligim? quia
iudee uoluit. & p'modū cuctis gentibs pdicari? Vt d
couti uocata rennueret. predicatores sci aduocatione

MS 484.9, f. 2v, France, s. XII[1]

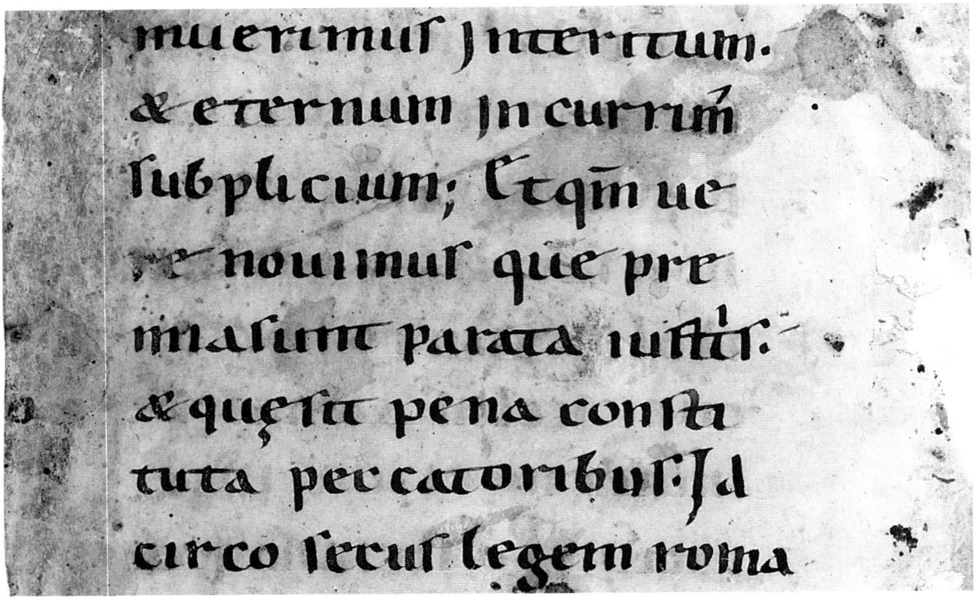

PLATE 145

nuerimuſ) nteritum.
& eternum)n currım
ſubplıcıum; Etqm ue
re nouımuſ que pre
ınaſunt parata ıuſtıſ:
& queſıt pe na conſtı
tuta peccatorıbuſ.)d
cırco ſecuſ legem roma

MS 484.10, f. 1v, Italy, s. XI/XII

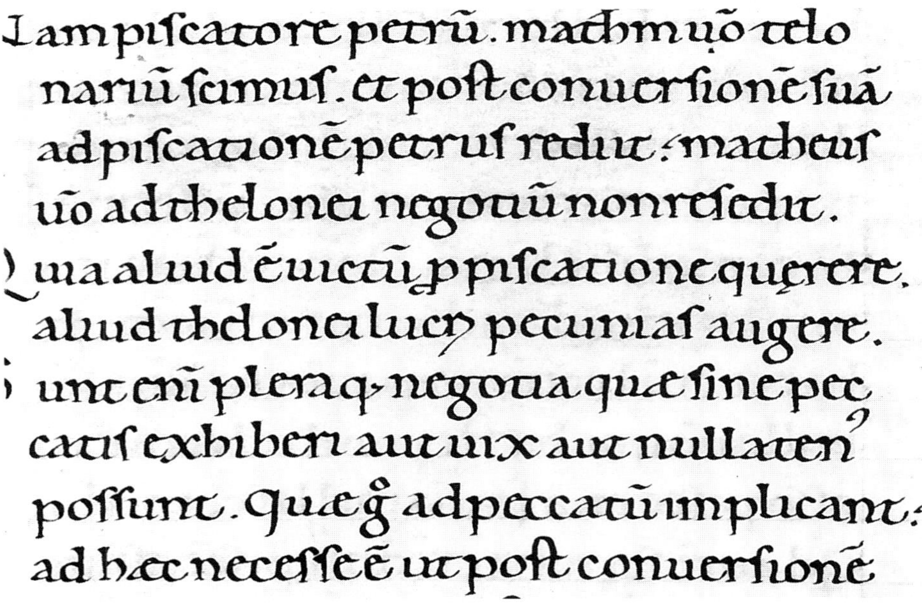

Iam piſcatore petru. mathm uo telo
nariu ſcimuſ. et poſt conuerſione ſua
ad piſcatione petruſ rediıt. matheuſ
uo ad thelonei negotiu non reſedıt.
Quia aliud é uictu p piſcatione querere.
aliud thelonei lucp pecuniaſ augere.
ſunt eni pleraq negotia que ſine pec
catıſ exhiberi aut uix aut nullaten
poſſunt. Que g adpeccatu implicant:
ad hec neceſſe é ut poſt conuerſione

MS 484.11, f. 1r, Italy, s. XII[1]

PLATE 146

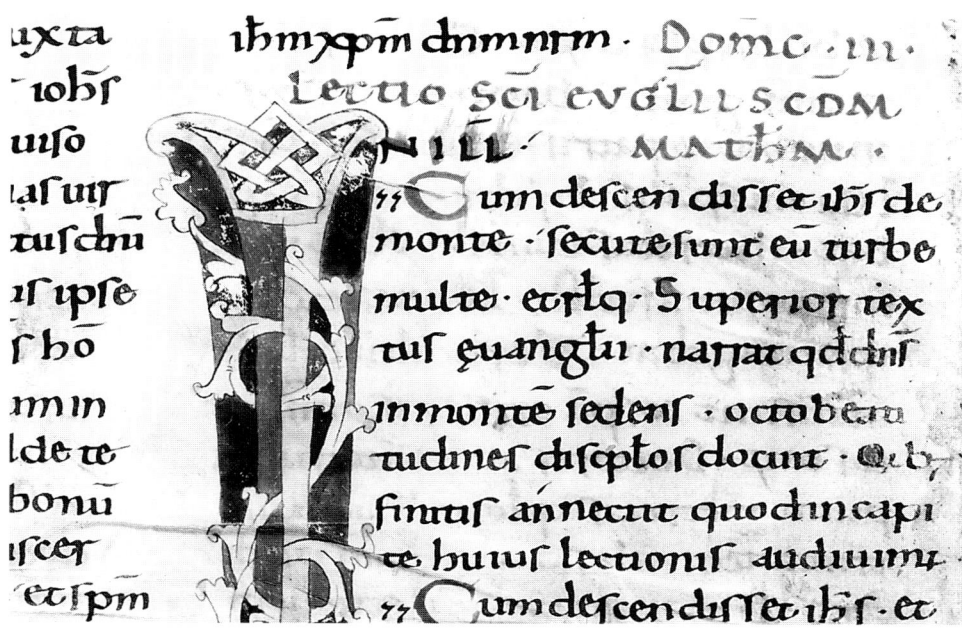

ihm xpm dnmnrm · Dome · in
lectio sci evglls cdm
MATHM ·

uxta
iohr
ulfo
lafuir
tufdnu
if ipfe
f ho
mm in
lde te
bonu
ifcer
et fpm

Cum defcen diffet ihf de
monte · fecutefunt eu turbe
multe · ecrtq · S uperior tex
tur euanglii · narrat qd dnf
in monte fedenf · octo bea
tudmef difcplof docuit · Q·hf
finitif annectit quod incapi
te huiuf lectionif audiuimr
Cum defcen diffet ihf · et

MS 484.12, f. 1v, Italy, s. XI/XII

cognofcetif eol. Nuqd colligunt defpinif
fic. Sic omif arbor bona. fruct bonof fac
t malof fac. Ni poteft arbor bona fruct m.
mala fruct bonof facere: Omif arbor qi
excidet & in igne mittet. Igr. exfructi
Sic omif qdic michi d d ittabit iregnu celo.
patrif mei qice lufe. ipfe itrabit iregr
tendit a falfif prophetif qui ueniunt ad uof inu
fecuf autem funt lupi rapacef a fructibuf eorum

MS 484.13, f. 1v, France or Italy, s. XI^{in}

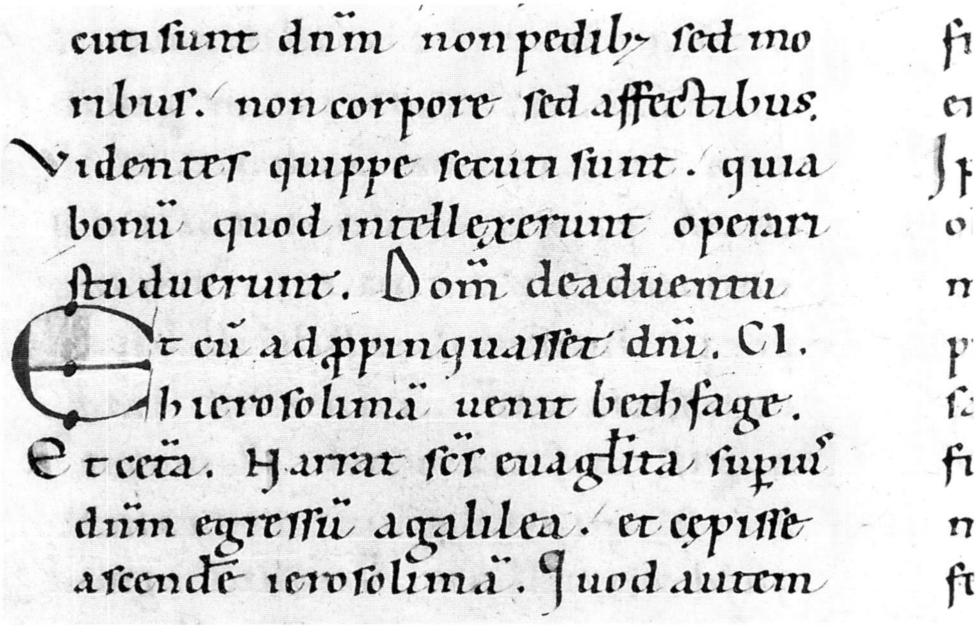

PLATE 147

cuti funt dñm non pedilz fed mo
ribuf. non corpore fed affectibus.
Videnter quippe fecuti funt. quia
bonũ quod intellexerunt operari
ftuduerunt. Dom deaduentu
Et cũ adppinquaffet dñi. CI.
Hierofolimã uenit bethfage.
Et cetã. Harrat fcr euãglita fupiuf
dñm egreffũ agalilea. et cepiffe
afcende ierofolimã. Quod autem

MS 484.14, f. 1v, Italy, s. XI/XII

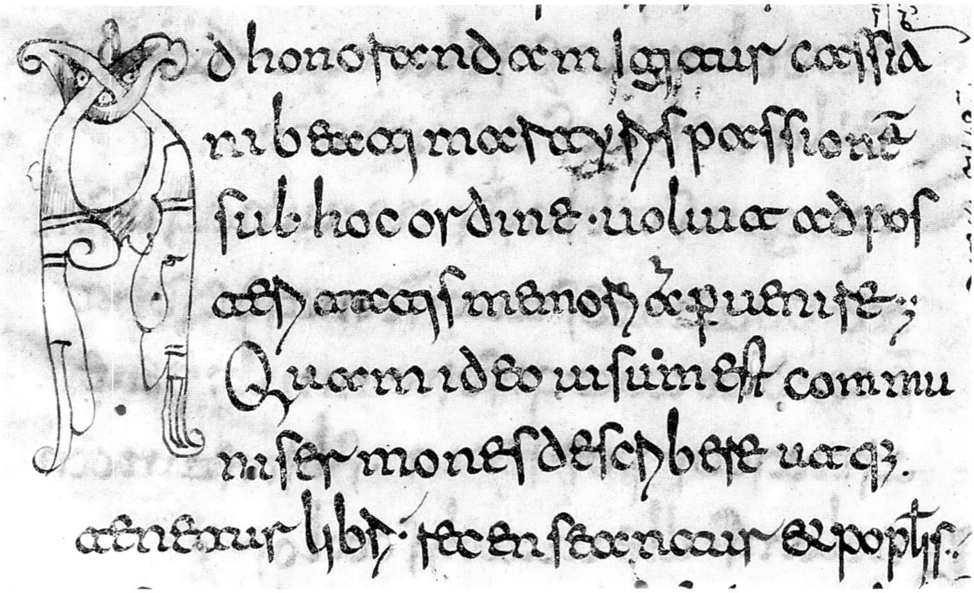

d honoreend ce m lgiciur coiîfta
rıbz ecoq mortyrdf poeffioné
fub hoc ordine · uoluic ced pof
ceaeccaf mänoq ocpuenife:;
Quam ideo uifum eft commu
ni ʃermonef defchbere uacq.
acnetur libr · ʃecen feoencair eexpoftʃ.

MS 484.15, f. 1v, Southern Italy, s. X/XI

PLATE 148

cem exhibere · et mea pficiendo con
scendite. Insistite opibus honis · ut p
ma aetna puenire possitis. Adiuti
gra xpi dni saluatoris. Item in nat
eiusdem beati martiris stephani.
omelia scī maximi epī.

ectio actuum aptor· quae
nobis hodie lectae dilmi frs. cūpluri
mum habeat inipsa specie ammiratio
nis· non minus tamn continet in miste

MS 484.16, f. 1r, Italy, s. XII^in

apatre spm ueritatis · ET RLc̄
omttueñ BEDE PRI de eadē Lec
XMUTIS
scī euglii Locis
inuenimus quiadi
scipuli ante aduen
tum scī sps · minus
capaces erant ad

MS 484.17, f. 1r, Italy, s. XII^med

PLATE 149

MS 484.18, f. 2v, France or Switzerland, s. XII^2

fuſ ſup cenſum ſalutiſ corporiſ. et non e ob
lettatio ſup cordiſ gaudium. Melior eſt ·
mors quam uita amara. et requieſ eterna
qͣua languor pſeuetranſ. Bona abſcondita
inore clauſo. quaſi appoſitioneſ epulaꝛ
circumpoſiṭ ſepulchro. Quid pͥderit li
batio ẏdolo. nec eni manducat. nec ho
dorabitur. Sic qui effugatur adno. et por
tanſ mercede iniquitatiſ. Videnſoculiſ
et ingemeſcenſ. ſicut ſpado coͣplectenſ

MS 484.19, f. 1r, Italy, s. XII^1

PLATE 150

MS 485.1, f. 1r (1/3 actual size), Italy, s. XVI; XIX/XX

MS 485.2, f. 1r (1/3 actual size), Northern Italy, s. XV

PLATE 150

MS 485.3, f. 1r (1/3 actual size), Spain, s. XVI

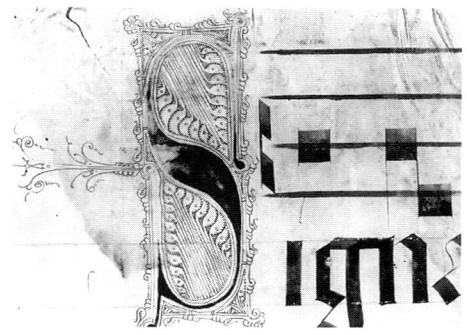

MS 485.4, f. 1r (1/3 actual size), Spain or Italy, s. XV

PLATE 150

MS 485.5, f. 1r (1/3 actual size), Spain, s. XVI or later

MS 485.6, f. 1v (1/3 actual size), Italy, s. XIV